METAPHYSICS, M
AND MEA

Metaphysics, Mathematics, and Meaning

Philosophical Papers I

NATHAN SALMON

CLARENDON PRESS · OXFORD

OXFORD
UNIVERSITY PRESS

Great Clarendon Street, Oxford OX2 6DP

Oxford University Press is a department of the University of Oxford.
It furthers the University's objective of excellence in research, scholarship,
and education by publishing worldwide in

Oxford New York

Auckland Cape Town Dar es Salaam Hong Kong Karachi
Kuala Lumpur Madrid Melbourne Mexico City Nairobi
New Delhi Shanghai Taipei Toronto

With offices in

Argentina Austria Brazil Chile Czech Republic France Greece
Guatemala Hungary Italy Japan Poland Portugal Singapore
South Korea Switzerland Thailand Turkey Ukraine Vietnam

Oxford is a registered trade mark of Oxford University Press
in the UK and in certain other countries

Published in the United States
by Oxford University Press Inc., New York

British Library Cataloguing in Publication Data

Data available

Library of Congress Cataloging in Publication Data

Salmon, Nathan U., 1951–
Metaphysics, mathematics, and meaning / Nathan Salmon.
p. cm.
Includes bibliographical references and index.
1. Metaphysics. 2. Mathematics—Philosophy. 3. Meaning (Philosophy). I. Title.
BD111.S28 2005   110—dc22   2005020153

Typeset by Newgen Imaging Systems (P) Ltd., Chennai, India
Printed in Great Britain
on acid-free paper by
Biddles Ltd., King's Lynn, Norfolk

ISBN 0–19–928176–9   978–0–19–928176–3
ISBN 0–19–928471–7 (Pbk.)   978–0–19–928471–9 (Pbk.)

1 3 5 7 9 10 8 6 4 2

These volumes are lovingly dedicated to my daughter,
Simone Becca Salmon,
the loveliest person it has been my honor to know.

Preface:
A Father's Message

The earliest philosophical thought I distinctly remember having was when I was a boy of around six. My mother (your grandmother) and her sister, Auntie Rae, were driving my cousins, my sister, and me to synagogue on the high holy day of Yom Kippur. My mother explained to the four of us sitting unsecured in the back seat (there were no car seat belts then) that God can do anything. She had taught me of God's omnipotence earlier. "Really absolutely *anything*?" I wondered. It was a challenge I could not resist: to come up with something that even He—the Big Guy in the Sky—can't do. I had already given the matter some thought, and had what I believed was a solution. The time had come for me to take a stand. I said triumphantly, "God can't stop time."

I meant that He cannot stop the passage of time. I explained that even though God might stop all motion—freezing everything and everyone dead in its tracks—time would still be passing for Him, and therefore, time would still be passing. I thought also that even if God then went into hibernation, freezing even Himself in thought as well as action, time would still be passing. However, I judged this further argument excessively subtle, so I kept it to myself. My father had dismissed my argument, insisting that God can even stop time. His tone implied that my attempt to find something God cannot do was heretical and therefore immoral. But my aunt's reaction was completely different. She turned to my mother and said, "That's amazing! That's *deep*!" Then she turned to me and said, "God can't stop time. That's very good, Nathan! Wow."

The incident impressed upon me several things. My father's reaction had made me feel depressed, though I knew even at that age that it was not an intellectually worthy rebuttal. My aunt's reaction made me feel vindicated. I was certain that any belief, even a religious belief, is rationally legitimate only if it can be subjected to critical assessment and only if it can withstand that sort of scrutiny. I also learned that theists typically do not share this attitude, at least not when it comes to their own religious beliefs. I also discovered that human beings (including myself) display a curious tendency to believe something not because they have good reason to think it true but because they need it to be true. I learned that those irrational beliefs are often among the beliefs that a person holds most strongly. Some go so far as to demand that others share those beliefs—as if one's beliefs are a matter of voluntary choice. And for the first time that I can remember, I felt that maybe my mind was capable of some substantial depth.

Later experiences seemed to confirm that theists resist all attempts to subject their faith to critical evaluation. It was not until I went to college that I encountered religious people who seemed to welcome the challenge of rational criticism. However, it still seemed to me that even those few philosophical theists are unwilling, maybe even unable, to look at religious belief in a completely detached and unbiased way. Today I religiously avoid discussing religious matters with religious people. Besides, I have become so thoroughly convinced that there are no gods that I find the issue completely uninteresting. Instead, I turned my attention to contemporary academic issues that are too abstract for anyone to take very personally.

I do philosophy. I investigate issues from a philosophical point of view, and try to achieve a deeper understanding using philosophical methods. My primary tool is reason, my primary criterion for success truth.

There will always be those who condemn reason as somehow excessively confining. There will also be those who hold that truth is over-rated, that it is somehow subjective, or even nonexistent, and that therefore it should not be the principal aim of rational inquiry. These people typically replace reason or truth with some favored practical, political, or social agenda, implicitly suggesting that the reasoned search for truth is immoral. Often, they misleadingly apply the word 'true' to any proposition that promotes or supports their substitute for genuine truth. These people are not merely mistaken; naturally understood, their stance is inconsistent. Worse, they devalue humanity's greatest intellectual achievements. Indeed they soil the noblest intellectual pursuit of which humanity is capable. Their stance is also dangerous. It is advisable to keep those who place little or no value on genuine reason and truth at a safe distance, at least intellectually (even though they frequently occupy positions of power and status). It is better to seek truth and miss than to aim elsewhere and hit the bull's eye. There is no sin in having erroneous beliefs, provided one endeavors not to.

My principal area is the philosophy of language. What is the meaning or content of a sentence—what is that which the sentence *says*, and which someone may believe or disbelieve? And how do the meanings of the individual words contribute toward forming the meaning of the sentence? I defend the *theory of direct reference*. According to direct-reference theory, the content of a name like 'Simone Salmon' is simply the person it stands for. This is *direct* reference because the name means directly what it stands for, rather than meaning some third entity that intervenes between the name and its bearer.

Direct-reference theory is saddled with serious philosophical problems. One set of problems concerns identifications. If direct-reference theory is correct, then a statement like 'Mark Twain is Samuel Clemens' simply says about Mark Twain that he is himself. So the sentence would mean the same thing as 'Mark Twain is Mark Twain.' But these two sentences do not appear to be synonymous. Everyone knows the information contained in the second sentence, but some people evidently don't know the information contained in the first: that Mark Twain and Samuel Clemens are one and the very same. This problem is called "Frege's puzzle," after the great philosopher who first used it to argue against direct reference. Frege held instead that the meaning of a word or expression is a concept of the thing referred to. Although both names stand for the same person, the name 'Mark Twain' means or expresses one concept, the name 'Samuel Clemens' another. I have become known for my defense of direct-reference theory against Frege's puzzle.

The other set of problems with direct-reference theory concerns names for individuals that do not exist. If the content of a name is just the thing for which it stands, as direct-reference theory holds, then a name like 'Harry Potter' should mean nothing at all, since it stands for a completely fictional character. If the name means nothing at all, then the sentences that make up the Harry Potter stories should be meaningless. But they are clearly meaningful. They make some sense, we understand them, and they entertain.

I have defended direct-reference theory against this problem. I argue that although Harry Potter is fictional, he is also every bit as real as you or me. What distinguishes a fictional character like Harry Potter is that he is not a real *person*. That is, Harry Potter is not actually a person. He is only a fictional person. A fictional person is a real *thing*, although not a real person. Harry Potter is an object—a real object—created by author J. K. Rowling. He is every bit as real as the novels themselves. In fact, he is a component part of those novels.

This sort of consideration does not lay the problem to rest finally. One can devise names that, unlike names from fiction, really do stand for nothing at all. The problem thus has a good deal of force and resilience. I have done much to bring the remaining problem into sharp focus, to pave the way for a full defense of direct reference.

My defense of direct reference points back to a theological theme. God, it turns out, is every bit as real as you or me. On the other hand, as an atheist I hold that God is also no more real than Harry Potter. God is depicted in modern mythology as an omnipotent, omniscient, benevolent, and divinely perfect being. In reality, He is an entirely mythical object, no more capable of real thought, action, intelligence, or even consciousness than any purely fictional character.

Those who are offended by this simple observation ought to look inside themselves and dispassionately ask "Why?". Most will not. Let us hope some will.

Acknowledgments

Each of the following is reprinted by permission of the original publisher.

1 'Existence,' in James Tomberlin, ed., *Philosophical Perspectives, 1: Metaphysics* (Atascadero, Calif.: Ridgeview, 1987), pp. 49–108.

2 'Nonexistence,' *Noûs*, vol. 32, no. 3 (September 1998), pp. 277–319, published by Blackwell Publishing.

3 'Mythical Objects,' in J. Campbell, M. O'Rourke, and D. Shier, eds., *Meaning and Truth*, Proceedings of the Eastern Washington University and the University of Idaho Inland Northwest Philosophy Conference on Meaning (Seven Bridges Press, 2002), pp. 105–123.

5 'Impossible Worlds,' *Analysis*, vol. 44, no. 3 (June 1984), pp. 114–117, published by Blackwell Publishing.

6 Critical Review of David Lewis, *On the Plurality of Worlds*, *The Philosophical Review*, vol. 97, no. 2 (April 1988), pp. 237–244 (re-titled); published by Cornell University.

7 'The Logic of What Might Have Been,' *The Philosophical Review*, vol. 98, no. 1 (January 1989), pp. 3–34, published by Cornell University.

8 'The Fact that $x = y$,' *Philosophia* (Israel), vol. 17, no. 4 (December 1987), pp. 517–518.

9 'This Side of Paradox,' in C. Hill, ed., *Philosophical Topics*, vol. 21, no. 2 (Spring 1993), pp. 187–197.

10 'Identity Facts,' in C. Hill, ed., *Philosophical Topics*, vol. 30, no. 1 (Spring 2002), pp. 237–267.

12 'Wholes, Parts, and Numbers,' in J. E. Tomberlin, ed., *Philosophical Perspectives, 11: Mind, Causation, and World* (Atascadero, Ca.: Ridgeview, 1997), pp. 1–15.

13 'The Limits of Human Mathematics,' in J. E. Tomberlin, ed., *Philosophical Perspectives, 15: Metaphysics, 2001* (Oxford: Blackwell, 2001), pp. 93–117.

14 'On Content,' *Mind*, vol. 101, no. 404 (October 1992; special issue commemorating the centennial of Gottlob Frege's '*Über Sinn und Bedeutung*'), pp. 733–751, published by Oxford University Press.

15 'On Designating,' in S. Neale, ed., *Mind*, special issue celebrating the centennial of 'On Denoting' (forthcoming 2005), published by Oxford University Press.

16 'A Problem in the Frege–Church Theory of Sense and Denotation,' *Noûs*, vol. 27, no. 2 (June 1993), pp. 158–166, published by Blackwell Publishing.

17 'The Very Possibility of Language: A Sermon on the Consequences of Missing Church,' in C. A. Anderson and M. Zeleny, eds., *Logic, Meaning and Computation: Essays in Memory of Alonzo Church* (Boston: Kluwer, 2001), pp. 573–595, published by Springer.

18 'Tense and Intension,' in A. Jokic, ed., *Time, Tense, and Reference* (Cambridge University Press, 2003), pp. 107–154.

19 'Pronouns as Variables,' *Philosophy and Phenomenological Research* (forthcoming 2005).

Volume I Contents

Introduction to Volume I

The present volume and its companion encompass most of the papers I wrote during the two decades since I left Ivy to return to sunnier shores. Together with my previous books, *Reference and Essence* (second edition, Amherst, NY: Prometheus Books, 1981, 2005) and *Frege's Puzzle* (second edition, Atascadero, Ca.: Ridgeview, 1986, 1991), these volumes represent my thought to date on a variety of topics philosophical. 'A Father's Message,' 'Modal Logic Kalish-and-Montague Style,' and 'Personal Identity: What's the Problem?' each appears here for the first time. I am grateful to Ernest Sosa, who first suggested that I compile the collection. With his suggestion came the realization: 'If not now, when?'

I have been deeply influenced by the writings of two dead, white, European males: Gottlob Frege and Bertrand Russell. I have also been deeply influenced by intellectual interactions with a number of remarkable American philosophers I have been privileged to know personally. Deserving of special mention are Tyler Burge, Keith Donnellan, Donald Kalish, and most especially, Alonzo Church, David Kaplan, and Saul Kripke. Standing on the shoulders of giants, the view has been breathtaking. For more than a quarter century I have strived—not always successfully—to strike a happy balance between independent thought and recognition of the fascinating and deeply significant insights of extraordinarily gifted minds. The pages that follow are a result of that endeavor.

In his second lecture on *The Philosophy of Logical Atomism*, Russell said, "the point of philosophy is to start with something so simple as not to seem worth stating, and to end with something so paradoxical that no one will believe it." Presumably, each of the transitions among the steps that lead from simple triviality to the paradoxically incredible must be like the starting point itself: so simple as not to seem worth stating. (Far too often in contemporary philosophy, this feature of the enterprise is undervalued, even ignored.) There is more to philosophy than the paradox of the heap, of course, and no one has demonstrated that better than Russell. Still, Russell's work often did conform to his succinct characterization of philosophy as the attempt to derive the incredible from the trivial. My own objective has often been similar to Russell's—more modest undoubtedly, but only somewhat. It has been to proceed by a sequence of obviously valid inferences (though not always uncontroversial) from clearly correct premises (though not generally indubitable) to a significant but unpopular thesis (though not typically incredible), or at least a rather surprising one.

In short, I have sought to establish (and insofar as possible, to prove) the surprising. If I should be accused of valuing this philosophical style because it is what I do, rather than the other way around, I shall take it as a compliment. I have argued for theses that fly in the face of conventional wisdom not because those theses are unfashionable, but because they are in each case, to the best of my ability to make a determination, the unrecognized, unappreciated truth of the matter. How far I have succeeded is for the reader to decide.

PART I

To be and not to be: These are the questions taken up in Part I. Here I stake out a position that concerns a variety of ontological issues and which, to my knowledge, had not been held before but which I am gratified to learn is now shared, or at least esteemed, by others. In 'Existence,' I reject Quine's dictum that *to be is to be a value of a variable* on the ground that variables range over nonexistents, and indeed must do so in order to yield the right results. Many things are such that there is no such thing; they do not exist. This observation does not entail *possibilism*—the doctrine that there are things that do not exist yet might have—and is consistent with *actualism*, the doctrine that everything there is exists. There were things and there will be things that do not now exist. There might have been things that do not actually exist. And to top it all, some things (examples are specified) could not have existed. All things existent and nonexistent—actual past things, actual present, actual future, merely possible, and even impossible—inevitably have properties. In this sense, predication precedes existence. Yet existence is itself a property, Kant not-withstanding. So is actuality. Only here the issue is more complex. The word 'actual' is ambiguous, having both an indexical use and a non-indexical use. Actuality$_1$ is simply the property of being of *this* possible world, as contrasted with the property of being of another. As such, actuality$_1$ has no special ontological or metaphysical significance. Actuality$_2$, by contrast, is the property of being of the way things *are*, as contrasted with the property of being of a way things are *not*. Metaphysically, this is the name of the game. Analytically, something is actual$_1$ if and only if it is actual$_2$. But it ain't necessarily so. The actual$_1$ world is necessarily thus, though it might not have been actual$_2$.

I argue in 'Nonexistence' that reference to, or designation of, the nonexistent is commonplace. And belief of nonexistent propositions is equally so. True, singular, negative existentials—true sentences of the form ⌜α does not exist⌝—come in a variety of shapes and sizes, varying by the semantic nature of the subject term or the ontological status of its designatum (referent). The most common sorts of true negative existentials involve names that genuinely designate nonexistent things—actual past things, actual future, merely possible, or impossible. Fiction does not provide a case in point, since fictional characters are real. Neither does error, which, fundamentally, is merely accidental fiction. The most interesting, and at the same time bizarre, instances of true negative existentials are those in which the subject term is genuinely non-designative. But such cases are exceedingly rare. And they are ambiguous, true on one reading, untrue (and unfalse) on the other.

In 'Mythical Objects' I invoke my account of error as accidental fiction to solve a notoriously difficult problem introduced by Peter Geach: How can it be correct to report that Hob and Nob have thoughts and beliefs concerning the same witch, when there are no such things as witches?

PART II

This part begins with 'Modal Logic Kalish-and-Montague Style,' which has circulated in unpublished form for a number of years among logic instructors who teach the natural-deduction techniques of Donald Kalish and Richard Montague from their textbook, *Logic: Techniques of Formal Reasoning* (second edition co-authored with Gary Mar). It extends that text's deductive apparatus to the most popular "normal" systems of modal propositional logic (*T, B, S4,* and *S5*)—the logic of what might have been—making significantly greater use of the Kalish-and-Montague "delightful system of boxes and cancels" (as Kalish had called it), than had been utilized in any of the earlier attempts of which I am aware.

'An Empire of Thin Air' criticizes the modal theory that David Lewis defended in *On the Plurality of Worlds* (Blackwell, 1986). According to Lewis, to say that John Kerry might have won the 2004 presidential election is to say that someone very similar to Kerry *does* win his presidential election in a parallel universe (in an alternative 'possible world'). This theory is indicative of a serious misunderstanding of such modal expressions as 'possibly' and 'necessarily', which are concerned not with any goings on in parallel universes but with what might have been. One need not disbelieve in possible worlds to recognize that they are not parallel universes. As I argue in 'Impossible Worlds,' and in greater detail in 'The Logic of What Might Have Been,' if there are merely possible worlds, then indeed there are also impossible worlds. Worlds are things, but impossible worlds are not impossible things. A *world*, in the sense in which the actual world is only one among many, is a maximal scenario, a total way for things to be—*all* things. The actual world is the way things are. Merely possible worlds are ways things might have been but are not. Impossible worlds are ways things could not have been. Some ways things could have been might instead have been ways things could *not* have been; they are only contingently possible worlds. Likewise, some impossible worlds are only contingently impossible. Equivalently put, there are counterexamples to *S5* modal propositional logic (which illegitimately assumes that any proposition that might have been true is necessarily such that it might have been true), and even to *S4* (which illegitimately assumes that any necessary truth is necessarily such). What about *B* (that for any truth, it is necessary that it might have been true)? Maybe the actual world, unlike some other possible worlds, could not have failed be a possible world. Though I know of no convincing grounds for supposing that even the actual world is only contingently possible, as far as the *logic* of modality is concerned (as opposed to the metaphysical reality), the actual world might instead have been impossible. The correct propositional logic of what might have been is simply *T* (any necessary truth is true). In 'This Side of Paradox' I defend my critique of the conventional wisdom concerning the logic of what might have been against a rejoinder by Timothy Williamson.

PART III

In Part II I stake out an extremely controversial position concerning modal propositional logic. In Part III I stake out an extremely controversial position concerning the prospect that identity is sometimes indeterminate. Though the reasoning in both cases is, to my mind, beyond reproach, the arguments have proved unpopular. While I remain hopeful that future generations will find my arguments as decisive as I take them to be, the current state of play leaves little cause for optimism. Orthodoxy is supported less by reason than by inertia.

If $x = y$, then the fact that $x = y$ is an *identity fact*. And conversely. (Of course, if $x \neq y$, then there is no fact that $x = y$.) Among the facts that obtain in every possible world are all the identity facts. As I argue in 'The Fact that $x = y$,' if there is such a fact, it bears a very special relation to the fact that $x = x$. They are *one and the same fact*. As an inevitable consequence, the fact that $x = y$, if such there is, enjoys a host of properties often denied of it: it obtains necessarily (or at least it necessarily obtains-if-x-exists); it obtains always (or at least as long as x exists); it is not a matter of decision, convention, or convenience, nor of elegance, simplicity, or uniformity of theory; it does not turn on any fact concerning anything other than x; it is the only purported fact that has any "claim" or "title" to be an identity fact involving x; it does not require any "criteria of identity"; it is not grounded in, or reducible to, other facts (such as facts concerning material origins, bodily continuity, psychological continuity, or memory), nor does it obtain "in virtue of" such facts; it is knowable solely on the basis of *a priori* reason by anyone who believes anything about or involving x; it is not known by knowing qualitative facts about x or y, such as facts concerning continuity, location, qualitative persistence, or similarity. Equally important, for any x there can be nothing y such that there is no fact concerning the identity/distinctness of x and y—i.e., no fact that $x = y$ and at the same time, no fact that $x \neq y$. For if there were, then y would differ from x in this respect: that there is no fact that x is it and no fact that x is not it. (By contrast, x is such that there is a fact that x is it.) Hence, y would be something other than x, in which case there would be a fact that $x \neq y$. Thus for any pair of entities x and y—for any persons, for any ships, for any sets or classes, for any sums of money, for *any* pair x and y—it is either a fact that they are identical, or else it is a fact that they are distinct. In short, identity is always determinate. 'Identity Facts' is a thorough defense of this argument against the most developed response to date. Part II closes with an application of this argument, combined with an application of the doctrine of impossible worlds, to a traditional problem in 'Personal Identity: What's the Problem?' (appearing here for the first time).

PART IV

Following Russell's paradigm of the point of philosophy, it would appear to be provable, as I show in 'Wholes, Parts, and Numbers,' that there cannot be exactly

2½ *F*'s, e.g., exactly two and a half oranges on the table. For the orange-half on the table is itself not an orange. An orange is a whole orange (or nearly enough so), whereas an orange-half, whatever else it is, is not a whole orange (nor even nearly so). Thus there are fewer than two and a half oranges on the table, *viz.*, exactly two, together with a third thing that (despite its color, taste, etc.) is no orange. Deviating from Russell's paradigm, I do not accept the paradoxical conclusion. Instead I opt for a non-classical understanding on which the numerical quantifier 'there are exactly *n*', surprisingly, creates a nonextensional context. Something is an orange on the table if and only if it is a (nearly) whole orange on the table. Yet there are two and a half *oranges on the table* and only two *whole (or nearly so) oranges on the table*, which comprise a sub-plurality of the two and a half oranges. The two and a half oranges on the table are three things (each a piece of fruit).

'The Limits of Human Mathematics' defends Gödel's claim that his famous incompleteness theorems yield the result, as a mathematically established fact, that the mathematical problem-solving capacity of the human mind either exceeds that of any finite machine or is incapable of solving all of mathematics' mysteries. The issue turns on the nature of mathematical proof by the human mind. Of particular relevance is the question of whether the deductive basis of human mathematics is decidable.

PART V

This part includes discussion of a host of issues regarding reference and semantic content. In 'On Content' I argue that Frege might be properly interpreted as having employed a notion of *logical content*—more fine-grained than his notion of *Bedeutung* (extension) yet more course-grained than *Sinn*—whereby expressions have the same logical content if they are logically equivalent. Strictly synonymous expressions (those having the same sense) have the same logical content, but the converse is not generally true (else, for Frege, all mathematical truths would be the same 'thought,' or proposition, e.g., that 2 is even and that $e^{\pi i} = -1$).

In 'On Designating' a new interpretation is proposed for the notorious "Gray's *Elegy*" passage in 'On Denoting.' On my interpretation, the "Gray's *Elegy*" passage is Russell's central argument in 'On Denoting' for the doctrine—surprising, yet crucial to Russell's philosophical program—that definite descriptions are not singular terms. The argument (later re-invented by others) goes as follows. If a definite description is a singular term, then besides its designatum ("denotation") it also has a content ("meaning"), which represents the description's designatum in propositions expressed by sentences in which the description occurs. But the attempt to form a singular proposition about a particular description's content, rather than its designatum, invariably fails. The would-be singular proposition collapses into a nonsingular proposition about the description's designatum. Thus any proposition about a description's content must be nonsingular, in which the content in question is represented by a new content. But this new content is not uniquely determined by the one it represents—"there is no backward road" from designatum to content—and this renders our comprehension of propositions about a description's content inexplicable. I offer a pair of possible responses to Russell's objection: one on behalf of Fregean theory, another on behalf of Millianism.

'A Problem in the Frege–Church Theory of Sense and Denotation' exposes an inconsistent triad to which Fregean theory, as expounded by Church, seems committed. The inconsistency consists of: (i) Frege's assertion that the sense that a sentence like 'Holmes has an older brother' expresses when it occurs within a propositional-attitude attribution—its *indirect sense*—is the customary sense of the corresponding phrase 'the proposition that Holmes has an older brother'; (ii) a Fregean solution, suggested by Church, to the traditional Paradox of Analysis, on which 'the proposition that Holmes has an older brother' and 'the proposition that Holmes has an older male sibling' differ in customary sense; and (iii) Church's observation that 'Holmes has an older brother' and 'Holmes has an older male sibling', even when expressing their indirect senses, can both be correctly translated, preserving sense, by means of a single sentence of another language (expressing its own indirect sense). The solution to this problem, I argue, is to reject (ii). This solution, however, threatens the very heart for the Frege–Church theory.

In 'The Very Possibility of Language,' I argue that several contemporary philosophers have missed entirely the fundamental point of Church's famous *Translation Argument* (which Church credits to C. H. Langford). A sentence like 'Chris believes that the Earth is round' certainly appears to mention a proposition—that the Earth is round—and to say something about it. But very many philosophers have argued that the sentence actually mentions particular *words* rather than any proposition, so that it might be more perspicuously paraphrased as 'Chris accepts "the Earth is round"'. Church demonstrates that this is incorrect by translating both the original sentence and its proposed paraphrase into another language. Doing so illustrates what was already evident even before translation, that the original sentence and its proposed paraphrase contain different information. The latter, at most, merely *describes* what it is that Chris is supposed to believe—specifying it as *the content, whatever that may turn out to be, of such-and-such words*—whereas the former *identifies* what Chris is alleged to believe. What Chris is said to believe is this: that the Earth is round. Michael Dummett's failure to appreciate this fundamental point leads to a dramatic collapse of his own theory, which has the preposterous consequence that language as we know it is altogether impossible.

'Tense and Intension' demonstrates how best to incorporate the traditional notion of a proposition as eternal and unvarying in truth-value into a semantic theory like that of David Kaplan by distinguishing among not three (as in Kaplan's work), but four levels of semantic value: extension, content, content base, and meaning. Unlike the semantic content, the *content base* of a sentence may be temporally neutral, and may thus vary in truth-value with time. This semantic theory supports the generally unrecognized fact that the semantic content of a predicate, like 'is reading', is a temporally indexed attribute (*reading at time t*), and hence changes as the predicate is evaluated with respect to different times. 'Pronouns as Variables' defends Peter Geach's view against the current orthodoxy that anaphoric pronouns that do not occur within the scope of their grammatical antecedent are not bound variables but definite descriptions, or rigidified variants.

PART I
ONTOLOGY

1

Existence (1987)

I shall discuss here the topics of existence and nonexistence, of what it is for an individual to be actual and what it is for an individual not to be actual. What I shall have to say about these matters offers little toward our primordial need to discover the Meaning of Existence, but I hope to say some things that will satisfy the more modest ambition of those of us who wish to know the meaning of 'existence'. I shall also say some things that bear on issues in the grandest traditions of Philosophy.

I

The questions I shall address here can be approached through the following thought-exercise: For every one of us, prior to our conception, the odds against the very gametes from which we in fact developed coming together to develop into a particular human individual are astronomical. There are countless billions of potential pairings of a human sperm cell with a human ovum that are never realized. Everyone of us is among the elite group of Elect whose gametes did manage, against all odds, to unite in the normal manner and develop into a human individual. Let S be a particular male sperm cell of my father's and let E be a particular ovum of my mother's such that neither gamete ever unites with any other to develop into a human zygote. Let us name the (possible) individual who would have developed from the union of S and E, if S had fertilized E in the normal manner, 'Noman'.[1]

Portions of the present chapter were presented at a symposium on problems of Existence and Identity at the University of North Carolina at Greensboro (April 1986); to the University of Padua, Italy; the University of Belgrade, Yugoslavia; the Analytic Section of the Philosophical Society of Serbia, Yugoslavia; the University of California, Santa Barbara; and the 1987 Alberta Philosophy Conference. It has benefitted from the discussions that followed, from comments by W. R. Carter, and from fruitful discussions with Robert Adams, Anthony Brueckner, William Forgie, David Kaplan, Ali Kazmi, and Timothy Williamson.

[1] I assume here that there is only one possible individual who would have resulted from the union of S and E, if S had fertilized E in the normal manner. (This assumption can be expressed through the judicious use of standard modal operators without the aid of a quantifier that purports to quantify over merely possible individuals, as follows: There might have existed an individual x such that x and actually necessarily only x actually would have developed from the union of S and E if S had fertilized E in the normal manner. This alternative formulation is somewhat cumbersome, though, and more difficult to grasp than the original formulation.) The intuition that this assumption is true is very widely shared. I am here relying on the assumption merely as a device to introduce the question that is the main topic of this essay. For further discussion of this and related

Noman does not exist in the actual world, but there are many possible worlds in which he (it?) does exist. This is just to say that Noman does not actually exist but he might have existed. Noman is, like all of us, a *possible individual*; it is true of him, and it is likewise true of each of us, that we might have existed. But something more can be said about us that cannot be said about Noman. There is a seemingly important difference between Noman and us. We are actual, Noman is not. Noman is *merely* possible. What does this difference between Noman and us consist in? What is it about us in virtue of which we, but not Noman, may be said to be 'actual'? What is it for something to have the ontological status of being actual, and is there any special metaphysical significance attached to something solely by virtue of its being actual? Is there such a thing as the *property* of existence, or the *property* of actuality—a property that Noman lacks, and that something has solely by virtue of the fact that it exists or is actual? Whatever actuality is, we seem to matter in a way that Noman does not seem to matter at all. (Noman does not matter even to *me*, and we are *brothers*! Well, at least we are brothers across possible worlds.)[2] Does this represent an objective fact about us *vis-à-vis* Noman and his kind, or is it ultimately a form of prejudice and discrimination on our part? Are we objectively better than, or objectively better off than, Noman by virtue of the fact that we have actuality, or solely by virtue of the fact that we exist, whereas he does not? Is it objectively better to have this ontological status called 'actuality' than to lack it? If so, what is it about actuality that makes us count for so much more than Noman? Is actuality something we might have lacked? Specifically, in those possible worlds in which we do not exist, are we not actual? Conversely, in those possible worlds in which Noman exists, is he actual? In a possible world in which Noman exists and I do not, which one of us inhabits the actual world? Does Noman have any properties? Does he lack every property? Do we have any properties in those possible worlds in which we do not exist?

In a sense, the question 'What is it for something to be actual?' has one simple, correct answer: For something to be actual is for it actually to be—that is, for it actually to exist. But this answer only trades one ontological question for two new ones. What is it for something to *be*, or to *exist*, and what is it for something *actually* to be the case? If we can answer these two questions satisfactorily, we will thereby have an answer to the question of what it is to be actual.

Let us begin with the question of existence. Consider first a slightly different question: What exists? Quine pointed out that this time-honored ontological question has its correct answer in a single word: Everything.[3] Does this observation help us with our slightly more difficult question of what existence is? It seems so. If the answer to the question of what exists is the universal quantifier 'everything', then for something to exist is for it to be one of everything. But does this constitute any

---

sufficiency principles of cross-world identity see my *Reference and Essence* (Princeton University Press, 1981), pp. 196–252, especially p. 209f; and 'Modal Paradox: Parts and Counterparts, Points and Counterpoints,' in P. French, T. Uehling, and H. Wettstein, eds., *Midwest Studies in Philosophy XI: Studies in Essentialism* (Minneapolis: University of Minnesota Press, 1986), pp. 75–120.

[2] *Cf.* Salmon, *Reference and Essence* pp. 116–133, on this and other cross-world relations.

[3] In the first paragraph of 'On What There Is,' in Quine's *From a Logical Point of View* (New York: Harper and Row, 1961), pp. 1–19.

sort of progress with respect to our question of what existence is? What does it mean to say that something is "one of everything"?

Modifying Berkeley's famous slogan, Quine gave substance to the idea that what exists is what is covered by the universal quantifier with his equally famous slogan 'To be is to be a value of a variable'.[4] Taken as a response to the question 'What is existence?', Quine's slogan seems at least extensionally correct. Every existing individual is indeed the value of some variable or other, under some cooperative assignment of values to variables, and it would seem that everything that is assigned to a variable as its value is "one of everything," i.e., it exists. But it cannot be seriously maintained that *being*, in the sense of 'existence', simply *is* the state or condition of *being the value of a variable, under some assignment of values to variables*. When Hamlet (pretending the play were nonfictitious) agonized over the question of whether to be or not to be, he was preoccupied with weightier matters than the question of whether or not to be the value of a variable. If there were no variables, would there be nothing? The dinosaurs had existence, but they didn't have variables. Perhaps there were no variables at the time of the dinosaurs for them to be the values of. To be sure, the geometric shapes and patterns that form the lower case italic '*x*', '*y*', and '*z*' existed even then, but were they *variables*, and were functions from them to objects *assignments of values to variables*? If it is supposed that they were, on the grounds that in some future language they are, then it probably should also be said that anything that might conceivably be used as a variable in a possible language is a variable (on the grounds that any such object is a variable in some possible language), and any singulary function from such objects is an assignment of values to variables. If Quine's slogan is understood to mean that for something to exist is for it to be in the range of a function whose domain is a set of objects that might someday serve as variables, one might as well skip the variables and their value-assignments altogether and say that to be is to be an element of a set. But then why not simply say that to be is to be the element of a singleton, or unit set? As explications of existence, these somehow fall flat. But I believe we have strayed from Quine's intended meaning.[5]

Taken literally, it is doubtful that Quine's slogan is even extensionally correct. The dinosaurs may be the values of some of today's variables, under some assignments,

[4] *Ibid.*, p. 15; and *Methods of Logic* (New York: Holt, Rinehart and Winston, Inc., 1972), p. 234.

[5] Quine's maxim does not directly concern the question of what things actually exist; it concerns the ontological commitments of this or that theory or piece of discourse (and by extension, the ontological commitments of this or that theorist or speaker), irrespective of whether the sorts of things to which the theory or discourse is ontologically committed actually exist. Quine's thesis is that a theory or piece of discourse is committed to the existence of things of a given *sort* (and, as a special case, to the existence of a given possible thing) if and only if some things of that sort (or that possible thing) must be counted among the values of variables in a suitable reformulation of the theory or the discourse if the reformulated theory or discourse is to be true. The ontological commitments of a theory or piece of discourse will thus include anything whose existence is explicitly affirmed, but I take it that the point of the thesis is that the ontological commitments of a theory or piece of discourse may outrun the explicit existence avowals. (Otherwise, it would be much simpler to say instead that a theory or piece of discourse is ontologically committed to all things, and to only those things, that are explicitly said to exist in a suitable reformulation of the theory or discourse.) A number of difficulties and problems for Quine's thesis could be raised, though only few will be mentioned here.

but none exist. (The dinosaurs once existed, of course, but sadly none exist today.)
Assignment of past dinosaurs to some present variables is required to give the correct
semantics for a suitable formalization of such sentences as 'There was a dinosaur that
this is a fossil of'[6] or the preceding sentence. If Hamlet (pretending the play were
nonfictitious) had decided not to be, he would not have ceased to be the value of a
variable. Quine's slogan might be understood instead as the claim that to be (or to
exist) at a time t in a possible world w is to be the value of a variable under some
assignment of values to variables *with respect to t and w*. At least this is extensionally
correct. But it puts the cart before the horse. The notion of a function being an
assignment of values to variables *with respect to* a time t *and* a possible world w is
defined in terms of the notion of existence: an assignment of values to variables is an
assignment with respect to t and w if and only if everything it assigns exists at t in w.

My claim that past individuals are the present values of variables even though
these past individuals no longer exist may conflict with the doctrine that to be is to
be a value of a variable, but it does not conflict with the alternative doctrine
(extracted from Quine's observation that the universal quantifier correctly answers
the question 'What exists?') that to be is to be "one of everything" (whatever that
means). The universal and existential quantifiers must not be confused with the
variables they bind.[7] A (typical) universal generalization $\ulcorner(\forall\alpha)\phi_\alpha\urcorner$ is true under an
assignment of values to variables s, with respect to a given time t, if and only if every

---

[6] *Cf.* David Kaplan, 'Bob and Carol and Ted and Alice,' in K. J. J. Hintikka, J. M. E. Moravcsik,
and P. Suppes, eds., *Approaches to Natural Language* (Dordrecht: D. Reidel, 1983), pp. 490–518,
appendix x, at pp. 503–505 and especially p. 516, note 15.

Quine's thesis mentioned above in note 5 appears to have the false consequence that if this
sentence concerning a particular fossil is true, then things that have been dinosaurs exist today.
(Immortal dinosaur souls?)

It has been suggested to me that Quine's actual proposed criterion of ontological commitment
avoids this difficulty since the criterion is restricted to one's commitments concerning *existence at
some time or other*, rather than to one's (stronger) commitments concerning existence *simpliciter*, i.e.,
commitments concerning what sorts of things are in the condition or state that something comes
into when it begins to exist and falls out of when it ceases to exist. Although I have been unable to
find an explicit and clear formulation of this restriction among Quine's writings on his proposed
criterion for ontological commitment, this tenseless construal seems truer to the spirit of his explicit
(and not altogether independent) views concerning canonical notation, verb tenses, and the regimentation of ordinary language. See for example 'Mr Strawson on Logical Theory,' in Quine's *The
Ways of Paradox* (New York: Random House, 1966), pp. 135–155, at pp. 143–146. (Thanks to
Peter van Inwagen for providing this reference.) If this restricted criterion accords better with
Quine's actual intent, his thesis would be less deceptively (albeit less neatly) encapsulated as follows:
'To-be-or-to-have-been-or-going-to-be is to be the value of a variable.'

Unfortunately, aside from ugliness of formulation, this leaves us with no criterion for one's
commitments concerning existence or being *per se*, as opposed to one's commitments concerning
existence-at-some-time-or-other. What is desired is a tense-sensitive criterion that commits one who
utters the past tensed sentence 'There used to be (things that at some time or other are) sea serpents'
at a time t to the existence *prior to* t of (things that at some time or other are) sea serpents, and one
who utters the present tensed 'There are (things that at some time or other are) sea serpents' at t to
the existence *at* t of (things that at some time or other are) sea serpents. Under the suggested
interpretation, Quine's criterion is insensitive to these differences in tense, assigning to utterers (at t)
of either tensed sentence the very same (timeless) ontological commitment (at t) to (things that at
some time or other are) sea serpents.

[7] Quine appears to fall into just this confusion, for example p. 13 (where he speaks of 'the
things over which the bound variable "something" ranges'), and elsewhere.

(past, present, or future) individual i that exists at t is such that ϕ_α is true under the assignment s', with respect to t, where s' is the assignment that assigns i to α and is otherwise exactly the same as s. The assignment s may already assign individuals that do not exist at t to certain variables; hence, the assignments s' may also assign individuals that do not exist at t to some variables, but not to α. The universal quantifier restricts its attention (typically) to assignments that assign existing individuals to the variable it binds. Existence *per se* matters nothing to the variables themselves or their value-assignments. Not only are past individuals the present values of variables, but future individuals are as well. Some possible assignments of values to variables even assign Noman as value to some variables. In fact, some modal constructions require such assignments, e.g., 'The gametes S and E might have been united in the normal manner to develop into an individual.'[8] It is the quantifier, and not the variable it binds, that insists on nothing but the existent. And it insists on nothing but the existent only as values for its adjacent variable, not as values for other variables in its less immediate vicinity.

It is a mistake in any case to attempt to explicate a metaphysical notion by means of essentially semantic notions. (Again, I believe this is not Quine's intent. See note 5.) One could say that to be is to be an element of the union of the extension of an English quantifier. Why not? One might as well say that to be a person is to be an element of the extension in English of 'person', to know a given proposition is to stand in the relation expressed by 'knows' in English to that proposition, and so on. For one thing, we are wrong: the attributes of existence, being a person, and knowing are not essentially semantic in nature. For another, we are still left wondering how the extension of a quantifier in English is secured. What feature must individuals possess if a class of them is to be an element of the extension of the English quantifier 'there is'? It need not be a mistake, however, to use (rather than to mention) an English quantifier in attempting to explicate existence. We need to find an adequate way to understand the slogan 'To be is to be one of everything'. Some progress is made toward answering the question 'What is existence?' if our concept of existence can be defined in terms of our concept of *everything*.

II

Philosophers who address the questions of what it is for an individual to exist, or what it is for an individual to be actual, often do so with reference to the fallacy they

---

[8] Quine's thesis mentioned above in note 5, if I understand it correctly, has the false consequence that if this sentence concerning S and E is true, then some individual who might have developed from the union of these gametes actually exists (at some time or other). *Cf.* note 6. These apparent consequences of Quine's thesis may demonstrate that his criterion of ontological commitment actually applies not to this or that theory, as Quine intends, but to the semantic metatheory for a suitable language in which this or that theory is formulated. Even thus construed, however, the criterion gives at most only a *sufficient* condition for ontological commitment of the metatheory *as augmented with the affirmation of the truth of the object theory*; no necessary condition is given. In fact, I believe that this condition is not even a sufficient condition. When I assign Noman to some variable as its value I commit myself to Noman's suitability as a value for variables, not to his actual existence.

have uncovered in the classical Ontological Argument for God's existence. Indeed, the Ontological Argument is useful as a vehicle by which this and other issues in ontology and the philosophy of logic may be introduced and sharpened. In what is perhaps its simplest form, the Ontological Argument is the following:

(1a) The divine individual is divine.
(1b) Any individual that is divine exists.

Therefore,

(1c) The divine individual exists.

Let us call this 'Version 1'. The term 'divine' serves here as a schematic term, which is to be interpreted relative to a context in which an argument of a particular Ontological Arguer is in question. If our concern is with Descartes's argument from his fifth *Meditation*, 'divine individual' is to be interpreted to mean *individual that has every perfection* (with 'perfection' interpreted in Descartes's sense). If our concern is with Anselm's instance of the argument schema (or at least the best known of Anselm's instances, as given in Chapter II of his *Proslogion*), 'divine individual' is to be interpreted to mean *individual whose magnitude of greatness exceeds any other possible magnitude of greatness* (with 'possible' interpreted in Anselm's sense of 'conceivable' and 'great' interpreted in his sense of 'great'). For present purposes, we may assume that, in each case, the relevant concept of divinity is such that it is provable, or otherwise manifest *a priori*, that there cannot be two or more divine individuals. The Ontological Arguer assumes premise (1a) as a logical or manifest truth, and contends that premise (1b) is likewise an analytic or conceptual or demonstrable truth.

Since the first premise is sometimes regarded by the Ontological Arguer as a logical truth, the argument may be formulated with the first premise left tacit, not included as an explicit premise of the argument and not supported by further, additional argument. Anselm provided an explicit argument in support of the premise, although his argument clearly indicates that he regarded the truth of the premise as manifest, a truth that even the atheist 'fool' is convinced of. When the premise is made explicit however, it should immediately strike the reader that there is a problem with it. The atheist and the agnostic doubt (by disbelieving and by suspending judgement, respectively) that there exists any divine individual in the first place. Why should they be expected to acquiesce in the assertion that the divine individual is divine?

The intended import of Version 1 is apt to be lost on the reader unless he or she understands a critical feature of the argument: it purports to involve quantification over more things than are dreamt of in Quine's philosophy of what exists. A more explicit and more sophisticated version of the Ontological Argument is the following:

(2a) The divine possible individual is a divine possible individual.
(2b) Any possible individual that is divine exists.

Therefore,

(2c) The divine possible individual exists.

Let us call this 'Version 2'. The difference between the two versions is that Version 2 explicitly involves, or at least explicitly attempts to involve, so-called *possibilist* quantification rather than so-called *actualist* quantification. That is, version 2 explicitly purports to employ quantification over all that might have existed, including what does not exist, rather than merely over all that does exist. The reader should take special note of the import of the premise of Version 2. The conclusion of the argument is supposed to be not merely that the divine possible individual *might have* been an existent divine individual, but that it *actually does* exist and *actually is* divine. Hence premise (2a) must be read in such a way that it asserts that the possible individual that *actually* is divine *actually* is divine, and premise (2b) must be read in such a way that it asserts that any possible individual that *actually* is divine *actually* exists. Both premise are intended to be taken in such a way as not to presuppose the real existence of any divine individual. So understood, whatever else may be problematic with the argument's first premise, it is not clear that it simply begs the question against the atheist or the agnostic. In fact, one of the philosophical issues raised by the Ontological Argument is precisely whether one can predicate a property (in this case, divinity) of a possible individual without presupposing the real existence of the possible individual. The argument cannot be summarily dismissed on the grounds of an uncontroversial prohibition against predicating properties of possible individuals whose existence is not to be presupposed. Indeed, there are some properties that can be predicated of possible individuals (such as Noman) without presupposing the existence of these individuals—for example the property of not existing, and its entailments.

Of course, in attributing Version 2 to a particular historical figure, such as Anselm or Descartes, some charity may be required in interpreting the modal locutions involved; the term 'possible' in the phrase 'possible individual' need not be interpreted to mean the modal logician's *metaphysical possibility* (although, it probably should be so interpreted for a contemporary Ontological Arguer). Anselm's instance of Version 2 is obtained by interpreting the phrase 'possible individual' in Anselm's sense of 'thing that exists *in intellectu*' (and by interpreting 'divine individual' to mean *individual whose magnitude of greatness exceeds any other conceivable magnitude of greatness*). We may assume here that the concept of divinity is such that it is provable or somehow manifest *a priori* that no two possible individuals are actually divine. We will return to the question of whether the atheist or the agnostic need deny that there is one possible individual who is actually divine.

Once possibilist quantification is admitted, we may pose Quine's ontological question in a new light: What possible individuals exist? Quine's simple and correct answer to the question 'What exists?', if resubmitted, apparently becomes simply incorrect—provided it is interpreted (contrary to Quine's intent) as the possibilist rather than the actualist universal quantifier. Not every possible thing exists. Or so it would seem. In any case, it is not necessary that everything actually exists; there might have been individuals that do not actually exist. Noman, for instance.

Is the English word 'everything' the actualist universal quantifier, or is it the possibilist universal quantifier? Is our ordinary, everyday concept of *everything* the concept of everything that exists, or is it the concept of everything that might have existed, including what does not actually exist? Is it somehow (ambiguously) both? Or is it none of the above? The doctrine that the standard quantifiers of natural language (the

English words 'everything', 'something', etc.) are possibilist quantifiers is sometimes called 'possibilism', and the doctrine that they are actualist quantifiers is sometimes called 'actualism'.[9] In observing that the standard English universal quantifier is the correct answer to the question 'What exists?', Quine proclaims his endorsement of actualism, and assumes his readers agree. I believe that actualism is indeed the predominant view among philosophers of logic and philosophers of language. My own view is that the quantifiers of English are *typically* actualist (and *presentist*, i.e., ranging with respect to a time *t* over only those things that exist at *t*)—that among potential restrictions on our use of quantification, restriction to existing things is, so to speak, the 'default value'—but that the domain of quantification may be, and very often is, adjusted either upward or downward in various ways, at the drop of a hat. (Consider our readiness to quantify over no longer existing objects in discourse about the past, and for instance in 'This is a fossil of some dinosaur'.) Still, I believe that our ordinary, everyday concept of *everything* (*simpliciter*) is the concept of everything that exists—no more and no less—and I shall assume this construal throughout most of this essay. In particular, then, I assume that it is legitimate to rely on the concept of actualist universal quantification in attempting to explicate what existence is, for we are merely relying on our ordinary concept of *everything*. (Indeed, unless we may rely on our prior grasp of actualist quantification, I doubt that a philosophically satisfactory definition or analysis of existence can be given. See note 16.) I shall not assume, however, that there is anything illegitimate about possibilist quantifiers *per se* or about the concept of *every possible individual*. Kit Fine has shown that the possibilist universal and existential quantifiers are fully definable using the standard modal operators in tandem with actualist quantifiers over both individuals and "propositions" *qua* sets of possible worlds, or alternatively, using standard modal operators in tandem with actualist quantification over both individuals and possible worlds together with a predicate for a possible world's being *realized*.[10] In fact, the import of a possibilist quantificational assertion can often be easily expressed using only first-order machinery through the judicious use of modal operators (including an operator for something's actually being the case) in tandem with actualist quantifiers only over individuals (excluding possible worlds). Occurrences of possibilist quantifiers in this essay are indicated throughout by modal adornment, in the manner of 'every possible individual', and so on. (Do not read 'there is a possible individual that is such-and-such' as meaning that there *exists* an individual that is both possible and such-and-such. Instead it means that there *might have existed* an individual that *actually is* such-and-such, etc.) Unadorned occurrences of English quantificational locutions are to be read actualistically (except in certain passages in Section VI below, where the phrase 'every object' takes on a distinctly Meinongian air).

The actualist universal quantifier 'everything' remains a correct answer to the question 'What possible individuals exist?', but it is not a very useful response. It

---

[9] These are not the only doctrines that go by these 'ism''s; nor are these the only 'ism''s that these doctrines go by.

[10] See Kit Fine, 'Prior on the Construction of Possible Worlds and Instants,' postscript to A. N. Prior and K. Fine, *Worlds, Times and Selves* (Amherst: University of Massachusetts Press, 1977), pp. 116–161. For example, the locution ⌜Some possible individual is ϕ⌝ may be defined as ⌜The possible world *w* that is realized is such that there might have existed an individual that, in *w*, is ϕ⌝.

does not tell us, for example, whether Noman is one of the possible individuals that exists—except by telling us that he exists if and only if he is one of everything. It is not yet clear what it means to say that a possible individual is "one of everything." Descartes's *cogito ergo sum* may be taken as specifying one possible individual that enjoys the ontological status of real existence (*viz.*, oneself). The Ontological Argument purports to specify another, as do existence proofs in mathematics. Unlike Quine's actualist–universal–quantifier response, however, these responses offer only particular instances, not an exhaustive specification. The question 'What possible individuals exist?' may be posed as a request for a *philosophical analysis* of the concept of existence, in the sense of an illuminating specification of a necessary and sufficient condition *C* such that, necessarily, a possible individual exists if and only if it satisfies *C*. This request is inextricably tied to our question of what existence is. What is it for a possible individual to be 'one of everything'?

The explicit use of possibilist quantification in Version 2 of the Ontological Argument may shift the critic's focus from the first premise of the argument to the second. Once possibilist quantification is admitted, it might be objected that premise (2b) is not a conceptual truth, on the grounds that it is logically possible for there to be a merely possible individual that is divine but does not exist. If premise (2a) is to be taken as manifest even to the atheist, and if premise (2b) is to be taken as strong enough to ensure validity for Version 2, then surely something needs to be said by the Ontological Arguer to assure the reader that premise (2b) is indeed a conceptual truth. In fact, historically, Ontological Arguers have offered support for their premise (2b) by means of another *a priori* argument. Sometimes this supporting argument is very brief and mentioned only in passing ('Existence is a perfection'). Sometimes it is the very heart of the Ontological Arguer's more general argument. Anselm's support for his premise (2b) came in the form of the notorious argument that, necessarily, the magnitude of greatness of any possible individual that exists exceeds its actual magnitude of greatness if it does not actually exist; hence, any possible individual whose actual magnitude of greatness exceeds any other possible magnitude of greatness, since it could exist, must exist—otherwise, its actual magnitude of greatness would not exceed its own possible magnitude of greatness. (Got it?) That should satisfy the fool who doubts that premise (2b) is conceptually or demonstrably true.

It would be in the spirit of the Ontological Argument, however, to reply to the objection that premise (2b) is not a conceptual truth by pointing out that, if the objector's concept of divinity does not already include the concept of existence as a necessary or entailed condition (so that the objector does not read premise (2b) as a conceptual or logically demonstrable truth), we may form the new concept of *exidivinity*, defined in terms of the objector's concept of divinity thus:

exidivine =$_{def.}$ divine and existent.

Now we replace the word 'divine' by 'exidivine' throughout Version 2, to obtain Version 3:

(3a) The exidivine possible individual is an exidivine possible individual.
(3b) Any possible individual that is exidivine exists.

Therefore,

(3c) The exidivine possible individual exists.

Using this simple strategy, the Ontological Arguer can remove any need to support the second premise by further *a priori* argument. Even the fool is convinced of the truth of (3b); the new second premise is beyond all reasonable doubt.

Well, premise (3b) is beyond all reasonable doubt provided we can be persuaded that the concept of exidivinity is a genuine and legitimate concept. Ay, there's the rub. In fact, in attempting to trivialize the argument's second premise in this way, the Ontological Arguer shifts the critical focus from the second premise back again to the first. Version 3 apparently attempts to treat existence in such a way that real existence may be proved of a possible individual simply by conceiving of it as existent.

The Ontological Argument may be useful as a device for introducing and discussing various philosophical issues, but taken polemically as a contribution to the debate over God's existence it is surely worthless. It is appropriate that Anselm should label his opponent 'the fool', since it is difficult to imagine a genuine atheist or agnostic who is not also a fool being converted to theism on the strength of this piece of sophistry. That the Ontological Argument (taken as a purported proof of God's existence) involves some error, there can be no doubt. This was conclusively established during Anselm's lifetime in a *reductio ad absurdum* by his formidable critic Gaunilo, who first observed that if the Ontological Argument succeeds in demonstrating its conclusion, then one can also prove the existence of a fantasy island by an exactly analogous argument.[11] Unfortunately, this *reductio* does not pinpoint the error in the Ontological Argument. The credit for having located the fallacy in the argument is often attributed to Kant, who purported to debunk the argument with his observation that existence is not a predicate that can be legitimately included in the definition or concept of something. Kant's refutation is widely regarded as conclusive, or at least sound, as regards the versions of the Ontological Argument discussed here. One exceedingly plausible idea that lends support to this refutation is that one cannot create new entities simply by defining them into existence. If existence were regarded as an admissible defining property or concept, exactly on a par with such mundane concepts as being green-eyed or being an island, then it would be possible to initiate merely possible individuals such as Noman into the elite club of Existence, simply by defining them as existing. Your next stop: the Twilight Zone.

Kant's observation that existence is not an admissible defining predicate was echoed by both of the two greatest figures of contemporary analytic philosophy, Gottlob Frege and Bertrand Russell—basking in the glow of their powerful, new quantification theory, with its precise and mathematically respectable notion of existential quantification. In the final footnote to '*Function und Begriff*' (1891) Frege wrote: 'The ontological proof of God's existence suffers from the fallacy of treating

---

[11] 'On Behalf of the Fool,' in A. Plantinga ed., *The Ontological Argument* (Garden City; Doubleday & Company, Inc., 1965), pp. 6–13, at pp. 11–12.

existence as a first-level concept.' This is essentially the same idea he advanced seven years earlier in his *Grundlagen der Arithmetik*, where he wrote: 'Because existence is a property of concepts the ontological argument for the existence of God breaks down' (section 53). Russell was even more emphatic in his lectures on logical atomism:

When you take any propositional function and assert of it . . . that it is sometimes true, that gives you the fundamental meaning of 'existence'. You may express it by saying that there is at least one value of x for which the propositional function is true. . . . Existence is essentially a property of a propositional function. It means that the propositional function is true in at least one instance. ('The Philosophy of Logical Atomism,' in Russell's *Logic and Knowledge*, ed., R. C. Marsh, at p. 232.)

. . . As regards the actual things there are in the world, there is nothing at all you can say about them that in any way corresponds to this notion of existence. It is a sheer mistake to say that there is anything analogous to existence that you can say about them. . . . There is no sort of point in a predicate which could not conceivably be false. I mean, it is perfectly clear that, if there were such a thing as this existence of individuals that we talk of, it would be absolutely impossible for it not to apply, and that is the characteristic of a mistake. (*ibid.*, 241.)

. . . there is a vast amount of philosophy that rests upon the notion that existence is, so to speak, a property that you can attribute to things, and that the things that exist have the property of existence and the things that do not exist do not. That is rubbish . . . (*ibid.*, p. 252. See also Russell's *A Critical Exposition of the Philosophy of Leibniz*, London: George Allen and Unwin Ltd, 1971, at pp. 174–175; and his *Introduction to Mathematical Philosophy*, London: George Allen and Unwin Ltd, 1953, at pp. 203–204.)

The problem with the Ontological Argument—according to Kant, Frege, and Russell—is that by invoking the alleged concept of exidivinity in talking about an *exidivine possible individual*, it illegitimately treats existence as an admissible concept or property of individuals, on a par with such mundane concepts or properties as being green-eyed or being an island, thereby violating its proper status (as a second-level property or concept of first-level concepts or of propositional functions, or as a pre-requisite for having any properties at all, or as something of the sort). Alas, the founders of mathematical logic would apparently cast out Descartes's lovely little *cogito ergo sum* alongside his Ontological Argument. The quest for an answer to the question 'What possible individuals exist?' begins to look more and more quixotic.

III

Schopenhauer gave expression to a very common reaction to the Ontological Argument when he called it 'a charming joke.'[12] The argument's propounders, however, do not offer the argument as a curious philosophical parlor trick or riddle; they advance it in all seriousness as a deductive proof of a thesis that most of us had been trained to believe since childhood, with very little in the way of rational

[12] In *The Fourfold Root of the Principle of Sufficient Reason*, in Plantinga, 1965, pp. 65–67.

justification. The thesis it purports to prove is extremely implausible—at least for (i.e., with respect to the epistemic situation of) those who are able to break free of their childhood religious training and for those who never had any—and for that reason alone the thesis needs something like evidence or argument for its epistemic justification. If there is any area in which philosophers are to be held to a higher standard than nonphilosophers, it is in providing justification for their otherwise implausible religious beliefs.[13] Whereas the Ontological Argument (taken polemically as a purported proof of God's existence) has always struck me as philosophy at its least dignified, I have never seen any merit whatsoever to the Kantian sort of reply recounted in the preceding section. Furthermore Descartes's *cogito* has always struck me as an excellent example of philosophy at its shining best. Let us distinguish three separate Kantian theses about existence:

(*i*)   The English verb 'exist' (and its cognates) represents, from the point of view of logic, not a first-order predicate of English, but a logical quantifier;

(*ii*) There is no property or concept of existence for individuals;

and

(*iii*) It is illegitimate to invoke the term 'exist' or the alleged property or concept of existence in forming the concept of something or in specifying one of the necessary conditions in the definition of something—so that one cannot legitimately define something as *the existent such-and-such*, or as *a such-and-such that exists*.[14]

---

[13] It is often argued (most notably by Alvin Plantinga) that belief in God is no less rationally justified that many other unproved and contestable philosophical beliefs that are widely shared and usually regarded as knowledge, such as the belief in other minds or the belief that there is an external, material world. See for example A. Plantinga, *The Nature of Necessity* (Oxford: Oxford University Press, 1974), at p. 221. The issue of the rationality of belief in God cannot be discussed adequately here, of course, but it should be noted that historically, the function and role of the Ontological Argument in philosophy is integrally related to the view that the hypothesis of God's existence requires substantial justification, in the form of something like proof, if it is to be rationally adopted. The observation that many external existence beliefs usually regarded as knowledge are based on very little in the way of decisive evidence seems both correct and epistemologically significant. However, there is an epistemologically important point of disanalogy between belief in God and belief in other minds or in the external world: The hypotheses of other minds and of the external world are extremely plausible (even with respect to the epistemic situation of someone who has not been philosophically indoctrinated since childhood concerning other minds or the external world), whereas the hypothesis of God's existence is fundamentally implausible (at least for those who are able to break free of their childhood religious indoctrination or who never had any), or at most, not significantly more plausible than the hypothesis of the real existence of the mythological Olympian gods of old, or than other superstitious or occult hypotheses. Indeed, it is difficult to imagine a nonphilosopher who did not believe in other minds or in the external world, yet there are masses of nonphilosophers who do not believe in God. It is not the contestability or unprovability of the hypothesis of God's existence as much as its intrinsic implausibility that renders the hypothesis in need of evidence or proof for its justification.

[14] In calling a thesis 'Kantian', I do not mean that it was in fact held or endorsed by Kant, only that it is in the spirit of theses often attributed to Kant.

There is, of course, the fourth Kantian thesis that the alleged property or concept of existence is not a predicate of German, or any other natural language, but it is difficult to see how this truism could be thought to offer any food for thought to the likes of Anselm and Descartes.

Insofar as Kant, Frege, or Russell, or their followers, have held any or all of theses (*i*), (*ii*), and (*iii*), it is virtually provable that they are completely mistaken.

It is widely recognized that thesis (*i*) is false. Any number of commentators have noted that the term 'exists' is fully and completely definable in formal logic as a first-order predicate of individuals, using standard, actualist, Frege-Russellian existential quantification. Its definition (which also employs the logical notions of identity and abstraction but nothing more) is the following:

$$(\lambda x)(\exists y)[x = y].$$

Less formally, the English word 'exists' may be regarded as being defined by the phrase 'is identical with something', or more simply, 'is something'. This yields an aternative way to give substance to the idea that to be is to be one of everything: To be one of everything is to be something. The phrase 'is something', in the sense of 'is identical with something', is paradigmatic of the sort of expression that, from the point of view of logic, would ordinarily be regarded as a first-order predicate of individuals. (Of course, it would not be regarded as a *simple* first-order predicate; it is a compound expression.) It satisfies every reasonable logical, grammatical, or semantic test or criterion for first-order predicatehood. In any case, the expression displayed above is unquestionably a logical first-order predicate. The fact that it (correctly) applies to every existing individual whatsoever, and does so by the rules of semantics alone, does nothing to threaten its status as a full-fledged predicate of individuals. On the contrary, the fact that the principles of classical semantics assign a class of individuals as an extension to this expression confirms that it is indeed a first-order predicate, and one of pure logic at that. Furthermore, the fact that its extension in any model is just the domain of individuals in that model confirms that it is the very predicate we want. If any individual in the domain of any model were left out of the predicate's extension, then whatever property or concept the predicate would be an expression for, it would not be an expression for the existence of individuals.

Although it has been less often noted, it should be equally obvious that there is a concept of existence for individuals, and that there is a special property—the property of existing—that an individual has only by virtue of the fact that it exists. Each of the notions involved in the definition of the predicate 'exists' is precise and mathematically respectable; each of the expressions making up the definiens has a definite sense or content. In fact, each of the three notions involved—existential quantification, identity, and abstraction—is precise in a way that many everyday notions are not. Existential quantification is fully definable in terms of the logical notions of *not* and *everything*, as follows:

$$(\lambda F)[\sim(\forall x) \sim Fx].$$

(More accurately, the occurrence of the existential quantifier in any existential generalization $\ulcorner(\exists \alpha)\phi_\alpha\urcorner$ may be contextually defined by $\ulcorner\sim(\forall_\alpha)\sim\phi_\alpha\urcorner$.) Identity is just the binary equivalence relation that each individual stands in to itself and to no other individual. Abstraction is just the formal operation by which a compound first-order predicate is formed from an open sentence of formal logic. The English expressions 'something' and 'is identical with' are paradigmatic of the sort of expression that is ordinarily regarded as expressing an attribute (property or relation) or concept as its sense or content. If any expressions express concepts or attributes as their sense or content, these do. Their senses or contents are easily specified. The sense or content of the second-order predicate (quantifier) 'something' is the property of classes of individuals of not being empty, the property of having at least one element. More accurately, the sense or content of 'something', with respect to a given time *t*, is the temporally indexed property or concept of not being empty at *t*. The sense or content of the phrase 'is identical with', with respect to a given time *t*, is the temporally indexed binary relation of being one and the very same thing at *t*, or the corresponding concept.[15]

If a set of expressions that express concepts or attributes as their sense or content are appropriately combined to form a new expression, the compound expression thus formed has a sense or content that is determined in a certain way by the senses or contents of the combined component expressions. Hence the phrase 'is identical with something', and the displayed expression, express a definite property or concept as their (shared) sense or content. This is the property or concept of *being identical with something* (or more simply, the property or concept of *being something*). It is this property or concept that is the sense or content of the predicate 'exists'. And it is this property or concept that we call 'existence'. We have here our answer to the question of what it is for something to be, or to exist. *To be is to be identical with something.*

I do not mean, of course, that the predicate 'exists' expresses the property or concept of being identical with some *particular* thing, such as Socrates or Russell. Such properties as these are nowadays called 'haecceities' or 'thisnesses' (Robert Adams), and are expressed by such phrases as 'is identical with Socrates' and 'is identical with Russell'. The property or concept of existence expressed by the predicate 'exists' involves existential quantification. It is the property or concept of being identical with *something or other*, the feature that an individual has only in virtue of the fact that not everything is distinct from it. More accurately, the sense or content of the term 'exists', with respect to a given time *t*, is the property of concept of being something at *t*, the property that an individual has only in virtue of that fact that, at *t*, not everything is distinct from it.

It stands to reason that the first-order concept of existence for individuals should involve the Frege-Russellian higher-level logical notion of *something or other*. To be is to be identical with something. Not to be is to be distinct from everything. More succinctly, to be is to be something, not to be is to be nothing. To be and not to be: these are the answers.[16]

---

[15] For an argument that the identity predicate is not vague, see Salmon, *Reference*, pp. 243–245; and the appendix to Salmon, 'Modal Paradox.'

[16] I have said that the quantifiers 'everything' and 'something' of standard English do not have a fixed domain, and may be restricted in various ways according to the context of use, but that the default value is restriction to existing things. This suggests a treatment of the English quantifiers on the model of the indexical phrases 'everything of *that* sort' and 'something of *that* sort', to be supplemented or completed by a contextual indication or 'demonstration' of the sort in question, where no explicit demonstration constitutes by default a contextual indication of the sort *existing thing*. On this picture, the "definition" provided by the slogan 'To be is to be identical with something' makes the 'is' of being an indexical predicate of individuals, shorthand for 'is identical

As far as I can see, there is nothing at all to be said for either thesis (*i*) or thesis (*ii*). In any case, despite their impressive credentials, neither Kant nor Frege nor Russell has any persuasive argument to offer for either of these theses.

Thesis (*iii*) is no better off. There is not a single plausible reason why the predicate 'exists', or the property or concept of existence, should be precluded from the definition of something or from the formation of some inclusive concept, such as the concept of an existent fantasy island or that of an existent lion. Why should *any* concept be precluded from the formation of more complex ones? The concept of an existent fantasy island is the concept of a fantasy island that is not distinct from everything, and the concept of an existent lion is that of a lion that is not distinct from everything. The concept of an existent lion is every bit as legitimate, *qua* concept, as the concept of a green-eyed lion. Similarly, we may define the term 'exiunicorn' as follows:

exiunicorn $=_{def.}$ unicorn that exists.

Let us call the procedure of forming such concepts or definitions as these 'existential definition'. What can possibly be wrong with existential definition? If there is anything illegitimate in our definition of an exiunicorn, it comes from 'unicorn', not from 'exists'.[17] Philosophers often form or invoke complex concepts that include existence as a necessary condition. We have the concept, for example, of a *temporary existent*, i.e., an individual that exists but does not always exist. We also have the concept of a contingent existent, i.e., an individual that exists but does not have necessary existence. These concepts are perfectly legitimate, and indeed, extremely useful for certain purposes.

Saul Kripke's powerful "schmidentity" form of argument can be applied here.[18] Suppose my claims that existence is the property or concept of being identical with something and that the English word 'exists' is a first-order predicate for this concept are mistaken. Then take instead the expression '$(\lambda x)(\exists y)[x = y]$'. As I have already said, this is unquestionably a logical first-order predicate. By the principles of semantics alone, this predicate (correctly) applies, with respect to any time t and possible w, to everything that exists at t in w, and to nothing else. Following Kripke, we may abbreviate this predicate by the word 'schmexists', and we may call the property or concept that is the sense or content of this predicate 'schmexistence'. There is absolutely no reason in the world why we cannot use this predicate in

with something of that sort'. Indeed, the 'is' of being in English does seem to display the same sort of context-sensitivity as the quantifiers 'everything' and 'something'. It is only when the demonstrative element takes its default value that the slogan becomes a 'definition' of the 'is' of *existence*. The result is a special sort of ostensive definition, rather than a nominal definition, one employing a peculiar sort of ostension-by-default. Given this picture of the inter-relations among the quantifiers, the 'is' of being, and the 'is' of existence, it is doubtful that a philosophically satisfactory nominal definition of the 'is' of existence can be given. (I have not said how far this picture should be maintained.)

[17] See Saul Kripke, *Naming and Necessity* (Harvard University Press, 1980), pp. 24, 156–158.

[18] *Ibid.*, p. 108; and 'Speaker's Reference and Semantic Reference,' in P. French, T. Uehling, and H. Wettstein, eds., *Contemporary Perspectives in the Philosophy of Language* (Minneapolis: University of Minnesota Press, 1979), pp. 6–27, at p. 16.

defining new expressions, or why we cannot invoke the concept of schmexistence in forming more complex concepts, as often as we like. The following expression, for example, is perfectly well-formed and meaningful:

$$(\lambda z)[(\lambda x)(\exists y)[x = y](z) \, \& \sim \Box (\lambda x)(\exists y)[x = y](z)].$$

This is a predicate for the concept of contingent existence. Exactly analogously, we may say that something is *schmexidivine* if it is divine and identical with something. We are perfectly free to use either of these defined notions in our reasoning. Who is to stop us?

If the best that Kant and the founders of mathematical logic can do to block the Ontological Argument is to prohibit existential definition, their response to the argument constitutes nothing more than an especially arrogant form of religious persecution. Let the Kantians scream 'Blue murder!' as often they please, existential definitions are perfectly legitimate.

It may be plausibly argued that there is no point in performing an existential definition. It is true, for example, that the concept of an existent lion is in some sense not very different from the concept of a lion, and as Kant pointed out, a hundred existent dollars is not worth one penny more than a hundred dollars. (I find it impossible to agree with him, however, that a hundred existent dollars is not worth one penny more than a hundred merely possible dollars. If all my dollar bills were merely possible, I would gladly trade them for just one existent dollar bill.) How does this show anything illegitimate about the concept of an existent lion or about that of an existent dollar? At most, it only shows that such concepts are superfluous, that they lack a *raison d'etre*, not that they are somehow illegitimately formed. I doubt that it even shows this much: Consider any class that has me as an element—{Nathan Salmon}, for example (the unit class that has me as its only element). When I am dead and gone, this class will no longer exist. It will not be an existent class. It is far from clear, however, that it will not be a class of any kind. I believe that it will still be a class after I am gone, and that I will still be an element of it (although, of course, since I will no longer exist, there will not be anything that is an element of it and it will not have any elements). Irrespective of one's philosophical disposition toward the (admittedly somewhat bizarre) question of whether an existent class can become an nonexistent one, the very fact that we can raise a substantive (albeit bizarre) question of whether a given such-and-such remains a such-and-such in certain circumstances in which it does not exist indicates that there is perfect legitimacy to the concept of an existent such-and-such, *qua* concept. My view that, at some time in the future, singleton me will still be a class but no longer an existent class, whether correct or incorrect, involves just such a concept, as does the view of anyone who denies that singleton me will ever be a nonexistent class.

Furthermore, if the Ontological Arguers were correct, there would be yet another, and no less significant, purpose that may be served by forming complex concepts that include the concept of existence. The charge that existential definition is pointless, in a sense, begs the question against Anselm, Descartes, *et al.*

IV

Version 3 of the Ontological Argument is unscathed by Kant's alleged refutation. Moreover, although its second premise is not beyond all possible doubt, it is beyond all reasonable doubt.

Well, its second premise is beyond all reasonable doubt provided we can make sense of the possibilist phrase 'any possible individual'. The use of possibilist quantification offends the sensibilities of some actualists, and may obfuscate the evaluation of the argument as valid or invalid. It would be desirable to eliminate somehow the possibilist quantification of Version 3.

That is something we can do (at least to the extent demanded for present purposes), through the judicious use of modal operators and standard actualist quantification over individuals (and by assuming Russell's Theory of Descriptions in order to explicate the description 'the exidivine possible individual' by means of quantification and identity).[19] In removing possibilist quantification from the argument, one must be sensitive to possible misinterpretations of the premise and conclusion. Recall the import of the premise of Version 2. The same is true of Version 3, replacing 'divine' by 'exidivine': conclusion (3c) is supposed to be not merely that the exidivine possible individual *might have* been an existent divine individual, but that it *actually does* exist and *actually is* divine. Hence premise (3a) must be read in such a way that it asserts that the possible individual that *actually* is exidivine *actually* is exidivine, and premise (2b) must be read in such a way that it asserts that any possible individual that *actually* is exidivine *actually* exists. An actualist rendering of Version 3, then, is the following:

(4a) There might have been an individual x such that: x, and actually necessarily only x, is actually exidivine.

(4b) Necessarily, every individual x is such that, actually, if x is exidivine then x exists.

Therefore,

(4c) There might have been an individual x such that: (*i*) x, and actually necessarily only x, is actually exidivine; and (*ii*) x actually exists.

Let us call this 'Version 4'. It is what Version 1 becomes when it is submitted to regimentation in accordance with contemporary standards of rigor, with an aim to satisfying, certain reasonable formal desiderata. Version 4 is a valid modal argument, one that involves actualist quantification. And its second premise is now beyond all reasonable doubt.

Yet Gaunilo demonstrated that the argument must involve some error. If existential definition is not the source of the error, what is?

---

[19] See note 10. Fine's results combined with Russell's Theory of Descriptions enable one to secure the effect of referring by definite description to possible but nonexistent individuals. The locution ⌜The possible individual that is ϕ is ψ⌝ may be defined as ⌜The possible world w that is realized is such that there might have been an individual x such that, x and in w necessarily only x is ϕ in w, and x is ψ in w⌝.

Here again, the correct answer has been noted by a number of commentators. As Kant himself pointed out (and others before him), the only conceptual truths that follow *directly* from concepts or definitions are hypothetical conclusions of the form 'If anything satisfies the concept or definition, then it has such-and-such properties' and 'Anything having such-and-such properties satisfies the concept or definition.' It is a conceptual *a priori* truth, for example, that if there is a green-eyed lion, then it is a lion and has green eyes, and that any lion that has green eyes is a green-eyed lion. Exactly analogously, it is a conceptual *a priori* truth that if there is an existent lion, then it is a lion and exists, and that any lion that exists is an existent lion. It is true by definition, if you will, that all and only exilions are lions that exist.[20] Analogously again, it is a conceptual *a priori* truth that all exiunicorns are unicorns and exist, and only unicorns that exist are exiunicorns.

The important point is that in this respect nothing changes when we move from actualist to possibilist quantifier logic. Even in possibilist quantifier logic, the conclusions that follow directly from definitions are always hypothetical in form. It is a conceptual *a priori* truth, for example, that if a possible individual is a green-eyed lion, then it is a possible individual that is a lion and has green eyes, and any possible individual that is a lion and has green eyes is a possible individual that is a green-eyed lion. It is similarly a conceptual *a priori* truth that if there is an exidivine possible individual then it is a divine possible individual and exists, and if there is exactly one divine possible individual that exists then it is the exidivine possible individual. It is true by definition that a possible individual is the exidivine possible individual if and only if it, and (among possible individuals) only it, is both divine and existent. It certainly is not a conceptual *a priori* truth, or true by definition, that some possible individual is an existent lion, that some possible individual is an exiunicorn, or that some possible individual is exidivine. For all that can be known merely by reflection on the concept of a such-and-such (or on that of an existent such-and-such), there may not be anything that fits the concept, not even a possible thing. Even if it can be known *a priori* that there is a possible thing that *might* fit the concept, there may not be any possible thing that *actually* fits the concept. There is not even a kernel of truth to the idea that if existence were treated as an admissible defining property or concept, then it would be possible to create entities by defining them into existence. The most we obtain directly from the existential definition of an existent such-and-such is that, *if* a possible individual is an existent such-and-such, then it exists and is a such-and-such.

The problem with the Ontological Argument (as it has been formulated here) is not that it involves existential definition, but that its expounders commit Meinong's fallacy of assuming that, for any formula ϕ, it is logically or trivially or manifestly true that the ϕ is a ϕ. (To put the matter less anachronistically, Meinong commits Anselm's fallacy.) Far from being a logical schema, this assumption is actually contradictory. In fact, the assumption is contradictory even if the range of the formula-variable ϕ is restricted to consistent formulas that may apply to possible

[20] Actualists claim that it is also a logical *a priori* truth that anything that is a lion is a lion that exists. If actualism is correct, it is a conceptual truth that all and only lions are exilions.

individuals. To see this, let ϕ_x be '$F(x)$ & p'. Now let ϕ_x be '$G(x)$ & $\sim p$'. Logic gives us only that *if there is exactly one* ϕ, then the ϕ is a ϕ.[21] Even in the strange land of possibilist quantification, logic—through its Law of Noncontradiction—rejects the claim that, for every (consistent) formula ϕ, the possible individual that is a ϕ is a ϕ. Possibilist quantifier logic gives us only that, *if* exactly one possible individual is a ϕ, then the possible individual that is a ϕ is a ϕ. Premise (2a) is no truth of logic. It is no piece of trivia either. Likewise for premise (3a). This much is obvious from its translation into actualist discourse via (4a).

The considerations raised in the preceding two paragraphs are both necessary and sufficient to expose the fallacy in ontological arguments in the style of Versions 1 through 4, whether for the existence of lions, fantasy islands, unicorns, or divine individuals. No doubt more is required to debunk more sophisticated versions, although I believe not much more. Certainly, one need not take the drastic measure of retreating to theses about existence that are demonstrably false (or nearly so).

In fact, Kant, Frege, and Russell all recognized explicitly in their writings that definitional truths are always hypothetical in form. Why, then, did each think it necessary to insist also on one or all of theses (*i*)–(*iii*)? I do not know. It is possible that they reasoned along the following lines: Conceptual or definitional truths concerning the such-and-such always have the hypothetical form 'If the such-and-such exists, then it is thus and so'. If it were legitimate to include the very concept of existence itself in the definition of the such-and-such, then we could satisfy the antecedent of this hypothetical by the very definition, thereby securing the consequent categorically, without the existential proviso, via *modus ponens*. And the consequent in this case includes existence as one of the conditions it ascribes. We would have obtained an analytic existential; we would have defined something into existence. But we cannot create new entities simply be defining them into existence. It is illegitimate, therefore, to include existence itself (or anything that entails existence, such as the concept of *necessary existence* or that of exidivinity) in forming a complex concept or in defining a term (thesis (*iii*)). If there were a concept or property of existence for individuals, or if there were a first-order predicate of

---

[21] In 'On Denoting' Russell notoriously raises a number of objections to Frege's theory of *Sinn* and *Bedeutung* that are apparently based on one or more confusions or misunderstandings. One particular objection in 'On Denoting' is quite powerful, but is briefly stated amid the other, mistaken criticisms, and consequently has been unduly neglected. In connection with his example of 'the present King of France' Russell writes: "Or again consider such a proposition as the following: 'If u is a class which has only one member, then that one member is a member of u', or, as we might state it, 'If u is a unit class, *the u is a u.*' This proposition ought to be *always* true ..." On Frege' theory, any English sentence containing the phrase 'the present King of France' (and free of oblique devices) is neither true nor false. Russell correctly points out that whereas Meinong's theory errs in one way by counting the sentence 'The present King of France is a present King of France' as logically true when in reality it is not even true, Frege's theory errs in another but equally objectionable way by discounting the weaker, conditional sentence 'If there is exactly one present King of France, then the present King of France is a present King of France', which is logically true, as not even true. By contrast with Frege, the 'secondary occurrence' or 'narrow scope' reading of the latter sentence is indeed a trivial theorem of *Principia Mathematica*. (This is not to say, though, that Russell's account of definite descriptions as contextually defined 'incomplete symbols' that are more analogous to second-order predicates than to singular terms is superior to an account of definite descriptions as complete, genuine singular terms.)

individuals that correctly applied to all and only existing individuals, then it would be perfectly legitimate to include this concept or property in forming more complex concepts, and it would be perfectly legitimate to use this predicate in defining other terms. Consequently, there is no concept or property of existence for individuals (thesis (*ii*)), and the word 'exists' is not a first-order predicate (thesis (*i*)). In fact, it is clear on independent grounds that existence is a second-level concept rather than a first-level concept. This further confirms thesis (*iii*).

The reasoning here is fallacious. The mistake occurs when it is argued that by building existence into the concept of the such-and-such, one would make it true by definition that the such-and-such exists. This is just Meinong's fallacy again. Whereas the Version 3 Arguer committed this fallacy is asserting premise (3a) as a logical or manifest truth, Kant and his followers may have committed the very same fallacy in attempting to locate the source of the illegitimacy.

One may defend the Kantian refutation of the Ontological Argument by claiming that what Kant and his followers have in mind is that it is illegitimate to include existence in the definition of something *in such a way that* it follows just from the definition that the thing categorically exists. If existence is to be legitimately included in the very definition of the such-and-such, it must be included in such a way that only hypothetical conclusions follow from the definition. If this is what they have in mind, then at least they do not commit the very same fallacy as their opponents. They are, however, guilty of *something*, even if only gross understatement. It is not that it is merely somehow illegitimate to include existence in the definition of something in such a way that its existence follows from the very definition. Though it is perfectly possible to include existence in the definition of something, it is quite literally *impossible* to do so in such a way that existence follows from the definition. If 'ought not' implies 'can', then it is false that one ought not to include existence in the definition of something in this way.

The fact that the first premise of the Ontological Argument is not a truth of logic and not manifestly true does not entail that it is not true at all. But do atheists and agnostics have any reason to suppose it true? Indeed, does the Ontological Arguer have any reason to suppose it true? Why should anyone believe that there is a divine possible individual?

One might infer that there is a divine possible individual from the observation that it is perfectly possible for there to be a divine individual. This is essentially Anselm's argument for his premise (2a).[22] It is fallacious, but it is understandable why so many writers have been convinced by it. In order to steer clear of the fallacy, one must distinguish sharply between the assertion that it is possible for there to be something that is such-and-such, and the separate assertion that it is possible that there is something that *actually is* such-and-such. In possibilist discourse, we must distinguish the assertion that there is a possible individual that *might have* existed having a certain property from the stronger assertion that there is a possible individual that *actually* has the property. That these are different assertions is confirmed by considering the (yet to be analyzed) property of existing without actually

---

[22] In Plantinga, *Ontological Argument*, at p. 4.

existing: There might have been something that does not actually exist (there is a possible individual that might have had the property of existing without actually existing), but there could not be something that actually exists but does not actually exist (there is no possible individual that actually has the property of existing without actually existing). Let us suppose for the moment that it is somehow manifest or knowable *a priori* that it is possible that there is divine individual. In possibilist quantifier logic, it follows that there is a possible individual that *might have been* both divine and existent. It does not follow that there is a possible individual that actually is both divine and existent. The fact that there might have been an individual that would have been divine does not entail that there might have been an individual that *actually is* divine. The latter is what is needed to legitimize premise (2a).

I am not making the common objection that the Ontological Arguer begs the question since one must establish or assume that the divine possible individual exists before it can be concluded that the divine possible individual is divine.[23] That may be true, but as far as the present objection goes, it need not be. It is open to the Ontological Arguer to attempt some neutral, non-question-begging way of establishing that there is a possible individual that is actually divine, without assuming that one actually exists. What I am pointing out is that, even if the atheist and agnostic have been persuaded on *a priori* grounds that there might have been a divine individual, the Ontological Arguer still owes them some *further* argument to convince them that there might have been an individual that actually is divine (before it can be concluded via premise (2b) that there actually exists a divine individual). Merely establishing that there is a possible individual that might have been divine doesn't cut it.

For the purposes of the Ontological Arguer, the additional argument must proceed from premise whose truth is *a priori*, or otherwise manifest. The additional argument must not depend in any way on the assumption that a divine possible individual actually exists, since this is what is supposed to be ultimately proved. Furthermore, the additional argument must be sound; it must be an argument that cannot be extended to fantasy islands and the like. Surely no such argument exists. There does not even possibly exist any possible such argument.

V

In a penetrating critique pf the Ontological Argument, David Lewis suggested one reason on behalf of the Ontological Arguer for supposing that some possible, individual not only might have been but actually is divine.[24] We were supposing, for the sake of argument (although it has not yet been established), that it is manifest that in some possible worlds there exists something that is divine. Hence, in some possible worlds the property of divinity is exemplified. Now, the actual world is generally thought to be a special possible world in that, unlike any other possible world, it alone is actual. If the special property of divinity is exemplified in any

---

[23] This objection was apparently first raised by Gaunilo. See Plantinga, *Ontological Argument*, at p. 11.   [24] 'Anselm and Actuality,' *Noûs*, 4 (1970), pp. 175–188.

possible world, it seems only fitting that it should be exemplified in the most special of the worlds, the actual world. Lewis writes:

This reason seems *prima facie* to have some force: whatever actuality may be, it is something we deem tremendously important, and there *is* only one world that has it . . . Therefore it may well seem plausible that the actual world, being special by its unique actuality, might also be special by being a [world in which divinity is exemplified]. This does not pretend to be a proof of [premise (2a)], but [I] do not demand proof; [I] wish to know if the ontological arguer has any reason at all to accept [(2a)], even a reason that does no more than appeal to his sense of fitness. (p. 184)

Lewis's suggestion is a Trojan horse. For he goes on to argue that actuality is not a special property at all. According to Lewis, the word 'actual' is, in its primary sense, an indexical term analogous to 'here' or 'now': its reference varies with the context in which it is uttered—treating possible worlds along with times and locations as relevant features of contexts of utterances.

The *fixed* meaning we give to 'actual' is such that, at any world w, . . . , in *our* language . . . 'the actual world' *denotes* or *names w;* the predicate 'is actual' *designates* or *is true of w* and whatever exists in w; the operator 'actually' *is true of* propositions true at w, and so on for cognate terms of other categories . . .

A complication: we can distinguish primary and secondary senses of 'actual' by asking what world 'actual' refers to at a world w in a context in which some other world v is under consideration. In the primary sense, it still refers to w, as in 'If Max ate less, he would be thinner than he actually is'. In the secondary sense it shifts its reference to the world v under consideration, as in 'If Max ate less, he would actually enjoy himself more'. (p. 185)

Lewis extracts from his theory that 'actual' is indexical the consequence that actuality is not a special property of the actual world, and that all possible worlds are equally significant, or equally insignificant, from an enlarged and objective modal point of view:

If I am right, the ontological arguer who says that [the actual] world is special because [it] alone is the actual world is as foolish as a man who boasts that he has the special fortune to be alive at a unique moment in history: the present. The actual world is not special in itself, but only in the special relation it bears to the ontological arguer. Other worlds bear the same relation to [their] ontological arguers. We should conclude, therefore, that [Version 2 of the Ontological Argument] is a valid argument from a premise [(2a)] we have no non-circular reason to accept . . . [Premise (2a)] derives its credibility entirely from the illusion that because [the actual] world alone is actual, therefore [the actual] world is radically different from all other worlds—special in a way that makes it a fitting place of [divinity]. But once we recognize the indexical nature of actuality, the illusion is broken and the credibility of [(2a)] evaporates. It is true of *any* world, at that world but not elsewhere, that that world alone is actual. (pp. 187–188)[25]

---

[25] Lewis is actually concerned with an alternative formulation of Anselm's Ontological Argument, and more specifically with the weaker premise that some possible individual is actually divine, in the particular Anselmesque sense of 'divine'. His arguments, though, extend straightforwardly to premise (2a), whether 'divine' is understood in the Anselmesque sense or in some other sense (such as the Cartesian), as well as to premise (3a).

We have arrived at last at the question of what it is for a possible individual to be actual. If I am right that *to be is to be identical with something*, then to be actual is actually to be identical with something. Lewis has provided us with an answer to the question of what it is for something actually to be the case.

Unfortunately, there is much in Lewis's analysis of actuality that commentators have taken exception to. Yet there is much in the account that has the ring of truth. It is important to sort these matters out if we are to be clear about what it is for a possible world or a possible individual to be "actual," properly so-called.

One immediate difficulty with Lewis's theory of actuality is that his statement of the theory presupposes his highly controversial view that the (standard) inhabitants of possible worlds are world-bound individuals, i.e., that each possible individual exists in one and only one possible world. This view, in turn, is connected with Lewis's idiosyncratic view that possible worlds are physical systems. Nowadays, philosophers more commonly regard possible worlds as abstract entities of a certain sort, such as maximal consistent sets of propositions that might have been jointly true (Robert Adams), maximal situations that might have obtained (Saul Kripke), maximal histories the cosmos might have had (Kripke), total states the cosmos might have been in (Kripke, Robert Stalnaker), maximal states of affairs that might have obtained (Alvin Plantinga), or maximal scenarios that might have been realized (myself). As with most of Lewis's commentators, I regard Lewis's presuppositions concerning the nature of modality as inessential to the main idea of his theory that the term 'actual' is indexical, and I propose to consider instead a version of the indexical theory that makes the considerably more plausible assumption that possible worlds are maximal abstract entities of one sort or another. (If Lewis's presuppositions concerning the nature of modality are essential in some sense to the *whole* of his indexical theory, then my concern here is with a proper part of that theory, especially with those aspects of the theory that have the ring of truth, supplemented with an abstract-entity conception of possible worlds.) On the abstract-entity conception of possible worlds, possible individuals need not be world-bound—although, for all that is demanded by the conception itself, it may turn out that an extreme version of the doctrine of essentialism is true, making every possible individual world-bound in some sense. (Logically, it could turn out that the actual world is the only possible world—extreme metaphysical determinism—so that the only possible individuals are both actual and world-bound.)

On the abstract-entity conception of possible worlds, in every possible world there will exist alternative possible worlds (unless extreme metaphysical determinism is true), but in any single possible world *w*, every world other than *w* itself is *merely* possible. If worlds are maximal compossible sets of propositions, then according to any single possible world, it is the only world whose elements are all *true*, and every other world is a set of propositions that are *not* all true. If worlds are maximal states the cosmos might have been in, then according to any single possible world, it is the only world that the cosmos is *in*, and every other world is a maximal state the cosmos is *not* in, and so on. We may abbreviate this by saying that in any single world *w*, one and only one possible world is *realized*, and that is *w* itself. The exact meaning of 'realized' depends on which abstract-entity conception of possible worlds one adopts. If worlds are maximal propositions, then 'realized' simply means "a true maximal proposition". If worlds are maximal states of affairs, then 'realized' simply means "a maximal state of affairs that obtains", and so on. Whatever particular abstract-entity conception is decided upon, it will be an analytic or conceptual truth that one and only one possible world is realized. One thing that should emerge from any proper account of indexicality is that the term 'realized' just introduced is *not* indexical, even if the term 'actual' is indexical.[26]

The notions of a world being actual and of a proposition being actual (i.e., of something actually being the case) are interdefinable. For the purposes of this investigation, it will be convenient to take the propositional operator 'actually' to be the fundamental term and various uses of the term 'actual' to be derivative. We may mark these various cognates of 'actually' by way of superscripts indicating the type of entity to which the term is applicable. A possible world is said to be *actual*^{w} (or an *actual world*) if it is actually realized. A possible individual is said to be *actual*^{i} (or an *actual individual*) if it actually exists, i.e., if it exists in the actual^w world. An individual is said to be an actual^p ϕ if it is actually ϕ (i.e., if the proposition that it is ϕ is actually the case), and so on. (Exactly analogously, a world is *possible*^{w} if it is possibly realized; an individual is *necessary*^{i} if it necessarily exists, etc.) Since the indexical theory of 'actually', as propounded by Lewis, admits a secondary, non-indexical sense of 'actually' and its cognates, for complete precision a subscript of '1' or '2' should be added to indicate the primary or secondary sense, e.g., 'actual$^i_1$'.

Whereas a number of objections have been raised against the theory that 'actually' (in its primary sense) and its cognates are indexical, every objection that I am aware of is based straightforwardly on one or more confusions. In some cases, the confusion belongs to some of the adherents and defenders of the indexical theory as well as to the theory's critics.

Perhaps the simplest confusion is the idea that, if one treats possible worlds along with times and locations as features of contexts of utterance, then any nonrigid definite description will emerge as an indexical expression, since the referent (in actual English) of any such description with respect to a world in which it is uttered varies with the world.[27] This confusion between indexicality and nonrigidity stems from a common misdescription, and a concomitant misunderstanding, of the semantic term 'indexical'. An *indexical* expression is usually defined as an expression whose referent (denotation) or extension with respect to a context varies with the context, so that there are possible contexts c and c' such that the referent or extension of the expression with respect to c is not the same as its referent with respect to c'. (Lewis misdefines indexicality in exactly this way in the passage quoted in the preceding section, thereby helping to foster the confusion I am discussing, although he is not guilty of this confusion.) The definition is too general; it fails to discriminate between genuinely indexical expressions, such as 'the present US president', and certain nonindexical expressions, such as 'the US president'.

---

[26] Contrary to Peter van Inwagen's interpretation of the indexical theory of 'actuality' in 'Indexicality and Actuality,' *The Philosophical Review*, 89, 3 (July 1980), 403–426, at p. 409 (and apparently contrary to Lewis, 1970, at the final footnote). It should also be remembered that Lewis admits a secondary, nonindexical sense of 'actual'.   [27] van Inwagen, 'Indexicality,' pp. 413–416.

A more accurate definition is this: An expression is *indexical* if its referent or extension with respect to a context of utterance *and* with respect to other semantic parameters of evaluation, such as a time and a possible world, varies with the context (holding the other parameters fixed).[28] An expression is nonindexical if its extension with respect to a context and with respect to a set of additional semantic parameters does not vary with the context. On the other hand, a singular term is (intensionally) *rigid*, with respect to a given context, if its referent with respect to the given context and with respect to other semantic parameters does not vary with the additional parameters. A singular term is (intensionally) nonrigid if its referent with respect to a context and with respect to a set of parameters varies with the set of semantic parameters.

It is common to distinguish between the *extension* and the *intension* of an expression. The *intension* of an expression, with respect to a given context of utterance, is the function that assigns to any time and possible world (and perhaps some further semantic parameters other than a context of utterance) the extension that the expression takes on with respect to the given context and with respect to those parameters. An alternative definition of the term 'indexical', then, is the following: An indexical expression is one whose *intension* with respect to a given context varies with the context, so that there will be possible contexts c and c' such that the intension of the expression with respect to c is not the same as its intension with respect to c'.[29] A singular term is (intensionally) *rigid*, with respect to a given context, if its intension with respect to that context is a constant function.

For example, the referent of 'the US president', with respect to my present context and with respect to the year 1978, is Jimmy Carter, since he was president in 1978. Carter remains the referent if one changes the context while retaining the year 1978 as the second parameter, although the referent changes as one changes the second parameter. The referent of 'the present US president', with respect to the same two parameters, is Ronald Reagan, since he is president at the time of the context. The referent varies if one changes the context, even if the time parameter is held constant at the year 1978. With respect to any actual context, the former expression is (temporally) nonrigid; yet it is also nonindexical, since it retains the same intension with respect to every context of utterance. The latter expression, being a true indexical, takes on different intensions with respect to different contexts, but with respect to any actual context it is (temporally) rigid.

The referent of a singular term with respect to a context c *simpliciter* (that is, with respect to c but not with respect to any other parameters) may be defined as the referent of the term with respect to c and with respect to various features of c (such as the time of c) to act as the needed extra parameters.[30] In the general case,

---

[28] See my 'Tense and Singular Propositions,' in J. Almog, J. Perry, and H. Wettstein, eds., *Themes From Kaplan* (Oxford University Press, 1989), pp. 331–392.

[29] The notion of the *character* of an expression introduced in David Kaplan, 'On the Logic of Demonstratives,' *Journal of Philosophical Logic*, 8 (1978), pp. 81–98 (also in P. French, T. Uehling, and H. Wettstein, eds., *Contemporary Perspectives in the Philosophy of Language*, Minneapolis: University of Minnesota Press, 1979, pp. 401–412, at p. 409) is defined (roughly) as the function that assigns to any context c the intension that the expression takes on with respect to c. In this terminology, an indexical expression is one whose character is not a constant function.

[30] See Kaplan, especially at p. 408 of French, Uehling, and Wettstein, 1979.

if one speaks of the referent of a term (or the truth-value of a sentence, etc.) with respect to a certain diminished or incomplete set of further parameters, it is understood that the diminished or incomplete set is to be augmented or completed by drawing additional parameters from the given context. Since the referent of 'the US president' with respect to a context and a time varies with the time, so does its referent with respect to a context *simpliciter* (since varying the context in this case involves varying the time parameter). The expression is nonindexical nevertheless. A singular term whose referent with respect to a context *simpliciter* varies with the context is either indexical or (intensionally) nonrigid. It may even be both (e.g., 'the political leader of this country'), but it can be one without the other.

The theory that 'actually' (in its primary sense) and its cognates are indexical claims that there is a similar difference between the expressions 'the US president in 1985' (nonindexical) and 'the person who actually$_1$ is US president in 1985' (indexical), by treating possible worlds along with times and locations as features of contexts of utterance. As such, the theory instructs us to index (i.e., relativize) the extensions of expressions both to a context, which is to include a possible world as one of its various features, and to an additional possible world, which is to be treated as an independent parameter of semantic evaluation.

It may seem that once possible worlds are included as features of contexts, there is no purpose to be served by doubly indexing extensions to both contexts and possible worlds, treating each as independent semantic parameters. We should be able to make do with the possible worlds of the contexts. We may say, for example, that a sentence of the form ⌜It is possible that S⌝ is true with respect to a context c if and only if S itself is true with respect to some context that is just like c in every respect other than in its possible world and whose possible world is accessible to that of c. This singly indexed account seems to yield the correct results until we consider sentences that embed one modal operator within the scope of another. Consider the following sentence:

(5) It is possible that the actual$^p_1$ US president be a woman.

According to the singly relativized account, this sentence is true with respect to a context of utterance c if and only if there is some world w' accessible to the world of c such that the US president in w' is a woman in w'. But this is the wrong truth-condition for the sentence. In fact, it is correct truth-condition for the wrong sentence, to wit, the nonindexical sentence.

(6) It is possible that the US president be a woman,
    or more idiomatically,

The US president might have been a woman,

on one of its readings (the Russellian secondary occurrence or small scope reading). Sentences (5) and (6) differ in their truth-conditions; if both sentences are uttered in a world in which the person occupying the presidency is essentially a man, sentence (5) is false whereas sentence (6) is true. Sentence (5) is true with respect to a context of utterance c (roughly) if and only if there is some world w' accessible to the world of the context c such that the US president *in the world of the context of utterance c*—rather than in w'—is a woman *in w'*, rather than in the world of c. The modal operator 'it is possible that' directs us to evaluate its operand sentence 'The actual$^P{}_1$ US president is a woman' with respect to worlds w' accessible to that of the context of utterance c. This sentence is true with respect to the same context c and a world w' accessible to that of c if and only if the description 'the actual$^P{}_1$ US president' refers with respect to c and w' to something to which the predicate 'is a woman' applies with respect to c and w'. In computing the referent of the description with respect to c and w', the indexical operator 'actual$^P{}_1$' directs us to seek an object to which its operand phrase 'US president' applies with respect to the very world of the context of utterance c itself, forgetting about the world w'. Thus in evaluating sentence (5) with respect to a world of utterance w (the world of its context of utterance c), we are concerned simultaneously with the extension of 'US president' with respect to w and the extension of 'is a woman' with respect to some world w' accessible to w. The truth-value of the whole depends entirely and solely on whether the unique object to which the phrase 'US president' applies with respect to w is something to which the predicate 'is a woman' applies with respect to an accessible world w'. It is for this reason that a systematic theory of the extensions of the expressions of a language containing indexical modal operators requires double indexing, i.e., in general the notion of the extension of an expression (e.g., the truth-value of a sentence) is relativized to both a context and a world, treated as independent semantic parameters. The notion of the extension of an expression with respect to a context c *simpliciter* is then definable as the extension of the expression with respect to the context c and the world of c.

A common objection to the indexical theory of 'actually' is that it requires a commitment to utterances or their producers being world-bound (existing in only one world), and thereby to Lewis's unpopular metaphysical view that individuals are world-bound.[31] The reasoning goes as follows: When we say of an expression that it is *indexical*, what we are saying is that different utterances of the expression may take on different semantic values (referent, truth-value, intension, etc.), so that it is not the expression *type* but its utterance (inscription, token) that is the proper object of these semantic values. An utterance of the indexical 'now' refers to the time of the utterance, an utterance of 'here' to the place of the utterance, an utterance of 'I' to the producer of the utterance, and so on. To say, then, that 'actual' (in its primary sense) is indexical is to say that an utterance of it designates the possible world in which the utterance takes place, or the possible world in which the producer of the utterance exists, or something like that. But whereas it is perfectly legitimate to talk about the time or place of an utterance (in a given world), it is illegitimate to talk about the *possible world* of an utterance or its producer, since one and the very same utterance is produced by one and the very same speaker in indefinitely many different worlds. If I utter the sentence

(7) Actually₁, a Republican will be elected US president in 2100 AD,

---

[31] See for example Adams, 'Theories of Actuality,' at pp. 195–199 of Loux, *Possible and Actual*; and van Inwagen, 'Indexicality,' at pp. 416–417.

I would have made the same utterance regardless of which party controls the presidency a hundred and fourteen years from now. The same utterance by me occurs in different possible worlds, true in some and false in others. No world may be singled out as *the* world of my utterance—unless (contrary to what has been said) utterances or their producers are world-bound. Yet the utterance is either true or false, and not both.

This piece of reasoning goes wrong when it is argued that to say that an expression is indexical is to say that its utterance is the proper object of semantic values. The proper object of semantic values is the expression (type) itself; but the semantic values are had only relative to a *context*, and may vary accordingly. To say that 'actual' (in its primary sense) is indexical is not to say that an utterance of it designates the world of the utterance; rather, it is to say that, with respect to any context, it designates the world of the context. This requires seeing the contexts of utterances, rather than the utterances themselves, as world-bound. The notion of context that is relevant here is such that, for any particular actual utterance of any expression by anyone, if any facts had been different in any way, even if only facts entirely independent of and isolated from the utterance itself, then the context of the utterance would *ipso facto* be a different context—even if the utterance is made by the very same speaker in the very same way to the very same audience at the very same time in the very same place. To put it another way, whereas a single utterance occurs in indefinitely many different possible worlds, any particular possible context of an utterance occurs in one and only one possible world, so that in every possible world in which the same utterance occurs, it occurs in a new and different context— even if the speaker, his or her manner of uttering, the time of the utterance, the location of the speaker, the audience being addressed, and all other such features and aspects of the utterance remain exactly the same. A single utterance occurs in many different contexts, each of which occurs in a different possible world. This is what it means to include a possible world as one of the features of a context.

Whereas utterances are not world-bound entities, it is nevertheless perfectly reasonable to treat their contexts as world-bound entities. Indeed, not doing so would be unreasonable. Suppose, for example, that it will come to pass that a Democrat is elected president in the year 2100, and consider a world *W* that is exactly like the actual world in every detail up to 1 January 2099, but in which a Republican is elected president in 2100. Suppose I here and now utter sentence (7). In the actual world, I thereby assert a proposition that is necessarily false. In *W*, on the other hand, I thereby assert a proposition that is necessarily true.[32] I utter the very same sequence of words of English with the very same English meanings in the two worlds, yet I assert different propositions, one proposition being necessarily false and the other being necessarily true. If we refuse to treat contexts as world-bound we are forced to say—quite mysteriously—that I utter the very same sentence with the very same meaning in the very same context in the two worlds, yet assert different things! The information content of sentence (7) would emerge as a semantic

---

[32] See Kaplan, 'Logic of Demonstratives,' and Allen Hazen, 'One of the Truths About Actuality,' *Analysis*, 39, 1 (January 1979), pp. 1–3.

function not only of the meaning of the sentence and the context of utterance, but also of the apparently irrelevant question of which political party wins the US presidency in the year 2100. Treating contexts as world-bound, we may say instead that the adverb 'actually$_1$' is indexical, and that the same utterance takes place in different contexts, resulting in different propositions asserted. We thereby assimilate this phenomenon to the sort of context-sensitivity that is familiar in cases of such sentences as 'A Republican is presently US president'.

The central thesis of the indexical theory of 'actually' and its cognates may thus be stated by saying that the extensional semantics governing 'actually' in its primary sense is given by the following recursion rule:[33]

A1 A formula of the form $\ulcorner$Actually$_1$ $\phi\urcorner$ (where ϕ is any formula) is true with respect to a context c, a possible world w, and other semantic parameters (such as a time t, and an assignment of values to variables s) if and only if ϕ is itself true with respect to the context c, the possible world of c rather than the world w, and the other semantic parameters.

The extensional semantic rules governing the cognates of 'actually$_1$' (in their primary senses) are easily derived from this clause governing 'actually$_1$' together with the definitions of the cognates in terms of 'actually$_1$' and some elementary modal semantics. For example, we thus obtain:

A^w_1 The predicate 'actual$^w_1$' (correctly) applies with respect to a context c, a possible world w, and other semantic parameters, to the world of c, rather than to the world w, and to nothing else.

and

A^i_1 The predicate 'actual$^i_1$' (correctly) applies with respect to a context c, a possible world w, and other semantic parameters (such as a time t), to a possible individual i if and only if i exists in the world of c (at t).

Another common objection to this theory of 'actually' and its cognates is that is clashes with our understanding of what it means to say that a world (or individual, or proposition) is 'possible.' For to say that worlds other than the actual world are possible is just to say that the world that happens to be actual might not have been actual and that some other world might have been actual instead. But if 'actual$^w_1$' is indexical, such a claim is ruled out as semantically incoherent. On the indexical theory, in any actual context of utterance, only the actual world may be properly called 'actual$^w_1$' with respect to any world, and every world other than the actual world is properly called 'nonactual$^w_1$' even with respect to itself. On the

---

[33] *Cf.* Kaplan, 'Logic of Demonstratives,' recursive definition 10 at p. 407 of French, Uehling and Wettstein, *Midwest Studies*.

In speaking of the 'extensional semantics' governing an expression, I mean the semantics of the expression at the level of extension (singular term reference, sentence truth-value, predicate application), rather than at some higher level, such as the level of content or proposition expressed. For more on the notion of different 'levels' of semantic values, see my *Frege's Puzzle* (Atascadero, Ca.: Ridgeview, 1986, 1991), chapter 2.

indexical theory, then, it is a necessary truth about the actual world that it is the actual world. In what sense are the other worlds *possible* if they could not have been actual?[34]

A closely related objection raised by Robert Adams is this: One may easily glean from the indexical theory's semantic rules A_1, A'_1, and A^w_1 that actuality (the property of being actual), on the indexical theory, is of no special metaphysical significance. Specifically, the fact that something is actually$_1$ the case, on the indexical theory, does not make it ontologically or metaphysically more substantial or important than if it were possibly the case but not actually$_1$ the case. For the fact that a certain proposition is actually$_1$ the case, on the indexical theory, is just the fact that it is the case in a particular possible world (which happens to be the world of the actual context of utterance)—in just the same way that the fact that some (recurring) event is occurring *now* is just the fact that it is occurring at a particular time (which happens to be the time of the context of utterance). From an objective point of view, the fact that a given time is the present time does not make it special in any way: it is just a time like any other time, one that happens to be the time of a particular utterance. The fact that the time in question happens to be the time of a particular utterance, by itself, is of no consequence. Any time is properly called 'the present' at that time and no other. Similarly, on the indexical theory, to call our world 'actual$^w_1$', *per se*, is not to attribute to it any metaphysically significant distinction. The fact that a given possible world is actual$^w_1$ is just the fact that it is this world rather than some other world. This does not constitute any special status; every world is the world it is and not another world. Indeed, this feature of the indexical theory is precisely what gives the point to Lewis's response to his envisaged Ontological Arguer. But it is greatly at odds with our ordinary thinking about actuality and mere possibility (nonactuality), especially as reflected in our ordinary value judgements in connection with actual and nonactual events. We judge it good that a cure for some terrible disease is actually discovered. We do not judge it good (indeed we probably judge it bad) that a cure might have been discovered but is not actually discovered. We condemn someone for actually committing assault. We do not condemn someone merely on the grounds that he or she *might have* committed assault in radically different circumstances. We might even applaud someone for actually resisting provocation to assault (unless it is Clint Eastwood). We feel pity for the victims of actual disasters. We do not feel pity for the would-be victims of disasters that might have occurred but did not actually occur. To quote Adams: "if we ask, 'What is wrong with actualizing evils, since they will occur in some other possible world anyway if they don't occur in this one?', I doubt that the indexical theory can provide an answer which will be completely satisfying ethically."[35]

These objections have considerable force. But they can be completely met while accommodating what truth they may contain by invoking Lewis's secondary,

---

[34] See Adams, 'Theories of Actuality,' at pp. 201–202 of Loux, *Possible and Actual*; Plantinga, *Necessity*, at pp. 48–51; van Inwagen, 1980, at pp. 423–425.

[35] Adams, 'Theories of Actuality', at pp. 194–195 of Loux, *Possible and Actual*.

nonindexical sense of 'actually' and its cognates.[36] The secondary-sense analogues to the three semantic rules given above are the following:

A_2 A formula of the form ⌜Actually$_2$ ϕ⌝ (where ϕ is any formula) is true with respect to a context c, a possible world w, and other semantic parameters (such as a time t, and an assignment of values to variables s) if and only if ϕ is itself true with respect to the context c, the possible world w (rather than the world of c), and the other semantic parameters.

A^w_2 The predicate 'actual$^w_2$' (correctly) applies with respect to a context c, a possible world w, and other semantic parameters, to the world w (rather than to the world of c) and to nothing else.

A^i_2 The predicate 'actual$^i_2$' (correctly) applies with respect to a context c, a possible world w, and other semantic parameters (such as a time t), to a possible individual i if and only if i exists in the world w (at t).

It is immediately apparent from these semantic rules governing the secondary sense of 'actually' and its cognates that the expressions in question are nonindexical in their secondary senses. By contrast with the semantic rules governing the primary senses, the context c plays no significant role in the semantic rules governing the secondary senses. More interesting, the propositional operator 'actually$_2$' itself plays no significant semantic role. It is completely superfluous, in that the truth-conditions (with respect to semantic parameters) of any formula of the form ⌜Actually$_2$ ϕ⌝, as given by A_2, are exactly those of the immediate subformula ϕ itself. To say that a proposition is actually the case in the secondary sense is just to say that it is true, no more and no less. This fully accords with Lewis's example of the secondary sense: 'If Max ate less, he would actually enjoy himself more'. It also helps to explain why the adverb 'actually' is often used as a device for emphasis or for indicating contrast between belief or expectation and reality, as in Lewis's example, rather than as a modal auxiliary. There can be little doubt that the adverb 'actually' has these two distinct uses.[37] The context of use—the point of the utterance—will generally favor one reading over the other, although it need not in every case. An exactly analogous ambiguity arises in the temporal mode with the world 'current'. Consider: 'In 1950 the current US president was a Democrat'.

Since a possible world is said to be actual if and only if it is actually realized and a possible individual is said to be actual if and only if it actually exists, to say that a possible world is actual in the secondary sense is just to say that it is realized and to say that a possible individual is actual in the secondary sense is just to say that it exists. Thus actuality$^w_2$ is just the property of being realized. This property was explained above in terms of the abstract-entity conception of possible worlds: If a possible world is a maximal compossible set of propositions, the property of being realized is the property of being a maximal set of true propositions; if a possible world is a maximal state of affairs that might have obtained, the property of being realized is the property of being a maximal state of affairs that obtains, and so on.

[36] *Cf.* Lewis, 'Postscripts to "Anselm and Actuality",' Postscript B, in Lewis, 'Anselm,' at p. 22.
[37] *Cf.* Hazen, 'Truths about Actuality', and Lewis, 'Anselm'.

Likewise, actuality$^i_2$ is just the property of existence. This property was analyzed in Section III above in terms of the logical notions of abstraction, negation, universal quantification, and identity. These construals of 'actual' in the secondary sense are complemented by the semantic rules A^w_2 and A^i_2, which impute the very same nonindexical extensional semantics to 'actual$^w_2$' and 'actual$^i_2$' as would be correct for 'realized' and 'exists', respectively.

The secondary sense of 'actual^w' is evidently the appropriate sense for understanding the truism that some possible world other than the actual world might have been "actual" instead. It is also in the secondary sense rather than in the primary sense that calling a world *possible* is to say that it might have been "actual." Each possible world is realized in itself and in no other world; hence every world is the actual$^w_2$ world in itself. But only this world—the way things happen to be—is actually realized in the primary sense, and in every world it is the one and only actual$^w_1$ world.[38]

By the same token, it must be said that actuality in the secondary sense, by contrast with actuality in the primary sense, is *in some sense* a special status. The feature of a proposition that it is true, and the feature of a state of affairs that it obtains, and the feature of a possible individual that it exists, are unlike the features of being true or obtaining or existing *in a particular world* (actuality in the primary sense) in that the latter are all more-or-less ordinary *extra-world* features having no metaphysically special entailments whereas the former are all special *intra-world* features that afford their possessors in a given world a metaphysically significant status *in that world*.[39] That actuality in the secondary sense is in some sense an objectively special sort of status is not the sort of fact that would ordinarily require a substantiating argument. In the sense in which it is true, it is also perfectly obvious and completely trivial.[40] Among propositions in a given world, those that are true are obviously special in a certain way. Likewise, if you were a state of affairs, would you rather obtain or not obtain? That existence is metaphysically more significant than nonexistence is hardly the sort of fact that could be open to question. Anyone who doubts or seriously questions whether existence is metaphysically more significant

[38] Here is a simple quiz question: On the indexical theory, is the expression 'the actual world' a (modally) rigid designator?

[39] An intra-world property is one that something has, or lacks, *in* a possible world (e.g., being a native Californian), whereas such relativization to possible worlds is unnecessary or superfluous in connection with extra-world properties (e.g., being a native-Californian-in-world-w). For more on the distinction between intra-world and extra-world attributes, see Salmon, *Reference*, section 13.2, pp. 118–120.

[40] Nevertheless, I believe it is denied by Lewis. This is due to the fact that Lewis does not endorse the abstract-entity conception of possible worlds, on which actuality in the secondary sense reduces to such properties as that of being true or that of obtaining. Instead, Lewis adopts a concrete or physicalistic conception of possible worlds as maximal, spatiotemporally self-contained, causally isolated physical systems, on which actuality in the primary sense reduces to something like the ontologically unimportant property of being part of a particular maximal causally and spatio-temporally isolated physical system and not another, and actuality in the secondary sense, if it reduces to anything, reduces to the equally unimportant (in the present context) binary relation between a part of such a physical system and the system of which it is a part. The maximal causally and spatiotemporally isolated physical system of which we are a part is, from an objective point of view, no more special ontologically than any other such physical systems that may exist.

than nonexistence simply does not understand the phrase 'metaphysically signific-ant', as it is used in the present context, or else misunderstands the word 'existence', or else is taking one or the other of these expressions in some nonstandard sense.

One final point about this theory of 'actually' and its cognates must be stressed. It is often claimed, by proponents and critics alike, that on the indexical theory, to say that a possible world (or a possible individual, or a proposition) is actual (in the primary sense) is to say merely that it is (or exists in, or is true in) the world of the context of utterance. Similarly, it is often said that the actuality (in the primary sense) of the actual world (or of an actual individual, or of a proposition that is actually the case) on the indexical theory is a property that is possessed only in relation to a speaker and his or her context. For example, in his original paper Lewis writes: "The actual world is not special in itself, but only in the special relation it bears to the ontological arguer.... It is true of *any* world, at that world but not elsewhere, that that world alone is actual."[41] More recently, he says that his indexical theory of 'actual' "makes actuality a relative matter: every world is *actual at* itself, and thereby all worlds are on a par.... The 'actual at' relation between worlds is simply identity.... Surely it is a contingent matter which world is actual... at one world, one world is actual; at another, another."[42] Similarly, in his critique of Lewis's theory Adams writes: "According to the indexical theory of actuality, the actuality of the actual world consists in its being... the world in which *this act of linguistic utterance occurs*.... According to the indexical theory, actuality is a property which the actual world possesses, not absolutely, but only in relation to us, its inhabitants."[43] These claims involve a confusion about the nature of indexicality in general, and may be traceable to a use-mention confusion. The claims are more appropriate for the property of being correctly *called* 'actual' in English, than for the property of actuality thereby attributed. Indexicality is a feature of expressions, not of the properties designated by these expressions. For this reason, it is better to speak not of the indexical theory of actuality, but of the indexical theory of 'actuality' in English. That actuality in the primary sense is neither context-relative nor contingent on the indexical theory can easily be seen from the semantic rules governing 'actually$_1$' and its cognates. On the indexical theory, to say that something is actually$_1$ the case is to say that it is the case in a particular possible world. The particular world in question is, of course, the world of the context of utterance, but that this is so is not part of what is asserted. Exactly analogously, the property of occurring now is not the property of occurring simultaneously with any speech act token, but the property of occurring at a particular time t. That time t is the very time at which I wrote the preceding sentence, but the property of occurring at t is not the same thing as the property of occurring when I wrote the preceding sentence. On any given occasion of utterance of 'occurring now', the property designated will be indexed to the very time of the utterance, so that what property is designated will vary from utterance to

[41] Lewis, 'Anselm,' at pp. 187–188. Ironically, just one page earlier (at pp. 186–187) Lewis cautions against a common confusion that is very closely related to the sort of confusion exhibited in the quoted passage.

[42] *On the Plurality of Worlds* (Oxford: Basil Blackwell, 1986), at pp. 93–94.

[43] Adams, 'Theories of Actuality,' at pp. 193–194 of Loux, 1979.

utterance. Also analogously, the property of being me is not the property of being the speaker or producer of a particular utterance. Rather, it is Nathan Salmon's haecceity, the property of being the very individual NS. The properties designated by such indexical expressions as 'occurring now' and 'being me' are not themselves context-relative in any straightforward sense. Quite the contrary; the property of occurring now is a temporally indexed property, and hence it is not the sort of property that something (a recurring event) has *relative to* some times and not to others. In the same way, the property designated by 'actual$^i_1$' is an extra-world property; if a possible individual has this property at all, it has this property relative to every world, and if a possible individual lacks the property, it lacks the property relative to every world. In fact, the property designated by the nonindexical 'actual$^i_2$' may be said to be context-relative in a way that actuality$^i_1$ cannot. The former property is just existence, which is an intra-world property that a possible individual has relative to any world in which it exists. The temporal analogue of this is equally true of 'current' in its nonindexical sense. Similarly, the property designated by the nonindexical phrase 'being the speaker' might be called 'context-relative' in that an individual has this property relative to any context in which he or she is the one doing the talking. By contrast, the property designated in the present context by the indexical phrase 'being me' is such that an individual has it relative to a given context if and only if he or she is Nathan Salmon, regardless of how much talking he or she may be doing in the context.

Actuality in the primary sense *per se* is of no special metaphysical significance; actuality in the secondary sense is in some sense metaphysically significant. Lewis's criticism of the Ontological Argument is that, since actuality$^w_1$ is no special distinction, it is a mistake to argue that if any possible individual is divine in any possible world, it is only fitting that some possible individual should be divine in the one and only possible world that is special by virtue of its actuality. We have just argued that even if the actual world is nothing special just for being uniquely actual$^w_1$, nevertheless it is trivially special and metaphysically distinguished by virtue of being actual$^w_2$, that is, by virtue of being realized. Lewis's acknowledged secondary sense of 'actual' thus seems to undercut his criticism of his suggested grounds or basis for premise (2a) of Version 2. (But see note 40 above.)

Does this mean that Lewis's suggested basis for (2a) is adequate after all? Surely not. Actuality in the secondary sense is metaphysically special in some sense, but it is not so special that any other property (of a given sort) that is special or important in some sense will *ipso facto* have some instance in actuality$_2$. Consider the very property in question: divinity. For Descartes divinity is the property of having all perfections. For Anselm it is the property of having a magnitude of greatness that exceeds any other conceivable magnitude of greatness. Whichever construal one chooses, divinity is no doubt in some way a very special status, one that enjoys very special religious significance. In the same way, the property of being the state of affairs of there being some possible individual that has divinity is itself very special, of considerable religious significance. The property of being a possible state of affairs that obtains is also special, but in a very different way. It is special in a distinctly secular and peculiarly metaphysical way. The fact that the state of affairs of there being some possible individual that is divine is special in the first way is no ground whatsoever for the hypothesis that it also has a property that is special in the second way, the metaphysically special property of obtaining. At most, it supports only the hypothesis that this state of affairs *deserves* or *ought* to obtain—in the sense that it would be good or 'fitting' if it did. What is wrong with Lewis's suggested basis for (2a) is not that actuality in any reasonable sense is not special; it is that the suggested basis is no basis at all. One might as well argue that, since being the best of all possible worlds is in some sense a very special property, it is only fitting, and therefore true, that the world that is special for its actuality$^w{}_2$ should also enjoy this other special property. It would follow from this line of reasoning (assuming that the property of being the best of all possible worlds is necessarily special) that *every* world is, according to itself, the best of all possible worlds. The incurable optimist, and the metaphysically deterministic pessimist, may be content with this argument. The rest of us know that, fitting though it may be, the actual$^w{}_2$ world is hardly the best of all possible worlds (even though it is indeed the most realized of all possible worlds), and that therefore, it is literally impossible for the actual$^w{}_1$ world to be the best of all possible worlds.

VI

I suggested in Section II above that nonexistent possible individuals, such as Noman, have properties—for example, the property of nonexistence and its entailments. These entailments include such negative properties as that of not being a philosopher. It does not follow that if you are asked to count up everything that is not a philosopher, Noman is to be included in the count. Nor should the dinosaurs be included in the count. Like the dinosaurs, Noman in not one of everything. Consequently, he is not one of everything that is not a philosopher. Indeed, not being one of everything is the very property of Noman we started with.

By contrast with Meinongians, I am not claiming that there are individuals that do not exist. If the quantifier 'there is' is actualist, that Meinongian claim is simply contradictory—and otherwise, it is trivial. What I am claiming is that there *might have* been individuals that do not actually₁ exist and that actually₁ have certain properties. Alvin Plantinga has given the name 'serious actualism' to the doctrine that necessarily, every individual is such that it must exist if it is to have any properties at all.[44] In Plantinga's terminology I am denying serious actualism while maintaining (a version of) actualism. But I am dead serious. My claim is philosophically quite moderate, not nearly as radical as it might seem. Exactly analogously, there have been individuals that do not now exist but that now have certain properties. Some past dinosaurs now have the property of being fossilized, and such immortal artists as Mozart and John Lennon are justly admired by millions today. Not to mention such posthumously acquired properties as arise from posthumous

[44] '*De Essentia,*' in E. Sosa, ed., *Essays on the Philosophy of Roderick M. Chisholm* (Rodopoi, Amsterdam, 1979), pp. 101–121, at p. 109; and 'On Existentialism,' *Philosophical Studies*, 44 (1983), pp. 1–20, at p. 11.

awards and the like. If nothing else, there are always such properties as having once existed and having been a musician. This is fundamentally the same phenomenon: An individual from one circumstance has certain properties in another circumstance in which it does not exist, as a result of the properties it has in its own circumstance.

In fact, so-called serious actualism is really quite a radical doctrine.[45] There is no ground for this doctrine that would not provide analogous grounds for denying present properties to such past individuals as John Lennon and dinosaurs. It might be thought that past individuals and past states of affairs are in some way more real than possible individuals that never come into existence and possible states of affairs that never obtain.[46] We are concerned much more with individuals and events from our past than with individuals and events that never come to pass, and this is sometimes taken as evidence of the greater degree of reality we attribute to the past over the possible-but-never. Those who see things this way usually attribute an intermediate degree of reality to future individuals and future states of affairs—more real than never existent individuals and never obtaining states of affairs, but less real than past individuals and past states of affairs. This is all a mistake. Past individuals *were* more real than merely possible individuals *are*, and events that occurred in the past *were* more real (in some sense) when they occurred than events that never occur *are now*. For that matter, future individuals *will be* more real than merely possible individuals *are*, and future events *will be* more real when they occur than events that never occur *are now*. The past reality of an individual or event may give us a present reason for concern in regard to that individual or event. Contrary to what one would expect according to the comparative reality view I am disputing, we are typically concerned more about future realities than about past realities, at least with regard to future realities we know of or anticipate. The bondage of causation to time's arrow gives us a present and pressing reason for concern about future generations and future events. What's done is done. We cannot change the past, but our present actions and inactions to a great extent determine the future. As far as the present is concerned, past individuals and states of affairs, future individuals and states of affairs, and forever merely possible individuals and states of affairs are on a par: they are now equally unreal. The future is nevertheless a topic of special present concern, because it *will be* real, and what we do *now* determines what it *will be*. Furthermore, we are all time-travellers, on a journey in the direction of time's arrow.

Of course, since such merely possible individuals as Noman have properties even though they do not exist, if our quantifiers are actualist, then the classical logical rules of universal instantiation and existential generalization are fallacious.[47] Instead we have

---

[45] *Cf.* Kit Fine, 'Plantinga on the Reduction of Possibilist Discourse,' and John Pollock, 'Plantinga on Possible Worlds,' in J. Tomberlin and P. van Inwagen, eds., *Alvin Plantinga* (Dordrecht: D. Reidel, 1985), pp. 121–186, at pp. 164–171 and pp. 126–129, respectively.

[46] See for example Robert Adams, 'Time and Thisness,' in P. French, T. Uehling, and H. Wettstein, eds., *Midwest Studies in Philosophy XI: Studies in Essentialism* (Minneapolis: University of Minnesota Press, 1986), pp. 315–329.

[47] In his 'Replies to my Colleagues,' section II.B, in Tomberlin and van Inwagen, *Alvin Plantinga*, pp. 316–323, Plantinga attempts a response to Pollock's denial of so-called serious actualism. Some of Plantinga's arguments for so-called serious actualism beg the question by critically relying (pp. 319, 322) on classical existential generalization. Also, in defending himself against Pollock's

free logical versions: $\ulcorner$Everything is ϕ. α exists. Therefore, α is $\phi\urcorner$ and $\ulcorner\alpha$ is ϕ. α exists. Therefore, something is $\phi\urcorner$. In addition to these we have the following possibilist variations: $\ulcorner$Every possible individual is ϕ. α is a possible individual. Therefore α is $\phi\urcorner$ and $\ulcorner\alpha$ is ϕ. α is a possible individual. Therefore, some possible individual is $\phi\urcorner$. If the singular term α is a simple individual constant (proper name) or variable and the possibilist quantifiers are defined in terms of the actualist quantifiers, then these possibilist versions of free logical UI and EG are tantamount to the following:

> Necessarily, everything actually$_1$ is ϕ.
> χ might have existed.
> Therefore, α is ϕ.

and

> χ is ϕ.
> χ might have existed.
> Therefore, there might have been something that actually$_1$ is ϕ.[48]

We could have something more. The original free logical versions of UI and EG are required by the presence of true sentences in which singular terms that do not refer to (denote) existing individuals occur (outside of nonextensional contexts, such as those created by quotation marks), whether or not these terms refer to possible individuals that do not exist. If we require that all our terms refer to possible individuals, we may retain the *form* of classical UI and EG using the possibilist quantifiers. If the possibilist quantifiers are defined in terms of the actualist quantifiers, this is tantamount to deleting the modal existential second premise from the possibilist free logical UI and EG rules displayed above. Unfortunately, not all singular terms that do not refer to existing individuals refer to possible individuals that do not exist, as witness Quine's 'the merely possible fat man in that doorway' and Meinong's 'the round square'.[49] No merely possible man is actually$_1$ fat or actually$_1$ in Quine's doorway, let alone both, and no merely possible individual is actually$_1$ round or actually$_1$ square, let alone both. And of course, there could not be any impossible individuals. These descriptions are thus *strongly* nonreferring, in that they not only do not refer to any existing thing, they do not even refer to any merely possible thing. Yet there seem to be true sentences in which such strongly nonreferring terms occur; for example, the negative existential 'The round square does not exist'. We could follow Frege's strategy and stipulate that all strongly

charge of fallacious modal reasoning Plantinga appears (at p. 319, first complete paragraph) to commit the very fallacy Pollock attributes to him. (Specifically, he appears to infer the falsehood 'Necessarily, everything is necessarily such that if it exemplifies nonexistence then it exists' from the truth 'Necessarily, everything is such that if it exemplifies nonexistence then it exists'.)

[48] Similarly, we also have such temporal versions as $\ulcorner$Every present or past individual is ϕ. α is a present or past individual. Therefore, α is $\phi\urcorner$ and $\ulcorner\alpha$ is ϕ. α is a future individual. Therefore, some future individual is $\phi\urcorner$, etc. (More accurate versions of these rules would include an additional premise requiring the inter-substitutability of α and the variable of generalization under any assignment of a value to the variable under which it and α are co-referential.)

[49] Quine, 'On What There Is,' at p. 4; Alexius Meinong, 'The Theory of Objects,' in R. Chisholm, ed., *Realism and the Background of Phenomenology* (New York: Free Press, 1960), pp. 76–117, at p. 82.

nonreferring terms shall hereafter refer to Noman. We could then have our classical UI and EG back, at least in form, by interpreting the quantifiers possibilistically. The negative existential 'The round square does not exist' would still be true, as would the modal sentence 'It is possible for the round square to exist'. Indeed, the latter would be logically true. But as Russell noted in discussing Frege's strategy, "this procedure, though it may not lead to actual$^P{}_2$ logical error, is plainly artificial, and does not give an exact analysis of the matter." Darn! Russell is right.

Does Noman have any positive properties in addition to such negative properties as not existing and not being a philosopher? Yes. For example, he has the modal property of possibly existing and its entailments. He also has the dispositional property that he would be male if he existed.

Does he have any nonnegative nonmodal properties, then? Yes he does. He has the property of being mentioned and discussed in these very passages. In fact, as was intimated two paragraphs back, he has the more fundamental semantic property of being referred to by the name 'Noman'. Indeed, Noman is *rigidly designated* by the name 'Noman'. Again, it does not follow that the name refers to something. Noman is not something, and hence, even though 'Noman' refers to him, there is nothing that 'Noman' refers to. Still, Noman might have been someone; he might have existed. Although 'Noman' does not refer to any actual$^i{}_1$ individual, it does refer to a possible individual. It is thus only a weakly nonreferring term. That is, although 'Noman' does not actually$_1$ refer to anything, there might have been someone x such that 'Noman' actually$_1$ refers to x.[50] Reference precedes existence. This is not to say that if Noman had existed, the name 'Noman' would have referred to him. Indeed, if he had existed, the name would not have been conferred onto him. The name only contingently refers to him. In fact, the name contingently rigidly designates him.

How does a name like 'Noman' come to refer to a merely possible individual like Noman? Through fixing its reference by description, in a standard Kripkean stipulation. Of course, the description operator involved must include merely possible individuals in its range, but we have already seen that this presents no problem. (See notes 10, 19 above.) The hard part is finding a property that uniquely identifies a particular merely possible individual. In Noman's case, that was not difficult: Noman is the only possible individual who would have developed from the union of the particular gametes S and E if S had fertilized E in the normal manner. Not all merely possible individuals are so easily pinned down.[51]

---

[50] Contrary to Monte Cook, 'Names and Possible Objects,' *Philosophical Quarterly*, 35, 140 (July 1985), pp. 303–310, at p. 309. See Kaplan, 'Bob and Carol and Ted and Alice,' at pp. 506 and 517, note 19. I once found these claims baffling. *Cf.* Salmon, *Reference*, p. 39n. I was confused. Once it is admitted that classical UI and EG are fallacious, and that an additional existential premise is all that is required in each case to correct the fallacy, what once appeared utterly mysterious becomes perfectly clear and straightforward. The claim that 'Noman' refers to Noman and yet does not refer to anything, properly understood, is really no more baffling than the claim that 'Shakespeare' refers to Shakespeare, who is long dead. When referring to merely possible individuals, it is somewhat more natural (although by no means mandatory) to allow one's quantifiers to go possibilist, thereby preserving the form of classical UI and EG. Likewise, when referring to past or future individuals, it is natural to allow one's quantifers to range over all past or all future individuals.

[51] See Kaplan, 'Bob and Carol and Ted and Alice,' appendix XI, at pp. 505–508.

Since 'Noman' refers to Noman even though he does not exist, a sentence containing 'Noman' might express a possible proposition about Noman even though the possible proposition does not exist. Consider the following:

(8) Noman is a native Californian.

This sentence expresses the possible proposition that Noman is a native Californian. It is arguable that this proposition is a Russellian *singular proposition* (David Kaplan) in which Noman himself occurs as a constituent.[52] In any event, by uttering (8) one asserts *of* Noman, *de re*, that he is a native Californian. Many philosophers would agree that in asserting *of* an individual, *de re*, that it has a certain property, one thereby asserts a singular proposition in which the individual in question occurs directly as a constituent.[53] Thus, in uttering (8) one may be regarded as asserting the possible singular proposition about Noman that he is a native Californian. This proposition is false. In fact, it does not even exist. (Recall the restriction on EG.) But it is possible, in two important senses. First, it might have existed. Second, it might have been true. (As a matter of fact, if it had existed, it very likely would have been true.) There is no proposition that sentence (8) actually$_1$ expresses, but there might have existed a proposition that the sentence actually$_1$ does express. This is the possible proposition about Noman that he is a native Californian. The fact that this possible proposition might have been true underlies the fact that the modal sentence

Noman might have been a native Californian

actually$_1$ is true.

In fact, some merely possible propositions are true despite the fact that they do not exist, for example, the possible singular proposition about Noman that he does not exist, and its entailments. Indeed, for any possible individual x, the possible singular proposition to the effect that x does not exist is necessarily such that if it is true, it does not exist. Its truth entails its nonexistence.

There is an especially remarkable anomaly that arises from these considerations. Let E_{NS} be the ovum from which I actually$_1$ developed. Consider now the possible individual who would have developed from the union of the sperm cell S from Noman's possible zygote with the ovum E_{NS} from my actual^1 zygote, if S (instead of the sperm cell from which I actually$_1$ developed) had fertilized E_{NS} in the normal manner. Let us name this possible individual 'Nothan'. It would seem that it is literally impossible for both Nothan and me to exist together. If one of us exists, the other cannot also exist. We are *incompossible* individuals. Nevertheless, Nothan and I stand in certain cross-world relations to one another. (In fact, we are incompossible brothers across possible worlds.) If Nothan had existed instead of me, he would have grown to reach some determinate height. It is either true that Nothan would have been taller than I actually$_1$ am, or else it is true that Nothan would not

[52] See Salmon, *Frege's Puzzle*, for a defense of singular propositions as the contents of sentences containing proper names.
[53] See Salmon, *Frege's Puzzle*, at pp. 4–6, for a defense of the claim that the objects of *de re* propositional attitudes are singular propositions.

have been taller than I actually$_1$ am. Suppose I utter the sentence

Nothan would have been taller than I actually$_1$ am,

thereby asserting *of* Nothan and myself, *de re*, that he would have been taller than I actually$_1$ am, and suppose Saul Kripke denies what I assert. Here again, it seems very likely that what are true or asserted are certain singular propositions in which Nothan and I occur directly as constituents, to wit, the singular proposition that he would have been taller than I actually$_1$ am or the singular proposition that he would not have been taller than I actually$_1$ am.[54] Although one of these singular propositions is true and the other false, and one of them asserted by me and the other by Kripke, if Nothan and I are incompossible individuals, neither singular proposition can possibly exist. In any possible world in which one of its individual constituents exists, the other individual constituent does not. Something exactly analogous is true of the complex dispositional states of affairs of it being the case that Nothan would have been taller than I actually$_1$ am, and it being the case that Nothan would not have been taller than I actually$_1$ am. One of these states of affairs obtains, yet neither can exist. Or consider instead the *de re* modal proposition concerning Nothan and me that it is impossible for both of us to exist simultaneously. This singular proposition is no more existent than the possible proposition that Noman might have existed, and it is no less true. But if it is true, it *cannot* exist. Its truth entails its *necessary nonexistence*. Thus, there would seem to be a sense in which there are some impossible objects (certain singular propositions or states of affairs) that have certain properties (being the case, obtaining, being asserted or denied, etc.), even though they *cannot* exist, and indeed in some cases, the very property in question entails the impossibility of existence.

Here again, I am not making the Meinongian claim that any description, even if logically contradictory, refers to some possible or impossible object. Quine's description 'the merely possible fat man in that doorway' does not refer to any sort of object, whether existent, merely possible, or impossible. It is a *very* strongly non-referring term. Similarly, Meinong's round square is not only not a possible object, it is not even an impossible object. What makes an impossible object impossible is not that it has contradictory or otherwise incompatible properties. No object—whether existing, past, future, forever merely possible, or forever impossible—has incompatible properties. An impossible object, such as the singular proposition that Nothan would have been taller than I actually$_1$ am, is a complex constructed out of possible objects. Any such object has a perfectly consistent set of properties; it is impossible only because some of its essential constituents are incompossible. An impossible object cannot exist, but it can and does have the properties it has.[55]

---

[54] The first of these propositions may be spelled out more fully as follows: The height that Nothan would have had if he had existed is greater than the height that I actually$_1$ have. The second proposition may be regarded as the negation of the first. See note 2 above.

[55] A simpler example of an impossible object that has properties is the pair set {Nothan, Nathan}, i.e., the set that a possible individual is an element of if and only if that possible individual is either Nothan or me. This impossible set has such properties as its membership, not being empty, being finite, and so on, all of which are perfectly compatible with one another. The term '{Nothan, Nathan}' may be regarded as a strongly nonreferring term that is not very strongly nonreferring; it

Present existence is not a pre-requisite for presently have properties. Nor is the disjunction of past and present existence, i.e., the property of either existing or have once existed. Nor even is the disjunction of past, present, and future existence, i.e., the property of existing at some time or other. Even *possible* existence seems not to be a pre-requisite for having properties, since it seems that in some sense, some impossible things have properties! The moral: The metaphysical condition of having properties is quite separable from the ontological condition of existing. Predication precedes existence. Of course, anything that exists has properties, but this is because having properties is metaphysically utterly unavoidable—in a way that even death and taxes are not. Noman is spared the latter, but no object, not even an impossible one, is spared the former. Such is the negative-existential predicament.

If nonexistence, and even necessary nonexistence, do not preclude having properties, what can be metaphysically so special or important about existence? How can actuality$^i_2$ be an important property when it is a necessary truth that everything has it, and even the possible individuals that do not have it, and the impossible individuals that could not have it, nevertheless have other properties? What is it about actuality in the secondary sense that makes it metaphysically important?

One reason that actuality$_2$ is metaphysically important might be that so many other significant properties depend upon it. If a possible state of affairs does not obtain, it cannot explain, or cause, or be the result of any other state of affairs. And unless a particular possible individual exists, it cannot be anywhere or do anything. Although Noman's properties are not restricted to negative properties and modal properties, they are severely restricted. Noman does not have experiences. A merely possible individual does not live and learn; it does not feel pleasure and pain, or know joy and sorrow; it does not laugh or cry; it does not even lie still at rest. (Let alone is any merely possible individual divine, in any significant sense.) The properties of merely possible individuals, and of impossible individuals, are inert; they include only such unimpressive credentials as being referred to, not being a native Californian, and possibly existing or necessarily not existing. Not an enviable resumé. The mere property of existing, once it is acquired, opens up a galaxy of new possibilities. The question of whether an actual$^i_2$ individual is better off than a nonactual$^i_2$ one probably depends on which properties the actual$^i_2$ individual has. Existence *per se* does not make one well off, except insofar as it opens the door to the potential for being well off. Unfortunately, it also opens the door to the potential for being badly off.

---

does not refer to any existing or merely possible thing, yet it does refer to an impossible thing. Similar remarks may be made in connection with the 'that'-clause, 'that Nothan would have been taller than Nathan actually$_1$ is'.

Here is a not-so-simple quiz problem: Find a way to make discourse involving quantification over impossible objects possibilistically acceptable, by defining, analyzing, or somehow reconstructing the superunrestricted impossibilist quantifiers—'every possible and every impossible individual' and 'some possible or some impossible individual'—in terms of the possibilist quantifiers and standard modal operators. (See note 10 above.) If this cannot be done, how are we to understand the claim that it is true (or I assert, or Saul Kripke denies) of Nothan and me that he would have been taller than I actually$_1$ am? What is it that is true (asserted, denied)?

2

Nonexistence (1998)

I

Among the most perennial of philosophical problems are those arising from sentences involving nonreferring names. Chief among these problems is that of true singular negative existentials. Consider, for example,

(0) Sherlock Holmes does not exist,

interpreted not as an assertion within the fiction (as might be made mendaciously by Professor Moriarty in one of the *Sherlock Holmes* stories), but as an assertion about reality outside the fiction. So interpreted, the sentence is evidently true. But how can any sentence with a nonreferring term in subject position be true? It seems as if (0) designates someone (by its subject term) in order to say (by its predicate) that he does not exist. But it entails that there is no such thing to be designated. G. E. Moore put the problem as follows:

[I]t seems as if purely imaginary things, even though they be absolutely contradictory like a round square, must still have some kind of *being*—must still be in a sense—simply because we can think and talk about them....And now in saying that there is no such thing as a round square, I seem to imply that there *is* such a thing. It seems as if there must be such a thing, merely in order that it may have the property of not-being. It seems, therefore, that to say of anything whatever that we can mention that it absolutely is *not*, were to contradict ourselves: as if everything we can mention must be, must have some kind of being. (*Some Main Problems of Philosophy*, London: George Allen & Unwin, 1953, at p. 289)

In 'On Denoting,' Russell trumpeted his Theory of Descriptions not only for its explanation (which I believe Russell saw as the theory's principal virtue) of how we gain cognitive access to the world beyond our immediate acquaintance, but also for its ability to handle a variety of puzzles that arise on his theory that the semantic

The present chapter is a result of the Santa Barbarians Discussion Group's ruminations on fictional objects, during Fall 1996, organized by C. Anthony Anderson. I am grateful to the participants, especially Anderson, for our extremely useful confusions. I also thank Alan Berger, Kevin Falvey, Steven Humphrey, David Kaplan, and Scott Soames for discussion or comments. Portions of the paper were presented at the universities of California, Irvine; California, Los Angeles; Southern California; and Yale. I am grateful to those audiences for their comments. The essay is dedicated to Noman, without whom it would not have been possible.

content of a singular term is solely its referent (denotation, designatum).[1] The puzzles are primarily: Frege's Puzzle about $\ulcorner \alpha = \beta \urcorner$; the more general problem of substitution failure in certain contexts, especially those ascribing propositional attitude; the question of content and truth-value for sentences involving nonreferring terms; and as a special case, true negative existentials. In previous writings I have discussed the first two problems from the perspective of *Millianism*, which I endorse, according to which the semantic contents of certain simple singular terms, including at least ordinary proper names and demonstratives, are simply their referents, so that a sentence containing a nonvacuous proper name expresses a *singular proposition*, in which the name's bearer occurs directly as a constituent.[2] It has been objected that the second two problems are sufficient by themselves to refute Millianism even if the first two problems are not. Here I shall discuss the problems of nonreferring names from a Millian perspective, and also from the less committal perspective of the *theory of direct reference*, according to which the semantic content of a name or demonstrative is not given by any definite description. I have also discussed the concept of existence in previous work.[3] I shall draw on these previous discussions.

Russell has us consider the English sentence

(1) The present king of France is bald,

which, given that France is no longer a monarchy, Russell deems 'plainly false' (p. 165). As he points out, if (1) is indeed false, then it would seem that its negation,

(2) The present king of France is not bald,

---

[1] *Mind*, 14 (1905), pp. 479–493. Page references are to the reprinting in Robert M. Harnish, ed., *Basic Topics in the Philosophy of Language* (Prentice-Hall, 1994), pp. 161–173.

[2] Principally in the following: *Frege's Puzzle* (Atascadero, Ca.: Ridgeview, 1986, 1991); 'Reflexivity,' *Notre Dame Journal of Formal Logic*, 27, 3 (June 1986), pp. 401–429; 'How to Become a Millian Heir,' *Noûs*, 23, 2 (April 1989), pp. 211–220; 'Illogical Belief,' in J. Tomberlin, ed., *Philosophical Perspectives, 3: Philosophy of Mind and Action Theory* (Atascadero, Ca.: Ridgeview, 1989), pp. 243–285; 'A Millian Heir Rejects the Wages of *Sinn*,' in C. A. Anderson and J. Owens, eds., *Propositional Attitudes: The Role of Content in Logic, Language, and Mind* (Stanford, Ca.: Center for the Study of Language and Information, Stanford University, 1990), pp. 215–247; 'How *Not* to Become a Millian Heir,' *Philosophical Studies*, 62, 2 (May 1991), pp. 165–177; 'Reflections on Reflexivity,' *Linguistics and Philosophy*, 15, 1 (February 1992), pp. 53–63; 'Relative and Absolute Apriority,' *Philosophical Studies*, 69 (1993), pp. 83–100; and 'Being of Two Minds: Belief with Doubt,' *Noûs*, 29, 1 (January 1995), pp. 1–20.

To correct a common misconception: Millianism does not entail that a proper name has no features or aspects that might be deemed, in a certain sense, intensional or connotive. Unquestionably, some names evoke descriptive concepts in the mind of a user. Some may even have particular concepts conventionally attached. Though the names 'Hesperus' and 'Phosphorus' have the same semantic content (the planet Venus), the former connotes *evening*, the latter *morning*. Barbarelli was called 'Giorgionne' because of his size, though the two names for the Venetian artist are semantically equivalent. There is no reason why there cannot be an operator that operates on this kind of connotation. Kripke mentions the particular construction 'Superman was disguised as Clark Kent'. The second argument position in '___ is disguised as ___' (or 'dressed as', 'appears as', etc.) is semantically sensitive to the physical appearance associated with the name occurring in that position. It does not follow that this connotive aspect of a name belongs to semantics, let alone that it affects the propositions semantically expressed by sentences containing the name.

[3] 'Existence,' in J. Tomberlin, ed., *Philosophical Perspectives, 1: Metaphysics* (Atascadero, Ca.: Ridgeview, 1987), pp. 49–108.

ought to be true. But (2) is as wrong as (1), and for the very same reason. By contrast, the singular existential

(3) The present king of France exists

is indeed false, and its negation,

(4) The present king of France does not exist

is true. In Russell's Theory of Descriptions, (1) is analyzed as:

(1') $(\exists x)[(y)(Present\text{-}king\text{-}of\text{-}France(y) \equiv x = y) \wedge Bald(x)]$,

in English as 'Something is both uniquely a present king of France and bald' (where to say that something is *uniquely* such-and-such is to say that it, and nothing else, is such-and-such). As with (1), Russell says that (1') is 'certainly false' (p. 170). In the English sentence (2), the existential quantifier of (1') together with its accompanying material joust with negation for dominant position. Sentence (2) may mean either of two things:

(2') $(\exists x)[(y)(Present\text{-}king\text{-}of\text{-}France(y) \equiv x = y) \wedge \sim Bald(x)]$

(2'') $\sim(\exists x)[(y)(Present\text{-}king\text{-}of\text{-}France(y) \equiv x = y) \wedge Bald(x)]$.

The former is the wide-scope (or *primary occurrence*) reading of (2), on which it expresses that some unique present king of France is not bald. This is false for the same reason as (1'). The latter is the narrow-scope (*secondary occurrence*) reading of (2), on which it expresses that no unique present king of France is bald. This genuinely contradicts (1') and is therefore true. In *Principia Mathematica*, instead of analyzing (3) by replacing '*Bald*(x)' in (1') with '$(\exists y)(x = y)$', Russell and Whitehead analyze it more simply as

(3') $(\exists x)(y)(Present\text{-}king\text{-}of\text{-}France(y) \equiv x = y)$,

i.e. 'Something is uniquely a present king of France.' This is equivalent to its analysis in the style of (1'), since '$(\exists y)(x = y)$' is a theorem of *Principia Mathematica*. Although Russell did not distinguish two readings for (4), he might as well have. The narrow-scope reading is equivalent to the reading given,

(4') $\sim(\exists x)(y)(Present\text{-}king\text{-}of\text{-}France(y) \equiv x = y)$,

while the wide-scope reading is straightforwardly inconsistent, and hence, presumably, cannot be what would normally be intended by (4). Russell extended his solution to sentences involving nonreferring proper names through his thesis that ordinary names abbreviate definite descriptions. The name 'Sherlock Holmes', for example, might abbreviate something like: *the brilliant but eccentric late 19th century British detective who, inter alia, performed such-and-such exploits*. Abbreviating this description instead as 'the Holmesesque detective', (0) is then subject to an analysis parallel to that for (4'), as:

(0') $\sim(\exists x)(y)(Holmesesque\text{-}detective(y) \equiv x = y)$.

Neither (0') nor (4') designates anyone in order to say of him that he does not exist.

Frege had defended a very different theory in '*Über Sinn und Bedeutung*' (1892) concerning sentences like (1) and (2).[4] On that theory—later championed in a somewhat different form by Strawson[5]—although the truth of (1) requires that there be a unique present king of France, (1) is not rendered false by the nonexistence of such a monarch. Instead, (1) *presupposes* that there is a unique present king of France, in the sense that (1) and (2) each separately entail (3'). Since this entailed proposition is false, neither (1) nor (2) is true. Though meaningful, (1) is neither true nor false.[6] Frege regarded this as a consequence of the Principle of Compositionality for Reference, according to which the referent of a compound expression—and as a special case, the truth-value of a sentence—is determined entirely by the referents of the component expressions and their mode of composition. On Frege's view, if a component lacks a referent, so does the whole.

In 'Mr Strawson on Referring,' published some fifty-four years after 'On Denoting,' Russell responds to the objection that (1) is neither true nor false.[7] Where he had earlier claimed that (1) is 'plainly' false, he now says that the issue of whether (1) is false 'is a mere question of verbal convenience' (p. 243). Though this seems to indicate a change of heart, I believe it may not actually do so. He goes on to say, 'I find it more convenient to define the word "false" so that every significant sentence is either true or false. This is a purely verbal question; and although I have no wish to claim the support of common usage, I do not think that he [Strawson] can claim it either.' Frege can indeed accommodate Russell's verdict that (1) is 'plainly false,' simply by understanding 'false' as coextensive with 'untrue'. One way for Frege to do this is to invoke a distinction between two types of negation, so-called *choice* and *exclusion* negation.[8] The difference between the two is given by their three-valued truth tables (where 'U' stands for 'undefined,' i.e., without truth-value):

p	$\sim_C p$	$\sim_E p$
T	F	F
F	T	T
U	U	T

Frege's Principle of Compositionality for Reference requires that exclusion negation be seen as an *ungerade* (oblique) operator. Where '$\sim_C$' is concerned with the customary referent of its operand sentence (i.e., its truth-value), '$\sim_E$' is concerned instead with the indirect referent of its operand, which is its customary sense. Exclusion negation is definable using choice negation. Let p be the proposition expressed by sentence φ. Then $\ulcorner\sim_E\varphi\urcorner$ means that p is not$_C$ true—or in Fregean

---

[4] Page references are to the reprinting in Harnish, pp. 142–160.

[5] In 'On Referring,' *Mind*, 59 (1950), pp. 320–344.

[6] Frege also speaks of a sentence like (1) as presupposing that the expression 'the present king of France' refers to something (pp. 151–152).

[7] In Russell's *My Philosophical Development* (London: Allen and Unwin, 1959), pp. 238–245.

[8] These are called 'internal' and 'external' negation, respectively, in D. A. Bochvar, 'On a Three-Valued Calculus and its Application in the Analysis of the Paradoxes of the Extended Functional Calculus,' *Mathematicheskii Sbornik*, 46 (1938), pp. 287–308.

terminology, that the thought p does not$_C$ determine the True. Hence, 'The present king of France is not$_E$ bald' may be regarded as shorthand for 'It is not$_C$ true that the present king of France is bald'. One might say this if one wishes to assert, cautiously, that either there presently is no unique king of France, or else there is such and he is not bald—i.e. that (2'').

One may understand the term 'false' so that to call a sentence 'false' is to say that its negation is true, where the relevant notion of the negation of a sentence is syntactic (rather than defined in terms of truth tables). The two notions of negation, choice and exclusion, thereby yield two notions of falsehood. Let us say that a sentence is *F-false*$_1$ (false in the Fregean primary sense) if its choice negation is true, and that it is *F-false*$_2$ (false in the Fregean secondary sense) if its exclusion negation is true. The latter term is coextensive with 'untrue'. By Frege's lights, (1) is neither true nor *F*-false$_1$, and therefore, plainly *F*-false$_2$.

So far so good. But Russell's response to Strawson suggests that not only could Frege and Strawson have chosen an alternative sense for 'false', and deem (1) 'false' in that sense, but Russell himself could have chosen a sense for 'false' on which (1') is neither true nor 'false.' Only in that case can it rightfully be said that the question of whether (1) is false is entirely terminological.[9] Is there a legitimate sense of 'false' on which (1) is neither true nor false given its analysis on the Theory of Descriptions?

Whatever 'false' means, it is something contrary to truth. Russell, as well as Frege, could understand falsehood as truth of the (syntactic) negation. Except that on Russell's theory, the negation of (1) is ambiguous. Let us restrict our focus for the time being to sentences none of whose definite descriptions occur within the scope of a nonextensional operator (including sentences with no definite descriptions). Let us call the reading of the negation of such a sentence on which each description is given narrowest possible scope the *outermost negation* of the original sentence, and let us call the reading of the negation on which each description is given widest possible scope the *innermost negation*. (*Cf.* note 8.) Let us say of a sentence of the sort under consideration that it is *R-false*$_1$ if its outermost negation is true, and that it is *R-false*$_2$ if its innermost negation is true. (A multitude of further Russellian notions of falsehood are definable in similar ways.) On the Theory of Descriptions, a sentence none of whose definite descriptions occur in a nonextensional context and all of whose definite descriptions are proper (i.e., such that there is exactly one thing answering to it) is *R*-false$_1$ if and only if it is *R*-false$_2$. Not so for sentences containing improper descriptions. In particular, (1) is *R*-false$_1$ by Russell's lights—and indeed, plainly so in the present absence of a king of France. But (1) is neither true nor *R*-false$_2$.

Russell's reply to Strawson has a good deal of merit. It is by no means obvious, however, that the issue of whether (1) is false is entirely verbal. Whereas both Russell and Frege may deem (1) 'false' in one sense and not 'false' in another, it appears that

---

[9] Echoing Russell, Michael Dummett argues, in 'Presupposition,' *Journal of Symbolic Logic*, 25 (1960), pp. 336–339, that Strawson has not shown that (1) is not false in an antecedently understood sense of the term, but has instead introduced a natural sense of 'false' different from that employed by Russell and on which the term, so understood, does not apply to (1). See also his *Frege: Philosophy of Language* (Cambridge, Mass.: Harvard University Press, 1973, 1981), chapter 12, especially pp. 419–429.

the particular senses Russell employs are not the same as Frege's. The distinction between innermost and outermost negation is not the same as the distinction between choice and exclusion negation. The Fregean treats (2) as involving a lexical ambiguity; Russell sees (2) instead as involving a scope ambiguity. The terms 'R-false$_1$' and 'R-false$_2$' presuppose the Theory of Descriptions, while 'F-false$_1$' and 'F-false$_2$' presuppose the opposing view (assumed by John Stuart Mill as well as Frege) that definite descriptions are singular terms. Insofar as the term 'false', in its standard sense, is identical in extension, and at least close in meaning, to one of these theoretically loaded terms (or to some appropriate variation), it cannot be close in meaning to any of the remaining three. To decide whether (1) is false in the standard sense, it would seem that one must first make a determination between Russell's theory and the Frege/Strawson view—or (perhaps most likely) in favor of some alternative account.

The nature of the divergence between Russell and Frege emerges more fully at a deeper level of analysis on which the four notions of falsehood are theoretically neutralized, to the extent that this is possible. The notions of R-falsehood$_1$ and R-falsehood$_2$ can be made more or less neutral by taking the former to be truth of the *de dicto* reading of the negation, the latter to be truth of the *de re* reading—where (2) read *de dicto* expresses that it is not true that the present king of France is bald, and read *de re* that the present king of France is such that not bald is *he*. One need not embrace the Theory of Descriptions to recognize the *de-re/de-dicto* distinction (problematic though this general distinction is on Fregean theory). R-falsehood$_1$ thus corresponds, closely enough, to F-falsehood$_2$—essentially the notion of untruth. All parties agree that (1) is plainly "false" in this sense. The relationship between R-falsehood$_2$ and F-falsehood$_1$ is not nearly this close. The Fregean agrees that (1) is not R-false$_2$, since it is plainly not true that the present king of France is nonbald. But this is different from the Fregean denial that (1) is F-false$_1$. F-falsehood$_1$ is falsehood in the sense of the 'F' invoked in three-valued truth tables. This notion, though Fregean, is not anti-Russellian. There could be untrue sentences in which all singular terms refer but which lack F-falsehood$_1$ for reasons unrelated to singular-term reference—for example, because of a partially defined predicate, or a category mistake, or a failed presupposition that is not existential in nature. It is perfectly consistent to acknowledge that such sentences are neither true nor F-false$_1$ (i.e., that they are U) while embracing the Theory of Descriptions. A decision would have to be made concerning whether the negation symbol '$\sim$' is a sign for choice or exclusion negation, but whichever decision was made (it is customary to use it for choice negation), a second negation sign could be introduced for the other notion. Even if the Russellian were to embrace the Principle of Bivalence—according to which every well-formed declarative sentence is either true or false (Russell says that he finds it convenient to use the term 'false' in such a way as to honor this principle)—this need not represent a rejection of F-falsehood$_1$. It may constitute a thesis that every well-formed sentence is either true or F-false$_1$—even category-mistake sentences and the rest, or that such "sentences" are not well-formed, etc.

F-falsehood$_1$ should be understood not merely as truth of the choice negation, but as truth of the choice negation *construed as the authentic contradictory of the original sentence*—in effect, as truth of the outermost choice negation. Readings or analyses of the choice negation that do not contradict the original sentence, or do not contradict an analysis of it, are irrelevant. If a category-mistake sentence is neither true nor F-false$_1$, then the outermost choice negation of it, and of any analyses of it, are likewise neither true nor F-false$_1$. The question is whether the untrue (1) is F-false$_1$. On Russell's theory, (1) is F-false$_1$ if and only if (2″) is true. The untruth of (2′) is not pertinent. To rebut the objection that (1) is neither true nor F-false$_1$ it is not sufficient for Russell to agree that (1) is neither true nor R-false$_2$. He must argue further that (1) is indeed F-false$_1$, and that in denying this Frege and Strawson have probably confused F-falsehood$_1$ with R-falsehood$_2$.[10]

II

Whereas Frege's Principle of Compositionality for Reference requires that sentences like (1) and (2) lack truth-value, his theory of sense and reference explains how such sentences nevertheless semantically express propositions. On the other hand, the same Principle of Compositionality creates a problem for Frege in connection with sentences like (3) and (4). It is natural to take these to be analyzable as:

$(3'')\ (\exists x)[(\imath y)Present\text{-}king\text{-}of\text{-}France(y) = x]$

$(4'')\ \sim(\exists x)[(\imath y)Present\text{-}king\text{-}of\text{-}France(y) = x],$

respectively. The intended truth-conditions for (3″) and (4″) are given by (3′) and (4′). But since the definite description lacks a referent, (3″) and (4″) must instead for Frege be neither true nor false—assuming the standard interpretation for existential quantification, identity, and negation (as Frege gave them in connection with his own notation) on which each is fully extensional.

---

[10] An analogous situation obtains in connection with verbs like 'know', 'realize', 'notice', etc. Is the untrue sentence 'Jones knows that the Earth is flat' false, or is it neither true nor false? The analogue of the Russellian view would be that this sentence is analyzable into a conjunction ⌜The Earth is flat and φ⌝, for some sentence φ concerning Jones's epistemic situation (e.g., 'Jones is epistemically justified, in a manner not defeated by Gettier-type phenomena, in believing that the Earth is flat'). This is the standard view in contemporary epistemology. The negation 'Jones does not know that the Earth is flat' may then be subject to an innermost/outermost scope ambiguity. The analogue of the Fregean view would be that the original sentence instead presupposes that the Earth is flat. This alternative to the Russellian view has been discussed by linguists. See Ed Keenan, 'Two Kinds of Presupposition in Natural Language', in Charles Fillmore and D. Terence Langendoen, eds., *Studies in Linguistic Semantics* (1971), Paul and Carol Kiparski, 'Fact,' and Charles Fillmore, 'Types of Lexical Information,' both in D. D. Steinberg and L. A. Jakobovits, eds., *Semantics* (Cambridge University Press, 1971), and Deirdre Wilson, *Presuppositions and Non-Truth-Conditional Semantics* (Academic Press, 1975). On this view, the negation of the original sentence may be subject to a choice/exclusion lexical ambiguity. Either view may thus regard the negation as true in one sense and untrue in another, making the original sentence false in one sense, unfalse in another. The two views nevertheless differ over the question of whether the original sentence instantiates F-falsehood$_1$. (The similarity between the issues concerning reference and factives can be made more than merely analogous, by taking ⌜α knows that φ⌝ as shorthand for ⌜α knows the fact that φ⌝, with ⌜the fact that φ⌝ a definite description that is proper if and only if φ is true.)

By way of a solution to this difficulty, Frege suggested that (3) and (4) are properly interpreted not by (3″) and (4″), but as covertly quotational. He wrote:

> We must here keep well apart two wholly different cases that are easily confused, because we speak of existence in both cases. In one case the question is whether a proper name designates, names, something; in the other whether a concept takes objects under itself. If we use the words 'there is a - - - - -' we have the latter case. Now a proper name that designates nothing has no logical justification, since in logic we are concerned with truth in the strictest sense of the word; it may on the other hand still be used in fiction and fable. ('A Critical Elucidation of some Points in E. Schroeder's *Algebra der Logik*,' published 1895, translated by Peter Geach in *Translations from the Philosophical Writings of Gottlob Frege*, Oxford: Basil Blackwell, 1970, p. 104)

Elsewhere Frege made similar remarks about singular existentials and their negations: "People certainly say that Odysseus is not an historical person, and mean by this contradictory expression that the name 'Odysseus' designates nothing, has no referent (*Bedeutung*)" (from the section on 'Sense and Reference' of Frege's 1906 diary notes, 'Introduction to Logic,' in H. Hermes, F. Kambartel, and F. Kaulbach, eds., *Posthumous Writings*, translated by P. Long and R. White,[11] University of Chicago Press, 1979, at p. 191). Earlier in his 'Dialogue with Pünjer on Existence' (pre-1884, also in Hermes, *et al.*), Frege observed: "If 'Sachse exists' is supposed to mean "The word 'Sachse' is not an empty sound, but designates something", then it is true that the condition "Sachse exists" must be satisfied [in order for 'There are men' to be inferred from 'Sachse is a man']. But this is not a new premise, but the presupposition of all our words—a presupposition that goes without saying" (p. 60).[12]

The suggestion would appear to be that (3) and (4), at least on one reading (on which the latter is true), are correctly formalized as:

(5) $(\exists x)$['the present king of France' refers$_{English}$ to x]

(6) $\sim(\exists x)$ ['the present king of France' refers$_{English}$ to x].

Notice that this semantic-ascent theory of singular existence is not disproved by the success of substitution of coreferential terms in existential contexts—as for example, in 'The author of *Naming and Necessity* exists. The author of *Naming and Necessity* is the McCosh Professor of Philosophy at Princeton University; therefore the Princeton McCosh Professor of Philosophy exists'.[13] Although positions within quotation marks are not typically open to substitution of coreferential terms, by the very nature of the particular context ⌜'___' refers$_{English}$ to x⌝ the position within its quotation marks respects such substitution. Assuming, as Frege did, that each instance of the metalinguistic schema

(F) (x)(['the' + NP refers$_{English}$ to x] $\equiv$ $(y)[\phi_y \equiv x = y]$),

---

[11] Except that I here render '*Bedeutung*' as 'referent'.

[12] Frege also suggests here that there may be an alternative reading for 'Sachse exists', on which it is tantamount to 'Sachse = Sachse', which Frege says is self-evident. He might well have said the same about '$(\exists x)$[Sachse = x]'.

[13] The term 'semantic ascent' is due to W. V. O. Quine. See his *Word and Object* (Cambridge, Mass.: MIT Press, 1960), §56.

is true where ϕ is a formalization in the notation of first-order logic for the English NP, (5) is true if and only if (3′) is, and (6) is true if and only if (4′) is. Frege can thus attain the same truth-conditions for (3) and (4) as does Russell.

Frege's semantic-ascent approach succeeds in capturing information that is indeed conveyed in the uttering of (3) or (4). But, to invoke a distinction I have emphasized in previous work, this concerns what is *pragmatically imparted* in (3) and (4), and not necessarily what is *semantically encoded* or *contained*.[14] Frege does not attain the same semantic content as Russell or even the same modal intension, i.e., the same corresponding function from possible worlds to truth-values. Indeed, that the semantic-ascent interpretation of (3) and (4) by (5) and (6), respectively, is incorrect is easily established by a variety of considerations. The semantic-ascent theory of existence is analogous to Frege's account of identity in *Begriffsschrift* (1879). Curiously, Frege evidently failed to see that his objection in '*Über Sinn and Bedeutung*' to the semantic-ascent theory of identity applies with equal force against the semantic-ascent theory of existence. Another objection to semantic-ascent analyses has been raised by Frege's most effective apologist and defender, Alonzo Church.[15] Translating (4) into French, one obtains:

Le roi présent de France n'existe pas.

Translating its proposed analysis into French, one obtains:

'The present king of France' *ne fait référence à rien en anglais.*

These two translations, while both true, clearly mean different things in French. So too, therefore, do what they translate.

A theory of singular existence statements that is equally Fregean in spirit but superior to the semantic-ascent account takes the verb 'exist' as used in singular existentials to be an *ungerade* device, so that both (3) and (4) concern not the phrase 'the present king of France' but its English sense.[16] This is analogous to the semantic-ascent theory of existence, except that one climbs further up to the level of intension. On the intensional-ascent theory of existence, (3) and (4) are analyzed thus:

(7) $(\exists x)\Delta(^{\wedge}(\imath y)\textit{Present-king-of-France}(y)^{\wedge}, x)$

(8) $\sim(\exists x)\Delta(^{\wedge}(\imath y)\textit{Present-king-of-France}(y)^{\wedge}, x),$

where 'Δ' is a dyadic predicate for the relation between a Fregean sense and that which it determines (that of which the sense is a concept) and the '$^{\wedge}$' is a device for indirect quotation (in the home language, in this case a standard notation for

[14] *Frege's Puzzle*, pp. 58–60 and elsewhere (especially 78–79, 84–85, 100, 114–115, 127–128). The distinction is developed further in other works cited in note 2 above.

[15] See Church's 'On Carnap's Analysis of Statements of Assertion and Belief,' *Analysis*, 10, 5 (1950), pp. 97–99. For a defense of the Church-Langford translation argument, see my 'The Very Possibility of Language: A Sermon on the Consequences of Missing Church,' in C. A. Anderson's and M. Zeleny, eds., *Logic, Meaning and Computation: Essays in Honor of Alonzo Church* (Boston: Kluwer, 1998).

[16] Church cites the particular sentence (4) as an example of a true sentence containing an *ungerade* occurrence of a singular term ('name'), in *Introduction to Mathematical Logic I* (Princeton University Press, 1956), at p. 27n. See note 58 below.

first-order logic with 'Δ').[17] Like the semantic-ascent theory, this intensional-ascent account of existence is not disproved by the success of substitution of coreferential terms in existential contexts. On a Fregean philosophy of semantics, indirect–quotation marks create an *ungerade* context—one might even say that they create the paradigm *ungerade* context as Frege understood the concept—so that any expression occurring within them refers in that position to its own customary sense, yet the position flanked by them in the particular context $\ulcorner\Delta(^\wedge\_\_\_^\wedge, x)\urcorner$ remains open to substitution because of the special interplay between indirect–quotation and 'Δ'. The intensional-ascent theory is not so easily refuted as the semantic-ascent approach by the Church translation argument.[18] In place of schema (F), we invoke the following:

$$(C) \ (x)[\Delta(^\wedge(\imath y)\phi_y^\wedge, x) \equiv (y)(\phi_y \equiv x = y)],$$

thereby attaining the familiar Russellian truth and falsehood conditions for (3) and (4). Unlike (F), every instance of (C) expresses a necessary truth. The intensional-ascent theory of existence thus also obtains the correct modal intensions for (3) and (4).

III

A singular term is *nonreferring* (with respect to a context c, a time t, and a possible world w), in one sense, if and only if there does not exist anything to which the term refers (with respect to c, t, and w). On Millianism, a nonreferring proper name is thus devoid of semantic content. A Millian, like myself, and even a less committal direct-reference theorist like Kripke, may not avail him/herself of the Theory of Descriptions to solve the problems of sentences with nonreferring names.[19] If α is a

---

[17] *Cf.* my 'Reference and Information Content: Names and Descriptions,' in D. Gabbay and F. Guenthner, eds., *Handbook of Philosophical Logic IV: Topics in the Philosophy of Language* (Dordrecht: D. Reidel, 1989), chapter IV.5, pp. 409–461, at 440–441 on Fregean sense-quotation. The idea comes from David Kaplan's 'Quantifying In,' in D. Davidson and J. Hintikka, eds., *Words and Objections: Essays on the Work of W. V. O. Quine* (Dordrecht: D. Reidel, 1969), pp. 178–214; reprinted in L. Linsky, ed., *Reference and Modality* (Oxford University Press, 1971), pp. 112–144, at 120–121. In English, the word 'that' attached to a subordinate clause (as in $\ulcorner$Jones believes that $\phi\urcorner$ or $\ulcorner$It is necessary that $\phi\urcorner$) typically functions in the manner of sense-quotation marks.

[18] On this application of the translation argument, see my 'A Problem in the Frege–Church Theory of Sense and Denotation,' *Noûs*, 27, 2 (June 1993), pp. 158–166, and 'The Very Possibility of Language: A Sermon on the Consequence of Missing Church.'

[19] Kripke does not officially endorse or reject Millianism. Informal discussions lead me to believe he is deeply skeptical. (*Cf.* his repeated insistence in 'A Puzzle about Belief' that Pierre does not have inconsistent beliefs—in A. Margalit, ed., *Meaning and Use*, Dordrecht: D. Reidel, 1979, pp. 239–283; reprinted in N. Salmon and S. Soames, eds., *Propositions and Attitudes*, Oxford University Press, 1988, pp. 102–148.) Nevertheless, Kripke believes that a sentence using a proper name in an ordinary context (not within quotation marks, etc.) expresses a proposition only if the name refers. Similarly, Keith Donnellan, in 'Speaking of Nothing,' *The Philosophical Review*, 83 (January 1974), pp. 3–32 (reprinted in S. Schwartz, ed., *Naming Necessity and Natural Kinds*, Ithaca: Cornell University Press, 1977, pp. 216–244), says, 'when a name is used and there is a failure of reference, then no proposition has been expressed—certainly no true proposition. If a child says, 'Santa Claus will come tonight,' he cannot have spoken the truth, although, for various reasons, I think it better to say that he has not even expressed a proposition. [*footnote:* Given that this is a statement about reality and that proper names have no descriptive content, then how are we to represent the proposition expressed?]' (pp. 20–21).

proper name, referring or not, it is not a definite description, nor by the direct-reference theory's lights does it 'abbreviate' any definite description. Direct-reference theory thus excludes application of the Theory of Descriptions in connection with the analogues of (1)–(4):

(1α) α is bald
(2α) α is not bald
(3α) α exists
(4α) α does not exist.

For similar reasons, the direct-reference theorist is also barred from using Frege's sense-reference distinction to solve the difficulties. How, then, can the theorist ascribe content to (1α)–(4α)? In particular, how can (4α) express anything at all, let alone something true? The semantic-ascent theory of existence is refuted on the direct-reference theory no less than on Fregean theory by the Church translation argument as well as by modal considerations (among other things). The *ungerade* theory hardly fares much better on direct-reference theory in connection with (3α) and (4α). On the Millian theory, it fares no better at all. Using the '^' now as a semantic-content quotation mark, the intensional-ascent theory yields

(7α) $(\exists x)\Delta(^\wedge\alpha^\wedge, x)$

(8α) $\sim(\exists x)\Delta(^\wedge\alpha^\wedge, x)$

as purported analyses for (3α) and (4α), respectively. But according to Millianism, if α is a proper name, then $\ulcorner{^\wedge}\alpha^\wedge\urcorner$ refers to α's bearer. Where α is a nonreferring name, $\ulcorner{^\wedge}\alpha^\wedge\urcorner$ is equally nonreferring.

Canvassing some alleged cases of true sentences of the form of (4α) with α a nonreferring name reveals that the so-called problem of nonreferring names, on closer examination, frequently vanishes.

First, let the α in (3α) and (4α) be a name for a possible individual that does not actually exist, i.e. for a merely possible individual. Though there is no bald man (we may suppose) in Quine's doorway at this moment, there might have been.[20] I hereby dub the merely possible bald man in Quine's doorway (if there is exactly one there) 'Curly-0'. Even though Curly-0 might have existed, this much should be clear: Curly-0 does not exist. But how can that be?

Contemporary philosophy has revealed that my little naming ceremony was an exercise in futility. For even if we countenance merely possible individuals, at least for the purpose of naming one of them, I have not yet singled any one of them out to be named. There are many different merely possible individuals who might have been bald men standing in Quine's doorway, but none of them are actually bald or standing in Quine's doorway. The problem is to distinguish one of them. Difficult though the task may be, David Kaplan has found a way to do it.[21] Gamete S is a particular male

---

[20] *Cf.* 'On What There Is,' in Quine's *From a Logical Point of View* (New York: Harper and Row, 1953, 1961).

[21] 'Bob and Carol and Ted and Alice,' in K. J. Hintikka, J. Moravcsik, and P. Suppes, eds., *Approaches to Natural Language*, Dordrecht: D. Reidel, 1973, pp. 490–518, at 516–517n19. Kripke has also described such a procedure.

sperm cell of my father's, and gamete E is a particular ovum of my mother's, such that neither is ever actually united with any other gamete. Following Kaplan's instructions, I have given the name 'Noman-0' to the particular possible individual who would have resulted from the union of S and E, had they united in the normal manner to develop into a human zygote.[22] Noman (as I call him for short) is my merely possible brother. He is a definite possible individual who might have been a bald man standing in Quine's doorway. Noman does not exist. But how can that be?

The apparent difficulty here is an illusion. Consider the following analogous situation. Let the α in (4α) be the name 'Socrates'. Then (3α) is true with respect to the year 400 BC, and (4α) false. With respect to the present day, these truth-values are reversed. Socrates is long gone. Consequently, singular propositions about him, which once existed, also no longer exist. Let us call the no-longer-existing proposition that Socrates does not now exist, 'Soc'. Soc is a definite proposition. Its present lack of existence does not prevent it from presently being true. Nor does its nonexistence prevent it from being semantically expressible in English. Notice that in 400 BC, the sentence 'Socrates does not exist' evidently did not express anything in English, and hence was not true or false, since the language itself had not yet come into being. Some might argue that the sentence did not yet even exist. Moreover, even if the language had come into being in 400 BC, the English sentence 'Socrates does not exist' might not have had the exactly same semantics then that it has today. Expressing a proposition (or being true or false, etc.) *with respect to* a given time t is not the same thing as expressing that proposition *at t*. Today the sentence 'Socrates does not exist' expresses Soc with respect to the present time. It does not follow that there exists a proposition that this sentence expresses with respect to the present time. There presently exists no such proposition, but there was such a proposition. 'Socrates does not exist' does indeed single out a definite past thing in order to say of it, correctly, that it does not now exist. It does not follow that there presently exists someone designated in the sentence (and said therein not to exist). There presently exists no one to whom the term 'Socrates', as a name for the philosopher who drank the hemlock, refers in English, but there did exist someone to whom the name now refers. The sentence 'Socrates does not exist' *now* expresses Soc, and Soc is now true. And that is why the sentence is now true in English (even though Soc does not now exist). This account of the truth of 'Socrates does not exist' applies *mutatis mutandis* to objects from the future as well as the past. Kaplan has named the first child to be born in the twenty-second century 'Newman-1'.[23] There presently exists no proposition expressed by 'Newman-1 does not exist'. But there will exist a particular proposition that is already so expressed, and it is true.

The principal facts about Socrates and Newman-1 are true as well of Noman. I call a nonreferring singular term *weakly nonreferring* if there might have existed something to which the term actually refers, and I call a nonreferring term *very weakly nonreferring* (at a time t) if (at t) there has existed, or is going to exist, something to which the term refers. 'Noman' is weakly nonreferring but not very

[22] In 'Existence,' cited above in note 3, at pp. 49–50. I draw heavily from the discussion there, especially at pp. 90–98, in the remainder of this section.
[23] In 'Quantifying In,' p. 135 of Linsky.

weakly. There exists no one to whom 'Noman' refers but there might have been a definite someone x such that 'Noman' *actually* refers to x. By the same token, there exists no proposition expressed by 'Noman does not exist', but there might have been a proposition that *actually is* expressed, and it is actually true.

Consider now *la pièce de résistance*. A *strongly nonreferring* term is one such that there could not have existed something to which the term actually refers. Curiously, an extension of the same solution may be made even for some strongly nonreferring terms. To see this, let E_{NS} be the ovum from which I actually sprang. I have introduced the name 'Nothan-0' for the merely possible individual who would have sprang from the union of S and E_{NS} had they been united in the normal manner. Like 'Noman-0', 'Nothan-0' is weakly nonreferring but not very weakly. It seems that Nothan (as I call him) and I are *incompossible*; we could not both exist since we each require the same ovum. Either it is true or it is false that Nothan might have been taller than I actually am. This is a truth-valued singular proposition about a definite pair of possible individuals. But unlike the proposition that Nothan is 6 feet tall, this proposition could not possibly exist; there is no possible world in which its two constituent possible people exist together. The term 'the proposition that Nothan-0 might have been taller than Nathan Salmon actually is' is thus strongly nonreferring. Still, there is in *some* sense a definite impossible thing to which the term actually refers: the very singular proposition in question, which is true if Nothan might have been taller than I actually am and is otherwise false. An analogous situation obtains in connection with the proposition, which I believe, that Plato was taller than I now am. There is no time at which this singular proposition exists. In particular, it does not now exist, yet I now believe it.[24] The negative existential 'The singular proposition that Nothan might have been taller than Nathan Salmon actually is, does not exist' is true, and its subject term is strongly nonreferring. In fact, the proposition expressed by this negative existential could not possibly exist. Yet there is in some sense a definite proposition that is in question, and it is true. Something analogous to this is true also in connection with the pair set, {Nothan-0, Nathan Salmon}; there is in some sense a definite set that is actually referred to by this piece of set-theoretic notation (assuming it is properly interpreted), yet that set could not possibly exist. Even if Nothan had existed, {Nothan, me} still could not do so. Neither could the singular proposition about the pair set that it does not exist. Yet that proposition is true, precisely in virtue of the fact that the pair set to which it makes reference does not exist. Analogously again, the pair set

---

[24] The same fate might befall Soc, if (as some believe) the present time did not itself exist when Socrates did. In order to facilitate the exposition I have pretended instead that times (like the present) exist eternally.

The sense in which there is a proposition that Nothan might have been taller than I actually am is troublesome. The fact that it seems to require quantification over objects that could not exist should give one pause. Still, it is difficult to deny that in *some* sense, there are such objects to be quantified over; the proposition that Nothan might have been taller than I actually am is one such. To deny this would be to undertake the burden of explaining how it is either true that Nothan might have been taller than I actually am or true that Nothan could not have been. Either way, the result seems to be a true singular proposition that exists in no possible world. A substitutional interpretation of 'there are' may be called for when impossible objects rear their ugly heads.

{Plato, me} does not exist, never did, and never will. Neither does the proposition that this pair set does not now exist. But it is a definite set with a definite membership, and the proposition is true.

It should be noted that the mentioned impossible objects are not like 'the round square,' which Alexius Meinong claimed had lower-class ontological status, a sort of being shy of existence due to its incompatible properties of shape.[25] What makes the pair set {Nothan-0, Nathan Salmon} and the proposition that Nothan might have been taller than I actually am impossible is not that they have inconsistent or otherwise incompatible properties. As a matter of pure logic, it is provable that nothing has inconsistent properties. An impossible object, like the mentioned pair set or singular proposition, is a complex entity composed of incompossible things. Any composite entity, even one whose components are incompossible, has a perfectly consistent set of attributes. An impossible object is not a Meinongian inconsistent Object. Though it cannot exist, an impossible object's properties are perfectly coherent.

Some might wish to object to the foregoing that, of the nonreferring names mentioned, only 'Socrates' refers to a definite individual, since the reference of the rest is not fixed by the entire history of the universe up to the present moment. There is not yet any objective fact, says the objector, concerning which future individual the name 'Newman-1' names.[26] This objection involves the issue of future contingencies. While a full response cannot be given here, I will provide a brief response that I think adequate to the task at hand. First, the particular example of Newman-1 could be replaced with the introduction of a name for the future result of an in-progress physically and causally determined process. Second, the objection confuses truth with a concept of unpreventability, which entails truth but is not entailed by it. The fact that 'Socrates' has the particular reference it does is now unpreventable. By contrast, perhaps it is still within our power (at least if free will is assumed) to influence who will be the first child born in the twenty-second century. Suppose it is not yet causally (or in some other manner) determined which future person will be born first in the twenty-second century. It does not follow that there is no fact of the matter, or that it is as yet neither true nor false that that future person will be born first in the twenty-second century. Many facts about the future are as yet causally open, still preventable. Suppose I am about to decide whether to listen to Beethoven or Beatles, but have not yet done so. I will either choose Beethoven or I will not. One of these two disjuncts obtains—one of them is a fact—though which one is not yet settled. There is no incompatibility between its not yet being settled which choice I will make and my eventually choosing Beethoven. On the contrary, it's not yet being settled entails that either I will choose Beethoven and it is not yet settled that I will, or else I will decide against Beethoven and that is not yet settled. Either way, there now is a fact concerning my future choice—as yet still preventable but a fact nonetheless. However I choose, although that future choice is still preventable the fact remains (however preventably) that I will make that decision instead of the other.

---

[25] 'The Theory of Objects,' in R. Chisholm, ed., *Realism and the Background of Phenomenology* (Glencoe, Ill.: The Free Press, 1960), pp. 76–117.

[26] Ilhan Inan brought this possible objection to my attention.

What follows from our assumption is that there is no unpreventable fact concerning whom 'Newman-1' now names, not that there is no fact at all. It is not yet *causally* (or in the other manner) fixed which future individual the name names, but the name's reference is *semantically* fixed. There is—or rather there will be—a fact concerning whom the name names, even if it is still preventable. That fact also does not yet exist, but it is already a fact, and eventually (not yet) it will even be unpreventable. Kaplan fixed the reference of 'Newman-1' *semantically* not by means of the description 'the future person who is unpreventably going to be born first in the twenty-second century', but by 'the future person who *will* be born first in the twenty-second century'. The name's reference is even *causally* fixed to the extent that, given the way in which Kaplan introduced the name, it is already settled that the name now refers to whichever future individual will turn out to be the first child born in the twenty-second century if there will be such an individual (and that the name is nonreferring otherwise). This much about the name is unpreventable (although, of course, the name's semantics can be changed from what it currently is). Though it is not yet causally fixed who will be born first in the twenty-second century, there already is (or rather, there will exist something that is now) a fact, as yet preventable, concerning who it will be. These two facts—one unpreventable, the other still preventable—entail a third fact, itself as yet preventable, concerning whom the name now names.[27] The possible causal indeterminacy, and our present ignorance, concerning who the first child born in the twenty-second century will

---

[27] The situation can be illustrated by means of a deductively valid argument:

(P1) The referent$_{English}$ of 'Newman-1' = the first child to be born in the twenty-second century.
(P2) The first child to be born in the twenty-second century = Newman-1.

Therefore,

(C) The referent$_{English}$ of 'Newman-1' = Newman-1.

Assume 'Newman-1' is used as a name of the future person who will be born first in the twenty-second century. (This assumption, of course, begs the question against the objector, but let that pass; I wish to clarify the objector's position from the perspective of one who is not persuaded by the objection.) Then the conclusion (C) specifies whom 'Newman-1' names; it states that the name names *that* particular future individual. Think of the argument as consisting not of these sentences, but of the propositions they express. The question at issue is whether (C) (the proposition) is already true. The truth or falsity of (P2), we are assuming, is not yet causally (or in some other manner) fixed. Equivalently, the result of prefixing the sentence (P2) with a temporal/modal operator 'It is unpreventable that' is false with respect to the present, and likewise the result of prefixing its negation. (Unpreventability is closed under logical consequence.) The objector reasons that since (P2) (the proposition) is still preventable, both it and (C) are as yet neither true nor false. (The objector will want to say this about (P1) as well.) This wrongly assumes that (for propositions of the class in question) truth is the same thing as unpreventability, thus making $\ulcorner$It is unpreventable that $\phi\urcorner$ truth-functional, equivalent in a three-valued logic to the double exclusion-negation of ϕ, $\ulcorner\sim_E\sim_E\phi\urcorner$. The truth of (P1) is already unpreventable. Contrary to the objector, (P2) is also true, even though that fact is still preventable. Therefore (C), though preventable, is true.

This same deductive argument illuminates other philosophically interesting issues. I have used it to argue that though (P1) is true by semantics done, and is also known by semantics alone, surprisingly (C)—which is established by this very argument—is neither. See 'How to Measure the Standard Metre,' *Proceedings of the Aristotelian Society* (New Series), 88, (1987/88), pp. 193–217, at 200–201n10; and 'Analyticity and Apriority,' in J. Tomberlin, ed., *Philosophical Perspectives 7, Language and Logic* (Atascadero, Ca.: Ridgeview, 1993), pp. 125–133, at 133n15.

turn out to be does not impugn the fact that whoever it turns out to be, that one is already the referent of 'Newman-1'. Nor does that future individual's present non-existence impugn this fact, any more than Socrates's present nonexistence impugns the fact that 'Socrates' refers to him. Socrates's pastness and unpreventability does not bestow on his name any more semantic factuality, or rigidity, than 'Newman-1' enjoys—nor, for that matter, than 'Noman-0' enjoys. There is no more justification for saying that 'Socrates' is semantically superior to 'Newman-1' because Newman-1 is preventable and Socrates is not, than there is for saying that 'Newman-1' is semantically superior to 'Socrates' because Socrates is dead and Newman-1 is not.

Followers of Quine dismiss merely possible objects like Noman on the ground of a lack of clear "identity conditions." It is worth noticing that it is causally determined which possible individual would have sprang from gametes S and E, had they united in the normal manner to form a zygote. If causal determination were important to semantic definiteness, the name 'Noman-0', and even the term '{Nothan-0, Nathan Salmon}', should be semantically definite to a greater degree than 'Newman-1'. Despite its actual nonexistence, there is no problem about the identity conditions of the proposition that Noman does not exist. Nor is there a problem about the identity conditions of Soc. Or at least there is no more problem than there is in the case of the ordered pair consisting of Socrates first, and the temporally indexed property (or concept) of present nonexistence second. A proposition is identical with Soc if and only if it consists of these very same two constituents. Indeed, Soc might even be identified with the ordered pair. If the Principle of Extensionality suffices for giving the 'identity conditions' of sets, then an exactly analogous principle is sufficient for propositions, presently existent and not. Quine and his followers also object to such intensional entities as properties and concepts, and on similar grounds. But the particular property of nonexistence creates no special problems. One may take it to be fully definable by means of the purely logical notions of abstraction, universal quantification, negation, and identity thus: $(\lambda x)(y)[x \neq y]$.[28] There is no legitimate reason for allowing a sentence of the form (4α) to be true by virtue of expressing Soc, but to disallow such a sentence from being true by virtue of expressing the analogous proposition about Noman.

Some may balk at my proposal on the grounds that it conflicts with the meta-physical principle that any object must exist in every conceivable circumstance in which that object has any properties. This principle that existence is a pre-condition for having properties—that existence precedes suchness—underlies the Kantian doctrine that existence is not itself a property (or 'predicate'). It, like the Kantian doctrine it supports, is a confused and misguided prejudice. Undoubtedly, existence is a pre-requisite for a very wide range of ordinary properties—being blue in color, having such-and-such mass, writing *Waverley*. But the sweeping doctrine that existence universally precedes suchness has very clear counterexamples in which an object from one circumstance has properties in another circumstance in virtue of the properties it has in the original circumstance. Socrates does not exist in my present circumstance, yet he has numerous properties here—for example, being

[28] *Cf.* note 24. The universal quantifier here cannot be substitutional. One of my central tasks in 'Existence' was to investigate the viability of an analysis of existence in terms of standard objectual quantification.

mentioned and discussed by me. Walter Scott, who no longer exists, currently has the property of having written *Waverley*. He did exist when he had the property of writing *Waverley*, of course, but as every author knows, the property of writing something is very different from the property of having written it. Among their differences is the fact that the former requires existence. On the doctrine that existence precedes suchness, Scott lacks the property of having written *Waverley* not because he did not write *Waverley* (since he did), but merely because he does not exist. Once it is conceded that Scott wrote *Waverley*, or that Socrates is admired by Jones, etc., what is gained by denying nevertheless that they have these very properties? To satisfy the prejudice, one may simply insist that objects like Socrates that no longer exist can no longer have properties. To do so is to concede that Socrates does not exist. One thereby falsifies the very position insisted upon, by bestowing on Soc the particular property of being conceded (or asserted, agreed upon, presupposed, etc.). As long as it is deemed now true that Socrates does not exist, that is sufficient for the present truth in English of 'Socrates does not exist', granted that 'Socrates does not exist' expresses in English (with respect *t*) that Socrates does not exist (at *t*). It matters little whether it is conceded that Soc has the property Truth—or for that matter whether it is conceded that 'Socrates does not exist' has the corresponding property of being a true sentence of English. And it matters not at all that Soc no longer exists.[29]

IV

Though the realm of "logical space" may fail to provide clearly problematic examples of true negative existentials, the realms of fiction and myth may fare better. Let the α

---

[29] *Cf.* 'Existence,' pp. 90–97. Alvin Plantinga calls the doctrine that everything exists in any possible world in which it has properties *serious actualism*, in 'De Essentia,' in E. Sosa, ed., *Essays on the Philosophy of Roderick M. Chisholm* (Amsterdam: Rodopi, 1979), pp. 101–121, at 108–109. By analogy, *serious presentism* would be the corresponding temporal doctrine that everything exists at any time at which it has properties. The doctrine that existence precedes suchness encompasses both serious actualism and serious presentism. Kripke says that the doctrine that existence is not itself a property but a pre-requisite for having any properties, though rather obscure, seems to him in some sense true. The doctrine seems to me erroneous on both counts. What can a pre-condition for a given property be if not another property?

Joseph Almog, in 'The Subject-Predicate Class I,' *Noûs*, 25 (1991), pp. 591–619, objects to my view that 'Socrates does not exist' is true in English in virtue of expressing a true singular proposition, on the ground that no sentence can be made true by Soc's being the case since Soc no longer exists. Instead, he asserts (influenced by Donnellan—see note 19) that the sentence is true because 'Socrates' refers to Socrates, who does not exist (pp. 604–607; *cf.* Donnellan, pp. 7–8). Far from solving the problem, skepticism about propositions only makes matters worse: A sentence that mentions Socrates but expresses nothing whatever about him cannot have truth-value, let alone truth. In order for a sentence to be true, what it expresses must be the case; this is what truth for sentences consists in. (Curiously, Almog seems to concede this, just one page after objecting to my view.) Further, as Frege and Church argued, 'Jones believes that Socrates does not exist', if true, requires something for Jones to believe. A genuine solution requires genuine semantic content. Worse still, Almog's purported solution is inconsistent. If Soc cannot be true only because it does not exist, then for exactly the same reason Socrates cannot be referred to—the name 'Socrates' *is* nonreferring, however weakly—and we are left with nothing that accounts for the truth in English of 'Socrates does not exist'. But Socrates is referred to, warts and all, and Soc is the case (and in addition is expressed, believed, known, etc.).

in (3α) and (4α) be a name from fiction, for example 'Sherlock Holmes'. It is a traditional view in philosophy, and indeed it is plain common sense, that (3α) is then false and $(4\alpha) = (0)$ true, when taken as statements about reality. For 'Sherlock Holmes', as a name for the celebrated detective, is a *very strongly* or *thoroughly nonreferring* name, one that does not in reality have any referent at all—past, present, future, forever merely possible, or even forever impossible. Bertrand Russell lent an eloquent voice to this common-sense view:

[M]any logicians have been driven to the conclusion that there are unreal objects. . . . In such theories, it seems to me, there is a failure of that feeling for reality which ought to be preserved even in the most abstract studies. Logic, I should maintain, must no more admit a unicorn than zoology can; for logic is concerned with the real world just as truly as zoology, though with its more abstract and general features. To say that unicorns have an existence in heraldry, or in literature, or in imagination, is a most pitiful and paltry evasion. What exists in heraldry is not an animal, made of flesh and blood, moving and breathing of its own initiative. What exists is a picture, or a description in words. Similarly, to maintain that Hamlet, for example, exists in his own world, namely in the world of Shakespeare's imagination, just as truly as (say) Napoleon existed in the ordinary world, is to say something deliberately confusing, or else confused to a degree which is scarcely credible. There is only one world, the 'real' world: Shakespeare's imagination is part of it, and the thoughts that he had in writing *Hamlet* are real. So are the thoughts that we have in reading the play. But it is of the very essence of fiction that only the thoughts, feelings, etc., in Shakespeare and his readers are real, and that there is not, in addition to them, an objective Hamlet. When you have taken account of all the feelings roused by Napoleon in writers and readers of history, you have not touched the actual man; but in the case of Hamlet you have come to the end of him. If no one thought about Hamlet, there would be nothing left of him; if no one had thought about Napoleon, he would have soon seen to it that some one did. The sense of reality is vital in logic, and whoever juggles with it by pretending that Hamlet has another kind of reality is doing a disservice to thought. A robust sense of reality is very necessary in framing a correct analysis of propositions about unicorns, golden mountains, round squares, and other such pseudo-objects.[30]

Contemporary philosophy has uncovered that, unlike 'Noman', a name from fiction does not even name a merely possible object. Thus Kripke writes:

The mere discovery that there was indeed a detective with exploits like those of Sherlock Holmes would not show that Conan Doyle was writing *about* this man; it is theoretically possible, though in practice fantastically unlikely, that Doyle was writing pure fiction with only a coincidental resemblance to the actual man. . . . Similarly, I hold the metaphysical view that, granted that there is no Sherlock Holmes, one cannot say of any possible person, that he *would have been* Sherlock Holmes, had he existed. Several distinct possible people, and even actual ones such as Darwin or Jack the Ripper, might have performed the exploits of Holmes, but there is none of whom we can say that he would have *been* Holmes had he performed these exploits. For if so, which one?

I thus could no longer write, as I once did, that 'Holmes does not exist, but in other states of affairs, he would have existed' (*Naming and Necessity*, Harvard University Press, 1972, 1980, pp. 157–158).

---

[30] *Introduction to Mathematical Philosophy* (London: Allen and Unwin, 1919), at pp. 169–170. *Cf.* Russell's *The Philosophy of Logical Atomism*, D. Pears, ed. (La Salle, Ill.: Open Court, 1918, 1972, 1985), at pp. 87–88.

It is not merely true that Sherlock Holmes does not exist, it is a necessary truth. On Kripke's view, the name 'Sherlock Holmes' is a rigid *non*designator, designating nothing—not even a merely possible thing—with respect to every possible world. In a similar vein, Kaplan says:

> The myth [of Pegasus] is possible in the sense that there is a possible world in which it is truthfully *told*. Furthermore, there are such worlds in which the language, with the exception of the proper names in question, is semantically and syntactically identical with our own. Let us call such possible worlds of the myth, '*M* worlds'. In each *M* world, the name 'Pegasus' will have originated in a dubbing of a winged horse. The Friend of Fiction, who would not have anyone believe the myth . . . , but yet talks of Pegasus, pretends to be in an *M* world and speaks its language.
>
> But beware the confusion of our language with theirs! If *w* is an *M* world, then *their* name 'Pegasus' will denote something with respect to *w*, and *our* description 'the *x* such that *x* is called "Pegasus" ' will denote the same thing with respect to *w*, but *our* name 'Pegasus' will still denote nothing with respect to *w*. . . .
>
> To summarize. It has been thought that proper names like 'Pegasus' and 'Hamlet' were like 'Aristotle' and 'Newman-1', except that the individuals denoted by the former were more remote. But regarded as names of *our* language—introduced by successful or unsuccessful dubbings, or just made up—the latter denote and the former do not.[31]

The passage closes with a 'Homework Problem': If the foregoing account of names deriving from fiction is correct, how could a sentence like (0) be true? Our task is to examine this very problem from a Millian perspective.

We begin with a plausible theory of fiction and its objects. Saul Kripke and Peter van Inwagen have argued, independently, and persuasively, that wholly fictional characters should be regarded as real things.[32] Theirs is not a Meinongian view—one of Russell's targets in the passage quoted above—on which any manner of proper name or definite description, including such terms as 'the golden mountain' and 'the round square', refers to some Object, though the Object may not exist in any robust

---

[31] From appendix XI, 'Names from Fiction,' of 'Bob and Carol and Ted and Alice,' at pp. 505–508. Kaplan credits John Bennett in connection with this passage. The same general argument occurs in Donnellan, at pp. 24–25, and in Plantinga, *The Nature of Necessity* (Oxford University Press, 1974), section VIII.4, 'Names: Their Function in Fiction,' at pp. 159–163.

[32] Kripke, *Reference and Existence: The John Locke Lectures for 1973* (Oxford University Press, unpublished); van Inwagen, 'Creatures of Fiction,' *American Philosophical Quarterly*, 14, 4 (October 1977), pp. 299–308, and 'Fiction and Metaphysics,' *Philosophy and Literature*, 7, 1 (Spring 1983), pp. 67–77. One possible difference between them is that van Inwagen accepts an ontology of fictional characters whereas Kripke is instead merely unveiling an ontology that he argues is assumed in the way we speak about fiction while remaining neutral on the question of whether this manner of speaking accurately reflects reality. My interpretation of Kripke is based partly on notes I took at his seminars on the topic of reference and fiction at Princeton University during March-April 1981 and on recordings of his seminars at the University of California, Riverside in January 1983. See also Kit Fine, 'The Problem of Non-Existence: I. Internalism.' *Topoi*, 1 (1982), pp. 97–140; Thomas G. Pavel, *Fictional Worlds* (Harvard University Press, 1986); Amie Thomasson, 'Fiction, Modality and Dependent Abstracta,' *Philosophical Studies*, 84 (1996), pp. 295–320; Nicholas Wolterstorff, *Works and Worlds of Art* (Oxford University Press, 1980). Various articles on the philosophy and logic of fiction are collected together in *Poetics*, 8, 1/2 (April 1979)—see especially Robert Howell, 'Fictional Objects: How They Are and How They Aren't,' pp. 129–177—and in Peter McCormick, ed., *Reasons of Art* (University of Ottawa Press, 1985).

sense and may instead have only a lower class ontological status (and, as in the case of the round square, may even have inconsistent properties).[33] To be sure, wholly fictional characters like Sherlock Holmes, though real, are not real people. Neither physical objects nor mental objects, instead they are, in this sense, abstract entities. They are not eternal entities, like numbers; they are man-made artifacts created by fiction writers. But they exist just as robustly as the fictions themselves, the novels, stories, etc. in which they occur. Indeed, fictional characters have the same onto-logical status as the fictions, which are also abstract entities created by their authors. And certain things are true of these fictional characters—for example, that the protagonist of the *Sherlock Holmes* stories was inspired in part by an uncannily perceptive person of Sir Arthur Conan Doyle's acquaintance.

On this theory, a negative existential like (0), taken as making an assertion about the fictional character and taken literally, denies real existence of a real fictional character, and is therefore false. Yes, Virginia, there is a Sherlock Holmes. In fact, Holmes may well be the most famous of all fictional characters in existence. The same sentence, understood as making an assertion about the fictional character, may be open to a more charitable and plausible interpretation, albeit a nonliteral one. Perhaps one may reinterpret the predicate 'exists', for example, to mean *real*, in something like the sense: *not merely a character in the story, but an entity of just the sort depicted.* Then (0) may be understood, quite plausibly, as making an assertion that the character of Sherlock Holmes is a wholly fictional man, not a real one. That is to say, there is a fiction in which Holmes is a man of flesh and blood, but in reality Holmes is merely a fictional character. On this Pickwickian reading, the sentence is indeed true. But it is then not an authentic negative existential, and thus generates no special problem for Millianism, let alone for direct-reference theory.[34]

Our homework problem is not yet solved. How can this talk about the fictional character of Sherlock Holmes as a real entity be reconciled with the passage from Kripke quoted above, in which he appears to agree with Kaplan and Russell that 'Sherlock Holmes' is nonreferring?

On Kripke's account, use of the name 'Sherlock Holmes' to refer to the fictional character is in a certain sense parasitic on a prior, more fundamental use not as a name for the fictional character. Kripke and van Inwagen emphasize that the author of a fiction does not assert anything in writing the fiction. Instead, Kripke, like Kaplan, says that Conan Doyle merely *pretended* to be referring to someone in using the name 'Sherlock Holmes' and to be asserting things, expressing propositions, about him. A fiction purports to be an accurate historical recounting of real events involving real people. Of course, the author typically does not attempt to deceive the audience that the pretense is anything but a pretense; instead the fiction merely goes through the motions (hoaxes like Orson Welles's radio broadcast of H. G. Wells's

---

[33] *Cf.* Terence Parsons, 'A Meinongian Analysis of Fictional Objects,' *Grazer Philosophische Studien*, 1 (1975), pp. 73–86, and *Nonexistent Objects* (New Haven: Yale University Press, 1980).

[34] *Cf.* Van Inwagen, at p. 308n11. Kripke argues against any interpretation of (0) on which the name is used as a name of the fictional character but 'exist' receives a Pickwickian interpretation on which the sentence is true. I am somewhat less skeptical. See below, especially note 48. (Van Inwagen's suggestion is neutral between this sort of account and the one proposed below.)

The War of the Worlds and the legend of Santa Claus being the exceptions that prove the rule). Frege expressed the basic idea as follows:

Assertions in fiction are not to be taken seriously: they are only mock assertions. Even the thoughts are not to be taken seriously as in the sciences: they are only mock thoughts. If Schiller's *Don Carlos* were to be regarded as a piece of history, then to a large extent the drama would be false. But a work of fiction is not meant to be taken seriously in this way at all: it's all play.[35]

According to Kripke, as the name 'Sherlock Holmes' was originally introduced and used by Conan Doyle, it has no referent whatsoever. It is a name in the make-believe world of storytelling, part of an elaborate pretense. By Kripke's lights, our language licenses a certain kind of metaphysical move. It postulates an abstract artifact, the fictional character, as a product of this pretense. But the name 'Sherlock Holmes' does not thereby refer to the character thereby postulated, nor for that matter to anything else, and the sentences involving the name 'Sherlock Holmes' that were written in creating the fiction express no propositions, about the fictional character or anything else. They are all part of the pretense, like the actors' lines in the performance of a play. It is only at a later stage when discussing the fictional character from a standpoint outside of the fiction, speaking about the pretense and not within it, that the language makes a second move, this one semantical rather than metaphysical, giving the name a new, nonpretend use as a name for the fictional character. The language allows a grammatical transformation, says Kripke, of a fictional name for a person into a name of a fictional person. Similarly van Inwagen writes, "we have embodied in our rules for talking about fiction a convention that says that a creature of fiction *may* be referred to by what is (loosely speaking) 'the name it has in the story'" (p. 307*n*). On this account, the name 'Sherlock Holmes' is ambiguous. In its original use as a name for a human being—its use by Conan Doyle in writing the fiction, and presumably by the reader reading the fiction—it merely pretends to name someone and actually names nothing at all. But in its nonpretend use as a name for the fictional character thereby created by Conan Doyle, it genuinely refers to that particular artifactual entity. In effect, there are two names. Though spelled the same, they would be better spelled differently, as 'Holmes$_1$' for the man and 'Holmes$_2$' for the fictional character. Neither names a real man. The latter names an abstract artifact, the former nothing at all. It is the original, thoroughly nonreferring use of 'Sherlock Holmes'—its use in the same way as 'Holmes$_1$'—that Kaplan, Kripke, and Russell emphasize in the passages quoted.

Kripke's theory involves a complex account of sentences from fiction and myth, like 'Sherlock Holmes plays the violin' and 'Pegasus has wings' (*cf.* (1α)). I shall call these sentences *object-fictional*, to be contrasted with *meta-fictional* sentences like 'According to the stories, Sherlock Holmes plays the violin'. On Kripke's view, object-fictional sentences are multiply ambiguous, as a result of the two uses of the

---

[35] 'Logic,' in Frege's *Posthumous Writings*, at p. 130. See also Kendall L. Walton, 'On Fearing Fictions,' *Journal of Philosophy*, 75 (1978), pp. 5–27; and *Mimesis As Make-Believe: On the Foundations of the Representational Arts* (Cambridge, Mass.: Harvard University Press, 1990).

names and of differing perspectives from within and without the fiction or myth. Using the name in 'Sherlock Holmes plays the violin' in the manner of 'Holmes₁' as the pretend name of a pretend man, and using the sentence to make a statement not within the pretense and instead about the real world outside the fiction, the sentence expresses nothing and is therefore not literally true. (See note 19.) But object-fictional sentences may also be used from within the fiction, as part of the general pretense of an accurate, factual recounting of real events, not to be mistaken as a 'time out' reality check. Interpreted thus, the sentence 'Holmes plays the violin' is a correct depiction, part of the storytelling language-game. So used, the sentence may be counted 'true' in an extended sense—truth *in the fiction*, as we might call it—conforming to a convention of counting an object-fictional sentence 'true' or 'false' according as the sentence is true or false in, or according to, the fiction. This is the sense in which the sentence should be marked 'true' on a true–false test in English Lit 101.³⁶ Alternatively, the name may be used in the manner of 'Holmes₂' as a name for the fictional character. With the name so used, and the sentence used as a statement not about the fiction but about reality, it is false; no abstract entity can play a musical instrument. On the other hand, according to Kripke, we also have an extended use of predicates, on which 'plays the violin' correctly applies to an abstract entity when it is a character from a fiction according to which the corresponding fictional person plays the violin. Giving the name its use as a name of the fictional character, and understanding the predicate 'plays the violin' in this extended sense, the sentence is true. According to the stories, Holmes₁ plays the violin. In virtue of that fact we may say that Holmes₂ 'plays the violin.' The truth-conditions of the sentence on this reading are exactly the same as the conventional truth-in-the-fiction conditions of the sentence interpreted as 'Holmes₁ plays the violin'. But they differ in meaning. The former invokes a new interpretation for both subject and predicate.³⁷

Viewing the negative existential (0) on this same model, it has various interpretations on which it is false. Interpreted in the sense of 'Holmes₁ does not exist', it is like 'Holmes₁ does not play the violin' in pretending to express a proposition that is false in the fiction. The sentence should be marked 'false' on a true–false quiz about

---

³⁶ Kripke recognizes that this is generally equivalent, in some sense, to treating an object-fictional sentence φ as implicitly shorthand for the meta-fictional ⌜According to the fiction, φ⌝, and evaluating it as true or false accordingly. But he says that he prefers to regard it as applying 'true' and 'false' in conventionally extended senses directly to object-fictional sentences themselves in their original senses. *Cf.* David Lewis, 'Truth in Fiction,' *American Philosophical Quarterly*, 15 (1978), pp. 37–46; reprinted with postscripts in Lewis's *Philosophical Papers: Volume I* (Oxford University Press, 1983), pp. 261–280.

³⁷ Kripke cautions that when one is merely pretending to refer to a human being in using a name from fiction, that pretense does not in and of itself involve naming a fictional character. On the contrary, such a pretense was involved in the very creation of the as yet unnamed fictional character. He also remarks that an object-fictional sentence like 'Sherlock Holmes plays the violin' would be counted true in the conventionally extended 'according to the fiction' sense even if the name had only its 'Holmes₁' use and the language had not postulated fictional characters as objects. Van Inwagen (pp. 305–306) invokes a notion of a fiction 'ascribing' a property to a character, but admits that his terminology is misleading. He does not explain his notion of *ascription* in terms of what sentences within the fiction express, since such sentences on his view (as on Kripke's) do not mention fictional characters and express nothing at all. Nor does he explain this kind of ascription in any other terms. Instead the notion is an undefined, primitive of the theory.

the *Sherlock Holmes* stories. Interpreted in the sense of 'Holmes$_2$ does not exist', the predicate 'exist' may be given its literal sense, or alternatively it may be given its extended sense on which it applies to a fictional character if and only according to the relevant fiction the corresponding person exists. Either way the sentence is false. The fictional character exists, and moreover the corresponding person exists according to the stories. But now read (0) again in the sense of 'Holmes$_1$ does not exist', and this time take it not as a statement within the fiction but as a statement about the real world. Then it is significantly unlike 'Holmes$_1$ does not play the violin', which expresses nothing about the real world outside the fiction. For 'Holmes$_1$ does not exist', according to Kripke, is in reality quite true. On this interpretation, the sentence is regarded by Kripke, as by traditional philosophy, as an authentic true negative existential with a thoroughly nonreferring subject term.

This was our primary concern. We have attempted to deal with the problem of negative existentials by concentrating on 'Holmes$_2$ does not exist'. But it is Holmes$_1$, not Holmes$_2$, who literally does not exist. The homework problem requires more work. Kripke says that it is 'perhaps the worst problem in the area.'

By way of a possible solution, Kripke proposes that (0) should not be viewed on the model of 'Holmes$_1$ plays the violin', understood as a statement about the real world—and which thereby expresses nothing—but instead as a special kind of speech act. Consider first the object-fictional sentence 'Sherlock Holmes does not play the violin', in the sense of 'Holmes$_1$ does not play the violin' construed as a statement about reality (*cf.* (2α)). One may utter this sentence even if one is uncertain whether Holmes$_1$ is a real person, in order to make the cautious claim that either there is no such person as Holmes$_1$ or there is but he does not play the violin. In that case, the assertion is tantamount to saying that either there is no proposition that Holmes$_1$ plays the violin, or there is such a proposition but it is not true. In short, the sentence is interpreted as meaning *there is no true proposition that Holmes$_1$ plays the violin*. A similar cautious interpretation is available whenever negation is employed.

Kripke extends this same interpretation to singular negative existentials. He proposes that whenever one utters any sentence of the form (4α) from the standpoint of the real world, what one really means is better expressed by ⌜There is no true proposition that α exists⌝. What is meant may be true on either of two very different grounds: (*i*) the mentioned proposition is not true; (*ii*) there is no such proposition. If α is 'the present king of France', so that (4α) is (4), then what one is really saying— that there is no true proposition that the present king of France exists—is true for the former reason; it is false that the present king of France exists. If (4α) is (0) with 'Sherlock Holmes' in its 'Holmes$_1$' use, then what one is really saying—that there is no true proposition that Holmes$_1$ exists—is true for the latter reason. Kripke's is not a theory that takes (4α) to express that (3α) is not true$_{English}$. Semantic-ascent theories are notoriously vulnerable to refutation (as by the Church translation argument). Instead Kripke takes (4α) to express that there is no true proposition of a certain sort, if only because there is no proposition. This is closer to the intensional-ascent theory of existence—with a wink and a nod in the direction of Millianism.

Kripke extends this account to mistaken theories. He explicitly mentions the case of the fictitious intra-Mercurial planet Vulcan, hypothesized and named by Jacques

Babinet in 1846 and later thought by Urbain Le Verrier to explain an irregularity in the orbit of Mercury. The irregularity was eventually explained by the general theory of relativity.[38] Though the Vulcan hypothesis turned out to be a mistake, it nevertheless bore existent fruit—not in the form of a massive physical object, but a man-made abstract entity of the same ontological status as Holmes$_2$. Vulcan even has explanatory value. It accounts not for Mercury's perihelion, but for the truth in English of 'A hypothetical planet was postulated to explain Mercury's irregular orbit'. In introducing the name 'Vulcan', Babinet meant to introduce a name for a planet, not an abstract artifact. His intentions were thwarted on both counts. Kripke holds that the dubbing ultimately resulted in two distinct uses of the name—in effect two names, 'Vulcan$_1$' and 'Vulcan$_2$'—the first as a name for an intra-Mercurial planet, and consequently thoroughly nonreferring, the second as a name of Babinet's creation. (Presumably these two uses are supposed to be different from two other pairs of uses, corresponding to the fire god of Roman mythology and Mr. Spock's native planet in *Star Trek*.) When it is said that Vulcan$_1$ does not influence Mercury's orbit, and that Vulcan$_1$ does not exist, what is meant is that there are no true propositions that Vulcan$_1$ influences Mercury or that Vulcan$_1$ exists.

The motivation for Kripke's intensional ascent is obscure. In any event, the account fails to solve the problem. The 'that' clauses 'that Holmes$_1$ plays the violin' and 'that Holmes$_1$ exists' are no less problematic than 'Holmes$_1$' itself. Kripke concedes, in effect, that if α is a thoroughly nonreferring name, then propositional terms like ⌜the proposition that α is bald⌝ are also thoroughly nonreferring. The account thus analyzes a negative existential by means of another negative existential, generating an infinite regress with the same problem arising at each stage: If α is a thoroughly nonreferring name, how can ⌜There is no proposition that α is bald⌝ express anything at all, let alone something true (let alone a necessary truth)? To give an analogy, a proposal to analyze (4α) as ⌜Either $\{\alpha\}$ is empty or it does not exist⌝ yields no solution to the problem of how (4α) can express anything true. Even if the analysans has the right truth-conditions (the first disjunct may be true if α is an improper definite description, the second is true if α is a nonreferring simple term), it also invokes a disjunct that is of the form of (4α) itself, and it leaves unsolved the mystery of how either disjunct can express anything if α is a thoroughly nonreferring name.[39]

---

[38] Babinet hypothesized Vulcan for reasons different than Le Verrier's. See Warren Zachary Watson, *An Historical Analysis of the Theoretical Solutions to the Problem of the Perihelion of Mercury* (doctoral dissertation, Ann Arbor, Mich: University Microfilms, 1969), pp. viii, 92–94; and N. T. Roseveare, *Mercury's Perihelion: From Le Verrier to Einstein* (Oxford University Press, 1982), at pp. 24–27. (Thanks to Alan Berger and Sidney Morgenbesser for bibliographical assistance. I also researched the Vulcan hypothesis on the Internet. When I moved to save material to a new file to be named 'Vulcan', the program responded as usual, only this time signaling a momentous occasion: **Vulcan doesn't exist. Create? Y or N.**)

[39] As Kripke intends the construction ⌜There is no such thing as α⌝, it seems close in meaning to (8α). In our problem case, α is 'the proposition that Holmes$_1$ exists'. Since the 'that' prefix is itself a device for indirect-quotation (see note 17), 'Holmes$_1$' would thus occur in a doubly *ungerade* context. It may be, therefore, that Kripke's intensional-ascent theory presupposes (or otherwise requires) a thesis that proper names have a Fregean *ungerade Sinn*, or *indirect sense*, which typically determines the name's referent, the latter functioning as both customary content and customary

There is more. On the account proposed by Kaplan, Kripke, and van Inwagen, object-fictional sentences, like 'Sherlock Holmes plays the violin', have no genuine semantic content in their original use. This renders the meaningfulness of true meta-fictional sentences like 'According to the *Sherlock Holmes* stories, Holmes plays the violin' problematic and mysterious. (See note 37.) On Kripke's account, it is true that according to the stories $Holmes_1$ plays the violin, and that on Le Verrier's theory $Vulcan_1$ influences Mercury's orbit. But how can this be if there is no pro-position that $Holmes_1$ plays the violin and no proposition that $Vulcan_1$ influences Mercury? What is it that is the case according to the stories or the theory? How can Le Verrier have believed something that is nothing at all? If object-fictional sentences like '$Holmes_1$ plays the violin' express nothing and only pretend to express things, how can they be true with respect (or 'according') to the fiction, and how can meta-fictional sentences involving object-fictional subordinate clauses express anything at all, let alone something true?

More puzzling still are such cross-realm statements as 'Sherlock Holmes was cleverer than Bertrand Russell', and even worse, 'Sherlock Holmes was cleverer than Hercule Poirot'. The account as it stands seems to invoke some sort of intensional use of 'Sherlock Holmes', whereby the name is not only ambiguous between '$Holmes_1$' and '$Holmes_2$', but also accompanying the former use is something like an *ungerade* use, arising in constructions like 'According to the stories, $Holmes_1$ plays the violin', on which the name refers to a particular concept—presumably something like: *the brilliant detective who performed such and such exploits*. Kripke acknowledges this, calling it a 'special sort of quasi-intensional use.' The account thus ultimately involves an intensional apparatus. Indeed, it appears to involve industrial strength intensional machinery of a sort that is spurned by direct-reference theory, and by the very account itself. Further, the intensionality seems to get matters wrong. First, it seems to give us after all a proposition that $Holmes_1$ plays the violin, a proposition that $Vulcan_1$ influences Mercury, etc.—those things that are the case (or not) according to stories or believed by the theorist. Worse, depending on how the *ungerade* use of '$Holmes_1$' is explained, it could turn out that if there were someone with many of the attributes described in the *Sherlock Holmes* stories, including various exploits much like those recounted, then there would be *true* propositions that $Holmes_1$ existed, that he played the violin, etc. It could even turn out that if by an extraordinary coincidence there was *in fact* some detective who was very Holmesesque, then even though $Holmes_2$ was purely fictional and not based in any way on this real person, there *are* nevertheless true propositions that $Holmes_1$ existed, played the violin, etc. The theory threatens to entail that the question of Holmes's authenticity (in the intended sense) would be settled affirmatively by the discovery of someone who was significantly Holmesesque, even if this person was otherwise unconnected to Conan Doyle. If the theory has consequences like these, then it directly contradicts the compelling passage of Kripke's quoted above, if not

referent, but which in the case of a thoroughly nonreferring name determines nothing. This would provide a reason for intensional ascent; one hits pay dirt by climbing above customary content. Kripke's theory would then involve Fregean intensional machinery that direct reference scrupu-lously avoids and Millianism altogether prohibits.

also itself. Kripke expresses misgivings about the theory, acknowledging that the required "quasi-intensional" use of a name from fiction needs explanation.[40]

V

One may well demur from these tenets of Kripke's otherwise compelling account. One need not claim, as Kripke does, that a name like 'Sherlock Holmes' is ambiguous. In particular, there is no obvious necessity to posit a use of the name by Conan Doyle and his readers that is nonreferring (in any sense) and somehow prior to its use as a name for the fictional character and upon which the latter use is parasitic. There is first a general methodological consideration. Once fictional characters have been countenanced as real entities, why hold onto an alleged use of their names that fails to refer to them? It is like buying a luxurious Italian sports car only to keep it garaged. I do not advocate driving recklessly, but I do advise that having paid for the car one should permit oneself to drive it, at least on special occasions.

There is a more decisive consideration. The alleged use of 'Sherlock Holmes' on which it is thoroughly nonreferring was supposed to be a pretend use, not a real one. In writing the *Holmes* stories, Conan Doyle did not genuinely use the name at all, at least not as a name for a man. He merely pretended to. Of course, Conan Doyle

---

[40] *Cf.* Gareth Evans, *The Varieties of Reference*, J. McDowell, ed. (Oxford University Press, 1982), at pp. 349–352. See also note 2 above. The kind of intensionality required on Kripke's account is not merely pragmatic in nature. Taking account of note 39, the account may be steeped in intensionality. The danger of entailing such consequences as those noted is very real. The theory of fiction in Lewis is similar to Kripke's in requiring something like an *ungerade* use for thoroughly nonreferring names from fiction. Lewis embraces the conclusion that "the sense of 'Sherlock Holmes' as we use it is such that, for any world *w* where the Holmes stories are told as known fact rather than fiction, the name denotes at *w* whichever inhabitant of *w* it is who there plays the role of Holmes" (p. 267 of his *Philosophical Papers, I*). A similar conclusion is also reached in Robert Stalnaker, 'Assertion,' P. Cole, ed., *Syntax and Semantics, 9: Semantics* (New York: Academic Press, 1978), pp. 315–332, at 329–331. These conclusions directly contradict Kripke's account of proper names as rigid designators. In the first of the Locke Lectures, Kripke argues that uniquely being Holmesesque is not sufficient to be Holmes. Further, Kripke also argues there that the phenomenon of fiction cannot yield considerations against this or that particular philosophico-semantic theory of names, since it is part of the fiction's pretense, for the theorist, that the theory's 'criteria for naming, whatever they are, are satisfied.' Why should this not extend to the thesis, from direct-reference theory, that names lack Kripke's hypothesized "quasi-intensional use"?

Donnellan regards negative existentials as unlike other object-fictional sentences, though his solution differs significantly from Kripke's and is designed to avoid intensionality. Donnellan provides a criterion whereby if α and β are distinct names from fiction, then (in effect) the corresponding true negative existentials, taken in the sense of $\ulcorner\alpha_1$ does not exist$\urcorner$ and $\ulcorner\beta_1$ does not exist$\urcorner$ as literally true statements about reality, express the same proposition if and only if α_2 and β_2 name the same fictional character. (I have taken enormous liberties in formulating Donnellan's criterion in terms of Kripke's apparatus, but I believe I do not do any serious injustice.) This proposal fails to provide the proposition expressed. In fact, Donnellan concedes that "we cannot . . . preserve a clear notion of what proposition is expressed for existence statements involving proper names" (p. 29; see note 19 above). This fails to solve the original problem, which is even more pressing for Donnellan. How can such sentences be said to "express the same proposition" when by his lights neither sentence clearly expresses any proposition at all? *Cf.* note 29.

wrote the name down as part of sentences in the course of writing the *Holmes* stories. In that sense he used the name. This is like the use that stage or film actors make of sentences when reciting their lines during the performance of a play or the filming of a movie. It is not a use whereby the one speaking commits him/herself to the propositions expressed. Even when writing 'London' or 'Scotland Yard' in a *Holmes* story, Conan Doyle was not in any robust sense using these names to refer. As J. O. Urmson notes, when Jane Austen, in writing a novel, writes a sentence beginning with a fictional character's name,

[i]t is not that there is a reference to a fictional object, nor is there the use of a referring expression which fails to secure reference (as when one says "That man over there is tall" when there is no man over there). Jane Austen writes a sentence which has the form of an assertion beginning with a reference, but is in fact neither asserting nor referring; therefore she is not referring to any character, fictional or otherwise, nor does she fail to secure reference, except in the jejune sense in which if I sneeze or open a door I fail to secure reference. Nothing would have counted on this occasion as securing reference, and to suppose it could is to be under the impression that Miss Austen was writing history. . . . I do not say that one cannot refer to a fictional character, but that Miss Austen did not on the occasion under discussion.

What I am saying is that making up fiction is not a case of stating, or asserting, or propounding a proposition and includes no acts such as referring. ("Fiction," *American Philosophical Quarterly*, 13, 2 (April 1976), pp. 153–157 at p. 155)

The pretend use of 'Sherlock Holmes' by Conan Doyle does not have to be regarded as generating a use of the name on which it is nonreferring. *Pace* Kaplan, Kripke, Russell, and traditional philosophy, it *should* not be so regarded. A name semantically refers to this or that individual only relative to a particular kind of use, a particular purpose for which the name was introduced. One might go so far as to say that a pretend use by itself does not even give rise to a real name at all, any more than it gives birth to a real detective. This may be somewhat overstated, but its spirit and flavor is not.[41] Even if one regards a name as something that exists independently of its introduction into language (as is my inclination), it is a confusion to think of a name as referring, or not referring, other than as doing so *on* a particular use. On this view, a common name like 'Adam Smith' refers to different individuals on different uses. The problem with saying that 'Sherlock Holmes' is nonreferring on Conan Doyle's use is that in merely pretending that the name had a particular use, no real use was yet attached to the name on which it may be said to refer or not to refer.

The matter should be viewed instead as follows: Conan Doyle one fine day set about to tell a story. In the process he created a fictional character as the protagonist, and other fictional characters as well, each playing a certain role in the story. These characters, like the story itself, are man-made abstract artifacts, born of Conan Doyle's fertile imagination. The name 'Sherlock Holmes' was originally coined by Conan Doyle in writing the story (and subsequently understood by readers reading the *Holmes* stories) as the fictional name for the protagonist. That thing—in fact

[41] C. J. F. Williams, in *What is Existence?* (Oxford University Press, 1981), argues that 'Sherlock Holmes' is not a proper name (pp. 251–255). This is what Kaplan ought to have said, but he did not. See his 'Words,' *Proceedings of the Aristotelian Society*, 64 (1990), pp. 93–119, especially section II, 'What are Names?' at pp. 110–119.

merely an abstract artifact—is *according to the story*, a man by the name of 'Sherlock Holmes'. In telling the story, Conan Doyle pretends to use the name to refer to its fictional referent (and to use 'Scotland Yard' to refer to Scotland Yard)—or rather, he pretends to be Dr. Watson using 'Sherlock Holmes', much like an actor portraying Dr. Watson on stage. But he does not really so use the name; 'Sherlock Holmes' so far does not really have any such use, or even any related use (ignoring unrelated uses it coincidentally might have had). At a later stage, use of the name is imported from the fiction into reality, to name *the very same thing* that it is the name of according to the story. That thing—now the real as well as the fictional bearer of the name—is according to the story a human being who is a brilliant detective, and in reality an artifactual abstract entity created by Conan Doyle.

The use of 'Sherlock Holmes' represented by 'Holmes$_2$', as the name for what is in reality an abstract artifact, is the same use it has according to the *Holmes* stories, except that according to the stories, that use is one on which it refers to a man. The alleged thoroughly nonreferring use of 'Sherlock Holmes' by Conan Doyle, as a pretend name for a man, is a myth. Contrary to Kaplan, Kripke, *et al.*, there is no literal use of 'Sherlock Holmes' that corresponds to 'Holmes$_1$'—or at least I know of no convincing reason to suppose that there is one. One might say (in the spirit of the van Inwagen-Kripke theory) that there is a mythical use represented by 'Holmes$_1$', an allegedly thoroughly nonreferring use that pretends to name a brilliant detective who performed such-and-such exploits. This kind of use is fictitious in the same way that Sherlock Holmes himself is, no more a genuine use than a fictional detective is a genuine detective. Instead there is at first only the pretense of a use, including the pretense that the name refers to a brilliant detective, a human being, on that use. Later the name is given a genuine use, on which it names the very same entity that it named according to the pretense, though the pretense that this entity is a human being has been dropped.

Literary scholars discussing the *Holmes* stories with all seriousness may utter the name 'Sherlock Holmes' as if to import its pretend use as the name of a man into genuine discourse—as when a Holmes 'biographer' says, 'Based on the evidence, Holmes was not completely asexual.' Even then, the scholars are merely pretending to use the name as a name for a man. There is no flesh-and-blood man for the name to name, and the scholars know that.[42] If they are genuinely using the name, they are using it as a name for the fictional character. The only genuine, nonpretend use that we ever give the name—of which I feel confident—is as a name for the character. And that use, as a name for that very thing, is the very use it has in the story—though according to the story, that very thing is a human being and not an abstract entity. Conan Doyle may have used the name for a period even before the character was fully developed. Even so, this would not clearly be a genuine use of the name on which it was altogether nonreferring. For it is at least arguable that if that was a

---

[42] What about a foggy headed literary theorist who maintains, as a sophomoric anti-realist or Meinongian philosophical view (or quasi-philosophical view), that Sherlock Holmes is in some sense no less flesh-and-blood than Conan Doyle? The more bizarre is someone's philosophical perspective, the more difficult it is to interpret his/her discourse correctly. Such a case might be assimilated to that of myths. See below.

genuine use by Conan Doyle, then it was very weakly nonreferring, in the sense used earlier. There would soon exist a fictional character to which *that* use of the name already referred.[43] In the same way, expectant parents may begin to use a name already decided upon even before the actual birth, perhaps even before conception, and readers of Kaplan may already use the name 'Newman-1' to refer. Once the anticipated referent arrives on the scene, to use the name exactly as before is to use it with reference to that thing. At that point, to use the name in a way that it fails to refer would be to give it a new use.

It seems at least as reasonable as Kripke's account to claim instead that once the name 'Sherlock Holmes' has been imported into genuine discourse, Conan Doyle's sentences involving the name express singular propositions about his character. One might even identify the fiction with a sequence of propositions, about both fictional and nonfictional things (e.g., Scotland Yard). To say this is not to say that Conan Doyle asserted those propositions. He did not—at least not in any sense of 'assert' that involves a commitment to one's assertions. He merely pretended to be Dr. Watson asserting those propositions. In so doing, Conan Doyle pretended (and his readers pretend) that the propositions are true propositions about a real man, not untrue propositions about an abstract artifact. That is exactly what it is to pretend to assert those propositions. To assert a proposition, in this sense, is in part to commit oneself to its truth; so to pretend to assert a proposition is to pretend to commit oneself to its truth. And the propositions in question entail that Holmes was not an abstract entity but a flesh-and-blood detective. Taken literally, they are untrue.[44]

This is not quite an offer one can't refuse. Some have reacted to this proposal with a vague feeling—or a definite feeling—that I have conscripted fictional characters to perform a service for which they were not postulated and are not suited. Do I mean to say that *The Hound of the Baskervilles* consists entirely of a sequence of mostly false propositions about mostly abstract entities? Is mine a view on which the essence of fiction is to pretend that abstract entities are living, breathing people? These misgivings stem from a misunderstanding of the nature of fiction and its population. The characters that populate fiction are created precisely to perform the service of being depicted as people by the fictions in which they occur. Do not fixate on the fact that fictional characters are abstract entities. Think instead of the various *roles* that a director might cast in a stage or screen production of a particular piece of fiction. Now think of the corresponding characters as the components of the fiction that *play* or *occupy* those roles in the fiction. It is no accident that one says of an actor

---

[43] On the view I am proposing there is a sense in which a fictional character is prior to the fiction in which the character occurs. By contrast, Kripke believes that a fictional character does not come into existence until the final draft of the fiction is published. This severe restriction almost certainly does not accord with the way fiction writers see themselves or their characters. Even if it is correct, it does not follow that while writing a fiction, the author is using the name in such a way that it is thoroughly nonreferring. It is arguable that the name already refers to the fledgling abstract artifact that does not yet exist. There is not already, nor will there ever be, any genuine use of the name as the name of a human being; that kind of use is make-believe.

[44] See note 37. If my view is correct, then van Inwagen's use of the word 'ascribe' in saying that a fiction ascribes a particular property to a particular fictional character may be understood (apparently contrary to van Inwagen's intent) quite literally, in its standard English meaning.

in a dramatic production that he/she is playing a "part." The characters of a fiction—the occupants of roles in the fiction—are in some real sense *parts* of the fiction itself. Sometimes, for example in historical fiction, what fictionally plays a particular role is a real person or thing. In other cases, what plays a particular role is the brainchild of the storyteller. In such cases, the role player is a *wholly* fictional character, or what I (following Kripke) have been calling simply a 'fictional character.' Whether a real person or wholly fictional, the character is that which according to the fiction takes part in certain events, performs certain actions, undergoes certain changes, says certain things, thinks certain thoughts. An actor performing in the role of Sherlock Holmes portrays Holmes$_2$; it is incorrect, indeed it is literally nonsense, to say that he portrays Holmes$_1$, if 'Holmes$_1$' is thoroughly nonreferring.

It is of the very essence of a fictional character to be depicted in the fiction as the person who takes part in such-and-such events, performs such-and-such actions, thinks such-and-such thoughts. Being so depicted is the character's *raison d'être*. As Clark Gable was born to play Rhett Butler in Margaret Mitchell's *Gone with the Wind*, that character was born to be the romantic leading man of that fiction. Mario Puzo's character of Don Corleone is as well suited to be the charismatic patriarch of *The Godfather* as Marlon Brando was to portray the character on film. Except even more so. The character was also portrayed completely convincingly by Robert De Niro. But only that character, and no other, is appropriate to the patriarch role in Puzo's crime saga. Likewise, the butler in Kazuo Ishiguro's *The Remains of the Day* would have been completely inappropriate, in more ways than one, as the protagonist of Ian Fleming's *James Bond* novels. It is of the essence of Flemings's character precisely to be the character depicted in the dashing and debonair 007 role in the *James Bond* stories—and not merely in the sense that being depicted thus is both a necessary and a sufficient condition for being the character of Bond in any metaphysically possible world. Rather, this is the condition that defines the character; being the thing so depicted in those stories characterizes exactly *what* the character of James Bond *is*.

In a sense, my view is the exact opposite of the traditional view expressed in Russell's pronouncement that "it is of the very essence of fiction that only the thoughts, feelings, etc., in Shakespeare and his readers are real, and that there is not, in addition to them, an objective Hamlet." To Russell's pronouncement there is Hamlet's own retort: "There are more things in heaven and earth, Horatio, Than are dreamt of in your philosophy." It is of the very essence of Shakespeare's *Hamlet* that there is indeed an object that is Hamlet. I am not urging that we countenance a person who is Hamlet$_1$ and who contemplated suicide according to the classic play but who does not exist. There is no sense in which there is any such person. The objective Hamlet is Hamlet$_2$—what plays the title role in the Bard's drama—and hence not a human being at all but a part of fiction, merely depicted there as anguished and suicidal. It is with the most robust sense of reality prescribed by the Metaphysician that I should urge recognition of this fictionally troubled soul.[45]

---

[45] In reading a piece of fiction, do we pretend that an abstract entity is a prince of Denmark (or a brilliant detective, etc.)? The question is legitimate. But it plays on the distinction between *de dicto* and *de re*. Taken *de dicto*, of course not; taken *de re*, exactly. That abstract entities are human beings is not something we pretend, but there are abstract entities that we pretend are human beings. Seen

It is an offer one shouldn't refuse lightly. Unlike Kripke's theory, a treatment of the sentences of the *Sherlock Holmes* stories on which they literally make reference (although their author may not) to the fictional character, and literally express things about that character (mostly false), yields a straightforward account—what I believe is the correct account—of the meaningfulness and apparent truth of object-fictional sentences like 'Sherlock Holmes plays the violin', and thereby also of the meaning and truth of meta-fictional sentences like 'According to the *Holmes* stories, Holmes plays the violin'. Following Kripke's lead in the possible-world semantics for modality, we say that 'Sherlock Holmes' is a rigid designator, referring to the fictional character both *with respect to the real world* and *with respect to the fiction*. The object-fictional sentence is not true with respect to the real world, since abstract entities make terrible musicians. But it is true with respect to the fiction—or true 'in the world of the fiction'—by virtue of being entailed by the propositions, themselves about fictional characters, that comprise the fiction, taken together with supplementary propositions concerning such things as the ordinary physical-causal structure of the world, usual societal customs, etc., that are assumed as the background against which the fiction unfolds.[46] When we speak within the fiction, we pretend that truth with respect to the fiction is truth *simpliciter*, hence that Holmes ($=$ Holmes$_2$) was a human being, a brilliant detective who plays the violin, and so on. Or what is virtually functionally equivalent, we use object-fictional sentences as shorthand for meta-fictional variants. The meta-fictional ⌜According to fiction *f*, ϕ⌝ is true with respect to the real world if and only if ϕ is true with respect to the mentioned fiction. In effect, the meta-fictional sentence receives a Fregean treatment on which the object-fictional subordinate clause has *ungerade* reference, referring to a (typically false) proposition about a fictional character. In all our genuine discourse about Holmes, we use the name in the 'Holmes$_2$' way. One may feign using 'Sherlock Holmes' as the name of a man, but this is only a pretend use. To say that according to the stories Holmes$_1$ plays the violin is to say nothing; what is true according to the stories is that Holmes$_2$ plays the violin.[47]

in the proper light, this is no stranger than pretending that Marlon Brando is Don Corleone. (It is not nearly so strange as Brando portraying a character in *The Freshman* who, in the story, is the real person on whom the character Marlon Brando portrayed in *The Godfather* was modelled.)

[46] *Cf.* John Heintz, 'Reference and Inference in Fiction,' *Poetics*, 8, 1/2 (April 1979), pp. 85–99. Where the fiction is inconsistent, the relevant notion of entailment may have to be non-standard. Also, the notion may have to be restricted to a *trivial* sort of entailment—on pain of counting arcane and even as yet unproved mathematical theorems true with respect to fiction. *Cf.* Lewis at pp. 274–278 of his *Philosophical Papers, I.*

[47] Philosophers have sometimes neglected to distinguish among different possible readings of an object-fictional sentence—or equivalently, between literal and extended (fictional) senses of 'true'. See, for example, Richard L. Cartwright, in 'Negative Existentials,' *Journal of Philosophy*, 57 (1960), pp. 629–639; and Jaakko Hintikka, '*Cogito Ergo Sum*: Inference or Performance,' *The Philosophical Review*, 71 (January 1962), pp. 3–32.

When we use an object-fictional sentence ϕ as shorthand for something meta-fictional, what is the longhand form? Perhaps ⌜There is a fiction according to which ϕ⌝, perhaps ⌜According to the fiction in which he/she/it/they is a character, ϕ⌝, perhaps ⌜According to *that* fiction, ϕ⌝, perhaps something else. Recognizing that we speak of fictional characters in these ways may to some extent obviate the need to posit a nonliteral, extended sense for all predicates. On the other hand,

Consider again sentence (0), or better yet, 'Sherlock Holmes does not really exist; he is only a fictional character'. Taken literally, this sentence expresses the near contradiction that Holmes$_2$ is a fictional character that does not exist. It was suggested above that the existence predicate may instead be given a Pickwickian interpretation on which it means something like: *is the very sort of entity depicted*. This suggestion, however, is questionable. In many cases, Russell's analysis (0′) seems closer to the facts. In uttering (0), the speaker may intend not merely to characterize Holmes$_2$, but to deny the *existence* of the eccentric detective. It may have been this sort of consideration that led Kripke to posit an ambiguity, and in particular a use of the name in the alleged manner of 'Holmes$_1$', a pretend-referring-but-really-nonreferring use on which the 'Holmes$_2$' use is parasitic (and which generates an intensional *ungerade* use). Kripke's posit, I believe, is also off target. There is a reasonable alternative. We sometimes use ordinary names, especially names of famous people, in various descriptive ways, as when it is said that so-and-so is a Napoleon, or a Nixon, another Hitler, no Jack Kennedy, or even (to segue into the fictional realm) a Romeo, an Uncle Tom, quixotic, Pickwickian, etc. I submit that, especially in singular existential statements, we sometimes use the name of a fictional character in a similar way. We may use 'Sherlock Holmes', for example, to mean something like: *Holmes more or less as he is actually depicted in the stories*, or *Holmes replete with these attributes* [the principally salient ones ascribed to Holmes in the stories], or best, *the person who is both Holmes and Holmesesque*. In uttering (0), one would then mean that the Holmes of fiction, Holmes as depicted, does not exist in reality, that there is in reality no such person—no *such* person, no person who is both Holmes$_2$ and sufficiently like *that* (as depicted in fiction).

Since this interpretation requires a reinterpretation of the name, it might be more correct to say that the speaker expresses this proposition than to say that (0) itself does. This is not a use of 'Holmes' as a thoroughly nonreferring name, but as a kind of description that invokes the name of the fictional character. In short, the name is used *a là* Russell as a disguised improper definite description. It is very probably a nonliteral, Pickwickian use of the name. It is certainly a nonstandard use, one that is parasitic on the name's more fundamental use as a name for the fictional character, not the other way around. It need not trouble the direct-reference theorist. The disguised-description use is directly based upon, and makes its first appearance in language only after, the standard use in the manner of 'Holmes$_2$' as (in Russell's words) a "genuine name in the strict logical sense." If an artificial expression is wanted as a synonym for this descriptive use, something clearly distinguished from both 'Holmes$_2$' (which I claim represents the standard, literal use of the name) and 'Holmes$_1$' (which represents a mythical use, no genuine use at all) is called for. Let us

---

something like Kripke's theory of extended senses may lie behind the use of gendered pronouns ('he') to refer to fictional people even in discourse about reality.

Perhaps the most difficult sentences to account for are those that assert cross-realm relations. Following Russell's analysis of thinking someone's yacht larger than it is, 'Sherlock Holmes was cleverer than Bertrand Russell' may be taken to mean that the cleverness that Holmes$_2$ had according to the stories is greater than the cleverness that Russell had. *Cf.* my *Reference and Essence* (Princeton University Press and Blackwell, 1981), at pp. 116–135, and especially 147n.

say that someone is a *Holmesesque-Holmes*$_2$ if he is Holmes$_2$ and sufficiently like he is depicted to be, in the sense that he has relevantly many of the noteworthy attributes that Holmes$_2$ has according to the stories. Perhaps the most significant of these is the attribute of being a person (or at least person-like) and not an abstract artifact. Following Russell, to say that *the* Holmesesque-Holmes$_2$ does not exist is to say that nothing is uniquely both Holmes$_2$ and Holmesesque—equivalently (not synonymously), that Holmes$_2$ is not Holmesesque. It is an empirical question whether Holmes$_2$—the character of which Conan Doyle wrote—was in reality like *that*, such-and-such a person, to any degree. The question of Holmes's existence *in this sense* is answered not by seeking whether someone or other was Holmesesque, but by investigating the literary activities of Conan Doyle.[48]

   These various considerations, and related ones, weigh heavily in favor of account of names from fiction as unambiguous names for artifactual entities.[49] In its fundamental use that arises in connection with the fiction—and I am inclined to think, its only literal use—'Sherlock Holmes' univocally names a man-made artifact, the handiwork of Conan Doyle. Contra Russell, *et al.*, names from fiction do not have a prior, more fundamental use. They do not yield true negative existentials with thoroughly nonreferring names.

VI

The account suggested here is extendable to sentences that are uttered in debunking myths, like 'Pegasus does not exist'. By 'myth' I mean any mistaken theory that has been held true. A mythical object is a hypothetical entity erroneously postulated by a theory. Like a fictional object, a mythical object is an abstract (non-physical,

---

[48] The notion of something being *sufficiently* like Holmes$_2$ is depicted may be to some extent interest-relative. Consequently, in some cases the truth-value of an assertion made using (3α), with α a name from fiction, may vary with the operative interests. Some scholars tell us, while not believing in vampires, that Bram Stoker's character of Count Dracula really existed. (This aspect of the theory I am suggesting raises a complex hornets' nest of difficult issues. Far from disproving the theory, however, some of these issues may tend to provide confirmation of sorts.)

   Kripke argues that the sentence 'Sherlock Holmes does not really exist; he is only a fictional character', properly interpreted, involves an equivocation whereby the name has its original nonreferring use and 'he' is a 'pronoun of laziness' referring to the fictional character—so that the sentence means that the man Holmes$_1$ does not exist and the fictional character Holmes$_2$ is just that. Kripke also says that one should be able to assert what is meant in the first clause of the original sentence without mentioning Holmes$_2$ at all. This is precisely what I believe cannot be done. The original may even be paraphrased into 'Sherlock Holmes does not really exist and is only a fictional character'. On my alternative hypothesis, the speaker may mean something like: *The Holmesesque-Holmes$_2$ does not really exist; Holmes$_2$ is only a fictional character*. This is equivalent to: Holmes$_2$ is not Holmesesque but a fictional character. Besides avoiding the putative 'Holmes$_1$' use, my hypothesis preserves an anaphoric-like relation between pronoun and antecedent. (Other possibilities arise if Kripke's theory of extended senses for predicates is applied to 'Holmesesque'.)

[49] In later work, and even in the same work cited *above* in note 32, Kripke argued persuasively against positing ambiguities when an alternative, univocal hypothesis that explains the phenomena equally well is available. *Cf.* his 'Speaker's Reference and Semantic Reference,' in P. French, T. Uehling, and H. Wettstein, eds., *Contemporary Perspectives in the Philosophy of Language* (Minneapolis: University of Minnesota Press, 1979), pp. 6–27, especially 19.

non-mental) entity created by the theory's inventor. The principal difference between myth and fiction is that a myth is believed whereas with fiction there is typically only a pretense.[50] An accidental storyteller, Le Verrier attempted in all sincerity to use 'Vulcan' to refer to a real planet. The attempt failed, but not for lack of a referent. Here as before, there is ample reason to doubt that 'Vulcan$_1$' represents a genuine use of the original name. Le Verrier held a theory according to which there is such a use, and he intended and believed himself to be so using the name. Had the theory been correct, there would have been such a use for the name. But the theory is false; it was all a mistake. Kripke says that in attempting to use the name, nineteenth-century astronomers failed to refer to anything. But this verdict seems to ignore their unintended relationship to the mythical planet. One might just as well judge that the ancients who introduced 'Hesperus' as a name for the first star visible in the dusk sky, unaware that the 'star' was in fact a planet, failed to name that planet. Nor had they inadvertently introduced two names, one for the planet and one thoroughly nonreferring. Plausibly, as the ancients unwittingly referred to a planet believing it to be a star, so Le Verrier may have unknowingly referred to Babinet's mythical planet, saying and believing so many false things about it (for example, that it affects Mercury's orbit). There may have been a period during which 'Vulcan' was mis-applied to the mythical planet before such application became enshrined as the official, correct use. It does not follow that there is a prior, genuine use of the name

[50] Donnellan says that myth is not analogous to fiction (at pp. 6–8). Almog agrees, and dismisses the idea of a mythical Vulcan (pp. 611, 618n13). I am convinced these philosophers are mistaken, and that this myth about myths has also led other philosophers astray. When storytellers tell stories and theorists hypothesize, fictional and mythical creatures abound. (An interesting possibility: Perhaps the myth invented by Babinet no longer exists, now that no one believes it. Can a myth, once it is disproved, continue to exist as merely an unbelieved theory? If not, then perhaps 'Vulcan' is nonreferring after all, though only very weakly.)

Kripke extends his account in the natural way also to terms for objects in the world of appearance (e.g., a distant spec or dot), and to species names and other biological-kind terms from fiction and myth, like 'unicorn' and 'dragon'. The theory should be extended also to general terms like 'witch', 'wizard', etc. There is a mythical species designated by 'dragon', an abstract artifact, not a real species. Presumably, if K is the mythical species (or higher-level taxonomic kind) of dragons, then there is a corresponding concept or property of being a beast of kind K, thus providing semantic content for the predicate 'is a dragon'. Kripke believes there is a prior use of the term, in the sense of 'dragon$_1$', which has no semantic content. But as before, on this point I find no persuasive reason to follow his lead.

Are there dragons? There are myths and fictions according to which there are dragons, for example the legend of Puff. Is Puff, then, a dragon? No, he is a fictional character—an abstract artifact and not a beast. Fictional dragons like Puff are not real dragons—though they may be said to be 'dragons,' if by saying that we mean that they are dragons in the story. (*Cf.* Kripke's hypo-thesized extended sense of 'plays the violin'.) Is it metaphysically possible for there to have been dragons in the literal (unextended) sense of the word? No; the mythical species K is not a real species, any more than Puff is a real beast, and the mythical species could not have been a species any more than Puff could have been a beast. It is essential to K that it not be a species. *A fortiori* there could not have been such beasts. The reasoning here is very different from that of Kripke's *Naming and Necessity*, at pp. 156–157, which emphasizes the alleged 'dragon$_1$' use (disputed here), on which 'There are dragons' allegedly expresses nothing (hence nothing that is possibly true).

The account of mythical objects as real abstract artifacts also yields a solution to P. T. Geach's famous problem about Hob's and Nob's hypothesized witch, from 'Intentional Identity,' *Journal of Philosophy*, 74, 20 (1967).

on which it is thoroughly nonreferring. I know of no compelling reason to deny that Babinet introduced a single name 'Vulcan' ultimately with a univocal use as a name for his mythical planet.[51] One might say that 'Vulcan$_1$' represents a mythical use of the name. As with 'Holmes$_1$', this kind of use is no more a genuine use than a mythical planet is a genuine planet.

It is unclear whether there are significant limitations here, and if so, what they might be. Even Meinong's golden mountain and round square should probably be seen as real mythical objects. Meinong's golden mountain is an abstract entity that is neither golden nor a mountain but as real as Babinet's Vulcan. Real but neither round nor square, Meinong's round square is both round and square according to Meinong's erroneous theory. Should we not also admit and recognize such things as fabrications, figments of one's imagination, and flights of fancy as real abstract entities? Where does it all end?

In the kingdom of France.

If one adopts a very inclusive attitude toward such applicants for Existence as fictional characters, mythical planets, fabricated boyfriends, and flights of fancy, then one is hardly in a position to urge a restrictive admissions policy when it comes to nonreferring names. We know that France has no emperor at present. But we do not know this *a priori*. We could even be mistaken. It is not *a priori* impossible that a fanatic, with the help of an underground army and the unanimous approval of the United Nations, has just seized control of the French government and declared himself the new emperor. I hereby introduce the name 'Nappy' to refer to the new emperor of France, whoever that might be, if there is one, and to refer to nothing otherwise. Take note: I do not introduce 'Nappy' as a name for a particular fictional character that I just created. I am not storytelling and I am not pretending to use 'Nappy' as a name of a person. Nor do I subscribe to any theory to the effect that France now has an emperor. Rather I introduce 'Nappy' as a name for the actual present emperor of France, provided—contrary to my every expectation—that there presently is an emperor of France. Barring a fairly radical skepticism, we know that there is no such person as Nappy. Nappy is not a fictional character, not a mythical character, not a fabrication, not a flight of fancy. There is a very good reason why Nappy is none of these things. Not to put too fine a point on it, Nappy does not exist.

Or consider again the name 'Curly-0', which I introduced above for the merely possible bald man presently standing in Quine's doorway. There is no such merely possible man. But the name itself, so introduced, is real. I introduced it. And it does not refer. It would have been a mistake to suppose that there might have been someone to whom the name actually refers. But I made no such mistake in introducing the name; I knew I had not succeeded in singling out any particular possible individual. This much, then, is not a mistake: Curly-0 does not exist.

---

[51] I am assuming throughout that in introducing 'Vulcan', Babinet presupposed the existence of an intra-Mercurial planet to be so named. In some cases of reference fixing, the description employed may have what I call a *Bad mock referential*, or *Ugly*, use—i.e., reference is fixed by an implicit description not coreferential with the description explicitly used. See my 'The Good, the Bad, and the Ugly,' in M. Reimer and A. Bezuidenhout, eds, *Descriptions and Beyond* (Oxford University Press, 2004), pp. 230–260. *Cf.* Kripke on 'Hesperus', in *Naming and Necessity*, at p. 80 n. 34.

Why do the introductions of 'Nappy' and 'Curly-0' result in thoroughly non-referring names when Babinet's introduction of 'Vulcan' results in a name for an existing abstract artifact? Because in inventing his theory, Babinet inadvertently invented a mythical planet, and though Babinet intended to target an independently existing planet, his referential arrow eventually struck the mythical object—not in exactly the same manner as the ancients' arrow that struck Venus despite its not being a star, but close. To the allegation that I have invented a fictional emperor of France, I plead Not Guilty. One should not suppose that to every improper definite description one might conjure up there corresponds a fiction, or mini-fiction, in which the description is proper. Even pulp fiction is not that easy to write.[52]

My contention has not been that there are no true sentences of the form (4α) with α a thoroughly nonreferring name. My point, rather, is that they are rare—and bizarre. The examples are not like an utterance of 'Sherlock Holmes does not really exist' to assert that Holmes$_2$ in reality is not sufficiently like the way he is depicted. The examples are also dissimilar from 'Socrates does not exist', 'Newman-1 does not exist', 'Noman does not exist', and even '{Noman-0, Nothan-0} does not exist'. In these other negative existentials, there is some sense in which the subject term refers to a definite nonexistent thing: a past, future, merely possible, or impossible object. The negative existentials say of these definite things, correctly, that they do not exist. By contrast, 'Nappy does not exist' and 'Curly-0 does not exist' have a completely different flavor and are true on altogether different grounds: In no sense is there a definite nonexistent thing referred to. Do these two sentences, then, deny existence of different things? If so, what things? How do they differ? 'Curly-0' is a different name from 'Nappy', but Curly-0 is not a different *thing* from Nappy. They are not *things* at all; they are nothing. Or perhaps I should say, there is no such thing as Curly-0, and likewise Nappy. As much as to say that Curly-0 and Nappy do not exist. That there are no such things is true, but what exactly is it?

One might be tempted to suppose that 'Nappy does not exist' expresses the proposition that there is no unique present emperor of France. This is essentially the approach of Russell. It directly conflicts with the theory of direct reference (entailing, for example, that 'Nappy' is not a rigid nondesignator), and has been discredited by the arguments supporting that theory. So with the Fregean semantic-ascent and intensional-ascent approaches to singular existentials. I shun the heavy-handed intensionality of these approaches, as well as the unexplained intensional machinery

[52] But see note 43. I introduced 'Holmes$_1$' as a name having the thoroughly nonreferring use that the name 'Sherlock Holmes' originally has according to Kripke's theory. That alleged use is mythical. My introduction of the name thus misfired; no genuine use was attached to the name on which it may be said either to refer or not to refer. I might have fixed the reference of a new name, say 'Holmes$_3$' (not a disguised description), by the description 'the Holmesesque-Holmes$_2$'. Analogously, I might have introduced a name 'Vulcan$_3$' as a name for the planet, if there is one, whose gravitational force (rather than general relativity) correctly explains the irregularities in Mercury's orbit, and nonreferring otherwise. I would exploit a certain myth to obtain the reference-fixing description, but would have introduced the name in such a way that it does not refer instead to Babinet's mythical planet. Had I done this, authentic true negative existentials with thoroughly nonreferring names would have been generated.

of Kripke's proposal to interpret 'Nappy does not exist' as a paraphrase of 'There is no true proposition that Nappy exists'. There is here a new homework problem.

Consider the slightly simpler issue of the meanings of sentences of the form of (1α) with α a thoroughly nonreferring name. Does 'Nappy is bald' express anything? Does 'Curly-0 is bald?' I believe the answer is clearly that they do. They are not mere strings of nonsense syllables. They have translations—very literal translations—into most natural languages (by resorting to use of the very names 'Nappy' and 'Curly-0'). Such translations preserve *something*. What? Not the proposition expressed, for these sentences express no proposition, or at least none that is a candidate for being true or false. I would propose that they be seen instead as expressing something severely disabled, the partially formed product of a failed attempt to construct a true-or-false proposition, something whose cognitive and semantic function is that of a truth-valued proposition but which is unable to fulfil its function for lack of an essential component. Think of the nondefective sentence 'Marlon Brando is bald' as expressing its semantic content in the manner of: 'This object is bald: Marlon Brando'. Then 'Nappy is bald' expresses the semantic content of 'This object is bald: '. 'Curly-0 is bald' expresses the very same thing. Let us call it a *structurally challenged proposition*. It may be thought of for the present purpose as an ordered pair, or rather a would-be ordered pair, whose second element is the concept or property of baldness and whose first element is nothing whatsoever.[53]

Granted sufficient leeway, expressions like 'the proposition that Nappy is bald' and 'that Curly-0 is bald' may be taken to refer to the structurally challenged proposition expressed in common by their complement clauses. This is one crucial respect in which the present view differs from that of Kripke, who contends that 'Nappy is bald' and 'Curly-0 is bald' express nothing, and that their corresponding 'that' clauses are consequently thoroughly nonreferring. (See note 19.) On the view I am proposing, although Nappy does not exist, the structurally challenged

---

[53] The set-theoretic representation can be made formally precise in an intuitive way (for example by invoking partial functions). *Cf.* my discussion of *open propositions* in *Frege's Puzzle*, at pp. 155–156n. (The alternative terminology of 'structurally impaired proposition' is implicitly structurist, hence contrary to the inclusive spirit of the present essay, which celebrates cognitive structural diversity. I also resist the temptation to use the abbreviation '*SC*-proposition', for fear it might be mistaken as shorthand for 'Southern California proposition' and the idea then summarily dismissed.)

It is reported in Almog, p. 618n15, that Kaplan, in an unpublished 1973 lecture commenting on Kripke, proposed that 'Vulcan does not exist' expresses a true 'gappy proposition.' Kaplan briefly mentions a similar idea in 'Demonstratives,' in J. Almog, J. Perry, and H. Wettstein, eds., *Themes from Kaplan* (Oxford University Press, 1989), pp. 481–563, at 496n23. Contrary to the view imputed to Kaplan, 'Vulcan does not$_C$ exist', taken literally, expresses on my view a false structurally *un*challenged singular proposition about the mythical planet (and may frequently be understood instead as expressing the true proposition that there is no Vulcanesque Vulcan$_2$).

Plantinga, in 'On Existentialism,' *Philosophical Studies*, 44 (1983), pp. 1–20, at p. 9, argues as part of a defense of serious actualism (note 29 above) that the singular proposition about William F. Buckley that he is wise might be regarded as existing but 'ill-formed or even maimed' in a possible world in which Buckley does not exist. This is decidedly different from my view. The only defect suffered by Soc is that it does not exist; it is neither 'ill-formed' nor 'maimed.' It is even true. In a possible world in which Buckley does not exist the proposition that he is wise is neither existent nor true, but it does not face the structural challenges of singular propositions about Nappy and Curly-0.

proposition that Nappy is bald exists, and is identical to the structurally challenged proposition that Curly-0 is bald. Not all sentences of the form (1α) with α a non-referring name or improper definite description express this structurally challenged proposition. 'Socrates is bald' expresses that Socrates is bald, a proposition that does not exist but once did. 'Newman-1 is bald' expresses a different proposition, one that will exist but does not yet. 'Noman-0 is bald' expresses a proposition that might have existed but never will, and '{Nothan-0, Nathan Salmon} is bald' (properly interpreted) a proposition that could never exist. 'Sherlock Holmes is bald' and (1) express existing propositions that are untrue. None of these propositions are structurally challenged in the manner of ⟨___, baldness⟩. But all sentences of the form (1α) with α a thoroughly nonreferring name express this same structurally challenged proposition, *this one is bald*: . None of these various propositions, structurally challenged and not, are true. I shall assume here that atomic structurally challenged propositions cannot be either true or false.[54]

Though both express the same structurally challenged proposition, 'Nappy is bald' and 'Curly-0 is bald' present their common semantic content to the mind of the reader in different ways. One presents it in the manner of 'This object is bald: the present emperor of France', the other in the manner of 'This object is bald: the possible bald man presently in Quine's doorway'. The reader takes the structurally challenged proposition differently, depending in this case on the actual words used to express it.[55] I have argued in previous work that the way in which a reader takes a given proposition has no bearing on semantics; what matters as far as semantics goes is the literal meaning of the sentence and what propositions are thereby semantically expressed. Though the way in which a proposition is taken is not semantics, it bears on cognitive psychology and plays an extremely important role in pragmatics, on which I have spoken elsewhere at some length. Structurally challenged propositions do not differ from their unchallenged cousins in this respect.[56]

---

[54] Frege's Principle of Compositionality for Reference, as he understood it, required that the usual truth-functional connectives observe their Kleene weak three-valued truth tables, on which any truth-functional compound with a non-truth-valued component is itself without truth-value regardless of the truth-values of the other components. Whereas Frege's argument for this may seem inconclusive at best, an analogous argument is more persuasive as regards truth-functional compounds with structurally challenged components. At the very least, atomic structurally challenged propositions do seem, intuitively, to lack the resources necessary to achieve truth-value. If it is incorrect to say that Nappy is bald, it is equally incorrect to say that Nappy is not$_c$ bald, and for the very same reason. Mimicking Russell, if we enumerated the things that are bald, and then the things that are not bald, we should not find Nappy in either list. Even Russell, who loved truth-value (and abhorred a synthesis), would probably have withheld falsity as well as truth from ⟨___, baldness⟩—unless he was prepared to label such things as Picadilly Circus and his own singleton false.

[55] The same point might be made by using Kaplan's '*dthat*' operator, on its originally intended interpretation. *Cf.* Kaplan's 'Afterthoughts' to his 'Demonstratives,' pp. 565–614, at 578–582. I am arguing that, on that original interpretation, the two sentences '*Dthat* [the present emperor of France] is bald' and '*Dthat* [the possible bald man presently in Quine's doorway] is bald' express the same thing, though each presents the structurally challenged proposition in its own special way.

[56] Thus one who believes that Curly-0 is bald thereby also believes (despite any denials) that Nappy is bald. *Cf. Frege's Puzzle*, at p. 7, and especially pp. 127–128. The present essay delivers on the promissory note issued there.

VII

Structurally challenged propositions provide content for the most intransigent instances of (4α). Even if (4α) does not express a nonexistent singular proposition (past, future, merely possible, or impossible), there is always the structurally challenged proposition. But if α is thoroughly nonreferring, all of (1α)–(4α) express structurally challenged propositions. It would seem that (4α) must then be neither true nor false, hence not true. But if α is nonreferring, (4α) is true. In philosophy, this is what is known as a *Headache*.[57]

I prescribe relief in the form of a new theory of singular existence, or rather of nonexistence. Although the intensional-ascent theory of existence improves upon Frege's semantic-ascent theory by capturing (or at least by approaching) the right modal intensions for singular existentials, there remains an intuitive difference between 'The present queen of England exists', which evidently mentions Queen Elizabeth II, and '$(\exists x)\Delta(^\wedge(_1 y)(Present\text{-}queen\text{-}of\text{-}England(y)^\wedge, x)$', which does not. There is an alternative to both approaches that, although still within the spirit of Fregean theory, has not to my knowledge been explicitly proposed before. We saw in Section I that the distinction between choice and exclusion negation reveals an ambiguity in (2) for which there is no corresponding ambiguity in (1). According to Frege, one who utters (2) using 'not' in the sense of choice negation erroneously presupposes that there presently is a unique king of France. But one may use 'not' in the sense of exclusion negation to commit oneself only to the significantly weaker claim that no unique present king of France is bald. This same ambiguity occurs wherever 'not' does. One may thus take (3) to be analyzed by (3″), as was the original idea, while taking (4) to be ambiguous between the following:

(9) $\sim_C(\exists x)[(_1 y)Present\text{-}king\text{-}of\text{-}France(y) = x]$

(10) $\sim_E(\exists x)[(_1 y)Present\text{-}king\text{-}of\text{-}France(y) = x].$

These correspond exactly to the two readings of the negation sign in (4″). In the general case, on this theory, (3α) receives its usual analysis (alternatively, the existence predicate may be regarded as primitive), while the 'not' in (4α) yields two readings. On one reading, (4α) means the same as ⌜α does not_C exist⌝, on the other the same as ⌜The proposition that α exists is not_C true⌝, or ⌜It is untrue that α exists⌝.

---

[57] David Braun, in 'Empty Names,' *Noûs*, 27 (December 1993), pp. 449–469, at 460–465, develops Kaplan's idea of gappy propositions in connection with sentences like 'Vulcan is bald' and 'Vulcan does not exist'. See note 53 above. To repeat: Vulcan does exist, and such sentences as these express ordinary, structurally unchallenged propositions. Aside from this, Braun illegitimately makes the problem too easy for himself, arguing by analogy (in effect) that since all structurally unchallenged propositions have truth-value so too do all structurally challenged ones, then asserting without further argument that atomic monadic singular propositions are false whenever there is nothing in the subject position that has the property in the predicate position—so that without any further ado, all atomic structurally challenged propositions are straightforwardly false. Against this, see note 54 above.

Let us call this analysis of singular existentials and their negations *the choice/exclusion theory of nonexistence.*[58]

The choice/exclusion theory still has the consequence by Frege's lights that (3) is neither true nor F-false$_1$, and hence not false. But at least it is thus judged untrue (F-false$_2$). The choice/exclusion theory also has the consequence that (4) has a true reading while (3) does not. This might be deemed satisfactory.

It might even be deemed insightful. There is something odd about (4). If one wishes to correct the view that France presently has a king, it is more natural to do so by saying 'There presently is no king of France' (accompanied with an explanation that France is no longer a monarchy) or 'There is no such thing as the present king of France'. The former suggests (4'), the latter something like (8). By contrast, (4) itself seems to involve a faulty presupposition. We can use (4) to say something acceptable, but when we do, we seem to mean that it is untrue that the present king of France exists—precisely what (10) expresses. (This is what we mean, that is, unless someone whom we wish to enlighten about international politics has inadvertently created a mythical king of France, so that the description in (4) is used with invisible scare quotes to mean *the mythical object that Smith believes is presently king of France, thus depicted*.) Some of (4)'s oddness is present also in (3), and even in true singular existentials. If (1) presupposes (3'), as Frege and Strawson claim, then how could (3) fail to do so? (Compare Frege's comments about the name 'Sachse'.) If Britain were to dissolve its monarchy during the present queen's lifetime, 'The present queen of England exists', uttered after the dissolution, would become untrue. But would it become straightforwardly false?

---

[58] As mentioned in note 16, Church cites (4) as an example of a true sentence in which a singular term has an *ungerade* occurrence. He also cites 'Lady Hamilton was like Aphrodite in beauty' and 'The fountain of youth is not located in Florida'. It is possible that Church held that the constructions '___ is located in Florida' and 'Lady Hamilton is like ___ in beauty' are (at least sometimes) *ungerade* devices. On such a view the un-negated sentences, 'The fountain of youth is located in Florida' and (3) would be F-false$_1$ sentences in which the subject terms have *ungerade* occurrences, the first expressing that the concept ^{s}the fountain of youth^s determines something with a certain location. But it seems at least as likely, assuming that 'the fountain of youth' is non-referring, that this sentence is neither true nor F-false$_1$, and the *ungerade* device in 'The fountain of youth is not located in Florida', and that in (4), is instead something common to both sentences.

In light of the fountain of youth's role in fable and myth (not to mention its impact on Ponce de Leon), Church's example might be better replaced with a sentence like 'The present king of France is not among the bald men of the world', which may be more readily accepted as true than (2). It is unclear whether Church would have held that this sentence, assuming it is true, means that the concept ^{s}the present king of France^s does not determine something that is among the bald men of the world (analogously to the intensional-ascent theory of existence), or instead that the proposition ^{s}the present king of France is among the bald men of the world^s is not true (analogously to the exclusion theory of nonexistence). Church's abstention from citing (2) itself as another example of the same phenomenon may suggest the former interpretation—on which such expressions as 'located in Florida' and 'among the bald men of the world' are distinguished from 'bald' as *ungerade* devices. (C. Anthony Anderson conjectures that the relational aspect of '___ is located in ___' and '___ is like ___ in beauty' may have played a role in Church's view that they are *ungerade* devices. This would involve assimilating them to '___ seeks ___', which on Church's view expresses a relation between an object and a concept, thus distinguishing them from '___ is bald'. Cf. *ibid.*, p. 8n20. Anderson notes that '___ is among ___' is likewise relational.) On the other hand, the mere juxtaposition of two examples involving negation may suggest the latter interpretation. (It is possible that relational phrases like 'located in Florida' and 'among the bald men of the world' have a greater tendency than 'bald' to induce the exclusion reading of their negation.)

I propose combining the choice/exclusion theory of nonexistence with structurally challenged propositions. The resulting theory applies across the board to sentences with improper definite descriptions, nonreferring proper names, or other non-referring terms. The negative existential 'Socrates does not exist' receives two readings: Soc, and *it is untrue that Socrates exists*. Neither proposition currently exists, but both are true. Similarly for 'Newman-1 does not exist' and 'Noman-0 does not exist'. The sentences 'Nappy does not exist' and 'Curly-0 does not exist' are also deemed ambiguous. On one reading, they each express the same structurally challenged proposition, one that is neither true nor false. On the other reading, they each express the same true proposition, that the structurally challenged proposition $\langle$___, existence$\rangle$ is untrue. Both readings, because of the involvement of structurally challenged propositions, are to some extent bizarre. The presence of distinct bizarre readings contributes towards the overall oddness of these negative existentials.

This theory relieves the Headache without capitulating to golden mountains. It also respects distinctions of content among intuitively nonsynonymous true negative existentials, like 'Socrates does not exist' and 'Noman does not exist'. And while it equates true negative existentials with thoroughly nonreferring names as expressing the same thing (or the same things), it respects their nonsemantic differences regarding how they present their common content. The theory diverges from Kripke's theory that a sentence like (2α) is sometimes true on the same ground as ⌜There is no proposition that α is bald⌝ and (4α) on the same ground as ⌜There is no proposition that α exists⌝—whatever that ground is. There is no true proposition that Nappy is bald, or that Nappy exists, but these propositions exist. Instead (2α) sometimes means the same as ⌜It is untrue that α is bald⌝ and (4α) as ⌜It is untrue that α exists⌝, where the 'that' clauses always refer. Unlike Kripke's account, mine makes no intensional concessions that run against the grain of direct-reference theory.[59]

More important, the theory is intuitively correct as applied to a very wide range of sentences with nonreferring terms. The theory also coheres with Millianism to form a unified theory of content for singular terms, referring and not, and for sentences, existential and not. If there remain problematically true negative existentials for which the present theory does not provide a plausible account, I do not know which ones they are. Most importantly, if there are such, it may be that the Unified Metaphysico-Semantic Theory that some of us have sought exists only in fable and myth.

[59] The choice/exclusion ambiguity may extend also to the negation in 'Nappy is nonexistent', and even to the negations in 'Nappy is innocuous, since he is nonexistent'. The theory may even be sufficiently flexible to accommodate those who remain unconvinced concerning the nonexistent propositions mentioned above, like Soc. A skeptic concerning a particular nonexistent proposition may replace the offending proposition with the corresponding structurally challenged proposition, which does exist. It is not always possible to do so, however, while preserving truth-value. The nonexistent proposition that Nothan, had he been born instead of me, would have been taller than I actually am is either true or false, but the corresponding structurally challenged proposition is evidently neither. Even if the latter is deemed to have truth-value, then so must be the structurally challenged propositions corresponding to the nonexistent propositions that Nothan would have been shorter than I actually am and that Nothan would have been exactly the same height as I actually am. At least one of these existing structurally challenged surrogates fails to preserve the truth-value of the nonexistent proposition it was put in to replace.

3

Mythical Objects (2002)

NOTIONAL AND RELATIONAL

It is widely recognized that a sentence like

(1) Ralph wants a sloop

is subject to a nonlexical ambiguity not duplicated in, for example,

(2) Ralph owns a sloop.

(1) may indeed be read analogously with (2): There is a sloop that Ralph wants/owns. This is what W. V. Quine calls the *relational* reading. On this reading, (1) is like (2) in logically entailing the existence of at least one sloop, and the author of (1), like that of (2), is thus ontologically committed to sloops. But (1) may be read instead as indicating an aimless desire on Ralph's part for the very state of affairs described by (2): Ralph's relief from slooplessness. Quine calls this the *notional* reading. Here (1) asserts not that a relation obtains between Ralph and a sloop, but that one obtains between Ralph and the generalized, nonspecific concept of *some sloop or other* (or some counterpart of this concept, like the property of being a class that includes some sloop or other among its elements). No sloop in particular need be the object of Ralph's desire; for that matter, all sloops everywhere may be destroyed. Ralph can still notionally want one. There is no analogous reading for (2). Sloop ownership is as commonplace as sloops. Whatever it would be to stand in the ownership relation to a concept, it is clear that (2) does not attribute such a state to Ralph.

The same asymmetry arises in connection with the following pair:

(3) Ralph believes a spy has stolen his documents.
(4) A spy has stolen Ralph's documents.

On its relational reading (3) asserts that there is a spy whom Ralph suspects of having stolen his documents—just as (4) asserts that there is a spy who has indeed taken the missing documents. This is the so-called *de re* reading of (3), what Russell (1905)

This chapter was presented at various venues before and after the turn of the millennium. I am grateful to Mark Fiocco, Steven Humphrey, Genoveva Marti, Michael McGlone, and Teresa Robertson for discussion, as well as my audiences and the participants in my UCSB seminar during Spring 2000.

calls the *primary occurrence* reading.[1] On this reading, some spy is under suspicion, and the speaker is logically committed to there being at least that one spy, in just the same way that the author of (4) is committed to the existence of at least one spy. On its notional reading, (3) reports Ralph's more generalized belief of the very proposition contained in (4): that some spy or other has made off with the documents. No one in particular need be under suspicion. There need not even be any spies anywhere, as long as Ralph believes otherwise. This is the *de dicto* reading, what Russell calls the *secondary occurrence* reading. It asserts a relation not between Ralph and a spy, but one between Ralph and the concepts of *some spy or other* and *stealing documents*. There is no analogous reading for (4). Concepts are not thieves, nor does (4) make any accusation against any concept. Underlying the relational/notional dichotomy in (1) and (3) is the pertinent fact that wanting and believing are psychological states that may be directed equally toward concepts or objects (or concepts that involve objects, or propositions that involve objects, etc.). Ownership and theft are not states of this sort.

Care must be taken not to confuse the notional/relational distinction with various alternative distinctions. One such alternative concerns different uses that a speaker might make of an indefinite descriptive phrase. Though 'a sloop' expresses the indefinite concept *some sloop or other*, there is no bar against using the phrase with reference to a particular sloop (as, for example, in 'I was in a sloop yesterday. Was it yours?'). Such a use flies in the face of the indefinite character of the concept semantically expressed by the phrase. We say something nonspecific and mean something specific; in effect, we say 'some sloop' but mean 'that sloop'. And yet life goes on relatively unperturbed. Keith Donnellan famously pointed out (as did some others independently) that definite descriptions are likewise used sometimes with a particular object in mind ('referential use'), sometimes not ('attributive'). Let us call a use of a definite or indefinite description in uttering a sentence *directed* when there is a particular object to which the use is relevantly connected (e.g., the speaker intends a specific object or person) and the speaker may be regarded as thereby asserting (or asking) something specific directly about that object, and let us call a use of a description *undirected* when the speaker instead merely intends something general to the effect that whatever (whoever) is the only such-and-such/at least one such-and-such or other.[2]

The distinction between directed and undirected uses is clearly genuine; of that there can be no legitimate doubt. What is subject to serious dispute is whether the

---

[1] W. V. Quine, 'Quantifiers and Propositional Attitudes.' *Journal of Philosophy* 53. Reprinted in Quine's *The Ways of Paradox* (New York: Random House, 1966), 183–94. B. Russell, 'On Denoting.' *Mind* 14 (1905), pp. 479–93. Russell would extend his primary/secondary occurrence distinction to (1) by rewriting it in sentential-operator form, for example, as ⌜Ralph desires that (2)⌝.

[2] K. Donnellan, 'Reference and Definite Descriptions.' *The Philosophical Review* 75 (1966), pp. 281–304. Donnellan's referential/attributive distinction for definite descriptions is a special case of the directed/undirected distinction, which also covers indefinite descriptions. A use of 'some atheist' in uttering 'Some atheist is a spy' may be undirected even if the speaker is regarded as thereby designating a higher-order entity relevantly connected to that same use (for example, the function from functions-from-individuals-to-truth-values that assigns *truth* to any function assigning *truth* to at least one atheist and otherwise assigns *falsity*).

distinction has a direct bearing on the semantics of descriptive phrases. In particular, is (2) literally true, even if only by dumb luck, when 'a sloop' is used directedly for a sloop Ralph does not in fact own, if Ralph nevertheless owns a sloop? Intuition strongly favors an affirmative response. Russell recognized the point, and urged it in favor of his theory (now generally taken for granted) that indefinite descriptions function univocally as existential quantifiers:

What do I really assert when I assert 'I met a man'? Let us assume, for the moment, that my assertion is true, and that in fact I met Jones. It is clear that what I assert is *not* 'I met Jones.' I may say 'I met a man, but it was not Jones'; in that case, though I lie, I do not contradict myself, as I should do if when I say I met a man I really mean that I met Jones. It is clear also that the person to whom I am speaking can understand what I say, even if he is a foreigner and has never heard of Jones.

But we may go further: not only Jones, but no actual man, enters into my statement. This becomes obvious when the statement is false, since then there is no more reason why Jones should be supposed to enter into the proposition than why anyone else should. . . . Thus it is only what we may call the concept that enters into the proposition.

More systematic considerations can also be brought to bear, discrediting the thesis that the directed/undirected distinction is relevantly relevant.[3] Still some remain unconvinced. Joseph Almog (pp. 77–81) has claimed that the distinction (or one like it in all relevant respects) is not only semantically significant, but indeed provides the basis for the notional/relational distinction.[4] The relational reading of (1), Almog contends, is generated by a directed use of the relevant indefinite description, the notional reading by an undirected use (1998, 79–81; Almog speaks of 'readings' rather than 'uses'). The account extends the notional/relational distinction to (2), portraying the undirected use of the indefinite as generating a notional reading. In fact, Almog explains the notional reading of (1) as the exact analogue of the reading generated by an undirected use of (2).

The fact that the directed/undirected distinction applies to sentences like (2) and (4), not just (1) and (3), is in itself reason for suspicion of the proposal. Almog's account gets things exactly reversed with the facts. It is the relational reading of (1), not the notional, that arises by reading it on the model of (2): There is some sloop or other that Ralph owns/wants. A genuinely notional reading of (2) should depict Ralph as somehow standing in the ownership relation to a nonspecific concept!

---

[3] See S. Kripke, 'Speaker's Reference and Semantic Reference.' In P. French, T. Uehling, and H. Wettstein (eds.), *Contemporary Perspectives in the Philosophy of Language* (Minneapolis: University of Minnesota Press, 1977).

[4] J. Almog, 'The Subject Verb Object Class.' In J. Tomberlin (ed.), *Philosophical Perspectives 12: Language, Mind, and Ontology* (Cambridge, Mass.: Blackwell, 1998). Others who also maintain that the directed/undirected distinction is semantically relevant include Barbara Partee ('Opacity, Coreference, and Pronouns.' In D. Davidson and G. Harman (eds.), *Semantics of Natural Language* (Boston: D. Reidel, 1972). Almog follows Partee in confusing relational/notional with directed/undirected); Jon Barwise and John Perry, *Situations and Attitudes* (Cambridge, Mass.: MIT Press, 1983); and Howard Wettstein ('Demonstrative Reference and Definite Descriptions.' *Philosophical Studies* 40 (1981), pp. 241–57; 'The Semantic Significance of the Referential-Attributive Distinction.' *Philosophical Studies* 44 (1983), pp. 187–96). I challenge Wettstein's account in Salmon). 'The Pragmatic Fallacy.' *Philosophical Studies* (1991), pp. 83–97.

Likewise, it is the relational reading of (3), not the notional, that arises by reading it on the model of (4): There is some spy or other who has stolen Ralph's documents— or whom Ralph believes has stolen them.[5]

The explanation for the collapse of the notional/relational distinction on Almog's account is straightforward. Consider the relational reading of (1): A sloop is such that Ralph specifically wants it. Whereas 'a sloop' may be used directedly, there is nothing to prevent the speaker from instead using the indefinite phrase undirectedly, and to mean by (1), understood relationally, that Ralph's desire is focused on some sloop or other: There is a very particular sloop—which sloop is not here specified— that Ralph has his heart set on. (I maintain that this accords with the literal meaning of (1), read relationally, regardless of whether the indefinite is used directedly or undirectedly, whereas the specific thought that Ralph wants *that sloop I have in mind* provides more information than is semantically encoded into the relational reading.) Exactly similarly for (3): There is a very particular spy—which spy is not here specified—to whom Ralph's finger of blame is pointed in a most *de re*, accusatory way. In neither case does an undirected use preclude the relational reading; read relationally, the indefinite may be used either directedly or undirectedly.

Ironically, an undirected use in fact evidently precludes the notional reading. If (1) is read notionally, the description 'a sloop' functions not to *express* the generalized concept of some sloop or other, but to *refer to* it, in order for (1) to

---

[5] Almog explains the notional reading of 'Madonna seeks a man' (misidentified with its undirected use) by saying that it is true if and only if Madonna seeks at least one instance of the kind *Man* ('Subject Verb Object,' pp. 57, 80). This is at best a tortured expression of Madonna's objective ('Mankind, schmankind. I'm just looking for a man.'). Worse, the formulation leaves the notional/relational ambiguity unresolved. In seeking at least one instance of mankind, is there anyone in particular who is the object of Madonna's desire, or is she merely seeking relief from her unbearable loneliness? Almog disambiguates in exactly the wrong direction, saying: (*i*) ' "Madonna met a man" . . . is true on this parsing [its undirected use] . . . iff Madonna met at least one man'; furthermore, (*ii*) 'no special treatment accrues intensional verbs. Thus to get the truth conditions of the [notional] reading of "Madonna seeks a man", simply substitute "seek" [in (*i*)]' (p. 80). Substitution of *seeking* for *having met* in Madonna's having met at least one man (or in Madonna's standing to mankind in the relative product, *x* met at least one instance of *y*) directly results in a targeted search by the diva.

Almog denies (pp. 53–54) that (2) logically entails (2′) 'There is a sloop that Ralph owns', on the grounds that (1), which has the same logical form as (2), can be true without (1′) 'There is a sloop that Ralph wants'—while conceding that it is nevertheless necessary and knowable *a priori* that if Ralph owns a sloop then there is a sloop that he owns. This argument carries no conviction. Logic can no more tolerate a divergence in truth-value between 'Ralph owns at least one sloop' and 'At least one sloop is such that Ralph owns it' than it can between 'The number of planets is such as to be not even' and 'It is not the case that: the number of planets is even'. The second pair are equivalent despite the fact that substitution of 'possibly' for 'not' yields a falsehood and a truth, respectively. There is a reading of (1) on which it evidently entails (1′)—*viz.*, the relational reading. In any event, on this reading (1) yields (1′) with the same sort of modality as between (2) and (2′)— whether the connection is deemed logical or only necessary, *a priori*, intuitive, conceptual, true by virtue of meaning, and whatever else (knowable by reason alone?). The relational/notional distinction may even be defined or characterized by contrasting the reading of (1) on which it is yields (1′) *via* the same sort of modality as between (2) and (2′), with that on which it instead attributes a desire for slooplessness relief compatible with (1′)'s denial. Owning and finding provide a template for wanting and seeking, but only for wanting and seeking in the relational senses. The desire for mere relief from slooplessness provides a new paradigm (familiarity of grammatical form notwithstanding).

express that Ralph stands to this very concept in the specified relation.[6] Analogously, on the notional reading of (3), the complement clause functions not to express the proposition that some spy or other has stolen Ralph's documents but to refer to the proposition, enabling the sentence to express that Ralph believes it. As Frege noted, in such cases the indefinite phrase does not have its customary content or reference, i.e., its customary *Sinn* or *Bedeutung*. Instead it is in *ungerade* ('oblique') mode. Insofar as the phrase is used to refer to a generalized concept, it is naturally used directedly for that very concept. The notional reading is thus generally accompanied by a directed use by the speaker (albeit an *ungerade* use), not an undirected one. Here again, Almog's account has matters exactly reversed with the facts.[7]

Taking (2) as a model for the notional reading of (1) inevitably yields exactly the wrong results. In effect, Almog attempts to capture the relational/notional distinction by contrasting directed and undirected uses of the relational reading, missing the notional reading altogether. The failure of the directed/undirected distinction as an analysis of the notional/relational is confirmed by Russell's insight that the latter distinction replicates itself in increasingly complex constructions. This is Russell's notion of scope. Thus the sentence.

Quine doubts that Ralph wants a sloop

yields not merely two, but three distinct readings: There is a sloop that Quine specifically doubts Ralph wants (*wide scope*); Quine doubts that there is any sloop that Ralph wants (*intermediate*); Quine doubts that Ralph seeks relief from slooplessness (*narrow*). The intermediate-scope reading is notional with respect to Quine and relational with respect to Ralph; the narrow-scope reading is doubly notional. The intermediate- and narrow-scope readings report Quine's doubt of the relational and notional readings, respectively, of (1). The wide-scope reading is the next generation of readings. Prefixing further operators introduces successive generations ('You understand that Salmon reports that Quine doubts...'). By contrast, the directed/undirected distinction does not reproduce with operators. The distinction naturally arises in the wide-scope reading, which is neutral between a directed and an undirected use of 'a sloop'. Each is permissible. ('A sloop [*that sloop I have in mind*

---

[6] This is not to say that Ralph wants to own a concept. There is no sloop or concept that Ralph specifically wants in virtue of wanting relief from slooplessness. Rather, Ralph stands in a certain relation to the generalized concept, *some sloop or other*. The relation is expressed in some English constructions by 'wants'. To say that Ralph notionally wants a concept is to assert that this same relation obtains between Ralph and a concept of a concept. *Cf.* Alonzo Church (*Introduction to Mathematical Logic I* (Princeton: Princeton University Press, 1956), p. 8n20).

[7] Almog depicts (2) on an undirected use as expressing (or at least as true exactly on the condition) that Ralph stands to the kind *Sloop* in the relative product, x owns at least one instance of y. This would suggest that, in such a use, the word 'sloop' refers to, and is directed toward, the kind *Sloop* while the words 'owns a' express the relative product (p. 79). Similarly for the analogous use of (1), yielding its relational reading (directly contrary to Almog's stated purpose; see note 5 above). The phrase 'a sloop' (as opposed to the word 'sloop' occurring therein) on such a use would refer neither to the kind nor to the relative product, nor to anything else. In effect, it is contextually defined away. (Alternatively, it might be taken as referring to a higher-order entity, e.g., $(\lambda F)[(\exists z)(z$ is an instance of the kind *Sloop* & $Fz)]$; *cf.* note 2 above. But Almog eschews such entities in his semantic analysis.) By contrast, 'a sloop' on the notional reading of (1) refers to, and its use is directed toward, the concept, *some sloop or other* (or if one prefers, *at least one instance of Sloop*).

vs. *some sloop or other*] is such that Quine specifically doubts that Ralph wants *it*.') In both the intermediate- and narrow-scope readings, 'a sloop' is in *ungerade* mode, and hence, insofar as it is used directedly or undirectedly, is presumably directed.[8]

GEACH'S PUZZLE

The notional/relational distinction may be tested by anaphoric links to a descriptive phrase. Consider:

Ralph wants a sloop, but it is a lemon

Ralph believes a female spy has stolen his documents; she also tampered with the computer.

These sentences strongly favor a relational reading. Appropriately understood, each evidently entails the relational reading of its first conjunct, even if the first conjunct itself is (somewhat perversely) read notionally. If, as alleged, it is a lemon, then there must be an *it* that is a lemon, and that *it* must be a sloop that Ralph wants. Similarly, if she tampered with the computer, then there must be a *she* who is a spy and whom Ralph suspects of the theft.

---

[8] The various considerations demonstrating the failure of the directed/undirected analysis of relational/notional are well known in connection with definite descriptions. *Cf.* Kripke (*Contemporary Respectives*, pp. 9–10). Analogous considerations are at least as forceful with regard to indefinite descriptions. In responding to Kripke's arguments against the alleged semantic significance of the directed/undirected distinction, Almog ('Subject Verb Object,' pp. 91–98) barely acknowledges these more decisive—and more fundamental—considerations against his proposal. Almog's defense of the semantic-significance thesis suffers furthermore from the confusions limned above, including, for example, the false premise that the notional reading of (1) asserts that one sloop or other has the property of being wanted by Ralph (something in fact entailed by the relational reading). Michael McGlone has pointed out (in conversation) that Almog might restrict his directed/undirected account of relational/notional to constructions like (1), not extending it to (3). (*Cf.* Almog, 'Subject Verb Object,' pp. 104n20.) Such a restriction would be both *ad hoc* and irrelevant. (The scope considerations apply equally to 'Diogenes wants to seek an honest man'.) The account fails for both sorts of cases, and for the same basic reason: The analogue for (1)/(3) of an undirected use of (2)/(4) is a straightforwardly relational reading, and hence fails as an analysis of the notional reading.

Perhaps Almog will recant and concede that verbs like 'want' and 'seek' do after all require special treatment to capture the elusive notional readings. On its notional reading, (1) is true iff Ralph is related to the kind *Sloop* by notionally wanting at least one instance of the latter, as opposed to relationally wanting one, as entailed by the discredited account. (See notes 5 and 7 above.) This of itself leaves the former condition unexplained. In particular, appealing to an alleged undirected use of 'a sloop' by the reporter yields the wrong reading. But Almog also explicitly rejects the Frege-inspired analysis (which I believe is essentially correct): that certain expressions including 'seek' and 'want' (not including 'find' and 'own') are *ungerade* operators, which induce 'a sloop' to refer to rather than to express the concept *some sloop or other*, eliciting a directed use by the speaker. (The relational reading of (1) is explicable on this analysis as a matter of wide scope/primary occurrence.)

A case can be made that the relational reading of (1) goes hand in hand with a directed use of 'a sloop', or a propensity toward a directed use, *on the part of Ralph* rather than the speaker, and the notional reading correspondingly with an undirected use, or a propensity thereto, by Ralph. A logico-semantic account of relational/notional along these lines, although not as conspicuously flawed as Almog's, is also significantly wide of the mark. (Suppose Ralph speaks no English. Consider also the Church–Langford translation test.) Almog anyway explicitly rejects the idea (p. 56).

The notional/relational distinction comes under severe strain, however, when confronted with Peter T. Geach's (1967) ingenious Hob/Nob sentence:

> (5) Hob thinks a witch has blighted Bob's mare, and Nob wonders whether she (the same witch) killed Cob's sow.[9]

This puzzling sentence seems to resist both a relational and a notional reading. If there is a *she* whom Nob wonders about, then that *she*, it would appear, must be a witch whom Hob suspects of mare blighting. But the sincere utterer of (5) intuitively does not seem committed in this way to the reality of witches. Barring the existence of witches, though (5) may be true, there is no actual witch about whom Hob suspects and Nob wonders. Any account of the notional/relational that depicts (5) as requiring the existence of a witch is *ipso facto* wrong. There is a natural reading of (5) that carries an ontological commitment to witches, *viz.*, the straightforward relational reading. The point is that the intended reading does not.

A tempting response construes (5) as fully notional, along the lines of

> (5_n) (i) Hob thinks: a witch has blighted Bob's mare; and (ii) Nob wonders whether: the witch that (Hob thinks) blighted Bob's mare also killed Cob's sow.

Yet this will not do; (5) may be neutral concerning whether Nob has a true belief about, let alone shares, Hob's suspicion. Nob's wondering need not take the form 'Did the same witch that (Hob thinks) blighted Bob's mare also kill Cob's sow?' It may be that Hob's thought takes the form 'Maggoty Meg has blighted Bob's mare' while Nob's takes the form 'Did Maggoty Meg kill Cob's sow?' If so, (5) would be true, but no fully notional reading forthcoming.

Worse, Hob's and Nob's thoughts need not involve the same manner of specification. It may be that Hob's thought takes the form 'Maggoty Meg has blighted Bob's mare' while Nob's wondering takes the form 'Did the Wicked Witch of the West kill Cob's sow?' This appears to preclude a neo-Fregean analysis along the lines of the following:

> (F) $(\exists\alpha)[\alpha$ **corepresents** for both Hob and Nob & Hob notionally-thinks ⌜α is a witch who has blighted Bob's mare⌝ & Nob notionally-thinks ⌜α is a witch⌝ and Nob **notionally-wonders** ⌜Did α kill Cob's sow?⌝].[10]

Geach himself argues (pp. 148–149) that since (5) does not commit its author to the existence of witches, it must have some purely notional reading or other.

---

[9] Peter Geach, 'Intentional Identity.' *Journal of Philosophy* 64: 627–32. Reprinted in Geach *Logic Matters* (Oxford: Basil Blackwell, 1972). Though the puzzle has generated a considerable literature, its general importance to the philosophy of logic and language remains insufficiently appreciated. (As will emerge, I believe Geach's moniker for the puzzle as one of 'intentional identity' is a likely misnomer.)

[10] *Cf.* David Kaplan ('Quantifying In.' In D. Davidson and J. Hintikka (eds.), *Words and Objections: Essays on the Work of W. V. Quine* (Dordrecht: D. Reidel, 1969), pp. 225–31). Contrary to Daniel C. Dennett ('Geach on Intentional Identity.' *Journal of Philosophy* 65 (1968), pp. 335–41), the intelligibility (indeed the fact) of Hob's and Nob's thoughts having a common focus, somehow on the same unreal witch, does not require that they agree on every possible issue regarding the witch in question—which would in any case entail their agreeing on every possible issue.

He suggests an alternative neo-Fregean analysis, evidently along the lines of the following:

(G) $(\exists\alpha)(\exists\beta)[\alpha$ is a witch-representation & β is a witch-representation & α and β **corepresent** for both Hob and Nob & Hob notionally-thinks ⌜α has blighted Bob's mare⌝ & Nob **notionally-wonders** ⌜Did β kill Cob's sow?⌝].[11]

This proposal faces certain serious difficulties, some of which are also problems for (F): The relevant notion of a *witch-representation* must be explained in such a way as to allow that an individual representation α (e.g., an individual concept) may be a witch-representation without representing any actual witch, and for that matter, without representing anything at all. More important, the relevant notion of *corepresentation* needs to be explained so as to allow the following: that a pair of individual representations α and β may co-represent for two thinkers without representing anything at all for either thinker. Geach does not explicitly employ the notion of corepresentation. I have included it on his behalf because it, or something like it, is crucial to the proposed analysis. Any analysis, if it is correct, must capture the idea that Hob's and Nob's thoughts have a common focus. Though there is no witch, Hob and Nob are, in some sense, thinking about the *same* witch. It is on this point that notional analyses generally fail. Even something as strong as (5_n)—already too strong—misses this essential feature of (5). On the other hand, however the notion of vacuously corepresenting witch-representations is ultimately explained, by contrast with (G), (5) evidently commits its author no more to corepresenting witch-representations than to witches. More generally, any analysis along the lines of (F) or (G) cannot forever avoid facing the well-known difficulties with neo-Fregean, notional analyses of relational constructions generally (e.g., the Twin Earth considerations).[12]

An alternative approach accepts the imposingly apparent relational character of (5) at face value, and construes it along the lines of the following:

(6) There is someone whom: (*i*) Hob thinks a witch that has blighted Bob's mare; (*ii*) Nob also thinks is a witch; and (*iii*) Nob wonders whether she killed Cob's sow.

---

[11] Peter Geach, 'Two Kinds of Intentionality.' *Monist* 59 (1976), pp. 306–20, pp. 314–18.

[12] Stephen Neale (*Descriptions* (Cambridge, Mass.: MIT Press, 1990), p. 221), proposes analyzing the relevant reading of (5) along the lines of: (*i*) Hob thinks: a witch has blighted Bob's mare; and (*ii*) Nob wonders whether: the *such-and-such* witch killed Cob's sow, where 'the *such-and-such* witch' is fleshed out by the context, e.g., as 'the local witch'. But (5) evidently does not attribute to Nob the particular thought 'Did *the local witch* kill Cob's sow?' nor any similarly descriptive thought. Worse, Neale's proposal fails to capture the crucial feature of (5) that Nob's wondering allegedly regards the very witch that Hob suspects. Michael McKinsey ('Mental Anaphora.' *Synthese* 66 (1986), pp. 159–75) argues that the only readings of (5) that do not commit its author to the existence of a witch (or to there being some real person whom Hob and Nob relationally suspect of witchcraft) are given by (5_n) (which he regards as ambiguous). Dennett apparently holds that the only such readings of (5) are either those given by (5_n) or else something similar to the less specific (F). *Pace* Geach, Dennett, McKinsey, and Neale, (5) is evidently relational yet free of commitment to witches (or to anyone who is a suspect). (Contrary to Dennett, the speaker's basis or justification for uttering (5) is mostly irrelevant.)

This happily avoids commitment to witches. But it does not provide a solution. Hob's and Nob's thoughts need not concern any real person. Maggoty Meg is not a real person, and there may be no one whom either Hob or Nob believe to be the wicked strega herself.

Some proposed solutions to Geach's puzzle make the unpalatable claim that Hob's and Nob's musings concern a Meinongian Object—a particular witch who is both indeterminate and nonexistent.[13] Many proposed solutions instead reinterpret relational attributions of attitude so that they are not really relational, i.e., they do not make genuine reference to the individuals apparently mentioned therein by name or pronoun. These responses inevitably make equally unpalatable claims involving relational constructions—for example, that Nob's wondering literally concerns the very same witch/person as Hob's belief yet neither concerns anyone (or anything) whatsoever, or that relational constructions mention or generalize over speech-act tokens and/or connections among speech-act tokens.[14] It would be more

---

[13] *Cf.* Esa Saarinen ('Intentional Identity Interpreted: A Case Study of the Relations Among Quantifiers, Pronouns, and Propositional Attitudes.' *Linguistics and Philosophy* 2 (1978), pp. 151–223). A variant of this approach imputes thoughts to Hob and Nob concerning a particular possible and fully determinate but nonexistent witch. This proposal cannot be summarily dismissed on the ground of an alleged ontological commitment to merely possibles. The proposed analysis may be understood instead as follows: There *might have existed* (even if there does not exist) a witch such that *actually*: (*i*) Hob thinks she has blighted Bob's mare; and (*ii*) Nob wonders whether she killed Cob's sow. Whereas this is in some sense committed to merely possible witches, it avoids commitment to their actual existence. The more serious difficulty is that neither Hob nor Nob (assuming they are real) is connected to any particular possible witch, to the exclusion of other possible witches, in such a manner as to have relational thoughts about her. How could they be? Witches do not exist. *Cf.* Kripke (*Naming and Necessity* (Cambridge, Mass.: Harvard University Press, 1972), p. 158) '. . . one cannot say of any possible person that he *would have been* Sherlock Holmes, had he existed. Several distinct possible people, and even actual ones such as Darwin or Jack the Ripper, might have performed the exploits of Holmes, but there is none of whom we can say that he would have *been* Holmes had he performed these exploits. For if so, which one?'

[14] The Hob/Nob sentence (5) is logically consistent with neither Hob nor Nob articulating his musings, explicitly or implicitly. Tyler Burge's ('Russell's Problem and Intentional Identity.' In J. Tomberlin (ed.), *Agent, Language, and the Structure of the World* (Indianapolis: Hackett, 1983), pp. 94–98) analysis seems to be roughly the following:

> Hob believes ⌈$(\exists x)(x$ is a witch who has blighted Bob's mare)⌉ & ∴ Hob believes ⌈(the$_{13}$ x) (x is a witch who has blighted Bob's mare) exists⌉ & Nob wonders ⌈y_{13} killed Cob's sow⌉.

Burge stipulates that the recurring subscript 'marks the anaphoric or quasi-anaphoric connection between the terms' (1983, 97), where 'a more explicit way of capturing the point of the subscripts' would explicitly generalize over communication chains, including both Hob's application of 'the$_{13}$' and Nob's application of 'y_{13}' (1983, 98).

Burge's apparatus is not explained sufficiently for this to qualify as a proposed solution to the problem. Aside from questions raised by the connective adjoining the first two conjuncts (how does a single statement contain an argument?), the analysis is inadequate on its most natural interpretations. An immediate problem is that (5), as intended, does not entail that Hob notionally thinks only one witch has blighted Bob's mare; the argument of the first two conjuncts is invalid. More problematic, if the special quotation marks indicate ordinary quotation (as seems to conform with Burge's intended interpretation), the analysis miscasts relational constructions as reporting dispositions toward sentences (e.g., purported utterances or implicit utterances) rather than the content of the attitudes thereby expressed and their relation to objects. Assuming instead (apparently contrary to Burge's intent) that the occurrence of 'y_{13}' is in bindable position, the variable remains free even assuming that the definite-descriptions operator 'the$_{13}$' is variable binding.

sensible to deny that (5) can be literally true on the relevant reading, given that there are no actual witches.[15] The problem with this denial is that its proponent is clearly in denial. As intended, (5) can clearly be true (assuming Hob and Nob are real) even in the absence of witches. Numerous postmodern solutions jump through technical hoops to allow a pronoun ('she') to be a variable bound by a quantifier ('a witch') within a belief context despite standing outside the belief context, hence also outside the quantifier's scope, and despite standing within an entirely separate belief context. These 'solutions' do not satisfy the inquiring mind as much as boggle it. It is one thing to construct an elaborate system on which (5) may be deemed true without 'There is a witch'. It is quite another to provide a satisfying explanation of the content of Nob's attitude, one for which the constructed system is appropriate. How can Nob wonder about a witch, and a particular witch at that—the very one Hob suspects—when there is no witch and, therefore, no particular witch about whom he is wondering? This is the puzzle in a nutshell. It combines elements of intensionality puzzles with puzzles concerning nonexistence and puzzles concerning identity, and has been deemed likely intractable.[16]

Burge's stipulation suggests the variable is to have a value assigned to it *via* Hob's alleged description 'the witch who has blighted Bob's mare', thus recasting the third conjunct into 'Nob wonders whether she—the witch who has blighted Bob's mare—killed Cob's sow'. (Otherwise, the 'y_{13}' evidently remains both free and value-less, leaving (5) without propositional content, hence untrue.) This, however, is evidently ambiguous between a reading on which the value-fixing is affected on the part of the author of (5)—call it *primary occurrence*—and a *secondary-occurrence* reading on which the value-fixing is allegedly affected on the part of Nob. (The terminology is intended to recall Russell's distinction. The ambiguity corresponds even more closely to two competing interpretations of David Kaplan's rigidifying operator '*dthat*'.) On the secondary-occurrence reading, the value-fixing description plays a representational role on Nob's behalf. On the primary-occurrence reading, the value-fixing is shielded from the shift-from-customary-mode function of the quotation marks, leaving the pronoun to carry the weight of representing for Nob. The analysans on the secondary-occurrence reading, like (5_n), commits not only Hob but also Nob to the existence of a witch who has blighted Bob's mare. Worse, the more likely primary-occurrence reading commits (5)'s author to the existence of such a witch. Neither is correct.

A further problem with the proposal is that the truth of (5) does not require that Nob make any pronominal application that is anaphoric on an application by Hob. The two might never communicate. Burge therefore offers something like the following as an alternative analysis ('Russell's Problem,' p. 96):

The community believes $\lceil (\exists x)(x$ is a witch wreaking havoc)$\rceil$ & $\therefore$ the community believes $\lceil$(the$_{13}$ x)(x is a witch who is wreaking havoc) exists$\rceil$ & Hob thinks $\lceil y_{13}$ has blighted Bob's mare$\rceil$ & Nob wonders $\lceil z_{13}$ killed Cob's sow$\rceil$.

This is subject to some of the same difficulties as the previous analysis and more besides, including some of the same defects as Neale's proposal (see note 12)—as well as some of the defects of the Fregean analyses that Burge eschews. By contrast, for example, (5) makes no claim regarding community-held beliefs, let alone regarding a specific alleged community belief that there is only one witch wreaking havoc.

[15] The account in Almog ('Subject Verb Object,' pp. 68, 75–76, and *passim*), extended to propositional-attitude attributions, apparently depicts (5) as modally equivalent on its intended reading to 'Hob thinks Maggoty Meg has blighted Bob's mare, and Nob wonders whether she killed Cob's sow', and depicts the latter as expressing a necessary falsehood in virtue of the failure of 'Maggoty Meg' to refer.

[16] Michael Clark ('Critical Notice of P. T. Geach, *Logic Matters*.' *Mind* 74 (1975), pp. 122–36, p. 124).

MYTHS

The solution I shall urge takes (5) at face value, and takes seriously the idea that false theories that have been mistakenly believed—what I call *myths*—give rise to fabricated but genuine entities.[17] These entities include such oddities as: Vulcan, the hypothetical planet proposed by Babinet and which Le Verrier believed caused perturbations in Mercury's solar orbit; the ether, once thought to be the physical medium through which light waves propagate; phlogiston, once thought to be the element (material substance) that causes combustion; the Loch Ness Monster; Santa Claus; and Meinong's Golden Mountain. Such *mythical objects* are real things, though they are neither material objects nor mental objects ('ideas'). They come into being with the belief in the myth. Indeed, they are created by the mistaken theory's inventor, albeit without the theorist's knowledge. But they do not exist in physical space, and are, in that sense, abstract entities. They are an unavoidable by-product of human fallibility.

Vulcan is a mythical planet. This is not to say, as one might be tempted to take it, that Vulcan is a planet but one of a rather funny sort, e.g., a Meinongian Object that exists in myth but not in reality.[18] On the contrary, Vulcan exists in reality, just as robustly as you the reader. But a mythical planet is no more a planet than a toy duck is a duck or a magician is someone who performs feats of magic. A mythical object is an imposter, a pretender, a stage prop. Vulcan is not a real planet, though it is a very real object—not concrete, not in physical space, but real. One might say that the planet Mercury is also a "mythical object," in that it too figures in the Vulcan myth, wrongly depicted as being gravitationally influenced by Vulcan. If we choose to speak this way, then it must be said that some 'mythical planets' are real planets, though not really as depicted in the myth. Vulcan, by contrast with the "mythical" Mercury, is a *wholly mythical* object, not a real planet but an abstract entity inadvertently fabricated by the inventor of the myth. I shall continue to use the simple word 'mythical' as a shorthand for the notion of something wholly mythical.[19]

The existence of fictional objects, in something close to this sense, has been persuasively urged by Peter van Inwagen and Saul Kripke as an ontological commitment of our ordinary discourse about fiction.[20] Their account, however, is significantly

[17] *Cf.* Salmon, 'Nonexistence.' *Noûs*, 32 (1998), pp. 277–319, pp. 304–5; especially 317n50.

[18] Geach, 1967b, 'The Perils of Pauline.' *Review of Metaphysics* 23, reprinted in Geach, *Logic Matters*, (Oxford: Basil Blackwell, 1972), pp. 153–65, misconstrues the claim in just this way.

[19] Sachin Pai asks whether there is in addition to Mercury a wholly mythical planet that astronomers like Le Verrier wrongly believed to be Mercury. I leave this as a topic requiring further investigation.

[20] P. van Inwagen, 1977, 'Creatures of Fiction,' *American Philosophical Quarterly* 14 (1977), pp. 299–308; Saul Kripke, 'Reference and Existence: The John Locke Lectures for 1973' (Oxford University Press, 1973, unpublished). Kripke does not himself officially either accept or reject an ontology of mythical objects. My interpretation is based partly on notes I took at Kripke's seminars on the topic of reference and fiction at Princeton University during March–April 1981 and on recordings of his seminars at the University of California, Riverside, in January 1983. Kripke's account of fictional and mythical objects is explicated and criticized, and my alternative theory defended, in Salmon, 'Nonexistence,' pp. 293–305.

different from the one I propose. Kripke contends that a mythical-object name like 'Vulcan' is ambiguous between two uses, one of which is parasitic on the other. It would be less deceptive to replace the ambiguous name with two univocal names, 'Vulcan$_1$' and 'Vulcan$_2$'. The name on its primary use, 'Vulcan$_1$', was introduced into the language, *sans* subscript, by Babinet as a name for an intra-Mercurial planet. Le Verrier used the name in this way in theorizing about Mercury's perihelion. In this use, the name names nothing; 'Vulcan$_1$' is entirely vacuous. Giving the name this use, we may say such things as that Le Verrier believed that Vulcan$_1$ affected Mercury's perihelion. Le Verrier's theory is a myth concerning Vulcan$_1$. The name on its secondary use, 'Vulcan$_2$', is introduced into the language (again *sans* subscript) at a later stage, when the myth has finally been exposed, as a name for the mythical planet erroneously postulated, and thereby inadvertently created, by Babinet. Perhaps it would be better to say that a new *use* of the name 'Vulcan' is introduced into the language. 'Vulcan$_2$' is fully referential. Using the name in this way, we say such things as that Vulcan$_2$ was a mythical intra-Mercurial planet hypothesized by Babinet. The difference between Vulcan$_1$ and Vulcan$_2$ could not be more stark. The mistaken astronomical theory believed by Babinet and Le Verrier concerns Vulcan$_1$, which does not exist. Vulcan$_2$, which does exist, arises from the mistaken theory itself. Vulcan$_2$ is recognized through reflection not on events in the far-off astronomical heavens but on the more local story of man's intellectual triumphs and defeats, particularly on the history of science.

Kripke's account is vulnerable to a familiar family of thorny problems: the classical problem of true negative existentials and the more general problem of the content and truth-value of sentences involving vacuous names. Vulcan$_1$ does not exist. This sentence is true, and seems to say about something (*viz.*, Vulcan$_1$) that it fails to exist. Yet the sentence entails that there is nothing for it to attribute non-existence to. Furthermore, on Kripke's account, Le Verrier believed that Vulcan$_1$ has an impact on Mercury's perihelion. What can the content of Le Verrier's belief be if there is no such thing as Vulcan$_1$? Furthermore, is the belief content simply false? If so, then it may be said that Vulcan$_1$ has no impact on Mercury's perihelion. Yet this claim too seems to attribute something to Vulcan$_1$, and thus seems equally wrong, and for exactly the same reason, with the claim that Vulcan$_1$ does have such an impact. Kripke is aware of these problems but offers no viable solution.

I submit that Kripke's alleged primary use of a mythical-object name is itself a myth. To be sure, Babinet believed himself to be naming a real planet in introducing a use of 'Vulcan' into the language, and other users like Le Verrier believed themselves to be referring to a real planet. But this linguistic theory of the name 'Vulcan' is mistaken, and is in this respect exactly like the astronomical theory that Vulcan is a real planet. The two theories complement each other, and fall together hand in hand. The situation should be viewed instead as follows: Babinet invented the theory—erroneous, as it turns out—that there is an intra-Mercurial planet. In doing this, he inadvertently created Vulcan. Indeed, Babinet even introduced a name for this mythical planet. The name was intended for a real planet, and Babinet believed the name thus referred to a real planet (notionally, not relationally!). But here again, he was simply mistaken. Other astronomers, most notably Le Verrier, became convinced of Babinet's theory, both as it concerns Vulcan (that it is a very real intra-Mercurial planet) and as it concerns 'Vulcan' (that it names the intra-Mercurial planet). Babinet and Le Verrier both believed, correctly, that the name 'Vulcan', on the relevant use, refers to Vulcan. But they also both believed, mistakenly, that Vulcan is a real planet. They might have expressed the latter belief by means of the French version of the English sentence 'Vulcan is a planet', or other shared beliefs by means of sentences like 'Vulcan's orbit lies closer to the Sun than Mercury's'. These beliefs are mistakes, and the sentences (whether English or French) are false.

Importantly, there is no relevant use of the name 'Vulcan' by Babinet and Le Verrier that is vacuous. So used, the name refers to Vulcan, the mythical planet. Le Verrier did *not* believe that $Vulcan_1$ is an intra-Mercurial planet—or, to put the point less misleadingly, there is no real use marked by the subscript on 'Vulcan' on which the string of words '$Vulcan_1$ is an intra-Mercurial planet' expresses anything for Le Verrier to have believed, disbelieved, or suspended judgment about. To put the matter in terms of Kripke's account, what Le Verrier believed was that $Vulcan_2$ is a real intra-Mercurial planet. Le Verrier's belief concerns the mythical planet, a very real object that had been inadvertently created, then named 'Vulcan', by Babinet. Their theory about Vulcan was completely wrong. Vulcan is in fact an abstract object, one that is depicted in myth as a massive physical object.

A common reaction is to charge my proposal with miscasting mythical objects as the objects with which myths are concerned. On the contrary, it is objected, if they exist at all, mythical objects enter the intellectual landscape only at a later stage, not in the myth itself but in the subsequent historical account of the myth. A robust sense of reality demands that the myth itself be not about these abstract objects but about *nothing*, or at most about representations of nothing. No one expresses this sentiment more forcefully than Russell (1919):

[Many] logicians have been driven to the conclusion that there are unreal objects . . . In such theories, it seems to me, there is a failure of that feeling for reality which ought to be preserved even in the most abstract studies. Logic, I should maintain, must no more admit a unicorn than zoology can; for logic is concerned with the real world just as truly as zoology, though with its more abstract and general features. To say that unicorns have an existence in heraldry, or in literature, or in imagination, is a most pitiful and paltry evasion. What exists in heraldry is not an animal, made of flesh and blood, moving and breathing of its own initiative. What exists is a picture, or a description in words. . . . A robust sense of reality is very necessary in framing a correct analysis of propositions about unicorns . . . and other such pseudo-objects.[21]

I heartily applaud Russell's eloquent plea for philosophical sobriety. But his attitude toward 'unreal' objects is fundamentally confused. To repeat, a mythical planet is not a massive physical object but an abstract entity, the product of creative astronomizing. Likewise, a mythical unicorn or a mythical winged horse is not a living creature but a fabricated entity, the likely product of blurred or fuzzy vision, just as mermaids are the likely product of a deprived and overactive imagination under the influence of liquor—creatures not really made of flesh and blood and fur

[21] Bertrand Russell, *Introduction to Mathematical Philosophy* (London: George Allen and Unwin, 1919), chap. 16, pp. 169–70.

or scales, not really moving and breathing of their own initiative, but depicted as such in myth, legend, hallucination, or drunken stupor.

It is frequently objected even by those who countenance mythical objects that the Vulcan theory, for example, is merely the theory that there is an intra-Mercurial planet, not the bizarre hypothesis that the relevant abstract entity is that planet. Babinet and Le Verrier, it is observed, did not believe that an abstract entity is a massive heavenly object. Quite right, but only if meant notionally. Understood relationally—as the claim that, even if there is such an abstract entity as the mythical object that is Vulcan, Babinet and Le Verrier did not believe it to be an intra-Mercurial planet—it turns mythical objects into a philosophical black box. What role are these abstract entities supposed to play, and how exactly are their myth-believers supposed to be related to them in virtue of believing the myth? In fact, this issue provides yet another reason to prefer my account over Kripke's. On my account, in sharp contrast, the role of mythical objects is straightforward: They are the things depicted as such-and-such in myth, the fabrications erroneously believed by wayward believers to be planets or the medium of light-wave propagation or ghosts, the objects the mistaken theory is about when the theory is not about any real planet or any real medium or any real ghost. It is not merely that being depicted as such-and-such is an essential property of a mythical object, a feature the object could not exist without. Rather, being so depicted is the metaphysical function of the mythical object; that is *what* it is, its *raison d'être*. To countenance the existence of Vulcan as a mythical planet while at the same time denying that Babinet and Le Verrier had beliefs about this mythical object, is in a very real sense to miss the point of recognizing Vulcan's existence. It is precisely the astronomers' false beliefs about the mythical planet that makes it a mythical planet; if no one had believed it to be a planet, it would not *be* a mythical planet. Come to that, it would not even exist.[22]

Another important point: I am not *postulating* mythical objects. For example, I am not postulating Vulcan. Even if I wanted to, Babinet beat me to it—though he postulated Vulcan as a real planet, not a mythical one.[23] Mythical objects would exist even if I and everyone else had never countenanced or recognized them, or admitted them into our ontology. Rather, I see myself as uncovering some evidence for their independent and continued existence, in something like the manner of the

[22] Mythical objects are of the same metaphysical/ontological category as fictional characters, and it is an essential property of any such entity that it be of this category. Perhaps a mythical object might instead have been a fictional character, or *vice versa*, but no mythical or fictional object could have been, say, an even integer. Some philosophers who accept the reality of fictional characters nevertheless reject mythical objects. The usual motivation is the feeling that whereas Sherlock Holmes is a real object, a character created by Sir Arthur Conan Doyle, the Vulcan theory was wrong precisely because Vulcan simply does not exist. This ignores the nearly perfect similarity between fiction and myth. Whatever good reason there is for acknowledging the real existence of Holmes extends to Vulcan. The Vulcan theory is wrong not because there is no such thing as Vulcan, but because there is no such *planet* as Vulcan as it is depicted. Or better put, Vulcan is no such planet. (Likewise, there was no such detective as Holmes, who is a fictional detective and not a real one.) Myths and fictions are both made up. The principal difference between mythical and fictional objects is that the myth is believed while the fiction is only make-believe. This difference does nothing to obliterate the reality of either fictional or mythical objects.

[23] *Cf.* Salmon, 'Nonexistence,' p. 315n38.

paleontologist who infers dinosaurs from their fossil remains, rather than the theoretical physicist who postulates a new category of physical entity in order to make better sense of things (even if what I am actually doing is in important respects more like the latter).[24]

Perhaps the most important evidence in favor of this theory of mythical objects is its logical entailment by our thoughts and beliefs concerning myths. We are sometimes led to say and think such things as, 'An intra-Mercurial planet, Vulcan, was hypothesized by Babinet and believed by Le Verrier to affect Mercury's perihelion, but there has never been a hypothetical planet whose orbit was supposed to lie between Mercury and Venus' and 'Some hypothetical species have been hypothesized as linking the evolution of birds from dinosaurs, but no hypothetical species have been postulated to link the evolution of mammals from birds.' The distinctions drawn cannot be made without a commitment to mythical objects, i.e., without attributing existence, in some manner, to mythical objects. No less significant, beliefs are imputed about the mentioned mythical objects, to the effect that they are not mythical. Being wrongly believed not to be mythical is just what it is to be mythical. Furthermore, beliefs are imputed to distinct believers concerning the very same mythical object.[25]

Further evidence—in fact, evidence of precisely the same sort—is provided by the Hob/Nob sentence. The puzzle is solved by construing (5) on its principal reading,

---

[24] I am aware some philosophers see no significant difference between the paleontologist and the theoretical physicist. But they are asleep, or blind.

[25] Linguistic evidence tends to support the general claim that if someone believes there is an F that is such-and-such when in fact there is no such thing, then there is a mythical F thereby believed to be such-and-such. It does not follow that whenever someone notionally believes an F is such-and-such, there is always something or someone (either an F or a mythical F) relationally believed to be such-and-such. That the latter is false is demonstrated by the believer who notionally believes some spy is shorter than all others. (Thanks to James Pryor and Robert Stalnaker for pressing me on this point.) If two believers notionally believe there is an F that is such-and-such when in fact there is no such thing, they may or may not believe in the same mythical F, depending on their interconnections. (This may help explain why it is more difficult to form beliefs about the shortest spy than about a mythical planet: Le Verrier and we are all *de re* connected to Vulcan.)

Mark Richard ('Commitment,' In J. Tomberlin (ed.), *Philosophical Perspectives 12: Language, Mind, and Ontology* (Cambridge, Mass.: Blackwell, 1998), pp. 262–64, 278–79n16) criticizes my account of mythical objects while defending a version of Kripke's. Richard objects (279) to the examples given here on the ground that, for example, the first quoted sentence is in fact untrue and is easily confused with a true variant that avoids attributing to Babinet and Le Verrier any ontological commitment to, or beliefs concerning, the mythical planet: 'It was hypothesized by Babinet that there is an intra-Mercurial planet, Vulcan$_1$, and it was believed by Le Verrier that Vulcan$_1$ affects Mercury's perihelion, but it has never been hypothesized that there is a planet whose orbit lies between Mercury and Venus'. (Richard denies, with Kripke, that Babinet and Le Verrier have beliefs concerning Vulcan$_2$.) Richard explains the alleged confusion as the product of an exportation inference from $\ulcorner\alpha$ believes that β is an F that is $G\urcorner$ to $\ulcorner\beta$ is an F that α believes is a $G\urcorner$, where β is a proper name. Richard says this inference pattern is valid if, but only if, the name β, as used by the referent of α (e.g., 'Vulcan' as used by Babinet and Le Verrier), has a referent. This explanation is dubious. For one thing, the particular exportation-inference pattern is invalid regardless of the logico-grammatical status of β. Moreover, it does not yield the quoted sentence. As will be seen shortly, Geach's puzzle demonstrates that Richard's substitute sentence does not do justice to the data. Babinet's and Le Verrier's beliefs concern *something*; indeed they each concern the *same* thing.

or at least in one of its principal readings, as fully relational, not in the manner of (6) but along the lines of:

> (7) There is a mythical witch such that (*i*) Hob thinks: she has blighted Bob's mare; and (*ii*) Nob wonders whether: she killed Cob's sow.[26]

This has the distinct advantage over (6) that it does not require that both Hob and Nob believe someone to be the witch in question. In fact, it allows that there be no one in particular whom either Hob or Nob believes to be a witch. It does require something not unrelated to this, but no more than is actually required by (5): that there be something that both Hob and Nob believe to be a witch—some*thing*, not some*one*, not a witch or a person, certainly not an indeterminate Meinongian Object, but a very real entity that Nob thinks a real witch who has blighted Bob's mare. Nob also believes this same mythical witch to be a real witch and wonders about 'her' (really: about *it*) whether she killed Cob's sow. In effect, the proposal substitutes ontological commitment to mythical witches for the ontological commitment to real witches intrinsic to the straightforward relational reading of (5) (obtained from (7) by deleting the word 'mythical'). There are other witch-free readings for (5), but I submit that any intended reading is a variant of (7) that equally commits the author to the existence of a (real or) mythical witch, such as:

> Hob thinks: some witch or other has blighted Bob's mare; and (*ii*) the (same) mythical witch that Hob thinks has blighted Bob's mare is such that Nob wonders whether: she killed Cob's sow.[27]

Significantly, one who accepts Kripke's account may not avail him/herself of this solution to Geach's puzzle. On Kripke's account it may be observed that

> Hob thinks: Meg_1 has blighted Bob's mare; and (*ii*) Nob wonders whether: Meg_1 killed Cob's sow.

---

[26] Quasi-formally:

$(\exists x)(x$ is a mythical-witch & Hob **thinks** $^\wedge x$ has blighted Bob's mare$^\wedge$ & Nob **wonders** $^\wedge x$ killed Cob's sow$^\wedge)$,

where ' $\wedge$ ' serves as an indirect-quotation mark. Note the quantification into both *ungerade* contexts. (*Cf.* note 13 above regarding the error of replacing 'mythical' with 'merely possible'.)

[27] This may better capture Geach's intent. The first conjunct is notional. The second is relational, and entails that there is exactly one mythical witch whom Hob relationally thinks has blighted Bob's mare. Quasi-formally:

Hob **thinks** $^\wedge (\exists x)(x$ is a witch & x has blighted Bob's mare$)^\wedge$ & $(\lambda y)[$Nob **wonders** $^\wedge y$ killed Cob's sow$^\wedge](\imath x)(x$ is a mythical-witch & Hob **thinks** $^\wedge x$ has blighted Bob's mare$^\wedge)$.

The principally intended reading of (5) is perhaps best captured by an equivalent formulation:

Hob **thinks** $^\wedge (\exists x)(x$ is a witch & x has blighted Bob's mare$)^\wedge$ & Nob **wonders** $^\wedge dthat[([(\imath x)(x$ is a mythical-witch & Hob **thinks** $^\wedge x$ has blighted Bob's mare$^\wedge)]$ killed Cob's sow$^\wedge$,

interpreting '*dthat*'-terms so that their content is their referent (*cf.* note 14 above). Elizabeth Harman has suggested (in conversation) a neutral reading on behalf of the speaker who remains cautiously agnostic on the question of witchcraft: replace 'x is a mythical-witch' with the disjunction, 'x is a witch $\vee$ x is a mythical-witch'.

The Hob/Nob sentence (5) is not obtainable by existential generalization on 'Meg$_1$', since by Kripke's lights, this name is supposed to be vacuous and to occur in nonextensional ('referentially opaque,' *ungerade*) position. Nor on Kripke's account can 'Meg$_2$' be correctly substituted for 'Meg$_1$'; Hob's and Nob's theories are supposed to concern the nonexistent witch Meg$_1$ and not the mythical witch Meg$_2$. Kripke might instead accept the following, as a later-stage observation about the Meg$_1$ theory:

Meg$_2$ is the mythical witch corresponding to Meg$_1$.

Here the relevant notion of *correspondence* places 'Meg$_2$' in extensional position. While 'Meg$_2$' is thus open to existential generalization, 'Meg$_1$' supposedly remains in a nonextensional position where it is not subject to quantification. It is impossible to deduce (5) from any of this. Geach's puzzle does not support Kripke's account. On the contrary, the puzzle poses a serious threat to that account, with its denial that Hob's and Nob's thoughts are, respectively, a suspicion and a wondering regarding Meg$_2$.

On my alternative account, we may instead observe that

Maggoty Meg is a mythical witch. Hob thinks she has blighted Bob's mare.

Nob wonders whether she killed Cob's sow.

We may then conjoin and EG to obtain (7). In the end, what makes (7) a plausible analysis is that it (or some variant) spells out in more precise language what (5) literally says to begin with. Babinet and Le Verrier provide a real-life case in which the thoughts of different thinkers converge on a single mythical object: Babinet thought he had seen an intra-Mercurial planet, and Le Verrier believed that it (the same 'planet') impacted Mercury's perihelion. The primary lesson of Geach's puzzle is that when theoretical mistakes are made mythical creatures are conceived, and in acknowledging that misbelievers are sometimes related as Nob to Hob, or as Le Verrier to Babinet, we commit ourselves to their illegitimate progeny.[28]

---

[28] It can happen that Hob misidentifies Maggoty Meg with, say, her mythical sister. Hob might thus notionally think that only one witch has blighted Bob's mare even though there are two mythical witches each of whom Hob relationally thinks has blighted Bob's mare.

One further note: The present analysis entails that (5) is committed to mythical witches. The analysis is not itself thus committed, and is consistent with the thesis that (5) is untrue precisely because of this commitment. Disbelief in mythical objects is insufficient ground for rejecting the analysis. It is a basis for rejecting the present solution to Geach's puzzle (which takes it that (5), so analyzed, can be true in the absence of witches, assuming Hob and Nob are real), but carries with it the burden of explaining the intuition that (5) can be true *sans* witches—a challenge that might be met by providing a plausible rendering of (5), as intended, that is free of mythical objects. (Good luck.)

PART II
NECESSITY

4

Modal Logic Kalish-and-Montague Style (1994*u*)

A natural-deduction apparatus for the propositional modal system *S5*, based on the nonmodal deductive apparatus of D. Kalish, R. Montague, and G. Mar, *Logic: Techniques of Formal Reasoning*, Second Edition (Oxford Univrsity Press, 1964, 1980), chapter 2, was given in Jordan Howard Sobel, 'A Natural Deduction System for Sentential Modal Logic,' *Philosophy Research Archives* (1979).[1] The Sobel system can be significantly improved, and made sufficiently flexible to accommodate other well-known modal systems, by utilizing additional natural-deduction techniques. Besides its more extensive reliance on the general approach of Kalish, Montague, and Mar (hereafter 'K&M'), the apparatus proposed below provides genuinely natural-deduction derivations not only for *T, S4,* and *S5*, but also for the unduly neglected modal system *B* (the *Brouwersche* or *Brouwerian* system), which I have argued is less vulnerable than *S5* and *S4* to counter-example.[2]

Specifically, we augment and modify the deductive apparatus of K&M as follows. The following clause is added to the characterization of the class of *symbolic formulas* given on p. 309.

(5′) If ϕ is a symbolic formula, then so are

$$\Box \phi$$

$$\Diamond \phi.$$

The following primitive inference rules for the new sentential connectives are added to the rules given in K&M, pp. 60–61.

Necessity instantiation (NI): $\dfrac{\Box \phi}{\phi}$

Modal negation (MN), in four forms:

$$\frac{\sim \Box \phi}{\Diamond \sim \phi} \qquad \frac{\Diamond \sim \phi}{\sim \Box \phi} \qquad \frac{\sim \Diamond \phi}{\Box \sim \phi} \qquad \frac{\Box \sim \phi}{\sim \Diamond \phi}$$

I thank Allen Hazen, Ilhan Inan, Andrrzej Indrzejczak, and Gary Mar for their comments and suggestions.

[1] Sobel's original system was unsound, and was later corrected in his 'Names and Indefinite Descriptions in Ontological Arguments,' *Dialogue*, 22 (1983), pp. 195–201, at 199–200.

[2] See my 'The Logic of What Might Have Been,' *The Philosophical Review*, 98, 1 (January 1989), pp. 3–34, concerning the philosophical superiority of *T* and *B* over *S4* and *S5*.

The rule of necessity instantiation and the third form of modal negation taken together yield the following derived modal rule.

Possibility generalization (PG): $\dfrac{\phi}{\Diamond\phi}$

These are known as the *modal inference rules*. We also introduce a new form of derivation, known as *strict derivation* (SD), which provides both a $\Box$-introduction rule and a sort of combination elimination-introduction rule for $\Diamond$, and which is subject to restrictions roughly analogous to those for universal derivation (UD in K&M, p. 143). Whereas all of the inference rules are available in each of the propositional modal systems *T, B, S4,* and *S5,* in each of these systems one rule is designated as that system's characteristic *strict importation rule*. A strict importation rule enables one to enter a necessary truth into a subsidiary strict derivation. The *T*-importation rule is NI. The *B*-importation rule is PG. The *S4*-importation rule, $\Box$R, is simply repetition (R in K&M, p. 15) applied to a symbolic formula of the form

$$\Box\phi.$$

And the *S5*-importation rule, $\Diamond$R, is repetition applied to a symbolic formula of the form

$$\Diamond\phi.$$

Each of the modal systems *B, S4,* and *S5* also admits NI as a primitive strict importation rule together with its own characteristic strict importation rule, thus admitting two primitive strict importation rules apiece.[3]

An *antecedent line* in an incomplete derivation is defined in K&M, p. 24, as a preceding line that is neither boxed nor contains an uncancelled occurrence of '*Show*'. Strict derivations are explained in terms of a distinction between two kinds

---

[3] The strict importation rules are usually called '(strict) reiteration rules'—a term that fits $\Box$R and $\Diamond$R better than the other two. The characteristic strict importation rules for *T* and *S4* were first given in Frederic Brenton Fitch, *Symbolic Logic: An Introduction* (New York: Ronald Press, 1952), chapter 3, pp. 64–80 (referring to the former system as 'almost the same as the system Lewis calls *S2*'). The *S5*-importation rule was first given in William A. Wisdom, 'Possibility-Elimination in Natural Deduction,' *Notre Dame Journal of Formal Logic*, 5, 4 (October 1964), pp. 295–298, at 298n2, wherein the rule is credited to Robert Price. The *B*-importation rule proposed here (which was discovered independently by the author) is a variation of the *B*-importation rule given by Fitch in 'Natural Deduction Rules for Obligation,' *American Philosophical Quarterly*, 3, 1 (January 1966), pp. 27–38, at 32. (I thank Max J. Cresswell and Allen Hazen for this bibliographical information.) Although PG is a derived modal rule, its role in *B* as a strict importation rule is not derived but primitive.

The admission of NI as a primitive strict importation rule is redundant in *S4* (as the reader will easily verify) and in *B* (though this is less easily verified and has not been noted before now). As C. Anthony Anderson pointed out to me, it is also redundant in *S5*. Indeed, the natural-deduction apparatus for *S5* given in G. E. Hughes and Cresswell, *An Introduction to Modal Logic* (London: Methuen and Co., 1986), at pp. 331–334, employs $\Diamond$R as the only primitive strict importation rule. However, the argument (pp. 333–334) for the apparatus's being at least as strong as *S5* (and hence for its completeness) fallaciously assumes that the axiomatic system whose basis is $\Box\phi \rightarrow \phi$ plus $\Diamond\phi \rightarrow \Box\Diamond\phi$ together with the classical rule of necessitation is sufficient without the *K* axiom $\Box(\phi \rightarrow \psi) \rightarrow (\Box\phi \rightarrow \Box\psi)$ for *S5*. (Strict derivation with NI as a strict importation rule does the work of necessitation and the *K* axiom simultaneously.)

of antecedent lines. Let us say that an antecedent line is *accessible* if there is at most one line of the form

$$Show \; \Box \phi$$

or of the form

$$Show \; \Diamond \phi,$$

where ϕ is a symbolic formula, and containing uncancelled '*Show*', subsequent to that antecedent line, and that it is *inaccessible* otherwise. As a derivation proceeds in stages, with the writing of new lines containing '*Show*' and the cancelling of previous occurrences of '*Show*', a single antecedent line that is accessible at one stage may become inaccessible at a later stage, and then become accessible again at a still later stage. There are two forms of strict derivation. The initial line of a strict derivation (which may be a subsidiary derivation wholly contained within a larger derivation) is either of the form

$$Show \; \Box \phi$$

or of the form

$$Show \; \Diamond \phi.$$

If the initial line is of the first form, no special assumption is made. If the initial line is of the second form, and a symbolic formula of the form

$$\Diamond \psi$$

occurs as an accessible line antecedent to the initial line, on the next line one may write the symbolic formula ψ as an assumption. In either case, one then proceeds by inference rules, subsidiary derivations, and citing of premises until the symbolic formula ϕ is secured. One may then cancel the occurrence of '*Show*' in the initial line and box all subsequent lines provided that there is no uncancelled occurrence of '*Show*' among those lines, and provided further that none of those lines (inclusive of boxed lines) was entered as a premise, by an application of an inference rule to an inaccessible line (inaccessible at the current stage, immediately prior to boxing and cancelling), or by an application of an inference rule other than an admissible strict importation rule to an accessible line (accessible at the current stage) antecedent to the initial line. In a strict derivation, any inference rule may be applied to any accessible lines subsequent to the initial line. The first form of strict derivation is known as *necessity derivation* (ND). The second form, invoking a special assumption, is known as *possibility derivation* (PD).

More accurately, besides the addition of the modal inference rules, the following new clause is added to the directions for constructing a *derivation* from given symbolic premises, as it appears in K&M, pp. 24–25:

(4′) *If ϕ is a symbolic formula such that*

$$Show \; \Diamond \phi$$

occurs as a line, then any symbolic formula

$$\psi$$

may occur as the next line, provided that the symbolic formula

$$\diamond\psi,$$

occurs as a preceding accessible line. [*The annotation should refer to the number of the preceding line involved, followed by 'Assumption for possibility derivation' or simply 'Assumption (PD)'.*]

In addition, clause (6) (the 'box and cancel' clause), as it appears in K&M, pp. 24–25, is replaced with the following:

(6') *When the following arrangement of lines has appeared*:

Show ϕ

χ^1

$\vdots$

χm,

where none of $\chi 1$ through χm contains uncancelled 'Show' and either

(i') *ϕ occurs unboxed among $\chi 1$ through χm, and $\chi 1$ does not occur as an assumption for possibility derivation,*
(ii') *ϕ is of the form*

$$(\psi 1 \rightarrow \psi 2)$$

and $\psi 2$ occurs unboxed among $\chi 1$ through χm,
(iii') *for some symbolic formula χ, both χ and its negation occur unboxed among $\chi 1$ through χm, and $\chi 1$ does not occur as an assumption for possibility derivation,*
or

(iv') *ϕ is either of the form*

$$\square\psi,$$

or of the form

$$\diamond\psi,$$

ψ occurs unboxed among $\chi 1$ through χm, and none of $\chi 1$ through χm occurs as a premise, by an application of an inference rule to an inaccessible line, or by an application of an inference rule other than an admissible strict importation rule to an accessible line antecedent to the displayed occurrence of

Show ϕ,

then one may simultaneously cancel the displayed occurrence of 'Show' and box all subsequent lines. [*When we say that a symbolic formula ϕ occurs among certain lines, we mean that one of those lines is either ϕ or ϕ preceded by 'Show'. Further, annotations for clause (6'), parts (i'), (ii), (iii'), and (iv') are 'DD', 'CD', 'ID', and 'SD', respectively, to be entered parenthetically after the annotation for the line in which 'Show' is cancelled.*]

Some of the virtues of this deductive apparatus become more evident upon performing the following.

EXERCISES

1. Construct a T-proof of K: $\Box(P \to Q) \to (\Box P \to \Box Q)$.
2. Prove that PG is derivable in each of the modal systems T, B, $S4$, and $S5$.
3. Prove that the following result obtains in each of the modal systems.

   N: If $\vdash \phi$, then $\vdash \Box\phi$.

4. Prove by induction that interchange of equivalents (IE in K&M, pp. 362–363) is derivable in each of the modal systems.
5. Prove that the T-importation rule of NI is redundant in $S4$ (i.e. that it is a derivable strict importation rule in the system that results by declassifying it as a primitive strict importation rule of $S4$).
6. Construct a T-derivation for the following argument: $\Box\Box(P \to Q)$. $\Box\Diamond P$. $\Box(\Diamond Q \to R \vee S)$. $\sim\Box R$ $\therefore$ $\Diamond S$
7. Construct an $S5$-derivation for the following argument: $\Box(P \to \Box Q)$. $\Diamond P$. $\therefore \Box Q$
8. Construct a B-derivation for the following argument: $\Box(P \to \Box P)$. $\Diamond P$. $\therefore \Box P$
9. Construct a B-proof of '$\Diamond\Box P \to P$'.
10. Construct an $S4$-proof of '$\Diamond\Diamond P \to \Diamond P$'.
11. Construct S5-proofs of the following. B: $P \to \Box\Diamond P$
     E: $\Diamond\Box P \to \Box P$
     4: $\Box P \to \Box\Box P$
12. Prove that the characteristic strict importation rules PG and $\Box R$ of B and $S4$, respectively, are derivable strict importation rules in $S5$.
13. Prove that the T-importation rule of NI is redundant in B.
14. Prove that the T-importation rule of NI is redundant in $S5$.

Exercises 9 and 11, part 3, are solved here for illustration.

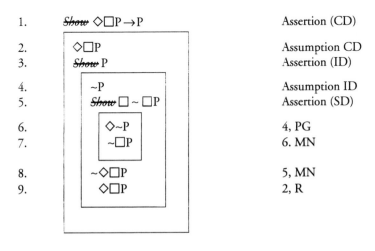

1.	~~Show~~ $\Diamond\Box P \to P$	Assertion (CD)
2.	$\Diamond\Box P$	Assumption CD
3.	~~Show~~ P	Assertion (ID)
4.	$\sim P$	Assumption ID
5.	~~Show~~ $\Box \sim \Box P$	Assertion (SD)
6.	$\Diamond \sim P$	4, PG
7.	$\sim\Box P$	6. MN
8.	$\sim\Diamond\Box P$	5, MN
9.	$\Diamond\Box P$	2, R

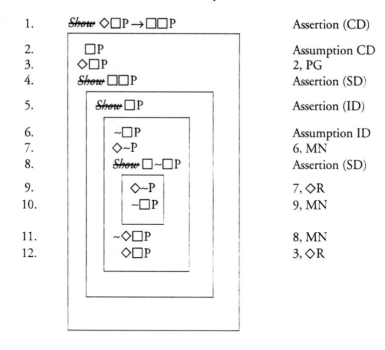

1.   ~~Show~~ ◇□P → □□P   Assertion (CD)

2.   □P   Assumption CD
3.   ◇□P   2, PG
4.   ~~Show~~ □□P   Assertion (SD)

5.   ~~Show~~ □P   Assertion (ID)

6.   ~□P   Assumption ID
7.   ◇~P   6, MN
8.   ~~Show~~ □~□P   Assertion (SD)

9.   ◇~P   7, ◇R
10.   ~□P   9, MN

11.   ~◇□P   8, MN
12.   ◇□P   3, ◇R

These proofs also yield solutions to exercises 12–14. The second proof illustrates several features of the deductive apparatus. Obtaining line 10 was sufficient for cancelling the occurrence of '*Show*' at line 8 and boxing lines 9 and 10, since those subsequent lines comply with the restriction of importing only from accessible lines in accordance with admissible importation rules. (They do not comply with the restrictions for strict derivation in any of the modal systems other than *S*5, since line 9 was imported by the *S*5-importation rule.) At the stage at which line 12 is imported into the subsidiary derivation beginning at line 5, line 3 (from which 12 is imported) is in fact inaccessible, since at that stage both of the lines 4 and 5 are of the form

$$Show\ \Box\phi\,,$$

with uncancelled '*Show*'. The subsidiary derivation beginning at line 5, however, is a (uniform) indirect derivation (K&M, pp. 20–21, 32) rather than a strict derivation, and is therefore not required to comply with the restrictions for strict derivation. When the occurrence of '*Show*' is cancelled in line 5, line 3 becomes accessible once again, so that, by that stage, the newly boxed line 12 now occurs by an application of ◇R to an accessible line. The boxed line 12 thus complies with the restrictions for the strict derivation beginning at line 4. It is important to notice also that it is permissible simply to repeat line 2 in place of the subsidiary derivation at lines 5–12 (or alternatively to repeat line 2 in place of the entire sequence of boxed lines 6–12). But had we done so, we would have been prevented from cancelling the occurrence of '*Show*' in line 4 and boxing the subsequent lines as we did, since application subsequent to line 4 of an inference rule other than an admissible importation rule to any line antecedent to line 4 disqualifies the subsidiary derivation beginning at line 4 from the boxing-and-cancelling privileges of a strict derivation.

In light of exercise 12, PG and $\Box$R may be admitted as derived strict importation rules of *S5*, thereby significantly increasing the ease of abbreviated *S5*-derivations (K&M, pp. 71–73).

To extend the deductive apparatus to quantified modal logic with identity, the inference rules of universal instantiation, existential generalization, and existential instantiation (UI, EG, and EI in K&M, pp. 140–141) should be replaced with the following free-logical forms.

Free universal instantiation (FUI)
$$\wedge\alpha\phi_\alpha$$
$$\frac{\vee\alpha\ \alpha = \beta}{\phi_\beta}$$

Free existential generalization (FEG)
$$\phi_\beta$$
$$\frac{\vee\alpha\ \alpha = \beta}{\vee\alpha\phi_\alpha}$$

Free existential instantiation (FEI)
$$\frac{\vee\alpha\phi_\alpha}{\phi_\beta \wedge\ \vee\alpha\ \alpha = \beta}$$

where ϕ_β comes from ϕ_α by *proper substitution* (K&M, p. 219) of the singular term β for the individual variable α, i.e. where ϕ_β is the same symbolic formula as ϕ_α except for having free occurrences of β wherever ϕ_α has free occurrences of α.[4] (In the case of FEI, the instantial term β must be a variable new to the derivation.) In addition, universal derivation (K&M, p. 143) should be replaced with a free-logical form. More precisely, besides the substitution of the free-logical quantifier inference rules, the following clause should be added to the old directions for constructing a *derivation* from given symbolic premise, as it appears in K&M, pp. 144–145, 199–200.

(4′) *If ϕ is a symbolic formula such that*

Show $\wedge\ \alpha_1 \ldots \wedge \alpha_k\psi$,

occurs as a line, then

$$\vee\beta_1\beta_1 = \alpha_1 \wedge \ldots \wedge \vee\beta_k\beta_k = \alpha_k,$$

may occur as the next line, where for each i, the variable β_i does not occur free in the term α_i. [Annotation: 'Assumption for universal derivation' or simply 'Assumption (UD)'.]

This extension of the apparatus excludes the Barcan Formula '$\wedge x\Box Fx \rightarrow \Box \wedge xFx$' and its converse, as well as '$\vee x\Box Fx \rightarrow \Box \vee xFx$', sometimes called *the Buridan*

---

[4] Compare UID and EGD in K&M, pp. 399–400; and my 'Existence,' in J. Tomberlin, ed., *Philosophical Perspectives, 1: Metaphysics* (Atascadero, Ca.: Ridgeview, 1987), pp. 49–108, at 92–93.

Formula, and its converse as theorems, replacing the converse Barcan Formula with the weakened version '$\Box \wedge xFx \rightarrow \wedge x\Box(\vee yx = y \rightarrow Fx)$' and the Buridan Formula with the weakened version '$\vee x\Box(\vee yx = y \wedge Fx) \rightarrow \Box \vee x\ Fx$'. In addition, the inference rule of Leibniz' law (LL in K&M, p. 270) is replaced with the following:

$$\Box\Box \ldots \Box\alpha = \beta$$
$$\frac{\phi_\alpha}{\phi_\beta},$$

where '$\Box\Box \ldots \Box$' represents a string of occurrences of $\Box$, and ϕ_β is the same symbolic formula as ϕ_α except for having free occurrences of the term β where ϕ_α has free occurrences of the term α. When each of the terms α and β is either an individual variable or an individual constant (i.e. a 0-place operation letter, or 'name letter' in K&M, pp. 119, 202), the string of occurrences of $\Box$ may be of any length, including 0. Otherwise the length of the string is subject to a lower-bound restriction: It must be at least as great as the largest number of occurrences in ϕ_α of symbolic formulas of the form

$$\Box\psi$$

or of the form

$$\Diamond\psi,$$

where ψ is a symbolic formula, such that there is a single free occurrence of α standing within each (i.e. the largest number of modal-operator occurrences having the same free occurrence of α in their scope). Other modifications are possible.[5] For example, the string of occurrences of $\Box$ in Leibniz' law might be taken to be subject to the same lower-bound restriction with regard to length if α or β is an individual constant.[6]

It is possible also to extend the natural-deduction apparatus to the separate modal systems obtained by adding a modal operator for 'actually' (in the indexical sense) to the logical vocabulary.[7]

[5] In 'Gödel's Ontological Proof,' in J. J. Thompson, ed., *On Being and Saying* (Cambridge, Mass.: MIT Press, 1987), pp. 241–261, at 259–260n, Sobel extends his K&M-based modal natural-deduction apparatus (see note 1 above) to QML in a significantly different manner from that proposed here. (In particular, Sobel rightly objects to the inclusion of the Barcan and Buridan Formulas and their converses as theorems, but adds modal inference rules that yield equally objectionable versions of the Buridan and Converse Barcan Formulas.) For alternative extensions to QML, see Andrzej Indrzejczak, 'Natural Deduction in Quantifier Modal Logic,' *Bulletin of the Section of Logic*, 23, 1 (March 1994), pp. 30–40.

[6] See my 'How to Become a Millian Heir,' *Noûs*, 23, 2 (April 1989), pp. 211–220, at 212–215, for an argument against so extending the lower-bound restriction.

[7] I provide some details in 'A Natural-Deduction Apparatus for Modal Logics with "Actually",' unpublished notes, University of California, Santa Barbara.

5

Impossible Worlds (1984)

In a recent commentary on my *Reference and Essence* (Amherst, NY: Prometheus Books, 2005), William R. Carter represents me as endorsing the first two of the following three modal propositions, which together constitute an inconsistent triad (following Carter's numbering scheme):[1]

(2) If a given table (ship, bicycle, etc.) x is originally constructed from a certain hunk of matter y, then it is a necessary or essential feature of x that it is originally constructed from y.

(3) If a given table (ship, bicycle, etc.) x is originally constructed from a hunk of matter (collection of material parts) y, then x could have originated from a hunk of matter z 98% (or more) of which overlaps with y; but x could not have originated from any hunk of matter z', such that less than 98% of z' overlaps with y.

(4′) If c is a material component (e.g., a molecule) of a hunk of matter y, then it is a necessary or essential feature of y that it has c as a material component.

In fact, I endorse (4′), but neither (2) nor (3). The strongest principle along the lines of (2) that I endorse is the following:[2]

(2′) If a given table (ship, bicycle, etc.) x is originally constructed from a certain hunk of matter y, then x could have been originally constructed from any hunk of matter z which is sufficiently like y (in mass, volume, composition, etc.) and which sufficiently substantially overlaps y; but x could not have been originally constructed from any hunk of matter z' which does not sufficiently substantially overlap y.

I offer (3) as one among uncountably many possible regimentations or sharpenings of (2′), one candidate for what is to count as *sufficiently substantial* overlap. I do not actually endorse (3), however, since I regard the vagueness of the phrase

---

[1] Salmon on Artifact Origins and Lost Possibilities', *The Philosophical Review*, 92, No. 2 (April 1983), pp. 223–231.

[2] Here I assume the following modal evaluation clause:

$\ulcorner \Box \phi \urcorner$ is true with respect to w iff ϕ is true with respect to every world determinately accessible to w and either true or neither true nor false with respect to any world neither determinately accessible nor determinately inaccessible to w.

For more on indeterminate accessibility, see *Reference and Essence*, pp. 247–252. The evaluation clause assumed here differs from the (strong) rule proposed there at p. 248, note 27.

'sufficiently substantial overlap' in (2′) as intrinsic to the epistemic situation. No precise principle, like (3), which removes the vagueness by substituting sharp cut-off points is knowably true. (*Cf. Reference and Essence*, pp. 240–252.)

A principle like (2′) is not the sort of proposition that merely happens to be true. If it is true at all, it is necessarily so. In fact, if it is true at all, then it is necessary that it is necessarily true, and it is necessary that it is necessary that it is necessarily true, and so on. From this observation, a sorites-type construction, the main idea of which has been exploited by Roderick Chisholm,[3] can be made to show that the generally accepted axiom schema of *S4* modal propositional logic,

$$\Box p \supset \Box\Box p$$

or equivalently, the notion that modal accessibility among worlds is transitive, should be rejected in its unrestricted form. Consider any hunk of matter z which is sufficiently like the hunk of matter y (in mass, volume, composition, etc.) that originally constitutes an artifact x, but which does not sufficiently overlap y. By (2′) it is necessary that artifact x is not originally formed from hunk z. But there is a (perhaps scattered) hunk of matter z_1 which includes some of the molecules of hunk z and which does sufficiently overlap hunk y, so that artifact x could have been formed from hunk z_1. Consider now yet another hunk of matter z_2 which includes still more of the molecules of hunk z and which sufficiently overlaps hunk z_1 (though perhaps does not sufficiently overlap hunk y). If artifact x could have been formed from hunk z_1, then (even if, in fact, x could not have been formed from z_2, still) it *might have been* that x could have been formed from z_2. Continuing in this vein, it will follow that, although it is necessary that artifact x is not formed from hunk z, still it might have been that it might have been that it might have been . . . that x is formed from z. More intuitively, if there is a possible world w_1 (possible relative to the actual world) in which artifact x is formed from hunk z_1, then there is a world w_2 possible relative to w_1 in which x is formed from z_2. Hence there is a world w_3 possible relative to w_2 in which artifact x is formed from a hunk of matter z_3 which includes still more molecules of hunk z and which sufficiently overlaps hunk z_2, and so on. Finally, there will be a world w which bears the ancestral of the accessibility relation to the actual world, and in which artifact x is formed from hunk z, though by hypothesis there is no world accessible to the actual world in which x is formed from z. World w is an *impossible world* from the point of view of the actual world.

Though the artifact x could not have been formed from hunk z, there is no reason why hunk z could not have been formed instead of hunk y into an artifact of exactly the same type and form as x in place of x itself. Thus there is a world w' possible relative to the actual world in which an artifact x', qualitatively just like x, is formed

[3] See his 'Identity Through Possible Worlds: Some Questions', *Noûs* 1 (March 1967), pp. 1–8; and *Person and Object* (La Salle: Open Court, 1976), pp. 148–149. Chisholm does not accept my conclusions concerning his argument, but instead rejects any principles like (2′) and (3) in favor of the inflexible essentialism of (2). See also Saul Kripke, *Naming and Necessity* (Harvard University Press and Basil Blackwell, 1980), at p. 51, note 18; and Hugh S. Chandler, 'Plantinga and the Contingently Possible', *Analysis* 36.1, January 1976, pp. 106–109.

from hunk *z*. World *w'* is, we may suppose, materially exactly like the impossible world *w* in every molecular, atomic, and sub-atomic detail. Given a complete accounting of the entire history of all of the matter in the worlds *w* and *w'*, with its causal interconnections and exact configuration through time, the two worlds are absolutely indistinguishable. Atom for atom, quark for quark, they are exactly the same. Yet they must be distinct, since *w'* is, and *w* is not, a *genuinely* possible world, i.e., a world possible relative to the actual world. (*Cf. Reference and Essence*, pp. 230–240.)

Carter objects to this "model of the situation" on the grounds of a principle of the identity of materially indiscernible worlds. If the phrase 'materially indiscernible' is understood in such a way that *w* and *w'* count as materially indiscernible, then what we have here is an example which gives the lie to this principle. It is important to notice that *w* and *w'* are indeed discernible, even if not materially discernible in this sense, and in fact discernible not only by their accessibility relations to the actual world. They also differ as regards which facts obtain in them. World *w* includes the fact that artifact *x* is formed from hunk *z*, whereas world *w'* exludes this. Some other artifact *x'*, distinct from *x*, is formed from hunk *z* in *w'*. In place of Carter's principle, I propose a principle of the identity of factually indiscernible worlds, worlds in which the very same facts obtain. (*Cf. Reference and Essence*, p. 238.) I also propose a principle of the identity of *mutually accessible* materially indiscernible worlds. (*Cf. Reference and Essence*, p. 240, and p. 249, note 28.) But an unbridled principle of the identity of materially indiscernible worlds is refuted by the sorts of considerations raised here.

Is this picture of impossible worlds and mutually inaccessible materially indiscernible worlds really acceptable? There are a number of conceptions of possible worlds presently in vogue. Possible worlds are variously construed as maximal compossible sets of propositions (Robert Adams), possible total histories or states of the world (Saul Kripke, Robert Stalnaker), total ways things or the world (cosmos) might have been (David Lewis, sometimes), maximal states of affairs (Alvin Plantinga). For present purposes, these need not be regarded as competing conceptions of possible worlds (except in the case of Lewis, who usually takes nonactual possible worlds to be something like immense concrete objects, someplace far, far away). On any of these conceptions, whatever grounds there may be for believing that there really are possible worlds yield the same, or related, reasons for believing that there are impossible worlds (maximal consistent though not compossible sets of propositions, impossible total histories of the world, impossible total states of the cosmos, total ways things could not have been, etc.), for believing that there are materially indiscernible worlds (materially indiscernible total histories of the cosmos, materially indiscernible total ways for things to be, etc.), for believing the identity of factually indiscernible worlds, and the rest.

[handwritten marginal notes:]

Are there total ways that no world things could have been?
— "necessarily" impossible worlds
— maximal inconsistent sets of propositions
— are these ways that they themselves even could not be?

6

An Empire of Thin Air (1988)

David Lewis's book, *On the Plurality of Worlds*, is derived from his 1984 John Locke Lectures, and is the latest word on possible worlds from the discipline's foremost champion of possibilia. It is a serious defense, *a priori*, of Lewis's notorious doctrines (here called 'modal realism') to the effect that there are tiny purple anthropologists who study human culture unobserved, colossal human-eating monsters 50 feet in height, professional philosophers earning annual salaries in excess of 37 million dollars (pre-inflation), and the like, and that these oddities reside in fabulous alternative universes that are never empirically detected by us (but that are empirically detectable by us).

The central idea of Lewis's theory is that whatever might have transpired involving individuals of our universe does indeed transpire in one of these alternative universes, involving counterparts of these individuals (p. 2)—'the principle of plenitude.' Equally critical to Lewis's project is the converse principle that everything that transpires in one of these alternative universes involving our counterparts is something that might have transpired involving ourselves. We may call this 'the principle of moderation.'[1] Together these two principles assert an isomorphism between total *ways things might have been* with regard to this universe and extant alternative universes, prompting Lewis to identify the former with the latter (p. 86). Lewis thus misleadingly calls his alleged alternative universes 'possible worlds,' and indeed they play a role in Lewis's theory of modal discourse similar in many respects to that of the intensional possible worlds invoked in contemporary philosophical semantics, as conceived of by such writers as Saul Kripke and Robert Stalnaker, that is, maximally specific states or histories.[2] These genuine possible worlds Lewis misleadingly labels 'ersatz worlds.' Like genuine possible worlds, Lewis's alternative universes allegedly "represent" possible events and states of affairs that might have occurred concerning the individuals of our universe; they are supposed to be entities *according to which*

---

[1] These principles are not explicitly articulated as I have them. My statement of plenitude is based on a plausible interpretation of Lewis's less explicit formulation. Lewis provides a version of moderation which is closely related to, but much weaker than, the principle formulated here, and which he derives from the trivial modal logical truth that whatever is the case might have been the case (p. 5). This weaker principle, however, is insufficient for Lewis's purposes.

[2] See Robert Adams, 'Theories of Actuality,' *Noûs*, 8 (1974), pp. 211–231; Kripke, *Naming and Necessity* (Cambridge, Mass.: Harvard University Press, 1980), at pp. 15–20, 44–48, and *passim*; Alvin Plantinga, *The Nature of Necessity* (Oxford, England: Oxford University Press, 1974), at pp. 44–45, and *passim*; Stalnaker, 'Possible Worlds,' *Noûs*, 10 (1976), pp. 65–75; and my 'Impossible Worlds,' *Analysis*, 44 (June 1984), pp. 114–117.

this or that total history that might have transpired involving us and our spatio-temporal surroundings does transpire. But, Lewis insists, they are not something like maximally specific scenarios or stories; they are 'something like remote planets' (p. 2), causally and spatiotemporally isolated physical systems, many replete with authentic tiny purple anthropologists and the like. By contrast with the canonical possible worlds of contemporary philosophical semantics, which are overtly intensional entities, Lewis's alternative universes and their inhabitants are supposed to possess their alleged function of representation entirely by virtue of similarity relations to us and our universe. Indeed, Lewis claims that an assertion that such-and-such might have transpired involving us is just the assertion that such-and-such does transpire involving counterparts of us in some alternative universe. Thus, according to Lewis, to say that Hubert Humphrey might have won the 1968 presidential election is to say that there is an alternative universe in which a Humphrey counterpart—someone sufficiently resembling our Humphrey in certain respects—wins his presidential election in a counterpart of our tumultuous year of 1968, and to say that there might have been tiny purple anthropologists is to say that there *are* tiny purple anthropologists in an alternative universe.

The theory's defense is pragmatic: It is argued that the postulation of alternative universes replete with authentic tiny purple anthropologists accomplishes useful things for us that the most likely rival theories do not. For example, Lewis argues, the postulation allows for a reductive analysis of modality, whereas the story-like entities of contemporary philosophical semantics require that modality be taken as primitive (pp. 150–157). Furthermore, conceptions of possible worlds as story-like entities whose constituents are restricted to actually existing entities cannot make certain modal discriminations, for example among qualitatively identical but numerically distinct possible but nonactual individuals (pp. 157–165).

The defense does not succeed. It is true that the conventional conception of possible worlds as story-like entities does not allow for an analysis of modality in terms of possible worlds; on the contrary, possible worlds are seen as story-like entities that *might have* been true. However, the conventional conception *per se* does not require that modality be taken as primitive. In fact, Lewis himself is compelled to provide something like an alternative analysis of modality, (implausibly) in terms of recombination, in a section (pp. 86–92) devoted to an attempt to give substance to the principle of plenitude—which, on Lewis's theory, is a trivial truism as stated. The conventional possible-world theorist, if so inclined, is free to propose similar (albeit similarly implausible) combinatorial analyses.[3] More importantly, it is entirely unclear that modality is not in fact a primitive concept.[4] Lewis's second

---

[3] More accurately, the conventional theorist is free to propose combinatorial *explications* of modality. Whether the proposed explication qualifies as a (purported) *analysis* depends on what counts as an analysis, properly so called. If Lewis's explication of modality by means of his principles of plenitude and moderation, coupled with his explication of counterparthood in terms of resemblance, constitutes a (purported) analysis of modality, then some conceivable combinatorial explications based on the conventional possible-world approach also constitute (purported) analyses.

[4] I discuss the issue of the order of analysis further, and offer additional criticisms of Lewis's arguments, in 'The Logic of What Might Have Been,' *The Philosophical Review*, 98, 1 (January 1989), pp. 3–34.

objection that the conventional conception lacks the resources to make required modal discriminations is more serious. But even if the point is well taken, it only argues for a need to quantify over all possible individuals, including nonactual individuals who *might have been* tiny purple anthropologists. It is no argument for the existence of things that *are* authentic tiny purple anthropologists, inhabiting authentic alternative universes spatiotemporally disjoint from our universe. Taken as a defense of Lewis's theory of alternative universes, the argument blurs the critical distinction between an assertion concerning a possible individual *x* that it might have been such-and-such and the much stronger assertion that *x* is *in fact* such-and-such.[5]

More to the point, even if the postulation of alternative universes replete with tiny purple anthropologists had the advantages that Lewis claims over more palatable hypotheses, these alleged advantages would be obtained only by means of an hypothesis that is too far-fetched to warrant serious consideration. And even if, miraculously, Lewis's principles of plenitude and moderation are correct, when we say that Humphrey might have won, what we say certainly has nothing to do with political goings-on in alternative universes, nor do those of us who believe that there just *might have* been tiny purple anthropologists typically believe also that there are bizarre alternative universes in which such creatures do indeed exist.[6]

It is tempting to conclude from the theory and its defense that Lewis officially endorses an extremely implausible cosmological theory and, believing this theory to be relevant to the content of modal discourse, does not understand what it means (in English) to say 'it might have been that such-and-such.' This reviewer conjectures that Lewis's highly eccentric views concerning alternative universes, counterpart

[5] *Cf.* my 'Existence,' in James Tomberlin, ed., *Philosophical Perspectives I: Metaphysics* (Atascadero, Calif.: Ridgeview, 1987), pp. 49–108.

[6] Lewis considers the objection that necessity and possibility do not concern what transpires in extant alternative universes but concern instead what transpires according to alternative scenarios involving the totality of whatever there is, including whatever alternative universes there may be—since this totality itself might have been different in some way or other—and that this fact leads to serious difficulty for his theory (pp. 97–101). Lewis formulates this objection so that it depends on a separate criticism, which I am not making, of Lewis's use of the terms 'actual' and 'world' as not covering all of what there is. Although Lewis's response is aimed primarily at defending his restrictive use of these terms, the question of their correct use is in fact completely inessential to the general point of the objection (with which I am entirely sympathetic). My objection here is that, even if there are alternative universes that exactly mirror all of the possibilities concerning things of this universe in which we live and breathe, and none mirroring the impossibilities—whether these universes are said to be of this 'world' or not—the fact (thought, belief, etc.) that our universe might have been different is obviously not a fact concerning any alternative universe. Exactly analogously, if everything that will ever take place on the planet Zartron is coincidentally exactly depicted in some tale or other told by Scheherazade, and conversely every tale told by Scheherazade coincidentally exactly depicts some series of events that will take place on Zartron, the fact that a volcano will erupt tomorrow on Zartron is still not a fact concerning Scheherazade's tales, or vice versa. (If an astronomer predicts the Zartron eruption, he or she does not thereby assert something about Scheherazade's tales, etc.) In response to the general point of the former objection, Lewis repeats his claim that 'might have' means *according to some alternative universe* (p. 98), and insists that although the things of our universe might have been different in various ways, the whole of whatever there is (including whatever alternative universes there are) is not something that might have been different (p. 101*n*). These claims provide further confirmation of the conclusion of this review, that Lewis seriously misunderstands what 'might have' means in English. (Thanks to Mark Johnston for suggesting that Lewis's remarks in this connection should be addressed here.)

relations, and their alleged role in modal discourse have their ultimate source in a conceptual confusion between the modal proposition that *x* might have been such-and-such (where *x* is a possible individual) and the nonmodal proposition that *x* is in fact such-and-such (and is in some 'world').[7] This conceptual confusion concerning such trivial assertions as that there might have been tiny purple anthropologists and that Humphrey might have been victorious, in combination with Leibniz's Law (and some finesse), leads more or less directly to Lewis's idiosyncratic account of the matter, and to a concomitant serious misunderstanding of the English phrase 'might have.'

The conjecture suggests that a nonliteral interpretation of Lewis's explicit theoretical pronouncements may be called for, in at least some contexts. Given Lewis's highly unusual theory of modal discourse, it is natural to construe his use of modal locutions ('might have,' 'necessarily,' etc.) as implicitly nonmodal, and concerned instead with the goings-on in alternative universes. However, if Lewis confuses possibility with a kind of actuality, then an alternative and potentially more illuminating tack is to construe much of his apparently nonmodal discourse concerning the plurality of universes as implicitly modal in import (at some deeper level). There is one such nonliteral interpretation that makes some (though not all) of Lewis's claims somewhat more reasonable than they sound to the naked ear. The alternative interpretation replaces reference to (and quantification over) possible individuals with reference to (alleged) entities that I have elsewhere called 'possible-world slices' of ordinary possible individuals.[8] These are, roughly, possible individuals *as they might have been*, for example Humphrey-having-won-the-election (-and-also-being-such-that-...., where the entire universe is described in every detail). Indeed, although the matter is extremely delicate, much of Lewis's discussion of individuals as existing in only one 'world' strongly suggests that, at least sometimes, he is actually discussing possible-world slices rather than ordinary, cross-world-continuant possible individuals.[9] If *i* is an ordinary possible individual and *w* is a (genuine) possible world according to which *i* exists, the possible-world slice *i*-in-*w* may be represented (for present purposes) by the ordered pair consisting of *i* together with *w*. The alternative interpretation of Lewis's discourse is obtained as follows: (1) We reinterpret ordinary proper names and indexicals so that each refers to the actual-world slice of its standard referent. Thus, for example, Lewis's uses of the first-person

---

[7] This mistaking of possibility for a type of actuality could have resulted from Lewis's having initially assimilated (correctly and contrary to his later theory) the modal proposition that *x* might have been such-and-such to the proposition that *x* is such-and-such in some possible world (that is, the proposition that *according to* some possible maximal scenario, *x* is such-and-such), and then mistaking the latter for the conjunctive nonmodal proposition that *x* is such-and-such and is literally *in* some "world," in something like the layman's sense (physical universe). My 'The Logic of What Might Have Been' discusses some relevant ambiguities in the phrase 'possible world.' (I am not suggesting that Lewis went through this fallacious line of reasoning explicitly.)

[8] *Reference and Essence* (Princeton, N.J.: Princeton University Press and Oxford, England: Basil Blackwell, 1981; Amherst, NY: Prometheus Books, 2005), at pp. 107–111.

[9] Compare for example Lewis's original explication of his notion of counter-parthood in 'Counterpart Theory and Quantified Modal Logic' (in Lewis's *Philosophical Papers I* (Oxford, England: Oxford University Press, 1983), pp. 26–46), wherein he remarks (at p. 28) that "your counterparts are men you *would have been*."

pronoun 'I' are interpreted as referring not to Lewis himself, but to his actual-world slice, Lewis-as-he-actually-is. (Lewis differs from his actual-world slice precisely in that the latter could not have been different in any way, and hence it exists in no possible worlds other than the actual world.) (2) We reinterpret quantifiers (and other variable-binding operators) so that their range with respect to a possible world w is typically the set of w-slices rather than the set of the cross-world-continuant possible individuals of which they are w-slices. (Thus, utterances of the modal locution 'there might have been' are typically interpreted to mean roughly *some possible-world slice*.) In meta-modal contexts (in which modality is itself a topic of philosophical discussion), we re-interpret the quantifiers as typically ranging over all possible-world slices rather than over all cross-world-continuant possible individuals. (Sentential connectives are not re-interpreted.) (3) Most importantly, we must reinterpret most, but not all, ordinary predicates in such a way that a typical n-place predicate applies (with respect to a possible world) to an n-ary sequence $\langle x_1, x_2, \ldots, x_n \rangle$ if and only if the x_i's are possible-world slices of cross-world continuants that stand, respectively, in the n-ary relation associated with the predicate in its use in standard English, across the worlds of the x_i's. Thus, for example, something is said to be 'victorious' (with respect to a possible world) if and only if it is a possible-world slice x of a cross-world continuant that is (literally) victorious according to x's world, and similarly for 'tiny,' 'purple,' 'anthropologist,' etc. Analogously, x is said to be 'taller than' y if and only if x and y are possible-world slices of cross-world continuants x' and y' such that x''s height in x's world is greater than y''s height in y's world.[10] Notice that this step involves interpreting most of Lewis's apparently nonmodal discourse as implicitly invoking modality. For example, an utterance of 'Nixon is a Republican' is interpreted to mean (roughly) that Nixon$_@$ is a possible-world slice of a cross-world continuant that *according to Nixon$_@$'s world* is a Republican—where 'Nixon$_@$' is a name for Nixon's actual-world slice. (4) For every possible world w, we consider the w-slice of the mereological sum of all possible individuals that exist according to w, and we re-interpret the term 'world' (as used in meta-modal contexts) as applying to these in place of genuine possible worlds. The meta-modal predicates 'possible,' 'actual,' and 'accessible,' as applied to worlds, are reinterpreted accordingly to be applicable to these 'worlds' in place of genuine possible worlds. (5) Finally, having done away with explicit reference to cross-world continuants, the relation of genidentity between possible-world slices is replaced by the next best thing: resemblance. Accordingly, modal operators (the box and diamond, 'must,' 'might,' and subjunctive mood) must be interpreted in accordance with a counterpart-theoretic semantics rather than in accordance with standard modal semantics. Thus an utterance of 'Humphrey might have been victorious' is interpreted to mean (roughly) that some possible-world slice x is both a counterpart of Humphrey$_@$ and a possible-world slice of a cross-world continuant that in x's world is victorious—where 'Humphrey$_@$' is a name for Humphrey's actual-world slice. This is equivalent (in some sense) to the assertion

---

[10] *Cf.* the discussion of cross-world relations in *Reference and Essence*, pp. 116–133. The mechanism described there for generating cross-world relations from the definitions or compositional analyses of binary relations is extendable to n-ary relations for arbitrary n.

that there might have been someone who sufficiently resembled Humphrey in certain respects, as Humphrey actually is, and who was victorious.[11]

This complex nonliteral interpretation makes such sentences as 'Humphrey exists at only the actual world' and 'There are worlds at which there exist tiny purple anthropologists' at least relevant to modality. It also makes their utterance not altogether unreasonable—provided the special predicate 'exists at' is not among those that have been reinterpreted. In fact, in a number of respects this nonliteral interpretation of Lewis seems the most charitable one available. Still, it does not make everything Lewis says acceptable. Many find quantification over all possible individuals objectionable, of course—let alone quantification over all possible-world slices of sums of possible individuals—although I do not. Whatever the objections are to possible individuals, it is clear (contrary to Lewis's defense, under this interpretation) that the theory of possible-world slices that this interpretation attributes to Lewis cannot have any significant advantages over the theory of ordinary possible individuals and genuine possible worlds, since these theories are (for most purposes) effectively the same—except for the supplementation of the former by counterpart-theoretic modal semantics. Like many others, I find counterpart-theoretic semantics completely implausible as a semantic theory of the English modal operators 'might have,' 'must,' etc.[12]

In any case, Lewis vigorously protests being re-interpreted along lines similar to these (pp. 210–220), and indeed he appears to doubt the existence of possible-world slices (p. 214n). Given the extreme implausibility of Lewis's explicit pronouncements concerning alternative 'worlds' (when these pronouncements are taken literally), and given their obvious irrelevance to modality, his protests do not constitute decisive evidence against the suggested interpretation (which otherwise fits most contexts remarkably well), but they do make it unclear how the Principle of Charity is to be applied. The proper conclusion to draw is this: Either (i) Lewis is to be taken literally, and he therefore officially endorses an extremely implausible and modally irrelevant cosmological theory of alternative universes and seriously misunderstands what such modal operators as 'might have' mean (in English); or

---

[11] This interpretation tends to support Kripke's original objection (in *Naming and Necessity*, at p. 45n) to Lewis's counterpart-theoretical treatment of this modal sentence concerning Humphrey. An alternative interpretation along similar lines is obtained if we leave names and indexicals alone, construe quantifiers as ranging over ordinary possible individuals, and provide a parallel re-interpretation of the predicates. This alternative nonliteral interpretation depicts Lewis as advocating a particularly inflexible essentialism with regard to ordinary possible individuals, with this endorsement of inflexible essentialism camouflaged by a counterpart-theoretic construal of modal operators. *Cf.* my *Reference and Essence*, at pp. 234–237.

[12] This issue is separate from Lewis's postulation of alternative "worlds," and several writers (such as Graeme Forbes, Anil Gupta, Allen Hazen, Kripke, and Stalnaker) who reject the postulation of alternative universes nevertheless favor, defend, or propose some form of counterpart-theoretic semantics for some contexts. (Kripke's suggestion of a counterpart-theoretic treatment for certain philosophical problems is made more or less in passing, amid an emphatic rejection of counterpart theory for most modal contexts. See his *Naming and Necessity*, at p. 51n.) Some of my objections to counterpart-theoretic modal semantics (in all contexts) are given in *Reference and Essence*, at pp. 232–246, and in more detail in 'Modal Paradox: Parts and Counterparts, Points and Counterpoints,' in P. French, T. Uehling, and H. Wettstein, eds., *Midwest Studies in Philosophy XI: Studies in Essentialism* (Minneapolis, Minn.: University of Minnesota Press, 1986), pp. 75–120.

(ii) something like the suggested interpretation is correct and Lewis's theory of other 'worlds' is therefore relevant to modality and more reasonable than it sounds, but he seriously misunderstands what ordinary names, indexicals, (most) predicates, quantifiers, and the modal operators refer to or mean (in English); or else (iii) some alternative interpretation (like the extreme-essentialist interpretation mentioned in footnote 11) is correct; or finally (iv) some combination of the above, for example, in some contexts Lewis is to be taken literally while in others something like the suggested interpretation is operative. Whichever is the case, Lewis seriously misunderstands what 'might have' means.

7

The Logic of What Might Have Been
(1989)

In earlier work I argued (following Hugh Chandler) that the conventionally accepted system *S5* of (first-order) modal propositional logic, and even the weaker system *S4*, embody an invalid pattern of modal reasoning; they are fallacious systems for reasoning about what might have been.[1] I argued, in fact, that the characteristic *S4* axiom schema, '$\Box \phi \supset \Box \Box \phi$'—or equivalently, the principle that for any necessarily true proposition *p*, the proposition that *p* is necessarily true is itself necessarily true—is not only not logically true, some instances are in fact untrue. I argued, that is, that for some necessary truths *p*—for example, that a certain table does not originate from a certain hunk of wood—the fact that *p* is necessary cannot itself be correctly deemed necessary. Instead, although any such proposition *p* is necessary, the claim that *p* is necessarily necessary is untrue, and indeed some claim of the form '$\Box \Box \ldots \Box p$' is altogether false.

While some of my audience have found these arguments against *S4* modal logic persuasive, many have found them unconvincing. I have repeatedly encountered two particular objections, which are probably best regarded as two parts of a single objection. This objection, however, betrays a serious misunderstanding of my position, or a failure to appreciate the full force of my (Chandleresque) arguments, or both, and is based on a confusion among concepts central to the foundations of contemporary semantics for modal logic. In this paper I shall present the objection(s) and my response. I shall also argue for the further claim (which I have not made elsewhere) that even the conventionally accepted system *B*, which is weaker than *S5* and independent of *S4*, has not been adequately justified as a fallacy-free system of reasoning about what might have been. The axioms characteristic of *B* are

This chapter was presented to an international conference on Meaning and Natural Kinds at the Inter-University Centre of Postgraduate Studies in Dubrovnik, Yugoslavia, September 1986. It has benefitted from a discussion with Timothy Williamson, and from comments by Hugh Chandler, Graeme Forbes, and the anonymous referees.

[1] Hugh Chandler, 'Plantinga and the Contingently Possible,' *Analysis*, 36 (1976), pp. 106–109. For my renderings of Chandleresque arguments, see *Reference and Essence* (Princeton, NJ: Princeton University Press and Oxford, England: Basil Blackwell, 1981), section 28, pp. 229–252; 'Impossible Worlds,' *Analysis*, 44 (1984), pp. 114–117; and 'Modal Paradox: Parts and Counterparts, Points and Counterpoints,' in French, Uehling, and Wettstein, eds., *Midwest Studies in Philosophy XI: Studies in Essentialism* (Minneapolis, Minn.: University of Minnesota Press, 1986), pp. 75–120. The last includes further bibliographical references.

sentences of the form '$\phi \supset \Box \Diamond \phi$.' That is, B is characterized by the principle that for any true proposition p, the proposition that p is possibly true is itself necessarily true. Here, however, I shall not argue for the strong claim (analogous to my claim in connection with $S4$) that some true proposition p is such that the proposition that p is necessarily possible is untrue. (I believe that the characteristic B principle may well have no such counterexamples.) I contend only that, even if the B axioms are in fact true, and even if they are necessarily true, it seems to be logically possible for some proposition p to be true while the proposition that p is necessarily possible is at the same time false. Thus, even if the B principle is necessarily true, its alleged status as a logical (or analytic) truth remains in need of justification. Similar arguments may be made against other proposed extensions of the weak modal system T. If I am correct, insofar as modal logic is concerned exclusively with the logic of metaphysical modality, and not also with other, nonlogical features of metaphysical modality, T may well be the one and only (strongest) correct system of (first-order) propositional modal logic.[2]

I

The case against $S4$ modal logic stems from the intuition (which many of my opponents share) that a particular material artifact—say, a particular wooden table which we may call 'Woody'—could have originated from matter slightly different from its actual original matter m^* (while retaining its numerical identity, or its *haecceity*) but not from entirely different matter. Wherever one may choose to draw the line between what matter Woody might have originated from and what matter Woody could not have originated from, it would seem that, by stretching things to the limit, we may select some (presumably scattered) matter m such that, although Woody could not have originated from m, m is close enough to being a possibility for Woody that if Woody *had* originated from certain matter m' that *is in fact* possible for Woody—matter differing in as many molecules from the actual original matter $m*$ as possible, and sharing as many molecules with m as possible, while remaining a possibility for Woody—then it *would have been* possible for Woody to have originated from m, even though it is not *actually* possible. Even if one denies that there is a sharp line to be drawn between what matter is and what matter is not possible for the origin of Woody, by stretching things to whatever sort of limit remains (such as an interval of vagueness and indeterminacy in lieu of a dividing line

[2] Metaphysical modal logic concerns metaphysical (or alethic) necessity and metaphysical (alethic) possibility, or necessity and possibility *tout court*—as opposed to such other types of modality as physical necessity, epistemic necessity, etc. The (strongest) correct system of logic for some other modality need not coincide with that for metaphysical modality. (The characteristic principle of T that any proposition that must be true is true must already fail in deontic modal logic, the logic of what is morally required to be the case and what is morally permitted to be the case.) Throughout this paper I am concerned primarily with metaphysical modality. Where I speak simply of 'modal logic,' the reader is to understand that only metaphysical modal logic is under discussion. My use of such modal locutions as 'necessary,' 'might have,' etc. is to be similarly construed throughout, unless otherwise indicated.

between what is and is not possible), there will still be some matter *m* such that Woody (just barely) determinately could not have originated from *m*, yet the claim that this is itself necessary is untrue (or not 'true to the maximum degree,' or whatever), and in addition, unfalse. Either way, the conditional claim (which is an axiom of *S4*) that if Woody necessarily does not originate from *m*, then it is necessary that Woody necessarily does not thus originate fails. (It suffers the same truth-value status as its consequent.) Also failing is the inference from the antecedent of this conditional to the consequent, since the premise of the inference is altogether true and the conclusion is not. *S4* modal logic is fallacious.

I supplemented my argument against *S4* with a particular conception of what possible worlds are—in conjunction with the standard identification of necessity with truth in every possible world and possibility with truth in at least one possible world. As with many contemporary philosophers of modality, I conceive of possible worlds as certain sorts of (in some sense) maximal abstract entities *according to which* certain things (facts, states of affairs) obtain and certain other such things do not obtain. Possible worlds are total *ways things might have been* (David Lewis). A possible world is something like a total history that might have obtained concerning everything in the cosmos (Saul Kripke), or a maximal property or state that the cosmos might have had or been in (Kripke, Robert Stalnaker), or a maximal state of affairs (Alvin Plantinga) or maximal scenario (myself) that might have obtained. For most purposes, one may conceive of a possible world as an infinitely long, complex, and detailed set of states of affairs or (potential) facts or statements (that is, an infinite set of structured propositions, more or less as Russell conceived propositions),[3] one that does not leave any question of fact undecided (Robert Adams). Since the actual world is itself a possible world, it too is conceived of as a maximal scenario or history; and may be conceived of as a maximally comprehensive set of statements, in this case the set of all statements that are in fact true.

More accurately, a possible world may be conceived of as a set of (potential) facts or statements that does not leave any of a very comprehensive range of questions of fact undecided. Some of the facts that are decided may in some cases determine that certain other statements are neither true nor false, owing to false presuppositions, category mistakes ('sortal incorrectness'), vagueness, or something else. If Frege was right, for example, the fact that there is no present King of France determines that the statement that the present King of France is bald is neither true nor false, so that neither this statement nor its negation is included in the set of statements corresponding to the actual world. More importantly, certain meta-facts (or facts about possible worlds and sets of facts) cannot be included in such a set for familiar reasons concerning cardinality problems, since there are at least as many such metafacts as there are subsets of any given infinite set of facts, and these subsets

---

[3] I mean to exclude here the modal logician's conception of a proposition as a set of possible worlds (or equivalently, as a characteristic function from possible worlds to truth-values). It is not a good idea to think of possible worlds as sets of propositions, and at the same time to think of propositions as sets of possible worlds. For more on my favored Russellian conception of propositions, see my *Frege's Puzzle* (Cambridge, Mass.: The MIT Press/Bradford Books, 1986).

outnumber the facts in the given set.[4] A possible world, then, may be thought of as a set of statements of a certain restricted but still very comprehensive sort.

Recall that it is (just barely) impossible for Woody the table to have originated from certain matter m. Woody cannot be in the state of originating from m. That is, originating from m is a state metaphysically unavailable to Woody; it is a way that Woody cannot be. But it is still a way for an individual to be. Likewise, there is a total way for all things in general to be—a "maximal" set of (potential) facts, if you will—according to which Woody originates from m. Let us call this maximal way for things to be 'W'. Since Woody originates from m according to W, and Woody metaphysically cannot do so, W is a total way things cannot be. A total way things cannot be is a total way for things to be such that things cannot be that way, a state or history for everything in the universe such that everything in the universe cannot be in that state or have that history, a maximal state of affairs or scenario that cannot obtain. Total ways things cannot be are thus also "worlds," or maximal ways for things to be. They are impossible worlds. In fact, although W is an impossible world, there is a possible world W' (assuming m was chosen carefully enough, and ignoring for the moment the prospect of vagueness and regions of indeterminacy) according to which Woody originates from the matter m' instead of its actual original matter m^*, and if W' had obtained (as indeed it might have), W would have been a way things might have been rather than a way things cannot be; W would have been possible instead of impossible. Although W is impossible relative to the actual world, it is possible relative to W', which is itself possible relative to the actual world. Thus W is a possibly possible world. Other impossible worlds may be not even possibly possible, but only possibly possibly possible, and so on. The binary relation between (possible or impossible) worlds of relative possibility—the modal relation of *accessibility*—is not transitive.

What are the limits on the admissibility of possible and impossible worlds? None to speak of. Any degree of variation and recombination qualifies. Some ways for things to be are not even possibly possibly . . . possible, for any degree of nesting. A world according to which Nathan Salmon is Henry Kissinger is such a world, for example, as is a world according to which Nathan Salmon is a Visa credit card account with the Bank of America. Since they are ways-for-things-to-be of a certain sort (*viz.*, such that things necessarily cannot be that way, and necessarily necessarily cannot be that way, and so on), these too are "worlds." As far as I can tell, worlds need not even be logically consistent. A world according to which there is both life on Mars and no life on Mars is a way things cannot be on logical grounds alone. Hence this too is a "world," a way for things to be. The only restriction on *worlds*, as opposed to lesser ways for things to be, is that they must be (in some sense) *maximal* (total, comprehensive) ways for things to be; for every statement of fact, either it or its denial must obtain according to a world—*modulo* cases of nonbivalence arising from presupposition failure, vagueness, etc., and subject to cardinality constraints if the totality of facts constituting a world are to form a set.

[4] See Selmer Bringsjord, 'Are There Set Theoretic Possible Worlds?' *Analysis*, 45 (1985), p. 64; Christopher Menzel, 'On Set Theoretic Possible Worlds,' *Analysis*, 46 (1986), pp. 68–72; and Patrick Grim, 'On Sets and Worlds: A Reply to Menzel,' *Analysis*, 46 (1986), pp. 186–191.

II

The first part of the standard objection to this account is summed up by David Lewis as follows:

Say I: This is no defence [of the essentialist doctrine that a table could not have originated from entirely different matter], this is capitulation [to radical anti-essentialism]. In these questions of haecceitism and essence, by what right do we ignore worlds that are deemed inaccessible? Accessible or not, they're still worlds. We still believe in them. Why don't they count? (*On the Plurality of Worlds*, Oxford: Basil Blackwell, 1986, p. 246)

This part of the objection may be spelled out further: Intransitive accessibility relations are introduced into modal semantics for the purpose of interpreting various 'real' or restricted types of modalities, such as nomological necessity. A proposition is *nomologically necessary* in an arbitrary possible world w if and only if it is true in every possible world in which all of the laws of nature in w are true. For convenience, we may say that a world w' is *accessible to*, or *nomologically possible relative to*, a world w if every natural law of w is true in w'. Then we may say more succinctly that a proposition is nomologically necessary with respect to a possible world w if and only if it is true in every possible world accessible to w. More restrictedly, perhaps, a proposition is *physically necessary* with respect to an arbitrary possible world w if and only if it is true in every possible world in which all of the laws of physics in w are true. Other restricted modalities require alternative accessibility relations: a proposition is said to be *necessary*, in the restricted sense in question, with respect to an arbitrary possible world w if and only if it is true in every possible world of such-and-such a restricted sort—the restriction in question depending on some appropriate relation to w. Such restrictions yield failures of the characteristic *S4* principle that any "necessary" truth is necessarily necessary, and even of the characteristic *B* principle that any truth is necessarily possible. Suppose, for example, that w and w' are worlds so different in their natural constitution that although every natural law of w is true in w' (so that w' is nomologically possible relative to w), some of these natural laws of w are not natural laws in w' but merely accidental generalizations, while certain other generalizations not even true in w are additional natural laws in w'. Then a natural law of w (which is automatically nomologically necessary in w) that is not also a natural law of w' will not be true in every world nomologically possible relative to w', and hence will not be nomologically necessarily nomologically necessary in w. Similarly, a proposition that is true in w but violates one of the additional natural laws of w' will not be nomologically necessarily nomologically possible in w. In this restricted scheme, accessibility between worlds is neither transitive nor symmetric. It remains reflexive, of course—as long as the natural laws of a given world are true in that world. The fundamental characteristic *T* principle that any "necessary" truth is true is thereby preserved.

By contrast, the objection goes, the hallmark of metaphysical (alethic) necessity or necessity *tout court*—its distinguishing characteristic—is that it is completely unrestricted. Metaphysical necessity and possibility is the limiting case of restricted necessity and possibility, the case with no restrictions whatsoever. A proposition is necessary in this unrestricted sense with respect to a possible world *w* if and only if it is true in absolutely every possible world whatsoever, no restrictions. By contrast with the case of restricted modalities, the objection continues, my conception of a *metaphysically impossible world* is incoherent. Any possible world is *possible* in the unrestricted, metaphysical sense. Since my account admits the existence of a world *W* in which Woody originates from *m*, even though I deem this world 'inaccessible' to the actual world, I implicitly acknowledge (contrary to my explicit pronouncements) that it is *not* necessary in the relevant, metaphysical sense of 'necessary' that Woody does not originate from *m*. Indeed, by admitting possible worlds of unlimited variation and recombination, I simply abandon true metaphysical essentialism. By my lights, any property is attached to anything in some possible world or other. I am a closet radical anti-essentialist.

This part of the objection brings with it an oft-used defense of *S5* modal logic. In the metaphysical, unrestricted senses of 'necessary' and 'possible,' the characteristic *S5* principle that any possible truth is necessarily possible may be easily proved. Suppose *p* is a possible truth, that is, a proposition true in at least one possible world *w*. Then relative to any possible world *w'*, without exception, there is at least one possible world in which *p* is true—namely, *w*. It follows (given our assumption that *p* is possible) that it is necessary that *p* is possible. For in the unrestricted sense of 'possible,' one possible world in which *p* is true is all that is required for *p* to be "possible" relative to any given world *w'*, with no further restriction as to what sort of world *p* is true in or how that world is related to *w'*. There are similar direct proofs of the characteristic *B* and *S4* principles.

There remains my claim that such a world as *W*, in which Woody originates from *m*, is inaccessible to the actual world. The first part of the objection more or less ignores this claim as irrelevant, a red herring. The second part of the objection focuses on this claim. When such restricted modalities as nomological necessity or physical necessity are under discussion, the phrase 'possible relative to' has a tolerably clear sense (given that we have a prior understanding of such notions as *law of nature* and *law of physics*). Such notions of accessibility are more or less sharply defined. My notion of *necessity* is also some restricted notion, since I deem some worlds inaccessible to others. Yet, the objection goes, I have not defined the restriction; I leave my use of the phrase 'possible relative to' with no tolerably clear sense. It does not seem to mean much of anything; it is simply an *ad hoc* device for sweeping a serious difficulty under the rug. To quote Lewis again:

[W]e look in vain, in ... many ... places, for an account of what it means to deny that some world is "relatively possible". I think it is like saying: there are things such that, ignoring them, there are no such things. Ignoring all the worlds where such-and-such obnoxious things happen, it is impossible that such things happen. Yes. Small comfort (*ibid.*, p. 248).

III

The objection presented in the preceding section confuses or conflates two notions that must be kept sharply distinct: the generic notion of a way for things to be and the peculiarly modal notion of a way things *might have* been. Confusion between these two notions probably stems from an analogous ambiguity in the phrase 'possible world.' The layman speaks of a 'world' almost exclusively as a planet, though sometimes as the whole physical universe of atoms, molecules, planets, stars, galaxies, superclusters, and what-have-you. By contrast, in the metaphysics of modality a *world* is an abstract entity according to which some things obtain and other things do not, such that all (or sort of all) such questions of fact are answered one way or the other. Modal worlds are not physical universes but intensional entities that represent things as being one way or another. Even Lewis, who in his metaphysical constructions idiosyncratically maintains the layman's conception of a *world* as a whole physical universe, combines this conception with the metaphysician's conception of a world as an entity *according to which* some states of affairs obtain (including, for Lewis, states of affairs concerning things not part of that world) and other such states of affairs do not, such that all (or sort of all) such questions of fact are answered by the 'world.'[5] It is awkward to call these things simply 'worlds,' since that term is so highly suggestive of the layman's notion. Fortunately (or rather unfortunately!) Leibniz provided a more descriptive term: 'possible world.'

There are two problems with this bit of Leibnizian terminology. The first problem concerns what the word 'possible,' as it occurs in the phrase 'possible world,' does not mean. In metaphysics when we call something a possible such-and-such, we generally mean that it is a such-and-such that might have existed, even if it does not. But whether or not possible worlds actually exist, in calling something a 'possible world' most of us do not mean a world (*qua* total way for things to be, or maximal entity according to which some states of affairs obtain and others do not) that might have existed, even if it does not. To think that the concept of a possible world is that of a world that might have existed is to misunderstand the function of the word 'possible' in the phrase 'possible world.'[6]

The second problem with the phrase 'possible world' concerns what the word 'possible' does mean there. For it means *something* there. Strictly speaking, a possible world is not a way for things to be that might have existed; it is a way for things to be such that things might have been that way. Similarly, a possible history or possible state for an individual is not a history or state that might have existed, but a history or state that the individual might have had or might have been in. Thus the word 'possible' contributes some special meaning to the phrase, and more meaning than is accommodated by the generic notion of a total way-for-things-to-be-even-if-things-could-not-have-been-that-way. Strictly speaking, a possible world is not any old total

---

[5] I criticize Lewis's views concerning the nature of possible worlds in my review of his *On the Plurality of Worlds*, in *The Philosophical Review*, 97 (1988), pp. 237–244.

[6] The objection of the preceding section need not depend in any way on this common misconstrual of the phrase 'possible world,' although it probably often does. One who misunderstands the phrase 'possible world' to mean *world that might have existed* will conclude that 'impossible worlds' cannot exist. Possible worlds would emerge as the only worlds there could be, so that a (possible) thing is a world if and only if it is a 'possible world.' It seems likely that this fallacy lies behind the common confusion of the generic notion of a world and the modal notion of a possible world.

way for things to be, but a modally special kind of total way for things to be, namely a total way that things *might have* been. A possible world is a total way for things to be that conforms to metaphysical constraints concerning what might have been. The generic notion of a total way for things to be is a notion without a proper term of its own. Aesthetic considerations aside, rather than let the phrase 'possible world' do double duty for this generic notion as well as for the modal notion, we would be better off reserving it exclusively for the modal notion—for which it is certainly more apt—and using my highfalutin hyphenated phrase 'total way-for-things-to-be-even-if-things-could-not-have-been-that-way' for the generic notion, or my modally unadorned phrase 'total way for things to be,' or if worse comes to worst, the simple unadorned word 'world.' In the best of all possible worlds, total ways for things to be are not called 'possible worlds,' unless they are total ways things might have been.

Whatever the source of the confusion between the generic notion of a way for things to be and the modal notion of a way things might have been, this confusion is very probably the primary source of the idea that metaphysical modality is the limiting case of restricted modalities, that metaphysical necessity and possibility is the unrestricted, and hence the least restricted, type of necessity and possibility. For metaphysical necessity is indeed truth in all ways things might have been (modal, not generic), and metaphysical possibility is indeed truth in at least one way things might have been (modal, not generic).

Metaphysical modality is definitely *not* an unrestricted limiting case. There are more modalities in Plato's heaven than are dreamt of in my critics' philosophy, and some of these are even less restrictive than metaphysical modality. One less restrictive type of modality is provided by *mathematical necessity* and *mathematical possibility*. A proposition is mathematically necessary if its truth is required by the laws of mathematics alone, and mathematically possible if its truth is not precluded by the laws of mathematics alone. Many metaphysical impossibilities are mathematically possible, for example, Nathan Salmon being a Visa credit card account with the Bank of America. Another type of modality less restrictive than metaphysical modality is provided by what is sometimes called 'logical necessity' and 'logical possibility,' to be distinguished from genuinely metaphysical necessity and possibility, or necessity and possibility *tout court*. A proposition is logically necessary if its truth is required on logical grounds alone, logically possible if its truth is not ruled out by logic alone (that is, if its negation is not logically necessary). Thus whereas it is logically necessary that Nathan Salmon is not somebody other than Nathan Salmon, and it is also logically necessary that either Nathan Salmon is a Visa credit card account with the Bank of America or he is not, it is not logically necessary that Nathan Salmon is not a credit card account. Although there is a way things logically could be according to which I am a credit card account, there is no way things metaphysically might have been according to which I am a credit card account. This illustrates the restricted nature of metaphysical modality. Some logically possible worlds must be 'ignored.' Metaphysical necessity is truth in every logically possible world of a certain restricted sort.

What is the restriction? To worlds that are metaphysically possible. (What else!) When we identify necessity with truth in every possible world, the word 'possible' means *something* there, and what it means there places a restriction on the sort of worlds under consideration. The metaphysical notion of possibility restricts the logical notion of possibility, in a manner exactly analogous to that in which the notion of *natural law* involved in the notion of nomological necessity restricts the metaphysical notion of possibility. Just as nomological possibility is a special kind of metaphysical possibility, so metaphysical possibility is a special kind of logical possibility.[7]

Even logical necessity may be seen as observing some restriction: a proposition is logically necessary (with respect to a world w) if and only if it is true in every *logically consistent* world (according to w), whether metaphysically possible or not—or every world in which the laws and rules of logic (in w) obtain (including the logical prohibition on inconsistency).[8] The logically inconsistent worlds do not count as regards what is logically necessary. Still, logical modality is considerably freer of restriction than metaphysical modality. With its freedom from the additional constraint of metaphysical possibility, logical necessity may be construed as accommodating all of the axioms and rules of S5. But if logical modality is unrestrictive enough to accommodate all of the axioms and rules of S5, it may not be restrictive enough to zero in on S5. Depending on what counts as logically possible, the interpretation of the diamond '$\diamondsuit$' as logical possibility instead of metaphysical possibility could turn $\ulcorner \diamondsuit \phi \urcorner$ into a logical truth for every logically consistent formula ϕ. It would then become a logical truth that Woody "might have" originated from m, and that Nathan Salmon "might have" been a credit card account. Even if we essentialists are wrong and metaphysical necessity does not extend beyond logical necessity, the logic of logical necessity can extend far beyond that of metaphysical necessity.[9]

---

[7] Timothy Williamson has pointed out that this may be strictly false, since (as David Kaplan has shown) there are sentences that are valid in the logic of indexicals and that do not express metaphysically necessary truths, for example 'If Saul Kripke is an anthropologist, then Saul Kripke is actually an anthropologist.' I believe, however, that insofar as propositions (as opposed to sentences) may be appropriately called 'logically valid' or 'not logically valid,' the propositions expressed by such sentences are not logically valid even though the sentences themselves are. (Conversely, some sentences that are not logically valid express propositions that are, for example, 'All bachelors are unmarried men.') Cf. *Frege's Puzzle*, pp. 132–151, and especially p. 177, note 1. The important point here is that some logically possible (that is, consistent) propositions are nevertheless metaphysically impossible.

[8] If w is itself logically consistent, this rules out worlds in which such logical truths as the Law of Noncontradiction do not obtain. What about an inconsistent world according to which there is both life on Mars and no life on Mars and yet (by logic) no proposition and its negation are both true? (I owe this marvelous example to Saul Kripke, who has used it for a different but related purpose.) This had better count somehow as a world in which the Law of Noncontradiction does *not* obtain, in the relevant sense. Otherwise, such contradictions will emerge as logical possibilities.

[9] Thus whereas it is metaphysically impossible on my view for Woody to originate from m, it may nevertheless be logically true (and hence logically necessary) that it is logically possible that Woody so originates. Whether the sentence 'It is logically possible that Woody originated from m' should itself count as a logical truth may depend on whether logical necessity and possibility are treated as attributes of sentences, or rather as attributes of propositional contents. See note 7 above. It is arguable that the logical (as opposed to metaphysical) possibility of truth for the proposition that Woody originated from m is itself a truth of pure logic. Alternatively, if logical possibility is an attribute of sentences rather than of their contents, it is arguable that the logic of logical necessity

If worlds include ways things metaphysically cannot be in addition to ways things metaphysically might have been, then the idea that metaphysical necessity corresponds to truth in every world whatsoever is flatly mistaken. If worlds include ways things logically cannot be, then no proposition is true according to every world and every proposition is true according to some world. I know of no standard or conventional sense of 'possible' on which even the proposition that Nathan Salmon is somebody other than Nathan Salmon is "possible." It is not clear that there would be any interest, other than purely formal interest, in a completely unrestricted notion of modality on which anything is possible and nothing is necessary—and there is not much purely formal interest in this unrestricted notion. Such a notion would preserve the characteristic *S4* axiom schema, but perhaps at the cost of turning $\ulcorner \Diamond \phi \urcorner$ into a logical truth for every formula ϕ, and thereby ruling out the inference rule of necessitation (which licenses the inference from a logical theorem ϕ to $\ulcorner \Box \phi \urcorner$) as well as the characteristic axiom schema of *B* and hence also that of *S5*. (The last, in fact, would be replaced by its negation.) Even if there is interest in such a notion, it has nothing to do with metaphysical modality. Surely it is metaphysically impossible that there should be life on Mars and no life on Mars at the same time. The failure of the characteristic *B* axiom schema in the case of the completely unrestricted interpretation of the modal operators demonstrates that there must be some fallacy in the 'proof,' presented in the preceding section, that unrestricted modality honors *S5*.

Do worlds, *qua* ways for things to be, include ways things cannot be in addition to ways things might have been? I know of no plausible grounds for denying that they do. Indeed, nearly any plausible argument for the existence of ways things might have been (including those arguments offered by my opponents)[10] affords an analogous and parallel argument for ways things cannot be, even ways things cannot be on logical grounds alone. Every argument I am aware of against impossible worlds in favor of only possible worlds confuses ways for things to be with ways things might have been, or worse, confuses ways things cannot be with ways for things to be that cannot exist—or worse yet, commits both errors. The fact that Woody cannot originate from *m* entails that originating from *m* is a way Woody cannot be. It follows from the latter that Woody originating from *m* and Socrates being wise and . . . (where 'all' questions of fact are fixed), is a maximal way that things (in general) cannot be. It follows from the fact that Woody cannot originate from *m*, therefore, that there is a maximal way things cannot be. Likewise, it follows from the fact that I cannot be somebody other than myself, that me being somebody other than myself and Socrates being wise, etc., is also a way things cannot be. We should

and possibility should take into consideration the logical possibility of the sentence 'Woody originates from *m*' being analytically false while retaining its logical form (expressing, for example, the proposition that Venus is distinct from Venus). In that case, it need not be a truth of logic (although it would still be true) that 'Woody originated from *m*' is logically possible. Even under this construal, however, *S5* may not be the appropriate (first-order) propositional logic of logical necessity. The rule of necessitation (which licenses the inference of $\ulcorner \Box \phi \urcorner$ from a subsidiary proof of ϕ) is inapplicable to such logical validities as 'If Saul Kripke is an anthropologist, then Saul Kripke is actually an anthropologist.' (See note 17 below.)

[10] *Cf.* 'Impossible Worlds,' pp. 116–117; and Margery Bedford Naylor, 'A Note on David Lewis's Realism About Possible Worlds,' *Analysis*, 46 (1986), pp. 28–29.

not resist these inferences; we should draw them, and see where they lead. At the very least we should refrain from asserting their premise while rejecting their conclusions, since they are valid.

An impossible world like W may be seen as merely a variation of a genuinely possible world. Consider the "maximal" set of statements that would have been true if m had been formed into a table and Woody had never been constructed at all. Let us call the (possible) table that would have been formed from m if m had formed a table 'Mia,' and let us call this set of statements 'K_{Mia}.' Now there is surely a "maximal," coherent set of statements K like K_{Mia} except that every statement in K_{Mia} concerning Mia (or concerning the table formed from m) is replaced by the corresponding statement concerning Woody, and every statement concerning Woody is replaced by the corresponding statement concerning Mia (or the table that actually would have been formed from m), with whatever further additions and deletions are required by these changes. The world W is simply the way-for-things-to-be determined by K. Indeed, W is just like the possible world W_{Mia} corresponding to K_{Mia} (the maximal scenario that would have obtained if m had been formed into a table and Woody had never been constructed), except for the substitution of certain 'components' (non-maximal scenarios, as it were). Since W is a world according to which Woody originates from m, and by hypothesis Woody cannot thus originate, we have here what so many philosophers have so often repudiated: an impossible world. But what is there to repudiate? World W is just the maximal way-for-things-to-be corresponding to a particular set of statements or (potential) facts, something of the same ontological category or sort as the genuinely possible world W_{Mia}. The key difference between W_{Mia} and W is modal rather than ontological-categorical. The former might have been realized whereas the latter could not have been realized; the former is a way things might have been whereas the latter is a way things could not have been. Both are ways for things to be, and in that sense, ontologically on a par.[11]

IV

Given this conception of metaphysically possible worlds as forming a restricted subclass of more things of the same ontological category, one cannot rely on the mere existence or nonexistence of worlds according to which it is the case that such-and-such in order to determine whether such-and-such is possible or impossible. It is metaphysically impossible for Woody to originate from m, yet there are many worlds according to which Woody so originates. On my conception, the notions of metaphysical necessity and possibility are not defined or analyzed in terms of the

---

[11] If anything, W_{Mia} is the more dubious of the two, since it directly involves Mia, which does not actually exist, in place of Woody, which actually exists. But let us not worry about this potentially significant ontological difference here. If the truth be told, my own view is that most of the worlds quantified over by modal semanticists do not actually exist, though they might have existed, or possibly might have existed, or possibly possibly might have existed, etc. I do not see this as a decisive reason not to quantify over them, as long as one keeps one's ontology straight. *Cf.* my 'Existence,' in J. Tomberlin, ed., *Philosophical Perspectives I: Metaphysics* (Atascadero, Calif.: Ridgeview, 1987), pp. 49–108.

apparatus of possible worlds. The order of analysis is just the reverse: a possible world is understood to be a total way things might have been (or a maximal scenario that might have obtained, etc.), relying on one's prior understanding of the modal notion of what *might have* been. What is possible and what is impossible according to a world is determined by the world itself. Recall that worlds are *maximal* or *total* ways for things to be, deciding all (or a very comprehensive class of) questions of fact. They are not silent concerning all questions of modal fact, since these too are questions of fact. If *p* is a nonmodal proposition, then one (partial) way for things to be is for *p* to be a necessary truth, and another is for not-*p* to be possible. Among the facts (or statements of fact, etc.) that constitute (or obtain according to) a world are such peculiarly modal facts, facts of the form "It is necessary that such-and-such" or "It is possible that such-and-such." It is a fact of the actual world, for example, that it is necessary that Woody does not originate from *m*, and this fact is included among the facts that constitute the actual world. Given this conception of what a world is, the relevant notion of relative possibility, or accessibility, is perfectly straightforward. If a definition is wanted, it is this: a world *w'* is *metaphysically possible relative to* a world *w* if and only if every fact of *w'* is a possibility in *w* (that is every proposition that is true according to *w'* is possible according to *w*). Equivalently, *w'* is metaphysically possible relative to *w* if and only if every necessary fact of *w* obtains in *w'* (that is, every proposition that is necessary according to *w* is true according to *w'*). If we assume that one question of fact decided by any maximal scenario (or total way for things to be) is the question of whether a given alternative maximal scenario is a scenario that might have obtained (a way things might have been), and we note that on every consistent maximal scenario it itself is the only maximal scenario that obtains, we may prove that every necessary fact of a consistent maximal scenario *w* obtains in a given alternative maximal scenario *w'* if and only if on scenario *w, w'* is a scenario that might have obtained. (If "maximal" scenarios are sets of such things as purported facts, then such facts as that an alternative maximal scenario is a maximal scenario that might have obtained will be meta-facts, which obtain according to the given set of facts not by being included directly as elements of the set but only implicitly by virtue of the facts that are included in the set.) If we confine our attention to consistent maximal scenarios, we may thus put our "definition" another way: to say that a maximal scenario (or total way for things to be) *w'* is *metaphysically possible relative to* a consistent maximal scenario *w* is to say that on scenario *w, w'* is a scenario that might have obtained (a way things might have been). More simply, a world *w'* is accessible to a consistent world *w* if and only if *w'* is possible in *w*. Being 'accessible to' or 'possible relative to' a consistent world is simply being possible *according to* that world, nothing more and nothing less. On this conception, what is possible and what is necessary at a given world is not imposed from above by a mysterious and unanalyzed accessibility relation among worlds; rather, a world's accessibility relations to other worlds is internal to the world, *via* the possibilities at that world.[12]

---

[12] Lewis's complaint that 'we look in vain, in . . . many . . . places, for an account of what it means to deny that some world is "relatively possible"' is unjustified. The definition I propose here of the accessibility relation is the natural one, and as Saul Kripke pointed out to me, it follows

It follows, given this conception, that a proposition is metaphysically necessary according to a consistent world w if and only if it is true in every world metaphysically possible relative to w, and a proposition is metaphysically possible according to a consistent world w if and only if it is true in at least one world metaphysically possible relative to w. These are not definitions of metaphysical necessity and possibility. They are theorems that follow from the definition of relative possibility. One must have a prior understanding of metaphysical modality in order to grasp the notion of it being the case that everything that *must* be so on one scenario is so on another scenario (the notion of one world being *possible relative to* another)—as well as the closely related notion of it being the case on one scenario that another scenario is a scenario that *might have* obtained (the notion of one world being *possible according to* another). The idea that the notion of a possible world comes first, and explains the notion of metaphysical modality, is of a piece with the same mythology that gave us the idea that metaphysical necessity is truth in every world whatsoever, without restriction. The notion of metaphysical modality comes first, and like every notion of modality, it is restricted.

There is one alternative yet to be considered. One may choose to ignore ways things could not have been, confining one's sights always and without exception to ways things actually might have been. One may stipulate that a proposition is necessary with respect to an arbitrary possible world w if and only if it is true in every world accessible to the actual world—never mind worlds accessible to w—and likewise that a proposition is possible with respect to an arbitrary possible world w if and only if it is true in at least one world accessible to the actual world. One may accordingly declare it impossible that Woody even *might have* originated from m, since one is ignoring possibly possible but impossible worlds like W, worlds that are once removed from the actual world on the scale of accessibility and in which Woody originates from m. One may then ignore accessibility altogether. We have finally zeroed in on $S5$ modal logic.

precisely the characterization of accessibility that he had offered originally in 'Semantical Analysis of Modal Logic I: Normal Modal Propositional Calculi,' *Zeitschrift für Mathematische Logik und Grundlagen der Mathematik*, 9 (1963), pp. 67–96, at p. 70; and again in 'Semantical Considerations on Modal Logic,' in L. Linsky, ed., *Reference and Modality* (New York, NY: Oxford University Press, 1971), pp. 63–72, at p. 64. There is no suggestion in these pioneering works that such subsystems as *T*, *B*, or *S4* arise from special restrictions on metaphysical modality; instead accessibility is explained in terms of propositions being (metaphysically) possible in worlds. Kripke has informed me (in discussion and personal correspondence) that he is sympathetic to many of the positions advanced in this paper, having seriously considered whether the conventional presupposition that the basic modal logic is *S5* is justified. He now believes he should have stressed both that his use of an accessibility relation does not make 'possible' (as applied to worlds) into a dyadic predicate any more than the natural treatment of baldness in possible-world discourse as a binary relation between individuals and worlds makes "is bald" into a dyadic predicate, and that unless we have *S4*, strictly speaking, many of the worlds are not "possible," but only "possibly possible," and so on. Whereas Kripke shares some of my controversial views concerning the logic of metaphysical modality, he is not fully convinced that *S4* modal logic is invalidated in cases like that involving Woody and m (though he tells me he is nearly convinced). *Cf. Naming and Necessity*, p. 51n. See also *Reference and Essence*, pp. 240–252; and 'Modal Paradox: Parts and Counterparts, Points and Counterpoints,' especially pp. 89–95.

This is the ostrich approach to metaphysical modality. It is not a very happy alternative.[13] The ostrich approach flies in the face of the very meanings of the words 'necessary' and 'possible.' On any standard or conventional sense of 'possible' in English, a sentence of the form 'It is possible that such-and-such' is true if there is a possible (in the same sense) scenario, a way things might have been, according to which it is the case that such-and-such. Certainly this is so with respect to the metaphysical sense of 'possible.' Likewise, in English, it is simply incorrect to say "It is necessary that such-and-such" when there is a possible scenario according to which it is not the case that such-and-such. In particular, therefore, as long as there is a possible scenario according to which it is possible for Woody to have originated from m, it is true (in English) to say 'It is possible that it is possible that Woody originates from m,' and one cannot correctly say (in English) 'It is necessary that it is necessary that Woody does not originate from m' (or 'It is impossible that Woody *might have* originated from m'). If the possible scenarios (such as W') that verify a possibility claim or falsify a necessity claim draw our attention to inaccessible worlds, then we are obliged to pay attention to those inaccessible worlds. We ignore them to our own detriment, counting what is true false and what is false true.

Surprisingly, the ostrich approach has nevertheless ascended to the status of orthodoxy. It is precisely the approach followed by my critics. The most obvious sign of the ostrich approach is the explicit denial of impossible worlds, but there are a number of additional signs, several of which manifest themselves in the objection presented in Section II above. If one ignores impossible worlds altogether, then ways things might have been are the only ways for things to be that are left. The distinction between the generic notion and the modal notion loses all significance. If one confines one's sights to genuinely possible worlds, disavowing the impossible worlds, then metaphysical modality emerges as the limiting case—the "unrestricted" modality that takes account of "every" world—and $S5$ emerges as its proper logic. Metaphysical modality appears unrestricted because the restriction to metaphysically possible worlds is already built into one's practice concerning which worlds to pay attention to and to quantify over. If certain entities are ignored entirely and always, then they are not even seen as things that are ignored. Since there is no possible world in which Woody originates from m, and possible worlds are the only worlds taken into consideration, one will insist that it is necessary that it is necessary that Woody does not originate from m, and that it is necessary that it is necessary that it is necessary... that Woody does not so originate, with as many iterations as one pleases. If some iconoclast comes along and argues that some worlds are inaccessible and that in some of these Woody originates from m, those who ignore impossible worlds altogether will be puzzled as to what this philosopher could possibly mean by 'inaccessible,' and hence by 'possible' and 'might have.' Whatever restricted sort of modality the modal iconoclast means by these terms, it would seem to be based on some completely unexplained restriction among the *possible* worlds, for these are the only worlds that are ever considered. When the modal iconoclast protests that in

---

[13] In *Reference and Essence* I referred (p. 239) to this philosophical position as 'a narrow-minded form of modal ethnocentrism.'

pleading for inaccessible worlds he is not talking about a special and peculiar sort of possible world but about worlds of a sort entirely ignored by the friends of *S5*, those who ignore these worlds will shrug and dismiss these protests as lacking in substance. For in restricting their quantifications over worlds always to possible worlds, they can hardly help but misconstrue the modal iconoclast's claims concerning worlds in general, misinterpreting them as puzzling claims concerning possible worlds. Since he maintains that there are worlds in which Woody does indeed originate from *m*, the modal iconoclast is seen by those who quantify over only possible worlds as capitulating to anti-essentialism. Any such worlds would have to be possible, no matter what the modal iconoclast may mean by calling them 'inaccessible,' since no other type of world is ever recognized and quantified over, no matter what anyone says. The situation is not unlike that of a philosopher who tries to persuade a pure set theorist, whose quantifiers range only over sets, of the existence of ur-elements (non-set elements), and who is misunderstood as rejecting Extensionality by postulating a plurality of empty sets.

The practice in modal semantics of ignoring worlds that are not possible according to the actual world leads theorists into understanding something different with the use of our terms 'necessary' and 'possible' from what they mean in English. Specifically, the ostrich approach misconstrues the simple modal term 'necessary' to mean the modally complex concept of *actual* necessity, or necessity according to $W_@$, where $W_@$ is the actual world. Likewise, the ostrich approach misconstrues 'possible' to mean *actual* possibility, or possibility according to $W_@$. The simple modal concepts of necessity and possibility *simpliciter*—the real meanings of the simple modal terms 'necessary' and 'possible'—are not the same as the concepts of actual necessity and actual possibility, necessity and possibility according to the actual world. In exactly the same way, the concept of a philosopher is not the same as that of an actual philosopher. The difference shows up in modal contexts. Whereas it was not necessary for Saul Kripke to have been a philosopher, he actually is a philosopher and hence (in the indexical sense of 'actually') it is necessary that he be *actually* a philosopher—since in every possible world, the actual world (indexical sense again) is one in which he is a philosopher. Likewise, whereas it is not necessary that it be necessary that Woody not originate from *m*, it is actually necessary that Woody does not so originate, and hence it is necessary that it be *actually* necessary that Woody does not so originate. In effect, the ostrich approach prevents us from speaking of nested modalities altogether, instructing us to misconstrue iterations of modal operators in our speech as redundant embellishments that make no significant contribution to cognitive information content, as mere stuttering. But ignoring impossible worlds does not make them go away, and reinterpreting someone's words to mean what they do not in fact mean does not make the actual meaning go away. Although Woody's originating from *m* is impossible, the presence of worlds such as *W*, in which Woody originates from *m* (and hence, which are impossible) but which are possible according to some possible worlds, makes *something* true as regards the prospect of Woody's so originating. This *something* is expressed in English by saying that the prospect in question is 'possibly possible.' The *S5* theorist's misconstrual of English makes nested modality unseen, but it does not make nested modality vanish. The modal iconoclast may echo the words of his colleague: In these questions of haecceitism and essence, by what right do we ignore worlds that are inaccessible? Accessible or not, they're still worlds. Why don't they count? Ignoring all the possibly possible worlds where such-and-such obnoxious things happen, it is impossible that such things even *might* happen. Yes. Small comfort.

The ostrich approach may offer comfort of sorts, but certainly no illumination. It is not I who ignore inaccessible worlds. I acknowledge them and give them their full due, no more and no less. It is my critic, the friend of $S5$, who ignores them altogether. In pleading for inaccessible worlds, I am not drawing an unexplained distinction among the worlds that my opponents recognize, and proposing to ignore those on one side of the undefined boundary line. I am calling attention to worlds to which my opponents pay no attention (other than to repudiate).

V

The world W, in which Woody originates from m, is a way things could not have been. Nevertheless, there is a way things might have been, W', in which Woody originates from m' instead of from m^*, and in (according to, relative to, from the point of view of) W', W is a way things might have been, as is the way things actually are. The denial of this is highly counterintuitive.[14] The impossible world W is thus only contingently impossible. No doubt it is an essential property of any way things could not have been that it is a way for things to be. And of course, some impossible worlds (such as a world according to which I am a credit card account) are essentially impossible. But others are not. Similarly, it is only a contingent fact about W' that it is a way things might have been rather than a way things could not have been. For there is some matter m'' that Woody might have originated from in lieu of m^*, and that differs considerably enough from m' (though overlapping just enough with the actual original matter m^* to remain a possibility for Woody's origin) that if Woody had originated from m'', it would then have been impossible for Woody to have originated from m'.[15] Let W'' be a possible world in which

---

[14] I am ignoring here the complications introduced by indeterminacies and regions of vagueness. These complications complicate, but do not significantly alter, the points I am making. Roughly, the idea is that it may in some cases be neither true nor false according to a world w (owing to vagueness in the notion of metaphysical necessity) whether a certain fact obtaining in w is necessary. This, in turn, would inject some indeterminacy into the accessibility relation, so that some worlds may be neither definitely possible nor definitely impossible relative to others. These complications are discussed in some detail in 'Modal Paradox: Parts and Counterparts, Points and Counterpoints.'

[15] As long as some overlap is required and total replacement prohibited, such matter is always possible. Since m' is a possibility for Woody, there will be some overlap between m^* and m'. Simply replace as much of m^*'s overlap with m' as allowable with completely new matter, while preserving the remainder of m^*, including the entire portion of m^* replaced in m'. The resulting matter is m''. It differs from m' by more than the difference between m^* and m', since it fully restores all of m^*'s matter that was replaced in m'—it duplicates the entire difference between m^* and m'—and in addition replaces some of the remaining matter of m' with new matter. If the proportion of required overlap is more than one-half (as seems reasonable), some overlap between m'' and m' will remain, but not enough. Since the matter in m^* that was replaced in m' has been restored in full, and the maximal replacement by new matter is effected entirely elsewhere in m', the resulting matter m'' exceeds the allowable nonoverlap with m' by exactly the restored matter of m^*.

Woody originates from m''. From the point of view of W'', W' is impossible. Perhaps the actual world is essentially possible. (That is, it may be that the actual world is possible relative to every world possible relative to it.) Even so, some possible worlds are like W', only contingently possible. Whether a world is possible or not can be a question of contingent fact like any other question of contingent fact.

This sort of consideration uncovers the fallacy in the "proof," presented in Section II, of the characteristic $S5$ principle that any possible truth is necessarily possible. The argument was that if a proposition p is true in some possible world w, then no matter what possible world one considers, from its point of view p is true in at least one possible world, namely w, so that in the metaphysical sense of 'possible' (in which one possible world in which p is true is all that is required for p to be possible with respect to any given world), if p is possible it is necessarily possible. This argument is framed with an ambiguous usage of the phrase 'possible world,' indiscriminately meaning either a way for things to be or a way things might have been. The argument is therefore susceptible to two conflicting interpretations. Since our concern is with the logic of what might have been, the argument is of considerably greater philosophical significance when it is interpreted as concerning genuinely possible worlds, rather than worlds in general. Under this interpretation the argument fallaciously presupposes that worlds that are possible in the actual here-and-now are also possible even according to alternative possible worlds.[16] This assumption, though perhaps understandable given the common confusion between possible worlds and worlds in general, is intuitively incorrect. The standard "proofs" of the characteristic B and $S4$ principles likewise involve equivocation between the generic and properly modal sense of the phrase 'possible world,' resulting in fallacious presuppositions concerning the essentiality of the property of being a possible world (B) or that of not being a possible world ($S4$).

Believers in $S5$ as a correct system of reasoning (in propositional logic) about what might have been must claim that it is an essential property of any way things might have been that things might have been that way. Similarly, believers in the weaker $S4$ modal logic (and hence also believers in $S5$) must claim that it is an essential property of any way things could not have been that things could not have been that way. Believers in B modal logic (and hence also believers in $S5$) must claim that it is an essential property of the way things actually are that things might have been that way. These claims are versions of essentialism. They are doctrines to the effect that certain properties (in this case, certain modal properties) of certain sorts of things (possible worlds, impossible worlds, and the actual world, respectively) are properties that these things could not fail to have. More than this, since their claim is that $S5$, $S4$, or B is a correct *logic* of what might have been and of what must be, the

---

[16] When the purported 'proof' of the characteristic $S5$ principle is interpreted instead (less interestingly) as concerning all worlds without exception, whether genuinely possible or not, it commits a similar error. Under this interpretation the argument fallaciously presupposes that worlds that are available in the actual here-and-now as ones in which a given proposition is true remain available as such even according to alternative impossible worlds. Let w be a world in which a given proposition p is true. One cannot correctly conclude that no matter what world one considers, possible or not, w is still one world in which p is true. There are radically impossible worlds according to which p is not true in w or in any other world.

essentialism espoused must be held to be not merely metaphysically true but true by the very *logic* of (metaphysical) necessity and possibility. The essentialism must be held to be not the metaphysically substantive sort of essentialism that requires Woody not to originate from *m* and me not to be a credit card account, but the minimal, vacuous, and trivial sort of essentialism that requires Woody to be such as to originate or not originate from *m*, that requires me not to be somebody other than myself, that requires Mars not to be such as to contain life and not to contain life at the same time. This does not weaken the import of the essentialist claims. On the contrary, the logical nature of the claims makes them extremely strong versions of essentialism. The claim is not merely that such-and-such worlds are essentially thus-and-so, but that they are essentially thus-and-so *by logic alone*. It is not merely by virtue of the laws of metaphysics that these worlds are supposed to be essentially thus-and-so, but by virtue of the very laws of logic and nothing more. The doctrine that some properties of some things are properties that on logical grounds alone these things could not fail to have is by itself the most trivial type of essentialism—because it is entirely nonspecific. The doctrine that *such-and-such* properties of *so-and-so* things are properties that on logical grounds alone these things could not fail to have is a horse of a different color. The logical essentialism concerning worlds that the friends of *S5, S4,* and *B* are committed to is some seriously committed essentialism. It is essentialism of the most committed type.

In fact, the logical essentialism concerning worlds that the friends of stronger modal logics are committed to seems intuitively false. At the very least, it requires substantial justification. The possible world *W'* is a way things are not but might have been; it is a way-for-things-to-be that is not realized, but might have been realized. This is just to say that it is a contingent or accidental feature of *W'* that it is a way things are not rather than the way things are. I have argued that the accidentalness of the property of being realized is extendible to the modal properties of possibly being realized and of not possibly being realized. Certainly it seems to be logically possible—not precluded by the principles of correct reasoning about modality—that a way-for-things-to-be that might have been realized might have been instead a way-for-things-to-be that could not have been realized, and that a way-for-things-to-be that could not have been realized might have been instead a way-for-things-to-be that might have been realized. The friends of *B* modal logic commit themselves to the loaded claim that it is logically true that the property of possibly being realized (or of being a way things might have been) is an essential property of the actual world. The friends of *S4* modal logic commit themselves to the similarly loaded claim that it is logically true that the property of not possibly being realized is always an essential property of those worlds that have it. The friends of *S5* modal logic commit themselves to the double-barreled claim that it is logically true that both the properties of possibly being realized and of not possibly being realized are always essential properties of the worlds that have them. Yet all admit that the property of being realized is merely an accidental property that possible worlds can have or lack. What, then, is the rationale for their extremely strong versions of logical essentialism? Why should the modal properties of possibly being realized and of not possibly being realized be any less contingent or accidental, from the point of view of pure logic, than the nonmodal properties of being realized and of not being realized? These alleged logical truths do not *seem* logically true. Indeed, the last two alleged logical truths, I have argued, are false. The first alleged logical truth, even if it is true, and even if it is necessarily true, does not seem logically true. Surely the burden of proof falls on the logical essentialists with respect to modal properties. We have just seen that the standard 'proofs' of the characteristic *B*, *S4*, and *S5* axioms are in fact fallacious, since they assume that any possible world is essentially a possible world (or, in the case of *S4*, that anything that is not a possible world is essentially not a possible world). Whereas this may be trivially true in the generic sense of 'possible world,' it simply begs the question in the modal sense. The reasoning involved in any purported justification of the contentious doctrine of logical essentialism with respect to modal properties cannot make use of such modal logics as *B*, *S4*, or *S5*—any more than induction can be justified to the Humean skeptic by citing inductive evidence. The systems *B*, *S4*, and *S5* for reasoning about what might have been are precisely what are at issue.

We friends of *T* modal logic are committed to the claim that it is logically true that the actual world has the property of possibly being realized, that as a matter of logic alone, the way things are is a way things might have been. Here we have something that is transparently logically true. Quite plainly, anyone who cannot recognize the validity of an inference from an assertion that it must be that such-and-such to the assertion that such-and-such, does not know how to reason correctly about what must be; and anyone who cannot recognize the validity of an inference from an assertion that such-and-such to the assertion that it might have been that such-and-such does not know how to reason correctly about what might have been. Even the characteristic *B* principle, which may well be necessarily true, does not seem logically true. A proper justification for *B* as a system of modal logic, as opposed to a justification for *B* as a *metaphysical theory* of modality, would require not merely a defense of the truth of the essentialist doctrine that the actual world is necessarily possible, and not merely a philosophical argument that the doctrine is indeed a necessary truth, but a convincing case that the doctrine is, like the characteristic principle of *T*, required by logic and nothing more. Until such a justification is provided, modal reasoning in accordance with *B* is not to be recommended—except, of course, insofar as one is prepared to accept a commitment to a certain metaphysical theory. Even then, the *B* "axioms" would not be logical axioms, properly so-called, but metaphysical postulates or premise.

If the modal logical systems *B*, *S4*, and *S5* have never been satisfactorily justified, why are they almost universally accepted as correct systems for reasoning about what must be and what might have been? I have already cited several sources of the present confused state of affairs in contemporary philosophical logic. First, there is the generic-modal ambiguity in the phrase 'possible world,' which has led to the widely accepted myths that the concepts of metaphysical necessity and possibility are defined in terms of, or constructed from, the concept of a possible world and that metaphysical modality is unrestricted modality. Equivocation between these two senses of 'possible world' has led to the fallacious "proofs" of the characteristic *B*, *S4*, and *S5* principles. These fallacious arguments very likely owe something also to another source of confusion in contemporary philosophical logic: the widely adopted ostrich approach to modality, with its consequent misconstrual of 'necessarily' as meaning actual necessity and 'possibly' as meaning actual possibility. In fact, if the indexical sentential operator 'actually' is added to the modal resources of a language, with appropriate logical axioms and restrictions governing its use in modal reasoning, while retaining only the weak modal system T for the underlying logic of 'necessarily' and 'possibly,' exact analogues to the characteristic axioms and rules of T, B, $S4$, and $S5$ emerge as trivial theorems for the special complex modal operators 'actually necessarily' and 'actually possibly.' In this sense, $S5$ (as the logic of 'actually necessarily' and 'actually possibly') is a subtheory of T plus the modal logic of 'actually.'[17] Given its misconstrual of 'necessarily' and 'possibly,' the ostrich approach thus inevitably leads to the acceptance of $S5$ as the correct logic for these modal operators.

My claim is this: the sort of consideration raised in Section I above *demonstrates* the invalidity of $S4$ modal reasoning. I am not proposing a rejection of $S4$ in an *ad hoc* manner, as merely an effective measure for avoiding the difficulty, with no further justification beyond the fact that it avoids the difficulty. The difficulty stems from a widely shared modal intuition, to the effect that some small variation in the origin of a material artifact is possible whereas complete variation is impossible. Even if one does not share this intuition, however, it should be quite obvious that the modal position of one (such as myself) who canonizes the intuition into metaphysical doctrine is at least coherent. The position cannot be summarily dismissed on logical grounds alone, as one would (rightly) dismiss the position of someone who proposes restricting the inference rule of *modus ponens* or denying the Law of Noncontradiction or rejecting the characteristic principles of T. If the modal position in question seemed not only false but incoherent, a proposal to reject $S4$

---

[17] The observation made in the last two sentences derived in part from a fruitful discussion in Dubrovnik with Timothy Williamson (who does not fully endorse the views defended in this article). Williamson correctly observed that although infinitely iterated necessity and infinitely iterated possibility are modal operators for which the analogue of $S4$ is derivable as a subtheory using only T as the underlying logic of 'necessarily' and 'possibly,' the analogues of B and $S5$ are not thus derivable, since the infinitely iterated modalities replace ordinary accessibility by its ancestral, which is automatically transitive but which is not logically required to be symmetric if ordinary accessibility is not. Williamson wondered whether, on my view, there is any modal operator that is definable in terms of 'necessarily,' and for which the analogue of $S5$ is derivable as a subtheory using only T as the underlying logic of 'necessarily.' The answer I proposed was: 'actually necessarily.' (See also note 9 above.)

One characteristic axiom schema of the logic of 'actually' is ⌜actually $\phi \supset \Box$actuallyϕ⌝. Another is ⌜$\phi \equiv$ actuallyϕ⌝. Application of the rule of necessitation must be restricted to subsidiary proofs that do not invoke the latter axiom.

Williamson's observation generates one serious difficulty for a claim that is often made in response to my arguments and which is closely bound to the myth that metaphysical modality is completely unrestricted: that the logic of necessity and possibility *has to* be $S5$ because 'necessarily' really means what I am calling 'infinitely iterated necessity' and 'possibly' really means what I am calling 'infinitely iterated possibility.' The logic of what I am calling the 'infinitely iterated modalities' would seem to be not $S5$ but $S4$. (A more immediate difficulty with the suggested interpretation is its intrinsic implausibility. For example, it rejects the intuition that, necessarily, Woody might have originated from any wood that is only one molecule different from its original wood but could not have originated from entirely different wood, as not merely false but literally inconsistent.)

modal logic solely on the basis of the modal intuition in question would indeed be drastic and poorly motivated. But the mere logical possibility, as opposed to the truth, of the modal intuition is beyond all reasonable doubt. Mere logical possibility, as opposed to truth, is what my argument against *S4* requires. The position outlined in Section I yields a *model* or *interpretation* that both respects the intended interpretation of the logical constants, including 'necessarily' (see note 2), and invalidates *S4*. Due consideration of this difficulty makes it *intuitively* plain that *S4* modal reasoning involves a fallacy. Every attempt that I am aware of to retain *S4* modal logic in the face of this difficulty is distinctly counterintuitive.[18] The sort of consideration raised in Section I *exposes* a certain modal *fallacy*, that of inferring the iterated necessity claim 'It must be that it must be that such-and-such' from the weaker claim 'It must be that such-and-such.' Elsewhere I have called this 'the fallacy of necessity iteration.' This fallacy is the very cornerstone of *S4* modal logic.

[18] By far the most popular such attempt is the proposal—made or suggested by Roderick Chisholm, Graeme Forbes, Anil Gupta, Saul Kripke, and Robert Stalnaker (to name but a few)—to replace standard modal semantics with some form or other of counterpart-theoretic modal semantics, as championed by David Lewis. (Kripke's suggestion of a counterpart-theoretic treatment for philosophical problems of the sort engendered by Woody *vis-à-vis* the matter *m* is made more or less in passing, amid an emphatic rejection of counterpart theory for less problematic modal contexts. See note 12 above.) This alternative system of modal semantics allows for the retention of *S5* modal propositional logic, at a considerable cost. For an accounting of the costs involved, see 'Modal Paradox: Parts and Counterparts, Points and Counterpoints.'

PART III

IDENTITY

8

The Fact that $x = y$ (1987)

The central objection raised by Cook in 'Difference at Origin'[1] against the position advocated by Hugh Chandler and me seems to depend on the plausible and philosophically popular metaphysical thesis that, where x is a possible individual from a possible world w_1 and y is a possible individual from a possible world w_2, if $x = y$ then there must be something in the qualitative nature of x and y, as they are in these worlds, that makes this so, some fact about the qualitative character of x in w_1 and y in w_2 in virtue of which they are identical. This thesis (which is one of various theses that go by the name 'anti-haecceitism') is false. In fact, despite its popularity and *prima facie* appeal, precisely the opposite is (virtually) provable: where x is a possible individual from a possible world w_1 and y is a possible individual from a possible world w_2, if $x = y$ then there is no fact about their qualitative character (as they are in these worlds) in virtue of which this is so, and there is nothing in the qualitative nature of x and y, other than their mere possible existence, that makes them identical. For surely there is no qualitative fact about x, other than the fact of its possible existence, in virtue of which $x = x$. That is, x is such that there is nothing in its qualitative character (in any possible world) that makes x identical with it. It follows by Leibniz's Law that if $x = y$, then y is also such that there is nothing in its qualitative character that makes x identical with it. Therefore, if $x = y$, then there is nothing in x's, i.e. y's, qualitative character that makes $x = y$. Q.E.D.

The very same proof applies *mutatis mutandis* against an almost universally accepted thesis which underlies the great bulk of the extant philosophical literature on identity over time with regard to artifacts and persons (and which might be called 'transtemporal anti-haecceitism'). This is the metaphysical thesis that, where x is a (past, present, or future) individual from a time t_1 and y is a (past, present, or future) individual from a later time t_2, if $x = y$ then there must be some qualitative transtemporal relation between x at t_1 and y at t_2 that makes this so, some transtemporal facts about x and y in virtue of which they are identical—such as facts concerning spatiotemporally "continuous" or gradual transitional change linking x to y during the period from t_1 to t_2, where x and y are physical objects, or facts concerning y's memories and continuation of past experiences that connect with x, where x and y are persons. No such transtemporal facts ground the identity of x with itself. Hence, if $x = y$, then y must be like x in the respect that no such transtemporal facts ground x's identity with it.

[1] *Philosophia* (Israel), 17, 4 (December 1987), pp. 126–132.

These conclusions are not as strange as they may appear. If $x \neq y$, then there is no such thing as the (possible) *fact* that $x = y$. The fact that $x = y$, if such a thing is indeed a *fact*, is just the fact that $x = x$. These are the very same fact, described two different ways. Described as 'the fact that $x = x$', it is quite obvious that this fact obtains solely in virtue of logic and logic's applicability to x, and not in virtue of any further fact concerning the possible qualitative character or history of x. The same thing is true of this fact (even if it is less obvious) when it is described as 'the fact that $x = y$', assuming there is such a (possible) fact.[2]

---

[2] The letters 'x' and 'y' are, of course, free variables throughout. The proofs apply no matter what values are assigned to these variables. The proofs can be extended unaltered to cases in which the variables are replaced with individual constants, indexicals, pronouns, or proper names (or any combination), but not to cases in which one (or both) of the variables is replaced with a definite description, because of a needed restriction on substitutivity (via Leibniz's Law or 'λ'-conversion) in such cases. For further relevant details see my 'Modal Paradox: Parts and Counterparts, Points and Counterpoints,' in P. French, T. Uehling, and H. Wettstein, eds., *Midwest Studies in Philosophy XI: Studies in Essentialism* (Minneapolis: University of Minnesota Press, 1986), pp. 75–120, and especially in the appendix thereto, at pp. 110–113.

9

This Side of Paradox (1993)

In his intriguing book, *Identity and Discrimination*, Timothy Williamson presents a modified version of a philosophical problem about modality sometimes called 'Chisholm's Paradox'.[1] Williamson proffers a solution based on the apparatus developed in the book, a solution that is at odds with an alternative solution to Chisholm's Paradox that I have defended and developed in a series of essays. Williamson argues[2] that his proposed solution is superior to mine, since it is tailored to handle a variety of philosophical difficulties involving identity, including the original version of Chisholm's Paradox, whereas my solution to the latter involves controversial general claims about modality that are altogether irrelevant to his own version of the paradox. Consider, then, a version of Chisholm's Paradox that I have presented in earlier work.[3] It proceeds from the following two modal principles:

(A) If a wooden table x is the only table originally formed from a hunk of matter y according to a certain plan P, and y' is any distinct (possibly scattered) hunk of matter that very extensively (sufficiently) overlaps y and has exactly the same mass, volume, and chemical composition as y, then x is such that it might have been the only table originally formed according to the same plan P from y' instead of from y.

(B) If a wooden table x is the only table originally formed from a hunk of matter y, and z is any hunk of matter that does not very extensively (sufficiently) overlap y, then x is such that it could not have been the only table originally formed from z instead of from y.

Principle (A) is a principle of modal tolerance; principle (B) is one of modal intolerance, or essentialism.[4] Chisholm's Paradox starts with the exceedingly

I thank John Birmingham, David Cowles, Graeme Forbes, Bernie Kobes, Michael White, Stephen Yablo, and my audience at Arizona State University for their insightful comments on an earlier draft. I am especially grateful to Timothy Williamson for correspondence.

[1] Timothy Williamson, *Identity and Discrimination* (Oxford: Basil Blackwell, 1990), pp. 126–143. A version of the paradox was apparently first noted by Saul Kripke, in *Naming and Necessity* (Cambridge, Mass.: Harvard University Press, 1980), p. 51n. 18, where it is briefly discussed. Something directly akin to this paradox was also noted and discussed by Roderick Chisholm in 'Parts as Essential to their Wholes,' *Review of Metaphysics*, 26 (1973), pp. 584–586. The paradox is highly reminiscent of Chisholm's paradoxical queries concerning cross-world identity in his seminal 'Identity Through Possible Worlds: Some Questions,' *Noûs*, 1 (1967), pp. 1–8.

[2] *Identity and Discrimination*, pp. 127, 135, and 142.

[3] Nathan Salmon, 'Modal Paradox: Parts and Counterparts, Points and Counterpoints,' *Midwest Studies in Philosophy XI: Studies in Essentialism* (Minneapolis: University of Minnesota Press, 1986), pp. 80–81. See the first endnote of that work for further bibliographical references.

[4] These are the principles labelled '(II)' and '(III)', respectively, in 'Modal Paradox.' See p. 75 of that work for further modal principles more fundamental than these two. (Thanks to Theodore Guleserian for pointing out the need for a more careful formulation than I had originally given.)

plausible assumption that these two modal principles are not true merely as an accidental matter of contingent fact, but are necessary truths. Furthermore, principle (A), at least, is such that if it is true at all, then it is necessary that it is necessarily true, and it is necessary that it is necessary that it is necessarily true, and so on *ad infinitum*. In fact, on the conventionally accepted system S5 of modal propositional logic, any proposition is such that if it is necessarily true, then it is necessary that it is necessarily true, and it is necessary that it is necessary that it is necessarily true, and so on. The paradox consists in a modal propositional argument, which I call '(CP)'. The argument, which is valid in S5, has numerous premises, all of which seem true, and an explicit contradiction as a conclusion. The first premise is the following:

(P_0) a is the only table originally formed from hunk of wood h_0 according to such and such a plan.

This is to be true by hypothesis. Let n be the total number of molecules in hunk h_0. We consider a sequence of (possibly scattered) hunks of wood $h_0, h_1, \ldots, h_n$, where each successive hunk of wood in the sequence differs from its predecessor by only one molecule, qualitatively identical to the one it replaces, in such a way that the final hunk h_n has not a single molecule in common with table a's original wood h_0. Premise (P_0) is then joined by n premises of the following form, each of which is derived on the basis of the necessitation of principle (A), where $0 \leq i < n$:

(P_{i+1}) Necessarily, if a is the only table originally formed from hunk h_i according to such and such a plan, then it is possible that a is the only table originally formed instead from hunk h_{i+1} according to the same plan.

These premises are followed finally by the premise,

(P_{n+1}) It is impossible for a to be the only table originally formed from hunk h_n according to such and such a plan,

which is derived from principle (B). The derivation of the contradictory conjunction of (P_{n+1}) together with that which (P_{n+1}) denies from the premises of (CP) is, in some sense, the canonical form of Chisholm's Paradox.

The solution I endorse (following Hugh Chandler) is based on a rejection of the S4 axiom, and hence also the S5 axiom, of classical modal logic.[5] In its absence, the premises of (CP) have no philosophically interesting consequences. A very interesting, and enlightening, consequence is generated, however, if each premise (P_{i+1}) is modified by replacing its initial single occurrence of the modal auxiliary 'necessarily' with i or more iterated occurrences—a switch that can be justified on the basis of the infinitely iterated necessitation of (A). In the absence of S4, the modified premises

[5] *Cf.* Hugh Chandler, 'Plantinga and the Contingently Possible,' *Analysis*, 36 (1976), pp. 106–109. The S4 axiom is, in effect, the claim that if it is possible that it is possible that p, then it is possible that p. The S5 axiom is the claim that if it is possible that it is necessary that p, then it is necessary that p. The B axiom is the claim that if it is possible that it is necessary that p, then p. The S5 axiom entails both the B axiom and the S4 axiom in the weak modal logic T. In 'The Logic of What Might Have Been,' *The Philosophical Review*, 98 (1989), pp. 3–34, I extend the fundamental argument against S4 (and S5) into a challenge to B propositional modal logic as well. (The work includes a lengthy bibliography.)

taken together with the initial premise (P_0) still do not have the consequence that it is possible for *a* to be the only table originally formed from hunk h_n, but a weaker consequence to the effect that the prospect of *a* being formed from h_n—which, according to (P_{n+1}), is impossible—is nevertheless possibly possibly possibly ... possible.

Williamson objects that we have no good reason to believe that any of the premises of the canonical version (*CP*) yield counterexamples to the *S4* axiom:

> For [the corresponding premise of analogous] temporal paradoxes are not counter-examples to the analogous principle that if it is at some time the case that it is at some time the case that *A* then it is at some time the case that *A*. They involve the failure of some other assumption; it will have a modal analogue; why should we suppose that the latter does not fail, and blame the *S4* principle instead? Salmon can point to the intuitive plausibility of the other modal assumptions, but he has not shown it to be any greater than the intuitive plausibility of their temporal analogues, at least one of which is false. For what it is worth, the present author's intuitions are equally strong in the two cases. Furthermore, the *S4* principle is not behind the modal paradox [presented here].[6]

The crucial wrinkle in Williamson's modified version of Chisholm's Paradox is that we do not begin with an actual artifact. This eliminates altogether the initial premise (P_0) of (*CP*). Instead we are asked to identify and distinguish merely possible artifacts that *would have been* constructed from various portions of matter.[7] A particular carpenter, whose job it is to construct a table from a single hunk of wood according to a specified plan, is repeatedly presented with the entire sequence of hunks $h_0, h_1, \ldots, h_n$ in rapid succession, alternating between sequential order and reverse sequential order. He need only pull a lever in order to select one hunk. Intending to choose at random, the carpenter dies suddenly just before making his selection.[8] Following Williamson's notation, let us abbreviate a modal description of the form 'the merely possible table that would have been the only table originally formed from hunk h_i, according to such and such a plan, had the carpenter selected that hunk and completed the job in that fashion' by '$o(h_i)$'. Intuitively, for each of the descriptions '$o(h_0)$', '$o(h_1)$', and so on, there is a unique possible table that the description designates (assuming each of the terms 'h_i' designates a specific hunk of wood, and ignoring any lingering doubts one may harbor about designating the nonexistent). Furthermore, in considering the differences between the would-be construction of a table from any hunk h_i and that from its immediate successor in the sequence, Williamson argues that, intuitively, such cross-world differences are

too slight to amount to the distinctness of their products. The very same [table] would be made in both cases, but out of marginally different material. ... The underlying intuition feels

---

[6] *Identity and Discrimination*, p. 142.

[7] Stephen Yablo informs me that John Drennan had presented a similar version of the paradox.

[8] Williamson's actual example involves fashioning a pair of semi-circular earrings by cutting along any diameter of a rotating metal disk. I have taken considerable liberties in modifying Williamson's example to make it more like the situation described in (*CP*). The various differences between Williamson's actual example and my modification of it are not differences on which Williamson places any emphasis. I believe that my modifications do not affect the philosophical points that either Williamson or I wish to make.

the same as that which gives plausibility to somewhat different principles such as Salmon's [modal principle (A)].[9]

Let (W) be the claim that the cross-world differences between the constructions of tables according to the same plan from neighboring hunks of wood are sufficiently slight to ensure the identity of their products. On its basis we obtain n equations of the form '$o(h_i) = o(h_{i+1})$' in place of the former premises (P_{i+1}). In place of the former final premise (P_{n+1}) we have '$o(h_0) \neq o(h_n)$'. Together these new premises entail a new contradiction in classical extensional logic, without any special modal axioms.

Williamson explicitly cites principle (A), seemingly approvingly, in support of the n equation premises. But recall that he also criticizes my solution to (CP), which challenges the modal reasoning involved, partly on the ground that analogous temporal paradoxes impugn the conjunction of modal assumptions involved in the premise of the argument. Williamson has confirmed that he accepts principle (B), and hence also the final premise (P_{n+1}) of (CP), while rejecting (A), or at least its necessitation, and hence also the conjunction of premises (P_1)–(P_n) of (CP) which are justified on its basis.[10] His solution to Chisholm's Paradox thus involves embracing a fairly intolerant form of mereological essentialism, in many respects similar to (though perhaps not as extreme as) Chisholm's own brand of essentialism.

Williamson likewise ultimately rejects the conjunction of the first n premises in his own version of the paradox. Indeed, in light of the extreme plausibility of the final premise (and the logic of identity), it should be clear that not all of the equation premises can be true.[11] The claim made by (W) must be mistaken. Williamson

---

[9] *Identity and Discrimination*, p. 129.   [10] In correspondence, January 1992.

[11] David Cowles has pointed out that the infinite necessitation of (B) is insufficient by itself to justify Williamson's final premise that $o(h_0) \neq o(h_n)$. It is logically possible (although very likely metaphysically impossible) that while (B) is necessary, and necessarily necessary, etc., the amount of variation possible in the original matter of a typical table exceeds one-half of the totality of its molecules. In that case, all of the first n premise may be true. Against this logical possibility, there are at least two ways that Williamson's final premise might be justified. One may simply note that the possible table that would have been the only table originally formed from hunk h_0 if *both* hunks h_0 and h_n had been simultaneously formed into two separate tables, both according to such and such a plan, is none other than $o(h_0)$, and likewise that the possible table that would have been the only table originally formed from hunk h_n if both h_0 and h_n had been simultaneously formed into two separate tables is $o(h_n)$. It immediately follows that $o(h_0) \neq o(h_n)$.

Stewart Cohen and David Cowles have pointed out that this argument does not also show that $o(h_0) \neq o(h_{n-1})$—unless $o(h_{n-1}) = o(h_n)$, or alternatively $o(h_0) = o(h_{-1})$, where h_{-1} is a hunk of matter just like h_0 except for the replacement of the one molecule common to both h_0 and $o(h_{n-1})$. In lieu of the above argument, one may invoke a suitable generalization of (B), such as the infinitely many principles given by the following schema:

> (B_i) If x is a wooden table and z is any hunk of matter that does not very extensively overlap any hunk of matter y such that it is possible^i that x is the only table originally formed from y, then x is such that necessarily$(^{i+1})$, it is not the only table originally formed from z instead of from y.

Here 'possibly^j' is a string of j occurrences of 'possibly', and similarly for 'necessarily^j'. (The original (B) corresponds to (B_0).) We now make the plausible assumption that the amount of variation possible in the original matter of a typical table is less than one-half of the totality of its molecules. (This assumption may even be strengthened to some extent without significant loss of plausibility.) Let w_0 be any of the 'nearest' possible worlds (those most like the actual world) in

utilizes his rich conceptual machinery to explain why that mistaken assumption seemed plausible.[12]

But he seriously overstates the case when he says categorically that *S4* modal logic is not behind this problem. There is a clear sense in which what I would deem untrue instances of the *S4* axiom are precisely what give the problem its air of paradox. I will explain.

Notice first a significant difference between (*CP*) and Williamson's version of the paradox. The latter, but not the former, is formulated in terms of the cross-world identity of possible tables, and indeed the elaborate apparatus that Williamson invokes to explain the intuitive appeal of the mistaken assumption (*W*) is explicitly designed for dealing with cases in which genuine identity is supplanted with certain sorts of approximations to identity. The primary question he poses is: 'Which portions of matter would constitute the same artifact?'[13] This is quite different from the questions posed at the beginning of his discussion of the modal and temporal paradoxes: 'How different could things have been, still being those things? How different could *they* have been?'[14] Although Chisholm originally cast his problem as one concerning identity across possible worlds, and although most others who have discussed the same or related problems (such as Kripke) have also posed those problems in terms of cross-world identity, identity is all but irrelevant to Chisholm's Paradox.[15] Certainly it is not a paradox *about* identity. In particular, the validity of (*CP*), unlike that of Williamson's replacement, does not depend in any way on the logic of identity. As I have argued elsewhere, Chisholm's Paradox is also not a sorites paradox, in the usual sense.[16] It is a paradox about modality.

What of the claimed analogy with the temporal paradoxes? Williamson's contention that the intuitive plausibility of the two modal principles involved in (*CP*) is no greater than that of their temporal analogues is incorrect. Williamson himself,

---

which the carpenter randomly selects hunk h_0. By our assumption, h_n does not sufficiently extensively overlap any hunk h_m that sufficiently extensively overlaps h_0. Hence, by the necessitation of (B_1), instantiated to w_0 (and the double necessitation of (B_0), doubly instantiated to worlds possible relative to w_0), there is no world possible relative to any world possible relative to w_0 in which the actual $o(h_0)$ originates instead from h_n. The actual world is clearly possible relative to w_0. Therefore, none of the nearest worlds in which the carpenter randomly selects hunk h_n is one in which the resulting table is $o(h_0)$.

[12] In the correspondence mentioned above in note 10, Williamson offered a similar account of the plausibility of the necessitation of (*A*). I sharply disagree not only with Williamson's rejection of modal tolerance, but also with this positive component of his account. The positive account includes the claim that each of the *n* equation premise of his own version of Chisholm's Paradox is neither determinately true nor determinately false, because all of the singular terms '$o(h_i)$'—and even much more basic terms like 'that table'— "fail of perfectly determinate reference" (pp. 133–134, 140–141). An alternative view is that each of the equation premises has a determinate truth-value, though it is not known which it has (over and above the knowledge that some or others are false). In the book Williamson dismisses this view as "scarcely credible" (p. 133). The former view, in fact, strikes the present writer as far less credible than the latter (partly in light of the central argument of the appendix to 'Modal Paradox,' pp. 110–114), though I am deliberately avoiding these issues here. (Williamson says that he is now more sympathetic to the latter view, though he continues to regard the former as a serious candidate.)   [13] *Identity and Discrimination*, p. 131.

[14] *Ibid.*, p. 126.   [15] *Cf.* 'Modal Paradox,' p. 93, last paragraph.
[16] 'Modal Paradox,' p. 89.

like many others, accepts principle (B). And he should; it is extremely plausible. In fact, it is surely true. Yet situations like that of the Ship of Theseus pose a very powerful intuitive challenge to a straightforward temporal analogue. Specifically, the familiar tale forcefully challenges the claim that the following is true even of a ship that will undergo extensive refurbishment:

If x is the only ship constituted (or the only ship originally constituted) by a hunk of matter y, and z is any hunk of matter that does not very extensively overlap y, then x is such that it is never the only ship constituted by z.

A great many philosophers share the view that temporal change is more tolerant than modal accident in regard to artifacts and organisms. A table or ship could not have originated from entirely different matter, but once it has been constructed, it is claimed, its material constitution could gradually change, as with a living body, into entirely different matter. Of course, some philosophers (and Williamson is evidently one) favor the status quo, by denying that artifacts have the capacity for total material change.[17] They embrace principles of temporal intolerance, like that displayed above, on intuitive grounds. But then such philosophers should, and probably would, automatically reject temporal analogues of the necessitation of (A), on the same grounds. Those grounds strike the present author as comparatively strikingly weak. Perhaps it is not altogether implausible that physical-object artifacts cannot undergo total material change. But just as it is an empirical question whether a living body routinely undergoes gradual total material change, we cannot rule it out *a priori* that tables and ships are forever undergoing rapid total refurbishment right under our very noses—perhaps because of the handiwork of very busy elves, or even of natural processes. By contrast, it does not seem implausible that we can rule it out *a priori* that a table that originated from a hunk of wood might have originated instead from entirely different matter. *A priori* or not, the conjunction of the necessitations of the original (A) and (B) is part of my own metaphysical doctrine. It is, at least, a coherent position. Its (relevant) temporal analogue is patently incoherent.

A better temporal analogy to the modal paradoxes arises by replacing the modal auxiliary 'necessarily' with a restricted temporal operator like 'at every moment within the interval from the preceding thirty minutes to the subsequent thirty minutes' and 'possibly' by 'at some moment within the interval from the preceding thirty minutes to the subsequent thirty minutes'.[18] One might then accept appropriate counterparts of the necessitations of both (A) and (B), even as applied to Theseus's ship.[19] At least they are consistent. Here, of course, the analogue of the *S4* principle clearly fails.

[17] This denial seems somewhat more plausible with regard to such things as languages, as with Williamson's Latin/Italian example (pp. 135–141). I find it considerably implausible with regard to living bodies, and altogether implausible with regard to Heraclitus's river.

[18] *Cf.* my 'Fregean Theory and the Four Worlds Paradox,' in *Philosophical Books*, 25 (1984), pp. 9–10. One may replace the word 'minute' by 'year' or even 'century', if doing so will help to make the point.

[19] In order to obtain the intended assumption, one must change the quantifier on 'y' in (A) to an existential, change the conditional to a conjunction, etc.

I accept the necessitations of both (*A*) and (*B*), and I argue from their joint truth—or merely from their joint coherence—to the invalidity of *S4* modal logic.[20] The rejection of *S4* is not supported merely on the grounds that it provides one way around Chisholm's Paradox. Even if there is a persuasive philosophical argument against principles like (*A*) and (*B*)—and I do not know of any—I would still argue that the position defined by the conjunction of the infinitely iterated necessitations of (*A*) and (*B*) is at least a coherent metaphysical position, and that *S4* modal logic is thereby *seen to be* fallacious. That metaphysical position demonstrates how it is logically possible for something to be possibly possible without being possible. The mere coherence of the position *exposes* the fallacy in *S4* modal logic—in something like the way that the overlooked possibility of empty general terms exposes the Aristotelian fallacy of inferring 'Some *S* are *P*' from 'All *S* are *P*'.

I have claimed that Williamson's version of the paradox is driven by the same logical fallacy that drives Chisholm's. Although the argument in Williamson's version of the paradox is classically valid in extensional logic, *S4* modal logic lies in hiding at the very heart of that paradox. The relevance of *S4* can be illustrated by means of a convenient (though by no means required) assumption. It is plausible that, although no hunk of wood is actually formed into a table by the carpenter, there is exactly one hunk $h_@$ such that if a selection had been made by the carpenter, it would have been of $h_@$. Notice that the fact that the carpenter would have selected 'at random' does not rule this out. Perhaps Williamson could construct the case in such a way as to rule it out (using quantum indeterminacies or some even stranger device) but pretend for the moment that there is a special such hunk of wood.[21] We may take the possible table that would have resulted from the selection of $h_@$ as having a special modal status—not quite actuality, but the next best thing: being nearest to actuality of all the possible tables in question. This allows us, given sufficient flexibility, to reduce Williamson's possible tables to 'the previous case'; i.e., to a case like (*CP*) in which we begin with an actual table.

Suppose we have the necessitation of the following essentialist principle:

(*A′*) If a wooden table *x* is the only table originally formed from a hunk of matter *y* according to a certain plan *P*, and *y′* is any hunk of matter that very extensively (sufficiently) overlaps *y* and has exactly the same mass, volume, and chemical composition as *y*, then there could not have been a table that is both distinct from *x* and the only table originally formed according to the same plan *P* from *y′* instead of from *y*.

Notice that this is a significantly strengthened variant of the original principle (*A*) of modal tolerance, asserting under the relevant hypotheses not merely that *x* might have been the table formed from *y′* according to plan *P*, but that *x* is the only

---

[20] *Cf.* 'The Logic of What Might Have Been.'

[21] Even if it is assumed instead that several distinct hunks are, so to speak, equally nearly-actual hunks of the carpenter's random selection, if they are close enough to each other in molecular composition (and it is plausible that they will be, as Williamson set up his example—see note 9 above), one may still go some considerable distance along the path we are now on. This is so, in fact, even if there are several such clusters of equally nearly-actual hunks of random selection.

possible table of which this is true.[22] Recall that $o(h_@)$ is the actual-but-for-the-grace-of-God table that would have been constructed had the carpenter lived long enough to finish the job. We may then be willing to say that a selection of a hunk of wood that differs only very slightly from $h_@$ (say by no more than a few molecules) would have resulted in this same nearly-actual table, $o(h_@)$, but that a selection of any hunk of wood that differs from $h_@$ by more than the required margin would have resulted in a different possible table. In fact, this follows from the necessitations of (A') and (B) above, taken together with plausible assumptions to the effect that if it would have been the case, if $o(h_@)$ had existed, that $o(h_@)$ would have been the only table originally formed from y' if y' had been formed into a table, then that actually *is* the case even though $o(h_@)$ does not actually exist; and likewise if it would have been the case, if $o(h_@)$ had existed, that $o(h_@)$ could not have been the only table originally formed from z, then that actually *is* the case even though $o(h_@)$ does not actually exist. One cannot consistently say this, of course, about all the possible tables that might have been constructed by means of a selection from the relevant sequence of hunks of wood. This is what I mean by saying that we are exploiting $o(h_@)$'s near-actuality as the next best thing to actuality. We are assuming that, since $o(h_@)$ is the possible table that would have existed, if any of the relevant possible tables had existed, the relevant limitations on $o(h_@)$'s would-be possibilities (its relevant would-be impossibilities) are also limitations on its actual possibilities. (Of course, one need not attempt to justify the above claims about whether $o(h_@)$ would have resulted from selections of various hunks of wood by means of (A') and (B).)

In saying that the selection of any hunk sufficiently overlapping $h_@$ would have resulted in $o(h_@)$ but that other selections would not have resulted in $o(h_@)$, we thereby reject (W)—an assumption which Williamson defends citing the original principle (A) but ultimately rejects. In fact, even if one rejects the facilitating claim that some hunk of wood is distinguished by being the one that would have been selected, the independent assumption that yields the n equation premises is, as I have already said, clearly untrue in any case. Suppose it were built into the case instead that no hunk in the sequence is distinguished by being a selected-but-for-the-grace-of-God hunk, and that each hunk is instead equally nearly-actual—because of quantum indeterminacies, or whatever. It might then be indeterminable which of the n equation premises is true and which false. But one can still rest assured that some of them are false.[23]

---

[22] Principle (A') is a strengthened variant of a sort of combination of principle (A) and principle (I) from 'Modal Paradox,' p. 75. Under the hypotheses of the principle, hunk y' might have been formed into a table according to plan P, since y' is just like hunk y in all relevant respects. Given (A') together with this observation, the original principle (A) follows. To this extent, (A') is a principle of modal tolerance (as well as a principle of intolerance, or essentialism). Strictly speaking, (A') does not cover Williamson's original example involving possible earrings. (See note 9 above.) In that example, possible artifacts formed by selections of different hunks of matter are not formed, in their respective worlds, according to precisely the same plan, as I had meant the term. But we may construe the term 'plan' more liberally here, so that the same 'plan' is realized in any two such worlds.

[23] This much accords to a significant extent with Williamson's current stance with respect to his problem. See notes 10 and 11 above.

This solution to the problem can be made very similar to—in fact, nearly the same as—the treatment I have proposed elsewhere for a variant of (CP) in which each of the n premises (P_{i+1}) is replaced by:

> $(P_{i+1}{}')$ If it is possible that a is the only table originally formed from hunk h_i according to such and such a plan, then it is also possible that a is the only table originally formed instead from hunk h_{i+1} according to the same plan.[24]

This is more like a genuine sorites, or 'slippery slope,' paradox. Here the difficulty is not with the reasoning involved in the argument (which is just *modus ponens*), but with the premises $(P_{i+1}{}')$, not all of which can be true. The suspect modal logical axiom *S4* remains behind this sorites version of Chisholm's Paradox, however. For one relies on *S4* in justifying the new premise $(P_{i+1}{}')$ on the basis of the necessitation of principle (A)—or alternatively, on the basis of the legitimately derived former premise (P_{i+1}).[25]

Williamson's argument is much more like this slippery slope variant of (CP). The original argument essentially involves nested modality. Williamson might have set up his version of Chisholm's Paradox by citing the necessitation of (A') in lieu of (W). In a sense, he should have. By setting it up in this way his problem would have involved nested modality, and thus, would have been significantly more like Chisholm's Paradox, in what I take to be its canonical form. If Williamson will permit it, I also take the result of substituting the necessitation of (A') for (W) to be the canonical form of what I hereby dub 'Williamson's Paradox'. It is a deeper, subtler, more paradoxical paradox. This is partly because the necessitation of (A') is enormously plausible—considerably more so than (W), which we both reject.

---

[24] The resulting argument is $(CP)'$ from section 4 of 'Modal Paradox,' pp. 87–89. See also p. 114 n. 3.

[25] Graeme Forbes suggests justifying the premise $(P_{i+1}{}')$ independently of *S4* by means of the following modal principle:

> (F) If y' is any (possibly scattered) hunk of matter that very extensively overlaps a distinct hunk of matter y, and y' has exactly the same mass, volume, and chemical composition as y, then if a wooden table x is such that it might have been the only table originally formed from hunk y according to a certain plan P, then x is also such that it might have been the only table originally formed instead from hunk y' according to the same plan P.

This principle, which comes very close to (W), is equally objectionable. Indeed, given the essentialist principle (B), Forbes's principle (F) is immediately highly suspicious—and for much the same reason as are the typical general principles from which genuine sorites paradoxes proceed. Compare, for example, the general claim that for any height h, and for any distinct height h' greater than but very close to h, if any adult human with height h is short then so is any adult human with height h'. One immediately worries about the 'borderline cases': heights h and h' at or near, or in between, the boundary between being short and not being short. Better yet, consider the claim that for any natural number n, if n straws did not break the camel's back, then neither will $n+1$ straws. (Remarks to be made in the final paragraph below concerning the relation between (W) and the necessitation of (A') apply, *mutatis mutandis*, to Forbes's principle (F) and the necessitation of the original principle (A). In particular, the sharp contrast between the very high degree of plausibility of (A) and the evident non-truth of (F) casts serious doubt on *S4*.)

This is ironic, since Williamson cites the plausibility of a close variant of (A') as part of the intuitive defense of (W), the assumption he ultimately rejects. It is precisely here that $S4$ comes into play. The necessitation of (A') entails the offending assumption—in $S4$ but not in T. One severs the connection between the switched assumptions by rejecting $S4$. I would suggest that the offending assumption (W) derives much of whatever appeal it may enjoy from the intuitive truth of the necessitation of (A'), and from a failure to distinguish between the two—perhaps as a result of implicitly committing what I call 'the fallacy of necessity iteration' or 'the fallacy of possibility deletion'; i.e., reasoning in accordance with $S4$. This is confirmed by Williamson's explicit citation of a close variant of (A') in his defense of the assumption. Rejecting $S4$ paves the way to rejecting the assumption while retaining the necessitation of (A'). And, of course, rejecting $S4$ provides a solution—indeed, I maintain, the correct solution—to what I take to be the canonical form of Williamson's Paradox.

10

Identity Facts (2002)

The history of philosophy is a story of agreements and of disagreements, often thoughtful disagreements among reasonable people. No doubt these agreements have reflected genuine convergence of opinion on matters of philosophical substance, and the disagreements genuinely clashing points of view. Often they have not. Too often an apparent disagreement is based on a serious misunderstanding of the very language in which the disagreement is couched, reflecting linguistic deviance more than a genuine difference of opinion, with any substantial conflict of viewpoint camouflaged by terminology and usage. Even more misleading, misunderstanding has concealed fundamental divergences in viewpoint behind a veil of apparent agreement. Through misunderstanding and misuse, apparent agreement masks underlying disagreement and *vice versa*. Sometimes the misunderstanding is explicit. Sometimes it is implicit. But too often it is simply unclear what view is actually being held. The phenomenalists spoke of 'tables' and 'chairs,' but such talk, they maintained, concerned the occurrence of *sensibilia*, both actual and would-be, rather than a strictly external world. Before them Bishop Berkeley believed in the real existence of tables and chairs, he said, but claimed they were made of ideas rather than matter. Did he believe in tables and chairs while holding an incorrect view as to their constitution? Or did he disbelieve in them, while deceptively mislabeling the ideas of tables 'tables' and the ideas of chairs 'chairs'?[1] That he sincerely denied doing the latter is, of course, no proof. For if he did mislabel ideas of tables 'tables', he likewise misused the phrase 'idea of tables' as a term for ideas of ideas of tables. His clarifications of his own meanings are subject to the same problem: if he misunderstands terms like 'table' and 'idea of a table', then his use of these terms in the metalanguage produces a mis-statement regarding his own usage. No one will explain his or her own usage by saying 'I use the word "table" for something other than tables'—including those who do so misuse the term. Given his pronouncements that 'tables and chairs are not material,' Berkeley's clarifications of his own

I am grateful to the participants in the Santa Barbarians discussion group and in my University of California, Santa Barbara seminar during winter 2002 for acting as the initial sounding board for the material presented here.

[1] This interpretation of Berkeley was proposed in a seminar by Saul Kripke at Princeton University around 1980. Though I prefer a slightly different interpretation of Berkeley, the present discussion is heavily indebted to Kripke's insights.

linguistic usage do not constitute evidence one way or the other. Perhaps (as I am inclined to think) he misidentified tables with perceptions or images of tables and used the word 'table' indiscriminantly, covering both tables and table perceptions. (Again, his protest that he did not do so, however sincerely made, is in itself no evidence one way or another.) Nor would this problem have been avoided if Berkeley had symbolized his pronouncements in *Principia Mathematica* notation. For we would still be left wondering about his non-logical propositional-function constants.

The problem of linguistic misuse in philosophy is not restricted to the controversy over the nature of tables and chairs. Wherever there is sharp disagreement, there is a serious potential for misuse and a resulting cloud of misunderstanding: theories of right and wrong, epistemologies (skepticism *vs.* anti-skepticism), theories of mind, theories of freedom, theories of the contents of proper names, theories of truth (correspondence *vs.* coherence *vs.* pragmatic), theories of essence, theories of reality (mind- or theory-dependent *vs.* mind-independent)—the list is as long as the history of philosophy. In all cases, attempts at clarification of one's terminology does not automatically solve the problem. For any such attempt is itself verbal, and hence subject to the very same misuse and misunderstanding, or to a related one (e.g., a corresponding metalinguistic misunderstanding). The potential for misuse and misunderstanding does not mean that we can never know whether we disagree on matters of substance. On the contrary, we surely *do* often know exactly that. What the problem of misusage does mean is that what passes superficially as an agreement on substance or as a disagreement is not always what it appears.

                                          II

One recent controversy that has been clouded in misuse and misunderstanding concerns the question of whether there can be a pair of objects for which there is no fact of the matter as to whether they are identically the same thing or instead distinct things. Fruitful discussion of this controversy calls for agreement at the outset concerning just what the issue of contention is about. Identity, in the relevant sense, is simply the relation of being one and the very same thing. This is sometimes called *numerical identity*, as opposed to *qualitative identity* or indiscernibility, i.e., the relation of being exactly alike. Numerical identity is the binary relation that obtains between x and y when they are not two things but one, when y just *is* x and not another thing. Identity is the smallest equivalence relation, the relation that each thing bears to itself and to nothing else, no matter how similar. I am identical with myself and nothing else. You are identical with yourself and nothing else. For each thing x, x is identical with x and with nothing else. The logical symbol for this relation is the equality sign, ' $=$ '. Numerically distinct things are not identical, not one thing but two.

Could there be a pair of objects for which there is simply no fact of the matter whether they are one and the very same? Philosophical puzzles about the identity of certain objects (e.g., questions of personal identity or of the persistence of an artifact over time) strongly invite the view that there is sometimes no fact as to identity or distinctness. Some years ago I discovered a simple proof that there is always a fact of identity or distinctness.[2] The following year there appeared a similar proof in a cryptic note by Gareth Evans.[3] Although there are significant difficulties in interpreting Evans's language—which can seem seriously confused and even inconsistent—his discussion is usually interpreted in such a way as to depict his proof and mine as near notational variants. Although many are persuaded by these disproofs of indeterminate identity, many others are not. The main idea underlying the proof is disarmingly simple: What would y have to be like in order for there to be no fact of the matter whether it just *is* x? One thing is clear: it would not be exactly like x in every respect. But in that case it must be something else, so that there is a fact of the matter after all.

Proof (Formulation I): (1) Suppose a pair, $<x, y>$, for which there is no fact of identity or distinctness. (2) By contrast, there is a fact of identity for the reflexive pair $<x, x>$. (3) It follows that $<x, y>$ is distinct from $<x, x>$. (4) Therefore, by standard set theory, $x \neq y$. (5) Consequently, there is a fact of the matter.

The preceding derivation proceeds along the lines of what Hans Reichenbach called the *context of justification*. The *context of discovery* may be somewhat more instructive.[4] The disproof of indeterminate identity occurred to me while considering how a semantics for indeterminacy should be engineered. Starting with the most basic sort of case, suppose there is a man of thinning hair, Harold, for whom there is no fact of the matter whether he is genuinely bald—or to put it alternatively, it is indeterminate whether, or neither true nor false that, Harold is bald. How is this reflected in the semantic structure of the sentence 'Harold is bald'? Nothing is amiss with the name 'Harold'; it simply designates the man in question. Any funny business is confined to the predicate 'is bald'. The predicate *applies to* those things of which it is true, i.e., to anything x for which there is a fact that x is bald. The predicate's choice predicate-negation 'is non-bald' (or 'isn't bald') applies to anything y for which there is a fact that y is not bald.[5] Let us say that a monadic predicate Π *applies against* (or *anti-applies to*) something when, and only when, its choice

[2] I discovered my proof in 1977 while working on my doctoral dissertation, later published as *Reference and Essence* (Princeton, N.J.: Princeton University Press, 1981; Amherst, NY: Prometheus Books, 2005). The proof appears at pp. 243–246. The proof does not entail, and was not taken to show, that every identity statement has truth-value. On the contrary, arguably if either α or β fails to refer, then $\ulcorner \alpha = \beta \urcorner$ is neither true nor false.

[3] 'Can There Be Vague Objects?' *Analysis*, 38 (1978), p. 208. See note 9 below.

[4] Reichenbach, *The Rise of Scientific Philosophy* (Berkeley and Los Angeles: University of California Press, 1951), at 231.

[5] The *choice sentential negation* of φ is true when φ itself is false, false when φ is true, and neither true nor false whenever φ is. Choice predicate-negation is the analogue for predicates. I indicate this operation by means of the prefix 'non-'. Choice negation contrasts with exclusion negation, which is like choice negation except that the exclusion negation of φ is true when φ is neither true nor false. The operation is captured in English by the phrase 'it is not true that'. Exclusion predicate-negation is the analogue for predicates. (An example might be the prefix 'un-' in 'undead', as the latter is used in vampire folklore.)

predicate-negation, *non-*Π, applies to that thing.[6] That is, a monadic predicate applies against those things of which it is false. The extension of a monadic predicate is the set (or class) of things to which the predicate applies. A predicate's *anti-extension* is the set of things against which the predicate applies, i.e., the set of things of which the predicate is false. The predicate 'is bald' is a witness to the fact that some predicates may be *partially defined*, in the sense that they are neither true nor false of some objects. Let us say that a monadic predicate is *inapplicable with respect to* something if and only if the predicate applies neither to nor against that thing (something of which the predicate is neither true nor false), and let us call the set of things with respect to which a monadic predicate is inapplicable the predicate's *syn-extension*. A predicate's extension, anti-extension, and syn-extension form a triad of disjoint sets which (barring a more radical kind of partial definition) together partition the relevant universe of discourse. Poly-adic predicates (dyadic, triadic, etc.) are then handled in the obvious way by taking ordered *n*-tuples. Now we may semantically characterize the English predicate 'is bald' *vis-à-vis* Harold: the words are inapplicable with respect to Harold. Harold is an element of the English syn-extension of 'is bald'.

This is not a fully developed semantic theory of non-bivalence. It is a plausible framework for a more detailed semantic development of non-bivalence, at least to the extent that any such development that enjoys significant intuitive force will accommodate analogues to the relevant notions (e.g., inapplicability). It is important to note that although the framework is non-classical, insofar as it includes a 'middle' that Aristotle's law excludes, the meta-theory is set out (or can be) in a completely classical metalanguage, one that is bivalent and fully extensional.[7] Of course, if one attempts to fix the English extension of 'is bald' by incorporating that very predicate into the metalanguage ('The predicate 'is bald' applies to something in English iff that thing *is bald*'), the resulting metalanguage will be non-bivalent. But there is no pressure to do so. On the contrary, it is advisable to invoke predicates in the metalanguage for *determinate* baldness and non-baldness, as in 'The predicate 'is bald' applies against something in English iff that thing is determinately-non-bald.' In theory (ignoring here the prospect of higher-order indeterminacy), one could fix the extension, the anti-extension, and the syn-extension of 'is bald' by specifying precise proportions of hair on the head (e.g., 25 percent or less hair: *bald*; 30 percent or more: *non-bald*). The meta-theoretic notions of application to, application against, and inapplicability are like determinate baldness and determinate non-baldness: bivalent one and all. Although 'Harold is bald' is neither true nor false, the meta-English sentence 'The English predicate 'is bald' applies to Harold' is simply false.

Let us now apply the framework to indeterminacy of identity. The relevant predicate is the dyadic logical symbol ' $=$ ', or the English 'is identical with' in the sense of *being numerically one and the very same object*. Classically, this predicate applies to

---

[6] A semantic notion of *dissatisfaction* may be defined in terms of application-to and application-against, for sufficiently well-behaved languages, with the result that an assignment of values to variables dissatisfies an open sentence φ iff it satisfies the sentential choice negation $\ulcorner \sim \varphi \urcorner$.

[7] A language is *extensional* if it generates no contexts that violate the principle of extensionality, according to which the extension of a compound expression (the reference of a compound singular term, the truth-value of a sentence, etc.) is a function of the customary extensions of its meaningful components and their mode of composition.

the reflexive pairing of any object x in the relevant universe of discourse with itself, and applies against any other pairs of objects in the discourse universe. But we are in a non-classical framework which makes room for inapplicability and non-bivalence. Suppose we have a pair of objects, $<x, y>$, for which there is no fact of their identity or distinctness. This pair is then an element of the identity predicate's syn-extension; the predicate is inapplicable with respect to $<x, y>$, and hence applies neither to nor against the pair. Still, the predicate *does* apply to the pair $<x, x>$. This latter pair is an element of the predicate's extension. The two pairs, $<x, y>$ and $<x, x>$, are thus different in this respect: ' $=$ ' applies to the latter and not the former. Hence, they are different pairs. They *have to be* different pairs. One is an element of the syn-extension of ' $=$ ' and the other is not. (It is instead an element of the extension.) But then x and y must be distinct after all, and $<x, y>$ is an element of the identity predicate's anti-extension rather than the syn-extension. The syn-extension is empty.

Once I saw that the very idea of indeterminate identity is semantically incoherent in this way, it was a simple matter to convert the observation into a disproof. And it was none too surprising to find that the disproof, or one very much like it, would be discovered independently. What has been very surprising, and disheartening, is the subsequent skepticism. Though the reasoning is, to my mind, beyond reproach, the disproof of indeterminate identity has proved controversial. While I remain hopeful that future generations will find the argument conclusive, as I take it to be, the current state of play leaves little cause for optimism. Orthodoxy is supported less by reason than by inertia. Cherished doctrine dies hard even in the face of disproof. The structurally identical refutation of contingent identity initially met with skepticism.[8] I long for the day when the determinacy of identity gains the same universal acceptance that the necessity of identity enjoys today.

The disproof I offered can be reformulated entirely in what Rudolf Carnap called 'the formal mode' through semantic ascent. I shall call the following derivation 'Formulation II':

(0') ' $=$ ' is inapplicable with respect to $<x, y>$ — assumption for *reductio ad absurdum*

(1') ' $=$ ' does not apply to $<x, y>$ — (0'), definition of 'inapplicable'

(2') ' $=$ ' applies to $<x, x>$ — semantic rule for ' $=$ '

(3') $<x, y>$ is determinately-distinct from $<x, x>$ — (1'), (2'), *the deteminate-distinctness of determinately-discernibles*

(4') x is determinately-distinct from y — (3'), set theory, logic

(5') ' $=$ ' applies against $<x, y>$ — (4'), semantic rule for ' $=$ '

(6') ' $=$ ' is not inapplicable with respect to $<x, y>$ — (5'), definition of 'inapplicable', logic

(7') ' $=$ ' is not inapplicable with respect to $<x, y>$ — (0'), (0'), (6'), *reductio ad absurdum*

---

[8] A number of provocative theses about identity (e.g., that personal identity is grounded in, or reducible to, some more complex relation between the identified persons, such as psychological

Both formulations proceed by distinguishing the putatively indeterminately identical pair $<x, y>$ from the determinately identical pair $<x, x>$, then inferring the distinctness of x from y. A more direct procedure distinguishes x from y directly in virtue of the different ways in which each is related to x. The former is such that it is determinate whether it is x; on the initial assumption, the latter is not. Since they differ from each other in this way, they are distinct after all. (The disproof offered by Evans appears to proceed along these lines.) This third formulation can be symbolized by introducing a truth-functional connective, '∇', for indeterminacy. Its truth table is the following:

φ $\nabla\varphi$
T F
F F
U T

We may also introduce a connective for determinacy (the dual of '∇'):

φ $\Delta\varphi$
T T
F T
U F

These truth tables provide the logic of 'Δ' and '∇'. Formulation III proceeds as follows. We first prove a lemma: that x is not something for which it is indeterminate whether it is x.

1. $x=x$ logical truth
2. $\Delta(x=x)$ 1, logic of 'Δ'
3. $\sim\nabla(x=x)$ 2, logic of '∇'

The main proof is then straightforward:

4. $\nabla(x=y)$ assumption for *reductio ad absurdum*
5. $x \neq y$ 3, 4, logic (including Leibniz's Law)
6. $\Delta(x \neq y)$ 5, logic of 'Δ'
7. $\sim\nabla(x=y)$ 6, logic of '∇'[contradicting line 4]
8. $\sim\nabla(x=y)$ 4, 4, 7, *reductio ad absurdum*, logic of '∇'[9]

congruence and continuity) are refutable by means of arguments of the same structure. *Cf.* my 'Modal Paradox,' in *Midwest Studies in Philosophy XI: Studies in Essentialism*, ed. P. French, T. Uehling, and H. Wettstein (Minneapolis: University of Minnesota Press, 1986), pp. 75–120, at 110–114. The conclusion follows from two auxiliary observations: (*i*) the fact that $x=x$ lacks the provocative property attributed to the fact that $x=y$ (e.g., contingency, indeterminacy, reducibility to psychological congruence and continuity, obtaining in virtue of a "criterion" of identity, etc.); whereas (*ii*) the fact that $x=y$ (assuming there is such a fact) just *is* the fact that $x=x$.

[9] This is not the proof Evans intended. Indeed, he might have rejected its conclusion. Evans evidently believed that there are pairs of proper names, α and β, such that the equation $\lceil\alpha = \beta\rceil$ lacks truth-value, but he also believed that this is invariably due to some ambiguity, imprecision, or incompleteness in the notation—i.e., in one or both of the names or perhaps in the identity predicate. (*Cf.* David Lewis, 'Vague Identity: Evans Misunderstood,' *Analysis*, 48 [1988], pp. 128–130. Lewis construes vagueness as a kind of semantic *indecision* among various precise potential

A word about *reductio ad absurdum*: The classical form is not valid in a non-bivalent logic. A valid derivation of a contradiction from an assumption φ shows that φ is untrue, not that it is false. The proper inference to draw from the demonstration that φ is inconsistent is to something disjunctive: $\sim\!\varphi\vee\nabla\varphi$. However, $\ulcorner\sim\!\nabla\nabla\Psi\urcorner$ is a logical truth. Hence when the *reductio* assumption φ has the particular form $\ulcorner\nabla\Psi\urcorner$ (as with line 4 above), a further application of *modus tollendo ponens* yields the classical conclusion. (This is the object-theoretic analogue to the feature of Formulation II that it is derived in a classical, bivalent metalanguage.)

contents—'precisifications'—perhaps whereby the task of fixing a particular extension for a lexical item remains unfinished. He reports that this was also Evans's construal.) Evans's concern in his cryptic note is to demonstrate that vagueness is a feature of our conceptual and/or notational apparatus for representing the world and not of the world represented thereby, that there cannot be a 'vague world' composed of 'vague objects.' He mistakenly equated this with the thesis that any imprecision or indeterminacy in questions of identity is a feature of our conceptual and/or notational apparatus rather than of the very objects in question. (Evans identifies the opposing thesis that there are 'vague objects' for which questions of identity have no answers with the thesis that there are objects "about which it is a *fact* that they have fuzzy boundaries." This appears to be a separate confusion, depending on the meaning of 'fuzzy boundary'.)

Unlike Formulations I–III above, Evans's argument does not invoke (objectual) variables ranging over objects. Instead his argument is entirely meta-theoretic, and concerns a particular object-theoretic proof. He proceeds by assuming for a *reductio* that we have a pair of objects at least one of which is a vague object (whatever that means), and completely precise names α and β (Evans's uses 'a' and 'b') for these objects, so that the lack of truth-value of the equation $\ulcorner\alpha=\beta\urcorner$ is entirely due to the vague object(s) named rather than to any imprecision or indeterminacy in the notation itself, which is assumed to be completely precise and non-defective. His first step, then, is the assumption that $\ulcorner\nabla\,(\alpha=\beta)\urcorner$ is true solely in virtue of some defect in the objects named, not in the notation. Since $\ulcorner\sim\!\nabla(\alpha=\alpha)\urcorner$ is also precisely true (albeit perhaps concerning a 'vague object'), it follows that $\ulcorner\alpha\neq\beta\urcorner$ is also true. (Lewis reports that Evans believed this inference requires the assumption that there is no vagueness in the notation involved, since it does not go through where $\ulcorner\nabla(\alpha=\beta)\urcorner$ is true because one of the names involved is itself imprecise.) This contradicts the initial assumption that $\ulcorner\alpha=\beta\urcorner$ lacks truth-value solely in virtue of the objects named. Instead, Evans believes, if it lacks truth-value, this must be traceable to vagueness or imprecision in the very notation itself, perhaps in one of the names. Converting the object-theoretic derivation into a classic *reductio* proof, Evans jumps through a technical hoop (committing a further confusion along the way) in order to validate the deduction of $\ulcorner\Delta(\alpha\neq\beta)\urcorner$ from $\ulcorner\alpha\neq\beta\urcorner$, together with $\ulcorner\sim\!\Delta(\alpha\neq\beta)\urcorner$ from the *reductio* hypothesis. (This even by itself constitutes compelling evidence that Evans did not construe the operators 'Δ' and '∇' to be the truth-functional connectives occurring in Formulation III, whereby the validity of lines 5–7 is completely trivial.)

My own view is that precisely because identity is totally defined (as I claim to prove), there cannot be referring proper names α and β such that $\ulcorner\alpha=\beta\urcorner$ lacks truth-value. Of course, one could attempt to fix the reference of a name by means of a vague definite description. One may say, 'Let 'Mary' name whoever happens to be the most beautiful woman in this room.' If there is exactly one woman whose pulchritude, by the operative standard, determinately exceeds that of every other woman in the room, the attempt succeeds and the name unambiguously refers to her. If there are two women present whose pulchritude determinately exceeds all others in the room but it is untrue that one is the more beautiful—either because it is false or because there is no fact of the matter—the attempt fails. The name is not indeterminate with respect to reference; it does not "indeterminately refer." Nor is the name imprecise or semantically unfinished. It simply fails to refer. (*Cf.* note 2 above.) I agree with Evans that the name does not refer to a vague woman—whatever such a thing might be. However, I believe the treatment of vagueness as akin to indecision among potential "precisifications" is misleading at best.

Ironically, Evans's willingness to suppose that $\ulcorner\alpha=\beta\urcorner$ lacks truth-value in virtue of indeterminacy in the very notation raises the prospect (which I claim to refute) that in some cases the culprit is the identity predicate. His paper gives no clear indication that he thought this impossible.

III

The resistance to these disproofs is widespread. The details vary. However, nearly every reply objects to the use of Leibniz's Law—in the inference that $<x, y> \neq <x, x>$ in Formulations I and II and/or in the move from lines 3 and 4 to 5 in Formulation III. The most extensively developed reply is that of Terence Parsons.[10] I provided in my original presentation what I took to be a decisive response to this general objection.[11] I here apply and extend that response to Parsons's specific objections.[12] I shall argue that the problem of linguistic misuse, as described in section I above, manifests itself in a manner leading to an ironic collapse in Parsons's theory of identity.

Commenting on my inference in Formulation I from (1) '$\nabla(x=y)$' and (2) '$\sim\nabla(x=x)$' to (3) '$<x, y> \neq <x, x>$', Parsons complains, "This is fallacious; if it is indeterminate whether $x = y$ then it is indeterminate whether the pair $<x, y>$ is identical with the pair $<x, x>$. No principle of bivalent logic or bivalent set theory (or ordered-pair theory) should be taken to validate the inference to (3), since the inference crucially involves non-bivalency" (*Indeterminate Identity*, p. 61). "... to assume the validity of the [contrapositive of Leibniz's Law] is to beg the question" (p. 38). He speculates that "a natural way to think of" attempting to justify the inference to (3) is by means of an illegitimate use of *reductio ad absurdum* reasoning, fallaciously inferring (3) from the fact that its negation is inconsistent with the initial hypothesis (1). "There is no way to derive (3) from (1) and (2).... Instead, we can show, using comprehension, that it is indeterminate whether $[<x, y> = <x, x>]$" (p. 185). In response to Formulation III Parsons objects, "The argument does not

---

[10] Parsons, 'Entities without Identity,' in *Philosophical Perspectives I: Metaphysics*, ed. J. Tomberlin (Atascadero, Calif.: Ridgeview, 1987), pp. 1–19; Parsons and P. Woodruff, 'Worldly Indeterminacy of Identity,' *Proceedings of the Aristotelian Society*, 95 (Winter 1995), pp. 171–191; Parsons and Woodruff, 'Indeterminacy of Identity of Objects and Sets,' in *Philosophical Perspectives XI: Mind, Causation, and the World*, ed. J. Tomberlin (Atascadero, Calif.: Ridgeview, 1997), pp. 321–348; and Parsons, *Indeterminate Identity: Metaphysics and Semantics* (New York: Oxford University Press, 2000). Parsons credits Peter Woodruff in *Indeterminate Identity* for much of his defense of the notion.

[11] "I have encountered a number of objections to the argument, but none that are convincing. Perhaps the most frequent objection is the idea that if we take vagueness and indeterminacy seriously, it is fallacious to infer that $<x, y> \neq <x, x>$ from the assumption that it is indeterminate or vague whether the first pair of objects stand in the identity relation, whereas it is fully determinate and settled that the second pair of objects so stand. The objection is usually based on the notion that where a term is applied to objects for which the term's applicability may be vague or indeterminate, classically valid inference patterns are no longer legitimate. But the inference drawn here is from a conjunction consisting of an *assumption*—something we are taking to be determinately the case for the sake of argument—together with something that is quite definitely the case. The inference pattern need only be valid, i.e., truth-preserving. There is nothing more to require of it." (*Reference and Essence*, p. 244n).

[12] My presentation here has benefitted from correspondence with Parsons from April 1985 to January 1986, in which I offered a more detailed version of the same response. His reply in *Indeterminate Identity* differs in a variety of respects from that in his earlier 'Entities without Identity,' as well as that in his and Woodruff's papers cited above in note 10. I here concentrate almost exclusively on Parsons's more recent reply.

use Leibniz's Law at all, but rather its contrapositive. This is the principle [I] discussed and rejected . . . . The argument thus begs the question" (*ibid.*, p. 47). Parsons summarizes his primary complaint against the disproofs as follows:

> . . . it is coherent to hold that identity statements might be indeterminate . . . all of the a priori proofs to the contrary are clearly question-begging. (*ibid.*, p. vii)
>
>   In my opinion the major cause of ongoing controversy regarding . . . indeterminacy of identity . . . is our tendency to take for granted contrapositive reasoning when using propositions that may lack truth-value. This type of reasoning is so natural to us when dealing with truth-valued claims that we instinctively pursue it when dealing with meaningful claims that may lack truth-value, where it is straightforwardly fallacious. (*ibid.*, p. 27)

Parsons develops a metaphysico-semantic theory for indeterminate identity within the framework of a non-bivalent object language that is otherwise antiseptic—i.e., fully extensional and in which all singular terms refer. His theory correctly blocks classical 'contrapositive reasoning'—whereby a correct derivation of ψ from φ is taken to validate the further inference of $\ulcorner{\sim}\varphi\urcorner$ from $\ulcorner{\sim}\psi\urcorner$—and *reductio ad absurdum* reasoning. In a non-bivalent logic, only weaker conclusions are derivable from $\ulcorner{\sim}\psi\urcorner$, e.g., $\ulcorner{\sim}\varphi \vee \nabla\varphi\urcorner$. (*Reductio ad absurdum* is the special case of contrapositive reasoning where φ is the *reductio* assumption and ψ is $\ulcorner\chi \wedge {\sim}\chi\urcorner$.)

IV

Leibniz's Law is typically given as a schema of classical logic:

$$\alpha = \beta \supset (\varphi_\alpha \equiv \varphi_\beta)$$

where φ_β is the same formula as φ_α except for having free occurrences of the singular term β where φ_α has free occurrences of the singular term α.[13] As with any schema of classical logic, this one has restricted application in a non-bivalent framework: Every instance *in which all atomic formulas have truth-value* expresses a logical truth. The classical schema as well as the corresponding classical-logical inference rule of Substitution of Equality (derived from the schema using *modus ponens*) are based upon Leibniz's principle of *the indiscernibility of identicals*, i.e., if *x* and *y* are one and the very same thing, then they are exactly alike in every respect. One might suppose that Leibniz's notion of indiscernibility—being exactly alike in every respect—might be defined as follows:

> *x* and *y* are *indiscernible* $=_{def}$ every property is a property of *x* iff it is also a property of *y*.

---

[13] The conditional involved here is true whenever the antecedent is false or the consequent true, false only when the antecedent is true and the consequent false, and neither true nor false in the remaining three cases. The biconditional (formed from either '$\equiv$' or 'iff') is true when both sides have the same truth-value, false when they have opposite truth-value, and neither true nor false whenever either side is. Disjunction and conjunction are defined in the customary manner in terms of '$\supset$' and choice-negation. A disjunction is true when one or both of its disjuncts is, false when both disjuncts are, and neither true nor false in the remaining cases. A conjunction is true when both conjuncts are, false when one or both of its conjuncts is, and neither true nor false in the remaining cases.

But if some properties are indeterminate with respect to some objects, this definition does not capture the relevant notion of indiscernibility. If it is indeterminate whether Harold is bald, it is equally indeterminate whether Harold is bald iff Harold is bald. But Harold is still Harold nonetheless, and exactly like himself in every respect. The following weakening of the classical schema better captures the intended *indiscernibility of identicals*. It is intuitively universally valid in any language that is extensional and in which all singular terms refer—even including instances where one or both of φ_α and φ_β lacks truth-value:

$$LL : \alpha = \beta \supset [(\varphi_\alpha \equiv \varphi_\beta) \vee (\nabla\varphi_\alpha \wedge \nabla\varphi_\beta)].$$

I shall use 'Leibniz's Law' in the following as an alternate name for this more cautious schema.

Parsons says he endorses Leibniz's Law (pp. 35–36), but the terminology is misleading. He in fact explicitly rejects *LL*, favoring instead a significantly weakened variant (pp. 92–94).[14] As well he may if he is prepared to pay the price for avoiding the disproofs of indeterminate identity. Appropriate instances of *LL*, taken in conjunction with logical laws and rules that are valid in non-bivalent logic, provide exactly what is needed to validate both of the disproofs, without any reliance on the non-bivalent fallacy of contrapositive reasoning. The intuitive validity of *LL*, and its nearly unanimous acceptance as a logically valid schema (within a fully extensional framework in which all singular terms refer), therefore render Parsons's diagnosis of the ongoing controversy over indeterminate identity extremely unlikely. Parsons prefers to reserve the name 'Leibniz's Law' for Substitution of Equality. It is only a name, and I defend to the death Parsons's right to use it for the inference rule instead of an axiom schema as his preference might be. (The name is frequently so used.) But then his complaint that the disproof "does not use Leibniz's Law at all" is deceptive at best. His further complaint that since the disproof involves what is tantamount to the contrapositive of Substitution of Equality, which he explicitly

---

[14] He is not alone. As mentioned, most respondents have replied to the disproofs by rejecting *LL* in an extensional language in which all singular terms refer, or by undertaking a commitment to do so. A position similar to Parsons's was first defended by John Broome, 'Indefiniteness in Identity,' *Analysis*, 44 (1984), pp. 6–12. Both Broome and Parsons claim to embrace 'Leibniz's Law,' even while rejecting *LL*. Neither contends that *LL* has false instances (in such a language), but both believe some instances are neither true nor false.

In lieu of the standard conditional $\ulcorner\varphi \supset \Psi\urcorner$ (as defined in note 13 above), Parsons generally prefers a weaker conditional $\ulcorner\varphi \Rightarrow \Psi\urcorner$—the so-called Łukasiewicz conditional—equivalent to $\ulcorner(\varphi \supset \Psi) \vee (\nabla\varphi \wedge \nabla\Psi)\urcorner$. The Łukasiewicz conditional is sufficiently weak to accommodate such things as 'The present king of France is bald $\Rightarrow$ the present king of France is not bald' as well as its converse. Even the Łukasiewicz conditional, however, is sufficiently strong to validate *modus tollens*. For this reason, Parsons rejects not only *LL* but also the result of replacing ' $\supset$ ' by ' $\Rightarrow$ ' (pp. 92–94). One weaker variant of *LL* that Parsons does accept (for the appropriate language) is $\ulcorner\Delta(\alpha = \beta) \supset LL\urcorner$, i.e.:

$$\Delta(\alpha = \beta) \supset [\alpha = \beta \supset (\varphi_\alpha \equiv \varphi_\beta) \vee (\nabla\varphi_\alpha \wedge \nabla\varphi_\beta)].$$

But as I shall argue, Parsons's endorsement of even this variation of *LL* is unjustified. (See note 29 below.) It should also be noted that not all theorems of classical bivalent logic must be weakened in the move to a non-bivalent logic by affixing antecedents of the form $\ulcorner\Delta\varphi\urcorner$, or disjuncts of the form $\ulcorner\nabla\varphi\urcorner$, for each atomic component φ. The clasical theorem '$(p \supset q) \vee (q \supset r)$', for example, goes simply into '$\Delta q \supset [(p \supset q) \vee (q \supset r)]$', or alternatively, into '$(p \supset q) \vee (q \supset r) \vee \nabla q$'.

rejects, it is thus "clearly question-begging" is completely unjustified—lest any valid argument begs the question against the opponent merely by virtue of relying on a package of premise that the opponent is committed to rejecting.[15] Nor did Achilles beg the question against the Tortoise by relying on *modus ponens*.[16] Like *modus ponens*, LL is nearly universally accepted as intuitively valid (within an extensional framework). The burden of proof lies squarely on the side of those who wish to reject the validity of either. And a large burden it is. It is not enough to demonstrate that weakening LL is sufficient to make room for indeterminate identity. One would need to *expose a fallacy* in the unrestricted form. One would need to show not only that the restriction blocks the disproofs, but also that it is independently intuitive, and that its historical omission was a logical oversight, akin to the Aristotelian logician's inadvertently overlooking the fact that the inference from ⌜All S are P⌝ to ⌜Some S are P⌝ is invalid without the tacitly assumed premise ⌜Some things are S⌝.

Although he endorses full Substitution of Equality in an extensional non-bivalent setting (calling it 'Leibniz's Law'; but see note 29 below), Parsons points out that this in itself does not license the contrapositive inference from substitution failure to non-identity. What, then, is his alternative logical introduction rule for '≠'? Parsons endorses a principle (which, following Woodruff, he calls 'DDiff') of *the determinate distinctness of determinately discernibles*. This licenses a restricted variant of the contrapositive of Substitution of Equality, tantamount to:

$$\Pi(\alpha)$$
$$\sim\Pi(\beta)$$
$$\therefore \quad \alpha \neq \beta,$$

where Π is a monadic predicate—or rather, where Π is a special sort of monadic predicate, one guaranteed to express ('stand for') a property.[17] The idea here is that, assuming the terms α and β are referring, if there is a property that the referent of the former determinately has and the referent of the latter determinately lacks, then the referents are determinately distinct.

---

[15] The most common mode of objection to a philosophical theory consists in exposing an implausible consequence. In broad outline, the objection takes the form of a *modus tollens* argument: $T \supset C$. $\sim C$ $\therefore$ $\sim T$. In his work, both on identity and on unrelated matters, Parsons sometimes turns this form of objection on its head, arguing for a controversial or otherwise implausible hypothesis C on the very ground that the theory T (which he is defending) is committed to it. In effect, the objector's *modus tollens* becomes Parsons's *modus ponens*. He sometimes couples this with the charge that the objection begs the question against T by asserting the denial of the consequence C. This involves a misunderstanding of the function of a philosophical argument, which is not to force the opponent to concede but to persuade an idealized, intelligent, philosophically educated, but unbiased third party who is otherwise agnostic. An argument *begs the question* not merely by employing a premise the opponent may doubt, but by employing one or more premises the idealized unbiased agnostic cannot reasonably be expected to accept because their rational justification is based precisely on the argument's conclusion (or on something even stronger).

[16] Lewis Carrol, 'What the Tortoise Said to Achilles,' *Mind* NS, IV, 14 (April 1895), pp. 278–280.

[17] Parsons might distinguish syntactically between those simple predicates within the scope of this contrapositive of Substitution from those outside its scope by using a two-sorted stock of simple predicates. It is to be understood that a compound monadic predicate legitimately formed by λ-abstraction on an open formula qualifies as expressing a property.

Some such restriction must be imposed on Substitution of Equality itself, as well as its contrapositive and *LL*, the moment one enters a nonextensional framework. Failures of unrestricted Substitution are commonplace even in a bivalent setting whenever nonextensional operators are present. Quotation marks notoriously play havoc with Substitution. And although it is necessary that the US President is president of the US, and George W. Bush is the US President, it does not follow that it is necessary that George W. Bush is president of the US. Furthermore, although it is necessary that the US President is president of the US and unnecessary that George W. Bush is, it does not follow that George W. Bush is not the US President. The legitimacy of the restriction to subject-predicate sentences (and their negations) in the present setting, however, is dubious. As Parsons recognizes (pp. 30, 50), the sentential indeterminacy operator and its dual are truth-functional, hence completely extensional. Here again, the restriction to subject–predicate is *ad hoc*, at least unless and until a persuasive, independent justification is provided, exposing the alleged fallacy in the unrestricted form as a logical oversight (within an extensional framework in which all singular terms refer).

In any event, the restriction is idle unless it is accompanied by an additional restriction on the formation of compound monadic predicates from open formulas. Unrestricted λ-conversion would simply welcome the contrapositive of unrestricted substitution in the back door. Formulation III, for example, is easily resurrected by the insertion of four additional lines to obtain Formulation IV:

0*a*.	$(\lambda z)[\nabla(x=z)](x)$	assumption for *reductio ad absurdum*
0*b*.	$\nabla(x=x)$	0*a*, λ-concretion
1.	$x=x$	logical truth
2.	$\Delta(x=x)$	1, logic of 'Δ'
3.	$\sim\nabla(x=x)$ [contradicting line 0*b*]	2, logic of '∇'
3*a*.	$\sim(\lambda z)[\nabla(x=z)](x)$	0*a*, 0*b*, 3, *reductio ad absurdum*, logic of '∇'[18]
4.	$\nabla(x=y)$	assumption for *reductio ad absurdum*
4*a*.	$(\lambda z)[\nabla(x=z)](y)$	4, λ-abstraction
5.	$x\neq y$	3*a*, 4*a*, logic (with restricted Leibniz's Law)
6.	$\Delta(x\neq y)$	5, logic of 'Δ'
7.	$\sim\nabla(x=y)$ [contradicting line 4]	6, logic of '∇'
8.	$\sim\nabla(x=y)$	4, 4, 7, *reductio ad absurdum*, logic of '∇'

The previous disagreements concerning contrapositive reasoning, Leibniz's Law, and the rest, would thus seem to be only so many red herrings. Parsons attempts to block this new derivation by imposing an additional restriction, this time on classical λ-abstraction (pp. 48–49, 54). The principal bone of contention between Parsons and myself thus apparently comes down to the question of validity of classical

[18] Any sentence of the form $\ulcorner\sim\nabla(\lambda\alpha)[\nabla\varphi_\alpha](\beta)\urcorner$ is a logical truth (assuming all singular terms refer), rendering the inference at line 3*a* legitimate.

λ-abstraction within a non-bivalent but extensional framework in which all singular terms refer.[19] Officially, in Parsons's theory one is barred from abstracting any compound predicate that would otherwise apply to an object *y* and apply against an object *x* indeterminately identical with *y* (as with lines 3*a*, 4, and 4*a*). Parsons would thus limit λ-abstraction to the formation of predicates that satisfy *the determinate distinctness of determinately discernibles*.

Parsons's restriction has the undesirable feature that it would make syntax—not only proof theory, but evidently even well-formedness—dependent upon semantics, if not indeed upon metaphysics. Worse, it does not cut any ice. The controversy over whether identity can be indeterminate must be settled in advance in Parsons's favor for the 'restriction' to amount to any limitation at all. In Formulation IV, one would first have to know whether line 4 is satisfied by any pair of objects in order to know whether line 4*a* may be legitimately inferred from it. On one view (my own), line 4 is unsatisfiable, making the inference to 4*a* valid even on the supposed restriction. A purely syntactic restriction would be clearly preferable for Parsons's purposes. He might, for example, decree that λ-abstraction is applicable only to formulas not containing the identity predicate, or its cognates. Alternatively, he might restrict λ-abstraction to formulas not containing either '∇' or its dual, or any cognates. Parsons's remarks (at pp. 50–51) are unsympathetic to the latter, but strongly suggest that he would favor some version or variant of the former.[20] Either restriction would block Formulation IV. But again, that it blocks the proof is no justification for either restriction. An overlooked fallacy must be exposed in the unrestricted form. Simply declaring the disproof invalid by fiat will not do.

[19] Both classical λ-abstraction and *LL* fail in the presence of non-referring terms. Consider for example 'It is indeterminate whether the present king of France is bald; therefore, the present king of France is someone such that it is indeterminate whether he is bald'; or 'If the present king of France is Nathan Salmon, then it is determinate whether the present king of France is bald iff it is determinate whether Nathan Salmon is'. The failures should not be blamed on the determinacy operator, since the same failures occur even without any such device, as in 'The present king of France does not exist; therefore, the present king of France is something that does not exist' and 'If the present king of France is Nathan Salmon, then either the present king of France exists iff Salmon does, or else it is indeterminate whether the present king of France exists and also indeterminate whether Nathan Salmon does'. *Cf.* note 2 above. The inferences may be validated by the inclusion of appropriate existential premises. The modification is avoided here in the customary way, engineering the object language so that all singular terms refer.

[20] In 'Entities without Identity,' Parsons explicitly proposes the latter restriction.

In the present case the problem arises from applying a version of property abstraction to a formula containing an indeterminacy operator. If this is prohibited, then [Formulation III] fails ... [Formulation III] does not force us to give up either the use of an indeterminacy operator or the use of property abstraction that is restricted to classical constructions. It does show us that we cannot extend property abstraction to formulas containing indeterminacy operators. (p. 14)

Yet in *Indeterminate Identity*, some fifteen years later, Parsons says of operators like '∇' and its dual that they "do not create non-extensional contexts; one may freely existentially generalize on terms within their scopes ..." (p. 50). Insofar as '$\nabla Bald(Harold)$' yields '$(\exists x)\nabla Bald(x)$' by Existential Generalization, it must also yield '$(\lambda x)[\nabla Bald(x)](Harold)$' by λ-abstraction (or at least it *should* also do so). Here Parsons attempts to turn the proofs that identity is determinate into an argument that (in effect) applying λ-abstraction to formulas containing identity is a form of impredicative definition and therefore suspect (*ibid.*, pp. 50–51). The argument is unpersuasive. See below.

Restricting λ-abstraction to formulas not containing ' $=$ ' is clearly excessive (and indeed Parsons explicitly allows λ-abstraction on equations, at p. 54). Insofar as it is a metaphysically necessary truth that Hesperus is Phosphorus, Hesperus has at least one metaphysically essential characteristic: that of being identical with Phosphorus. And insofar as King George IV wished to know who wrote *Waverley*, correctly speculating that it might be Sir Walter Scott, that very feature of Scott—his being identical with the author of *Waverley*—was one that piqued the curiosity of King George IV, an accomplishment of the poet about which the monarch wondered. Worse, merely restricting λ-abstraction to formulas not containing ' $=$ ' or its cognates is inadequate for Parsons's purposes. Even a restriction to formulas not simultaneously containing both ' $=$ ' and 'Δ' (implausible though such a restriction may be) is inadequate without any further ado. Parsons holds that whenever it is indeterminate whether $x=y$, there is some property P that is determinate with respect to one of the pair but not determinate with respect to the other, i.e., P is either determinately a property of x or determinately not a property of x but is neither determinately a property, nor determinately not a property, of y, or vice versa (p. 31). This in itself yields a determinate difference between x and y. For suppose (without loss of generality) there is a property P that is determinate with respect to x but indeterminate with respect to y. Let α refer to x and β refer to y, and let Π be a predicate that expresses P. Then both $\ulcorner\Delta\Pi(\alpha)\urcorner$ and $\ulcorner\nabla\Pi(\beta)\urcorner$ are true. Hence, so are $\ulcorner\sim(\lambda z)[\nabla\Pi(z)](\alpha)\urcorner$ and $\ulcorner(\lambda z)[\nabla\Pi(z)](\beta)\urcorner$. (See note 18.) The property expressed by $\ulcorner(\lambda z)[\nabla\Pi(z)]\urcorner$—the property of being something with respect to which P is indeterminate—is thus determinately a property of y and determinately not a property of x. But then x and y are distinct even according to the weaker version of the contrapositive of Substitution of Equality that Parsons accepts, contradicting the hypothesis that it is indeterminate whether $x=y$. To block this disproof Parsons needs to block the formation of $\ulcorner(\lambda z)[\Delta\Pi(z)]\urcorner$ from Π. Unless he has some further syntactic restriction to impose on the predicates that express properties P of the sort described, Parsons thus needs to restrict λ-abstraction further to formulas containing neither 'Δ', '∇', nor their cognates.

Such a restriction is every bit as excessive as the previous restriction to formulas not containing ' $=$ '. (*Cf.* note 20.) It is indeterminate whether Harold is bald. In light of this, one cannot correctly attribute either baldness or non-baldness to Harold. But there is another property that can be correctly inferred—the property of being indeterminate with respect to baldness. What is one to make of the claim that although it is indeterminate whether Harold is bald, this fact about Harold does not generate, or yield, or point to (etc.), any particular feature of Harold? Surely Harold's indeterminacy with respect to baldness is a noteworthy feature of him— especially so in the present context.

The situation is worse. As Parsons recognizes, the restrictions on λ-abstraction that he needs do not stop with formulas involving either '∇' or ' $=$ ' or their cognates. Even if a subtle fallacy is plausibly and intuitively exposed in the application of λ-abstraction in Formulation IV (an enormous 'if'), there can be no similar fallacy in the formal-mode Formulation II. Insofar as ' $=$ ' applies to $<x, x>$ and not to $<x, y>$, there is a property of the former pair that is not a property of the latter: that of being applied to by ' = '. The relevant property in this case is not formed by abstracting on a metalinguistic formula involving both the identity predicate and the indeterminacy operator simultaneously, nor by abstracting on a formula involving identity, nor by abstracting into the indeterminacy operator. The abstraction is on a simple sentence of semantics proper. Formulation II proceeds entirely within a classical, bivalent, extensional metalanguage. This particular respect in which $<x, x>$ differs from $<x, y>$—that ' = ' applies to the former and not the latter—is no more airy fairy than the property of being named 'John Jacob Jingleheimer Smith'. (If anything, it is less so.) Parsons explicitly argues that the phrase ⌜is referred to by α⌝, mentioning a singular term α, is "a paradigm case of predicate that does not stand for a property" (p. 152). He would undoubtedly argue the same for 'is applied to by ' = '.' But exactly the opposite is true: Being named such-and-such is a paradigm case of a property. Being named 'Adolf', for example, is one property that most of us are relieved at having been spared.

Parsons rules against all of these properties at once, on the ground that they are incompatible (*via* his preferred version of the contrapositive of Substitution of Equality) with indeterminate identity. In effect, Parsons attempts to prohibit by decree any disproof of indeterminate identity via Leibniz's Law. One is barred in his system from forming any predicate by λ-abstraction that would discriminate between objects for which there is no fact concerning their identity by applying to one while simultaneously applying against the other. The attempt fails, as it must. Logical proof has a special force that cannot be countered by simple fiat. Consider an analogy to the standard proof of the necessity of identity.

> Suppose for a *reductio* that it is contingent that $x = y$. Then y is unlike x, in that x is necessarily, and hence non-contingently, x; hence by Leibniz's Law $x \neq y$, contradicting the *reductio* assumption.

Parsons's proposed restriction on λ-abstraction is analogous to—and no more legitimate than—a proposal to save contingent identity by restricting Leibniz's Law to those properties that do not discriminate between contingently identical objects. Suppose a believer in contingent identity replies to the above proof by rejecting the application of Leibniz's Law to the property of being non-contingently identical with x. And suppose the rejection is not on the ground that this application of Leibniz's Law is intuitively fallacious (since it is not), nor on the ground that, like the property of being a property that is not a property of itself, the crucial property of necessarily being x can be proved not to exist (since it cannot be). Suppose the objection is merely on the ground that, given Leibniz's Law, such properties as necessarily being x and non-contingently being x would preclude contingent identity. Which party begs the question and carries the burden of proof? Is it the theorem prover who employs intuitively valid and (nearly) universally accepted reasoning to establish a metaphysically significant result? Or is it the gainsayer who objects to the crucial logical step in the proof, not on the ground that nothing can be necessarily identical with x (since, as the gainsayer concedes, x is thus) nor on the ground that the inference is intuitively invalid (since it is not), but because the crucial step is incompatible with contingent identity? (See note 15.)

Parsons's objection to the property of determinate identity with x is not on the ground that nothing can be determinately x. On the contrary, he concedes that x itself is exactly that. Nor does he object to the property on the ground that it can be proved not to exist. For it cannot be. His objection is just that such a property would mark out a difference between x and anything indeterminately identical with x, thus precluding indeterminate identity altogether. This is not a rebuttal as much as it is a refusal to concede, exactly analogous to the contingent-identity theorist's refusal to acknowledge that his position has been refuted.

Parsons announces in an early chapter of *Indeterminate Identity* that if it is indeterminate whether $a = b$, then he will prove that the predicate 'is something such that it is indeterminate whether it is b' fails to express a property (p. 15n). After providing the proof, Parsons remarks, "In the discussion above it became clear that some abstracts, such as the one employed in [Formulation IV], cannot stand for one of the properties in terms of which we define identity" (p. 54). But what Parsons actually proves is something conditional: if $\nabla(a = b)$, then '$(\lambda x)\ [\nabla(x = b)]$' fails to express a property. His proof is a simple variation on Formulation IV of the disproof of indeterminate identity: If there were such a property, a and b would be distinguishable by means of it, and hence distinct rather than indeterminately identical (pp. 48–51). (The proof here employs the contrapositive of Substitution of Equality, but in the form Parsons accepts.) Contrary to Parsons's spin on his theorem, it does not yield the result that the predicate in question expresses no property ("in terms of which we define identity"). One can likewise prove using Leibniz's Law that if x is contingently identical with y, then there is no property of necessarily being x. Properly understood, this weaker theorem casts no doubt on the necessity of identity. For it is a trivial corollary. One need only observe that the predicate '(λx) $[\nabla(x = b)]$' expresses the property (unpossessed, as it turns out) of being a thing such that it is indeterminate whether it is b to draw the proper conclusion from Parsons's theorem.[21]

The disproofs of indeterminate identity are remarkably resilient. Like the disproofs of contingent identity, they enjoy a force irresistible by anyone who is prepared to accept the deliverances of logic.

V

Parsons writes:

> ...given that the language contains no non-extensional contexts, Leibniz's Law holds. Indeed, if Leibniz's Law were not to hold for such an extensional language, this would cast

---

[21] Parsons believes there are pairs of objects, a and b, such that $\nabla(a = b)$. Given his theorem, it follows that the predicate 'is indeterminately identical with b' fails to express a property. But this is no proof of the latter thesis. Here again, Parsons's *modus ponens* is another's *modus tollens*. (See note 15.) Nor does the assertion that the predicate in question expresses the property of indeterminately being b beg the question against Parsons. By contrast, Parsons's argument that the predicate fails to express any property *does* beg the question, since it relies on the premise that for some a and b, $\nabla(a = b)$, and this is the very question at issue.

serious doubt on whether our sign of identity were actually expressing identity, as opposed to some weaker relation." (*ibid.*, p. 36)[22]

Parsons is referring by 'Leibniz's Law' to Substitution of Equality. Ironically, however, even when the name is taken instead as referring to *LL* (contrary to Parsons's intent), his words retain a great deal of their force, if not indeed all of it. Might it be that Parsons uses ' = ' and its cognates (e.g., 'identical', 'distinct', etc.) in some non-standard way—perhaps also the word 'property' and its cognates (e.g., 'differ')? Might he mean by these words something different than their English meanings? He categorically denies doing so:

> I mean by 'identical' exactly what others mean by it; this is the only way I know to guarantee that we are discussing the same issue. . . . I use 'distinct' for 'not identical' (p. 32).

> I intend my terminology to be completely normal. When I speak of identity, and when I use the sign ' = ', or use 'is' in the sense of identity, I mean exactly what everyone else means. . . . The same is true of my use of the words . . . 'property', 'object', 'refer', . . . (p. 108)

However, as with the protests of Berkeley and his heirs that they mean by 'table' and by 'chair' exactly what these words mean in English, Parsons's own explanations of his usage, taken by themselves, provide no evidence one way or another. By contrast, some crucial remarks provide compelling evidence that he uses words like 'identical' and 'property' non-standardly.

Parsons endorses definitions for 'identical' and 'distinct' in terms of indiscernibility and discernibility, respectively, equivalent to the following (pp. 31–32):

> *x* and *y* are *identical* = $_{def}$ every property is either (*i*) a property of *x* iff it is a property of *y*; or else (*ii*) indeterminate with respect to each of *x* and *y*;

> *x* and *y* are *distinct* = $_{def}$ *x* and *y* are not identical (as just defined), i.e., there is a property that is both (*i*) either a property of *x* or a property of *y* but not a property of both; and (*ii*) determinate with respect to *x* or *y* or both.

Without doubting either of Leibniz's principles of *the indiscernibility of identicals* or *the identity of indiscernibles*, many would question whether identity can be defined or analyzed in terms of indiscernibility. We may sidestep this issue for present purposes by supposing that Parsons's "definitions" are meant to capture a metaphysically necessary and epistemologically *a priori* equivalence, nothing more. The disjunctive nature of Parsons's definition of identity is another red flag. The result of deleting the disjunct (*ii*) altogether expresses a simpler notion of indiscernibility. But as we have seen, the simpler notion is unintended and far less useful. If there is even a single property *P* that is indeterminate with respect to *x*, it is indeterminate in that case whether *x* has *P* iff *x* has *P*. It does not cease to be true merely on this ground,

---

[22] Similarly in 'Worldly Indeterminacy of Identity,' Parsons and Woodruff write: "In fact, the notion of identity that we are discussing validates Leibniz's Law: if a and b are identical for us, then their names are interchangeable in all extensional contexts. We agree that if this principle does not hold (for extensional contexts) then true identity is not under discussion. Leibniz's Law holds for the identity we discuss" (p. 174n) . . . "a determinately true identity should sanction interchangeability of its terms (assuming that there are no non-extensional contexts at issue). We agree completely, and we note that the metaphysical account of identity sketched above sanctions this version of Leibniz's Law" (p. 177).

however, that *x* is indiscernible in the intended sense from itself. The more inclusive, disjunctive notion of indiscernibility applies to anything and itself, regardless of the properties indeterminate with respect to it.

So far, so good. But there is a striking anomaly. Parsons explicitly restricts his use of the word 'property' to include only properties of a special kind—contradicting his assurance that he means by the word 'property' "what everyone else means" (p. 108)—and he explicitly stipulates that his definitions for 'identical' and 'distinct' are to be understood as employing his restricted use of 'property':

> [I have] talked about properties and relations "in the world"; this is an ontological notion of property. People sometimes talk about properties in another way, using 'concept' and 'property' interchangeably, sometimes even construing properties as the *meanings* [i.e., the semantic contents] of predicates. Suppose there are two sorts of things that are commonly called properties: real things in the world, on the one hand, and parts of our conceptual apparatus for representing the world, on the other. . . . If the distinction can be made, then it is clear that the theory I am discussing sees real identity in the world as arising with the worldly properties, not the conceptual ones. When people feel that [λ-abstracts] *must* stand for properties, they may be thinking of the other sorts of properties, those that are part of our conceptual apparatus. We can happily admit that [the λ-abstract, $\ulcorner(\lambda z)[\nabla(x=z)]\urcorner$, occurring in Formulation IV] expresses a *conceptual* property. But there is no reason that I know of for assuming that conceptual properties validate the contrapositive of [Substitution of Equality], which involves [only] the worldly sort of properties.
>
> . . . When I say without qualification that a predicate does not stand for a property, it will be the worldly sort of property that I have in mind. (p. 55)

My own view is that Parsons's attempt to draw a distinction between properties that form "part of our conceptual apparatus for representing the world" and those special properties that are "real parts of the world" is a determinate non-starter. Concepts are no less real than properties—and, for that matter, no more real. (Parsons concedes that his distinction is a difficult one to make.) But there are various distinctions that might be mis-characterized along such lines as "worldly" *vs.* "conceptual." There is the distinction between natural and nonnatural properties, for example. There is the distinction between empirical and innate concepts. Parsons may have one of these distinctions in mind, or some related one. Whichever distinction he intends, Parsons believes it underlies an ambiguity in the word "property", and he specifies that his use of the word is restricted to properties of the "real" or 'worldly' sort, excluding "conceptual" properties.

It is important to note something that Parsons is not claiming. One might say that some apparent properties are only *pseudo-properties*, in the following sense: that some expressions that function grammatically as monadic predicates do not assert or affirm anything about the referent of the attached singular term, but instead affirm something about some other, related thing. Clear examples are not ready to hand, but artificial examples are easy to construct. If we define the adjective 'pseudonymous', deviously enough, so that a sentence of the form $\ulcorner\alpha$ is pseudonymous$\urcorner$ is true if and only if the term α itself is a pseudonym, then the object of which we affirm something in the true sentence 'Mark Twain is, but Samuel Clemens is not, pseudonymous' is not Twain himself (i.e., Clemens). The word 'pseudonymous' does not express an aspect or feature of the author, but at best a property of his penname.[23] Parsons does not claim that a candidate for which there is no fact of identity or distinctness with Theseus's ship is not itself something such that there is no fact of the matter whether it is *the Ship of Theseus*. On the contrary, he maintains, or at least allows, that the candidate ship is exactly so, and that the predicate 'is something such that it is indeterminate whether it is *the Ship of Theseus*' expresses a concept that the candidate ship itself fits. Parsons's reason for dismissing the concept expressed in making a determination of identity or distinctness is very different. It is that the concept is in some manner part of our conception of the world rather than part of the world itself. This is considerably more vague than the complaint that the concept yields a pseudo-property in the foregoing sense, but it is clear that the alleged defect, whatever it is, is not that the relevant object somehow fails to fall under the concept.

Suppose there is a special subclass of properties that Parsons intends. We should avoid the potentially ambiguous word 'property'. I shall hereby coin the term '*w-characteristic*' for the special "real worldly" things that Parsons means by 'property'. And let us use the word 'feature' as a general term covering both *w*-characteristics and the "conceptual" things that Parsons excludes.

Insofar as there is a distinction between two sorts of features—the *w*-characteristics and the non-*w*-characteristics—and insofar as logic is concerned with extremely general features of the world and the things that populate it, logic should be concerned not merely with a thing's *w*-characteristics but with all of its features, from the ridiculous to the sublime. Logic should no more confine itself to a thing's *w*-characteristics than it should restrict its monadic predicates to, for example, natural-kind terms. (Indeed, Parsons acknowledges a need to allow for monadic predicates that express non-*w*-characteristic features, at p. 16.) On the basis of Parsons's description, the distinction between *w*-characteristics and other features would appear to be a distinction in metaphysics, rather than a distinction in pure logic. Yet Parsons's definition of identity is explicitly framed in terms only of *w*-characteristics. This gives rise to a peculiar collapse in Parsons's account of indeterminate identity.

Consider the binary equivalence relation of *sharing exactly the same w-characteristics*, i.e., coincidence in *w*-characteristics. Let us call this '*w-indiscernibility*', to be contrasted with indiscernibility *simpliciter*, i.e., coincidence in *all* features, mundane and other-worldly alike. The natural definitions are the following:

x and *y* are *w-indiscernible* $=_{def}$ every *w*-characteristic is either (*i*) a characteristic of *x* iff it is also a characteristic of *y*, or else (*ii*) indeterminate with respect to each of *x* and *y*;

x and *y* are *w-discernible* $=_{def}$ *x* and *y* are not *w*-indiscernible (as just defined).

---

[23] Or perhaps a relation between the author and his penname. By contrast, the phrase 'is believed by Ralph to be a spy' expresses a genuine property attributed to the object referred to by any attached term. Even W. V. O. Quine's predicate 'was so-called because of his size', when positioned in the appropriate context, arguably expresses a genuine property of Barbarelli: that of being called 'Giorgione' because of his size. *Cf.* Quine, 'Quantifiers and Propositional Attitudes,' in his *The Ways of Paradox* (New York: Random House, 1966), 183–194, at 184–189; and 'Reference and Modality,' in his *From a Logical Point of View* (New York: Harper & Row, 1953, 1961), pp. 139–159, at 139–140.

The definitions are legitimate if the notion of a w-characteristic is. Notice also that insofar as there may be no fact of the matter whether a given object has or lacks a given w-characteristic, the definitions make room for the prospect of a pair of objects, x and y, that are indeterminate with respect to w-discernibility—provided, of course, that x's feature of being determinately w-indiscernible from x (and the like) are not themselves w-characteristics. In essence, this is Parsons's reason for thinking that identity can be indeterminate: Identity is defined as w-indiscernibility, which can be indeterminate.

Using the newly introduced terminology, and taking Parsons literally and at face value, his position may be characterized thus: There can be an object x that determinately has some features determinately not shared by another object y, which in turn determinately has features determinately not shared by x, and although x and y are thus determinately discernible from one another, if x and y are not determinately w-discernible from one another—i.e., unless there is a w-characteristic that is determinately a characteristic of one and determinately not a characteristic of the other—logic does not license the inference that x and y are distinct things. Instead, logic declares that under the circumstances, *despite* their not being exactly alike in every respect, there is no fact of the matter whether x and y are one and the very same thing or instead two distinct things. Moreover, according to Parsons, although *LL* (or an appropriate monadic-predicate version of *LL* together with the classical rule of λ-abstraction) would support the conclusion that x and y cannot be one and the very same thing, this casts not the slightest doubt on the philosophical thesis that there is no fact of the matter. Instead this only shows that classical logic begs the question against the philosophical thesis. In particular, while Parsons is prepared to allow that the λ-abstract $\ulcorner(\lambda z)[\nabla(x=z)]\urcorner$ expresses a feature—one that is determinately not a feature of x itself but is determinately a feature of anything indeterminately identical with x—he maintains that the predicate fails to express ("stand for") a w-characteristic. This on the ground that otherwise indeterminate identity is impossible.

Again I ask: Which position begs the question and carries the burden of proof? The one that relies on intuitively valid axioms and inference rules to refute an exotic, provocative, and peculiarly philosophical thesis? Or the one that relies on the exotic thesis (instead of exposing any fallacy) to support the rejection of the axioms and inference rules?

One might reply that Parsons will understand such expressions as 'alike' and 'unlike' not in terms of features, but more strictly in terms of w-characteristics, and consequently he will understand the phrase 'exactly alike in every respect' to mean w-indiscernibility rather than general indiscernibility *simpliciter*, i.e., coincidence in all features—w-characteristics and non-w-characteristic features alike. But he does not, at least not consistently. For example, he contends that there is an empty set, $\emptyset$, with no determinate or indeterminate elements ('the emptiest set'), and that this set $\emptyset$ is indeterminately identical with various other 'empty sets.' Of these latter sets, he says 'they, unlike $\emptyset$, have indeterminate (individual) members' (p. 187). Yet Parsons must hold, on pain of inconsistency, that a set's feature of having indeterminate members is not a *w*-characteristic.[24] And indeed, Parsons evidently uses the word 'other'—normally a synonym of 'distinct'—at least occasionally (as I did three sentences back) for an object with different features (i.e., discernible *simpliciter*) from a given object. Thus, discussing the question of how to count how many ships have left port when only one *determinately* left port and that one is indeterminately *w*-discernible from two ships that did not determinately leave port, he says, "we point at the ship leaving port and say'one'—because it is determinately leaving port—and we do not count the other ships [i.e., the two with which it is indeterminately identical] because we know that they are not determinately ships that left port" (p. 137). Never mind the question of whether, and how, we are supposed to know that a ship neither determinately left port nor determinately did not. And never mind the question of how indeterminately identicals are to be counted.[25] Parsons's use of the word 'other' cannot be consistently intended in the sense of 'distinct', given his explicit explanation of his use of the latter. The justification for his use of 'other'—which, aside from his philosophical position, is perfectly natural—is closely related to the fact that the ships in question do not share all of their features, and therefore each ship differs from the . . . well, the *other*.[26]

VI

Parsons endorses unrestricted Substitution of Equality as a logically valid rule of inference in an extensional language even while rejecting its contrapositive as invalid. His endorsement of unrestricted Substitution is an acknowledgement of a

---

[24] Parsons develops a non-bivalent set theory based on the idea that for some sets, there is no fact of the matter whether a given object is an element (pp. 181–192). Suppose some sets are "fuzzy" in this sense of having indeterminate elements. Suppose there is a pair of sets, K and K', that share exactly the same determinate elements, but some object x is determinately not an element of K whereas it is indeterminate whether x is or is not an element of K'. Parsons thinks it is obvious that it is indeterminate whether K is K'. Quite the contrary, K' is fuzzy with respect to x's membership whereas K is not; hence, they must be different sets. Parsons bases his contrary conclusion on a variant of extensionality according to which sets are indeterminately identical whenever there is an object such that it is determinate whether that object is an element of one but indeterminate whether it is an element of the other, adding "I assume that any non-bivalent theory of sets will adopt this as a basic axiom" (pp. 181–182). This assumption is unwarranted, especially since the "axiom" is provably inconsistent, *via LL*, with the idea that a set's membership may be indeterminate. Considerably more plausible is the alternative axiom that sets (fuzzy and otherwise) are identical when, and *only when*, they coincide in determinate membership as well as in determinate nonmembership. This identity condition flows directly (assuming *LL*) from the idea that a set is extensional (unlike a property) but can have indeterminate membership.

[25] N. Angel Pinillos criticizes Parsons on this matter in 'Sets, Counting and Parsons' Vague Objects' (forthcoming).

[26] Similarly, in 'Worldly Indeterminacy of Identity,' Parsons and Woodruff say that whenever there is no fact of identity for a pair of objects a and b, "there is some property that one of them has or lacks and such that the other is indeterminate with respect to having it" (p. 181). Compare this with a context like the following: 'Samuel Clemens's barber erroneously believed Clemens was not Mark Twain; yet he knew that one shaved the other'. Here the word seems to be used in a kind of *substitutional* sense (as opposed to an *objectual* one).

fundamental fact about identity. This is *the indiscernibility of determinately identicals*.[27] That is, if x and y are determinately one and the very same thing, then they are exactly alike in every respect. This fundamental fact about identity makes no exceptions for any features, including those that are not w-characteristics. For everything is determinately identical with itself and nothing else, and any single thing is exactly like itself in *every* respect—w-characteristics and other features alike. This is why Parsons concedes that if unrestricted Substitution were not validated in an extensional language, "this would cast serious doubt on whether our sign of identity were actually expressing identity, as opposed to some weaker relation" (p. 36; *cf.* also note 22 above). It is precisely here that the anomaly rears its head. The definition of identity that Parsons embraces does not automatically accord with his acknowledgment of this fundamental fact about identity. Instead of *the indiscernibility of determinately identicals* the definition directly yields only *the w-indiscernibility of determinately identicals*.[28] Insofar as w-characteristics form a proper subclass of features generally, we so far have no guarantee that w-indiscernibles will be indiscernible *simpliciter*, and hence no guarantee that determinately identicals will be indiscernible. Even determinate w-indiscernibility is by itself no guarantee of indiscernibility *simpliciter*. Ironically, for this reason, contrary to Parsons's intentions, the semantics he provides for his antiseptic language, taken in conjunction with his definition of identity, fail to validate unrestricted Substitution. Instead he validates a weakened variant subject to the very same restrictions (whatever they may be) that he needs to impose on λ-abstraction. Specifically, if the formula $\ulcorner(\lambda x)[\varphi_x]\urcorner$ expresses a feature that is not a w-characteristic, Parsons's semantics does not exclude models in which φ_α and $\ulcorner\alpha = \beta\urcorner$ are both true while φ_β is false, since $\ulcorner\alpha = \beta\urcorner$ is made true by mere w-indiscernibility. But if the inference is invalid even though φ contains no non-extensional operators of any kind, then whatever else $\ulcorner\alpha = \beta\urcorner$ means, it does not affirm genuine identity. By his own standards, Parsons's antiseptic framework strongly supports the charge that he does not mean genuine identity by ' $=$ ', and instead he means the weaker relation of w-indiscernibility. By those standards, it is reasonable to charge his framework with being irrelevant.

Parsons attempts to prove from his semantics for ' $=$ ' that Substitution must automatically be valid within his non-bivalent, extensional semantic framework (pp. 35–36). But given his definition of identity, the proof is fallacious and the "theorem" false. Nor is it immediately obvious how his semantics is best modified to validate unrestricted Substitution without also validating its contrapositive.[29] Unless

---

[27] Parsons explicitly endorses this principle at pp. 93–94.

[28] Not to be confused with *the w-indiscernibility of identicals*, which Parsons does not accept (as it is intended here).

[29] Parsons concedes that his proof in some sense begs the question by employing Substitution in the metalanguage. But there is a more egregious error: The reasoning is fallacious. The "proof" is by induction on the complexity of $\varphi\alpha$. Treating ' $=$ ' as a sign for w-indiscernibility in accordance with Parsons's semantics, the argument concerning the base case where φ_α is an atomic monadic formula, $\ulcorner\Pi(\alpha)\urcorner$, goes through only on the assumption that every simple monadic predicate Π (one not formed by λ-abstraction) expresses a w-characteristic (or else the semantic feature of *being applied to by Π* is itself a w-characteristic). Analogously for the argument concerning the case where φ_α is the negation of an atomic monadic formula, $\ulcorner\sim\Pi(\alpha)\urcorner$. But Parsons explicitly stipulates that some simple monadic predicates do not express w-characteristics (p. 16). (He also specifies, at 152, that semantic

an object's entire résumé of features modally supervenes on its narrower résumé of determinate *w*-characteristics and determinate *w*-non-characteristics,[30] it is meta-physically possible for there to be determinately *w*-indiscernible objects that are not determinately indiscernible—and hence, that are determinately discernible.[31] And even if this is metaphysically impossible, unless an object's résumé of features is not only supervenient on its determinate *w*-résumé, but analytically *reducible* to the latter, it remains *logically* possible for there to be a pair of discernible objects that determinately share all the same *w*-characteristics and all the same *w*-non-characteristics. Parsons's endorsement of unrestricted Substitution of Equality as a logically valid inference rule thus stands in pressing need of justification. Likewise his endorsement of the equivalent *indiscernibility of determinately identicals.* It is no justification of the reducibility hypothesis that Substitution in conjunction with indeterminate identity requires it. (See note 15.) Quite the contrary, this very fact, in the absence of any useful characterization of a *w*-characteristic, raises a serious doubt whether Parsons's theory can plausibly embrace Substitution. Substitution is unjustified on Parsons's account even as an inference rule of metaphysics, let alone as one of pure logic.

Whereas determinate *w*-indiscernibility is no guarantee of indiscernibility *simpliciter,* indeterminate *w*-indiscernibility is a guarantee of discernibility. If *x* and *y* are indeterminately *w*-indiscernible, *ipso facto* they determinately differ in some of their features—e.g., the feature of being indeterminately *w*-indiscernible from *x*. In the absence of any useful characterization of the class of *w*-characteristics, there is no *a priori* disproof of the possibility of indeterminate *w*-discernibility. What *is* provable, *via* Leibniz's original principle of *the indiscernibility of identicals,* is that if *x* and *y* are indeterminately *w*-discernible, then $x \neq y$. If *x* and *y* are indeterminately *w*-indiscernible, then there is determinately a feature that is a feature of one and not of the other, and hence there is determinately at least one respect in which they differ.

---

properties like that of being applied to by a particular predicate are not *w*-characteristics.) Given his definition of identity, meta-Substitution thus fails to preserve meta-truth in these very cases. For a similar reason, some of the inductive cases (e.g., the case for negation) fail wherever *λ*-abstraction is restricted.

The semantics can be modified to validate unrestricted Substitution without also validating its contrapositive, which Parsons deems invalid. But if it is logically possible for determinately *w*-indiscernible objects to differ in some of their non-*w*-characteristic features, any such modification will rely on some thesis or other that is not pure semantics or is philosophically wrong-headed, or both. (Let 'F' express some feature that logically might discriminate between some pair of determinately *w*-indiscernibles, and consider 'F(*x*) · *x*=*y* ∴ F(*y*)'.) Substitution would be derivable from the independent assumption that, as a matter of logic, *w*-indiscernibles have all their features in common. But Parsons cannot accept *the indiscernibility of w-indiscernibles,* since it also validates the contrapositive of unrestricted Substitution. Parsons's derivation of Substitution can be validated instead by banishing all simple monadic predicates from his object language that do not express *w*-characteristics, and imposing obvious related restrictions (e.g., on *λ*-abstraction; *cf.* note 17). But this does nothing to allay the worry that ' = ' is misleadingly used as a sign for *w*-indiscernibility instead of genuine identity. On the contrary, the discriminating predicates that would otherwise reveal the deception have been suppressed by decree precisely in order to maintain the facade of indiscernibility.

[30] A *w*-non-characteristic of an object is a *w*-characteristic the object lacks.

[31] Suppose there is a feature *P* that *x* determinately has (lacks) but *y* does not. Then *x* determinately has, while *y* determinately lacks, the feature of determinately having (lacking) *P*.

Parsons rejects this proof, insisting as he does that x and y are indeterminately w-discernible if and only if they are indeterminately identical. He explicitly rejects Leibniz's principle as neither true nor false—unless it is understood in a sense equivalent to the claim that either $x \neq y$ or they are exactly alike *or else there is no fact of the matter whether $x = y$ and at the same time no fact of the matter whether they are exactly alike*. He rejects even the putatively weaker principle of *the w-indiscernibility of identicals*, unless it too is understood in a similarly weak sense.

At any rate, he *seems* to. But does he really do so? Taking his words literally, Parsons is committed to holding that even if x and y determinately differ from one another, they cannot be deemed distinct unless they are determinately discernible by means of a special kind of feature, a w-characteristic. Instead he holds that in the absence of determinate w-indiscernibility, the affirmation of x's distinctness from y must be deemed neither true nor false, despite the determinate differences between them. At least Parsons does say that in that case the affirmation of the identity of x and y is untrue. But taking his words at their face value, even this consolation claim stands in need of a theoretical justification. Unless and until a plausible case is presented that an object's entire résumé of features supervenes on its determinate w-résumé, Parsons cannot justifiably rule out the bizarre prospect that x and y are one and the very same thing after all, despite determinately differing from one another. This very notion does not merely defy commonsense. It is scarcely comprehensible.

As we have seen, by his own standards an alternative interpretation is invited. And indeed an alternative interpretation of Parsons's pronouncements does seem appropriate. The obvious hypothesis is that he misunderstands the sign '$=$' and the word 'identity', and their cognates (e.g., 'same thing'), taking them as terms for w-indiscernibility rather than genuine identity. This hypothesis fits perfectly with Parsons's ostensible rejection of *the indiscernibility of identicals*, understood in the relevant stronger sense, as well as his rejection of *LL* and of the unrestricted contrapositive of Substitution of Equality. It even fits with his ostensible rejection of the w-indiscernibility of identicals, understood in the corresponding sense. He will also reject *the w-indiscernibility of w-indiscernibles* as untrue (and that all bald men are bald men, etc.), similarly understood, since he holds that statements of the form $\ulcorner(x)[F(x) \supset F(x)]\urcorner$ lack truth-value when 'F' is inapplicable with respect to some object. The hypothesis fits equally nicely with Parsons's insistence that there can be objects for which there is no fact of the matter concerning their "identity" (read: *their w-indiscernibility*). Coupled with his explicitly restricted use of the word 'property' as a term for w-characteristics, the hypothesis fits equally nicely with his proposed restrictions on λ-abstraction and on the contrapositive of Substitution of Equality, and with his responses to the purported disproofs of indeterminate "identity." And of course, the hypothesis turns what is otherwise a scarcely comprehensible anomaly into a piece of trivia.[32]

---

[32] The very availability of this interpretation of Parsons's use of '$=$' and 'identical' and their cognates demonstrates that, in some sense, Parsons's position is coherent. Insofar as there is a legitimate restriction on features comprised by the alleged w-characteristics, the suggested interpretation, in effect, yields something akin to a *model* that satisfies Parsons's pronouncements, by reinterpreting his use of 'identity' to mean 'w-indiscernibility'. It does not follow, however, that the

An alternative, and perhaps more likely, hermeneutical hypothesis is that Parsons uses such expressions as ' = ', 'identical', 'same thing', etc., indiscriminantly both for w-indiscernibility and for genuine identity. Since he believes the latter is 'defined' by the former, he would have no reason to differentiate between the two relations in his usage. On this alternative hypothesis, Parsons's endorsement of unrestricted Substitution is understandable, perhaps even alongside his proposed restrictions on the contrapositive of Substitution and on λ-abstraction. But on either hypothesis, his endorsement of unrestricted Substitution remains in pressing need of justification. Is there any plausible ground at all (other than confusion resulting from equivocation) to suppose that if x and y are determinately w-indiscernible, then *ipso facto* they are exactly alike in every respect?

VII

Set aside for the moment the question of the proper use of pre-established signs and words. Kripke coined the term 'schmidentity' for the equivalence relation that holds between a thing x and x but nothing else. Let us temporarily usurp Kripke's artificial term, and use it here as a term for the equivalence relation of indiscernibility *simpliciter*.[33] Any object x is schmidentical with x. And given unrestricted feature-abstraction (permitting the abstraction of such features as *being Nathan Salmon*), anything schmidentical with x *ipso facto* has x's feature of *being x*—the feature (whatever it is) expressed by the predicate '___ is x'.[34] As we have seen, Parsons is committed to the thesis that determinately w-indiscernible objects are *ipso facto* schmidentical—though there is no obvious justification for the thesis. He must concede, however, that *in*determinately w-indiscernible objects are *not* schmidentical; they are discernible by means of their determinate features. For if it is indeterminate whether x and y are w-discernible, then y lacks x's feature of determinate w-indiscernibility from x.

The notion of indeterminate schmidentity is provably inconsistent. Objects are either determinately discernible from one another, or else they are determinately indiscernible; and the only thing that x is indiscernible from is x itself. Parsons

position literally (i.e., semantically) expressed in Parsons's pronouncements is logically consistent. For the term 'identical' is a term of logic, alongside the other logical operators and connectives of philosophical English ('not', 'and', 'or', 'iff', 'something', etc.), and as such its meaning remains constant among the logically admissible models. The putative 'model' generated by the interpretation is not logically admissible.

[33] Saul Kripke, *Naming and Necessity* (Cambridge, Mass.: Harvard University Press, 19), p. 108. The present argument is essentially Kripke's. In 'Indeterminacy of Identity of Objects and Sets,' Parsons and Woodruff say that 'how identity behaves *in the world* is . . . characterized in terms of properties and relations, not in terms of concepts or meanings' (p. 330). If Parsons insists that schmidentity, in the present sense, is a "conceptual" relation rather than a "worldly" one, then let it be such. It makes no difference. (Still it is worth noting that, intuitively, and *contra* Parsons, insofar as x and y are genuinely the very *same* thing, they are *one* thing rather than two, and hence they fall under the very same concepts and share the very same features—w-characteristics and otherwise.)

[34] We could also say that x is *schmdistinct* from anything that is not x—if only the word 'schmdistinct' were sayable.

must concede *the indiscernibility of schmidenticals*. This Leibnizian principle has no exceptions—no false instances and no neither-true-nor-false instances. Parsons "happily admits" that although $\ulcorner(\lambda x)[\nabla(a = x)]\urcorner$ does not express a *w*-characteristic, it does express a feature (p. 55). I imagine he will concede the same for 'is indeterminately schmidentical with *the Ship of Theseus*'. He must then concede also that nothing has this feature, and that *nothing can*.

Perhaps Parsons will reply that all this shows only that such expressions as ' = ' and 'identical' are ambiguous between *w*-indiscernibility and indiscernibility *simpliciter*. If so, his theory introduces a bizarre twist on Bishop Joseph Butler's famous distinction.[35] Here we have instead a distinction between *identity in the loose and philosophic sense* and *identity in the strict and popular sense*.

Which one are we typically concerned with—either when doing philosophy or when living life—when we are concerned with a question of *the very same thing*. Do we settle for *w*-indiscernibility as what we really intend, or do we hold out for schmidentity? Consider an unscrupulous but philosophically sophisticated watch repairman who repairs a precious gold timepiece, removing the gold and replenishing the missing matter with cheap material painted a golden hue. He returns the family heirloom to a customer, who eventually notices the modification and returns to the repairman.

"This isn't my watch," the customer complains.

"That's not a fair and accurate statement, sir," comes the reply, "and I resent the implications of your remark. This watch determinately has exactly the same *w*-characteristics that the original watch has, and it determinately lacks exactly the same *w*-characteristics that the other one lacks. In a word, this watch and the original are *w*-indiscernible. Therefore, they're the same watch in the philosophic sense."

"What are you talking about? This is a very different watch. What are you, some kind of crook?"

"Mind your manners, sir. I admit this watch does not have all the same features that the original one has. I make no warranty that this watch and the original are exactly like in every respect. I guarantee only identity with the original in the philosophic sense, and for that *w*-indiscernibilty is necessary and sufficient."

"This one's giving me a rash. My wrist is discolored."

"So there are a few minor differences between this watch and the other one. But the warranty guarantees you only a watch *w*-indiscernible from the original. Good day, sir."

"The paint is coming off this watch. Look at my wrist. It's green. Look at these welts."

"I can recommend a reputable dermatologist. He's not so good at philosophy, but . . . "

"Hey, you're wearing my watch!"

"No, I am wearing *my* watch. I grant you, it happens to have many of the features the original watch has. But I assure you my watch also has at least one *w*-characteristic that the original watch does not have. This watch that I have returned to you has exactly the same *w*-characteristics as the original one, and is therefore identical with it in the philosophic sense."

"Identical, scmidentical! This is a piece of junk."[36]

---

[35] Butler, 'Of Personal Identity,' from his *The Analogy of Religion;* reprinted in *Personal Identity,* ed. J. Perry (Berkeley and Los Angeles: University of California Press, 1975), pp. 99–105.

[36] *Cf.* Francis W. Dauer, 'How Not to Reidentify the Parthenon,' *Analysis,* 33, 2 (December 1972), pp. 63–64.

Pace, Parsons, insofar as identity is logically tied to a notion of indiscernibility, the operative notion is indiscernibility *simpliciter*, i.e., coincidence in all features, w-characteristics and non-w-characteristic features alike. Indiscernibility in terms of a restricted range of features is no substitute for genuine identity. The two are not exactly alike in every respect. There may be no fact of the matter whether x and y are w-indiscernible, as opposed to being identical, and this only when there *is* a fact that x and y are discernible and hence distinct. The restriction to w-indiscernibility may be a rebel with a cause, but it is also an *ad hoc* epicycle, and its cause a theoretical dead end.

11

Personal Identity: What's the Problem?[1]
(1995*u*)

I

We are gathered here to pay homage to a great genius. Saul Kripke is a phenomenon, nothing less, and the discipline of Philosophy is much the better for
his contribution to it. My own intellectual development has benefitted immeasur-
ably from my association with Kripke. I begin with a pair of quotes from another
great contemporary philosopher. Woody Allen said, "I do not wish to achieve
immortality through my work; I wish to achieve it through not dying." Like
Allen, Kripke will live on through his work long after most of the rest of us are
forgotten.

Woody Allen's semi-autobiographical movie, *Stardust Memories*, includes a brief
sketch in which Allen's character says the following:

> I've never been able to fall in love. I've never been able to find the perfect woman. There's
> always something wrong. And then I met Doris. A wonderful woman, great personality.
> But for some reason, I'm just not turned on sexually by her. Don't ask me why. And then I
> met Rita. An animal, nasty, mean, trouble. And I love going to bed with her. Though
> afterward I always wished that I was back with Doris. And then I thought to myself, 'If
> only I could put Doris's brain in Rita's body. Wouldn't that be wonderful?' And I thought,
> 'Why not? What the hell, I'm a surgeon.' . . . So I performed the operation, and everything
> went perfectly. I switched their personalities. . . . I made Rita into a warm, wonderful,
> charming, sexy, sweet, giving, mature woman. And then I fell in love with Doris.

This little tragedy raises a host of philosophical issues. The central issues
concern the irrational nature of human sexual attraction and romantic love, and the
often-troubling relationship between the two. The dialogue also raises moral issues
about the treatment of people as means rather than as ends in themselves, the
objectification and victimization of women, and related issues. The passage also

[1] The present essay incorporates portions of my "Trans-World Identification and Stipulation,"
Philosophical Studies, 84 (1996), pp. 203–223. The essay is dedicated to the memory of a
remarkable woman, Sandy Shaffer. It was delivered (in part) at the University of San Marino
International Center for Semiotic and Cognitive Studies Conference on Saul Kripke's Contribution
to Philosophy, May 1996; and at the University of Haifa Conference on Naming, Necessity, and
More, June 1999. I am grateful to those audiences for their reactions, and to Anthony Brueckner
and Jill Yeomans for their astute observations.

concerns the traditional philosophical problem of the identity of a person through change. With profound apologies to the reader, the present essay is concerned exclusively with personal identity. I shall argue that the traditional philosophical problem dissolves. Recent discussion has tended to focus on the question of 'what matters' in survival, with less attention paid to the original question of what makes someone the very same person even through change. This may be because it is widely believed that strict survival—genuine personal *identity*—is not what is fundamentally important and not what ought to concern us. Though I remain doubtful that this has been successfully argued, I shall not discuss the issue here. If I am correct, there is a better reason for dismissing the question of what personal identity consists in.

Others before me have rejected the problem of personal identity (or more generally, the problem of the identity of a thing through change) as a pseudo-problem, on the ground that it presupposes the questionable doctrine that a person is constituted by *stages* (*phases, temporal parts*), which are supposed to be portions of that person's life history.[2] Once this doctrine is rejected, it is argued, it follows immediately that there is no genuine problem about formulating principles of unification that specify which series of person stages constitute genuine persons, as opposed to gerrymandered non-persons. My objection to the alleged problem of personal identity has virtually nothing to do with this one, which seems to me to be wide of the target. I have no quarrel to make against stages or phases. No doubt much of what has been supposed about them is simply wrong, but that is not sufficient reason to doubt their existence.[3] More important, the typical puzzle cases for personal identity can easily be set out without any appeal, explicit or implicit, to the notion of a person stage (or anything similar). Something different must be

---

[2] For an elegant presentation of the problem of personal identity by means of person stages, see John Perry's introduction, 'The Problem of Personal Identity,' to his valuable edited collection, *Personal Identity* (Berkeley: University of California, 1975), pp. 3–30.

[3] Those who frame the problem of personal identity in terms of person stages tend towards the view that stages are conceptually prior to, or metaphysically more fundamental or real than, the continuants that they constitute through time. They often base their view on Leibniz's Law: *If x is the same thing as y, then x is exactly like y in all respects.* Being a law, this holds for any time t. The stage theorist presupposes an alternative, incorrect temporal generalization: For any *pair* of times t and t', if x is at t the same thing that y is at t', then x is at t exactly like y is at t'. Alternatively (or in addition), some stage theorists misunderstand what it is to have a property at a time t. The stage theorist presupposes that to be such-and-such at t, for any time t, entails being such-and-such *simpliciter* (whereas, in fact, to be such-and-such *simpliciter* is to be such-and-such at the present time). The erroneous temporal over-generalization of Leibniz's Law, and equally the misunderstanding of what it is to have a property at a time, exclude the possibility of genuine change in an enduring object. Each thus raises a pseudo-issue of how, or in what sense, a single thing can be such-and-such at t and not be such-and-such at t'. The stage theorist's answer is that only part of the thing is such-and-such, while another part is not such-and-such. *Cf.* David Lewis, *On the Plurality of Worlds* (Oxford: Basil Blackwell, 1986), at pp. 202–204; and Mark Johnston and Graeme Forbes, 'Is There a Problem about Persistence?' *Proceedings of the Aristotelian Society*, supplementary v. 61 (1987), pp. 107–155. Forbes defends an account that I favor of what it is to have a property at a particular time (pp. 140–142). *Cf.* my *Frege's Puzzle* (Atascadero, Ca.: Ridgeview, 1986, 1991), at pp. 24–43; and 'Tense and Singular Propositions,' in J. Almog, J. Perry, and H. Wettstein, eds., *Themes from Kaplan* (Oxford University Press, 1989), pp. 331–392. While opposed to Lewis's postulation of stages, Johnston joins Lewis in objecting to the account I take, on the ground that

said—or at least something more—if the problem, so formulated, is to be rejected as illegitimate.

The aspect of the problem that I discuss here is connected to a couple of doctrines recently brought into prominence by Saul Kripke's influential monograph, *Naming and Necessity* (Cambridge, Mass.: Harvard University Press, 1972, 1980). First is the doctrine of *individual essentialism*, according to which some properties of individuals are such that those individuals could not exist without those properties. To put it another way, there are properties that certain individuals have in every possible world in which those individuals exist. Second is Kripke's claim that possible worlds are not discovered like planets but "stipulated." In previous work, I have defended the idea that in whatever sense it is correct and useful to recognize possible worlds as entities, it is equally correct and useful to acknowledge that there are also *impossible worlds*.[4] My doctrine of impossible worlds has proved controversial, at least partly because it has seemed unclear whether such an apparatus has any philosophical utility. I here apply the doctrine, in a manner that I hope will prove its mettle, to the traditional problem of personal identity. I shall also bring the controversy of Haecceitism vs. Anti-Haecceitism, and the distinction between reducibility and supervenience, to bear on the problem.

To see how the alleged problem of personal identity might be presented without appealing to person stages and principles of unification, one need only look to the nonphilosopher who does not know from person stages. Woody Allen's character tells us that he has performed a complex surgical procedure on Doris and Rita, interchanging the brains between their two bodies, and consequently interchanging

any time, past or future, is as real as the present. I respond that the past *was* real but is so no longer, and the future *will be* real but is not so yet. The present is currently real in a way that the past and the future are not. This truism is unaffected by the context-relativity of the words 'now', 'past', 'present', etc. *Cf.* my 'Existence,' in J. Tomberlin, ed., *Philosophical Perspectives*, 1 (Atascadero, Ca.: Ridgeview, 1987), pp. 49–108, especially at 73–90.

Johnston defends an account according to which having a property at *t* is having the property in a certain manner (being such-and-such "in the *t*-mode," as it were). Though this is virtually derivable as a special case from the account that Johnston joins Lewis in rejecting, Johnston instead takes his account to be superior in allegedly according the past and the future the same ontological status as the present. Johnston's account has the significant disadvantage that it applies only to temporal qualifications of subject-predicate sentences, e.g. 'In 1987, *a* was such-and-such', and does not directly provide an interpretation for sentences like 'It will rain tomorrow', 'In 1987, there was something such that . . . it . . .', etc. For those sentences to which his account applies, Johnston ultimately falls back on familiar tense-logical semantics (p. 128). The latter holds that to be such-and-such *simpliciter* is to be such-and-such at the present time, and more generally, that truth *simpliciter* (i.e. in reality) is truth at the present time, whereas Johnston evidently means to reject the very idea of being such-and-such *simpliciter*. Why then not also reject the idea of reality, and replace it with different ways of being real (truth in the *t*-mode, truth in the *t'*-mode, etc.)?

[4] 'How *Not* to Derive Essentialism from the Theory of Reference,' *Journal of Philosophy*, 76, 12 (December 1979), pp. 703–725, at 723–724n; *Reference and Essence* (Princeton University Press, 1981; Prometheus Books, 2005), section 28 (especially pp. 238–240); 'Impossible Worlds,' *Analysis*, 44, 3 (June 1984), pp. 114–117; 'Modal Paradox: Parts and Counterparts, Points and Counterpoints,' in P. French, T. Uehling, and H. Wettstein, eds., *Midwest Studies in Philosophy XI: Studies in Essentialism* (Minneapolis: University of Minnesota Press, 1986), pp. 75–120; 'The Logic of What Might Have Been,' *The Philosophical Review*, 98, 1 (January 1989), pp. 3–34; 'This Side of Paradox,' *Philosophical Topics*, 21, 2 (Spring 1993), pp. 187–197.

also what I shall call their 'psychologies'—that is to say, their personality and character traits, their beliefs, attitudes, wishes, hopes, fears, memories, abilities, talents, habits, mannerisms, and the like. The standard philosophical question raised by the incident involving Doris and Rita—*the D/R Incident*, as I shall call it—is sometimes framed in terms of how one of the two person stages at some time *t* immediately after the surgery should be related to various person stages prior to the surgery in order for the stages to qualify as stages of a single person. But the question may be framed instead in terms of the identities of the two women to emerge from the surgery. Consider the woman with whom Allen has now fallen in love—she who now occupies what used to be Doris's body but who now has what used to be Rita's brain. Is that woman Doris? Is she Rita? Or is she perhaps someone else—call her 'Dorita'—who was created in the process, while Doris and Rita were destroyed?

At least three philosophical questions must be distinguished here. The issue of whether the woman in question is Doris or Rita, or neither, is *the primary question* about the D/R Incident.[5] In addition there is the question of how the correct answer to the primary question is determined. This meta-question is often put by asking for (and very often by demanding) a *criterion*, or *criteria*, that settle the primary question. The question bifurcates into two separate questions, which, although they may call for distinct answers, have often been blurred together. First, there is *the epistemological question* of how, or by what means or evidence, one is supposed to come to know or to discover the answer to the primary question about the D/R Incident. Second, and more fundamental, is *the metaphysical question* concerning the correct answer to the primary question, of what makes it the correct answer. In virtue of what fact or facts is it, and not its rivals, the right answer to the primary question? In short, what is it to be the same person? Although each of the three questions has been posed as 'the problem of personal identity,' it is the metaphysical question that has the strongest claim to being *the* problem of personal identity, as the phrase is traditionally meant.[6]

Although the demand for a criterion of personal identity is frequently made, the relevant notion of an identity criterion is usually not made precise. One way of understanding what a personal-identity criterion is that seems to fit much of the literature takes it to be a *trans-temporal link* that connects a person from one time to a person of another and thereby determines that they are the same. More precisely, on this interpretation a *criterion for personal identity* is an ordered triple consisting of a sortal property F and a pair of binary relations R and R', other than personal identity itself, such that it is necessary that for any persons x and y and any times t and t' such that x exists at t and y exists at t', x is the same person at t that y is at t' if there is some F (i.e. something of sort F) to which x bears R at t and to which y bears R' at t'. In most cases, but not all, the intent is better captured by strengthening the 'if' to 'if and only if'. Either way, the particular F is supposed to serve as the link (*via* the relations R and

[5] The classical discussion of this question is Sydney S. Shoemaker, *Self-Knowledge and Self-Identity* (Ithaca: Cornell University Press, 1963), pp. 23f. See also Shoemaker's 'Personal Identity and Memory,' *Journal of Philosophy*, 56 (1959), pp. 868–882; reprinted in Perry, ed., *Personal Identity*.   [6] *Cf.* Shoemaker, *Self-Knowledge and Self-Identity*, pp. 2–3ff.

R') that determines personal identity.[7] A memory-based criterion results by letting F be the sortal *experience token* letting R be the relation of *remembering*, and letting R' be the relation of *experiencing*. According to this criterion, by necessity, x is the same person as an earlier person y if (and only if) x remembers having some experience token of y's. Here the remembered experience links x to y across time.[8] A body-based criterion, by contrast, results by letting F be the sortal *body*, and both R and R' be the relation of *being the functional owner of*—in this case, the relation *u is the person whose body is v*. According to this criterion, by necessity, x and y are the same person if they are linked by having the same body across time. (The reader is invited to verify whether other criteria that have been proposed can also be put into the same general form involving the existence of a trans-temporal link.)

The ambiguity in the meta-question may be traced to a choice regarding the kind of necessity involved in the notion of a personal-identity criterion. The epistemological meta-question results by taking the necessity to be epistemic. The metaphysical meta-question results by taking the necessity to be alethic rather than epistemic. In the former case, the trans-temporal link is the epistemic basis for the judgment of personal identity over time. In the latter case, the link is the *metaphysical* basis for the *fact* of personal identity. Personal identity would thus *consist in* the existence of an appropriate trans-temporal link.

II

Allen says that he made Rita into the ideal mate he was seeking, and so, naturally, he has fallen in love with Doris. By putting things this way, he is evidently presupposing the body-based criterion for personal identity, according to which the woman who now has what was previously Doris's body is Doris, and the woman who now has what was previously Rita's body is Rita. If Allen had instead presupposed a psychology-based criterion—such as the memory-based or a personality-based criterion—he should have described the outcome of the D/R Incident by saying that he has made *Doris* into an ideal mate, but (alas) has fallen in love with *Rita*. Allen

---

[7] The resulting condition for personal identity is the *relative product* of R and the converse of R'. Although the relation of personal identity between x and y is here taken to be a trans-temporal relation, holding between objects across times (more accurately, holding among a quadruple of a person x, a time t, a person y, and a time t'), each of the criterial relations R and R' obtains between objects at a single time. For discussion of an analogous account of cross-world relations, see my *Reference and Essence*, section 13, pp. 116–135. With some ingenuity, other sorts of identity criteria, even criteria for identity at a time (as opposed to identity across time), might also be put into the same general form. For example, the traditional criterion for the identity of sets may be put: $x = y$ iff there is a particular membership m such that x has m and y has m.

[8] This memory-based criterion is not a counter-instance to the observation made in the preceding note that each of the criterial relations R and R' obtains between objects at a single time. The remembering of the experience takes place at a single time when the experience is already past. Although the remembered experience is no longer current, and hence in some sense no longer "real," the person remembering it enters into a relation with it while remembering it, precisely by remembering it. (Alternatively, one might let F be the sortal *biographical event*, R' be the relation of *being the principal figure involved in* a particular event, and R be the relation of *remembering being the principal figure involved in*.)

puts things as he does not because he is a closet materialist, but because he is a brilliant humorist. For some reason, putting things the other way spoils at least some of the humor of the monologue. This may reflect a natural tendency to identify people by their bodies. This tendency may obtain among most people, evidently including even the cleverest and most philosophical of non-philosophers.

In order not to beg the primary question in setting out the philosophical conundrum, philosophers have invented an artificial terminology better suited to philosophical debate. Philosophers call the person who now has what used to be Rita's brain in what used to be Doris's body 'the Doris-body-person', and we call the person who now has what used to be Doris's brain in what used to be Rita's body 'the Rita-body-person'. We may then pose the question: Is the Rita-body-person Rita, or is she Doris? Allen presupposes that the Rita-body-person is still Rita and the Doris-body-person is still Doris. The artificial terminology allows for a way of putting things that neither presupposes nor excludes any criterion of personal identity. We may say, neutrally, that the Rita-body-person is now an ideal mate, but Allen has fallen in love with the Doris-body-person. The primary question may be posed by asking whether Allen has fallen in love with Doris or Rita. That's not comedy; it's philosophy. The joke has been butchered, but the conundrum has been given life.

The different ways of making the identifications are conceptually at odds. They carry with them different conceptions of the changes that have taken place in Allen's victims. On the psychology-based identifications, Doris and Rita retain their brains intact, and therefore also their psychologies. They have *exchanged bodies*. More accurately, their bodies have been interchanged by Allen. Body swapping would no doubt require a variety of adjustments in one's life, some quite radical. Other than the ensuing psychological adjustments, however, on the psychology-based identifications Doris and Rita remain fundamentally unaltered psychologically. This way of making the identifications is committed to making sense of the alleged phenomenon of re-embodied minds or spirits—or to put it perhaps less tendentiously, of re-embodied persons. (It does not require the possibility of altogether disembodied persons, let alone of persons without brains.) By contrast, on the body-based identification, Doris and Rita retain their bodies while having exchanged brains. Each of their individual psychologies has thereby undergone a radical transformation. Although the two women have the same bodies, they are not at all the same as they used to be. One might even say (as Allen does) that the women have traded personalities. Doris now has the personality that was previously Rita's while Rita now has the personality that was previously Doris's. As persons, they have been psychologically *altered* or *modified*. Rita has been transformed into an ideal mate, and Doris has been modified to such an extent that Allen is now obsessed with thoughts of her. This is a very different interpretation or conceptualization of the changes in Doris and Rita. The psychology-based identifications carry with them the ideology of relocation, Allen's body-based identifications the ideology of transmutation. And, of course, the Dorita hypothesis carries with it the ideology of annihilation.

The two different ways of making the identifications are not merely alternative descriptions differing in conceptual flavor but otherwise equally acceptable. The two conceptualizations are logically incompatible. In effect, they present entirely different scenarios. At least one of them is mistaken. One is a misdescription of the situation. This is proved by the transitivity of identity. On the body-based identification Doris = the Doris-body-person, whereas on the psychology-based identifications Doris = the Rita-body-person. Yet it is clear that the Doris-body-person ≠ the Rita-body-person. Therefore at least one of the criteria gets things wrong. Or again, on the body-based identifications the victims retain their bodies while exchanging psychologies, whereas on the psychology-based criteria the victims retain their psychologies while exchanging bodies. Since it is logically impossible to retain one's body (or one's psychology) while also trading it for another, of necessity one or the other of these accounts of the D/R Incident is incorrect. Whichever description is correct (if either is), there is indeed an alternative but equally correct description. For whether it is correct to say of Doris and Rita that they have retained their bodies while switching their psychologies or *vice versa*, it is equally correct to say that the Doris-body-person has what was previously Doris's body and what was previously Rita's psychology whereas the Rita-body-person has what was previously Rita's body and what was previously Doris's psychology. This is the philosophically neutral way of describing the D/R Incident. It is neutral because it is incomplete. It fails to state all the relevant facts. In particular, it does not identify either the Doris-body-person or the Rita-body-person with either Doris or Rita. By design it leaves the identities of the Doris-body-person and the Rita-body-person wide open. To identify is to risk error.

The incompatibility between the two ways of making the identifications will perhaps strike the reader as trivial. That is for the good. The point *is* trivial. But it is often obscured in discussions on the topic—and that is reason enough for me to emphasize it here. It is extremely important to be clear on this point if we are to make any progress toward solving the problem of personal identity.[9]

Allen's joke exploits the body-based identifications. We, however, are not writing comedy; we are doing extremely serious philosophy. And fortunately, though not always easy to do, philosophy is always a good deal easier to do than comedy. Philosophically, the psychology-based identifications seem considerably more plausible than the body-based identifications—not as funny, but more plausible.

---

[9] Derek Parfit claims, in *Reasons and Persons* (Oxford University Press, 1986), at pp. 242–243, 259–260, that the different ways of making the identifications in puzzle cases of personal identity are "merely different descriptions of the same outcome," while explicitly denying that the competing descriptions are incompatible. His argument evidently assumes that if facts of one kind (e.g., personal identity) are reducible to, and hence not "further facts" beyond, those of another kind (psychological and/or bodily continuities), then the former are somehow illusory or unreal—or at least less real—so that the latter are compatible with utterly different ways of fixing the former. I disagree. If facts of one kind reduce to facts of another, then the latter determine the former. And if one sort is real, then so is the other.

Bernard Williams, in 'The Self and the Future,' *The Philosophical Review*, 79, 2 (April 1970), also in his *Problems of the Self* (Cambridge University Press, 1973), pp. 46–63, presents a rich account (pp. 52–55 in *Problems of the Self*) of the conceptual distinctions between the two different ways of making the identifications in a case like the D/R Incident. He notes that a description of the incident in completely neutral terms seems to lead naturally to the psychology-based identifications, but he also says of the situation given by the body-based description that it is in fact the same incident "differently presented." Unlike Parfit, Williams explicitly adds that the two "presentations" thus lead to contrary conclusions (p. 61). Indeed, Williams sees the incompatibility of these otherwise plausible presentations of the incident as producing a philosophical quandary.

This is not to say that some psychology-based criterion is correct in general. Even if it is taken as settled that the body-based identifications are clearly incorrect, it is arguable that the person who now has what had been Rita's brain in what had been Doris's body is neither Doris nor Rita but Dorita. Even if the psychology-based identifications are not decidedly vindicated in the D/R Incident, the body-based identifications seem decidedly refuted. Moreover, the psychology-based identifications do not seem at all implausible. If the D/R Incident presented all there were to the problem of personal identity, we might as well move on to discuss the more intriguing issues raised by the D/R Incident. But it does not.

III

Suppose that instead of transplanting brains, Allen had made use of the BW device. Although it is sometimes referred to as 'the brain washer,' the initials 'BW' actually refer to the device's inventor, Bernard Williams. As Williams describes the device, it extracts "information" from a person's brain—or, as we might put it nowadays, it extracts the operating system, the memory, and all the stored data and software. Exploiting the latest in digital technology, the device stores that information while the brain is repaired. Once the brain is repaired, the device is set it in the reverse mode, whereby it copies the information back into the brain, restoring the brain to exactly the same state it was in when the information was extracted.[10] The BW device is especially useful when removing a brain tumor that is located perilously close to brain areas intricately tied to certain higher cognitive phenomena (including certain abilities, long-term memories, vocabulary, and capacity for speech, sense of humor, and various other aspects of a personality). On one or two occasions, the BW device successfully extracted information from a dying brain and replaced it in an artificial brain that had been surgically implanted in place of the old one. The BW device also has the capability simply to render the brain a *tabula rasa*. If the information had been correctly extracted and stored, the washed brain can be restored to its former state. Although the prospect has been condemned as unethical by extremists, it is theoretically possible using two BW devices simultaneously to interchange all of the information of two brains.

Suppose Allen had done exactly that to Doris and Rita. Let us call the original D/R Incident 'D/R-1' and this new scenario 'D/R-2'. We may pose our three questions with regard to D/R-2: Which way of making the identifications, if either, is right about D/R-2? How is one supposed to settle the primary question? Finally, whichever way of making the identifications is correct, by virtue of what facts is it, rather than the alternative way, the right way?

D/R-2 seems to make our problem of personal identity less tractable than it first seemed. For now the body-based identifications do not seem as implausible. Interestingly, they may even seem more plausible in this case than the psychology-based identifications. Anyone who does not find them so is urged to reread Williams'

---

[10] *The Problems of the Self,* p. 47. Parfit's 'Branch-Line Case of the Teletransporter,' described in his *Reasons and Persons,* at pp. 199–201, is a variant of the BW device.

discussion, in which he deftly uses a puzzle case like D/R-2 to argue that one cannot legitimately dismiss the body-based criterion as cavalierly as one might be inclined to do.[11] Intuitive support for the body-based identifications is provided by supposing that one's own brain were drastically altered through a BW device, and considering how one views the further prospect of the resulting person's being painfully tortured. Perhaps Allen's body-based identifications are the right ones after all. The two meta-questions seem more pressing.

The very fact that our intuitions may diverge between D/R-1 and D/R-2 is itself an extremely important aspect of the problem. Presented in the right light, D/R-1 and D/R-2 bring our intuitions into direct conflict, thereby creating an especially perplexing conceptual difficulty. The tension between the intuitions that are operative in D/R-1 and D/R-2 shows that the problem of personal identity is not so easily laid to rest.

If D/R-1 stacks the deck in favor of psychology-based criteria and D/R-2 stacks the deck in favor of the body-based criterion, we can make our problem even more intractable by considering a case that does not stack the deck at all. In D/R-3, something mysterious happened to Doris and Rita while they slept, with the result that the Doris-body-person awoke with what was previously Rita's psychology and the Rita-body-person awoke with what was previously Doris's psychology. Allen did not interchange their brains. He did not apply BW devices to exchange information between their brains. He did not do anything to them. Someone else—or something else—did. Perhaps it was the fruition of a curse against their ancestors in ancient Egypt. Perhaps space creatures zapped them with alien rays. Perhaps it was the magic fulfillment of a mutual wish to trade places. Never mind what it was. Allen has fallen in love with the Doris-body-person. But who is that?

Consider now the primary question and the two meta-questions concerning D/R-3. Our intuitions seem to offer decidedly less assistance in this case than they did before.

---

[11] Williams argues that a neutral "presentation" of cases like D/R-1 and D/R-2 leads to the psychology-based identifications, whereas a specially designed alternative presentation leads to the opposite identifications. He evidently concludes that the case for psychology-based identifications is deeply inconclusive. (See note 9 above.) In noting the conceptual differences between the alternative presentations, Williams emphasizes two aspects that are prominent in his own presentations: First, in presenting the scenario in neutral terms the victims are referred to using the third-person, whereas the body-based scenario is presented as addressed to one of the victims using the second-person pronoun (and as understood by the victim using the first-person); and second, in presenting the body-based scenario, Williams makes little mention of the other victim. Williams creates the impression that these differences are crucial to the philosophical issues. These differences, however, are largely stylistic, reflecting different perspectives that Williams chose, perhaps at least in part, for dramatic effect. He could have provided a body-based presentation using the third-person perspective, or a neutral presentation using the second-person (and even the first-person, as by 'the my-body-person'), and still raise the principal philosophical questions on that basis. A more significant difference is given by the very fact that the body-based presentation explicitly includes particular identifications. By contrast with Williams, I believe that the proper lesson of his investigation is that the psychological evidence in favor of the psychology-based identifications—which is the focus in Williams's neutral description—has no force, since the very same psychological reactions would arise in Doris and Rita even if the body-based identifications prevailed. (Compare Kripke's 'schmidentity' argument strategy, in *Naming and Necessity*, at pp. 107–108, elaborated on in Kripke's 'Speaker's Reference and Semantic Reference,' in P. French, T. Uehling, and H. Wettstein, eds., *Contemporary Perspectives in the Philosophy of Language* (Minneapolis: University of Minnesota Press, 1977), pp. 6–27, especially at 16–18.)

Whatever conviction one may have had when considering D/R-1 that Doris and Rita have exchanged bodies is considerably weakened. The opposite intuitions tapped by D/R-2 now seem equally legitimate. And conversely, whatever conviction one may have had when considering D/R-2 that Doris and Rita have retained their bodies while becoming psychologically altered is also considerably weakened, in light of the equal legitimacy of the intuitions tapped in D/R-1. Concerning D/R-3, both intuitions seem equally legitimate, or equally illegitimate. There seems to be little to recommend the psychology-based criteria over the body-based criterion, or *vice versa*. The metaphysical meta-question concerning D/R-3 in some sense represents the traditional problem of personal identity in its purest and least tractable form.

Some philosophers maintain that there is no determinate, objective fact of the matter (independently of any decision we may make about the case) as to whether the Doris-body-person is identical with Doris or Rita, or neither. This position, however, is not a viable option. Let us name the Doris-body-person 'Doris-bod'. There is a fact of the matter concerning whether Doris-bod is identical with Doris-bod. The fact that Doris-bod is Doris-bod is an instance of a law of logic. If there is no objective fact of the matter as to whether Doris is Doris-bod, then that yields one respect (at least) in which Doris differs from Doris-bod. For on this hypothesis, Doris-bod has the feature that there is a fact as to whether she is Doris-bod while Doris lacks this feature. But if Doris and Doris-bod are not exactly alike in every respect—if they differ in any respect whatsoever—it follows by Leibniz's Law that they are distinct persons. (Or if one prefers, it follows by the contrapositive of Leibniz's Law—see note 3 above.) And if they are distinct, then there is a determinate, objective fact of the matter after all as to whether they are identical. The same argument may be made concerning Rita and Doris-bod. As desperate as the Dorita hypothesis seems, one may be inclined at this point to run with it.[12]

---

[12] Parfit takes the position that there is no determinate, objective fact of the matter in some of the puzzle cases of personal identity. See for example his 'Personal Identity,' *The Philosophical Review*, 80 (January 1971), pp. 3–27; and *Reasons and Persons*, at pp. 236–243. The motion is seconded by Johnston, in 'Fission and the Facts,' *Philosophical Perspectives, 3: Philosophy of Mind and Action Theory* (Atascadero, Ca.: Ridgeview, 1989), pp. 369–397, throughout and especially at 371–373, 393; and again in 'Reasons and Reductionism,' *The Philosophical Review*, 101, 3 (July 1992), pp. 589–618, at 603. (Curiously, Parfit also says that in puzzle cases of personal identity, different ways of making the identifications are "different descriptions of the same outcome," and furthermore that for reasons of symmetry, the best description of the standard fission case has it that the original person is distinct from each of the two subsequent people. Each of these claims seems incompatible with Parfit's doctrine of indeterminate identity, as well as with each other. See note 9 above.) I urged a version of the proof just given against Parfit in *Reference and Essence*, at pp. 242–246 (see especially p. 242n). Philosophers who embrace, or otherwise defend, the logical possibility of indeterminate identity have gone to extreme lengths to ward off the counter-proof. Typically, they have responded by accepting that the objects in question (in our case, Doris and Doris-bod) differ from each other in the respect cited while rejecting the Leibniz's-Law inference from '*a* and *b* are not exactly alike' to '*a* and *b* are not the same thing', on the ground that the conclusion may lack truth-value even when the premise is true. In his *Reasons and Persons*, Parfit endorses such a response (pp. 240–241). The response, however, requires a fundamentally counter-intuitive departure from classical reasoning. For it should be agreed that, of necessity, any *one* thing has every property it has, without exception. It follows by classical reasoning that if Doris lacks some property that Doris-bod has, then they cannot be *one* person. But if they are not one person, then they are two. (They are certainly not one and one-half persons, for example. *Cf.* my 'Wholes, Parts,

IV

D/R-1, D/R-2, and D/R-3 are distinct possibilities. Technically, though, they are not genuine, full-fledged possible worlds. Possible worlds are fully specific with respect to all questions of fact, down to the finest of details. There are numerous alternative

and Numbers,' in J. Tomberlin, ed., *Philosophical Perspectives, 11*, Atascadero, Ca.: Ridgeview, forthcoming 1997.) [*Homework exercise:* Formalize and derive the preceding argument. What inference rules and/or logical axioms are involved in the derivation? Notice also my use of the plural form '*objects* in question' and of the phrase 'differ from each *other*' in stating the typical response to the original proof. Is this usage consistent with the position stated thereby? If not, is there a coherent way to state the position, in its full generality?]

Parfit says furthermore that even if the proof that there is always a fact of the matter is correct, it only shows that in those cases in which there is no fact of the matter, it is incumbent upon us, if we wish to avoid incoherence, to create a fact by making a decision about the case at hand. This betrays a serious misunderstanding of the proof—and indeed, I believe, a fundamental confusion concerning such things as facts, decisions, and incoherence. The proof demonstrates that there is *already* a fact of the matter, quite independently of any decisions one may wish to make. In addition, a slight variation of the argument shows that it is quite impossible to make a pair of things identical (or distinct) by decision. Doris and Doris-bod are already what they are, and no decision on anyone's part can possibly affect their status with regard to the question of identity.

Johnston argues instead that even if the notion of personal identity (the notion of *same person*) is taken to be strict numerical identity restricted to persons, and even if strict identity is determinate for every pair of objects, there are nevertheless cases in which it is indeterminate whether a is the same person as b owing to an ambiguity in the word 'person'. His position appears to be that there are (at least) two distinct kinds, or notions, of a person—let us call these $person_1$ and $person_2$—such that, in such cases, each of a and b is a $person_1$ and also a $person_2$, but because the two kinds differ in the identity conditions they specify for their members, a is (determinately) the same $person_1$ as b yet not the same $person_2$ (so that neither is essentially a $person_2$). This position, however, implies that $a = b$ and $a \neq b$. (The same inconsistency occurs in Johnston's 'Human Beings,' *Journal of Philosophy*, 84, 2 (February 1987), pp. 59–83, at 76. See also his 'Is There a Problem about Persistence?' at p. 123, bottom. Although Johnston opposes the Cartesian-dualist position that persons exist "separately" from their bodies, his view that kinds specify identity conditions for their members, with different kinds specifying differing conditions, leads him to a position even more radical than the dualism he rejects: that we are not organisms, or indeed biological life forms of any kind.) A consistent variant would be this: a is both a $person_1$ and a $person_2$ at a time t_1, b is the same $person_1$, at a later time t_2 that a is at t_1 but b is *not* a $person_2$ at t_2 and consequently not the same $person_2$ at t_2 that a is at t_1. Since Johnston concedes that personal identity is strict identity restricted to persons, this alternative position reduces to the following: a is both a $person_1$ and a $person_2$ at t_1, whereas a is only a $person_1$ and no longer a $person_2$ at t_2. Whatever this prospect may mean for our ordinary concept of a person, it does not warrant the dramatic conclusion that the notion of personal identity is indeterminate for a. The alleged ambiguity may render some confusion over the issue of whether a is still a "person," but there is no lingering issue, and there should be no problem, concerning whether the thing at t_2 (whether or not it is still a person) is still the *same thing*, and if so, what makes it so. In the usual puzzle cases of the traditional problem of personal identity (including Johnston's favored puzzle case of fission), there is typically no serious question about the status of any of the relevant individuals as persons. Instead it is *given* that the principal individuals in question are persons. Typically, a is stipulated to be a person [man, woman] by hypothesis, while b is given descriptively as "the *person* who emerges from such-and-such a process" (e.g., as 'the a-body-person,' or as 'the *man* who now has the left hemisphere of what was previously a's brain,' etc.). The primary question concerns a's identity with, or distinctness from, b—not whether b is a person at t_2, or whether the erstwhile person a (whose identity with b is in question) is still a person at t_2. Indeed, the prospect that a is determinately no longer a person at t_2 (and for that reason alone, not the same person as b) is typically ignored altogether. (See note 29 below. Curiously, even Johnston does not consider this prospect in his cataloging of potential solutions to the problem.)

conceptions of what a possible world is. (Not all of these need be thought of as competing conceptions.) The conception I favor is that of a maximally specific scenario that might have obtained.[13] On this conception (and on suitably closely related conceptions), each of the puzzle-case scenarios is the intersection of an infinite plurality of possible worlds, i.e. a constituent 'mini-world,' or sub-scenario, common to each. Each of the three puzzle cases may be regarded as representing a distinct class of worlds. D/R-1, for example, represents the class of worlds in which Allen performs brain transplants with the result that the Rita-body-person is now an ideal mate and Allen has fallen in love with the Doris-body-person. The primary question for each of these scenarios is which identifications obtain in the worlds represented by that scenario.

Viewing the puzzle cases as representing classes of worlds, there appears to be some kinship between the problem of personal identity and another identity problem of contemporary philosophy: *the problem of cross-world identification*, i.e. the problem of identifying individuals in different possible worlds. Consider the possibility of Richard Nixon having continued as United States president for the duration of his second term in office. We may ask: Would the Democrats have regained the presidency, as they did in the actual world? Would they have nominated Jimmy Carter? And so on. But before we can answer, a philosopher interrupts. What determines whether the President in the possible world under discussion is Nixon? How can we know that it is Nixon rather than someone else who resembles Nixon in a variety of important respects, except for having finished out his presidency rather than resigning in disgrace? And furthermore, what does being Nixon consist in for someone in another possible world? In short, what is the *criterion*, or *criteria*, of cross-world identity that settles the question of whether someone in another possible world is Nixon? In a celebrated critique, Kripke has exposed the alleged problem of cross-world identity as a pseudo-problem (Kripke, pp. 15–20, 42–53, 76–77). He counters that possible worlds are not like independently existing planets with features to be investigated. " 'Possible worlds' are *stipulated*, not *discovered* by powerful telescopes," he says. "There is no reason why we cannot *stipulate* that, in talking about what would have happened to Nixon in a certain counterfactual situation, we are talking about what would have happened to *him*" (p. 44).

Kripke's contention that possible worlds are "stipulated" has been seriously misunderstood.[14] Many philosophers take it as thesis a about the ontological and/or

---

[13] *Cf.* my 'The Logic of What Might Have Been,' cited above in note 4.

[14] A dramatic case in point is Allen Hazen, in 'Counterpart-theoretic Semantics for Modal Logic,' *Journal of Philosophy*, 76, 6 (June 1979), pp. 319–338. Hazen asserts (pp. 334–335) that when Kripke says that possible worlds are stipulated rather than discovered, what he means, in part, may be explained by saying that a possible world is a combination of a purely qualitatively specified world together with a particular stipulated choice among various similarity correspondences or mappings (which need not be one-one) between individuals in other worlds and individuals of the qualitatively specified world. Hazen thinks of the similarity correspondences as schemes that represent an individual in some other world by means of a selected counterpart in the qualitatively given world. Hazen's entire apparatus is decidedly anti-Kripkean. Kripke adamantly insists that possible worlds need not be purely qualitatively specified, and that the very same individuals may exist in different possible worlds rather than being represented in another world by "counterparts" in that world.

epistemological status of possible worlds, about how they came into being and how we come to know of them. They see Kripke as a *modal conceptualist*, who believes that possible worlds are somehow created by us with the properties that we assign to them (a position analogous in certain respects to constructivism about mathematical entities). Readers have thought that Kripke holds that we are the masters of metaphysical modality, in the sense that it is entirely for us to decide, by "stipulation," what is metaphysically possible and what is not. These are serious misinterpretations. Kripke's observation that "possible worlds are not discovered but stipulated" is simply his endorsement of a version of the doctrine that David Kaplan calls *Haecceitism*. The *haecceity* of an individual x is the property of being identical with x, i.e. the property of being *that very individual*. Kaplan defines Haecceitism as the doctrine that

we can meaningfully ask whether a possible individual that exists in one possible world also exists in another without taking into account the attributes and behavior of the individuals that exist in the one world and making a comparison with the attributes and behavior of the individuals that exist in the other world . . . [the] doctrine that holds that it does make sense to ask—without reference to common attributes and behavior—whether *this* is the same individual in another possible world, that individuals can be extended in logical space (i.e., through possible worlds) in much the way we commonly regard them as being extended in physical space and time, and that a common "thisness" may underlie extreme dissimilarity or distinct thisnesses may underlie great resemblance, . . . [15]

Despite the usual gloss on Kaplan's explanations, the central doctrine of Haecceitism is not concerned primarily with the identification of individuals in distinct possible worlds—although the doctrine does have important consequences concerning cross-world identifications. The central doctrine primarily concerns an issue of *legitimacy*. It concerns the question of whether it is 'meaningful' to stipulate the facts about particular individuals in particular possible worlds, including such facts as that the individual with such-and-such properties in a given world w is a particular individual a, or is not the particular individual a, as the case may be. Haecceitism holds that it is perfectly legitimate when introducing a possible world for consideration and discussion, to specify the world explicitly in terms of facts directly concerning particular individuals, designating those individuals directly by name if one chooses to.

An extreme version of the doctrine—*Extreme Haecceitism*, as I shall call it—combines Haecceitism in the preceding sense with a further doctrine: that facts concerning the particular individual a are in some relevant sense primitive, not reducible to any more general facts, such as that the individual with such-and-such properties is thus-and-so. Extreme Haecceitism holds that it is legitimate to stipulate facts concerning particular individuals in a world, identifying those individuals by name, precisely *because* such facts about a world are held to be *separate* facts that are not fixed by, and cannot be logically inferred from, facts that do not specify which individuals are involved. I shall use the term 'Reductionism' for the opposing doctrine that any such facts about a world w as that the individual with such-and-such

[15] Kaplan, 'How to Russell a Frege–Church,' *Journal of Philosophy*, 72 (1975), pp. 716–729, at 722–723.

properties is *a*, or is not *a*, if indeed such facts exist, are reducible to such qualitative facts as that the individual with such-and-such properties in world *w* is the individual with so-and-so properties in world *w'* (where the so-and-so properties are similar, or closely related, to the such-and-such properties).

Unfortunately, it is unclear what it means to say that facts of one kind are *reducible* to facts of another—or using alternative terminologies, that facts of the first kind "consist in," or are "nothing over and above," facts of the second kind, or that facts of the one kind are "grounded in," "derived from," "based upon," "constructed out of," or "constituted by" facts of the other kind. The central idea seems to be that any fact of the first kind is a *logical* or *conceptual* consequence of facts of the second kind. An example would help enormously here. But there are precious few, if any, uncontroversial examples. One example from the philosophy of language may do. On Frege's philosophy of semantics, the referential (denotative, designative) facts concerning a language are reducible to other sorts of facts—in particular to intensional-semantic facts about what the sense of an expression is together with extra-linguistic facts about what a given sense *metaphysically determines*. To illustrate, the English noun 'water', in its use as a name for the familiar liquid, semantically expresses a certain concept (or property) *c* as its English sense, perhaps *the colorless, odorless, potable liquid found (with varying amounts of impurities) in lakes, rivers, and streams.*[16] This is a fact in the theory of meaning—a fact concerning the semantics of sense—and not a fact in the theory of reference. The concept *c*, in turn, metaphysically determines the chemical compound H_2O, in the sense that the compound exactly fits *c* and (let us suppose) no other substance does. This fact is completely independent of language. It is a straightforward logical consequence of these two—the meaning fact and the metaphysical fact—that there is some concept or other such that the word 'water' expresses that concept as its English sense and that concept in turn determines H_2O. The latter, according to a Fregean philosophy of semantics, just *is* the fact that 'water' refers in English to H_2O. This fact is thus partly semantic and partly metaphysical in nature.[17] In this sense, the fact that the English noun 'water' refers to H_2O is "nothing over and above" (consists in, is grounded in, is derived from, etc.) the two facts that the English noun 'water' expresses *c* and that *c* determines H_2O.[18]

---

[16] I use the word 'concept' here in the same sense as Alonzo Church, which is decidedly distinct from that of Frege's artificial use of the German '*Begriff*'.

[17] In the terminology and conceptual apparatus of my 'Analyticity and Apriority,' in J. Tomberlin, ed., *Philosophical Perspectives, 7: Logic and Language* (Atascadero, Ca.: Ridgeview, 1993), pp. 125–133, the fact in question is (according to Frege's theory of it) a fact of *applied* rather than *pure* semantics, since it involves some extra-linguistic metaphysics.

[18] The notion of reducibility involved here will be clarified further in Section VI below. An alternative notion of reducibility results by replacing the relation of logical consequence with the notion (metaphor?) of part-whole constitution. We may say that a fact *f* is *mereologically reducible* to a class of facts *c* if *f* is literally composed, without remainder, of the elements of *c*. Thus a mereologically complex fact is mereologically reducible to its constituent sub-facts. This notion is suggested by a more literal construal of the terminology of one fact being nothing over and above, or consisting in, etc., a plurality of other facts. The notion presupposes a picture of compound facts as complex wholes resulting from an assemblage of other facts. This picture raises baffling questions about the relationship between mereological reducibility and the logical or conceptual notion of

A doctrine more extreme than simple Reductionism opposes simple Haecceitism. *Anti-Haecceitism* is the doctrine that in introducing a possible world for consideration and discussion, one may not legitimately specify facts while mentioning the individuals involved by name (or by something similar, such as by a demonstrative uttered while pointing to an actual individual). Instead, one may specify only the general, qualitative sorts of facts to which the facts concerning a particular individual (if there are any such facts) are reducible according to Reductionism. Specifying the facts concerning a particular individual *a*, explicitly identifying *a* by name, is regarded as a form of cheating—or rather, it is held to be meaningless. Some Anti-Haecceitists go so far as to reject the very existence of such facts about a world as that the individual with such-and-such properties is, or is not, the very individual *a*. They hold that one may not legitimately specify such facts in giving a possible world for the simple reason that there are no such facts to be specified. This view might be called 'Extreme Anti-Haecceitism'. Less extreme Anti-Haecceitists embrace Reductionism, holding that while there are facts directly concerning specific individuals, they are reducible to general facts to the effect that the individual with such-and-such properties is, or is not, the individual with so-and-so properties. Extreme Haecceitism, in contrast to Anti-Haecceitism, and in sharp contrast to Extreme Anti-Haecceitism, holds that the former facts are *further* facts over and above general facts, not reducible to or constructed out of the latter. Along with the general facts, these separate facts concerning specific individuals are held to be built into the very fabric of the possible worlds themselves.

Little or no notice has been made in the extant literature on Haecceitism of the distinction between the moderate and extreme versions of these various doctrines. I have endeavored to make my usage correspond as closely as possible to established usage of the terms 'Haecceitism' and 'Anti-Haecceitism'. That is why I have introduced the special terms, 'Extreme Haecceitism' and 'Reductionism', for the opposing doctrines concerning the question of reducibility (which is less often the primary focus), and a third term, 'Extreme Anti-Haecceitism', for what may be the most controversial of the doctrines. Extreme Haecceitism and Reductionism are

---

reducibility explicated in the text. On Frege's meta-semantical theory, is the fact that the English word 'water' refers to H_2O mereologically reducible to other facts? In particular, does it mereologically reduce to the pair of facts that 'water' expresses c and that c metaphysically determines H_2O? Is it supposed to be obvious that it does? Suppose 'water' had expressed a different concept in English, but one which also determines H_2O. Would the fact that 'water' refers in English to H_2O then be a different fact, consisting of different sub-facts? Let us say that the proposition that such-and-such, if it is true, *corresponds to* the fact that such-and-such. On some theories, this relation of correspondence is simply identity restricted to true propositions. Suppose that a proposition p corresponds to a mereologically reducible fact f, and that propositions $q_1, q_2, q_3, \ldots$ correspond to the sub-facts to which f mereologically reduces. Is p then logically equivalent to the conjunction (q_1 and q_2 and q_3 and . . .)? Or is p merely a logical consequence of the conjunction? Or might the two even be logically independent?

Lacking answers to these and other questions, I shall rely in the text primarily on the conceptual notion of reducibility that invokes logical consequence rather than the part-whole relation. It may be useful, however, to bear in mind the possibility that a particular author may instead mean the mereological notion, or something else. Where appropriate, one should distinguish between Mereological Reductionism and Conceptual Reductionism (the notion explicated in the text), as I shall do in some notes below.

the exact denials of one another. Extreme Haecceitism, therefore, might also be called 'Anti-Reductionism'. One may consistently combine Haecceitism (*simpliciter*) with Reductionism by holding that it is legitimate to introduce a possible world for consideration by stipulating which facts concerning particular individuals obtain in the world even though such facts are reducible to, or nothing over and above, other sorts of facts. (It is possible that Kripke takes this position. See note 24 below.)

The various versions of Haecceitism and Anti-Haecceitism are perhaps best formulated by invoking a concept from the theory of propositions, that of a *singular proposition*. A singular proposition is a proposition in which at least one individual or object that the proposition is about occurs directly as a constituent, and the proposition is about that individual by virtue of directly including it, rather than a concept by which the individual is represented (determined, denoted). In introducing the terminology of 'singular propositions', Kaplan equates Haecceitism with the acceptance of singular propositions (*ibid.*, pp. 724–725). More accurately, Haecceitism is the doctrine that one may legitimately cite singular propositions in specifying the propositions that are true in a possible world introduced for discussion. Extreme Haecceitism is the stronger doctrine that the truth-values of any and all manner of singular propositions are among the primitive, brute facts about which propositions are true and which are false in a given possible world. If one conceives of possible worlds as maximal compossible sets of propositions, then Haecceitism holds that possible worlds include singular propositions among their elements in addition to non-singular, or general, propositions, and Extreme Haecceitism holds that the entire subset of nonsingular propositions included in a world to the effect that the F is such-and-such, for particular properties F, logically entails no singular proposition to the effect that x is such-and-such. Reductionism holds that the subset of singular propositions, assuming one countenances such propositions at all, is fixed by the subset of nonsingular propositions. Anti-Haecceitism (*simpliciter*) holds that possible worlds include *only* general propositions to begin with, leaving open the question of the truth-values of any singular propositions, and Extreme Anti-Haecceitism denies that there are any singular propositions to be concerned about.

Kaplan points out that one should strictly speak of Haecceitism, Anti-Haecceitism, and their variants as relativized to a particular kind of entity K, as for example, *Anti-Haecceitism with regard to concrete things, Reductionism with regard to social institutions*, etc. Reductionism with regard to political nations, for example, is the often-cited doctrine that facts involving political nations are reducible to other sorts of facts, such as the actions and histories of particular persons. Extreme Haecceitism regarding political nations is the denial of this alleged reducibility. Haecceitism with regard to a kind K is logically independent of Haecceitism with regard to any logically independent kind K'. One may consistently combine Haecceitism regarding human bodies with Anti-Haecceitism regarding persons, for example, by holding that it is legitimate to specify which bodies exist in introducing a possible world for consideration but not to specify which persons exist in that world.

The astute reader will have noticed that I have described the various versions and variants of Haecceitism and Anti-Haecceitism without mentioning the alleged problem of cross-world identification, focusing instead on the role of facts concerning specific individuals in presenting a possible world. How does the cross-world identity problem come in? On Anti-Haecceitism regarding individuals, possible worlds do not include specific individuals themselves. Instead they provide a structure and framework, given purely qualitatively, in which individuals are represented by means of individual concepts. It is not labeled which individual a given individual concept represents. For the Anti-Haecceitist, then, there is a special problem about how the individuals thus represented in distinct possible worlds are to be identified with, or distinguished from, one another. If identification is your game, some assembly is required. And all one has to go on are the individual concepts that represent the individuals. One thus needs criteria of cross-world identity. There is no like problem for the Haecceitist, since facts concerning specific individuals may be given directly in specifying the possible worlds under discussion. This is what Kripke means when he says that a possible world need not be given purely qualitatively. Haecceitism holds that facts concerning the haecceities—or in more ordinary parlance, the identities—of specific individuals may be taken as given in introducing a possible world for consideration, and Extreme Haecceitism holds that all facts concerning specific individuals are directly settled by the internal make-up of the possible worlds themselves. Possible worlds come already equipped with identification labels for the individuals that exist in them. No assembly is required, no identity criteria needed.

Kripke's assertion that possible worlds are not discovered but stipulated is a somewhat less felicitous way of stating what I take to be the central doctrine of Haecceitism *simpliciter*, or a closely related doctrine. Criteria for cross-world identity are to be replaced by stipulations. In fact, in this respect possible worlds are no different from anything else that might come under discussion. Suppose I say, "Some cities have monuments made of marble," as a prelude to saying something about some or all such cities. It would be silly (at best) for someone to object that while there are indeed marble monuments in *this* city (the city we are in), I must justify my claim that the monuments in the other cities I have in mind are really made of marble—instead of, say, some other material that was fashioned to look the way marble looks around here. I am discussing cities with marble monuments. I do not have to specify the relevant class of cities purely qualitatively and then provide a criterion for inter-city identity of material. I simply select the class of cities that I wish to discuss by specifying that they have monuments made of . . . , well, *marble*. Kripke contrasts possible worlds, which he says are stipulated, with planets, which are discovered. This may have given the wrong impression. Even independently existing planets may be stipulated in the sense that Kripke intends. One astronomer says to another, "There are undoubtedly thousands of planets that, like Earth, have significant amounts of oxygen in their atmospheres. What is the temperature range for such a planet?" Suppose a philosopher who has been eavesdropping interrupts, "Not so fast. How do you know, and what makes it true, that the atmospheric gas on the planet in question is oxygen, rather than some other element that superficially resembles oxygen? After all, you're not on that planet; you're in no position to send up a weather balloon or to conduct other atmospheric experiments. Are you supposing that, say, atomic number provides a criterion for interplanetary identity of elements? If so, why atomic number? Why not some other feature, like that of having its source in the particular portion of ancient post-Big-Bang material from which our Earth-bound oxygen was originally formed?" A reaction by the astronomers of eye-rolling annoyance would be completely justified. The astronomer simply *stipulated* that he discussing planets that have significant amounts of oxygen in their atmospheres. Even if interplanetary identity criteria for elements are readily available, our astronomer is under no obligation to specify the planets he has in mind purely qualitatively and then ensure that they contain significant amounts of oxygen by providing the available criteria. It is in this sense that even planets are "stipulated." When Kripke says that we do not discover but stipulate possible worlds, he is not making a special claim about their peculiar ontological or epistemological status, or about our peculiar status *vis-à-vis* possible worlds. Nor is he claiming that we decree what is possible and what is not. Instead what he means is that the question of which class of possible worlds is under discussion (and in particular the question of which individuals exist in those worlds) is like the matter of which class of entities of any sort is under discussion—whether they be animals, vegetables, minerals, sticks, stones, or even planets. It is a matter that is entirely open to, and may be entirely governed by, the stipulations of the discussants. The possibility of simply stipulating which individuals are involved renders cross-world identity criteria unnecessary.

V

Does the debate about Haecceitism have any bearing on the problem of personal identity? The problems of cross-world identification and of personal identity differ from each other in at least one relevant respect. The personal-identity puzzle cases begin with the stipulation that Doris and Rita are present in each. There is no question of identifying the Doris of D/R-1 with the Doris of D/R-2 or the Doris of D/R-3. For one thing, we are given that it is the same Doris in each scenario. For another, that does not help. We are not attempting to identify individuals across possible worlds. Instead we are attempting to identify individuals within a possible world (or within each of the possible worlds represented by the scenario under discussion). Kripke's observation about the stipulatory character of cross-world identifications appears to offer little help.

This appearance is deceptive. We are attempting to determine the identity (haecceity) of the Doris-body-person in D/R-1. This may be thought of as an attempt to identify an individual in an arbitrary possible world w of type D/R-1 with an individual of a possible world w', where the former is given qualitatively by means of the individual concept *the woman who now occupies such-and-such body*, and the latter is given directly, i.e. haecceitally, as either Doris or Rita. It happens that $w = w'$. This may be regarded as a special limiting case of the problem of cross-world identification in which the worlds in question are identical. Seen in this light, it emerges that the issue of Reductionism and the controversy between Haecceitism and Anti-Haecceitism are relevant to the problem of personal identity.

One point about the traditional problem of personal identity is perhaps obvious to anyone familiar with the topic. The problem presupposes a version of Reductionism regarding persons. It is safe to say that nearly all writers on the topic of personal identity are Reductionists. Nearly everything in the literature on the topic simply assumes Reductionism regarding persons without mentioning it as such.

It is therefore ironic that Reductionism regarding persons entails the Dorita hypothesis. This is shown by a variation of the proof given in Section III above that for any pair of objects x and y, there is a determinate, objective fact of the matter as to whether $x = y$. Consider D/R-1. Let us name the Doris-body-person in D/R-1 'Doris-bod$_1$'. Suppose first, for the sake of argument, that Doris-bod$_1$ is Rita rather than Doris. Reductionists who make this identification claim that the fact that Doris-bod$_1$ = Rita is grounded in the fact that Doris-bod$_1$, and no one else, now has exactly such-and-such a psychology, which used to be Rita's psychology before the brain transplant. If this hypothesis is correct, then it yields one respect in which Doris-bod$_1$ differs from Rita. For the fact that Rita = Rita is a fact of logic, grounded in her existence perhaps but not in facts about her psychological history. Rita therefore lacks Doris-bod$_1$'s property that the fact that she is Rita is reducible to in her psychological history. Conversely, Doris-bod$_1$ lacks Rita's property that the fact that she is Rita is independent of psychological features of Doris-bod$_1$'s biography. Either way, it follows by Leibniz's Law that Rita $\neq$ Doris-bod$_1$, contradicting our hypothesis. But the alternative hypothesis that Doris-bod$_1$ = Doris is subject to refutation by an exactly analogous argument, employing reducibility to facts about Doris-bod$_1$'s bodily history in lieu of reducibility to facts about her psychological history. Either way, whether it is judged that Doris-bod$_1$ is Rita or Doris, the Reductionist is driven, or at least committed, to giving up that judgment. And this leads to the Dorita hypothesis. An exactly similar argument may be made in connection with D/R-2 and D/R-3.

This is an uncomfortable result for Reductionists. Insofar as the Dorita hypothesis is regarded as implausible with regard to any of the puzzle-case scenarios, so to that same extent is the Reductionist assumption that personal identity is grounded in such matters as psychological or bodily continuity. Assuming that one or the other of the rival hypotheses is correct, the thesis that the haecceity of Doris-bod$_1$ is metaphysically reducible to other facts—facts about her psychological or alternatively facts about her bodily history—is thereby disproved.

In fact, a version of Extreme Haecceitism (Anti-Reductionism) is susceptible of a variation of the same proof. Suppose, for a *reductio*, that there is an object x from a possible world w and an object y from a possible world w' such that the fact that $x = y$ is reducible to (or consists in, is nothing over and above, is derived from, etc.) general facts about x in w and y in w'. Their identity might be reducible, for example, to x's bearing the relation R in w to the same F to which y bears R' in w', for appropriate intra-world relations R and R' and an appropriate cross-world sortal F. It is evident, by contrast, that the fact that $x = x$ is not similarly reducible to general facts about x in w or in w'. For the fact that $x = x$ is a fact of logic. If it is grounded in any other fact at all, it is grounded only in x's existence (in w or in w'). But then x differs from y in at least one respect. For x lacks y's feature that its identity with x is grounded in general (cross-world) facts about x and it. Conversely, y lacks x's feature that its identity with x is a primitive fact, not grounded in any general facts about *x* other than its existence. Either way, it follows by Leibniz's Law that *x* and *y* are different objects, contradicting the hypothesis that they are identical.[19]

Can we simply *stipulate* that the Doris-body-person in D/R-1 is, say, Rita? Haecceitism regarding persons implies an affirmative answer. And indeed on Extreme Haecceitism regarding persons, the matter of whether the Doris-body-person is Doris or Rita *should* be stipulated, since the identity (haecceity) of the Doris-body-person is a *further* fact, not reducible to such qualitative facts as that the Doris-body-person now has such-and-such a psychology (formerly characteristic of Rita). If we can simply stipulate that the Doris-body-person is Rita, then we should be equally free to stipulate instead that the Doris-body-person is Doris. Again, Haecceitism regarding persons implies that this is indeed so. Of course, the Doris-body-person cannot be both Doris and Rita. But we are not considering making both stipulations simultaneously. We are considering selecting one of them. And why not?

There is no particular reason why not. We *can* legitimately do this. As we have seen, the particular scenario D/R-1 represents a class of worlds. That class, it turns out, is diverse. The primary question concerning D/R-1 presupposes that in each of the worlds represented by that scenario, the identifications go the same way. This presupposition is erroneous. In some of the worlds represented by D/R-1, the Doris-body-person is Rita. In others of those worlds, the Doris-body-person is Doris. It is illegitimate to ask whether the Doris-body-person in D/R-1 is Doris or Rita. This is a matter to be settled by a stipulation concerning which worlds of the D/R-1 type are under discussion. We may say, "Consider a world of type D/R-1 in which Allen performs brain transplants on Doris and Rita with the result that they have exchanged bodies. In any such world, Allen thereby made Doris into an ideal mate, but fell in love with Rita." We may also say, "Consider another world of type D/R-1, different from the last one, in which again Allen performs brain transplants on Doris and Rita, only in this case their individual consciousnesses remain with their bodies, so that they have exchanged their brains and their psychologies. In any world of this alternative sort, Allen thereby made Rita into an ideal mate, but fell in love with Doris." Given Extreme Haecceitism, both sorts of worlds—both of these scenarios—are equally legitimate. They are equally legitimate *qua* scenarios. Neither is incoherent.

When a philosopher poses the D/R-1 scenario (or the D/R-2 or the D/R-3 scenario), and asks whether the Doris-body-person is Doris or Rita, and how this is supposed to be determined, the Extreme Haecceitist response—what I believe to be the correct response—goes something like this: You tell us who the Doris-body-person is. Until you do, you have not provided a scenario that is specified fully enough to settle the question. In response to your meta-question(s), it is not for us to *determine* which way the identifications go. It is up to you to *stipulate* which class of scenarios you have in mind. As stated, your questions presuppose that the identifications automatically go the same way for all scenarios of the relevant type. Since the identifications you seek are not reducible to the facts you have given us, that presupposition is false. Until you make the necessary stipulations, your primary question

---

[19] See my 'The Fact that *x* = *y*,' *Philosophia* (Israel), 17, 4 (December 1987), pp. 517–518. For a variety of controversial, but similarly proved philosophical theses concerning identity, see the appendix to my 'Modal Paradox,' pp. 110–114. (*Cf.* especially T6 and T7 listed there.)

is unanswerable in principle. And once you make the necessary stipulations, the answer is then trivial.[20]

VI

Given Haecceitism regarding persons, or at least given its Extreme cousin, the traditional problem of personal identity does not get off the ground. Yet an alternative version of the problem obstinately remains. Imagine that Allen actually *does* perform the operation on Doris and Rita. Imagine this really happening. Imagine that Allen really does—right here and now—implant what had been Doris's brain in what had been Rita's body and conversely. The Rita-body-person is now an ideal mate. Allen has fallen in love with the Doris-body-person. Who now has Allen fallen in love with?

This is not in any way a matter to be settled by stipulation. Surely there already is some fact of the matter concerning the Doris-body-person's identity. And it is not subject to our control what that fact is. If she is Rita, that is not at all a result of my (or of our) stipulating that this should be so. No one has made any such stipulation, nor would it have the slightest effect on things if one did. Instead the Doris-body-person's identity with Rita—the fact that Doris and Rita have exchanged bodies— seems to be somehow a result of the way the surgery was performed, somehow a result of the fact that the Doris-body-person now has what used to be Rita's brain and consequently also what used to be Rita's psychology. The whole business of identity criteria being replaced by Kripkean stipulations seems beside the point, if not completely wide of the mark.

One may feel uneasy about the idea of going beyond mere consideration of the possibility of a given situation, and instead imagining it to be actual. We know it is not actual. Why pretend that it is?

For a simple reason. The point is to mobilize intuitions concerning what *would* be the case if D/R-1 *had* occurred. If, counterfactually, Allen had performed brain transplants on Doris and Rita, then there would be a resulting fact as to whether the Doris-body-person was Rita or Doris, and that fact would not be a matter of our stipulating what is so. Kripke's observation that "possible worlds are stipulated," properly understood, is simply a recognition of the fact that in considering certain possibilities, we are free to stipulate which possibilities we have in mind by specifying which individuals are involved in them. As we have already seen, it is not a thesis to the effect that what is possible with respect to those individuals is subject to our decision. Nor is it a thesis to the effect that we decide what *would* be the case under certain counterfactual circumstances. There is already a fact of the matter, independently of us, as to who the Doris-body-person would be if D/R-1 had occurred.

Let us suppose again that the Doris-body-person would be Rita. If this hypothesis is correct, it appears to be a direct result of the fact that the Doris-body-person has what was previously Rita's brain with Rita's psychology relatively intact. Insofar as it is true that if D/R-1 had occurred, the Doris-body-person would be Rita, something

---

[20] *Cf. Reference and Essence*, at pp. 242–243.

significantly stronger is equally true. It is not as if the D/R-1 scenario might have had different results. If the Doris-body-person would have been Rita had D/R-1 occurred, then it is in fact metaphysically *impossible* for D/R-1 to occur with the Doris-body-person being Doris, or anyone else other than Rita. In a word, it is *necessary* that the Doris-body-person in D/R-1 is Rita.

Earlier I said that the class of worlds represented by the D/R-1 scenario was diverse, that there are possible worlds in which the D/R-1 scenario is realized and the Doris-body-person is Rita and other worlds in which the D/R-1 scenario is realized and the Doris-body-person is Doris. Now I am saying that the latter outcome is impossible, that there are no possible worlds in which the Doris-body-person is Doris. I seem to have contradicted myself.

I have not. It is at this juncture that I invoke impossible worlds. Haecceitism does not entail that it is in some way for us to decide what is, and what is not, metaphysically possible. Even Extreme Haecceitism does not entail this. Haecceitism simply holds that in introducing a world for consideration and discussion, we are free to stipulate the facts that obtain in the world. Depending on what we stipulate, the world, or worlds, we so introduce may turn out to be impossible rather than possible. This is so even if it was our intent to stipulate a possible world. We decide which individuals exist and what properties they have in the world we wish to consider, but Metaphysics decides, under its own authority, whether such a world is possible or impossible. The latter issue is completely out of our hands. There are indeed D/R-1 worlds in which the Doris-body-person is Rita, and there are indeed other D/R-1 worlds in which the Doris-body-person is Doris. For that matter, there are D/R-1 worlds in which the Doris-body-person is Madonna (altered to have Rita's psychology), and still other D/R-1 worlds in which the Doris-body-person is Ethel Merman resurrected (and psychologically altered). This is a consequence of Extreme Haecceitism. The question of the Doris-body-person's haecceity—the question of who the Doris-body-person is—is not to be found among, and does not reduce to or consist in, the facts that are given in the D/R-1 scenario. There are many different ways for the identifications to go. But most of those ways are quite impossible. In all of the genuinely *possible* D/R-1 worlds, the Doris-body-person is Rita. This is fixed by law but not by legislation. It is fixed by Metaphysical law.

It emerges from this analysis that there are two very different ways of interpreting the problem of personal identity, depending on whether Reductionism is presupposed. A puzzle case like D/R-1 is first set out, and the primary question and the two meta-questions then posed. If the questions are put forward under the presupposition of Reductionism, it is assumed that one has been given all the facts that are required for deciding the primary question, taken as a question about *all* the worlds represented by the puzzle-case scenario, possible and impossible. One may restrict one's focus to possible worlds, but there is no need to do so. The same answer will obtain for the impossible worlds as well, or at least for the logically consistent ones. For the Reductionist, so-called criteria of identity are reductionist analyses or definitions of what it is for a pair of individuals at different times or in different worlds to be identical—or at least analytic sufficient conditions for cross-circumstantial identity. The metaphysical meta-question is concerned with the presupposed reduction of personal-identity facts to facts about psychologies or about bodies. It is, in effect, a demand to be given a reductionist analysis for personal identity through change. We may call this *the Reductionist problem of personal identity*. It is the orthodox or canonical form of the problem.[21] As an Extreme Haecceitist, I reject this alleged problem as bogus (along with the alleged problem of cross-world identification).

If the primary question and the two meta-questions are put forward without presupposing Reductionism, one is then presumably being asked to confine one's attention to genuinely possible worlds. In those *possible* worlds in which D/R-1 (or D/R-2 or D/R-3) is realized, who is the Doris-body-person? In particular, if D/R-1 *were* realized, who *would* the Doris-body-person be? This question is perfectly legitimate. The facts of that case are sufficient to zero in on one metaphysically necessary outcome. That is to say, even if the Doris-body-person's identity (haecceity) is not *reducible* to the sorts of facts that one is given in D/R-1, the Doris-body-person's identity does *supervene modally* on exactly such facts. For present purposes, the relevant notion of supervenience may be defined as follows:

Properties of kind K *modally supervene on* properties of kind $K' =_{def}$ For any class c of K-properties and for any class c' of K'-properties, if it is metaphysically possible for there to be something whose K-properties are exactly those in c and whose K'-properties are exactly those in c', then it is metaphysically necessary that anything whose K'-properties are exactly those in c' is such that its (his/her) K-properties are exactly those in c.

Thus, to say that K-properties modally supervene on K'-properties is to say that either it is metaphysically necessary that anything that has exactly such-and-such K'-properties also has exactly so-and-so K-properties or else it is metaphysically impossible for anything to have exactly such-and-such K'-properties and also have exactly so-and-so K-properties. Or put another way, which K-properties a thing has is metaphysically necessitated by which K'-properties it has. For example, to say that a person's psychology modally supervenes on his/her brain and its physical states is to say that a complete accounting of the facts concerning a person's brain and its physical states leaves room for only one possible outcome concerning his/her psychology, in the sense that it would be metaphysically impossible for the person's brain to be in exactly those physical states while the person has a different psychology (even one that is only slightly different). What I am claiming here is that

---

[21] I have borrowed the terms 'Reductionism' and 'further facts' from Parfit, who explicitly calls himself a 'Reductionist' in rejecting the idea that identity facts are further facts (*Reasons and Persons*, at p. 255). In 'Are Persons Bodies?', in his *Problems of the Self*, pp. 64–81, Williams defends his setting out the problem of personal identity by means of the BW device thus: "Such a process may, perhaps, be forever impossible, but it does not seem to present any purely logical or conceptual difficulty" (p. 79). The exact intent of these remarks is perhaps unclear, but on one natural interpretation, Williams is prepared to allow for the prospect (putting the matter in terms of my apparatus) that all of the logically or conceptually possible worlds in which the D/R-2 scenario occurs are metaphysically impossible. Never mind; there is still supposed to be a problem. On this interpretation, the resulting "problem of personal identity" is a problem only on the assumption of Reductionism.

the Doris-body-person's haecceity modally supervenes on, but is not reducible to, exactly the sorts of biographical facts given in D/R-1.[22]

One may define a notion of reducibility by means of a simple adjustment in the above definition of supervenience, changing the metaphysical modalities to *conceptual* (or properly *logical*) modalities. It may be assumed here that conceptual necessity entails metaphysical necessity but not *vice versa*. What is conceptually necessary is true in every conceptually possible world, including such worlds as are metaphysically impossible. To say, then, that properties of kind K are *conceptually reducible to* properties of kind K' is to say that for any class c of K-properties and for any class c' of K'-properties, if it is conceptually (or logically) possible for there to be something whose K-properties are exactly those in c and whose K'-properties are exactly those in c', then it is conceptually (logically) necessary that anything whose K'-properties are exactly those in c' is such that its (his/her) K-properties are exactly those in c. The idea here is that either it is conceptually necessary (a logical or analytic truth) that anything that has exactly such-and-such K'-properties also has exactly so-and-so K-properties or else it is conceptually incoherent (logically inconsistent) for anything to have exactly such-and-such K'-properties and also have exactly so-and-so K-properties. Or put another way, which K-properties a thing has is a logical consequence of which K'-properties it has. For example, on Frege's meta-semantical theory, the referential semantics for a language is reducible to the language's intensional semantics (i.e., its semantics of sense) together with some metaphysics, in that the referential properties of a language are reducible to the language's sense properties taken together with the extra-linguistic matter of what objects are determined by those senses. Given that conceptual necessity entails metaphysical necessity but not *vice versa*, it follows that conceptual reducibility entails modal supervenience but not *vice versa*.[23] A claim to the effect that K-properties supervene on K'-properties therefore normally carries the implicature that K-properties are *not* reducible to K'-properties. And indeed, when philosophers explicitly advocate a supervenience thesis, they often explicitly contrast that thesis with the corresponding reducibility thesis, which they reject, or at least decline to endorse. I am doing exactly that here.

On the modal-supervenience interpretation of the problem of personal identity, the two meta-questions about "criteria for personal identity" are distinct. The

---

[22] Jaegwon Kim defines some non-equivalent notions of supervenience in 'Concepts of Supervenience,' *Philosophy and Phenomenological Research*, 65 (1984), pp. 257–270. The notion defined in the text corresponds to Kim's favored notion of *strong supervenience* (where the modality involved is metaphysical modality).

If I am correct, recognition of the distinction between supervenience and reducibility is crucial if we are to make significant progress toward solving the traditional problem of personal identity. The Reductionist regarding personal identity typically supposes that the haecceity of the Doris-body-person ought to be not merely supervenient on the sorts of facts about her that are given in D/R-3, but reducible to them. The weaker doctrine that personal identity modally supervenes on, but is not reducible to, such biographical features of a person as his/her psychological or bodily history may be what Parfit means when he speaks of what he calls *the Further Fact View* (p. 210). (Presently I shall deny that the haecceity of the Doris-body-person even modally supervenes on the facts given in D/R-3.)

[23] Given a certain kind of mereological essentialism, it follows that mereological reducibility of the sort described in note 18 above likewise entails modal supervenience but not *vice versa*.

metaphysical question is the deeper of the two—or at least, the more metaphysical. It is a demand for a metaphysical principle, or principles, that entail the answer to the primary question. It is, in effect, a demand for an individual person a's *essence*, in the sense of a property such that it is metaphysically necessary that someone has the property if and only if he or she is the very individual a and no other. Or perhaps it is a demand merely for a modally *sufficient* property for a's haecceity, i.e. a property such that necessarily, anyone with that property is the very individual a and no other. Or at the very least, it is a request for an *essential* property of a, i.e. a property that a has necessarily. The sought-after modal property must be adequate to the task of answering the primary question, interpreted now as a question about genuinely possible worlds in which the puzzle-case scenario obtains. This is *the Essentialist problem of personal identity*, to be distinguished from the Reductionist problem. The Essentialist problem does not presuppose that the sort of fact sought in answer to the primary question is reducible to, or is nothing over and above, facts of some other sort. The problem is perfectly compatible with the Extreme Haecceitist thesis that identity facts are further facts. Even by the Extreme Haecceitist's lights, it may be seen as a legitimate, and nontrivial, philosophical problem.[24]

We have seen that modal supervenience differs from reducibility (in one sense) over the type of modality involved. The two interpretations of the problem of personal identity carry with them correspondingly different notions of necessity that are involved in the explication given in Section I above of the concept of a criterion of personal identity. We said that a criterion of personal identity was a triple consisting of a sortal property F and a pair of binary relations R and R', other than personal identity itself, such that it is somehow necessary that x is the same person at t that y is at t' if (or perhaps iff) there is some trans-temporal link of sort F to which x bears R at t and to which y bears R' at t'. A purely epistemological criterion emerges by taking the necessity involved to be epistemic, e.g., knowability *a priori*, or perhaps the weaker notion: *given what we know, it must be that* (i.e., the dual of epistemic possibility: *for all we know, it may be that*). This would answer the epistemological meta-question. The Essentialist problem of personal identity takes the necessity involved to be metaphysical necessity, i.e. truth in all metaphysically possible worlds.

---

[24] Kripke (pp. 50–53) describes a version of the problem of cross-world identification that he finds legitimate, adding explicitly (p. 51) that there is a similarly legitimate problem concerning identity over time. The alleged problem is concerned with identifying physical objects in different possible worlds given only the facts concerning the relevant molecules (or other, more basic components). Insofar as Kripke is distinguishing between a pseudo-problem of cross-circumstantial identification that presupposes Reductionism with a genuine problem that instead presupposes mere modal supervenience, I am here echoing his sentiments specifically in regard to the traditional problem of personal identity. The textual evidence inconclusively suggests, however, that Kripke's remarks concern the Reductionist problem (which I dismiss as bogus), as opposed to the Extreme-Haecceitist/Essentialist problem. See my 'Trans-World Identification and Stipulation.'

It is possible that Kripke endorses a Mereological Reductionism of the sort described in note 18 above, and that his problem of cross-world identification presupposes this kind of Reductionism rather than Conceptual Reductionism. Although Kripke advocates Haecceitism in its moderate form, discussions I have had with him (subsequent to the appearance of *Naming and Necessity*) make me doubtful whether he is prepared to hold, as I do, that haecceities are separate from, or facts over and above, such facts about individuals as their molecular composition (though he may be). *Cf. ibid.*, at p. 51n; and my 'The Logic of What Might Have Been,' at p. 20n.

The Reductionist problem of personal identity takes the necessity involved to be truth in all logically possible worlds, whether metaphysically possible or metaphysically impossible. (The phrase 'criterion of identity' may not be entirely appropriate on the Essentialist interpretation of the problem, since it seems to carry with it in connotation an acceptance of the Reductionist construal. But I shall continue to use it.)

The literature on personal identity has suffered from a failure to distinguish sharply between the Reductionist and the Essentialist interpretations of the problem. Philosopher A provisionally proposes a solution that is (or that at least might be) appropriate to the Essentialist problem, only to have it dismissed by philosopher B, noting that the proposed criterion does not work for every conceivable case, and thus construing it as a solution to the Reductionist problem. It even happens sometimes that A and B themselves bear the relation of personal identity.[25] When the distinction between the two interpretations is not emphasized, there is also the opposite danger that a Haecceitist who rejects the (*sic.*) problem of personal identity as unreasonably demanding, construing it Reductionistically, will miss the significance of the Essentialist problem.

VII

Let us reconsider the primary question and the metaphysical meta-question concerning D/R-1, interpreted now as concerning the class of possible worlds (excluding the impossible worlds) incorporating that scenario. At the end of Section II, it seemed as though the psychology-based identifications were correct—or at least that the body-based identifications were clearly incorrect. We may now go further. It is

[25] I take Johnston's 'Human Beings' to be an example of the converse situation. Johnston sees the problem of personal identity in the standard Reductionist way. (His Reductionism regarding persons is evidenced by his emphasis in 'Fission and the Facts' on conceptual possibility and conceptual necessity, and by his use of such phrases as 'that in which personal identity consists' in 'Human Beings' and 'the core relations that actually constitute personal identity' throughout 'Reasons and Reductionism.' Unlike the typical Reductionist, though, Johnston does not claim that the haecceity of the Doris-body-person is reducible to the sorts of facts given in D/R-3. See note 22 above.) Frustrated by an alleged conflict of intuitions regarding scenarios like D/R-2 and by the failure of previous attempts to solve the problem of personal identity, Johnston concludes, erroneously in my view, that the standard philosophical methodology of putting hypothetical cases to the test of intuition is somehow misguided. He argues that one should address the metaphysical meta-question instead with an eye to the epistemological meta-question. This procedure may make sense from the Reductionist standpoint, since whatever else identity facts are, they are knowable. Johnston opts for a solution to the metaphysical meta-question which, while it may be appropriate for the Essentialist problem, would be proved mistaken from the Reductionist standpoint by the questioned method of testing cases against intuition. Johnston's failure to distinguish between the Reductionist and Essentialist interpretations of the problem is further evidenced by his complaint that, according to the challenged methodology, "the supposition that I could survive my body's petrification implies that the relations that tie me to my body are contingent" ('Human Beings,' p. 71). The phrase 'supposition that I could' here means conceptual possibility, while 'contingent' evidently means metaphysical contingency. Johnston also conflates reducibility and mere supervenience in 'Reasons and Reductionism,' at pp. 590–591. See also his 'Fission and the Facts,' at p. 381.

evident that, necessarily, in D/R-1 the psychology-based identifications are indeed correct. There are D/R-1 worlds in which the Doris-body-person is Doris, but such worlds are one and all impossible. In every *possible* world in which D/R-1 occurs, Doris and Rita have simply traded bodies (apart from their brains). To this extent, our original intuitions about this case are correct.

It does not follow that some psychology-based criterion for personal identity (such as the memory-based criterion) yields a correct answer to our metaphysical meta-question, interpreted on the Essentialist scheme. Psychology-based criteria are not the only criteria according to which Doris and Rita have exchanged bodies in D/R-1. A brain-based criterion would issue the same identifications. A brain-based criterion usually echoes the psychology-based criteria in the identifications it makes, but there is divergence in cases of brain damage. If a person's brain is damaged to an extent that significantly affects his/her psychology—such as by significantly altering his/her personality and/or memories of past events—corresponding psychology-based criteria deem the resulting person to be numerically distinct from the person prior to the brain damage. If the brain nevertheless continues to function sufficiently to produce consciousness and a psychology adequate for being a person, the brain-based criterion judges the resulting person to be literally and numerically the same as the person before the damage—only now not the same as he/she used to be.

Given what science informs us about the importance of the brain to consciousness, there does not seem to be much room for debate. The brain-based criterion, construed as an Essentialist criterion for personal identity, is intrinsically more plausible than either the body-based or the psychology-based criteria. I am not my body. But neither am I my psychology *as such*—my thoughts, my personality, my memories, my beliefs. I am more closely bound to my *consciousness* than to any of these other things. Not to my "stream of consciousness," mind you—the flow of thoughts, feelings, sensations, experiences, etc.—but the consciousness itself, the arena through which the flow flows. I may not be strictly identical with my consciousness. I continue to exist even through periods of unconsciousness (e.g. when asleep), even if not through all such periods. But there seems to be some connection between my consciousness and myself that is more intimate than that between my body and myself.[26] The brain is the organ that produces consciousness. Perhaps no one can say exactly how the brain does it. It may be that, at some sufficiently deep level of understanding, it is *impossible* to know how the brain does it. But somehow the brain does it, and that is something we do know. This knowledge provides forceful intuitive support for a brain-based Essentialist criterion for personal identity.

The body-based and psychology-based criteria each yield the same identifications in D/R-2 as they did in D/R-1. But the brain-based criterion has a special problem with D/R-2. Here the Doris-body-person has what was previously Doris's brain as well as what was previously Doris's body, but her brain now holds the information that was extracted from Rita's brain. Even if one has decided to make the identifications by attending to the brains rather than to the bodies or the psychologies, one

---

[26] The identification of a person with a consciousness, as opposed to a stream of consciousness, probably lies behind Descartes's proof of his own existence *via* his '*Cogito ergo sum*'. Ironically, it also lies behind Hume's denial of his own existence.

still has to decide whether the person's identity goes with the brain itself or instead with the information held within the brain. In D/R-2 these two come apart. The brain-*qua*-organ-based criterion is obtained by letting the sortal *F* in our explication of a personal-identity criterion be *brain* and letting both *R* and *R'* be the relation of *being the functional owner of*—which in this case may be taken to be the relation *u is the person whose brain is v*. The brain-information-based criterion is obtained instead by letting the sortal *F* be *brain-information* (operating system and RAM, etc.) and letting both *R* and *R'* be the relation: *u is a person whose brain holds exactly the information v*. According to the brain-*qua*-organ-based criterion, *x* is the same person as *y* if they have the same brain across time. According to the brain-information-based criterion, *x* is the same person as *y* if their brains store the same information across time. The brain-*qua*-organ-based criterion goes with the body-based criterion in D/R-2, the brain-information-based criterion with the psychology-based criteria.

Williams says that the primary advantage of setting out the problem of personal identity by means of the BW device rather than by means of brain transplants comes from the fact that D/R-2 is less radical than D/R-1 in the way it secures the condition that the Doris-body-person is appropriately connected to Rita so that the Doris-body-person's apparent memories of Rita's past are not automatically disqualified from being genuine memories. This remark of Williams' strongly suggests—and indeed much of the literature on personal identity assumes—that the identifications should come out exactly the same in both D/R-1 and D/R-2. (See note 11 above.) But it is at least potentially a mistake to assume this at the outset, without any argument or further ado. This is especially true since D/R-2 forcefully challenges the psychology-based criteria that seem so fitting when considering only D/R-1. It is logically possible, for example, that although the Doris-body-person is Rita in D/R-1, the Doris-body-person is instead Doris in D/R-2. This would have the consequence that the Doris-body-person of D/R-1 is numerically distinct from the Doris-body-person of D/R-2. But this is a logical possibility.[27]

I believe this logical possibility is philosophical reality. The primary question not only about D/R-1, but equally about D/R-2, when interpreted on the Essentialist scheme, is legitimate. In any genuinely possible D/R-1 world, the Doris-body-person is Rita, owing to the fact that the Doris-body-person in D/R-1 has what had been Rita's brain, still functioning in a normal manner. By contrast, in any possible D/R-2 world the Doris-body-person is Doris. And this is a result of the fact that the Doris-body-person in D/R-2 has what had been Doris's brain, still functioning in a normal manner. One noteworthy feature of the brain-*qua*-organ criterion—and an important argument in its favor—is that it discriminates between D/R-1 and D/R-2. It does indeed seem possible for a person to be given a different body by transplanting his/her brain into it. And it seems equally possible for a person to have his/her psychology radically altered by inducing substantial changes in his/her brain.

---

[27] The expressions 'the Doris-body-person' and 'the Rita-body-person' are definite descriptions (where a *Doris-body-person* is defined as being a person who now occupies what was Doris's body before the relevant procedure). There is therefore nothing about their semantics, as such, that requires them to be rigid designators, in the sense of Kripke.

Indeed, it is not an uncommon occurrence for someone's psychology to become significantly altered with brain damage. What seems impossible is for a person to take possession of a new body merely by having his/her psychology replicated in the new body's brain while his/her old brain is destroyed, or for a person's psychology to be modified by transplanting someone else's brain, with its readymade psychology, into his/her body. Of the several personal-identity criteria considered so far, the brain-*qua*-organ-based criterion is the only one that captures all of these intuitions. If one views the Essentialist problem of personal identity as a multi-partied election, then at this stage of the campaign at least, given our current state of knowledge, the brain-*qua*-organ-based criterion probably deserves one's vote. One thing seems clear: the rival criteria do not.

The solution I favor for the Essentialist problem of personal identity is to look neither to the body nor to the psychology, but to the organ of consciousness: the brain. I tentatively submit a pair of modal principles concerning persons and their brains. As a first approximation, consider the following essentialist principle:

> Necessarily, for any person P and any person-brain B, if B is P's brain at some time t (i.e. if P's consciousness is produced at t by B, etc.), then necessarily, for any time t' at which P is not brain-dead, P's brain at t' is B, so that if P is conscious at t', his/her consciousness is produced at t' by B.

The idea is that a person's brain is an essential property of the person, in the sense that as long as he or she is not brain-dead, his or her brain must be *that very brain* and no other. A different person-brain (for example, an artificial brain), no matter how extensively it replicates a person's original brain, cannot take the place of the original brain for that person. If the new brain produces consciousness, it is not that person's consciousness. Let us call this principle *the essentiality of one's brain*. The principle does not entail that a person's brain cannot undergo change. A person's brain might become damaged or undergo various surgical improvements (e.g., removal of tumors). The principle does not even deny that parts of a brain might be replaced with artificial components. What the principle entails is that whatever changes a brain undergoes, it must remain the same, numerically identical brain if its functional owner is to remain the same, numerically identical person. Replacement of a functional brain is homicide.

Kripke and others have proposed other essentialist principles concerning individuals, e.g. that the original material out of which an artifact was constructed is an essential feature of the artifact, and that any natural kind (e.g. the species) to which a creature belongs is an essential feature of the creature. As with these other principles, the essentiality of one's brain is *a posteriori*. It is subject to falsification and adjustment by the empirical facts. And as with other *a posteriori* essentialist principles, there is some more general, *a priori* essentialist principle from which the essentiality of one's brain is obtained. This may be the principle that if there is a single organ that is responsible for a person's consciousness, then it is essential to the person that he/she have that very organ (and not, for instance, a transplanted organ of the same type from someone else). The essentiality of one's brain derives its aposteriority from that of the supplementary observation that the organ of consciousness among persons is the brain. The latter observation is subject to falsification by the improbable empirical discovery of a person lacking a brain.

The general principle itself is also subject to revision through critical inquiry, perhaps even through empirical findings. Philosophers often ponder the prospect of fission, whereby a single person is divided into two people by bisecting his/her brain and transplanting one or both of the brain-halves into a brainless body. It may be that anything that might be reasonably called a *person* must, as a matter of actual physiology, have more than one-half of an ordinary brain.[28] The loss of a smaller portion of one's brain might in some cases be regarded as damage that the brain survives—that is, as the brain's losing a part without thereby ceasing to exist as a functional brain. But if it should turn out that (as is frequently supposed in the relevant literature) enough of a person's psychology and consciousness can be retained with only one-half (or even somewhat less) of a brain, we may decide to replace the principle of the essentiality of one's brain with a weaker principle of *the essentiality of some sufficient portion or other of one's brain*. According to this essentialist principle, a person could survive the destruction of his/her brain by retaining a sufficiently functional portion. An Essentialist version of the fission problem might then arise.[29] It is difficult to conjecture about what the limitations are. Perhaps gradual bionicization is a real possibility. Perhaps different brain functions, including different aspects of consciousness, can be gradually taken over by different artificial devices, making the brain itself dispensable, thus requiring further modification in the essentiality of one's brain. But suppose the discarded brain were refurbished. Who would its functional owner be?[30]

If it is assumed that Doris and Rita continue to exist in both D/R-1 and D/R-2 after the relevant procedure, then the essentiality of one's brain answers the primary questions, as interpreted on the Essentialist scheme. Given Doris's and Rita's survival, the principle entails that they have exchanged bodies in D/R-1 and have

---

[28] So argues John Robinson in 'Personal Identity and Survival,' *Journal of Philosophy*, 85 (1988), pp. 319–328.

[29] The fission problem is analogous in some respects to a similar problem concerning artifacts, as illustrated by the famous Ship of Theseus. The former problem, interpreted on the Essentialist scheme, may be amenable to an analogue of the solution I proposed to the latter in *Reference and Essence*, pp. 219–229. There are alternative solutions to the fission problem which are not usually considered but which, if sound, would save the principle of the essentiality of one's brain. One is the claim that what survives the removal of a brain hemisphere is not the original person, but only what had been a part of that person and what is now a full-fledged (though perhaps impaired) person in his/her own right. In this case, the two persons who emerge from fission were formerly not persons at all, but two halves of the original person, who was destroyed. A variant of this solution holds that the original person continues to exist even after the fission, but only as the scattered aggregate of two separate persons, and therefore not itself a person. The fission would in that case constitute a radical metamorphosis whereby what had been a person is transformed from a solo act into a duo. On both of these solutions, any person who loses one of his/her brain's hemispheres is distinct from the person (or from each of the persons) who emerges from the procedure with only the remaining hemisphere. Both of these prospects are worthy of more serious attention.

[30] One carefully guarded variation of the principle in the text is the following: Necessarily, for any person P and any person-brain B, if B is P's brain at some time t, then necessarily, for any later time t' at which P is not brain-dead and such that P has a functioning brain throughout the period from t to t', P's brain at t' is a portion of B.

exchanged psychologies in D/R-2. In both cases they retain their individual brains. Indeed, according to the principle, they *must* retain their individual brains if they are to survive the relevant procedure, whether it is a brain transplant or a BW-exchange. This suggests an complementary essentialist principle:

> Necessarily, for any person-brain B and any person P, if B is P's brain at some time t, then necessarily, for any time t' at which B is functioning roughly normally, the person whose brain at t' is B is P, so that if B is producing consciousness at t', the consciousness produced is P's.

The idea is that a brain's functional owner is an essential property of the brain, in the sense that, as long as the brain is functioning in a substantially normal manner (allowing for some malfunctioning due to brain damage, etc.), the brain's functional owner must be *that very person* and no other. (It is assumed that necessarily, for any time t, any person-brain that is functioning substantially normally has exactly one functional owner at t, i.e. there is exactly one person whose brain it is at t.) No matter how much the psychology may have been altered—due to brain washing, under the influence of drugs or religious fanaticism, etc.—if the same brain is still producing consciousness in a more-or-less normal manner, it is the same person, even if he/she has been psychologically deeply altered in the process. We may call this principle *the essentiality of a brain's ownership.*[31]

Seen in one light, the twin principles of the essentiality of one's brain and the essentiality of a brain's ownership are the same but for a different focus. The two principles may be combined into a single principle of the *essentiality of brain ownership*:

> Necessarily, for any person P and any person-brain B, if B is P's brain at some time t, then necessarily, for any time t' at which either P is not brain-dead or B is functioning substantially normally, P is the person whose brain at t' is B.

A couple of points bear repeating here. First, the issue of whether this principle is correct is one that is appropriately settled partly by reference to empirical facts and partly by philosophical inquiry. Second, whether it is the essentiality of brain ownership or some alternative essentialist principle that is supported by empirical facts and philosophical analysis, the resulting "criterion" for personal identity solves the Essentialist problem, not the Reductionist problem. The necessity involved in any brain-based criterion cannot be conceptual or logical necessity. It is manifestly not conceptually or logically necessary (e.g., it is clearly not an analytic truth) that persons have brains at all, let alone that a person has the same brain as long as he/she has the capacity for consciousness. Just as it is logically possible for a tin man to lack a heart yet live, it is likewise logically possible for a brainless scarecrow to be magically conscious, even impressively clever.[32]

---

[31] By the definition of supervenience given in Section VI, if one's haecceity modally supervenes on the original ownership of one's current brain, it follows that for any person x, no other than x can possibly currently have what was originally x's brain. This is, in effect, the principle of the essentiality of a brain's ownership.

[32] *Cf.* David Wiggins, *Identity and Spatio-Temporal Continuity* (Oxford: Basil Blackwell, 1967), at p. 55. Williams evidently denies the principle of the essentiality of one's brain. In 'Are Persons Bodies?', he asserts that "it seems pretty clear that under these circumstances [in which the BW device is used to copy information extracted from one brain into another] a person could be

An essentialist principle is a principle of modal intolerance; it imposes limitations on the variety of genuinely possible worlds. The essentiality of brain ownership does not concern impossible worlds. I am not proposing that a person's identity is *reducible* to (or that it is nothing over and above, or that it consists in, or is grounded in, derived from, etc.) facts about brains and their former owners. I maintain that the matter of the haecceity of a person given qualitatively as *the person who now functionally owns brain B* is a further fact. The traditional, canonical form of the problem of personal identity is correctly solved by rejecting it as a spurious pseudo-problem. One is free to stipulate that one is considering worlds in which the person who now has what used to be *a*'s brain is not *a* but someone else. There is a price to be paid for doing so: the worlds under consideration will be metaphysically impossible worlds. But there is absolutely no problem with that.[33]

counted the same if this were done to him, and in the process he were given a new brain . . . here we have personal identity without the same brain, though of course we have identity of the rest of the body to hold onto" (*Problems of the Self*, p. 80). Parfit argues similarly in *Reasons and Persons* (see note 10 above) that retaining some or all of one's brain is not what fundamentally "matters" in survival. Although Williams may be a Reductionist (see note 21 above), his claim here is framed using the subjunctive construction "if this *were* done to him, . . .", suggesting, perhaps, that if it is metaphysically possible to extract and restore brain information, then it is also metaphysically possible for someone to be given a new brain. Williams might be interpreted here as denying even the essentiality of a portion of one's brain. (As a Reductionist, however, Williams would be forced to regard personal identity in such a case as consisting in something else—hence the remark about the identity of the rest of the body as something to "hold onto.")

John Perry suggests a principle similar to the essentiality of one's brain and proceeds to criticize it, in his *A Dialogue on Personal Identity and Immortality* (Indianapolis: Hackett, 1978), at p. 47. Perry is also a Reductionist regarding persons (see, for example, pp. 21–22 of the same work), and his criticisms suggest that his intended target is a principle supporting a brain-based criterion of personal identity as a solution to the Reductionist problem.

[33] The combined principle of the essentiality of brain ownership is similar to what Parfit, in *Reasons and Persons*, p. 204, calls *the Physical Criterion* (although the latter is actually a principle of the essentiality of unique ownership of some sufficient portion or other of a brain). The thesis I am proposing is significantly different from the view of Thomas Nagel in *The View From Nowhere* (Oxford University Press, 1986). Nagel is at least tempted to identify a person with his/her brain, while denying that the connection is *a priori*. On his view, the sentence 'Jones = Jones's brain', and likewise the sentence 'Jones = B' where 'B' names Jones's brain, express necessary *a posteriori* truths. I am claiming that though a person and his/her brain are not identical, they are essentially related to each other by functional ownership. On my view, the sentence 'Jones's brain = B'—or more cautiously, the sentence 'If Jones has a functioning brain, then it is a portion of B'—expresses a necessary *a posteriori* truth, whereas Nagel's allegedly necessary *a posteriori* sentences are not even true.

On the other hand, Nagel describes the identification of person and brain as a 'mild exaggeration' (p. 40). Nagel's actual view may thus be closer to the view defended here. Parfit reports (*ibid.*, pp. 289–293, 468–477), that in then unpublished work (possibly a draft of chapter 3 of *The View From Nowhere*), Nagel rejects the Extreme Haecceitist thesis that the identity of a person, given qualitatively, is a further fact about the person given thus. Nagel reportedly defends a brain-*qua*-organ-based criterion as a solution to the meta-question for a Reductionist problem of personal identity. It is possible, however, that Nagel endorses a Mereological Reductionism of the sort described in note 18 above. Being an Extreme Haecceitism, I reject the traditional Reductionist problem of personal identity as a pseudo-problem. I similarly reject the idea that the identity of the person having a particular brain is mereologically reducible to facts about the brain. Whatever force Parfit's objections may have against Nagel's reported view, they carry little or no weight against my proposed essentialist principles. Another account having important points of contact with the account presented here is that in Peter Unger, *Identity, Consciousness, and Value* (Oxford University Press, 1990)—with the significant difference that Unger (p. 42) declines to endorse any nontrivial essentialism of the sort that is central to the present view.

VIII

The twin principles of the essentiality of one's brain and the essentiality of a brain's ownership yield answers to the metaphysical meta-question on the Essentialist version of the problem of personal identity. They also yield answers to the primary questions about D/R-1 and D/R-2, interpreted on the Essentialist scheme, different answers to each. Scenario D/R-3 is another matter. The essentialist principles seem not to help at all in settling the primary question about D/R-3—even when interpreting it as a question about the genuinely possible worlds represented by the scenario. We are not told whether the changes that have taken place in D/R-3 are the result of brain transplants, or information extraction by means of a BW device, or alien rays, or magic (if such is possible), or something else. The body-based and the psychology-based criteria go about their business in D/R-3 just as they do in D/R-1 and D/R-2, making the same identifications in all three scenarios. But the brain-*qua*-organ criterion comes up short in D/R-3. The criterion is not up to the task of answering the primary question about the most puzzling of puzzle cases, interpreted on the Essentialist scheme. There seems to be nothing in this neutral scenario for the criterion to take hold of.

There is something. The brain-*qua*-organ criterion discriminates between D/R-1 and D/R-2, making opposite identifications in each. That in itself, I have argued, is an important feature of the criterion. And it is a feature that the criterion brings with it to D/R-3. D/R-3 is neutral regarding the sort of facts in virtue of which D/R-1 and D/R-2 differ from each other. The reason the brain-*qua*-organ criterion is unable to settle the primary question in D/R-3 is that D/R-3 is silent where D/R-1 and D/R-2 are specific. D/R-3 fails to specify the sort of facts that the brain-*qua*-organ criterion needs in order to identify the post-switch body-persons. If D/R-3 is brought about by brain transplants performed by alien surgeons, then the identifications go the same way as in D/R-1. If D/R-3 is brought about instead through an alien version of the BW device, then the identifications go the same way as in D/R-2. Some facts or other of this sort must obtain in any scenario that realizes D/R-3. Yet D/R-3 fails to specify what they are.

The difficulty encountered in the attempt to answer the primary question creates the impression that one is confronting a deep philosophical conundrum for which the brain-*qua*-organ criterion's effectiveness breaks down and is seen to be inadequate. But the difficulty (indeed impossibility) of answering the primary question about D/R-3 is not due to a defect in the brain-*qua*-organ criterion. It is due to a defect in the scenario. It is under-specified, and for that very reason the brain-*qua*-organ criterion yields no answer to the primary question. In truth, D/R-3 is not so much a particular puzzle-case scenario for the Essentialist problem of personal identity as it is a generic *category* or *classification* of puzzle cases. It represents a *class* or *type* of genuinely possible scenarios. In some possible scenarios of that type, Doris and Rita exchange bodies while retaining their brains, and consequently also their psychologies. In other possible scenarios *of the very same type*, Doris and Rita exchange their psychologies while retaining their bodies, including their brains.

In some possible D/R-3 scenarios the Doris-body-person is Doris; in other possible D/R-3 scenarios the Doris-body-person is Rita. The reason the best criterion yet considered does not yield a single, unequivocal answer to the primary question, interpreted on the Essentialist scheme, when asked of D/R-3 itself, is that no answer is correct for all such cases. Any criterion that provides a single answer for all genuinely possible puzzle cases of that type is *ipso facto* mistaken. This would include both the body-based and the entire array of psychology-based criteria.[34]

This is true to a lesser extent about D/R-1 and D/R-2 as well. D/R-1 and D/R-2 are also under-specified, indeed in infinitely many respects. D/R-1 fails to specify, for example, the details of the surgical procedure that Allen performs on his victims. And D/R-2 does not specify very much at all about how the marvelous BW device works. The Doris/Rita incidents are not so much particular puzzle-case scenarios for the Essentialist problem of personal identity as they are *types* of puzzle cases. But there is an important difference between D/R-1 and D/R-2 on the one hand, and D/R-3 on the other. Arguably, all possible D/R-1 cases yield the same identifications, and all possible D/R-2 cases also yield the same identifications, exactly opposite to those of D/R-1 cases. The class of genuinely possible worlds represented by D/R-1 is a uniform class in regard to the relevant identifications. Similarly for the class of genuinely possible worlds represented by D/R-2. D/R-3, by contrast, defines a remarkably mixed bag. D/R-3 fails to specify the very sorts of facts upon which the answer to the primary question supervenes—to wit, the matter of whether the Doris-body-person's consciousness is being produced by what had been Doris's brain or by what had been Rita's. The class of genuinely possible worlds represented by D/R-3 remains diverse, in the same way as the class of all worlds, possible and impossible, represented by either D/R-1 or D/R-2. The primary question about D/R-3, even when interpreted on the Essentialist scheme, is thus a 'wife-beating' question. It remains unanswerable because of its false presupposition that the answer modally supervenes on facts concerning psychologies and/or bodies.

---

[34] For related discussion, see *Reference and Essence*, at pp. 242–246.

PART IV

PHILOSOPHY OF MATHEMATICS

12

Wholes, Parts, and Numbers (1997)

If it's not one thing, it's two.
James B. Ledford

I present here a puzzle that arises in the area of overlap among the philosophy of logic, the philosophy of mathematics, and the philosophy of language. The puzzle also concerns a host of issues in metaphysics, insofar as it crucially involves wholes, their parts, and the relation of part to whole. Almost entirely nontechnical, the puzzle is disarmingly simple to state. What little technicality I introduce below is mostly of a purely logical nature, and mostly inessential to the puzzle's central thrust. I discovered the puzzle nearly twenty years ago. (See note 4 below.) It had been my intention since that time to publish the puzzle together with its solution, but finding a solution that I was strongly inclined to accept proved difficult. I have presented the puzzle orally and informally to a number of philosophers, including several of the world's greatest thinkers in the philosophy of logic and the philosophy of mathematics. None offered a solution that strikes me as definitively striking to the heart of the matter. Indeed, I was in no position to make others appreciate the full philosophical significance of the problem. I present here a couple of my own proposals for its solution, an acknowledgment of some shortcomings of those proposals, and a final nod in the direction of the solution I currently think is best.

The Problem: There are several pieces of fruit, including exactly three whole oranges, on top of the table.[1] I cut one of the oranges exactly in half, eat one of the halves, and leave the remaining half on the table. Consider now the following question:

Q Exactly how many oranges are there remaining on the table?

Any schoolboy is able to calculate that the correct answer to (Q) is:

A There are exactly 2½ oranges remaining on the table.

But there is a proof that (A) is incorrect: Consider the orange-half (as it may be called) that remains on the table, and whose Siamese twin I have eaten. By Excluded Middle, either it is itself an orange on the table, or else it is not itself an orange on the table. If the former, then there are not only 2½ oranges on the table but 3—the two whole oranges together with the orange-half. If the latter, then there are not as many as 2½ oranges on the table but only 2—together with something that is not itself an

---

[1] Throughout, in saying that there are exactly *n* *F*'s, I mean that there are at least and at most *n* *F*'s, no more and no fewer.

orange on the table. Of course, there are many additional non-oranges on the table: four whole apples, two pear slices, and a kiwi fruit. The presence of non-oranges does not alter the fact that (on this horn of our dilemma) the correct answer to (Q) is:

A′ There are exactly 2 oranges remaining on the table.

In either case, then, the exact number of oranges on the table is not a number between 2 and 3. We seem forced to the conclusion that the schoolboy's answer (A) to question (Q) is incorrect, specifying either too few or too many.

One should note that the first horn of our dilemma, on which there are exactly three oranges on the table, may be eliminated by changing the example slightly. Suppose I go on to eat exactly half of the remaining orange-half, so that the schoolboy's answer to (Q) now becomes that there are exactly 2¼ oranges on the table. Surely an orange-quarter is not itself an orange; it is only a fractional portion of an orange.[2] On this modified version of the problem, we may construct a simpler proof that the correct answer to (Q) is in fact (A′).

The problem is that common sense tells us the correct answer to (Q) is not (A′). It is (A).

One solution: A solution to the problem lies somewhere in the very meaning, or perhaps what is called the 'logical form', of sentences like (A) and (A′). These sentence have, or at least appear to have, the common form:

F There are exactly *n* objects *x* such that ϕ_x.

There is a tradition in philosophical logic and the philosophy of mathematics of glossing the phrase 'there are exactly *n*', as it occurs in (F), as a special kind of quantifier: a *numerical quantifier*. The traditional logicist conception of number fits perfectly with the notion that the numerals '1', '2', '3', etc. are quantifiers (hence, not singular terms), thought of now as second-order predicates. As is well known, in the case of whole numbers, the corresponding numerical quantifiers are contextually definable in first-order logic by making use of the traditional quantifiers '∀' and '∃' in combination with '='. For example, the sentence '2*xFx*' (read 'There are exactly 2 objects *x* such that *Fx*') may be taken as shorthand for:

$$\exists x \exists y[Fx \wedge Fy \wedge x \neq y \wedge \forall z(Fz \supset x = z \vee y = z)].$$

---

[2] By contrast, a quarter of any (non-negligible sized) portion of an orange is another portion of an orange. One might say of an orange-quarter, with justification, that it is "an orange," in order to distinguish it, for example, from a pear (or a pear-portion). But it seems likely that this is a special use of the predicate 'is an orange' by the speaker to mean *orange-portion* (as opposed to a portion of some other kind of fruit). In saying that an orange-quarter is not itself an orange, I am relying on the intuition (which many, including myself, share) that an orange-quarter is not an element of the semantic extension of the count noun 'orange' in English. One does not produce many oranges from a single orange simply by slicing; instead one produces orange-slices. Although I will often assume in what follows that orange-halves are likewise not themselves oranges, I must emphasize here that nothing I say depends crucially on this assumption. Each of the arguments can be made, *mutatis mutandis*, on the opposite assumption that proper portions of oranges are themselves oranges (elements of the English extension of the noun 'orange')—and even (e.g. by a dilemma form of argument) on the assumption that the noun 'orange' is ambiguous, having one English meaning that includes, and another that excludes, proper orange-portions.

And the sentence '3*xFx*' may be taken as shorthand for:

$$\exists x \exists y \exists z [Fx \wedge Fy \wedge Fz \wedge x \neq y \wedge x \neq z \wedge y$$
$$\neq z \wedge \forall w (Fw \supset x = w \vee y = w \vee z = w)].$$

The sentence '3*xFx*' thus says something particular about the class of *F*'s: that it has exactly three elements. (Or if one prefers, the sentence says the corresponding thing about the Fregean characteristic function λxFx, which assigns truth to *F*'s and falsity to non-*F*'s.) If we follow the Frege-Carnap-Church tradition in distinguishing for expressions of every type between reference/extension on the one hand and content/intension on the other, then the numeral '3' itself may be taken as expressing the property of classes (or alternatively the concept) of having exactly three elements (the content of '3'), and as referring to the class of all such classes (the extension). This directly yields the Frege-Russell conception of number.[3]

The number 2½ is not a whole number, and (*A*) cannot be taken as shorthand in the same way for any first-order sentence whose only nonlogical component is a predicate for being an orange on the table. But not to despair. We may simply introduce a new expression, say '2.5', as a primitive numerical quantifier, giving (*A*) the particular form '2.5*xFx*', and similarly for other rational numbers. The question 'Exactly how many *F*'s are there?' may now be taken as an instruction to provide the particular numerical quantifier *Q* such that ⌜*QxFx*⌝ is true.

One immediate problem with this proposal is that, as we have seen, besides '2.5' there is another numerical quantifier *Q* such that ⌜*Qx* (*x* is an orange on the table)⌝ is true, namely '2'. Perhaps we must take the question 'Exactly how many *F*'s are there?' instead as an instruction to provide the *greatest* numerical quantifier *Q* such that ⌜*QxFx*⌝ is true, in the standard numerical ordering of numerical quantifiers. As any schoolboy knows, 2.5 > 2.

One remaining problem is that this proposal does not provide any reason to hold that (*A'*) is actually false. On the contrary, on the proposal now before us, both (*A*) and (*A'*) are deemed literally true. Why, then, does the latter not count, along with the former, as an alternative but equally accurate answer to (*Q*)?

There is a more serious problem. In classical formal semantics, a quantifier *Q* in a formula ⌜*QxFx*⌝ may be regarded as a second-order predicate, one that says something quantitative about the class of *F*'s (or about its characteristic function). The standard universal quantifier '∀'—or alternatively the English word 'everything'—expresses the concept of *universality*; '∀*xFx*' says that the class of *F*'s is universal. The

---

[3] It is often said that the theory of classes (or sets), if it is consistent, offers a selection of equally legitimate constructions for the sequence of whole numbers (the von Neumann construction, the Zermelo construction, etc.), no one of which may be singled out as the "right" one, exactly capturing metaphysically the actual, genuine numbers 0, 1, 2, 3, etc. However, only the Frege-Russell construction fits as well as it does with the treatment of whole-number numerals as first-order quantifiers. Philosophically, this gives the traditional logicist construction a stronger *prima facie* claim than its rivals to capturing the authentic numbers, since number terms ('two', '2½', etc.) are like color terms ('blue', etc.) in that the noun form (singular term) seems essentially parasitic on the adjective form (predicate or quantifier), which is fundamental. (In the final section of this paper, however, I shall present a new challenge to the claim that the logicist conception fits well with the treatment of numerals as quantifiers.)

standard existential quantifier '∃'—or 'something'—expresses the concept of being non-empty. The quantifier 'nothing' expresses the complementary concept of being empty. Similarly for the whole-number numerical quantifiers. They specify the cardinality of the class; '$2xFx$' says that the class of F's has exactly two elements, '$3xFx$' that the class has exactly three elements, and so on. This is precisely how the whole-number numerical quantifiers yield the Frege-Russell conception of number. But what exactly does the '2.5' in '$2.5xFx$' say about the class of F's? That it has exactly 2½ elements? What is that supposed to mean? How does an element of a class come to be counted merely as one-half, rather than as one, in determining the class's cardinality?

It does not. The class of oranges on the table has exactly two elements, no more and no less. The orange-half on the table is not an orange, and hence is not in the class of oranges on the table. It therefore cannot affect the cardinality of that class in any way. (Alternatively, if it is an orange, then the class of oranges on the table has exactly three elements, no more or no less. *Cf.* note 2 above.)

This point may be sharpened by considering an alternative first-order contextual definition of '2', *qua* numerical quantifier. We may contextually define the *lower-bound quantifiers* 'there are no fewer than 2' and 'there are no fewer than 3', respectively, as follows:

$$\geq 2xFx =_{\text{def}} \exists x \exists y (Fx \wedge Fy \wedge x \neq y).$$
$$\geq 3xFx =_{\text{def}} \exists x \exists y \exists z (Fx \wedge Fy \wedge Fz \wedge x \neq y \wedge x \neq z \wedge y \neq z).$$

Consider now the conjunction:

$$\geq 2xFx \wedge \sim \geq 3xFx,$$

i.e., there are no fewer than two F's but it is not the case that there are no fewer than three F's. Letting the predicate letter 'F' mean *orange on the table*, this conjunction is in fact true (assuming that the orange-half is not itself an orange). Since $2 \leq 2.5 < 3$, the conjunction may appear to cohere with the truth of '$2.5xFx$'. But the conjunction is in fact provably equivalent (in first-order logic, using no nonlogical hypotheses) to '$2xFx$', as contextually defined above. Once again, analysis in terms of numerical quantifiers leads us to (A'), rather than (A), as our answer to (Q).[4]

The lesson is this: Insofar as (A), not (A'), is the correct answer to (Q), the '2½' in (A) does not say, or does not merely say, something quantitative about the class of oranges on the table. If it says anything quantitative at all about that class, it also says something more, something not about the class.

An Alternative Solution: Have we construed our question (Q) excessively literally? Perhaps it asks something not merely about the class of oranges on the table,

---

[4] I discovered the puzzle, quite by chance, when teaching my logic students at Princeton University how to express the numerical quantifiers in terms of the lower-bound quantifiers, and how to express the latter in terms of '∀', '∃' and '='. One student, who failed to see the various connections clearly, innocently asked how the conjunction 'There are at least 2, but there are not at least 3, F's' (as defined in the text), requires that there be no more than 2 F's, rather than some number between 2 and 3, like 2½. Pondering what it means to say that there are exactly two and one-half F's, I realized that the student's confusion was not only hers, and not unwarranted.

properly so-called, but about the class of (proper and improper) pieces or portions of orange on the table. No; the latter class has exactly three elements, not two and one-half. Unless one counts undetached orange-parts as pieces of orange. And in that case, the class of pieces of orange on the table has some very large cardinality, far greater than 2½. If (A) is the correct answer to (Q), then (Q) does not ask for the number of objects that are pieces of orange remaining on the table.

Perhaps (Q) is concerned not with how many, but with *how much*. The question may be this: Exactly how much orange-stuff is there on the table? Certainly this is a legitimate question. It is the sort of question one might ask if one needs to make a specific amount of orange juice. It is not so much the quantity of oranges that matters as the quantity of orange-stuff. One should probably see this how-much question as asking for a measure of mass or weight. But since oranges do not typically vary greatly in size and weight—unlike, say, pumpkins—in some contexts (A) may yield a correct answer to the question of how much orange-stuff there is on the table.

Perhaps. But there is another way to construe the question. The *count* (how many) construal is at least as legitimate as the *mass* (how-much) construal, if no more so. (Some questions may even require the count construal, e.g. 'How many oranges make up three pounds of orange-stuff?') If there are exactly two pumpkins in the yard, one of which weighs a few ounces and the other six hundred pounds, it is still correct to answer the question 'Exactly how many pumpkins are there in the yard?' by saying that there are exactly two—even though this does not yield an answer to the question of how much pumpkin there is (which in this case is the equivalent of a substantial number of middle-sized pumpkins). Even when our question (Q) is explicitly put forward as a count question, and not as a mass question, the correct answer still appears to be (A) rather than (A'). Ask the schoolboy, 'Never mind how much orange-stuff there is on the table, exactly how many oranges are there?' The answer comes back: Two and a half.

A Preferable Solution: Let us write (A) out in longhand, replacing all mathematical notation with genuine English:

There are exactly two and one-half oranges remaining on the table.

With a modicum of word-processing magic, and some finesse, this might be rewritten as the following conjunction:

A'': There are exactly two oranges remaining on the table and there is exactly one orange-half remaining on the table.

We are now in a position to grant that there is something right about this alternative analysis of (A). There are indeed two objects such that each is an orange on the table, and no more than two. In addition, there is indeed one orange-half on the table, and in *some* sense, no more than one. As we have seen, there are also thousands of undetached orange-halves on the table. When we say that there is exactly one orange-half on the table, we mean that there is exactly one detached orange-half (or at least that there is exactly one mostly detached orange-half, or something similar).

There are serious difficulties with our new proposal, though. The shuffling around of characters that transformed (A) into (A'') produced a sea change in logical form.

Our new answer (A'') is evidently not a numerical-quantifier generalization of the form '$nxFx$' at all, but a conjunction of distinct generalizations. It is in fact the conjunction of our formerly rejected answer (A') with something else. What else? A new numerical-quantifier generalization of the particular form '$1xGx$', where 'G' stands in for the phrase 'orange-half on the table' (or perhaps I should say, for the phrase 'mostly detached orange-half on the table'). The patient has undergone massive surgical reconstruction. The numeral '2' occurring in (A) has been separated from its accompanying fraction, and now performs as a solo numerical quantifier. The fraction itself has been severely mutilated. The numeral '1', which appears as the fraction's numerator in (A), has ascended to the status of an antonymous quantifier, functioning independently both of its former denominator and of the quantifier in the first conjunct. At the same time, the word 'half' appearing in the longhand version of (A) has been reassigned, from quantifier position to predicate position. In effect, the mixed-number expression '2½', occurring as a unit in (A), has been blown to smithereens, its whole integer now over here, the fraction's numerator now over there, the fraction's denominator someplace else. Even those of us who have survived major earthquakes need some time to adjust to reconfiguration on this scale.[5]

Of particular philosophical interest is the word 'half', which on this proposal is attached by a hyphen to a count noun like 'orange' (*qua* noun rather than adjective) to form a new count noun with a new extension (and hence, of course, with a new intension as well). One may well doubt that this device can be sensibly attached to each and every count noun. If one cuts a television set down the middle, for example, does one thereby obtain two television-set-halves (or two half-television-sets)? Well, perhaps one does. In either case, the device seems clearly applicable at least to a great many nouns, especially the names of a wide variety of fruits and vegetables, and perhaps to such expressions as 'cup of coffee'. ('Exactly how many cups of coffee are there on the table? Two and a half.') And indeed, one advantage of this account of the English word 'half' is that it may provide a semantically-based explanation (of a sort, anyway) for the uneasiness one feels in such weird constructions as 'There are exactly two and one-half television sets in the storage room'.

On the other hand, the word 'half' occurring in the pure-English version of (A) is evidently the English counterpart of the fraction's denominator in the original (A). Can it be that one obtains a correct analysis of fractional quantifiers by stripping the denominator in numerical-quantifier position of a numeral's customary status as quantifier, and reclassifying it altogether as a special non-mathematical operator on nouns? If so, the apparent unity of the fraction is a mirage. Fractions emerge as fragmented entities, comprised by both a numerical quantifier (the numerator) and a noun operator (the denominator)—hybrid entities that are part mathematical and part non-mathematical in form and function. What are entities like that doing in a purely deductive discipline like mathematics? The whole things smells fishy.

[5] Living in Santa Barbara, my family was spared the great trauma that my friends at Cal State Northridge and their loved ones have had to endure since January 17, 1994. Although our own experience of the great Northridge Quake amounted to little more than an inconvenience, we are no strangers to massive deconstruction, having endured the full fury of Hurricane Iniki in a demolished condo on the south shore of Kauai only a few years before. And now this.

Even the schoolboy knows that the phrase 'and a half' in the sentence 'There are exactly two and a half oranges on the table' goes with the 'two' and not with the 'orange'.

A related problem: As we have seen, (A'') is the conjunction of (A') with 'There is exactly one orange-half on the table'. But (Q) asks simply for the number of oranges on the table. On the proposal under consideration, (A') correctly specifies that number. The second conjunct '$1x$ (x is an orange-half on the table)' merely provides extraneous information, information that was not explicitly requested. Why, then, do we not simply give (A') in answer to (Q), holding the second conjunct in reserve, in case we are later asked exactly how many orange-halves there are on the table? Instead, we persist in giving (A) as our answer, even though no one has asked separately for the number of orange-halves on the table.

There is a more concrete problem. Our new proposal puts (A'') forward as an analysis of the schoolboy's answer (A) to (Q). This analysis is subject to direct disproof. For (A'') to be a correct answer to (Q), it would have to be true. And this would require its first conjunct, (A'), to be true. Now for any pair of numbers n and m, if there are exactly n F's, no more and no less, and also exactly m F's, no more and no less, then n and m must be exactly equal. But $2\frac{1}{2} \neq 2$. The two alternatives, (A) and (A'), are not teammates but competing rivals. Hence, since it entails (A'), if (A'') is a correct answer to (Q), then (A) is not. In a word, (A'') and (A) are incompatible. Therefore, the former cannot provide a correct analysis of the latter.

Instead of precluding (A)'s rival, (A'), by entailing its negation, (A'') does exactly the opposite, directly asserting (A') itself and then something further. Suppose one were to ask a question for which something analogous to (A'') would be a correct reply—such as, for example, 'Exactly how many *whole* oranges are there remaining on the table, and exactly how many orange-halves?'. Here one might well reply, 'Exactly two of the former and exactly one of the latter.' A response instead of only the first conjunct would be regarded as compatible with the right answer, correct as far as it goes but essentially incomplete.[6] Even if one were to ask a question for which something analogous to (A'') is only part of the correct reply ('What portions of oranges are there remaining on the table, and exactly how many of each?' 'Exactly two whole oranges, exactly one orange-half, and nothing more'), we should still regard the first conjunct as compatible with the right answer. But in giving (A) as our answer to the original question (Q), we also reject (A')—not merely as incomplete, but as flatly incorrect. There are *not* exactly two oranges remaining on the table. On the contrary, there are exactly two and one-half.

In fact, (A) may also clash with the second conjunct of (A''). For (A) does not, or at least need not, pretend to specify the total number of orange-halves on the table. Suppose I cut one of the whole oranges exactly in half, placing the two

---

[6] I assume here that there are exactly two whole oranges remaining on the table, not exactly two and one-half. The phrase 'two and one-half whole oranges' is taken here to be an oxymoron. This is largely a matter of terminology. Call them what one will, there are exactly two (rather than two and one-half) of *something* orange-like remaining on the table. The orangey things of which there are exactly two on the table are what I call *whole oranges*. (Modifying Ledford, if it's less than one F but more than none, there's some sort G such that it's no G.)

orange-halves back on the table. Now there is only one whole orange together with three orange-halves on the table. Our current proposal would answer (Q) under these circumstances by saying that there are one and three-halves (1½) oranges on the table. But one might still answer our original question (Q) with the same old answer (A), adding now that one of the oranges has been cut in half. And indeed, 1½ = 2½. It is especially tempting to count (A) as still a correct answer since two of the three orange-halves on the table do indeed come from the same orange. While no longer whole, the orange in question might still be deemed to exist as a (slightly scattered) orange on the table. The configuration of the oranges on the table has changed, but not their number. By contrast, (A″) is not in any way a correct description of the new situation. There is not only one orange-half on the table. Rather, there are exactly three orange-halves on the table (together with one whole orange). This further demonstrates that (A) and (A″) are not equivalent.

Return to the original situation, with two whole oranges and a single orange-half on the table. As the schoolboy knows, 2½ = ⁵⁄₂. Substituting into (A), we obtain, as an alternative answer to (Q), that there are exactly five-halves oranges on the table. Special care must be taken here to distinguish syntactically between 'there are five-halves oranges' and 'there are five half-oranges'. The proposal under consideration regards the distinction as purely syntactic, a distinction without a difference. On that proposal, the claim that there are exactly five-halves oranges on the table amounts to the claim that there are exactly five orange-halves on the table—the sort of thing that would be true if there were one orange-half from each of exactly five different oranges on the table. The proposal cannot suppress the inevitable protest that there is only one orange-half on the table, not five—together, of course, with two whole oranges. Can we, as it were, *grok* two whole oranges alternatively as four orange-halves, without actually cutting into them? The four orange-halves would have to be undetached orange-halves. Well, then, which four undetached orange-halves? There are a great many undetached orange-halves *in* those two whole oranges. Why do we say only four? Is it not at least as accurate to say instead that there is one detached orange-half on the table and in addition hundreds, perhaps thousands, of undetached orange-halves on the table?

Perhaps we mean something like this: Cut them up into orange-halves any way you like, there will be exactly five *non-overlapping* orange-halves on the table. But probably we do not. Certainly the original schoolboy's answer (A) does not literally and explicitly make any dispositional assertion about what *would* result from performing certain hypothetical cutting procedures. The mere substitution of the notation '⁵⁄₂' for '2½' cannot introduce any counterfactual or dispositional notions that were not there to begin with. It is far more likely that our latest proposal errs in equating the claim that there are exactly five-halves oranges on the table with the (apparently false) claim that there are exactly five orange-halves on the table.[7]

---

[7] Frank McGuinness points out that since the expression '2½' is not a singular term on this solution, but a mishmash of numerical quantifiers, a truth-functional connective, and a predicate operator, the solution effectively blocks any straightforward application of Leibniz's Law (Substitutivity of Equality) in the manner proposed. This observation illustrates the extent to which the solution fails to respect the import of standard mathematical notation. Indeed, the solution

What, then, does the former claim mean? If it is correct, it can only mean something mathematically equivalent to (*A*)—which is, or at least seems, incompatible with anything mathematically equivalent to (*A'*). The meaning of (*A'*) is reasonably clear. But the exact meaning of (*A*) still is not.

The Preferred Solution? We considered some fairly definite phenomena that led us to dismiss the numerical-quantifier analysis. That proposal should now be re-evaluated in light of our dissatisfaction with alternative analyses. We have already acknowledged that the alleged mixed-numerical quantifier '2.5' is not contextually definable in first-order logic. Maybe it is *sui generis*. We are not compelled to say that the sentence '2.5x (*x* is an orange on the table)' says something quantitative about the class of oranges on the table. Surely (*A*) does not say anything primarily about the *class* of oranges on the table. The number 2½ is not the number of elements of the class of oranges on the table. It is a mixed number, while finite classes have only whole-number cardinalities. Mixed number though it is, it is also exactly how many oranges there are on the table.

Perhaps our numerically quantified sentence '2.5x (*x* is an orange on the table)' says something quantitative not about the class of oranges on the table, nor anything similar (like the characteristic function of that class), but about... well, ... *the oranges on the table*—the property, if you will, of being such an orange, or better, the *plurality* (group, collective), i.e. the oranges themselves. There are not only two, but two and one-half, of *those things*.

Pluralities are what plural terms like 'the oranges on the table' and 'those things', and conjunctive-enumerative terms like 'Sid and Nancy', refer to. A plurality is essentially not one but many. It is well known that pluralities differ in various ways from the separate individuals, taken individually, and also from their corresponding unity, the class of the individuals. When, in one of my fondest fantasies, C. Anthony Anderson, Anthony Brueckner, and I lift the Philosophy Department's photocopier to throw it out the window, no one of us lifts the machine individually (although it does seem that Brueckner and I put forth more than our fair share of effort). Still less does the class of all three of us—a causally inert abstract entity—lift the machine. It is not a unity but a threesome that lifts the machine. Note, however, that the threesome is not a fourth entity over and above the three of us. It *is* the three of us— or better put, the three of us are not a single entity at all but three, and therefore not a fourth entity. Talk of 'pluralities' may be regarded as a manner of speaking. The crucial idea is that some properties are exemplified or possessed by individuals taken collectively, in concert, rather than taken individually and rather than by the corresponding class. The property of lifting the photocopier is such a property.[8]

makes a complete mystery of equations like '2½ = ⁵⁄₂'. What is this equation supposed to mean, if not something that licenses the substitution of '⁵⁄₂' for '2½' in an ordinary extensional context (like 'There are exactly ___ gallons of fuel remaining in the tank', as opposed to 'Anderson believes that there are exactly ___ gallons of fuel remaining in the tank')?

[8] This idea also seems to lie behind our tendency to anthropomorphize groups, as when it is said, for instance, that the public favors one policy over another. A plurality should not be confused with the mereological sum or fusion of individuals. A mereological sum is a unit composed of many, the plurality is/are the many of which the sum is composed. The former is one, the latter essentially more than one. One might cash out the collective exemplification of a property in terms of the

On my proposal, yet another respect in which a 'plurality'—a many rather than a one—may differ from its (more accurately, from their) corresponding class is in regard to number. What numbers number are not classes but pluralities, things taken together, collectively and not individually. The class of objects that are oranges on the table has cardinality 2. Each individual orange on the table has a different number, namely 1. The class itself is also one. But the oranges themselves number some 2½.

How does the plurality of oranges on the table come to have a mixed number rather than a whole number? The orange-half is not itself an orange. Nor, therefore, is it one of the oranges on the table. And yet it is included, by virtue of its quantity of orange-stuff, in the plurality of oranges on the table. When sizing up a plurality, different individuals are given different weight. Some may have fractional shares, counting for less than one but more than none. Though not itself an orange on the table, the orange-half is counted among the oranges on the table. It is not *one* of those things. But it is *of* those things. And among those things, it counts for less than one—for one-half, in fact.[9] To be sure, this is not at all how the cardinality of a class is measured; instead, each element counts equally as one. The quantity of a plurality is measured differently. Among the F's, a part of a whole F counts for part of a whole number, i.e. it counts for a fraction.

Strictly speaking, on this proposal numbers are not merely properties of pluralities *simpliciter*, but relativized properties. They are properties of pluralities *relative to* some sort or counting property. Typically, the sort or counting property to which the number of a plurality is relativized is a sort or property of the individuals so numbered. The oranges on the table are two and one-half in number, but the detached orange-portions, proper and not, on the table are three—even though these are the very same things. The orange-half counts for 1 if one is counting detached orange-portions, but only counts for one-half if one is counting oranges—and only counts for zero if one is counting *whole* oranges, since it is not among the whole oranges.[10] One may also define an absolute notion of the number of a plurality, in terms of the number relative to a counting property, by taking the counting property

holding of a relation among the participants. Lifting a particular photocopier would appear to be a property, not an n-ary relation for any $n > 1$. Yet it may happen that two individuals, or three, or more, co-operate to lift the photocopier in concert. If lifting a photocopier is a relation, the relation must be *multigrade*, allowed to be n-ary for any of a wide range of whole numbers n (unary, binary, ternary, etc.). Property or multigrade relation, there is a difficulty either way. Given only a predicate (monadic or multiadic) for the attribute of lifting a photocopier, a monadic predicate for the property of being a full professor in the UCSB philosophy department holding a doctorate degree from UCLA, and the full resources of standard first-order logic, it is not possible to write a sentence saying that the UCSB full professors of philosophy with doctorates from UCLA are lifting the photocopier. A mechanism for plural reference is needed.

[9] The fact that it does not count for one may be why it is itself not *an* orange. An orange is one orange. The orange-half is not one orange; it is only *one-half* of an orange. These points are not essential to the solution proposed here, however, whose core ideas are compatible also with the opposing view that the orange-half is an orange, as long as it counts not for one but for one-half. See note 2 above.

[10] See note 6. Husserl held, against Frege, that numbers are properties of 'multiplicities' (*Mannigfaltigkeit*). Peter M. Simons cites Husserl while defending the view that numbers are properties of the referents of plural terms, in his 'Numbers and Manifolds,' in B. Smith, ed., *Parts*

to be fixed as the universal property of *being an object* or *being a thing*. The two and one-half oranges on the table are three things. The number of oranges that are on the table is two and one-half, whereas the number of things on the table that are oranges is two.[11] The number of things that are such-and-such is always a whole number. The sort *orange* includes a provision for fractional shares; the sort *thing* does not. Ledford's variant of Murphy's Law may be generalized as follows: If it's not one thing, it's a plurality of n for some whole number $n > 1$. But if it's not one fruit, it could be less.

If something along the lines of this proposal is right, then there is a serious rift between (A') and the first-order formula that had been given as a definition for its formal counterpart '$2x$ (x is an orange on the table)':

$$\exists x \exists y [x \text{ is an orange on the table} \wedge y \text{ is an orange on the table} \wedge x \neq y \wedge \forall z (z$$
$$\text{is an orange on the table} \supset x = z \vee y = z)].$$

This first-order formula is true. There are exactly two objects such that each is an orange on the table. This is, or is at least tantamount to, a statement of the cardinality of the class of oranges on the table.[12] The first-order formula does not attempt to specify the quantity of the plurality of oranges on the table. That is precisely what (A') does, and it does so unsuccessfully. (A') is false; the number of oranges on the table is correctly given by (A).

Given this rift, it is left for us to decide whether the quasi-formal sentence '$2x$ (x is an orange on the table)' is to mean the same as (A') or instead the same as the formula displayed above. Since we already have a way to symbolize the latter (namely, the latter itself), it would be better to let the numerically quantified sentence symbolize the former. On this solution, not only the mixed-number quantifier '2.5' but even whole-number quantifiers like '2', as they occur in numerically quantified sentences like (A'), are strictly not definable using the traditional universal and existential quantifiers together with identity. Any quantified statement of

and Moments: Studies in Logic and Formal Ontology (Munich: Philosophia Verlag, 1982), pp. 160–198. See also Glenn Kessler, 'Frege, Mill, and the Foundations of Arithmetic,' *Journal of Philosophy*, 77, 2 (February 1980), pp. 65–79; and Simons' reply, 'Against the Aggregate Theory of Number,' *Journal of Philosophy*, 79, 3 (March 1982), pp. 163–167. Kessler defends the view that numbers are properties relativized to properties. However, Kessler treats numbers as properties of aggregates (rather than pluralities), relativized to "individuating properties" of parts of those aggregates. Byeong-uk Yi endorses the view that numbers are properties of pluralities, although he does not accept my proposal that they are relativized to counting properties or that pluralities like the oranges on the table have mixed numbers. Instead he believes the correct answer to (Q) is (A'). Simons (p. 160) also restricts his account to whole numbers. One significant advantage of treating numbers as properties of pluralities, however, is precisely that doing so in the way I propose here—with some individuals of a plurality counting for more than none but less than one, relative to a counting property—justifies, and seems to underlie, our giving (A) as the correct answer to (Q) while rejecting (A'). (Thanks to Ronald McIntyre, Kevin Mulligan, and Yi for scholarly references.)

[11] See again note 2 above. One may substitute here the claim that there are exactly three things on the table that are oranges.

[12] Like the property of being a thing, the property of being an element of a set does not include a provision for fractional shares. There are exactly two and one-half oranges that are elements of the class of detached pieces of fruit on the table, but only two elements of that class are oranges (or alternatively, in accordance with the preceding note, all three elements are).

classical first-order logic concerns classes rather than pluralities. And it would appear that the quantity of a plurality may sometimes diverge, at least by a fraction, from the cardinality of the corresponding class. Another blow to traditional logicism.

One way to represent plural descriptions of the form 'the F's' would be by means of a variable-binding plurality-abstraction operator. We may read '$\mathcal{P}xFx$' as 'the objects x such that Fx'. (Note the plural form 'objects'.) This expression may be regarded as being of a special logico-syntactic type, which may be called a *plural term* (as opposed to a singular term). Conjunctive-enumerative terms and plural indexicals should count equally as plural terms. On the proposal I am making here, it may be said that numerical quantifiers like '2.5' are what some philosophers have called 'plural quantifiers'.[13] Given an appropriate numerical predicate, our numerical quantifier '2.5' might be contextually defined so that '$2.5xFx$' is taken to mean the same as '$\mathcal{P}xFx$ are 2½ in number'. A full treatment should introduce plural variables (corresponding to the English pronoun 'they'). Doing so would allow for the formalization of a plural description like 'the individuals who lifted the photocopier' using the variable-binding definite-description operator attached to a plural variable, in the manner of 'the plurality of individuals who are such that they lifted the photocopier'. (Notice that it would be incorrect to attempt to capture this plural description by means of the plurality-abstraction operator '$\mathcal{P}$' attached to a singular variable, since no one of the threesome who lifted the machine did so individually. See note 8.)

A couple of interestingly odd (though, I think, not unacceptable) consequences, or possible consequences, should be noted. First, if an orange-half from a fourth orange is placed alongside the two and one-half oranges already on the table, and question (Q) is posed anew, it is difficult (although not impossible) to resist the conclusion that the answer becomes that there are exactly three oranges on the table, since $2½ + ½ = 3$, despite the fact that the two detached orange-halves now on the table do not come from a single orange. Insofar as one is inclined to reject this answer, and to claim instead that there are only two oranges on the table (together with two orange-halves which do not comprise a third orange), one might likewise proffer (A') in place of (A) as the correct answer to the original question (Q), as posed before the placement of the second orange-half on the table. My own intuitions balk at (A') as the correct answer to (Q) in the original circumstances much more strongly than they balk at the answer 'exactly three' in the new circumstances—although a solution that avoids both would clearly be preferable. If (A') rather than (A) is the correct answer in the original circumstances, then one wonders whether there can be any true statement of the form 'There are exactly two and one-half F's'. Surely, for example, there can be exactly two and one-half gallons of orange juice in the tank. And if another half-gallon of juice is added to the tank, there will then be exactly three gallons. But then why not exactly three oranges on the table when the new orange-half is placed alongside the two and one-half oranges

[13] For valuable discussion of plural quantification, see George Boolos, 'To Be is To Be the Value of A Variable (or To Be Some Values of Some Variables),' *Journal of Philosophy*, 81 (1984), pp. 430–449; 'Nominalist Platonism,' *The Philosophical Review*, 94, 3 (July 1985), pp. 327–344; and David Lewis, *Parts of Classes* (Oxford: Basil Blackwell, 1991), at pp. 62–71.

already there? Perhaps because comparing gallons of orange juice to oranges is comparing apples and oranges. If one puts two half-gallons of juice together in the same tank, the result is a single gallon. But put two orange-halves from different oranges together on the same table, and the result is . . . what? Two orange-halves put together. Is that a scattered orange?[14]

Second, if we follow this path, numerical quantifiers like '2' may emerge as *nonextensional* operators. The phrase 'there are exactly 2' in (A') does not express a numerical property that is attributed to the semantic extension of the phrase (general term) 'orange on the table', i.e. to the class. Instead (A') assigns that number to the plurality semantically determined by the phrase, relative to the property expressed by the phrase. Since the orange-half counts itself among the plurality but is not itself an element of the phrase's extension, that extension does not determine the plurality. Nor, as we have seen, does the extension determine the property relative to which the elements are two and one-half in number. The nonextensionality of the numerical quantifier '2' manifests itself in the fact that although the phrase 'orange on the table' has exactly the same extension as the phrase 'whole orange on the table', the sentence 'There are exactly two whole oranges on the table' is true of the original example whereas the sentence 'There are exactly two oranges on the table' is false. The truth-value of a statement of the form ⌜There are exactly n F's⌝ depends not on some feature (e.g. the cardinality) of the class of F's, but on a feature of the F's themselves, taken collectively *qua* F's—or if one prefers, on a feature of the property of *being an F*. A numerical-quantifier phrase ⌜there are exactly n objects x such that⌝ is thus less like the phrase 'the class of objects x such that' than it is like the phrase 'the property of *being an object x such that*'.[15]

---

[14] Some, though not all, of the discomfort one feels in answering that there are now exactly three oranges on the table may stem from an inclination to interpret this answer as meaning that there are exactly three *whole* oranges on the table. This answer is presumably false of the expanded example. If it is true there are exactly three oranges on the table, then one of the three is the scattered mereological sum of two orange-halves, and hence not a whole orange. (This issue may be partly terminological. See again note 6. An inclination to interpret the answer 'exactly three oranges' as concerning whole oranges may be a result of the fact that 3 is a whole number.)

Robin Jeshion urged in discussion that one, such as me, who favors the preferred solution in the text should resist the inference that there are exactly three oranges when there are exactly two together with exactly two orange-halves. I am inclined to agree. But I remain troubled by the nagging fact that $2\frac{1}{2} + \frac{1}{2} = 3$. Why does this mathematical equation apply straightforwardly to gallons of orange juice but not to oranges, to yards but not to yardsticks, etc.?

[15] See again note 2. See also note 10. If instead the orange-half is included in the semantic extension of the phrase 'orange on the table', then that class is also the extension of the phrase 'proper or improper detached orange-portion on the table'. The quantity of the plurality determined by the latter phrase, relative to the property expressed, is 3. This is greater by $\frac{1}{2}$ than the quantity of the plurality determined by the former phrase relative to the property expressed (i.e. the number of oranges on the table). The plurality-abstraction operator '$\mathscr{P}$' is therefore likewise a nonextensional operator.

One may want to distinguish here between the singular phrase 'orange on the table' and its pluralization 'oranges on the table'. It may be held, for example, that the latter phrase does not have an extension, as a single unified object, but instead applies to the plurality, i.e. to the oranges themselves, including the orange-half in its second-class status. Pluralization may thus emerge as a nonextensional operation.

Notice that the nonextensionality of numerical quantifiers 'there are exactly n objects x such that' induces failures of substitution of co-extensional expressions only within the numerical quantifier's

Insofar as either, or both, of these alleged consequences is deemed genuine and undesirable, an alternative solution to the original problem is wanted. I have canvassed here all of the promising solutions I can think of, and in each case I have noted consequences that strike me as being at least as undesirable as the two possible consequences just noted. It is possible, of course, that there is some alternative solution that is free of all such difficulties. The reader is hereby invited to discover that solution. I would welcome hearing from you.[16]

operand matrix. More precisely, there are formulas ϕ_α and ψ_α, containing α as a free variable, such that ⌜there are exactly n objects α such that ϕ_α⌝ and ⌜$\forall_\alpha(\phi_\alpha \equiv \psi_\alpha)$⌝ are both true whereas ⌜there are exactly n objects α such that ψ_α⌝ is false. This does not entail that there are failures of substitution *within* the quantifier phrase. That is, we have no reason to deny that if ⌜there are exactly n objects α such that ϕ_α⌝ and ⌜$n = m$⌝ are both true, then so is ⌜there are exactly m objects α such that ϕ_α⌝. (Contrast with note 7 above.)

[16] A version of the present essay was delivered as the fifth annual *Philosophical Perspectives* Lecture at California State University, Northridge. I thank that institution for its invitation. As indicated above, I have discussed the problem presented here with a number of philosophers. Though I found their proposals unconvincing, I am grateful to them for their reactions. I am especially grateful to Ilhan Inan for discussion, and to Takashi Yagisawa and Byeong-uk Yi for correspondence concerning the favored solution proposed in the final section, and to my audience at CSUN for their helpful comments.

13

The Limits of Human Mathematics (2001)

I

What, if anything, do Gödel's incompleteness theorems tell us about the human intellect? Do they inform us, for example, about human insight and creativity? Or perhaps about the human mind's capacity for *a priori* certainty? Ernest Nagel and James R. Newman write:

> Gödel's conclusions bear on the question whether a calculating machine can be constructed that would match the human brain in mathematical intelligence. . . . as Gödel showed in his [first] incompleteness theorem, there are innumerable problems in elementary number theory that fall outside the scope of a fixed axiomatic method . . . The human brain . . . appears to embody a structure of rules of operation which is far more powerful than the structure of currently conceived artificial machines. . . . Gödel's proof [of the first incompleteness theorem] . . . does mean that the resources of the human intellect have not been, and cannot be fully formalized, and that new principles of demonstration forever await invention and discovery. . . . The theorem does indicate that the structure and power of the human mind are far more complex and subtle than any nonliving machine yet envisaged.[1]

More recently, Roger Penrose has declared that "from consideration of Gödel's theorem . . . we can see that the role of consciousness is non-algorithmic when forming *mathematical* judgments, where calculation and rigorous proof constitute such an important factor."[2] J. R. Lucas provided an argument in support of a similar (if slightly stronger) conclusion:

> Gödel's [first incompleteness] theorem must apply to cybernetical machines, because it is of the essence of being a machine, that it should be a concrete instantiation of a formal system. It follows that given any machine which is consistent and capable of doing simple

The present chapter grew out of meetings of the Santa Barbarians Discussion Group, organized by C. Anthony Anderson. I am indebted to the participants for encouraging my thoughts on the topic and for their comments on an early draft, and especially to Anderson for his valuable assistance.

[1] Nagel and Newman, *Gödel's Proof* (New York University Press, 1958, 1967), at pp. 100–102.

[2] In *The Emperor's New Mind: Concerning Computers, Minds, and the Laws of Physics* (Oxford University Press, 1989), at p. 416. Penrose revisits some of the issues in *Shadows of the Mind: A Search for the Missing Science of Consciousness* (Oxford University Press, 1994), and 'Beyond the Doubting of a Shadow: A Reply to Commentaries on *Shadows of the Mind*,' *Psyche*, 2, 23 (1996).

arithmetic, there is a formula which it is incapable of producing as being true—i.e., the formula is unprovable-in-the-system—but which we can see to be true. It follows that no machine can be a complete or adequate model of the mind; that minds are essentially different from machines.

...The conclusions it is possible for the machine to produce as being true will... correspond to the theorems that can be proved in the corresponding formal system. We now construct a Gödelian formula in this formal system. The formula cannot be *proved-in-the-system*. Therefore the machine cannot produce the corresponding formula as being true. But *we* can see that the Gödelian formula is true: any rational being could follow Gödel's argument, and convince himself that the Gödelian formula, although unprovable-in-the-given-system, was nonetheless—in fact, for that very reason—true. Now any mechanical model of the mind must include a mechanism which can enunciate truths of arithmetic, because this is something which minds can do...But...for every machine there is a truth which it cannot produce as being true, but which a mind can. This shows that the machine cannot be a complete and adequate model of the mind. It cannot do *everything* that a mind can do, since however much it can do, there is always something which it cannot do, and a mind can....The Gödelian formula is the Achilles' heel of the cybernetical machine. And therefore we cannot hope ever to produce a machine that will be able to do all that a mind can do: we can never, not even in principle, have a mechanical model of the mind.[3]

Anticipating this argument, Hilary Putnam exposed an apparently fatal fallacy.[4] We are to suppose, for a *reductio ad absurdum*, that we have been given in full detail a complex logistic ("formal") system that adequately and completely formalizes the mathematical abilities of a human mind. It is by no means a foregone conclusion that the mind can prove the proposition expressed by the Gödelian sentence for this system—a sentence that indirectly says of itself (in a well-defined sense) that it is not provable-in-the-given-logistic-system. What is proved is conditional: that the proposition is true *provided the logistic system is consistent*. Indeed, this much is provable within the very logistic system in question. Proving that the system is consistent (free of contradiction) would yield the target proposition as an immediate corollary. Gödel's second incompleteness theorem states that the logistic system, if it is consistent, cannot in this sense prove its own consistency. (The second theorem itself is proved precisely by noting the corollary that would otherwise result.) For some relatively simple logistic systems of arithmetic, we may know with mathematical certainty, even though this is not provable within the system, that its primitive deductive basis (the axioms and primitive rules of inference) does not generate any contradiction. In these cases, there may be a sense in which it is true that the human mind relevantly "sees" the truth expressed by the Gödelian sentence, since this provably follows from the system's consistency. But there are other logistic systems for mathematics with respect to which the system's consistency is anything but

---

[3] Lucas, 'Minds, Machines and Gödel,' *Philosophy*, 36 (1961); reprinted in A. R. Anderson, ed., *Minds and Machines* (Englewood Cliffs, NJ: Prentice-Hall, 1964), pp. 43–59, at 44, 47. A conclusion opposite in thrust from that of Lucas, Nagel and Newman, and Penrose is urged by Judson Webb, *Mechanism, Mentalism and Meta-mathematics* (Dordrecht: D. Reidel, 1980).

[4] Putnam, 'Minds and Machines,' in Sidney Hook, ed., *Dimensions of Mind: A Symposium* (New York: New York University Press, 1960); reprinted in A. R. Anderson, ed., *Minds and Machines* (Englewood Cliffs, NJ: Prentice-Hall, 1964), pp. 72–97, at 77.

obvious. In particular, the second incompleteness theorem calls into serious question whether the human mind is capable of a proof of consistency for a logistic system sufficiently complex to capture all of humanly demonstrable mathematics, i.e. a logistic system adequate to formalize the human capacity for proving mathematical theorems.[5]

Perhaps a more guarded conclusion can be legitimately drawn. In his 1951 Josiah Willard Gibbs Lecture to the American Mathematical Society, Gödel himself derives from his second incompleteness theorem a disjunctive conclusion which, though weaker than the conclusions of Newman and Nagel, *et al.*, Gödel says is a "mathematically established fact which seems to me of great philosophical interest":

> Either mathematics is incompletable in this sense, that its evident axioms can never be comprised in a finite rule, that is to say, the human mind (even within the realm of pure mathematics) infinitely surpasses the powers of any finite machine, or else there exist absolutely unsolvable diophantine problems of the type specified (where the case that both terms of the disjunction are true is not excluded, so that there are, strictly speaking, three alternatives).[6]

This disjunction is evidently not subject to the same response that Putnam made to Nagel and Newman and company. For Gödel judges only that the human mind surpasses any theorem-proving machine *provided that the mind is in principle capable of solving any purely mathematical problem, including the question of its own mathematical consistency.* This more cautious conclusion is nevertheless philosophically substantive. Gödel proceeds to draw disjunctive philosophical conclusions from it, by inferring consequences of the first disjunct about the human mind's capacity for outperforming any finite computing machine, including whatever theorem-proving machinery there is in the human brain, and consequences of the second disjunct about the independence and objectivity of pure mathematics. If the theorem-proving machinery of the human brain is a computer, then either the human mind surpasses the human brain or humankind does not deserve credit for creating pure mathematics (or as some might see it, humankind does not deserve the blame). Thus, the human mind either surpasses the very organ in which it evidently resides or else it is not responsible for the existence of pure mathematics—or both, as Gödel himself

---

[5] Lucas has replied, in 'Minds, Machines, and Gödel: A Retrospect,' in P. J. R. Millican and A. Clark, eds., *Machines and Thought: The Legacy of Alan Turing, Volume 1* (Oxford University Press, 1996), that the mechanist's claim that the proposed logistic system captures human mathematical reasoning is otiose unless the mechanist concedes that the system is consistent, and it is from this premise that Lucas derives the Gödelian sentence (p. 117). But unless the premise is itself proved mathematically, Lucas's derivation does not constitute a proof, or anything close to a proof. Given Lucas's objective, it is not sufficient for him to argue merely that mechanism cannot be proved.

An assessment of the arguments and assertions of Lucas and Penrose is provided in Stewart Shapiro, 'Incompleteness, Mechanism, and Optimism,' *The Bulletin of Symbolic Logic*, 4 (September 1998), pp. 273–302.

[6] 'Some Basic Theorems on the Foundations of Mathematics and Their Implications,' in Gödel's *Collected Works, III: Unpublished Essays and Lectures*, S. Feferman, J. W. Dawson, Jr., W. Goldfarb, C. Parsons, and R. N. Solovay, eds. (Oxford University Press, 1995), pp. 304–323, at 310. See also Hao Wang, *A Logical Journey: From Gödel to Philosophy* (Cambridge, Ma.: MIT Press, 1996), especially chapters 6 and 7, pp. 183–246.

believed (and I agree).[7] Here follows the relevant passage in which Gödel derives the disjunction:

> It is [the second incompleteness theorem] which makes the incompletability of mathematics particularly evident. For, *it makes it impossible that someone should set up a certain well-defined system of axioms and rules and consistently make the following assertion about it: All of these axioms and rules I perceive (with mathematical certitude) to be correct, and moreover I believe that they contain all of mathematics.* If someone makes such a statement he contradicts himself. [*Gödel's note*: If he only says "I believe I shall be able to perceive one after the other to be true" (where their number is supposed to be infinite), he does not contradict himself. (See below.)] For if he perceives the axioms under consideration to be correct, he also perceives (with the same certainty) that they are consistent. Hence he has a mathematical insight not derivable from his axioms. However, one has to be careful in order to understand clearly the meaning of this state of affairs. Does it mean that no well-defined system of correct axioms can contain all of mathematics proper? It does, if by mathematics proper is understood the system of all true mathematic propositions; it does not, however, if one understands by it the system of all demonstrable mathematical propositions. I shall distinguish these two meanings of mathematics as mathematics in the objective and in the subjective sense: Evidently no well-defined system of correct axioms can comprise all [of] objective mathematics, since the proposition which states the consistency of the system is true, but not demonstrable in the system. However, as to subjective mathematics, it is not precluded that there should exist a finite rule producing all its evident axioms. However, if such a rule exists, we with our human understanding could certainly never know it to be such, that is we could never know with mathematical certainty that all propositions it produces are correct; [*Gödel's note*: For this (or the consequence concerning the consistency of the axioms) would constitute a mathematical insight not derivable from the axioms and rules under consideration, contrary to the assumption] or in other terms, we could perceive to be true only one proposition after the other, for any finite number of them. The assertion, however, that they are all true could at most be known with empirical certainty, on the basis of a sufficient number of instances or by other inductive inferences. . . . If it were so, this would mean that the human mind (in the realm of pure mathematics) *is* equivalent to a finite machine that, however, is unable to understand completely its own functioning. [*Gödel's note*: Of course, the physical working of the thinking mechanism could very well be completely understandable; the insight, however, that this particular mechanism must always lead to correct (or only consistent) results would surpass the powers of human reason.][8]

There appears to be the following sort of argument: Suppose that the human mind's capacity for conceiving proofs is an effectively describable phenomenon, like the deterministic workings of a Turing machine, so that the very process by means of which the mind attains, or can attain, purely mathematical knowledge with

---

[7] If the second alternative obtains—that there are purely mathematical questions of a certain sort that the human intellect is in principle unable to prove or disprove—this would seem to indicate that truth in pure mathematics is not reducible to provability (demonstrability), since the two are not even co-extensional. This conclusion relies on the assumption that if there are humanly undecidable purely mathematical propositions, at least some have truth-value. In fact, the propositions that are produced in Gödel's proof as undecidable in the logistic system in question are true (their negations false) provided the system is consistent, and are otherwise false. Any analogous propositions that are undecidable in human mathematics are likewise truth-valued, so that truth in pure mathematics would provide no guarantee of certainty, or even potential certainty.

[8] *Ibid.*, pp. 309–310.

mathematical certainty is thus fully captured by some finite effective rule (even if it is very long). It is a consequence of the second incompleteness theorem that the mind cannot know with mathematical certainty that this rule generates only correct results, or even that its results are internally consistent. For if the mind can know with mathematical certainty of all the propositions of pure mathematics it is able to prove that all of them are true, then it can also know with mathematical certainty that they are formally consistent—something that is precluded by the theorem. Since the consistency of the system of theorems can be recast as a purely mathematical proposition, it follows that if the mind, in its theorem-proving capacity, is a finite machine, then there are purely mathematical truths it cannot know with mathematical certainty; in particular, it cannot prove its own consistency, and hence cannot completely understand its own functioning.

George Boolos has claimed that Gödel's disjunction—that either the human mind is not equivalent to a finite machine or there exist absolutely undecidable mathematical propositions—though it is weaker than the conclusions of Nagel and Newman, *et al.*, is still not validly derivable from the incompleteness theorems.[9] Boolos deems the above argument inconclusive owing to obscurity in the idea that "the human mind is equivalent to a finite machine." Even assuming, for the sake of argument, that the theorem-proving aspect of the human mind is mechanistic, it does not straightforwardly follow that in that case the mind's theorem-proving mechanism meets the conditions for being a Turing machine and is therefore incapable of proving its own consistency. For it is in the first place excessively unclear what is meant by saying (or by denying) that *the* human mind, or even that a single mind, simply *is* a Turing machine. And if what is meant is that the theorem-proving aspect of the mind, or of a single mind, is (or is not) *represented* by a Turing machine, Boolos objects, Gödel does not specify exactly how the representation is supposed to go.

The argument does indeed raise troubling questions of this sort, and more. A Turing machine is the formal counterpart of a deterministic computational process. It does much more than merely represent a recursive function in the abstract, mathematical sense. The function is fully represented by the machine's input and output, and may be aptly represented equivalently by a set of ordered sets of numbers. By contrast, a Turing machine is the program that produces a specific output for a given input; it represents the process of *calculating* the value of the function for any argument. In the opening paragraph of the Gibbs Lecture, just before arguing for his disjunction, Gödel cites Turing machines as providing the most satisfactory way of defining the concept of an effective calculation or algorithm (a 'finite procedure')—thereby indicating his acceptance of Church's thesis (at least as restricted to numerical functions, and sets characterizable by numerical functions). Is the 'finite machine' of which Gödel speaks in the quoted passage supposed to mirror, in the manner of a Turing machine, the method and procedures by which the human mind is able to construct or discover (as the case may be) mathematical

[9] Boolos, 'Introductory Note to *1951,' in Gödel's *Collected Works, III: Unpublished Essays and Lectures*, S. Feferman, J. W. Dawson, Jr., W. Goldfarb, C. Parsons, and R. N. Solovay, eds. (Oxford University Press, 1995), pp. 290–304, at 294.

proofs? If so, we need to know exactly how, and exactly to what extent, the finite machine does this in order to assess Gödel's conclusion. Lacking this additional information, the most that can be justified is the supposition that the machine delivers the same theorems that the mind is able to prove, though perhaps by a completely different construction.

Filling in the gaps, Boolos proposes a reconstruction of Gödel's argument culminating in a circumscribed conclusion concerning not the actual process of proving theorems, but just the results thereby obtained. Though still somewhat vague, Boolos grants that the following is a consequence of the second incompleteness theorem: If there is a theorem-proving Turing machine whose output is the set of sentences expressing just those mathematical propositions that can be proved by a mind capable of understanding all polynomials with integer coefficients (and therefore capable of understanding a mathematical sentence tantamount to the meta-theoretic observation that the mind's theorem-proving mechanism is consistent), then there is a true mathematical proposition that can be understood but cannot be proved by that same mind—namely, the mathematically recast assertion of its own consistency. (See note 10 below.) Thus, any mind whose theorem-proving capacity is representable by some Turing machine *in terms of the theorems it proves (as opposed to the proofs it produces and/or the process by which it conceives those proofs)* is in principle incapable of solving certain mathematical problems indirectly about its own theorem-proving capacity. On Boolos's reconstruction, the machine passively represents the mind's potential output of theorems. Boolos's conclusion concerns those theorems only in the sense that it is about that *class* of theorems, not their production. The machine does not necessarily represent the mind's potential proofs of that potential output, let alone the active process by which the mind can generate those proofs.

Boolos's conclusion is comparatively strikingly narrow. It is a trivial, disappointingly anti-climactic restatement of the second incompleteness theorem's corollary that no theorem-enumerating Turing machine prints a sentence tantamount to an assertion of its own consistency. Any possible generating activity whose output coincides, for whatever reason (or for no reason at all), with that of a theorem-enumerating Turing machine fails to produce a mathematical proposition tantamount to the consistency of that output—regardless of whether the activity is teleologically assisted by an understanding of the output, hence even if it is a room full of monkeys at typewriters.[10] One might also point out, in much the same spirit,

---

[10] Boolos misformulates his conclusion by saying that if there is a Turing machine whose output is the set of sentences expressing just those mathematical propositions provable by a mind capable of understanding all propositions expressed by any sentence of the form $\ulcorner(\forall x)(\exists y)\phi(x, y) = 0\urcorner$, where x and y are sequences of integer variables and $\phi(x, y)$ is a polynomial with integer coefficients, then there is a true mathematical proposition *of this same technical sort* that cannot be proved by that same mind. It is evident that the conclusion Boolos intends is, rather, that if there is a Turing machine that produces exactly the mathematical truths provable by a mind with such comprehension, then there is a mathematical truth *that such a mind understands* (never mind what technical sort it is) but cannot prove. The latter carries with it the suggestion that the mind's incapacity, under the envisaged circumstances, does not result from a lack of understanding.

The suggestion, however, is misleading. It is built into the case that the mind's theorem-proving capacity, by hypothesis, does not exceed the output of some theorem-enumerating Turing machine

that anyone whose feats in manipulating geometric figures, as it happens, do not exceed those geometric tasks that can be performed using only a compass and straightedge, does not trisect an angle. In confining his attention to the mathematical theorems themselves, setting aside the epistemological character of their potential proofs by the human mind, Boolos disengages his conclusion from the philosophical issues that drive Gödel's. Gödel's argument does not concern hypothetical minds of a precisely delimited capacity. It concerns the capability of the human mind, such as it is, to attain certainty in mathematics. It is about human mathematics at its edges—both the initial starting points and the ultimate upward limits. Does the obscurity of the very idea that the human mind is equivalent to a machine block us from any such sweeping conclusion, and force a disappointingly restrictive retreat? I believe it does not and that, *contra* Boolos, Gödel's argument about the limits of human mathematics is reasonably secure, or can be made so.

II

Gödel's principal argument does not make any essential detour through Turing machines, or machines of any sort. One can dispense with machines altogether and make an end run for a disjunctive conclusion of just the sort from which Gödel draws philosophical conclusions about the human mind and the objectivity of mathematics.

Following Gödel, let us distinguish between mathematics proper (i.e., all the truths of pure mathematics) and what I have called *human mathematics* (Gödel's 'subjective mathematics')—that portion of mathematics that the human mind, or any intelligence (whether biological or artificial) that is epistemologically similarly situated to human intelligence, is capable of knowing with mathematical certainty ('mathematical certitude'). It is useful for this purpose to introduce some artificial terminology. Let 'HuMath' designate the class ('system') of all true propositions of human mathematics. This is a subclass of the class **Math** of all purely mathematical truths. **HuMath** almost certainly extends well beyond all the mathematics that will ever have been known with mathematical certainty by humans—by some human or other at some time or other. Take note: it is not assumed that **Math** and **HuMath** are distinct, nor is it assumed that they are identical. It is not even assumed that **HuMath** include every purely mathematical proposition that mathematicians take to be true. **HuMath** is restricted to those purely mathematical propositions that are knowable,

---

or other. This in itself says nothing about *why* the mind's mathematical prowess is thus limited. No logical inconsistency results by adding that the mind's limitations do not result from any lack of understanding. But neither has it been argued that the prospect of such a human mind—whose theorem-proving capacity coincides exactly with the output of Turing machine but nevertheless capable of fully understanding that which, as a consequence of the second theorem, it therefore cannot prove—is a real psychological possibility. These issues are in any case irrelevant. Boolos's intended conclusion follows from the second incompleteness theorem in the same way as the misformulated conclusion. Any possible generating activity whose potential output happens to coincide with the actual output a Turing machine—human or alien, animate or inanimate, with understanding or without—cannot in the relevant sense prove its own consistency.

hence true. If (contrary to our expectation) there should be any false purely mathematical propositions of which mathematicians have been persuaded (e.g. by a subtly fallacious argument), they are excluded from **HuMath**. Since all of **HuMath** are true, **HuMath** is *a fortiori* consistent, i.e. no contradiction is correctly deducible from it. Notice also that **HuMath** excludes any purely mathematical truths that are only knowable by the human mind to some degree short of mathematical certainty.[11]

HuMath's definition invokes the generic notion of knowability by the human mind, and this notion is somewhat obscure. What is knowable by one human mind may be unknowable by another. It may be that no single, existent human mind (past, present, or future) is capable of knowing everything that the human mind is capable of knowing. It may even be that no *possible* human mind can know all of the facts each of which, taken individually, the human mind is capable of knowing.[12] As Boolos notes, it does not follow that no proposition involving the notion of human knowability is validly deducible from a mathematical theorem. Boolos cites the particular inference: *91 is composite therefore, it is not humanly knowable that 91 is prime.* This instance depends on the fact that knowledge entails truth. Gödel's derivation of his disjunction, by contrast, depends on the fact that knowledge entails epistemic *justification*. But this does not, in itself, provide a reason to doubt that Gödel's argument is sound. The basic epistemological assumption is that, whatever differences there are among humans, certain epistemic mechanisms—ways of coming to know—are is principle accessible to the human mind.[13] At a minimum, there is an epistemic mechanism that is characteristically human, in this sense, and yields mathematical knowledge with mathematical certainty. The principle does not require that one be able to determine with any certainty whether a particular alleged phenomenon (e.g., telepathy) is a human epistemic mechanism, in this sense, or whether a particular alleged fact is knowable by a human mechanism. It may well be that this fundamental epistemological principle is not itself known with

---

[11] **HuMath** is a proper subclass of the class of propositions, purely mathematical or otherwise, humanly knowable with mathematical certainty (i.e., with the same degree of certainty attainable in pure mathematics). It is not assumed that **Math**, or **HuMath**, is a set in the classical sense. Rather, the use of these terms in bold typeface in a sentence is to be regarded as an abbreviation for statements employing predicates that apply, respectively, to all purely mathematical truths and all purely mathematical truths humanly knowable with mathematical certainty. To say, for example, that a proposition p is one of (or an "element of," or "belongs to") **Math** is to say no more (or less) than that p is one of *these* propositions [the truths of pure mathematics], and to say that **HuMath** is a proper subclass of **Math**, is to say that all of *these* propositions [the truths of pure mathematics that are humanly knowable with mathematical certainty] are among *those* propositions [the truths of pure mathematics] but not *vice versa*. From the former it follows that *if* there is a set M of all truths of pure mathematics then $p \in M$, from the latter that again if there is such a set as M then the subset HM consisting of those elements humanly knowable with mathematical certainty is proper. Neither the antecedent of these conditionals nor its negation is presupposed.

[12] One may take Heisenberg's Uncertainty Principle to entail this.

[13] There may be other epistemic mechanisms, or potential epistemic mechanisms, that are, by contrast, precluded by a mind's being human, i.e. by the nature and biology of humanity. One such may be the ω-rule of inference, which licenses the inference from premises, $\phi(0)$, $\phi(1)$, $\phi(2)$, and so on, to their generalization in $\ulcorner(\forall n)\phi(n)\urcorner$. Unless the human mind can reason with infinitely premises in a finite time span, it may be unable to draw inferences in accordance with this rule.

mathematical certainty, and to the extent that Gödel's argument presupposes the principle, the derived disjunction is also not so known. But the principle is known (even if not with mathematical certainty), and is not typically subject to doubt. If a proposition is validly inferred from a mathematical theorem using this epistemological principle, it is not unreasonable to say that the inferred proposition is a mathematically established fact.

The epistemic mechanism by which the elements of **HuMath** are knowable with mathematical certainty by humans is evidently that of mathematical *proof*. Gödel notes that if any purely mathematical knowledge is obtained by proof on the basis of truths antecedently known with mathematical certainty, then some purely mathematical knowledge is not.[14] For proofs must have starting points, and knowledge obtained by proof is derived ultimately from knowledge of those starting points. The latter knowledge Gödel calls the 'evident axioms.' (It includes axioms of both logic and mathematics proper.) This epistemic mechanism for attaining certainty in pure mathematics is aptly represented by the logistic method.[15] There is a proper subclass **Ax** of **HuMath** consisting of epistemologically foundational axioms—purely mathematical "first truths" each knowable with mathematical certainty by the human mind (i.e., by some possible human mind) without proof from other purely mathematical truths but through direct mathematical intuition or insight ("perception"), or perhaps derived from something more fundamental than pure mathematics (including logic)—while the rest of **HuMath** are knowable with mathematical certainty only by proof, i.e. only by deductive derivation ultimately from the mathematical axioms, using logical (primitive) rules of inference together perhaps with purely mathematical rules of inference over and above the axioms. **HuMath** is the deductive closure of **Ax** under the rules of human mathematical reasoning. In this sense, the union of **Ax** with the rules of human mathematical inference form the deductive basis of human mathematics. Let us call it '**Basis**'.[16]

---

[14] p. 305.

[15] This observation is to be taken in a sense in which it is beyond reasonable dispute. Some writers have mistakenly taken the incompleteness results to cast doubt on it. Thus Penrose writes: 'Gödel's theorem ... established ... that the powers of human reason could not be limited to any accepted preassigned system of formalized rules'. It is incumbent on one who denies the observation to specify how the phenomenon of proof in mathematics might be otherwise understood while avoiding mathematical mysticism.

Contemporary holistic empiricism holds that even knowledge of mathematical axioms is inextricably interconnected with all human knowledge taken as a whole, and thus ultimately empirical and fallible. Epistemological holism, however, is not inconsistent (as suggested by Shapiro) with the observation—well confirmed by actual practice—that knowledge in mathematics, unlike other disciplines, is furthered by an epistemologically special tool: mathematical proof from axioms, themselves humanly knowable with certainty without proof. Certainty, even mathematical certainty, does not entail immunity from error, let alone the absolute impossibility of human fallibility. (Some holists have proved their own fallibility on the very point in question.) Holistic empiricism maintains that the principles governing mathematical reasoning are ultimately judged, and conceivably might be revised, on ordinary empirical grounds. Whatever the shortcomings of this epistemological stance, it is not committed to denying the obvious role of mathematical proof in extending knowledge with certainty.

[16] Axioms may be regarded as special rules of inference permitting inferences *ex nihilo*. On this conception, the deductive basis of a logistic system consists entirely of primitive inference rules. It is

Ax may extend beyond all those fundamental truths of pure mathematics that will ever have been known by humans with mathematical certainty without independent mathematical proof, i.e. without proof from antecedently known purely mathematical truths. It is not assumed that any particular human mathematician, or even any possible human mathematician, can know all the elements of **Ax**. However, each of the axioms, taken individually, must be humanly knowable with mathematical certainty without independent mathematical proof. If we cannot know an axiom, then we also cannot know anything derived from it—except by some independent epistemological means. Genuinely inferential knowledge requires knowledge of that from which it is inferred. Moreover, each of the rules of inference of human mathematical reasoning must be not only valid (i.e., such as to preserve truth in any model), but also of a sort that transfers, through the cognitive act of immediate inference, the sort of epistemic justification that yields mathematical certainty. It is not independently required that we know each of the inference rules to be valid (let alone that we know this with mathematical certainty), but knowing this may be inextricably bound up with the rules' being such as to transfer mathematical certainty to the immediately inferred conclusion from that from which the conclusion is immediately inferred. In any event, it is reasonable to suppose that we can know of each inference rule of the required sort, with mathematical certainty and without independent mathematical proof, that it is indeed valid.

It is frequently assumed in discussion of Gödel's incompleteness results (especially of their philosophical implications) that they entail that any well-defined deductive basis for arithmetic, if consistent, is incomplete and fails to decide in particular a recast assertion of its own consistency. From this it would follow directly that, contrary to David Hilbert, there are purely mathematical truths the human mind is incapable of proving, including an assertion of its own mathematical consistency. (Recall that **Ax** is a subclass of **HuMath**, which is restricted to truths, and that the rules are valid; hence **Ax** is consistent.) But the assumption often involves a mistake, and Gödel did not believe its conclusion. There exist deductive systems for arithmetic (in a broad sense of 'deductive system') that are both consistent and complete—Gödel's theorems notwithstanding. This simple fact, although sometimes overlooked, is essential to a proper understanding of Gödel's disjunction and the argument for it. One way to obtain a consistent deductive system for arithmetic whose theorems are exactly those sentences of the language that express truths of arithmetic is to take all and only those sentences as axioms.[17] No object-theoretic Gödelian sentence indirectly asserting its own unprovability-in-this-system exists. On the other hand, the axiom set is unwieldy—as unwieldy as possible without allowing for the deduction of falsehoods. It is all over the map. Each expressible truth of arithmetic, regardless of how complex or abstract, is provable in this system

common, on the other hand, to minimize the set of primitive (non-axiom) inference rules by taking *modus ponens* as the only such rule, replacing every other inference rule,

From $\phi_1, \phi_2, \ldots,$ and $\phi_n,$ to infer ψ

with all instances of the corresponding axiom schema $\ulcorner(\phi_1 \supset (\phi_2 \supset (\ldots (\phi_n \supset \psi)) \ldots)\urcorner$.

[17] Notice that the resulting axiom set is defined by a precise, finite rule. See note 23 below.

in a single line. We are currently in no position to determine whether certain sentences are axioms of this system—for example, the sentence expressing Goldbach's Conjecture. By contrast, the elements of **Ax** are narrowly confined to those purely mathematical truths that are humanly knowable with mathematical certainty without independent mathematical proof. The envisaged complete, consistent system does not come close to adequately representing the way the human mind achieves knowledge with mathematical certainty in arithmetic. Part of the significance of Gödel's incompleteness results derives from the fact that they obtain for deductive systems that do at least approach the way the human mind attains mathematical knowledge.

A requirement that the axioms be written out in full would be excessive, since it excludes the possibility of a logistic system with infinitely many axioms. Instead, it is customary to consider deductive systems whose primitive bases are recursively enumerable (if not indeed primitive recursive)—so that even if there are infinitely many axioms there is an effective procedure by which theoretically one could enumerate them (allowing repetitions) and calculate what the nth axiom is for any natural number n. This condition (or something that entails it, perhaps given Church's thesis) is typically built into the definition of a *logistic* or *formal* system or theory.[18] It is only in that case that the deductive system can be effectively specified (in an intuitive sense) in a finite description. Moreover, if the deductive basis is effectively decidable, then so is the notion of a proof. Suppose that the elements of **Ax** constitute a *recursively enumerable set of propositions*, in the following sense: that there is a recursive numerical function from whole numbers onto a set A of Gödel numbers of sentences of a possible formal language expressing each of the elements of **Ax** in that possible language—so that there is an effective procedure by which theoretically one could calculate what the nth element of **Ax** is for any natural number n.[19] Suppose also that the rules of inference are analogously recursively enumerable. (See note 16.) Gödel showed how, in that case, the notions of a proof-from-**Ax** and of contradiction, and therewith the statement of **HuMath**'s consistency (which is meta-theoretic), can be put into object-theoretic form. Specifically, if the

---

[18] Under this restriction, the deductive system that takes all sentences expressing truths of arithmetic as axioms (though it exists) is disqualified as a logistic or formal system or theory. Thus Wang—the expositor who more than any other brought Gödel's philosophical views into the public domain—gives the following informal statement of the first incompleteness theorem (p. 3): *No formal system of mathematics can be both consistent and complete*; or alternatively, *Any consistent formal theory of mathematics must contain undecidable propositions*. Similarly, C. Smorynski, 'The Incompleteness Theorems,' in J. Barwise, ed., *Handbook of Mathematical Logic* (Amsterdam: North Holland, 1977, 1983), pp. 821–865, states the theorem as follows: *Let T be a formal theory containing arithmetic. Then there is a sentence φ which asserts its own unprovability and is [undecidable by T if T is ω-consistent]* (p. 825).

[19] The possible formal language in question should satisfy certain minimal constraints. As a matter of clarity, for example, ambiguity is precluded. The language is assumed to contain denumerably many expressions, to be bivalent (i.e., every sentence is either true or false and never both), and also such that a version of Tarski's theorem about truth holds for it. The language must also include the resources to express any mathematical concept that figures in any element of **HuMath**—including such concepts that have not yet been, or will never be, discovered or apprehended. (It is not assumed that the language contains only a finite number of logical or mathematical primitive constants.)

elements of **Ax** form a recursively enumerable set, and so do the inference rules, then there is a purely mathematical binary relation *Proof* which is designated by an open formula $\phi_{Proof}(x, y)$ of a possible formal language suitable for arithmetic and which provably holds between a pair of numbers n and m if and only if n is the Gödel number of a sequence of formulae that collectively express, in that same formal language, a proof from **Ax**, by way of the inference rules, of the proposition expressed, in that language, by the formula whose Gödel number is m. Likewise, there is a purely mathematical relation *Contradict*, designated by an open formula $\phi_{Contradict}(x, y)$ of the same language, which provably holds between a pair of numbers if and only if they are the Gödel numbers of formulae one of which is the negation of the other. There is then a corresponding sentence φ_{Cons} of the form $\ulcorner \sim(\exists x)(\exists y)[\phi_{Contradict}(x, y) \wedge (\exists z)\phi_{Proof}(z, x) \wedge (\exists z)\phi_{Proof}(z, y)]\urcorner$, which is mathematical code *via* Gödel numbering for the consistency of the logistic system generated by the set A of axioms and the inference rules. The sentence φ_{Cons} expresses a mathematical proposition *Cons* which we know with mathematical certainty to be equivalent to the logistic system's formal consistency.[20] On the assumption that the elements of **Ax** and the rules constitute recursively enumerable sets, Gödel's second incompleteness theorem implies that φ_{Cons} is not provable from **Ax**. For the theorem (as extended by Barkley Rosser) states that if an axiomatic basis suitable for arithmetic is both recursively enumerable and consistent, then the corresponding object-theoretic statement (constructed thus *via* Gödel numbering) of the theory's consistency, though true, is not provable from those axioms.[21] Since each of the

---

[20] Gödel showed how to construct a formula along the lines of ϕ_{Cons} roughly for any logistic system suitable for arithmetic that includes the resources to designate any recursive function of integers and whose primitive deductive basis is recursive. For details, see Elliot Mendelson, *Introduction to Mathematical Logic* (New York: D. Van Nostrand, 1979), chapter 3, especially pp. 161–162. (See also the following note.) The notion of a mathematical *axiom*, in the sense of a fundamental, purely mathematical truth that is humanly knowable with mathematical certainty without independent mathematical proof, is not itself a purely mathematical notion and is not directly expressible in the language in question. Instead, assuming the elements of **Ax** are recursively enumerable, those propositions may be indirectly specified within the formula ϕ_{Proof} and hence within ϕ_{Cons}, by means of a direct, purely mathematical specification of the recursive function f that enumerates the Gödel numbers of sentences expressing those very propositions. As a corollary of Gödel's first incompleteness theorem, there can be no expression of the language that extensionally specifies **Math** in an analogous manner. (This is Tarski's theorem about truth; see the preceding note.)

The formulae ϕ_{Proof} and ϕ_{Cons} do not strictly speaking semantically express the notions of proof from such-and-such axioms (those generated by recursive function f) and the consistency of such-and-such axioms and inference rules, respectively. The mathematical notions that are semantically expressed are, however, provably equivalent to these meta-theoretic notions. Indeed, the relationship is closer than mere provable equivalence; in a sense, the formulae are a code for the meta-theoretic notions. It is useful in the present context to think of the language of ϕ_{Proof} and ϕ_{Cons} as consisting of integers (Gödel numbers) functioning directly as expressions, and of the expression of a proof within the language—i.e., of a "proof" in the syntactic sense of a sequence of formulae—as a sequence of such integers-*qua*-formulae (rather than as its encoded representation by a single integer *via* the integer's prime factorization). Then ϕ_{Cons} semantically expresses that there are no such proof-sequences of integers culminating in integers one of which is the number-theoretic negation of the other (or something trivially equivalent to this).

[21] Rosser, 'Extensions of Some Theorems of Gödel and Church,' *Journal of Symbolic Logic*, 1 (1936), pp. 87–91. It follows from the result obtained by William Craig in 'Axiomatizability

propositions expressed by the elements of A is knowable, *a fortiori* each is true. And since all of the them are true and the rules are valid, A is *a fortiori* consistent. Thus, if the elements of **Ax** constitute a recursively enumerable set, and so do the rules, then *Cons* is a purely mathematical truth that does not belong to **HuMath**.

In this sense, either the axiomatic basis of human mathematics (i.e., the purely mathematical truths knowable by the human mind with mathematical certainty without independent mathematical proof, together with the rules of human mathematical inference) is not reducible to a recursively enumerable set (and thus they do not yield a logistic or formal system, in the technical sense), or else some purely mathematical truths—including a mathematical encoding of the consistency of human mathematics—are in principle unknowable by the human mind with mathematical certainty. This result already goes significantly beyond Boolos's conclusion that any mind capable of understanding all polynomials with integer coefficients and whose provable theorems exactly coincide with the output of a theorem-proving Turing machine is incapable of proving a mathematical truth that it apprehends. But Gödel takes matters further still.

Enter the argument about a "finite rule" and the prospect of the human mind being "equivalent to a finite machine." Against the interpretation placed on this by Boolos and others, the imagined rule, as it is understood and intended by Gödel, does not generate proofs of the elements of **HuMath**—let alone does it capture the method or procedure by which the mind constructs or discovers proofs.[22] Whereas Gödel's argument is concerned with the epistemological character of potential proofs by the human mind, the actual cognitive process whereby the human mind might conceive or discover its proofs is irrelevant. Let it be by a mechanistic process or let it be utterly non-mechanistic, by an indescribable mathematical inspiration, by a vital, non-deterministic spark of creativity. Let it be by supernatural revelation, or by divine intervention. It makes no difference to the argument.

Nor is the envisaged "finite rule" merely supposed to produce the mathematical theorems provable by the human mind—the elements of HuMath—even if by a potentially different construction. What the speculated rule *is* supposed to generate are the "evident axioms," i.e., not the elements of **HuMath** themselves but their axiomatization in **Basis**. If **Basis** is recursively enumerable, there is an effective procedure that enables one to enumerate its elements (possibly with repetitions). According to Church's thesis (construed so as to include the effective enumeration of a set of propositions), the converse obtains as well. Suppose there is a finite rule that produces all the elements of **Basis**—for example, finite instructions enabling one automatically to write out the sentences of a possible mathematical language, one

Within a System,' *Journal of Symbolic Logic*, 18, 1 (March 1953), pp. 30–32, that if **Ax** is recursively enumerable, then even if **Ax** is not itself recursive, **HuMath** is primitive recursively axiomatizable. (Thanks to C. Anthony Anderson for calling my attention to the relevance of Craig's result.)

[22] Shapiro, explains the first disjunct of Gödel's disjunction as the denial of the thesis that "all human arithmetic procedures are effective algorithms," and says that Gödel inclined instead to hold (with Lucas and Penrose) that "some of the routines and procedures that humans can employ . . . cannot be simulated on a Turing machine. There are inherently *non-computational* human arithmetic *procedures*" (pp. 277, 290, emphasis Shapiro's).

after another, which express just the elements of **Ax** as well as the inference rules. Mathematical certainty that the rule, properly characterized, generates no inconsistencies would then be unattainable. It follows from the second incompleteness theorem (and Church's thesis) that if there are such instructions, then even though each of the propositions expressed by the sentences they produce is true and humanly knowable with mathematical certainty without proof, and even though each of the generated rules are valid and such as to transfer mathematical certainty *via* the immediate inference, we cannot know of the instructions, with the same certainty, that their product is even consistent. Therefore, either there is no such rule—equivalently, no recursive function that enumerates the elements of **Basis**—or again there are purely mathematical truths of a certain type that are humanly unprovable. This is, nearly enough, Gödel's disjunction. It is, in effect, a trivial transformation in propositional logic of the following: *If the elements of **Basis** constitute a recursively enumerable set, then **HuMath** is a proper subclass of **Math**.*[23]

Gödel expands on his first disjunct—that there is no effective procedure producing exactly the axiomatic basis of human mathematics—by drawing an inference concerning the human mind *vis-à-vis* a finite machine. If indeed there is no such rule, then the human mind's capacity for attaining certainty in mathematics surpasses that of a theorem-proving computer—at least insofar as the computer's theorem-proving capacity is restricted to procedures that correspond to a recursive notion of proof. There is no assertion here that the theorem-proving mechanism of the human brain is not a computing machine (if 'machine' is the right term to use) whose theorem-proving capacity is not restricted in this way. Boolos's worries about the vagueness of the general notion that "the human mind is equivalent to a finite machine," while they may be an appropriate reaction to an attempt to derive some such more sweeping conclusion than this, are not pertinent here. The difficulty of likening the theorem-proving capacity of the human brain to a computer is not so much that the brain's cognitive processes are not mechanistic. Nor is it that a machine cannot know the fundamental axioms of human mathematics. (Although it cannot. Strictly speaking, it is a person, and not the person's brain, that knows things.) The difficulty comes in the very *design* (let alone the construction) of a theorem-proving machine when there is no effective procedure for delimiting its proofs' admissible starting points. Either there is no such procedure with regard to

---

[23] Gödel says in the passage quoted that his second incompleteness theorem "*makes it impossible that someone should set up a certain well-defined system of axioms and rules and consistently make the following assertion about it: All of these axioms and rules I perceive (with mathematical certitude) to be correct, and moreover I believe that they contain all of mathematics.* If someone makes such a statement he contradicts himself.... [For] no well-defined system of correct axioms can contain... all true mathematical propositions..." (The thrust of this remark is evidently better conveyed if the italicized phrase 'I believe' is deleted.) A similar remark is reported by Wang (p. 187): "There is a vague idea that we can find a set of axioms such that (1) all these axioms are evident to us; (2) the set yields all of mathematics. It follows from my incompleteness theorem that it is impossible to set up an axiom system satisfying (1) and (2), because, by (1), the statement expressing the consistency of the system should also be evident to me.—All this is explicitly in my Gibbs lecture." In order for someone to "set up" (i.e., fully specify) an infinite system of axioms, there would have to be an effective procedure for enumerating them. The term 'well-defined' is evidently a synonym in this context for 'recursively enumerable'.

the human mind's capacity for attaining knowledge with mathematical certainty in pure mathematics, or else there are purely mathematical problems of a certain sort that are in principle unsolvable by the human intellect. This is Gödel's disjunction.

III

Gödel remarks in passing (in effect) that the correctness of a set of propositions (i.e., truth of all the elements) entails their formal consistency, and hence knowledge with mathematical certainty of the former yields knowledge with mathematical certainty of the latter. Call this 'Gödel's thesis'.[24] It follows that knowledge with mathematical certainty of a proposition p (which may be a conjunction of propositions) yields the knowledge, with the same certainty, that p is consistent. Insofar as **Ax** consists of propositions that the human mind is capable of knowing with mathematical certainty, one might expect the mind to be able to know the conjunction of those axioms (perhaps by repeated applications of a familiar logical rule of inference). From the latter, according to Gödel's thesis, we could deduce the conjunction's consistency, and from this the Gödelian undecidable proposition. Does Gödel's thesis provide support for Lucas's assertion that the mind can after all see the truth of Gödel's undecidable proposition, which indirectly says of itself that it is not provable from the axioms?

Not without further argument. **Ax** is presumably infinite. The conjunction of its elements would then be an infinite conjunction. But there is a question of whether there even exist such propositions. If such propositions do exist, there is still a question of whether the human mind can comprehend them. Furthermore, though each element of **Ax** is knowable with mathematical certainty without independent proof, it does not follow that the conjunction of all the axioms is itself knowable with mathematical certainty—even assuming that this conjunction is humanly comprehensible. In order for a proof to confer knowledge with mathematical certainty, one must know each of the axioms employed in the proof with the same certainty. Even if one is thus capable of knowing with certainty the conjunction of axioms used in any proof that one may construct or discover, since proofs are finite this yields knowledge with certainty of conjunctions of finite subsets of elements of **Ax**, not yet knowledge with certainty of the conjunction of *all* elements of **Ax**.[25]

---

[24] 'For if he perceives the axioms under consideration to be correct, he also perceives (with the same certainty) that they are consistent' (in the passage quoted above from p. 309). Trivially, no contradiction is validly deducible from a set of truths. The casual manner of Gödel's remark creates the impression that this triviality is sufficient for the thesis, whereas strictly speaking, this justification is incomplete. Given a class of putative inference rules, one must know with mathematical certainty that every element of the class is valid in order to know with the same certainty that no falsehood, and hence no contradiction, is derivable from truths by their means. The validity of each inference rule of human mathematical reasoning is humanly knowable with mathematical certainty. Assuming the inference rules constitute an effectively decidable set, it is reasonable to suppose further that those very rules can be known with mathematical certainty to be one and all valid. Gödel's thesis then follows.

[25] The argument I attribute to Gödel is significantly different from that to which Boolos's criticisms apply. Still other interpretations have been proposed. Wang (p. 185) apparently construes

Suppose the human mind were able to know the conjunction of all of **Ax** at once. Suppose the inference rules are finite. According to Gödel's thesis, we could then know with mathematical certainty that if the conjunction of such-and-such axioms is correct, then the conjunction of such-and-such axioms (these same ones) is formally consistent. The fact concerning **Ax**—that if all those propositions are correct then they are consistent—is something we would be able to know with mathematical certainty if we were capable of apprehending **Ax** all at once, and if we are capable of any mathematical knowledge at all. Hence, if we could but know the conjunction of all elements of **Ax** with mathematical certainty, we could infer their consistency by *modus ponens* (an inference rule of just the sort required). But if the elements of **Ax** constitute a recursively enumerable set, then we cannot know *Cons* (which is provably equivalent to the consistency of **Ax**) with mathematical certainty. Therefore, by *reductio ad absurdum*, either the elements of **Ax** are not recursively enumerable, or else their conjunction is not humanly provable. Or to put the point somewhat differently from Gödel: Though each of the elements of **Ax**, taken individually, is humanly knowable with mathematical certainty, if those elements are recursively enumerable, then even though they are, their conjunction is not humanly knowable with mathematical certainty. This result does not advance the position of Nagel and Newman, *et al.*

By Gödel's thesis, if the elements of **Ax** are recursively enumerable, then the human mind is barred from knowing their conjunction with mathematical certainty. This does not mean that if the elements of **Ax** are recursively enumerable, then the human mind is barred from knowing with mathematical certainty the general meta-theoretic proposition that *all the purely mathematical propositions knowable with mathematical certainty by the human mind without independent mathematical proof are true*. On the contrary, the latter proposition appears to be something of which we are certain (setting aside worries about the so-called paradox of the knower), on the basis of the analytic truth that whatever is known is true. (See note 25.) What it does mean is that if the elements of **Ax** are recursively enumerable, we are barred from knowing *of* those propositions (*de re*) with mathematical certainty that all are true, by inference from anything of the form ⌜Every x such that $\phi(x)$ is true⌝ where ⌜$\phi(x)$⌝ designates **Ax** in a manner provably equivalent to its designation in ϕ_{Proof} and ϕ_{Cons}.

Gödel as arguing that if the axioms and inference rules of human mathematics were finite in number, then we could not know those very propositions and rules to be the basis of human mathematical knowledge, since otherwise we could know something about that basis (by confirming each element individually) that is not deducible from it—its consistency—and hence they would not be *all* the axioms and rules of human mathematics.

I believe for a variety of reasons that this cannot be Gödel's argument. Curiously, Wang notes that the same line of argument yields another conclusion—one that is, in fact, significantly stronger—namely, that the basis of human mathematics is infinite. Wang might mean to attribute to Gödel a somewhat different argument: We cannot know any finite basis to be the basis of human mathematics; for otherwise we could prove (by individual confirmation) something mathematical that is not deducible from that basis: that the basis (and hence all) of human mathematical knowledge is consistent. But this will not do either. That the basis of human mathematical knowledge—whatever it is, and whatever its size—is internally consistent is trivial and as certain as any mathematical theorem. This, however, is not reducible to a mathematical truth. It is an epistemological truism.

In particular, even if the elements of **Ax** are recursively enumerable, we cannot know with mathematical certainty of any recursive function that enumerates it, that it generates only Gödel numbers of true sentences—with the enumerating function characterized so as to yield a formula $\ulcorner \phi(x) \urcorner$ of the indicated sort.

Again suppose there is a finite rule that produces exactly the axioms of human mathematics. Under certain circumstances (e.g., where one fully understands the possible language in question), knowing of the envisioned effective instructions that they produce only sentences expressing truths is tantamount to knowing those propositions expressed to be consistent. It follows that if there are such instructions, then even though each of the propositions expressed by the sentences they produce is true and humanly knowable with mathematical certainty without proof, we cannot know of the instructions, with the same certainty, that their product is correct. If there are effective instructions that produce sentences expressing exactly the axioms of human mathematics, we are incapable of knowing of those instructions with mathematical certainty that they do so. If we were to stumble upon such a rule we could not prove it to be such, or even that it produces only truths.[26]

Lucas, like Nagel and Newman and others who have discussed the philosophical import of Gödel's incompleteness results, evidently tacitly assumes that insofar as the mathematical capabilities of a human mind is represented by a deductive system at all, the axioms constitute a recursively enumerable set, if not indeed a recursive set.[27] It follows from this assumption, taken together with Gödel's thesis, that though each of the axioms is humanly knowable with mathematical certainty, the mind is incapable of deducing their conjunction. This in itself does not refute Lucas's argument. The position of Nagel and Newman, *et al.*, appears to be that, whatever one's axioms for mathematics may be at a given time, the human mind, unlike the logistic system it instantiates at that time, is capable of augmenting its primitive deductive basis through a non-mechanistic mathematical insight that goes beyond what is strictly provable from those axioms. The mind can both prove that the axioms cannot prove their own consistency, and at the same time *see* (without proving this from the current axioms) that those same axioms *en toto* are correct, hence consistent. The mind thereby expands its deductive basis, empowering itself to prove the incompleteness of the previous axioms from the new set. The mind can then repeat the maneuver with respect to its new deductive basis, and then again with the yet newer basis, and so on in an ongoing dialectic. More important, the vital

---

[26] This probably yields the intent behind the following remark of Gödel's, reported by Wang (p. 186): "The incompleteness results do not rule out the possibility that there is a theorem-proving computer which is in fact equivalent to mathematical intuition. But they imply that, in such a— highly unlikely for other reasons—case, either we do not know the exact specification of the computer or we do not know that it works correctly." If **Ax** is recursively enumerable, so that a computer program might be written for proving theorems from it, then even if we were to write such a program, we could not know that its product is correct; otherwise we would also know what, according to the second incompleteness theorem, we cannot prove: its consistency.

[27] Lucas (p. 44 of the reprinting in Anderson, *Minds and Machines*), declares that Gödel's results obtain for any formal system that is consistent and contains the natural numbers and the operations of addition and multiplication. In a later footnote (p. 52n6), he explicitly mentions the restriction that the primitive deductive basis be recursively enumerable.

mathematical faculty or insight that fuels the dialectical progression also yields knowledge with mathematical certainty of its own correctness, and hence consistency, and thereby of the correctness, and consequent consistency, of the entire system generated by the initial axioms and inference rules taken together with the special non-mechanistic faculty itself. The hypothesized vital mathematical insight would strikingly set the human mind apart from any machine or mechanistic process that lacks it.

Unfortunately, this view of human mathematics as a dynamic process of continuing discovery fueled by a unique kind of non-mechanistic and self-validating mathematical insight does not solve the problem. **Ax**, by definition, includes every purely mathematical truth that is humanly knowable without proof from other purely mathematical truths. If there is any special, self-validating faculty or intuition of the sort hypothesized, whatever is humanly knowable by its means is thus already included in **Ax**. The only way for the mind to come to know a purely mathematical truth with mathematical certainty that does not belong to **Ax** is to prove it ultimately from **Ax** (i.e., to prove it from **Ax**, or to prove it from theorems proved from **Ax**, or from theorems proved from theorems proved from **Ax**, etc.). **HuMath** is completely axiomatized by **Basis**, i.e., **Ax** together with the inference rules. In light of Gödel's second theorem, if **Basis** is recursively enumerable, the recast assertion of its consistency is not humanly knowable with mathematical certainty. Rather than making the case for the position of Nagel and Newman, *et al.*, this result spells trouble for it.

Assume for the moment, with Hilbert, that the human mind is capable, in principle, of solving any purely mathematical problem. It then follows from Gödel's disjunction that the mind's capacity for proving theorems surpasses that of any theorem-proving computer whose primitive deductive basis is recursively enumerable. The mind's superiority over any such machine (in this sense) is explained not so much, or not directly, by the mind's being able to "see" that which cannot yet be proved, but instead by the fact that its primitive deductive basis is essentially richer than the computer's. The richness of human mathematics would in that case result from some human faculty or intuitive insight—which would indeed separate man from those machines without it—but this special mathematical faculty or intuition might be the very same faculty that provides us with even the simplest axioms, not something further and different. Moreover, its consistency may not be reducible to any purely mathematical proposition, and therefore it need not be self-validating to be mathematically complete.[28] In any event, there remains the unproven assumption that the human mind can prove every purely mathematical truth.

IV

Gödel's derivation pointedly places a special focus on a question that is ignored in Lucas's argument: Are the elements of **Basis** recursively enumerable? Or put another

---

[28] Gödel evidently believed that the human mind does possess some self-validating insight of this sort. *Cf.* Wang, pp. 187–189.

way (under the assumption of Church's thesis, applied to the effective enumeration of a set of propositions): Is there an effective procedure for enumerating the rules of human mathematical inference together with those purely mathematical truths that the human mind is capable of knowing with mathematical certainty without independent mathematical proof? If there is not, then the mathematical capacity of the human mind surpasses that of any mathematics machine whose deductive basis is subject to such a procedure; and otherwise, the human mathematical mind is, in a certain sense, in principle incapable of resolving the question of its own consistency.

In particular, could it be that **Ax** is not effectively enumerable? Many logicians would regard this prospect as quite impossible. Church argued, in effect, that nothing should count as a genuine *proof* unless the totality of axioms form a recursively enumerable set, indeed a recursive set. He posed his argument in the context of a logistic system, construed syntactically. Church imposed as an inviolable restriction on any logistic system that "the specification of the axioms shall be effective in the sense that there is a method by which, whenever a well-formed formula is given, it can always be determined effectively whether or not it is one of the axioms."[29] Unless there is an effective procedure for deciding whether a given formula is or is not one of the axioms, the notion of proof itself will not be effective. Church's justification for the restriction is given with characteristic eloquence and force:

> There is then no certain means by which, when a sequence of formulae has been put forward as a proof, the auditor may determine whether it is in fact a proof. Therefore he may fairly demand a proof, in any given case, that the sequence of formulae put forward is a proof; and until this supplementary proof is provided, he may refuse to be convinced that the alleged theorem is proved. This supplementary proof ought to be regarded, it seems, as part of the whole proof of the theorem, and the primitive basis of the logistic system ought to be so modified as to provide this, or its equivalent. Indeed it is essential to the idea of a proof that, to any one who admits the presuppositions on which it is based, a proof carries final conviction.[30]

Lecturing on Gödel's incompleteness theorems in 1974, Church gave the following related argument, as reconstructed from my notes (edited and approved by Church at the time for distribution to the class):

> The initial reaction to an incompleteness proof for a logistic system is to search for additional axioms, postulates, or rules of inference which, when added to the incomplete system, yield a complete system. But there does not seem to be any way of doing this for the logistic system A^2 [a formalization of second order Peano arithmetic]. The Gödel proof does not make great use of the particular axioms, postulates, and rules of inference of A^2. The proof is of such generality that it is easily extended to a logistic system obtained from A^2 by the addition of particular axioms, postulates, and rules of inference.
>
> The reason for the incompleteness of A^2 does not lie in the axioms, postulates, or rules of inference, but rather in the notion of mathematical proof. A proof must carry conviction; one who accepts the axioms and rules of inference, if he has once seen a proof of a particular theorem, must then not be able justifiably to doubt the theorem. But if axiom schemata or rules of inference are non-effective, the situation can arise that one who has seen a proof

---

[29] Church, *Introduction to Mathematical Logic, I* (Princeton University Press, 1956), at pp. 50–51. See note 18 above.   [30] *Ibid.*, pp. 53–54.

may still doubt, because he is unable to verify that what is before him is in fact a proof. Thus the notion of proof must be effective, that is, there must be an effective procedure for determining whether an alleged proof is a proof. Presumably this means that the notion of proof must be general recursive, since there is no known effective check which is not general recursive. Even if we were to add an axiom schema to the logistic system A^2, the set of instances of this axiom schema must be general recursive, if not indeed primitive recursive, in terms of their Gödel numbers. One need only show that the notion of mathematical proof which is obtained by adding this axiom schema to A^2 is expressible in A^2 by means of Gödel numbering in order to carry through an incompleteness proof along the lines given above, and this should be possible in virtue of theorems connecting general recursion and primitive recursion (for example, that any general recursive relation can be expressed by means of quantifiers and primitive recursive relations).

Thus in a general way, the Gödel proof is not only a proof of incompleteness, but also a proof of incompletability. Since the only known way of making precise the notion of mathematical proof is the logistic system, the usual conclusion drawn from the Gödel proof is that any precise formulation of arithmetic cannot be complete—a conclusion which shatters one of the hopes of the Hilbert program.

A genuine mathematical proof is not merely a sequence of formulae satisfying certain purely syntactic conditions (*viz.*, every element of the sequence is either an element of the recursively specified set of "axioms," or else follows from formulae occurring earlier in the sequence by means of one of the recursively specified set of "rules of inference"). Rather, a genuine proof is what such a sequence of formulae semantically expresses: a line of reasoning, consisting of propositions, that conclusively demonstrates a proposition. Church's argument that since a proof must "carry final conviction" the notion of proof must be effective, if sound, applies directly to authentic proofs, and only derivatively, by extension, to their syntactic expression within a logistic system. If sound, the argument supports the broad conclusion that there must be an effective procedure that enables one to decide of any mathematical proposition whether it is or is not an element of **Ax**. In fact, assuming Church's thesis (in the form indicated above), his argument, if sound, supports the conclusion that the elements of **Ax** must *constitute a recursive set of propositions*, in the sense that there is a recursive numerical function that exactly characterizes a set of Gödel numbers of sentences of a possible formal language expressing each of the elements of **Ax**—e.g., a recursive function that yields 1 for the Gödel number of any axiomatic sentence and 0 for the Gödel number of any other sentence of the language in question. (See note 19.)

Church's argument, however, does not itself carry conviction. First, the fact that an auditor may justifiably doubt whether a purported proof is correct (and is thus a genuine proof) does not entail that the line of reasoning in question does not after all conclusively demonstrate its conclusion with mathematical certainty (i.e., is not a genuine proof). A proof provides potential epistemic justification for conviction; the carrying of conviction is a horse of a different color. Whether the horse drinks from the water to which it is led is up to the horse. It is not unusual for a theorem to be proved before it is confirmed that the reasoning is thoroughly sound—sometimes well before this is confirmed even to the original author's satisfaction. In such cases, a potential epistemic justification for conviction is provided before conviction is carried—perhaps even before conviction is actually justified by its potential justification. Church's concern is with the auditor who questions whether a purported proof that has been spelled out in full, with a justification provided for each step, is correct. Often one can know that a given object has a given property even in the absence of an effective test for the property in question. Often one can even prove this. In particular, a given proof's correctness can be verified without applying any general test capable of verifying the correctness of any proof whatsoever. It is typically sufficient to re-check each step of the particular proof in question, and to verify that those particular steps are legitimate. One can do this by applying certain sufficient conditions for the justification of a step, even in the absence of a complete set of such conditions, let alone a complete set of effectively decidable necessary and sufficient conditions. Where one auditor may doubt whether a particular piece of reasoning is a proof, another auditor may correctly see, without the benefit of an effective test, that the reasoning is perfectly sound. In that case, the reasoning can decisively establish its conclusion, at least for the second auditor.[31]

For that matter, even if there is an effective test, its mere existence does not put an end to the infinite regress of demanding a proof, then demanding a proof that the first proof is correct, then demanding a proof that the second proof is correct, and so on.[32] Nor does the existence of an effective test for proofs eliminate the possibility of justified doubt in a given case. To quell such doubt the test has to be applied to the proof in question. One may then question whether the test has been applied correctly. And even if one is satisfied that it was, one may justifiably doubt whether the purported test itself is correct. If an auditor wonders whether a particular proposition employed as an axiom in the proof is indeed antecedently known, it is no answer to point out that the formula expressing the proposition in question was written under the heading 'AXIOMS' in setting up the primitive basis of a particular logistic system for mathematics (or is generated by an effective procedure for producing the logistic system's "axioms"). The auditor's question is not whether the formula is playing the role of an axiom in the purported proof, or whether it is called an 'axiom'; the question concerns the proposition expressed, whether it is genuinely known with mathematical certainty without independent mathematical proof. The so-called test simply assumes it is so, as it were, by stipulative fiat. The prospects are dim for an effective procedure for deciding whether it really is so. If such a procedure is required for there to be proof, mathematical ignorance is considerably wider than is currently realized.

On the contrary, the general issue of whether the entire line of reasoning in question is a proof is separate from the issue the proof itself is intended to settle: whether the theorem in question is true. The reasoning, if it is correct, enables an auditor to know the theorem with mathematical certainty. This is the purpose of the

---

[31] C. Anthony Anderson makes a related objection in 'Alonzo Church's Contributions to Philosophy and Intensional Logic,' *Bulletin of Symbolic Logic*, 4, 2 (June 1998), pp. 129–171, at 130–131.

[32] *Cf.* Lewis Carroll, 'What the Tortoise Said to Achilles,' *Mind*, NS 4, 14 (April 1895), pp. 278–280.

proof, its *raison d'etre*. To ask whether the purported proof is correct is to raise a separate, further question, an epistemological meta-question related to the issue of whether one knows that one knows—a question that the auditor need not consciously consider in order to gain knowledge of the theorem with mathematical certainty on the basis of the proof. If the assumptions employed in the line of reasoning are *in fact* already known with mathematical certainty, and the inference rules are of the right character (so as to transfer mathematical certainty to the inferred conclusion), the reasoning can be of the right sort to establish its theorem conclusively, and to confer mathematical certainty for an auditor, even if the question of whether it does so is never raised—perhaps even if the question is raised and answered incorrectly, as long as the auditor continues to believe the theorem on the basis of the proof.

Church's argument is fundamentally Cartesian in character. It assumes that knowledge with mathematical certainty precludes the possibility of a certain kind of justifiable doubt. Church supposes that in order genuinely to know something in mathematics one must be able to prove it beyond all possible justifiable doubt, and in order to do this one must be able to prove beyond justifiable doubt that one has done so, by applying an effective test. Descartes took this assumption a step further, requiring that all knowledge, mathematical or otherwise, be obtained by proof that is not subject to doubt of this sort. But the same mistake occurs even when the assumption is restricted to knowledge in mathematics with mathematical certainty. Despite the astounding feats of its champions, the assumption inexorably leads to skepticism. One may legitimately wonder, for example, how one knows (and in particular, whether by direct mathematical insight) that if integers n and m have the same successor then $n = m$. It is doubtful that anything other than Descartes's *Cogito* is completely immune from the kind of doubt raised by demanding indubitable proof that one's proof is a proof. One may even doubt whether the *Cogito* is.

None of this diminishes the epistemological power of mathematical proof. That power is awesome. Though not immune from Cartesian doubt, mathematical proof provides a way—indeed, the only way—to extend human knowledge with mathematical certainty beyond the severely narrow confines of **Ax**. Few epistemological mechanisms can achieve the kind of certainty that mathematical proof confers. In any event, even if Church's argument is not cogent, it does not follow that his conclusion is incorrect.

Though severely narrow, **Ax** may be remarkably diverse. As noted, **Ax** includes fundamental mathematical truths that no one in the entire history of human life will have ever apprehended—let alone believed, let alone known. Some elements of **Ax** involve concepts that are humanly apprehendible but of which no one will have ever formed a grasp. Some elements of **Ax** may be knowable only through modes of thought which are humanly possible but in which no one will have ever engaged. It may be that, though each element of **Ax** taken individually is humanly knowable with mathematical certainty, no possible human mind could apprehend all of them—let alone believe all of them, let alone know all of them with mathematical certainty. As far as Godel's theorems go, the question is left open whether **Ax** is effectively decidable, or at least effectively enumerable, or enumerable at all—even whether the elements constitute a set. Hao Wang has reported that, though Gödel derives only a disjunction from his second incompleteness theorem, he believed Hilbert was correct in rejecting the second disjunct.[33] In light of Gödel's first theorem (and Church's thesis), Hilbert's optimism that the human mind is capable of solving any purely mathematical problem carries with it the view that the axioms of human mathematics are not effectively decidable. If every purely mathematical problem is humanly solvable in principle, then there is no effective procedure for listing the axioms of human mathematics. This would not mean that the human brain is not (among other things) an organic machine. It does mean that, insofar as Hilbert's optimism is correct, the theorem-proving capacity of the human mind far exceeds that of any theorem-proving mechanism whose deductive basis is effectively enumerable—a restatement of Gödel's disjunction. But one does not have to be optimistic to appreciate that if the human brain is a machine, then it is a remarkable one—or else Gödel was not human (or both).

[33] Wang, *From Mathematics to Philosophy* (London: Routledge and Kegan Paul, 1974), at pp. 324–326.

PART V

THEORY OF MEANING AND REFERENCE

14

On Content (1992)

I

Frege introduces his powerful theory of cognitive content in 'Über Sinn and Bedeutung', observing that $\ulcorner a = a \urcorner$ and $\ulcorner a = b \urcorner$ are obviously statements of differing 'Erkenntniswerte'—literally 'knowledge worth'—since the former is *a priori* and, following Kant, to be called 'analytic' whereas, for many distinct terms *a* and *b*, the latter contains an *a posteriori*, and indeed a very valuable, extension of knowledge. How is this possible? Prolonging the reader's suspense until the final paragraph, Frege explains that the sense of a sentence, i.e. the thought expressed by it, is no less relevant to the purpose of acquiring knowledge than the *Bedeutung*, i.e. the truth-value. Since $\ulcorner a = a \urcorner$ and $\ulcorner a = b \urcorner$ express different thoughts when *a* and *b* differ in sense, the two sentences will then differ in *Erkenntniswerte*.

The significance of these passages to the history of the philosophy of semantics can hardly be overstated. Yet there remains widespread disagreement concerning their proper interpretation.[1] Perhaps the most natural interpretation sees Frege as proposing that the *Erkenntniswerte* of a sentence be identified with the thought, or proposition, expressed. I have come to believe that this interpretation may be incorrect. Frege may be proposing instead that the *Erkenntniswerte* of a sentence be seen as a special feature of the thought expressed. The crucial wrinkle would be that whereas different thoughts often yield different *Erkenntniswerte* (as with the thoughts expressed by $\ulcorner a = a \urcorner$ and $\ulcorner a = b \urcorner$), they do not do so invariably. The *Erkenntniswerte* of a sentence would emerge as an intermediate semantic value: something that is determined by the thought but not *vice versa*, something that determines truth-value but not *vice versa*. If we posit *Erkenntniswerte* also for singular terms, the *Erkenntniswerte* of a singular term would likewise be a semantic value more coarsely grained than sense yet more finely grained than reference.

I am indebted to Jan Alnes for pointing out to me that Frege seemed to have in his *Begriffsschrift* a distinct notion of content, which is supposed to be that respect in which logically equivalent sentences are the same. Most of the ideas presented here emerged in the course of discussions with Alnes.

[1] See David Coder, 'The Opening Passage of Frege's "Über Sinn und Bedeutung"'. *Philosophia*, 4 (1974), pp. 339–343; Gregory Currie, *Frege: An Introduction to his Philosophy* (Sussex: The Harvester Press, 1982), pp. 108–112, especially 110. Rod Bertolet, in 'Conventions and Coreferentiality' (unpublished), issues a provocative reply to the interpretation I offered in my (1986, at pp. 51–54).

Is there a significant semantic value that is intermediate in this way between cognitive content and extension? One obvious candidate which is widely employed in philosophical semantics is what is sometimes called the 'intension', that is, the function from possible worlds to extensions—or what comes to the same thing in the case of sentences, the set of possible worlds with respect to which the sentence is true. (The former is the characteristic function of the latter.) The intension of a sentence yields one interpretation of the oft-used phrase 'truth conditions' as the maximal conditions which might have obtained and with respect to which the sentence is true. More than a few philosophers have misidentified the proposition expressed by a sentence with the sentence's intension. Our ordinary attributions of belief and other propositional attitudes leave little option but to differentiate among numerous beliefs sharing the same intension. There are additional reasons to distinguish between a proposition and its corresponding intension, some of essentially the same sort as the reason that Frege cites in distinguishing the *Erkenntniswerte* of $\ulcorner a = a \urcorner$ from that of $\ulcorner a = b \urcorner$. Indeed, it is clear that Frege should not identify the *Erkenntniswerte* of a sentence with its intension. For the sentences 'Either Socrates is wise or he is not' and 'Socrates is the only person to have developed from s and e', where 's' and 'e' name the particular gametes from which Socrates sprang, obviously differ in *Erkenntniswerte*. The first is analytic and its cognitive content *a priori*; the second is synthetic and contains an *a posteriori* extension of knowledge. Yet it is at least arguable that the two sentences share a common intension. Contingent and purely *a posteriori* examples of the same phenomenon abound: 'Mary is a Capricorn', 'Mary is either a Capricorn or an individual retirement account', and 'Mary is a Capricorn but not an individual retirement account' all coincide in intension yet clearly differ in *Erkenntniswerte*. To this extent, epistemology is more discriminating than metaphysics.[2]

Whatever Frege meant, or did not mean, in his use of 'Erkenntniswerte', if ordinary propositional-attitude attributions are a guide to the individuation of propositions, they also provide important reasons to posit an intervening semantic value that intercedes between the proposition and its intension. Doing so provides the means for solving a philosophical problem noticed by Ali Kazmi.[3] Some

---

[2] It must be acknowledged that in correspondence with Edmund Husserl, Frege offered a version of logical equivalence as his only criterion for two sentences expressing the same thought. See his *Philosophical and Mathematical Correspondence*, G. Gabriel, *et al.*, eds. (Chicago: University of Chicago Press, 1980), pp. 70–71. *Cf.* Frege's 'Compound Thoughts,' in his *Collected Papers on Mathematics, Logic and Philosophy* (Oxford: Basil Blackwell, 1984), pp. 390–406. I shall follow other commentators in assuming that Frege's pronouncements in this connection, since they are inconsistent with what seem to be the fundamentals of his theory of *Sinn* and *Bedeutung* (for example, his doctrines that the *Bedeutung* of the 'that' clause in 'Galileo believed that the Earth moves' is its customary *Sinn*, and that the truth-value of a sentence is a function of the *Bedeutungen* of the sentence components), represent a significant theoretical lapse, oversight, or perhaps a very crude over-simplification. Elsewhere Frege acknowledges that certain true arithmetic equations differ in sense—even though, given his logicism, all true theorems of arithmetic are logically equivalent (indeed, logically valid). See for example G. Frege, *Posthumous Writings*, H. Hermes, *et al.*, eds. (Chicago: University of Chicago Press, 1979), pp. 224–225. See also p. 211.

[3] Ali Kazmi, 'Reference, Structure and Content', unpublished comment on Richards 1990. (Delivered to a symposium of the American Philosophical Association, 1988). See M. Richard,

propositions have been given special labels. We say such things as 'Michael doubts Church's Theorem'. Exactly which proposition is Michael being said to doubt by that sentence? Kazmi points out that if propositions are individuated finely enough, then there is no nonarbitrary way to decide whether Church's Theorem is the proposition that first-order logic is undecidable, or instead the proposition that it is not the case that first-order logic is decidable. It is arguable that the two versions are distinct propositions strictly speaking. On the other hand, both formulations, and others as well, in some sense, clearly contain *the same theorem*. Someone who proffered an unusual formulation of Church's Theorem as a discovery of his own, one that should be placed alongside Church's Theorem in importance, would be properly dismissed as a desperate plagiarist. How can this conflict be resolved?

The general problem here cannot be eliminated satisfactorily by individuating propositions along the lines of their corresponding intensions. Church's Theorem is not the same proposition as Gödel's Completeness Theorem, yet both are true in every possible world. A more discriminating notion is needed. But propositions *qua* objects of belief, doubt, and other propositional attitudes seem to be excessively discriminating. Someone might come to believe that it is not the case that first-order logic is decidable while momentarily suspending judgment whether first-order logic is undecidable. As Mark Richard points out, Kazmi's problem is fuelled by the same forces from propositional-attitude discourse that pressure philosophers to individuate propositions more finely than their intensions.[4]

Let us take another example. Consider Murphy's Law, which is usually formulated: *Whatever can go wrong will*. There are numerous variants: *Whatever might not go right will not; Whatever does not go wrong cannot*, etc. All of these formulations share the same intension. More than that, they are logically equivalent. But it is very doubtful that they all express precisely one and the very same proposition. Some of the propositions involve the notion of something's going right, others the notion of something's going wrong. Some involve negation, others do not. Which of these nearly identical propositions is Murphy's Law? Perhaps the proposition expressed by the standard formulation has some special claim to the name, but it cannot be wrong to call the others 'Murphy's Law'. Each of the formulations, in some sense, contains *the same law*.

To take yet another example, consider Leibniz's Principle of the Identity of Indiscernibles. This principle can be formulated in a number of ways:

For all things x and y, if x has P iff y has P for all properties P, then $x = y$;[5]
Any two things are qualitatively different;
Anything exactly like a given thing is that thing itself;

Propositional Attitudes: An Essay on Thoughts and How We Ascribe Them (Cambridge: Cambridge University Press, 1990), pp. 161, n15, pp. 171–173. Richard defends his theory against Kazmi's problem, in part, by noting that it is a problem that every theory of propositions seems to face.

    [4] Richard, *Propositional Attitudes*, p. 172.
    [5] In order to forestall certain difficulties, it may be assumed here that the properties being quantified over do not include so-called haecceities, i.e. properties of being numerically identical with this or that particular thing. The same (or corresponding) restriction should be made for each of the formulations to be given.

Things that are the same in every respect are the very same thing;
Distinct things are always different from one another in some respect;
If things do not differ in any respect, then they are one and the same;
The only thing exactly like a given thing is itself; etc.

Some of these propositions involve the notion of things being exactly alike, while others involve the complementary notion of things being different in some respect. Some involve the notion of two things, others the notion of a single thing. Although they are different propositions, they are intimately related, so much so that no one of them can plausibly be singled out as *the* Principle of the Identity of Indiscernibles, to the exclusion of all the others. All of them qualify equally well.

Are there many different Principles of the Identity of Indiscernibles, each distinct from the others? No; that would miss the point. The solution that I propose lies in the recognition that such things as the Principle of the Identity of Indiscernibles are not themselves propositions. The Identity of Indiscernibles is something generic, something that is common to each of the distinct propositions formulated above. It is ... well, the *principle* which is embodied in each of the propositions. A similar point may be made in connection with any number of such items as Goldbach's Conjecture, the Heisenberg Uncertainty Principle, Kepler's Laws of Planetary Motion, the Principle of Sufficient Reason, and a host of ism's (dualism, logicism, behaviourism, pragmatism, logical atomism, functionalism, etc.).

There is something which all sentences logically equivalent to a given sentence share, even when they do not express a single proposition, and which is not shared by logically unrelated sentences. This something is what Frege in his *Begriffsschrift* (§3) called the 'conceptual content' (*begrifflichen Inhalt*) of the given sentence—a notion that may have been a precursor to his later notion of *Erkenntniswerte*.[6] To use an overworked and multiply ambiguous term, each of the formulations of the Principle of the Identity of Indiscernibles displayed above contains, in the relevant sense, the same *information*. The operative notion of information cannot be the traditional notion of *cognitive* or *propositional content* (Frege's notion of *Sinn*, Russell's notion of meaning), since the various formulations express different propositions, different thoughts. Nor is it the modal notion of *intension*. We have already seen sentences which are logically unrelated, and which therefore contain different information in the relevant sense, but which share the same intension. I have elsewhere used the phrase 'information content'[7] interchangeably with 'propositional content'. Since the latter expresses a notion that I am here distinguishing from the notion we seek, I shall introduce a different terminology. Let us tentatively call the primary semantic value that a sentence shares with all of its logical equivalents, but does not share with logically unrelated sentences, the *logical content* of the sentence. We may also speak of logical content in connection

---

[6] Frege's word for his logical formalism, 'Begriffsschrift', may be translated as 'Conceptual Notation'. He says in his preface to *Begriffsschrift* that it was his exclusive interest in "conceptual content" that led to the title of the work.

[7] Compare the explanation of my use of 'information' in my *Frege's Puzzle* (Atascadero, CA: Ridgeview, 1986), p. 154n2. I acknowledge there that the use of 'information content' as a term for propositional content "constitutes a departure from at least one standard usage, according to which the information content of a sentence is perhaps something like a class of [propositions], closed under logical consequence".

with singular terms. The key criterial idea is that expressions of a given sort have the same logical content if they are logically equivalent.

I mean 'logical equivalence' in a fairly common but not overly strict sense, so that, for example, the two sentences 'Michael is a husband' and 'Michael is male and Michael is married' count as logically equivalent. This use of 'logical equivalence' is perhaps nonstandard. The logical content of a sentence, as I intend the phrase, is not something that is strictly dependent on the very words (or other subsentential expressions) involved. Sentences of different languages, even some that do not have the same cognitive content, can share the same logical content relative to those languages. In some sense, the logical content of an expression is actually a feature of the expression's cognitive content, its sense. The operative notion of *logical equivalence* is that of an equivalence relation between propositions, thoughts. We have already seen that sentences with the same logical content may yet differ in the propositions they express. But those propositions must be equivalent. And sentences that express equivalent propositions *ipso facto* share the same logical content.[8]

Some sentences that are arguably logically equivalent in a straightforward sense do not even share the same intension. The two sentences

(1) Saul Kripke is an anthropologist

and

(2) Saul Kripke is actually an anthropologist

are equivalent in the modal logic of 'actually' (in its indexical sense), but they express propositions, or thoughts, that differ dramatically in intension. The latter proposition, but not the former, is concerned with the goings-on in a specific possible world. Both sentences are false, but where (1) contains a proposition that might have been true, (2) contains a proposition that could not have been true. These two propositions are not related to one another in the same way the various propositions containing Murphy's Law are related.

This goes to the very heart of the difference between the classical, sentential notion of validity and the propositional notion that we are limning. Unlike (1), exactly which proposition (2) contains with respect to a context of its utterance depends crucially on the context. But no matter what the range of possible contexts, with respect to every such context—even possible contexts in which Kripke is an anthropologist—(2) contains a proposition that has the same truth-value that the proposition contained in (1) has in the possible world of the context. Given the meaning of 'actually', it is no accident, then, that (1) and (2) share a common truth-value. It is in this sense that they are logically equivalent. Things are very different with respect to the propositions they contain. Since the proposition contained in (1) could have been true and the proposition contained in (2) could not, it is very much an accident, in the only relevant sense, that they happen to coincide in truth-value. If Kripke had gone into anthropology, they would not have. In that case, (2) would have been true, but only because it would have expressed a different proposition

---

[8] This notion of logical equivalence is thus closer to what I have called the *derivative notion of equivalence*. See my *Frege's Puzzle*, appendix A, p. 131.

altogether. The proposition expressed by (2) with respect to the present, actual context would still have been false. This is as much as to say that whereas 'actually' is a logical operator, in the logic of indexicality, its cognitive content with respect to a given context is not a logical operator. This should not be surprising. The first-person pronoun 'I' has its own logic, but I am not a logical anything.

Sentences that differ intensionally are not equivalent in their cognitive contents; the propositions they express are not themselves equivalent in the relevant, pro-positional sense. When such sentences can be called 'equivalent', they are equivalent in some other semantic value, one not determined by cognitive content. Sentences (1) and (2), for example, are equivalent in what David Kaplan calls 'character', i.e. in their respective functions that assign cognitive contents to contexts of utterance.[9] In the special sense used here, sentences sharing the same logical content must also share the same modal content. The picture is this: Cognitive content determines logical content; logical content determines intension; and intension determines extension for any possible world. But extension does not determine intension; intension does not determine logical content; and logical content does not determine cognitive content. Logical content is, in this sense, something intermediate between cognitive content and intension.

II

Frege's celebrated distinction between *Sinn* and *Bedeutung* is very likely a bifurcation of, and hence a replacement for, his earlier notion in *Begriffsschrift* of conceptual content.[10] My proposal here is to retain three distinct semantic values: cognitive content; extension; logical content. The emphasis of Frege's classic 1892 publication—even its very title—suggests that he saw his two-way distinction as fundamental. On the other hand, his employment of the term 'Erkenntniswerte' in addition to 'Sinn' and 'Bedeutung' might indicate that he had in fact drawn a three-way distinction, of exactly the sort I am proposing here. This would be significant in more than one way. First, if the proposal has merit, it would constitute yet another philosophical discovery of note by the genius from Jena.[11] In addition, if the notion of logical content that

---

[9] This is not to say that the two sentences share a common character. In fact, their separate characters assign distinct propositions to every context. But as has already been said, no matter what the range of possible contexts, the respective characters always assign propositions that coincide in truth-value in the possible world of the context in question.

[10] See the editor's preface to '*Begriffsschrift*' (G. Frege, '*Begriffsschrift*', in *From Frege to Gödel: A Source Book in Mathematical Logic, 1879–1931*. J. van Heijenoort, ed. (Harvard: Harvard University Press, 1967), p. 4). Frege explicitly acknowledges, in his May 24, 1891 letter to Edmund Husserl (*Philosophical and Mathematical Correspondence*, p. 63), and more reliably, in the introduction to his *Grundgesetze der Arithmetik, begriffsschriflich abgeleitet*. Jena: H. Pohle; tr. M, Furth (Berkeley: University of California Press, 1893), pp. 6–7, that his distinction between thought and truth-value is a bifurcation, as a consequence of distinguishing between *Sinn* and *Bedeutung*, of his earlier notion of judgeable content (*beurtheilbarer Inhalt*)—i.e., the content of a sentence.

[11] Tyler Burge argues in 'Sinning Against Frege'. *Philosophical Review*, 58 (1979), pp. 398–432 that Frege recognized a three-way distinction, among *Sinn*, *Bedeutung*, and what would be more properly termed 'linguistic meaning'. The last, a variant of Kaplan's notion of character, is

I am proffering yields something closer to the correct interpretation of Frege's use of 'Erkenntniswerte' in the opening and closing passages of 'Uber Sinn und Bedeutung,' then the argument in those passages proceeds quite differently—or at least could proceed quite differently—from what many, including myself, have thought.

In *Frege's Puzzle*, I portrayed Frege as arguing that since $\ulcorner a = b \urcorner$ does, but $\ulcorner a = a \urcorner$ does not, contain a valuable extension of knowledge, for some co-referential proper names a and b, the resulting difference in cognitive content between the two sentences in such cases traces to a difference in cognitive content between the names a and b. From this it would follow that so-called Millianism is false, i.e. that the cognitive content of a proper name is not always its bearer. I analysed this argument as relying on a plausible principle of compositionality for thoughts together with what I called 'Frege's Law':

If two sentences S and S' have the same cognitive content, then S contains a valuable extension of knowledge if and only if S' does.

Most adherents of Millianism would probably reject Frege's Law. I offered a different Millian reply. I objected that whereas Frege's Law is ultimately a special case of Leibniz's Law of the Indiscernibility of Identicals, and as such is unassailable, Frege's innocuous looking minor premise—that for some pair of co-referential proper names a and b, $\ulcorner a = b \urcorner$ contains a valuable extension of knowledge—is unsubstantiated and unsubstantiatable.

Suppose instead that Frege's notion of *Erkenntniswerte* corresponds more closely to logical content than to cognitive content. Then both Frege's Law (so-called) and the minor premise to which I objected become inessential to the argument. Frege may argue for the distinctness of the cognitive contents of $\ulcorner a = a \urcorner$ and $\ulcorner a = b \urcorner$ instead by noting that those two sentences are obviously inequivalent. Certainly it would be correct—and to Frege's purpose in the opening passages of 'Uber Sinn und Bedeutung'—to point out that pairs of sentences like

The point of intersection of lines a and b is the point of intersection of lines a and b

and

The point of intersection of lines a and b is the point of intersection of lines b and c

differ in logical content.[12] As Frege notes, the first is analytic, the second synthetic. It immediately follows that these two sentences differ in cognitive content, in the thoughts expressed. From this it would follow further—assuming that a definite description is a singular term whose *Bedeutung* is the individual uniquely described

something like a function, or rule, that determines the *Sinn* of a context-sensitive expression (like 'today') for any possible context of its use. I remain sceptical of Burge's argument for this interpretation, since Frege's remarks concerning the incompleteness of context-sensitive expressions, taken together with his doctrines concerning the distinction between function and object, seem to render this notion of meaning an idle wheel in Frege's philosophy of semantics. In any event, this notion of meaning, Fregean or not, is quite distinct from my notion of logical content.

[12] Notice that they probably do not differ in modal intension.

(if there is one)—that the cognitive content of a singular term is not its *Bedeutung*. Or at least, not always. One may then argue, by parity of form and function, that the cognitive content of a singular term is never its *Bedeutung* (unless by a certain sort of coincidence, as with the phrase 'the cognitive content of the definite description quoted parenthetically in the second-to-the-last sentence of §II of Nathan Salmon's "On Content"'). This argument calls for a different reply.

III

I have said that the criterial idea of logical content is that two expressions have the same logical content if they are logically equivalent, in a special but fairly standard sense. While this constrains the notion of logical content, it does not yet specify what the logical content of a sentence (or other expression) is. For those of us who share Frege's philosophical scruples pertaining to definitions, this is simply inadequate.[13]

Our question is this: Given that expressions have the same logical content if and only if their cognitive contents are logically equivalent, and given the further constraints that have been laid down on the relevant notion of logical equivalence, what exactly is the logical content of an expression? If laws like Murphy's Law and principles like Leibniz's Principle of the Identity of Indiscernibles are not propositions, then what exactly are they? It is not a trivial matter to provide objects, independently specifiable, to fill the role of logical contents. But the notion of logical content depends for its philosophical legitimacy on our doing just that.

Employing Frege's and Russell's idea in their implementation of logicism, one might take the logical content of a sentence to be the class of sentences logically equivalent to it. One variation on this theme would take the logical content of a sentence to be instead the class of propositions logically equivalent to the cognitive content of the given sentence. Other variations would take instead the class of sentences logically entailed by the given sentence, or the class of propositions logically entailed, in a propositional sense, by the given sentence's cognitive content. These proposals are not strictly circular, as long as the relevant notion of logical equivalence or logical consequence is definable independently of logical content. But there is an obvious sense in which these proposals put the cart before the horse. It is very much like identifying the meaning of an expression with the class of the expression's synonyms. Expressions are synonymous *in virtue of* the existence of an object that is their shared meaning, not *vice versa*.[14]

Indeed, the paradigm equivalence relations are those that are expressible in English by means of some phrase of the form ⌜VP the same NP⌝ ('expresses the same meaning as', 'is a sample of the same liquid as', 'is an animal of the same species as', etc.). Such phrases may be properly symbolized along the following lines:

$$(\text{the } z)[F(z) \wedge R(x, z)] = (\text{the } z)[F(z) \wedge R(y, z)].$$

---

[13] *Cf.* G. Frege, *Die Grundlagen der Arithmetik*, tr. Austin J.L., *The Foundations of Arithmetic* (Oxford: Basil Blackwell, 1959), §66.

[14] *Cf.* T. Williamson, *Identity and Discrimination* (Oxford: Basil Blackwell, 1990), pp. 81–82.

This literally asserts an identity between certain intermediate objects, *viz.* the *F*s to which the relata *x* and *y* are themselves suitably related by *R*.[15] In the case of synonymy, '*F*' symbolizes 'meaning' while '*R*' symbolizes 'expresses'. Just as synonymy is identity of expressed meaning, so logical equivalence, in the sense sought here, is identity of logical content. Expressions (more accurately, their cognitive contents) are logically equivalent in virtue of having the same logical content, not *vice versa*. Identification with equivalence classes may have a special justification in the case of numbers, but it sheds no illumination in the present instance.[16] It certainly provides no philosophical foundation for the notion of logical content.

A more promising approach is to look to the definition of logical equivalence in classical model theory for some entity that is shared by all and only those sentences logically equivalent to a given sentence. Equivalence may be defined in terms of validity of argument: A pair of sentences are equivalent if and only if the arguments that take one as premise and the other as conclusion are both valid. Validity of argument, in turn, is understood as the preservation of truth in passing from premise to conclusion, irrespective of the contributions to truth-value by the nonlogical components. Equivalent sentences thus emerge as those that share truth-value irrespective of the contributions to truth-value made by the nonlogical components. The relevant notion of contribution to truth-value is represented by a *model*. If models are to be called 'interpretations'—as they sometimes are—they are interpretations only in an austere sense. A model provides a semantics for the nonlogical lexicon, but only as much as is required (roughly) to determine mere truth-value for any sentence of the language, on the basis of the fixed semantics for the logical lexicon. Thus in the simplest sort of structure for an extensional object language, a model is an assignment both of a domain of individuals over which the individual variables range and of appropriate extensions to the nonlogical vocabulary for the language, keeping fixed the interpretations of the logical constants, like 'not' and 'some'.[17] Within the framework of model theory, to say that sentences of a given language are *logically equivalent* is to say that they have exactly the same models. The logical content of a sentence might thus be identified with the class of its models, i.e. the class of minimal 'interpretations' under which the sentence is true. If we wish

---

[15] A symbolization closer to the English phrase is given by:

$R(x, (\text{the } z)[F(z) \wedge R(y, z)])$.

Given the obvious premise, the two symbolizations are inter-derivable. That the symbolizations define an equivalence relation is also easily proved. For further discussion of the nature of such relations, and especially their involvement with intermediate entities (meanings, liquid substances, etc.), see *Reference and Essence*, pp. 116–148.

[16] If numerals are taken to be quantifiers, or second-order predicates—as Frege and Russell made plausible—then the Frege–Russell equivalence classes (or their characteristic functions, Frege's "concepts") would seem to be exactly the right entities for numerals to designate.

[17] Even in the nonextensional environment of standard modal logic, the models go minimalist, *qua* interpretations, by relativizing extensional semantic values like truth and reference to possible worlds. Such models provide intensions, but not yet cognitive contents, as the contributions to truth-value made by expressions lying within the scope of a modal operator. On the other hand, if there are such things as doxastic or epistemic logic, their models are pressed to provide full-blown propositions, or thoughts, as the cognitive contents of sentences that may appear within the scope of a doxastic or epistemic operator.

to extend this idea to expressions other than sentences, the logical content of an arbitrary well-formed expression E could be identified with the corresponding function that assigns to any model M, the extension (or other contribution to truth-value) of E in M. The logical content of a sentence S would thereby become a characteristic function that assigns a truth-value—either truth or falsehood—to any model M (*viz.* the truth-value of S in M).

This idea mirrors the idea of modal intension. And as we shall see, logical content and intension, though different, are intimately related. But the models differ from possible worlds in critical respects. We have already seen that there are pairs of sentences that are true with respect to exactly the same possible worlds while differing in their models. We have also seen sentences that share the same models (in the logic of indexicality) while differing in intension. The latter difference points up a feature of the class of a sentence's models that fails to capture the desired notion of logical content.

A further problem with the proposal is that it is confined to a single language. The central idea behind logical content is that a principle like Murphy's Law is not the proposition expressed by the sentence 'Whatever can go wrong will', but a coarser type of content shared by that formulation and any of its logical equivalents. This type of content is expressible in any number of different languages. The English and French sentences 'Either snow is white, or else snow is white and grass is green' and 'La neige est blanche' have the same logical content. We cannot say that they have the same models, however, without drastically modifying the classical notion of a model, which is a notion of an "interpretation" for a single language. Even if this problem can be avoided by considering "models" for two languages combined—interpretations respecting the interlanguage synonymies of French-*cum*-English, for instance—we could not say that 'Snow is white' has the same models as both its French and German translations without modifying the notion of a model even further to accommodate combinations of three languages, and so on (or by considering models for theories made up entirely of Carnapian 'meaning postulates' for combinations of languages and their consequences). The notion of *logical content* is such that nonsynonymous sentences of arbitrarily many distinct languages may nevertheless share the same logical content; they may contain the same principle, the same law, the same information.

At bottom, the problem with this approach is its focus on sentences and their components, rather than on their cognitive contents. As has already been said, the notion of logical content that we are seeking to clarify is that of a feature of propositions.

IV

Here again, Frege provides at least the beginnings of a possible solution. In the opening paragraph of 'Compound Thoughts' he makes the following observation:

> It is astonishing what language can do. With a few syllables it can express an incalculable number of thoughts, so that even if a thought has been expressed by an inhabitant of the

Earth for the very first time, a form of words can be found in which it will be understood by someone else to whom it is entirely new. This would not be possible if we could not distinguish parts in the thought corresponding to the parts of a sentence, so that the structure of the sentence can serve as a picture of the structure of the thought. (1984, p. 390)

If a proposition has essentially a sentence-like structure—with propositional constituents corresponding, at least roughly, to the grammatical components of the sentence for which it is the cognitive content—then propositions no less than sentences are subject to model-theoretic analysis. The central idea is to provide a kind of "semantics" for propositions, like the semantics that is more standardly provided for sentences, by treating the cognitive contents of expressions as the expressions themselves are treated in classical model theory.[18] In the simplest structure, a propositional model would consist of both a nonempty domain of individuals, to serve as the range of the variable-binding operators, and an assignment of extensions, based on the domain of the model, to logically simple propositional constituents that fill the role of cognitive content for nonlogical, unstructured first-order n-adic predicates and for nonlogical, unstructured n-adic functors, for any finite number n (including the limiting case of $n = 0$). If, for example, the cognitive content of a first-order dyadic predicate is assumed to be a binary relation between individuals, then the extension-assignment component of such a propositional model would assign an appropriate extension to every simple, nonlogical binary relation between individuals—not to every simple, nonlogical dyadic predicate like 'is to the left of', but to every relation that lacks any logical component, like the relation of being-to-the-left.[19] No separate assignment is made to logical compounds of attributes (e.g. being-to-the-left-of-if-larger-than). As a special case, no separate assignment would be made to the binary relation of (numerical) identity, since that relation is the cognitive content of a logical dyadic predicate, the 'is' of identity. Identity is a logical relation; its extension therefore remains fixed for all propositional models.

A first-order 0-adic predicate is a sentence. If there are corresponding nonlogical, propositions lacking the structure of an attribute-together-with-its-arguments (e.g., perhaps the proposition that it is raining), a propositional model of this simple type would assign a truth-value to any such proposition. A first-order 0-adic functor is an individual constant. If it is assumed that an unstructured individual constant may have a special sort of cognitive content, antecedently recognizable as being unlike the cognitive content of a definite description in its internal composition, then the extension-assignment component of a simple propositional model should also assign to every such cognitive content a single member of the model's domain as the cognitive content's extension in the model. The Millian theory that the cognitive content of a proper name is simply its bearer is the paradigm of the sort of theory on which entities that might serve as cognitive contents for individual constants (*viz*, the

---

[18] I illustrated this idea in *Frege's Puzzle*. The basic idea is described at p. 177n1. (See also the remarks on pp. 8–9.)

[19] The extension appropriate to a dyadic predicate, or to a binary relation, may be taken to be a set of ordered pairs of elements of the domain over which the variables range, or any variation thereof, e.g. a (possibly partial) function from ordered pairs to truth-values.

individuals themselves) thus play the same role in propositional models that primitive individual constants play in classical models. The orthodox Fregean theory that all individual constants invariably express a descriptional sense is the paradigm of the contrasting theory. Within the framework of orthodox Fregean theory, the extension of a singular-term sense in a propositional model is not imposed directly and independently by the model's extension-assignment, but as with any complex cognitive content, is determined indirectly and systematically by the extension in the model of the sense constituents. Likewise, the truth-value of any standard proposition in a model is determined in a systematic fashion by the extensions in the model of the proposition constituents, chiefly by the application of function to argument. (Compare how the truth-value of a structured sentence, or how the extension of a definite description, is fixed in classical model theory.) The general method of propositional models can be applied with respect to any theory of cognitive content (Fregean, Millian, etc.), as long as standard propositions are sufficiently sentence-like in structure to allow for the application of classical model-theoretic techniques.[20]

The method of propositional models yields distinct notions of logical validity for arguments consisting of propositions (rather than sentences) and hence also of validity for propositions taken individually and of logical equivalence between propositions. A propositional argument is valid, in this sense, if and only if its conclusion is true in every propositional model in which each of the premises is true. A proposition is valid if and only if it is the conclusion of a valid premise-free argument, i.e. if and only if it is true in every propositional model. Propositions are equivalent if and only if they are true in exactly the same propositional models.

This propositional notion of equivalence differs from the corresponding classical notion of equivalence among sentences, in exactly the ways discussed in §I. The propositions expressed by (1) and (2) are not equivalent, in the sense just defined, even though the sentences themselves are equivalent in (more or less) the classical sense. On the other hand, the proposition that Michael is a husband and the proposition that Michael is male and Michael is married are equivalent, in the relevant sense, even though the two sentences are not equivalent in a standard sense (in the absence of "meaning postulates").

This points the way to a response to the interpretation suggested in §II for the argument in the opening passages of '*Uber Sinn und Bedeutung.*' Although ⌜$a = a$⌝ and ⌜$a = b$⌝ are obviously inequivalent sentences when a and b are distinct terms, it begs the question against Millianism to assume that therefore the cognitive contents of those sentences are inequivalent thoughts. Millianism holds that the two sentences

---

[20] There is also the possibility of a compromise theory according to which at least some unstructured individual constants, although none of them are Millian terms, have cognitive contents that are significantly unlike the structured senses of definite descriptions—perhaps something like point individual concepts, not comprising the cognitive content of the definite-description operator together with an accompanying property, occurring as separately identifiable constituents. (These would be individual-concept analogues to simple, unstructured propositions.) Although such a theory seems in crucial respects more Fregean than Millian (some argue that Frege in fact held such a theory), the cognitive contents of individual constants are treated the same on such a theory as on the Millian theory.

share the same logical content, and indeed the same cognitive content, despite their sentential inequivalence, when the co-referential terms *a* and *b* are both proper names. On my own Millian view, both sentences are in that case analytic, or true as a consequence of meaning alone.[21]

On the other side of the coin, the notion of logical content may provide a solution to the closely related Paradox of Analysis. For it is arguable that philosophical analyses are unlike synonymy definitions precisely in that the former typically seek to provide an analysans that shares the same logical content, but not necessarily the same cognitive content (sense), as the analysandum.[22]

V

One may well wonder whether the logical contents we have been seeking can really be classes of propositional models, or functions from propositional models to extensions. The sense of artificiality has two principal sources. It stems partly from erroneously thinking of propositional models on the model of a linguistic interpretation, and partly from a genuine artificiality intrinsic to model-theoretic analysis. Standard models are contrived artifacts, set-theoretic constructs put forward to represent a logico-semantic idea in a mathematically tractable way—in much the same way that the logico-mathematical idea of a function is represented by means of a set of ordered pairs, or the way that an expression is represented by its Gödel number in the arithmetization of syntax. Model theory is the set-theoretization of semantics. If there is an intuitive idea that the model-theoretic definition of validity correctly captures, it is something like the following: Irrespective of what the variables range over, and irrespective of what contributions the simple nonlogical expressions make to truth-value, if the premise are true sentences, then so is the conclusion. This is a notion from what may be called the *Pure Theory of Validity*. The relevant notion of *irrespectiveness* is that of a modality—and indeed a logical modality (as opposed to, say, a metaphysical modality), but one relevant to Logic for Sentences. The class of all models represents meta-logical space, the totality comprising every *logically possible* range for the variables together with contributions to truth-value for the nonlogical lexicon.[23]

<hr>

[21] I argue for this in *Frege's Puzzle*, pp. 131–138, and, on different grounds, in N. Salmon, 'Relative and Absolute A Priority', *Philosophical Studies* (1992), p. 65.

[22] This seems to be true, for example, of the contextual-definition analysis that Russell gave for sentences involving definite descriptions. In various places he offered any of at least three different versions of his analysis of 'The φ is a ψ'; 'Some φ is a ψ, and every φ is the same'; 'There is at least one φ; there is at most one φ; and every φ is a ψ'; and 'There is something x such that something is a φ iff it is x and x is a ψ'. In 'On Denoting' he also preferred to eliminate the existential quantifier in terms of negation and universal quantification. These various versions of his analysis evidently differ in cognitive content—as Russell himself might have recognized—though, of course, they are always logically equivalent. For a penetrating discussion, see Anthony C. Anderson, 'Some Difficulties Concerning Russellian Intensional Logic'. *Noûs*, 4 (1986), pp. 35–43, at 40–42.

[23] I distinguish here between logic and metalogic. Logic proper asserts only such humdrum things as that if it is raining, then it is not the case that it is not raining. By contrast, the notion mathematically represented by the class of models is a metatheoretic notion from the Pure Theory

The propositional models we are considering are significantly different. They too are representational artifacts, but they are not *semantic* entities in the usual sense. They assign extensions not to bits of language, but directly to such entities as logically simple properties and logically simple relations, and perhaps to individuals and to logically simple propositions. Propositional models indirectly assign extensions also to logical compounds of attributes, etc., by means of the fixed extensions of the logical operations. The basic idea of propositional validity is something like the following: Irrespective of what objects there are, and irrespective of which of those objects have which logically simple non-logical properties or stand in which logically simple non-logical relations to one another, if the propositions contained in the premise are truths, then so is that contained in the conclusion. The relevant notion of irrespectiveness is a modality relevant to Logic for Propositions. The class of all propositional models represents the totality comprising every logically possible

of Validity, roughly that of the entire space of logically possible contributions to truth-value for the variables and the nonlogical lexicon. John Etchemendy, *The Concept of Logical Consequence* (Harvard: Harvard University Press, 1990) presents a sustained criticism of the classical model-theoretic definition of validity. In his central objection, Etchemendy argues by means of examples that the classical definition makes validity dependent on such factors as the minimum size of the universe, as determined by the axiom of infinity or the pair-set axiom of the theory from which the models are imported, and that such factors go beyond mere truths of logic. This objection (or some variant of it) may be warranted against an excessively unsubtle reading of the classical definition. The principal thrust of the critique, however, shows insufficient appreciation of certain facts: First, the invalidity of, for example, 'It is raining' is not a truth of logic proper, but one of metalogic. The mere fact that a proposed definition makes validity depend on matters that go beyond logic proper does not make that definition illegitimate, unless those matters also go beyond metalogic. More importantly, the classical definition of validity constitutes a model-theoretic reconstruction—a mathematical representation—of our intuitive concept. The representation itself, as opposed to the idea it represents, is not genuinely a matter of pure metalogic. This might be demonstrated, quite independently of such factors as the minimum size of the universe, by noting that the Pure Theory of Validity for English declares the sentence 'It is raining' invalid without strictly entailing the existence of any function (in the set-theoretic sense) that assigns falsehood to it. Models, and their extension assignments, are sets of sets of sets. The Pure Theory of Validity, by contrast, is not concerned with actual sets but with logically possible ranges for the variables together with contributions to truth-value for the nonlogical lexicon. The availability of a rich variety of models provides the basis of the suitability of the mathematical representation, in the same way that various facts of arithmetic provide the basis of the suitability of Gödel numbers as surrogates for expressions, though the things represented are strictly distinct from such matters. (Analogously, an excessively unsubtle reading of Tarski's celebrated definition of truth makes it seem as if the nontruth of 'Snow is green' depends on the irrelevant ontological question of whether there are set-theoretic sequences. The objection that the definition is therefore illegitimate is misplaced. Compare also the misguided criticism that Gödel's arithmetization of syntax is defective because it makes syntax dependent on arithmetic.) Far from being discredited by its reliance on set theory, the model-theoretic definition of validity can arguably be credited with having sharpened our grasp of the metalogical notion it represents, by revealing the nature of the relevant notion of truth preservation. Clearly, validity does not consist merely in the material conditional fact that the conclusion is true if the premise are true, since many invalid arguments share that feature. But neither is it the criterion of validity that this material conditional should be metaphysically necessary, nor even that it should be knowable *a priori*. Indeed, neither of these claims is correct about valid arguments in natural language, since the very meanings of the premise and conclusion are a contingent, *a posteriori* matter. The utility of the classical definition derives, in part, from its indicating that the point of validity is rather that truth is preserved irrespective of the contributions of the variables and the simple nonlogical components.

ontology together with a cosmology. Propositional models thus emerge as constructs that are more representational of possible worlds than of linguistic interpretations. Correspondingly, logical contents emerge as entities that are very much like intensions; the "genuine" logical content of an expression, if one insists, is something like a function from logically possible worlds to extensions (or to contributions to propositional truth-value). A sentence's propositional models may be regarded as representing the sentence's cognitive content's *logical truth conditions*: the maximal conditions which are logically possible and with respect to which the proposition is true. The crucial difference between logical contents and intensions is this: the former are limited not by the laws of metaphysics, but by the more permissive laws of logic. The worlds represented by propositional models include metaphysically impossible worlds, as long as they are *logically* possible.[24]

VI

The method of propositional models has sufficient flexibility to accommodate additional notions of content, notions even less discriminating than logical content but still more discriminating than intension. The solution to Kazmi's problem so far consists in taking Church's Theorem to be not a proposition, but the logical content of, e.g., the sentence 'First-order logic is undecidable'. But now a more resilient problem arises at the level of logical content. Mathematicians use the label 'Church's Theorem' freely in connection with differing formulations. Church's Theorem may be formulated as 'The set of deducible sentences of first-order logic is undecidable'. But it is also sometimes formulated as 'The set of valid sentences of first-order logic is undecidable'. Is Church's Theorem the logical content of the former, or is it instead the logical content of the latter? By Gödel's Completeness Theorem, the two are equivalent; so it would seem not to matter which one is selected as *Church's Theorem*. The two formulations, and anything logically equivalent to either, embody the same result. That result is what mathematicians often refer to using the phrase 'Church's Theorem'. Yet the two formulations differ in logical content as well as cognitive content; the propositions expressed are not logically equivalent. The Completeness Theorem inextricably links the two very different notions of first-order deducibility (derivability from the empty set of premise) and first-order validity. But the Completeness Theorem is a metatheorem; it is not itself a truth of logic.[25]

[24] In N. Salmon, 'The Logic of What Might Have Been', *Philosophical Review* (1989), 98, pp. 3–34, I discuss some of the various differences between these other types of worlds, as these differences bear on the question of what is the correct modal logic.

[25] Interestingly, in the original publication of his result, Church sharply distinguished between the two, pointing out that although the proof of the undecidability of the set of first-order theorems is constructive, the proof of Gödel's Completeness Theorem is nonconstructive, thus making the undecidability of the set of first-order valid sentences less certain. See the final two paragraphs of A. Church, 'A Note on the Entscheidungsproblem'. *Journal of Symbolic Logic* (1936), 1, 1 and 3. At the time of writing, Church might have regarded his theorem as a particular proposition concerning deducibility (or perhaps as a set of various propositions logically equivalent to that proposition), and not the alternative proposition concerning validity. Most mathematicians today would

Church's Theorem, if it is the common result embodied in both of the formulations above, cannot be the logical content of one and not the other. It must therefore be the logical content of neither. If Church's Theorem is a single result contained in both formulations, we should not say that it is a logical content at all. But neither is it a proposition; that, I have argued, is the proper lesson of Kazmi's problem. What kind of thing, then, is Church's Theorem, as the label is (at least sometimes) used by mathematicians?

While the Completeness Theorem that links the two formulations is not a truth of logic, it is a truth of something. It is a proven result from the restricted portion of the meta-theory for first-order logic that includes some proof theory (syntax) and some model theory (semantics), but nothing, for example, from recursive-function theory proper. Let us call this limited meta-theory 'M'. One thing the two formulations of Church's Theorem have in common is the set of propositional models that honour the truths of M and with respect to which the sentence in question is true. Either formulation will be false in some nonstandard propositional models for M—those which make extension assignments in such a way that the set assigned to the property of first-order theoremhood is among those in the set assigned to the property of decidability. But the two formulations will not differ in truth-value with respect to any propositional model for M, no matter how nonstandard. They are not logically equivalent—they differ in truth-value with respect to propositional models that do not respect the truths of M—but they are equivalent *within the framework of M*. We might say, therefore, that while the two formulations differ in logical content, they share the same M-content. That is to say, they have the same M-models; they are true in exactly the same logically possible M-worlds.

We may likewise say that various versions of the Axiom of Choice have the same ZF-content. For they are provably equivalent, once we are allowed to assume the axioms of Zermelo-Fraenkel set theory. If the setting is sufficiently liberal, one might even go so far as to identify the Axiom of Choice with the relevant class of ZF-models. This would be to equate Zorn's Lemma, for example, with the Axiom of Choice in a more thorough way than is customary, assuming the former is also identified with its ZF-content. There is similar variation in the phrase 'Church's Theorem', which is perhaps more often used in a restrictive sense on which the formulation in terms of validity is said to be not exactly Church's Theorem, but something equivalent to it by Gödel's Completeness Theorem. (See note 26 above.) I would suggest that this type of variation in usage typically reflects different kinds of content acting as denotations for labels like 'Choice' and 'Church's Theorem'. In short, such labels are often used ambiguously.

One difficulty with the various proposals made here arises from the fact that we use labels like 'Murphy's Law' in ascribing propositional attitudes, as if such labels referred to propositions. We say such things as 'Mary believes the Identity of Indiscernibles' and 'Michael doubts Church's Theorem'. It is unclear how best to accommodate this. Perhaps we should construe such remarks in accordance with a

---

probably not distinguish between the two on these grounds, and would instead regard either as the same mathematical result.

Principle of Charity, as meaning that Mary believes some proposition whose logical content is the Identity of Indiscernibles and that Michael doubts some proposition whose *M*-content is Church's Theorem. Alternatively, perhaps we should liberalize the philosopher's notion of belief and other so-called propositional attitudes. The things we are said to believe or to doubt, in common parlance, are a mixed bag. To be sure, we believe, or fail to believe, propositions; belief of propositions is doubtless the fundamental form of belief. But we are also said to believe, or not to believe, such things as signposts, omens, inscriptions, warning signs, sentences, other people, our own eyes. We are even sometimes said to believe, or not to believe, seemingly stranger things than these ('Michael could not believe the size of Mary's house'). In addition, we are said to believe, or not to believe, *in* a bewildering array of (alleged) phenomena and other things: magic, divine revelation, ghosts, demonic possession, miracles, destiny, heaven, America, love at first sight. Why not simply accept that logical contents—or more generally, theoretical contents—are also among the nonpropositional things we believe and fail to believe? It seems likely that all of these apparently nonpropositional forms of belief may be reducible in one way or another to belief of propositions.[26] If we harbour propositional attitudes toward the logical contents of propositions, that psychological fact may yield part of the explanation for the historical fact that propositions, or thoughts, are sometimes misidentified with their intensions.

[26] There might even be reason to hold that 'that'-clauses are also used ambiguously, serving as terms typically for propositions, but sometimes for their logical or other theoretical contents. In the absence of compelling evidence, however, this hypothesis should probably be resisted.

15

On Designating (2005)

I

One of the most important contributions to philosophy of the previous century was made when the century had barely begun. Few articles in philosophy have been studied as carefully as Russell's 'On Denoting,'[1] even if its insights have not always been sufficiently appreciated. And few passages have received as careful scrutiny as the famous sequence, eight paragraphs in all, in which Russell presents his argument involving 'the first line of Gray's *Elegy*' and 'the center of mass of the Solar System'. The argument presents objections to the semantic theory that ascribes to expressions a distinction between 'meaning,' i.e., semantic content (sense, John Stuart Mill's 'connotation,' Frege's *Sinn*), and 'denotation,' i.e., designation (semantic reference, Frege's *Bedeutung*). Russell's own emphasis demonstrates that the argument plays an important role in the article. Yet the presentation is garbled and confused, almost to the point of being altogether inscrutable and incomprehensible. Alonzo Church commented that Russell's objections in the passage in question 'are traceable merely to confusion between use and mention of expressions, of a sort that Frege was careful to avoid by the employment of quotation-marks. Russell applies quotation-marks to distinguish the sense of an expression from its denotation, but leaves himself without any notation for the expression itself; upon introduction of (say) a second kind of quotation-marks to signalize names of expressions, Russell's objections to Frege completely vanish.'[2] This has proved to be a challenge few can resist.

I present here a new, detailed interpretation of that paradigm of obscure philosophy and discuss specific issues raised by the argument. I believe that previous attempts to

I have had the essentials of the interpretation provided here since 1972, but many others have greatly influenced my thought on the topic, too many others to list here. No one influenced me more than David Kaplan. The Santa Barbarians Discussion Group patiently worked through my edited version of the crucial passage in 1997. I am indebted to them, especially C. Anthony Anderson, for their comments and our efforts. By not venturing to challenge the interpretation, the group shares at least some responsibility for the final product—how much responsibility depends upon the success or failure of the project. I am also especially grateful to Teresa Robertson and to the participants in my seminars at UCSB and UCLA during 1998–99 for their insightful comments, notably Roberta Ballarin, Stavroula Glezakos, David Kaplan, and D. Anthony Martin. Thanks to Matt Griffin for correcting an error.

[1] *Mind*, 14 (October 1995), pp. 479–493.

[2] In Church's review of Carnap's *Introduction to Semantics*, *The Philosophical Review*, 52 (1943), pp. 298–304, at 302.

decipher the difficult passage fail to capture important aspects of the principal thrust of the argument, as Russell intended it.[3] Commenting on one previous interpretation, David Kaplan (p. 143) said that 'the complete justification of any analysis of Russell's argument clearly awaits a fully annotated version of the two pages.' Yet after listing various interpretations for Russell's use of the phrase 'denoting complex', he added that 'all these (indeed all possible) views regarding the meaning of "denoting complex" are supported by the text' (p. 144). I do not claim that my interpretation is the correct one. The textual evidence is insufficient to warrant such a conclusion about any possible interpretation. The interpretation I provide is not merely supported by the text in Kaplan's weak sense; it is strongly suggested by the text. As is to be expected, there are areas of overlap between my interpretation and some previous efforts, but there remain significant differences, while other interpretations have little in common with mine. I will argue that Church's dismissive remarks have greater merit than subsequent interpreters have recognized, but I also hope to show that Church's assessment is fundamentally mistaken.

My objective is by no means purely, or even mostly, historical. My primary purpose, rather, is almost entirely philosophical and ahistorical. It is unimportant philosophically whether my interpretation is faithful to Russell's intent (though I aspire to make it largely so); what is important is whether the main elements of the argument I attribute to Russell succeed or fail, and why they do. I believe the

---

[3] Discussions subsequent to Church include the following, in chronological order: Ronald J. Butler, 'The Scaffolding of Russell's Theory of Descriptions,' *The Philosophical Review*, 63 (1954), pp. 350–364; John Searle, 'Russell's Objections to Frege's Theory of Sense and Reference,' *Analysis*, 18 (1958), pp. 137–143; Peter Geach, 'Russell on Meaning and Denotation,' *Analysis*, 19 (1959), pp. 69–72; Ronald Jager, 'Russell's Denoting Complex,' *Analysis*, 20 (1960), pp. 53–62; David Kaplan, reviews of Butler, Searle, Geach, Jager, and Garver, *Journal of Symbolic Logic*, 34, 1 (March 1969), pp. 142–145; A. J. Ayer, *Russell and Moore: The Analytic Heritage* (London: Macmillan, 1971), at pp. 30–32; Chrystine E. Cassin, 'Russell's Discussion of Meaning and Denotation: A Re-examination,' in E. D. Klemke, ed., *Essays on Bertrand Russell* (University of Illinois Press, 1971), pp. 256–272; Michael Dummett, *Frege: The Philosophy of Language* (London: Duckworth, 1973), at pp. 267–268; Herbert Hochberg, 'Russell's Attack on Frege's Theory of Meaning,' *Philosophica*, 18 (1976), pp. 9–34; Simon Blackburn and Alan Code, 'The Power of Russell's Criticism of Frege: "On Denoting" pp. 48–50,' *Analysis*, 38 (1978), pp. 65–77; Geach, 'Russell on Denoting,' *Analysis*, 38 (1978), pp. 204–205; Blackburn and Code, 'Reply to Geach,' *Analysis*, 38 (1978), pp. 206–207; A. Manser, 'Russell's Criticism of Frege,' *Philosophical Investigations*, 8 (1985), pp. 269–287; Peter Hylton, *Russell, Idealism and the Emergence of Analytic Philosophy* (Oxford University Press, 1990), at pp. 249–264; Pawel Turnau, 'Russell's Argument against Frege's Sense-Reference Distinction,' *Russell* (New Series), 2 (1991), pp 52–66; Michael Pakaluk, 'The Interpretation of Russell's "Gray's *Elegy*" Argument,' in A. D. Irvine and G. A. Wedeking, eds., *Russell and Analytic Philosophy* (Toronto: University of Toronto Press, 1993), pp. 37–65; Russell Wahl, 'Russell's Theory of Meaning and Denotation and "On Denoting",' *Journal of the History of Philosophy*, 31 (1993), pp. 71–94; Michael Kremer, 'The Argument of "On Denoting",' *The Philosophical Review*, 103, 2 (April 1994), pp. 249–297; Harold Noonan, 'The "Gray's *Elegy*" argument—and Others,' in R. Monk and A. Palmer, eds., *Bertrand Russell and the Origins of Analytic Philosophy* (Bristol, UK: Thoemmes, 1996), pp. 65–102; Gregory Landini, ' "On Denoting" Against Denoting,' *Russell* (New Series), 18, 1 (September 1998), pp. 43–80; William Demopoulos, 'On the Theory of Meaning of "On Denoting",' *Noûs*, 33 (September 1999), pp. 439–458; Gideon Makin, *The Metaphysics of Meaning* (London: Routledge, 2000), pp. 22–45, 206–222; James Levine, 'On the "Gray's *Elegy*" Argument and its Bearing on Frege's Theory of Sense,' *Philosophy and Phenomenological Research*, 69 (September 2004), pp. 251–295. (I make no attempt to address these discussions, though some comparisons will be made, especially in note 34 below.)

intended argument is significantly more germane and forceful—and therefore more pressing—to very contemporary philosophical concerns than has been appreciated. I shall present a sketch of what I believe to be the correct reply to the argument as here interpreted.

Here is the chestnut in a nutshell: The seemingly innocuous thesis that definite descriptions are singular terms is untenable. For the attempt to form a proposition directly about the content of a definite description (as by using an appropriate form of quotation) inevitably results in a proposition about the thing designated instead of the content expressed. I call this phenomenon *the Collapse*. In light of the Collapse, Russell argues, the thesis that definite descriptions are singular terms must accept that all propositions about a description's content are about that content indirectly, representing it by means of a higher-level descriptive concept. And this, according to Russell, renders our cognitive grip on definite descriptions mysterious and inexplicable.

'On Denoting' is concerned with the semantics—specifically with the designation, the semantic content, and the logical classification—of expressions of a certain grammatical category, what Russell calls the *denoting phrase*. This is a noun phrase beginning with what linguists call a *determiner*, like 'every', 'some', 'no', or 'the'. A *definite description* is a determiner phrase whose determiner is the definite article 'the', or alternatively a possessive adjective, like 'the author of *Waverley*' or 'my favorite son'. A definite description is said to be *proper* if there is something that uniquely answers to it, and is otherwise *improper*. (To say that something is *uniquely* such-and-such is to say that it and nothing else is such-and-such.) An *indefinite description* is a determiner phrase whose determiner is the indefinite article 'a' or 'an', or alternatively 'some'. Russell calls semantic content *meaning*. This has misled some readers, notably P. F. Strawson, who argues in opposition to Russell that an expression like 'the present queen of England' has the same 'meaning' in every context ('occasion') of use, and this meaning fixes whom or what the speaker 'refers to' in using the description, so that the designation may vary with the context.[4] In response, Russell correctly notes that this is utterly irrelevant.[5] It is perfectly consistent with Russell's views to posit a separate semantic value of a designating expression that determines for any given context whether the expression has a content, and if so what that content is.[6] In order to guard against confusing this semantic value with Russell's notion of 'meaning,' I shall consistently use the word 'content' for the latter.[7]

Russell's principal topic is the question: How do determiner phrases get at the objects of which we speak when we use those phrases? A *singular term* is an

---

[4] Strawson, 'On Referring,' *Mind*, 59, 235 (1950), pp. 320–344, §II.

[5] 'Mr. Strawson on Referring,' in Russell's *My Philosophical Development* (London: Allen & Unwin, 1959), pp. 238–245, at 238–240. In this article and also in 'On Denoting' Russell scores additional points against the Fregean theory that Strawson advocates, though I believe Russell does not gain a decisive victory over Frege-Strawson. *Cf.* my 'Nonexistence,' *Noûs*, 32, 3 (1998), pp. 277–319.

[6] *Cf.* Kaplan's notion of *character* as distinct from content, in his 'Demonstratives,' in J. Almog, J. Perry, and H. Wettstein, eds., *Themes from Kaplan* (Oxford University Press, 1989), pp. 481–563, at pp. 505–507.   [7] Fregeans may insert the word 'sense' wherever I use 'content'.

expression with the semantic function of designating a single individual or thing.[8] The very terminology that Russell uses for determiner, phrases raises an intriguing possibility: Are determiner phrases perhaps singular terms? In *The Principles of Mathematics*, Russell answered this question affirmatively. In 'On Denoting,' he is dissatisfied with his previous effort. Indeed, some determiner phrases are clearly not singular terms. Which single individual or thing would the 'no minor' in 'No minor will be admitted unless accompanied by an adult' designate?[9] Another class of determiner phrases, the indefinite descriptions, sometimes seem to function as singular terms, sometimes not ('*A colleague* has invited me to dinner' *vs.* 'No minor will be admitted unless accompanied by *an adult*'). Still other determiner phrases— the definite descriptions—appear always, or nearly always, to be singular terms.[10] So many theorists, including Frege and the author of *The Principles of Mathematics*, have taken them to be.

One of the central tenets of 'On Denoting' is that determiner phrases are never singular terms. According to the general Theory of Descriptions, presented in 'On Denoting,' a universal sentence like

Every author is a genius

is properly analyzed as:

$(x)(x$ writes $\supset x$ is ingenious$)$

or in plain English, *Everything is such that if it writes, then it is ingenious.* The analysans expresses about the conditional property (or 'propositional function') of *being ingenious if a writer* that it is universal. By Russell's lights, the original sentence therefore expresses a proposition that may be seen as consisting of two things: this conditional property and the second-order property of universality. The proposition predicates its second component of its first. There is nothing here—no unified entity—that can be identified as the distinct object contributed to the proposition by the phrase 'every author'. The first half of the phrase contributes one of the proposition components, and the other half only contributes toward part of the other proposition component. In Russell's words, the phrase itself 'has no meaning in isolation,' though the sentences in which it figures do have content. Nor therefore does the phrase 'every author' have the semantic function of designating. At best, it corresponds to an 'incomplete' quantificational construction: 'Everything is such that if it writes, then . . . it . . .'. Similarly, a sentence like

Some author is a genius

---

[8] The context-sensitivity of such terms as 'I' and 'you' does not disqualify them as singular terms. An expression may have the semantic function of designating a single individual even though the matter of which single individual it designates varies with context. Also, an expression may have the semantic function of designating a single individual without necessarily fulfilling its function. Hence, 'the present king of France' is not disqualified simply because France is no longer a monarchy (and would not have been disqualified even if France had never been a monarchy).

[9] Russell's theory of determiner phrases in *The Principles of Mathematics* omits the determiner 'no'. The omission is rectified in 'On Denoting.' This suggests that its earlier omission was an oversight.

[10] One possible exception would be such definite descriptions as 'the typical woman', which may be a paraphrase for something like 'most women', which is a determiner phrase that, like 'no minor', is clearly not a singular term. There are other exceptions.

is properly analyzed as:

$(\exists x)(x$ writes $\wedge$ x is ingenious$)$

or *Something both writes and is ingenious*. The indefinite description 'some author' is also relegated to the status of an incomplete symbol for which there is no corresponding proposition component—no 'meaning in isolation'—and consequently, no designation. That it does not designate any particular author said to be a genius is confirmed by the fact that, semantically, the English sentence is true as long as some author or other is a genius—any one will do (even if the particular author that the speaker means is not one). A sentence like 'No author is a genius' may be analyzed either as the denial of the proposition just analyzed, or equivalently as a universal proposition, *Everything is such that if it writes, then it is not ingenious*. Either way, the determiner phrase 'no author' is seen to lack the status of a singular term.

The special Theory of Descriptions concerns definite descriptions. On this theory, a sentence like

(1) The author of *Waverley* is a genius

is properly analyzed as follows:

(2) $(\exists x)[(y)(y$ wrote *Waverley* $\equiv x = y)$ $\wedge x$ is ingenious$]$

or *Something both uniquely wrote Waverley and is ingenious*. By Russell's lights, sentence (1) expresses a proposition consisting of the conjunctive property of *both uniquely having written Waverley and being ingenious* and the second-order property of *being instantiated*, i.e., *being a property of something or other*. There is nothing in this proposition that can be identified as the object contributed by the phrase 'the author of *Waverley*', any more than there is a component contributed by the phrase 'every author' to the proposition that everything is ingenious-if-a-writer. Even a definite description, therefore, does not have the semantic function of designating a single individual. In fact, on Russell's analysis the definite description 'the author of *Waverley*' is completely replaceable, with no change in the proposition expressed, by an indefinite description: 'a unique author of *Waverley*'.

Although the description 'the author of *Waverley*' is analyzed in such a way that it is not a singular term, the proposition that some unique author of *Waverley* is a genius may still be said to be *about* the author of *Waverley*—to wit, Sir Walter Scott. Since Scott is not actually designated, the proposition is 'about' him only in an extremely tenuated sense. The proposition is straightforwardly about the conjunctive property of *both uniquely having written Waverley and being ingenious*, and it is only through the sub-property of *uniquely having written Waverley* that the proposition 'gets at' the author himself, *qua* unspecified property instantiator. Though the definite description is not a singular term, there is an obvious sense in which it *simulates* designating Scott. Like a name for Scott, it is completely interchangeable with any genuine singular term designating Scott, with no effect on grammar and for the most part with no effect on truth-value—but for contexts like those of propositional attitude in which not mere designation, but the content itself, is at issue. For that matter, the indefinite paraphrase 'a unique author of *Waverley*' also simulates designating Scott. In presenting the Theory of Descriptions, Russell coins (or usurps) a cover term for the disjunction of designation with its simulation. He calls either *denoting*. He should have called the latter *pseudo-denoting*. I believe Russell saw this kind of simulated designation as the chief virtue of his Theory of Descriptions. For him, the simulation of designation of individuals through the genuine designation of properties, and the resulting attenuated *aboutness* of propositions, is the epistemological conduit by which we gain cognitive access to the world beyond the narrow confines of our 'direct acquaintance.' Though we cannot actually designate those things with which we are not immediately acquainted, sometimes, often in fact, we can 'get at' them by describing them as *a such-and-such* or as *the so-and-so*, pseudo-designating them by these descriptions, knowing them the only way we can: 'by description.' The propositions we know are directly about properties that we know to be instantiated, not the instantiators themselves.

II

The 'Gray's *Elegy*' argument must be viewed against this background to be properly grasped. My interpretation of the argument differs from previous attempts in the fundamental issue of exactly what theory is Russell's primary target. Previous commentators have disagreed concerning whether Russell is arguing against Frege's theory of *Sinn* and *Bedeutung* (as Church, Searle, and Blackburn and Code contend), or instead against the particular theory of designating developed in Russell's own *Principles* of a short time before 'On Denoting' (Geach, Cassin, Hylton, Pakaluk, Kremer, Noonan, Landini, Levine, Makin). Some interpreters have maintained that Russell criticizes an arcane and baroque theory that few have held (Jager, Pakaluk). Some reconstruct Russell's argument in such a way that he primarily attacks a straw-man theory that no one actually held (Butler, Searle). I believe Russell's target is not exactly any of these.

In one sense, each of the hypotheses that Russell's intended target was Frege's theory, or instead that of Russell's earlier self, is too broad. The main issue over which these theories differ concerns propositions of a certain stripe. If a proposition p is genuinely *about* an object x, in the sense that x is actually designated (and not merely in the way that (2) gets at Scott), then the proposition is about x (roughly speaking) in virtue of some proposition component. A *singular proposition* is a proposition that is about one of its own components by virtue of containing it. If p is a singular proposition about an object or individual x, then the component in virtue of which p is about x is simply x itself and the proposition is about x by containing x directly as a constituent. By contrast, if p is a general proposition about x, then the component in virtue of which p is about x is some sort of conceptual representation of x, like the content of a definite description to which x uniquely answers, and the proposition is thereby about x only indirectly. I shall say of the component of a proposition p in virtue of which the proposition is about x (whether directly or indirectly) that it *represents* x in p. A singular proposition about x, then, is a proposition in which x occurs as a self-representing component. The 'Gray's *Elegy*' argument proceeds by considering the prospect of certain singular propositions. The theory of the earlier Russell accepted singular propositions. Frege did not. Yet the 'Gray's *Elegy*' argument is not applied specifically against the earlier Russell's acceptance of singular propositions. Russell still accepts them in 'On Denoting,' and thereafter. Nor is it applied specifically against Frege's broad prohibition on singular propositions. (Whereas the 'Gray's *Elegy*' argument assumes the existence of singular propositions, it does not require the reader to accept them.) When explicitly criticizing Frege (and also when criticizing Alexius Meinong), Russell focuses on the truth-conditions of sentences containing improper definite descriptions, arguing that Frege gets the actual truth-values wrong. The 'Gray's *Elegy*' argument, is not concerned with such matters.

In a more significant sense the hypothesis that the 'Gray's *Elegy*' argument targets Frege's theory, and the rival hypothesis that it targets Russell's earlier theory, and even the conjunction of the two hypotheses, are too narrow in scope. Russell's target is instead a much broader and more basic account of one kind of expression: the definite description. The 'Gray's *Elegy*' argument explicitly targets the theory that a definite description has a semantic content, a 'meaning,' and that this content determines the description's designatum. The argument is not concerned more generally with theories that ascribe a content/designation distinction to other types of expressions, e.g., proper names or sentences. But even the tightly restricted theory that definite descriptions in particular have a content/designation distinction (whether or not proper names, pronouns, demonstratives, etc. do as well) is only the tip of an iceberg. It is a virtual corollary of a more basic theory that Russell wants to displace.

Russell's ultimate aim in 'On Denoting' is to supplant the view that a definite description is a singular term. This view is by no means peculiar to Frege or the earlier Russell. It was also held, for example, by John Stuart Mill and Meinong. And it remains commonplace among language scholars today. It seems obvious that the phrase 'the author of *Waverley*' designates a single individual, *viz.*, whoever it is who wrote *Waverley*. The burden of 'On Denoting' is to depose this very basic, and seemingly innocuous, account of definite descriptions. (Since 'On Denoting,' this account is no longer uncontroversial. Still, I myself am strongly inclined to accept the view—with respect to English at any rate.)

It is one thing to persuade an audience that the determiner phrases 'every author' and 'no author' are not singular terms, and quite another to argue convincingly that even the indefinite description 'an author' is not a singular term. Assuming one can overcome that hurdle, there is a still higher order of difficulty involved in arguing that even the definite description 'the author of *Waverley*' is not a singular term. Russell is aware of the almost irresistible force of the view he opposes, and of the magnitude of the daunting task before him. His logistical strategy is typically bold, and intimidating. He first presents his alternative account, the Theory of Descriptions, admitting that 'This may seem a somewhat incredible interpretation; but I am not at present giving reasons, I am merely *stating* the theory.' Only then does he present objections to the rival accounts of Meinong and Frege (as he interprets them). Russell explicitly labels these objections as evidence favoring his own theory. (In fact, he labels them as *the* evidence favoring his theory, although in the third paragraph of the article he says that the material following his discussion of Meinong and Frege—which includes the 'Gray's *Elegy*' argument—gives the grounds in favor of his theory.) Russell also explicitly characterizes both Frege's theory and his own earlier theory as versions of precisely the sort of theory that, before long, he will attack in the 'Gray's *Elegy*' argument. Thereupon follows a list of puzzles against which he proposes to test any theory of designating that might be proposed, including the Theory of Descriptions. Before showing how his theory solves the puzzles, however, he pauses to present the 'Gray's *Elegy*' argument. Afterward, he shows how the Theory of Descriptions solves the puzzles. He closes by challenging the reader to come up with a simpler theory of designating before daring to reject this one of Russell's invention.

If the best defense is a good offense, then the optimality of Russell's defense is questionable. Not the audacity. The very placement of the 'Gray's *Elegy*' argument, however, raises a question about Russell's overall strategy. If the argument were targeting the theory of Frege, or that of his earlier self, or even both of these, its coming after the presentation of the test puzzles rather than before would constitute a careless lapse in an otherwise impressively brave and aggressive campaign. I submit that Russell places the argument where he does because the puzzles he has just listed presuppose a much broader theory—the theory that definite descriptions are singular terms—and the same puzzles appear to be (indeed, in some sense, they *are*) solvable on that theory, simply by drawing the distinction between content and designation as a corollary.

It is exactly this basic, and seemingly innocuous, account—nothing less—that I believe Russell is ultimately attempting to refute in his 'Gray's *Elegy*' argument. Rather than apply the puzzle-test to the theory (which if fairly applied, would result in a clear pass), Russell aims to refute the theory once and for all. This preempts any solution to the puzzles that is predicated on the puzzles' own assumption that definite descriptions are singular terms. With that assumption out of the way, he proceeds to show how the Theory of Descriptions—itself immune from the kinds of problems developed in the 'Gray's *Elegy*' argument—fares under the proposed test. He thus intends to overthrow by his argument *both* Frege and his former self. But not only these two. Far from attacking a straw man, the 'Gray's *Elegy*' argument effectively aims to debunk Mill, Frege, Meinong, and every other philosopher of language to have come down the pike—including the author of *The Principles of Mathematics*. The 'Gray's *Elegy*' argument is both crucial and central to Russell's overall project and strategy in 'On Denoting.' This is reason enough to attempt to unravel its mysteries.

Russell characterizes his target in the 'Gray's *Elegy*' argument as the theory that attributes content, as distinct from designation, to determiner phrases. This characterization is misleading on two counts. First, the argument concerns only definite descriptions (although a similar objection may be made with at least equal force with respect to indefinite descriptions). Second, the argument does not really target the proposition that definite descriptions have a content/designation distinction. To illustrate: It has been suggested that, contrary to Russell's pronouncement, his proposed analysis together with his higher-order logic provide a 'meaning in isolation,' overlooked by Russell, for definite descriptions.[11] For the proposition Russell offers in analyzing (1) may be recast as the proposition that *being ingenious* is a property of someone or other who uniquely wrote *Waverley*. The description 'the author of *Waverley*' contributes to this proposition the second-order property of *being a property of a unique author of Waverley*, making the proposition indirectly about Scott. Thus, it is argued, on Russell's analysis, even though the description does not designate Scott, it has a content after all, since it designates the second-order property of *being a property of a unique author of Waverley*, which is predicated of *being ingenious*.

The suggestion is, in effect, that Russell analyzes definite descriptions as restricted existential quantifiers. There are differences between this view and the Theory of Descriptions. The propositions attached to the sentence by the two theories, though equivalent, are not the same. Arguably, the recast proposition is directly about the property of *being ingenious*, not the property of *uniquely having written Waverley*, and hence the proposition is not about Scott in exactly the same way that (2) is. For these reasons, it is possible that Russell would have none of it. Although the theory that definite descriptions are restricted existential quantifiers is not exactly the theory Russell proffers, it *is* a very close approximation to it. Close enough, in fact, that it is clearly *not* the sort of theory under attack in the 'Gray's *Elegy*' argument. As far as that argument is concerned, determiner phrases might as well be restricted existential quantifiers. Yet the theory that they are is a theory according to which definite descriptions have both a content and a designation. What saves the theory from the fangs of the 'Gray's *Elegy*' argument is the denial that the description 'the author of *Waverley*' designates the author of *Waverley*. On the theory, the description may be reinterpreted as what Russell would later call a *logically proper name* (or a *genuine name in the strict, logical sense*) for the second-order property of *being a property of a unique author of Waverley*. That is, its content is simply what it designates. Alternatively, it may be interpreted as (non-rigidly) designating the corresponding class of Scott's properties—with the added feature that the description then has a full-fledged content/designation distinction. Still it is not breakfast for; the 'Gray's *Elegy*' argument.[12]

Why, then, does Russell characterize his target in the 'Gray's *Elegy*' argument as the theory that ascribes a content/designation distinction to definite descriptions? Because he takes it for granted (as against the theory that definite descriptions are restricted existential quantifiers) that if a definite description designates at all, it designates the individual or thing that uniquely answers to it. He also takes it for granted that a definite description, even when proper, is not a logically proper name, i.e., it does not merely contribute the thing that uniquely answers to it to the propositions expressed with its help. Even one as Millian about singular terms as

---

[11] David Kaplan, 'Opacity,' in L. E. Hahn and P. A. Schilpp, eds., *The Philosophy of W. V. Quine* (La Salle, Ill.: Open Court, 1986), pp. 229–289, at 268.

[12] By contrast, suppose it were judged—perversely—that the description designates Scott, by virtue of expressing the second-order property of *being a property of a unique author of Waverley* and by virtue of Scott's literary activities. This theory (which is not theory that definite descriptions are restricted existential quantifiers) *does* fall under the jurisdiction of the 'Gray's *Elegy*' argument.

Mill recognized that though there may be a single thing uniquely answering to both of a pair of descriptions—for example, 'the inventor of bifocals' and 'the author of *Poor Richard's Almanac*'—the descriptions themselves need not be synonymous. For though it is true, it is no *analytic* truth that if exactly one person invented bifocals, and exactly one person wrote *Poor Richard's Almanac*, then the inventor in question and the author in question are one and the same. Given these assumptions, the theory that there is a content/designation distinction for definite descriptions in particular (whether or not other there is such a distinction also for proper names, pronouns, demonstratives, etc.) is tantamount simply to the theory that definite descriptions are singular terms. Not only Frege, his followers (like Church and Searle), Meinong, and the earlier Russell, but even Mill and many of us who are numbered among Mill's heirs embrace this general account of definite descriptions, which Russell now sets out to refute.

There is a more graphic way to get at the particular theory that the 'Gray's *Elegy*' argument aims to disprove. There is an alternative kind of theory that may be seen as denying the equivalence between the theory that definite descriptions are singular terms and the theory that they have a content/designation distinction. Keith Donnellan argues that what he calls the *referential* use demonstrates how a definite description might be a logically proper name, and might even designate something other than the thing that uniquely answers to it.[13] It is safe to say that Russell would not have accepted this as a plausible contender regarding the semantics of definite descriptions. Indeed, Donnellan's original objection to Russell was precisely that he failed to acknowledge the possibility of a definite description as a singular term with no content/designation distinction. Saul Kripke has defended Russell against Donnellan's arguments by considering a variety of hypothetical languages that are exactly like English except that Russell's theory, and certain variations of it, are stipulated to be true of them.[14] Though Kripke does not explicitly address the issue, ironically two of his hypothetical languages pave the way for a strikingly similar argument *against* the Theory of Descriptions. Kripke writes:

> By 'the weak Russell language', I will mean a language similar to English except that the truth conditions of sentences with definite descriptions are *stipulated* to coincide with Russell's: for example, 'The present king of France is bald' is to be true iff exactly one person is king of France, and that person is bald. On the weak Russell language, this effect can be achieved by assigning semantic reference to definite descriptions: the semantic referent of a definite description is the unique object that satisfies the description, if any; otherwise there is no semantic referent. A sentence of the simple subject–predicate form will be true if the predicate is true of the (semantic) referent of the subject; false, if either the subject has no semantic referent or the predicate is not true of the semantic referent of the subject.
>
> Since the weak Russell language takes definite descriptions to be primitive designators, it is not fully Russellian. By 'the intermediate Russell language', I mean a language in which sentences containing definite descriptions are taken to be abbreviations or paraphrases of their Russellian analyses: for example, 'The present king of France is bald' *means* (or has a

---

[13] 'Reference and Definite Descriptions,' *The Philosophical Review*, 75, 3 (1966), pp. 281–304.
[14] Kripke, 'Speaker's Reference and Semantic Reference,' in P. French, T. Uehling, and H. Wettstein, eds., *Contemporary Perspectives in the Philosophy of Language* (University of Minnesota Press, 1979), pp. 6–27.

'deep structure' like) 'Exactly one person is at present king of France, and he is bald,' or the like. Descriptions are not terms, and are not assigned reference or meaning in isolation. (p. 16)

This yields two competing hypotheses concerning English, as it is actually spoken: that it *is* Kripke's weak Russell language—or WRL, as I shall call it—and that it is Kripke's intermediate Russell language, IRL. As Kripke notes, the phrase 'weak Russell language' is technically a misnomer for WRL. In proffering the Theory of Descriptions, Russell maintains that WRL ≠ IRL, that English is IRL rather than WRL, and that English merely duplicates the truth-conditions of WRL without duplicating its entire semantics. Yet WRL itself seems, at least at first blush, to be a perfectly possible language. The mere possibility of WRL forcefully raises a particular difficulty for Russell's IRL hypothesis. How is one to decide between the two hypotheses? More specifically, what evidence can Russell provide to support the hypothesis that English is IRL rather than WRL? Other things being equal, that English = WRL is probably the more intuitively natural hypothesis. Russell needs to produce some data or other evidence favoring the IRL hypothesis. Yet he can find no difference in truth-conditions between English sentences and sentences of WRL. The problem he faces does not concern truth-conditions; it concerns *propositional structure*. Moreover, it is difficult to imagine any pragmatic phenomenon that Russell might cite about English that would not also arise, and in exactly the same way, in a hypothetical community of WRL speakers. Lacking such support, the hypothesis that English = IRL is no more compelling than the rival hypothesis that English = WRL. On the contrary, the widespread linguistic intuition that definite descriptions are contentful singular terms provides some measure of support for the latter. *Ceteris paribus*, that English = WRL is probably the preferred hypothesis.

As I interpret it, the 'Gray's *Elegy*' argument is meant to provide exactly what Russell needs to solve this problem. Faced with the challenge posed here, I believe Russell would point to the very phenomena that he cites in the 'Gray's *Elegy*' argument to show that English cannot be WRL, perhaps even that WRL is not a possible language that might be spoken and understood by human beings (or relevantly similar creatures).

In short, for Russell it is clear from the outset, and not subject to dispute (at least as far as 'On Denoting' is concerned), that if a definite description designates anything, it designates the thing that uniquely answers to it. It is equally clear for Russell that a definite description is not a logically proper name. Given this, the theory that definite descriptions are singular terms (as nearly all language theorists have taken them to be) is tantamount to the following:

ST: A definite description designates by virtue of the description's semantic content, which fixes the designatum of the description to be (if anything) the individual or thing that uniquely answers to the description; further, when the definite description occurs in a sentence, the description's content represents the description's designatum in the proposition expressed.

The hypothesis that English = WRL is a version of *ST*. The 'Gray's *Elegy*' argument, as I interpret it, is meant to refute this theory, and with it the WRL hypothesis.

III

What is the alleged fatal flaw in the theory *ST*? On my interpretation, Russell may be seen as arguing in eight separate stages (at least), as follows: At stage (*I*) he argues that there is some awkwardness in so much as stating the very theory *ST* in question. At stage (*II*) he argues that once a way of stating *ST* is found, the theory, so stated, gives rise to a peculiar phenomenon: The attempt to form a singular proposition about the content of a definite description inevitably results instead in a general proposition about the individual designated by the description. This is the Collapse. At stage (*III*) the Collapse leads to a preferable formulation of *ST*. At stage (*IV*) Russell shows that the Collapse remains a feature of the reformulated theory. At stage (*V*) Russell argues that the Collapse commits *ST* to a very sweeping conclusion: that no singular term designating the content of a definite description can be what Russell will later call a *logically proper name*; instead any such term must be itself a definite description, or function as one. As Russell puts it, on our theory *ST*, 'the meaning cannot be got at except by means of denoting phrases.' At stage (*VI*) he argues furthermore that the content of a definite description cannot be a constituent of the content of any definite description of it. Russell proceeds to complain at stage (*VII*) that the results of the preceding two stages are philosophically intolerable. At stage (*VIII*) he provides a complementary argument for the conclusion that *ST* ignores that which, by its own lights, is philosophically most significant about propositions.

The stages of the argument do not parallel the paragraph breaks. Following Blackburn and Code, the eight paragraphs of 'On Denoting' beginning with the words 'The relation of meaning to denotation involves certain rather curious difficulties' will be labelled '(*A*)' through '(*H*)', respectively, ending with 'Thus the point of view in question must be abandoned'. Paragraph (*A*) is entirely preliminary. The eight stages then occur in sequence. Stage (*I*) by itself takes up all of paragraphs (*B*)-(*D*), ending with the words 'Thus we have failed to get what we wanted'. Stage (*II*) occurs in an initial fragment of paragraph (*E*), beginning with the words 'The difficulty in speaking of the meaning of a denoting complex may be stated thus'. These infamous words are following by a brief presentation of the Collapse. Stage (*III*) occupies the rest of (*E*). The development of the Collapse for stage (*IV*) occurs in (*F*), which progresses through stage (*VI*). Stage (*VII*) takes up only an initial fragment of (*G*). The rest of (*G*) and all of (*H*) are devoted to stage (*VIII*). (See the appendix to this essay for an annotated translation of the full eight paragraphs with the eight stages indicated.)

Given the space that Russell devoted to both the initial stage (*I*) and the final stage (*VIII*), one must assume that he placed great weight on them. This is unfortunate, since both of these stages are completely unpersuasive. They are also completely unnecessary, given the reasoning in the intervening stages. Although the reasoning through stages (*IV*)–(*VII*) takes up only (*F*) and part of (*G*), it forms the heart of the 'Gray's *Elegy*' argument. The alleged flaw in *ST* is exposed early on at stage (*II*), but even by stage (*VI*) at the end of (*F*) it is presented only as a feature that the theory cannot avoid and not yet as a defect. And indeed, the feature in question is one to which some theorists in Russell's cross-hairs—Frege and many of his followers—explicitly subscribe, though others, like Mill, the earlier Russell, myself, and even some Fregeans like Rudolf Carnap and Michael Dummett, do not do so. Previous commentators have tended to see the reasoning within (E) and (F), by itself, as already presenting an objection. By contrast, on my interpretation, the alleged philosophical problem with the feature derived in (F)—the claim that it is a defect—is not argued until the first part of (G). I believe Russell makes his case in the latter part of (F) and the first part of (G) more persuasively than has been recognized, though less persuasively than he might have.

Unlike previous interpreters of the 'Gray's *Elegy*' argument, I shall rewrite the entire passage, annotating as I go and using an alternative terminology less liable to ambiguity and other difficulties. I do this in the belief that any interpretation that might be proposed, if it is to carry conviction, must be accompanied by plausible interpretations for each individual sentence, which, taken collectively, support the proposed interpretation of the entire passage. Moreover if these interpretations, taken individually, do not make sense of the transition between successive sentences, some plausible explanation (e.g., confusion of use and mention) must be provided. Russell introduces a special terminology for the theory that definite descriptions are singular terms as depicted by *ST*. A definite description of a given language is said to *mean*—in a more standard terminology, it expresses—a *denoting complex c* as its *meaning*, i.e., its sense or semantic content. The denoting complex, *c*, in turn, *denotes*—in Church's terminology, it is a concept of—an object as its *denotation*. Russell does not use any special term for the binary relation between a definite description and the object of which the expression's content in the language is a concept. Instead Russell speaks of 'the denotation of the meaning,' saying that a definite description α 'has a meaning which denotes' an object x. Sometimes he says that α itself (as opposed to its content) denotes x. In deconstructing and reconstructing Russell's argument, I shall translate 'meaning' as 'content'. I shall also avoid Russell's term 'denote'. Instead I shall use 'determine' for the relation between a complex c and the object x of which c is a concept, and I shall call x the 'determinatum' of c. I shall use 'designate' for the relation between the expression α and x (i.e., for Kripke's semantic reference, or Frege's *Bedeutung*, the relative product of expressing and determining), and I shall call x the 'designatum' of α.

Before presenting my analytical translation of the passage, a word about variables and quotation: *Caution.* Russell uses the upper case letter 'C' as a variable ranging over determining complexes, though he sometimes uses 'C' instead as a meta-linguistic variable ranging over determiner phrases. Though it is seldom recognized, Russell sometimes (frequently, one fears) uses 'C' instead—more accurately, he uses it *as well*—as a schematic letter (equivalently, as a substitutional variable). Any sentence, or string of sentences, in which 'C' occurs in this manner is strictly speaking a *schema*, of which Russell means to assert every instance. Worse, the schematic letter sometimes apparently stands in for an arbitrary definite description, sometimes apparently for a term designating an arbitrary determining complex. This multiply ambiguous usage of technical notation makes some use-mention confusion virtually inevitable. Interpretations that do not depict Russell as confused (some do not) fail to acknowledge an essential feature of the situation—or else themselves commit the same confusion. On the other hand, it would be to the serious detriment of philosophy that we discount the argument as therefore utterly hopeless—witness certain points made in Russell's argument that have had to be rediscovered independently in more recent years. Fortunately, with a little finesse, Russell's purely philosophical import can be conveyed while minimizing use-mention confusion by replacing some occurrences of '*C*' with a variable (objectual) ranging over definite descriptions, and other occurrences with a variable ranging over determining complexes, and still other occurrences with a schematic letter standing in for an arbitrary definite description—though doing so may not preserve the textual *gestalt*, in its full historical context. I shall use 'α' as a metalinguistic variable, and upper case '*D*' as a schematic letter standing in for an arbitrary definite description. I shall use lower-case '*c*' as a determining-complex variable. I shall use Quine's quasi-quotation marks, '$\ulcorner$' and '$\urcorner$' in combination with 'α'. In quasi-quotation, all internal expressions are quoted (i.e., mentioned) except for metalinguistic variables, whose values are mentioned. Russell suggests using standard quotation marks ("inverted commas") as indirect-quotation marks, which quote not expressions but their content, but he does not consistently use them that way. I shall use single quotation marks for direct (expression) quotation. Following Kaplan, I shall use superscripted occurrences of '*m*' as indirect-quotation marks, and superscripted occurrences of '*M*' as indirect-quasi-quotation marks.[15] In indirect-quasi-quotation, the contents of all internal expressions are mentioned, except for determining-complex variables, whose values are mentioned. Here I avoid double quotation marks, except when quoting Russell's use of them or as scare-quotes when using another's words.

Paragraph (*A*) is straightforward, announcing that the relation of content to designatum involves 'rather curious difficulties,' which we will now examine. Paragraph (*B*) initiates stage (*I*) of Russell's attack It reads:

(*B*) When we wish to speak about the *meaning* of a denoting phrase, as, opposed to its *denotation*, the natural mode of doing so is by inverted commas. Thus we say:
  The centre of mass of the Solar System is a point, not a denoting complex;
  "The centre of mass of the Solar System" is a denoting complex, not a point.
Or again,
  The first line of Gray's *Elegy* states a proposition.
  "The first line of Gray's *Elegy*" does not state a proposition.
Thus taking any denoting phrase, say *C*, we wish to consider the relation between *C* and "*C*," where the difference of the two is of the kind exemplified in the above two instances.

The importance of this paragraph is frequently overlooked. In it Russell introduces a use of inverted commas as indirect-quotation marks, a use he thinks is natural on the theory *ST*. Not being a subscriber himself, Russell is not abandoning the alternative use of inverted commas as direct quotation. (Indeed, just three paragraphs after the 'Gray's *Elegy*' argument he affirms his allegiance to the direct-quotation use.) From this point to the end of the argument, standard quotation marks might be used either

---

[15] Kaplan, 'Quantifying In,' in L. Linsky, ed., *Reference and Modality* (Oxford University Press, 1971), pp. 112–144, at 120–121. (Kaplan there calls indirect-quotation marks *meaning-quotation marks*.) The reader who is unfamiliar with these devices is advised to look them up.

way—or indeed as quasi-quotation marks, or even indirect-quasi-quotation marks. Worse yet, Russell may omit quotation marks where they are needed, especially where both types of quotation ought to occur together. And in one instance, he seems to include quotation marks where they do not belong. Using my safer notation, we distinguish three things: the center of mass of the Solar System, which is a point; 'the center of mass of the Solar System', which is a determiner phrase; and ^{m}'the center of mass of the Solar System'^{m}, which is a determining complex, the content expressed in English by 'the center of mass of the Solar System'.

The proper interpretation of the last sentence of (*B*) is unclear. Do we wish to consider the relation between a determining complex and its determinatum, i.e., the relation of ^{m}'the center of mass of the Solar System'^{m} to the center of mass of the Solar System, of ^{m}'the first line of Gray's *Elegy*'^{m} to the first line of Gray's *Elegy*, and so on? Or do we wish to consider the relation between ^{m}'the center of mass of the Solar System'^{m} and the definite description 'the center of mass of the Solar System'? Or perhaps that between the indirect quotation '^{m}'the center of mass of the Solar System'^{m}' and the definite description 'the center of mass of the Solar System'? The first is the relation of *determining*, the second that of *being the content*, the third that of *designating the content*.

The fact is that Russell wishes to consider all three of these relations. In general, taking any definite description α, we wish to consider the relation of *being determined* between the designata of α and of $\ulcorner{}^m\alpha^m\urcorner$, the relation of *expressing* between α and the designatum of $\ulcorner{}^m\alpha^m\urcorner$ and the relation of *expressing the designatum of* between the expressions α and $\ulcorner{}^m\alpha^m\urcorner$ themselves. In each case the difference between the two relata is, in some sense, 'exemplified' in Russell's two examples. The displayed instances directly concern the contrast between a definite description and its indirect quotation. The remaining paragraphs, (*C*)-(*H*), support the answer that Russell is primarily concerned with the relation between these expressions, i.e., the relation: *the content of x is designated by y*. And this is indeed the most important of the three relations for stages (*I*)-(*VII*).

Paragraph (*C*) begins in such a way as to support an interpretation on which Russell wishes primarily to consider a relation between expressions.[16] I translate the paragraph as follows:

(*C'*) We say, to begin with, that when α occurs it is the *designatum* [of α] that we are speaking about; but when $\ulcorner{}^m\alpha^m\urcorner$ occurs, it is the *content*. Now the relation of content [to] designatum is not merely linguistic through the phrase [i.e., it is not merely the indirect relative product of the semantic relations of *being the content of* a phrase and *designating*]:[17]

---

[16] No previous interpretation to my knowledge interprets the final sentence of (*B*) this way. Typically interpreters take the 'Gray's *Elegy*' argument to be primarily concerned with the relation of *determining* between the designata of $\ulcorner{}^m\alpha^m\urcorner$ and α. To repeat: I do not claim that this interpretation is incorrect while mine is correct. Rather, the text itself, and the available evidence, is inconclusive. In the present instance, since Russell is concerned with each of the three relations I mentioned, I do not find the orthodox interpretation at all counter-intuitive. I am here exploring the consequences of an unorthodox interpretation on which Russell's announced principal concern is instead the relation between a definite description and a term for its content.

[17] See note 34 below. An alternative interpretation of Russell's phrase, 'not merely linguistic through the phrase' that fits with my overall interpretation of the entire passage was suggested by David Kaplan. One might hold that the relation between a determining complex and its determinatum is a ternary

there must be a [direct, non-semantic, logico-metaphysical][18] relation involved, which we express by saying that the content *determines* the designatum. But the difficulty which confronts us is that we cannot succeed in *both* preserving the connexion of content [to] designatum *and* preventing them [the content and the designatum] from being one and the same; also that the content cannot be got at except by means of determiner phrases. This happens as follows.

The penultimate sentence of (*C*), beginning with 'But the difficulty which confronts us is that . . .', is undoubtedly crucial to a proper understanding of the remaining paragraphs. Using his later terminology, it might have been more perspicuous for Russell to formulate his objection this way:

We cannot succeed in both preserving the connection of content to designatum and *allowing* the content and the designatum to be one and the same. Moreover we cannot even succeed in both preserving the connection of content to designatum and *disallowing* the content and the designatum from being one and the same *unless* the content cannot be got at except by means of determiner phrases.

That is, if we preserve the connection whereby the designatum of a definite description is determined by the description's content which is distinct from the designatum itself, then the content cannot be designated by means of a logically proper name, i.e., by a genuine name in the strict, logical sense. This reformulation more or less captures, with a minimum of violence to Russell's actual wording, the thrust of the Collapse which will figure in (*E*) and (*F*). The 'unless', which is a term for a form of disjunction, strongly suggests a classical dilemma form of argument. Instead of 'unless', Russell uses 'also', a term for a form of conjunction. This may be explained by supposing that Russell initially *assumes* that anything can in principle be designated by means of a logically proper name, including a determining complex. Thus we cannot prevent the named complex and the object it represents from being one and the same, thereby violating the connection between content and designatum. This assumption yields the first disjunct: since we cannot prevent the complex from representing itself, we also cannot do this while preserving the complex's representational role posited by *ST*. This is followed (with Russell's usual stylistic flare) by a semi-colon. Anticipating that the believer in *ST* will not accept the conclusion just stated, Russell writes the words 'also that', and then draws the

relation that obtains through an expression, in such a way that a complex may determine one object relative to one expression and another object relative to another expression. This theory diverges sharply from *ST*, which sees the designation of an expression as the relative product of the semantic relation between the expression and its content and the non-semantic, logico-metaphysical relation between the content and its (absolute) determinatum. In particular, the former theory is not vulnerable in the same way as *ST* to the 'Gray's *Elegy*' argument. When Russell says that on the theory he is criticizing, 'the relation of meaning and denotation is not merely linguistic through the phrase: there must be a logical relation involved,' he may mean that the determining relation is not relative to a phrase but absolute. (This alternative interpretation is closely related to one proposed by Demopoulos, though if I am correct, Demopoulos misses the central point of the Gray's *Elegy* Argument: It is not merely that a singular proposition about a determining complex cannot be the semantic content of an understandable sentence, though it can be a supplementary semantic value of the sentence; rather, it is incoherent to suppose that such a proposition can even exist.)

[18] Russell says simply 'logical'. This has probably also led some interpreters astray.

modus tollendo ponens inference on the theorist's behalf to the second disjunct: We *can* after all prevent the complex from representing itself, thus preserving the posited representational role, but only by insisting that the complex can be designated only by description.

Paragraph (D) divides into two parts. We attempt here to designate the content of a determiner phrase α. Russell adeptly demonstrates that we cannot use a simple phrase like ⌜the content of α⌝ without resorting to quotation, or something like quotation. In most cases, this would make no sense; we cannot, for example, use 'the content of the author of *Waverley*' to designate a determining complex, since whatever virtues (or vices) Sir Walter Scott may have had, semantically expressing a determining complex was not among them. Russell deliberately uses a different example—one designating a sentence instead of a person—for which the incorrect phrase formed by simply prefixing 'the content of' without the assistance of quotation makes perfect sense. The problem in this case is that we then get at the wrong content. Sub-paragraph (D_i) concludes with the words:

Thus in order to get the meaning we want, we must speak not of "the meaning of C", but of "the meaning of 'C'", which is the same as "C" by itself.

Russell is arguing here for the conclusion that enclosing a determiner phrase within inverted commas renders the words 'the meaning of' (or 'the content of') completely superfluous. But where before we hungered for quotation marks, we now have quotation marks coming out of our ears.[19] Russell observes that in order to designate the content of our determiner phrase α, besides prefixing the functor 'the content of' we must also enclose α itself within inverted commas. He is correct; we should do this, provided that the inverted commas are understood as ordinary, direct quotation marks, in outright defiance of Russell's explicit explanation of their natural use as indirect-quotation marks on the theory he is attacking. Very well, but how can this be tantamount, as Russell says, to enclosing α itself within inverted commas without the prefix? It can, at least to the extent of forming a co-designating term, but only if the inverted commas are functioning as indirect-quotation marks, *in conformity with* Russell's explanation for them. Russell is in fact giving them this use in both attempts. The use as ordinary, direct quotation marks has been pre-empted by the indirect-quotation use, which Russell thinks is the "natural" use on the theory in question. This leads to the following translation of sub-paragraph (D_i). (Recall that, unlike Russell, I consistently use single quotes for direct quotation.)

(D'_i) The one phrase α was to have both content and designation. But if [in an effort to designate the content,] we speak of ⌜the content of α⌝, that gives us the content (if any) of the designatum [of α]. 'The content of the first line of Gray's *Elegy*' [designates] the same complex as 'The content of ′″The curfew tolls the knell of parting day″′', and . . . not the same as 'The content of ′″the first line of Gray's *Elegy*″′'. Thus in order to get the content we want, we must speak not of ⌜the content of α⌝, but of ⌜the content of ″α″⌝, which [designates] the same as ⌜″α″⌝ by itself.

[19] More terrifying still, different reprintings interchange single and double quotation marks (and vary the placement of un-quoted punctuation marks inside and outside quotation marks).

I am here attributing to Russell a serious equivocation, resulting from his dual use of inverted commas both as direct quotation marks and as indirect-quotation marks. He appears to believe that he has derived from the theory he is attacking the consequence that in order to designate ᵐthe center of mass of the Solar Systemᵐ, rather than using the phrase 'the content of the center of mass of the Solar System' (which Russell has shown is inappropriate) we must use 'the content of ᵐthe center of mass of the Solar Systemᵐ'—a phrase Russell fails to distinguish sharply from the perfectly appropriate 'the content of 'the center of mass of the Solar System''. This alleged consequence yields the awkward (to say the least) result that 'ᵐThe center of mass of the Solar Systemᵐ = the content of ᵐthe center of mass of the Solar Systemᵐ' is true. We thus ascribe a content to a determining complex itself, which is identified with its content. This interpretation casts the final clause of (D_i), as well as some of the more puzzling phrases yet to come in (E) and (F), in a new and very different light.[20]

This admittedly remarkable interpretation of (D_i) is corroborated by both (D_{ii}) and (E). In (D_{ii}), Russell attempts to support his derivation of the awkward alleged consequence by deriving an analogous consequence in connection with the functor 'the denotation of' in place of 'the content of', again carefully selecting a phrase (this time 'the denoting complex occurring in the second of the above instances') for which the prefix yields something that makes perfect sense but designates the wrong object. (D_{ii}) may be rewritten as follows:

(D'_{ii}) Similarly ⌜the determinatum of α⌝ does not [designate] the determinatum we want [the determinatum of α's content], but means something [i.e., expresses a determining complex] which, if it determines [anything] at all, determines what is determined by the determinatum we want. For example, let α be 'the determining complex occurring in the second of the above instances'. Then ⌜α = ᵐthe first line of Gray's *Elegy*ᵐ⌝ and ⌜The determinatum of α = 'The curfew tolls the knell of parting day'⌝ [are both true].[21] But what we *meant* to have as the determinatum was ᵐthe first line of Gray's *Elegy*ᵐ. Thus we have failed to get what we wanted [from ⌜the determinatum of α⌝].

---

[20] There is a strong temptation to interpret (D_i) as using only direct quotation:
'The content of the first line of Gray's *Elegy*' [designates] the same complex as 'The content of 'The curfew tolls the knell of parting day'', and ... not the same as 'The content of 'the first line of Gray's *Elegy*''. Thus in order to get the content we want, we must speak not of ⌜the content of α⌝, but of ⌜the content of 'α'⌝...

Russell's remarks then become unequivocally correct. This interpretation completely misses the point, however, of the final clause of (D_i), 'which is the same as "C" by itself': that on ST the words 'the content of' when followed by a quotation are superfluous. The phrase 'The content of 'the first line of Gray's *Elegy*'' is equivalent not to its truncated form ''the first line of Gray's *Elegy*'', which is a direct quotation, but to the indirect quotation 'ᵐthe first line of Gray's *Elegy*ᵐ'. More important, the interpretation I suggest provides a key to unlock the otherwise impenetrable wording of (E)–(F).

[21] In the original text, Russell here uses 'C' as a schematic letter standing in for a term designating a determining complex. The preceding two sentences should read:

For example, let 'C' [stand in for] 'the determining complex occurring in the second of the above instances'. Then C = ᵐthe first line of Gray's *Elegy*ᵐ, and the determinatum of C = 'The curfew tolls the knell of parting day'.

I have reformulated this in the metalinguistic mode using 'α', quasi-quotation, and the predicate 'is true'.

As a criticism of *ST*, and even as a neutral description, the entire paragraph (*D*) is a crimson red herring. The theory entails that one may designate ^{m}the center of mass of the Solar System^m using the functor 'the content of' in combination with 'the center of mass of the Solar System' and direct quotation, not indirect. *Pace* Russell, his implicit observation that in order to designate the designatum of α we should use $\ulcorner$the determinatum of $^m\alpha^m\urcorner$ rather than $\ulcorner$the determinatum of $\alpha\urcorner$, though correct, provides no support whatever to his apparent conclusion that, analogously, in order to designate the content of α, rather than using $\ulcorner$the content of $\alpha\urcorner$ we must use $\ulcorner$the content of $^m\alpha^m\urcorner$, which is in fact equally inappropriate. Instead we can designate α's content using $\ulcorner$the content of 'α'$\urcorner$ or $\ulcorner{}^m\alpha^m\urcorner$. Analogously, we can equally designate α's designatum by using $\ulcorner$the designatum of 'α'$\urcorner$ or α itself.[22]

Perhaps Russell believes that *ST* inevitably interprets all quotation as indirect quotation, and that there is no appropriate place for direct quotation marks on the theory. If so, he no longer has any legitimate ground for supposing that the theory under attack would attempt to designate contents using the functor 'the content of' in conjunction with quotation marks. Church's dismissive remarks concerning the 'Gray's *Elegy*' argument are in fact nearly completely correct when restricted to stage (*I*) (raising the suspicion that Church interpreted this stage similarly, and thought it best not to attempt to decipher the rest of the argument). Church's assessment requires slight emendation. For many purposes, the indirect-quotation marks themselves render the 'content of' functor superfluous, but they do not rob *ST* of the resources to designate expressions. And where it is necessary to designate an expression and attribute content to it—when doing genuine semantics, for example, or when giving the 'Gray's *Elegy*' argument—in principle the theory can get by with such locutions as 'the expression displayed below', followed by a suitable display of the expression in question, or if worse comes to worst, with cumbersome constructions like 'the determiner phrase that results by writing the 20th letter of the alphabet, followed by the 8th letter, followed by the 5th letter, followed by a space, followed by . . .', or even by exploiting an empirical property of the expression, as with 'the sentence written on the blackboard in Salmon's office' or 'the first line of Gray's *Elegy*'. More to the point, if there is any difficulty about using direct-quotation marks on the theory, it derives from a tenet entirely of Russell's own devising, which he imposes on a theory that did not ask for it.[23] Contrary to Church, however, Russell has a much stronger criticism to make in stages (*II*)–(*VII*), though

---

[22] Following Quine's explanation of quasi-quotation, the quasi-quotation $\ulcorner$the content of 'α'$\urcorner$ designates, under the assignment of the expression 'the center of mass of the Solar System' as value for the syntactic variable 'α', the phrase 'the content of 'the center of mass of the Solar System' ' (and not the infelicitous 'the content of 'α' ', which mentions the variable 'α' instead of its value).

[23] It is possible that Russell construed the theory as identifying an expression with what might be called an *interpreted expression*, i.e., an expression-*cum*-content, in effect, the ordered couple of the expression paired with its content. Inverted commas would then emerge as a natural mode of designating interpreted expressions, leaving us with no similar device for designating the syntactic component by itself. One could designate the content component using the functor 'the content of' together with quotation marks. But this would designate a component of the designatum of the quotation itself; it would not designate the *same* entity as the quotation.

his presentation in stages (*II*) and (*IV*) (at least) is colored in varying degrees by the red herring.

IV

Many a lance has been broken on paragraph (*E*). The paragraph should also be broken into parts corresponding to argument stages (*II*) and (*III*). In (*C*) and (*D*) we have been attempting to designate the determining complex that is the content of a determiner phrase. In (*E*) Russell speaks about the content not of a phrase but of a complex. He sometimes spoke in *The Principles* (and in intervening writings) of 'the meaning of a concept.' But not in 'On Denoting'—not until now (aside from a single footnote about Frege). Did Russell commit a slip of the pen, writing 'denoting complex' where he means 'denoting phrase'? Or has the determining complex expressed by a definite description given rise without notice to a new entity: a content of its own? If the latter, there are four entities in all: the phrase; its designatum; the complex expressed by the phrase; and the complex's content. Commentators have tended to divide themselves between these two theories. I accept neither.

On my interpretation, Russell believes he has just shown in the preceding paragraphs that on the theory under attack the content of the phrase is designated by speaking of the content ('meaning') of a complex. The opening sentence of (*E*) is explained by supposing that Russell is relentlessly flogging a dead horse. Mercifully, his intent in sub-paragraph (*E_{ii}*) is to provide a preferable phraseology, a mode of speaking that allows one to designate a determining complex without speaking of it as itself the content of a complex. But first he shows at stage (*II*) that the former mode of speaking already leads to the Collapse:

(*E'_i*) The difficulty in speaking of the content of a [determining] complex [i.e., in using a phrase of the form ⌜the content of $^m\alpha^m$⌝] may be stated thus: The moment we put the complex in a proposition, the proposition is about the determinatum; and [hence] if we make a proposition in which the subject [component] is ^{M}the content of c^M [for some determining complex c], then the subject [represents] the content (if any) of the determinatum [of c], which was not intended.

(*E'_{ii}*) This leads us to say that, when we distinguish content and determinatum [of a determining complex as we did in the preceding paragraph], we must be dealing [in both cases] with the content: the content has a determinatum and is a determining complex, and there is not something other than the content, which can be called [⌜the complex $^m\alpha^m$⌝], and be said to *have* both content and a determinatum. The right phrase[ology], on the view in question, is that some contents have determinata.

There is, in addition to the Collapse set out in (*E_i*), a more immediate problem with the phrase ⌜the content of $^m\alpha^m$⌝ and its accompanying terminology. We are attempting to express a proposition about a particular determining complex, say ^{m}the center of mass of the Solar System^m, using a sentence of the form 'The content of "the center of mass of the Solar System" is . . .'. But if the inverted commas are given their natural construal (according to Russell) as content quotation marks, this gives a proposition about the content of the target complex—the putative fourth entity—rather than the complex itself. Sub-paragraph (E_{ii}) sets out stage (III) of the argument, explicitly rejecting the four-entity theory in favor of a three-entity theory, while supplying the preferred phraseology: When we express a proposition using a sentence containing a definite description, the determining complex in the proposition does not have a separate content; rather, it is itself the content of the description. The content of the complex is not a fourth entity but (if anything) simply the complex itself, whereas the determinatum is what the proposition is about. We can designate the content of a definite description α simply by its content quotation $\ulcorner {}^m\alpha^m \urcorner$, dropping the useless prefix 'the content of'. Determining complexes *are* the contents of definite descriptions, and it is these very contents—some of them, at any rate—that represent their determinata in propositions.

By the end of stage (III) Russell has, with a helping of notational errors and use-mention confusions, drawn some trivial consequences of our theory ST, highlighting the feature (which theorists like Frege and Church readily accept) that propositions are not about the determining complexes that occur in them, but instead about the determinata of those complexes. This, presumably, is the "connexion of meaning and determinatum" that we are attempting to "preserve" while "preventing the meaning and determinatum from being one and the same." What is more important is the stage (II) argument laid out in (E_i). This marks the first appearance, as I interpret the entire passage, of the Collapse and also the first appearance of Russell's variable 'C' as ranging over determining complexes rather than determiner phrases. Moreover, the quotation marks here are indirect-quasi-quotation marks. The quotation ^{M}the content of c^{M} designates the determining complex that results from joining the content of the functor 'the content of' with the complex c. Russell cites a particular phenomenon that arises, as a consequence of the connection just noted between content and determinatum, when one attempts to form a singular proposition about a determining complex: inevitably the result is a general proposition about the complex's determinatum rather than a singular proposition about the complex itself. The reason is that, on ST, as soon as we put a determining complex in a proposition, by using a sentence involving a singular term whose content is the complex, the proposition is about the complex's determinatum. This generates the Collapse. Let c be a particular determining complex, say ^{m}the first line of Gray's *Elegy*^{m}. When we attempt to form a proposition about it—say, that it is intriguing—by using a sentence containing the indirect quotation '^{m}the first line of Gray's *Elegy*^{m}' (Russell supposes, for a *reductio*, that one way to do this on ST is by means of the sentence 'The meaning of "the first line of Gray's *Elegy*" is intriguing'), if the quotation functions as a logically proper name of the determining complex, in that its own content simply is the designated complex, then the resulting proposition is that (the content of) the first line of Gray's *Elegy* is intriguing, rather than a proposition about the intended determining, complex itself. This is one particular form of the Collapse: In attempting to form a proposition about a determining complex c by using a sentence containing a content quotation $\ulcorner {}^m\alpha^m \urcorner$, where α is a definite description that expresses c, we generate a proposition not about c but about its determinatum.

Some previous interpreters do not so much as mention what I am calling *the Collapse*. Others have extracted the alleged phenomenon from (E_i), but place little or no importance on it. Some have depicted its occurrence in the 'Gray's *Elegy*' passage as little more than a clever observation, characteristic of Russell but one that he makes only in passing and is of limited significance in the grand sweep of the overall argument. In sharp contrast, on my interpretation the Collapse is the very linchpin of the 'Gray's *Elegy*' argument, and will play a pivotal role in later stages that constitute the heart of the argument.[24]

By the end of (E), Russell acknowledges that to express a proposition about c itself we may use the simple content quotation $\ulcorner{}^m\alpha^m\urcorner$, or something like it, in lieu of the more cumbersome (to say the least!) determiner phrase $\ulcorner$the content of ${}^m\alpha^m\urcorner$. Alternatively, we may use $\ulcorner$the content of 'α'$\urcorner$. But having assimilated this to $\ulcorner$the content of ${}^m\alpha^m\urcorner$, or failing to distinguish the two, Russell believes he has just shown that use of such a phrase inevitably comes to grief, *via* the Collapse. In any event, the objective in (D) was to form a singular proposition about a determining complex, not a proposition in which the target complex is represented as the content of this or that phrase. Not surprisingly, the move to simple, unadorned indirect quotation is of no help whatsoever: the very same phenomenon arises. Stage (IV) presses this point. Paragraph (F) divides into three parts. In (F_i) Russell shows how the Collapse arises even when designating the complex c by using the simple content quotation $\ulcorner{}^m\alpha^m\urcorner$. This uncovers a significant difference between *ST* and the Theory of Descriptions (and thus between the WRL and IRL hypotheses), since the latter does not assign content "in isolation" to determiner phrases, and hence does not generate the Collapse. This is an extremely important point. Regrettably, the presentation is not altogether free of the red herring, though thankfully, its former luster is now mostly subdued. I rewrite sub-paragraph (F_i) as follows:

(F'_i) But this only makes our difficulty in speaking of contents more evident For suppose c is our [target] complex [and let 'D' represent in what follows a determiner phrase that

[24] Blackburn and Code mention the Collapse only after presenting their rival interpretation, which does not rely on the Collapse ('Russell's Criticism of Frege,' p. 76, crediting Kaplan for showing them that the Collapse refutes the earlier theory of designating in Russell's *Principles*). In sharp contrast to my interpretation, they express uncertainty whether Russell is even aware of the Collapse by the time he writes 'On Denoting.' As against the hypothesis that he was, they say that 'although this *is* a problem as to how one refers to senses [contents], the obvious solution is not to attack Frege, but rather to insist that his three-entity view [distinguishing among an expression, its content, and its designatum] applies to *all* referring [designating] expressions.'

There are at least five problems with this. First, Russell was explicitly aware of the Collapse already in the lengthy and rambling 'On Fundamentals', begun not two months prior to 'On Denoting' and posthumously published in A. Urquhart, ed., *The Collected Papers of Bertrand Russell 4: Foundations of Logic: 1903–1905* (London: Routledge, 1994), pp. 359–413, at 363, 382, and *passim*. Indeed, some passages of 'On Fundamentals' appear virtually *verbatim* in the 'Gray's *Elegy*' argument, which is in certain respects a streamlined version of the convoluted reasonings of the former. Second, whereas one might hope to solve the problem by insisting that any singular term that designates a content always has its own content distinct from its designatum, the same distinction does not have to be extended. to all terms (including names for concretes objects) in order for the solution to work. Third, though Russell was aware of the possibility of a theory like the one Blackburn and Code call 'the obvious solution' (as is shown by a passage they quote from *Principles*), he did not unequivocally endorse it. Fourth, on the contrary, a central purpose of 'On Denoting' is precisely to reject Frege's "three-entity view" in regard to all singular terms, and replace it with a two-entity view. Finally, and most importantly, the very point of (F) and (G) (to be interpreted more fully below) appears to be precisely that the very proposal in question utterly fails to solve the problem.

expresses c]; then we are to say that [$^mD^m$, *i.e.*,] c is the content of the [phrase 'D', instead of saying that $^mD^m$ itself has a content]. Nevertheless, whenever 'D' occurs without [indirect-quotation marks], what is said is not [about $^mD^m$], the content [of 'D'], but only [about D], the designatum [of 'D'], as when we say: The center of mass of the Solar System is a point.

Russell argues as follows. Consider a determiner phrase like 'the center of mass of the Solar System', and let us attempt to form a singular proposition about its content, ^{m}the center of mass of the Solar System^m, for example, the true proposition that this is a determining complex. Clearly, we do not succeed by writing 'The center of mass of the Solar System is a determining complex', for this expresses a necessarily false, general proposition about a particular point. In order to express the singular proposition we want, we should use a *genuine name* "in the strict, logical sense" for the complex, perhaps the indirect-quotation '^{m}the center of mass of the Solar System^m'. But supposing the indirect-quotation is a genuine name, to the extent that its sole semantic value—its content—is simply the designated complex, if we write '^{m}The center of mass of the Solar System^m is a determining complex', our new attempt also fails. Instead we thereby obtain precisely the same proposition as before, since the subject and predicate terms of the new sentence have precisely the same contents, respectively, as those of the old setence. The attempted true, singular proposition has collapsed into a false, general proposition. In fact, the proposition expressed by the new sentence is necessarily false, its negation necessarily true.

Russell continues at stage (*V*), converting the Collapse into a *reduction ad absurdum* argument for the conclusion that our theory *ST* (and thus the WRL hypothesis) entails that determining complexes cannot be genuinely *named*. Sub-paragraph (F_{ii}) is rewritten as follows:

(F'_{ii}) Thus to speak of $^mD^m$ itself, i.e., to [express] a proposition about the content [of 'D'], our subject [component] must not be $^mD^m$ [*itself*], but something [else, a new determining complex,] which determines $^mD^m$. Thus $^{mm}D^{mm}$—which [iterated indirect quotation] is what we use when we want to speak of the content [of '$^mD^m$']—must be not the content [of 'D', i.e., not $^mD^m$ itself], but something which determines the content.

Russell is arguing here by means of the Collapse that, on *ST*, $^{mm}D^{mm} \neq {}^mD^m$, where 'D' stands in for any definite description.[25] We may designate a particular complex, say ^{m}the center of mass of the Solar System^m, in order to express a proposition about it. However, any proposition in which the complex itself occurs is about the center of mass of the Solar System, i.e., the determinatum of the target complex rather than the complex itself. A singular proposition about a determining complex is an evident impossibility; hence any proposition that is about a complex must involve a second-level determining complex that determines the target complex. Hence, any term for a complex must function in the manner of a definite description. Even our indirect quotation, '^{m}the center of mass of the Solar System^m' (the closest thing there is to a *standard name* of the complex), must be a disguised definite description, expressing a second-level determining complex, $^m\,{}^m$the center of mass of

---

[25] The expression '$^m\,{}^mD^{m\,m}$' may stand in for the iterated indirect quotation '$^m\,{}^m$the center of mass of the Solar System$^m\,{}^m$', which designates the content of the indirect quotation, '^{m}the center of mass of the Solar System^m'.

the Solar System$^{m\ m}$, as its content. Furthermore, $^{m\ m}$the center of mass of the Solar System$^{m\ m}$ is distinct from, and in fact determines,^{m}the center of mass of the Solar System^{m}. It is in this very concrete sense that on *ST*, "the meaning cannot be got at except by means of determiner phrases." The only way to designate a determining complex is by expressing a higher-level determining comlex.[26]

Russell has thus far argued that the theory *ST* is committed, by the Collapse, to denying the very possibility of singular propositions about contents. Some commentators have construed this argument as an objection to Frege's theory, which rejects singular propositions.[27] Such an argument would be a howler. On the contrary, Fregeans should welcome the conclusion derived at stage (*V*), which provides a *reductio* argument against *ST in conjunction with singular propositions of unrestricted subject matter*—a theory like Mill's or that of Russell's *Principles*. The incoherence of these non-Fregean versions of *ST* may even be given a kind of proof, using the principle of *Compositionality* (which Russell relied on at least implicitly and Frege explicitly endorsed), according to which the content of a compound expression is an effectively computable function of the contents of the contentful components. Compositionality is subject to certain restrictions. For example, the content of a compound expression containing a standard (direct) quotation is a function of the content of the quotation itself, together with the contents of the surrounding subexpressions, but not of the content of the quoted expression. Subject to such restrictions as this, Compositionality evidently entails a similarly restricted principle of *Synonymous Interchange*, according to which substitution of a synonym within a larger expression preserves content. (I here call a pair of expressions *synonymous* if there is something that is the content of both.) To give the argument its sharpest focus, we consider Russell's example:

(3) The center of mass of the Solar System is a point.

According to *ST*, the grammatical subject of (3), 'the center of mass of the Solar System', expresses the determining complex ^{m}the center of mass of the Solar System^{m} as its English content. According to the non-Fregean version of *ST*, the content of the indirect quotation '^{m}the center of mass of the Solar System^{m}' itself is this same determining complex, and sentences containing the indirect quotation express

---

[26] This does not rule out that the content can also be "got at" by means of an indefinite description, even if it is deemed not a singular term. Since *ST* is neutral regarding indefinite descriptions, it is equally consistent with the view that definite and indefinite descriptions alike are singular terms. The latter view makes indefinite descriptions subject to the argument from the Collapse. On the Theory of Descriptions, by contrast, a definite description is analyzed as a special kind of indefinite description, neither being a singular term.

The interpretation of this stage of Russell's argument is strongly supported by the fact that he also gives this argument in writings just prior to "On Denoting" (posthumously published). *Cf.* his "On Fundamentals," *loc. cit.* preceding note; and "On Meaning and Denotation," also in A. Urquhart, ed., *The Collected Papers of Bertrand Russell 4: Foundations of Logic: 1903–1905*, (London: Routledge, 1994), pp. 314–358, at 322.

[27] Searle (*op. cit.*, p. 139–140) depicts Russell as arguing that in order for a term to designate, the designated object must, if we are not to "succumb to mysticism," occur in the propositions expressed with the help of the designating term; but then the Collapse excludes the possibility of designating determining complexes. Searle complains that the whole point of Frege's theory, which Russell is attacking, is to deny Russell's premise. It is possible that Church construes the argument similarly.

singular propositions about the complex. Hence, the description and the indirect quotation are synonymous according to the non-Fregean version of *ST*. Therefore, by Synonymous Interchange, so also are (3) and

(4) ᵐThe center of mass of the Solar Systemᵐ is a point.

But (3) is true while (4) is necessarily false, indicating that they do not express the same thing. The content of (4) must invoke the second-level complex ᵐ ᵐthe center of mass of the Solar Systemᵐ ᵐ to represent the first-level complex. (The same argument may be given using the free variable '*c*' in place of the indirect quotation. On the supposition that the content of the variable under the established assignment is its value, the variable has the very same content as the definite description 'the first line of Gray's *Elegy*'. The Collapse then follows directly by Synonymous Interchange. This refutes the assumption that the variable under its assignment is a logically proper name for the complex in question.) The theory *ST* is thus committed to extending its content/designation distinction for definite descriptions to *all* terms that designate determining complexes.

The argument can be repeated in connection with the content of the indirect quotation itself. The argument is thus converted into an argument by mathematical induction for an infinite hierarchy of contents associated with 'the first line of Gray's *Elegy*'. Indeed, the postulated second-level complex ᵐ ᵐthe first line of Gray's *Elegy*ᵐ ᵐ is, for Frege, the content that the description expresses when occurring in *ungerade* ("oblique") contexts, like the contexts created by 'believes that' and by indirect quotation marks.[28] He called this the *indirect sense* of 'the first line of Gray's *Elegy*'. The series beginning with 'The curfew tolls the knell of parting day', followed by ᵐthe first line of Gray's *Elegy*ᵐ, ᵐ ᵐthe first line of Gray's *Elegy*ᵐ ᵐ, ᵐ ᵐ ᵐ the first line of Gray's *Elegy*ᵐ ᵐ ᵐ, and so on, is precisely Frege's infinite hierarchy of senses for the definite description (treating designation as the bottom level in the hierarchy). Not all of Frege's disciples have followed the master down the garden path to Frege's jungle. Two noteworthy deserters are Carnap and Dummett.[29] But Church has followed Frege even here.[30] In fact, at least one of the loyal opposition has as well. Russell's argument *via* the Collapse for *ST*'s commitment to the hierarchy was independently reinvented closer to the end of the previous century by Tyler Burge.[31]

---

[28] In "*Über Sinn und Bedeutung*" (translated as "On Sense and Reference," in Robert M. Harnish, ed., *Basic Topics in the Philosophy of Language*, Prentice-Hall, 199, pp. 142–160, at 149), Frege identified the indirect sense of a sentence ϕ with the customary sense of ⌜the thought that ϕ⌝, which phrase may be presumed synonymous with ⌜ᵐϕᵐ⌝.

[29] Carnap, *Meaning and Necessity* (University of Chicago Press, 1947, 1970), at pp. 118–137, especially 129–133. Carnap may be profitably interpreted as rejecting singular propositions about individuals, while accepting that *ungerade* constructions (as occur in belief attributions, modal claims, etc.) express singular propositions about the contents of their complement clauses. *Cf.* Dummett *op. cit.*; and Terence Parsons, "Frege's Hierarchies of Indirect Senses and the Paradox of Analysis," in P. French, T. Uehling, and H. Wettstein, eds., *Midwest Studies in Philosophy* (University of Minnesota Press, 1981), pp. 37–58.

[30] Church disagrees with Frege on some details, and may have been inconsistent regarding the issue of the hierarchy. See note 37 below.

[31] Burge, "Frege and the Hierarchy," *Synthese*, 40 (1979), pp. 265–281. Burge argues (pp. 271–272), as follows, specifically that Frege's theory of *Sinn* and *Bedeutung* is committed to hierarchies of sense, when coupled with Church's methodology of eliminating ambiguity-producing devices (like

Russell clarifies the nature of the hierarchy at stage (VI), which makes up the final third of (F). Sub-paragraph (F_{iii}) is translated as follows:

(F'_{iii}) And $[^mD^m$, i.e.,] c must not be a constituent of this [higher–level] complex $^m{}^mD^{m\,m}$ (as it is of ^{M}the content of c^M); for if c occurs in the complex, it will be its determinatum, not [the] content [of 'D', i.e., not c itself], that will [be represented] and there is no backward road from determinata to contents, because every object can be designated by an infinite number of different determiner phrases.

A feature of (F_{iii}) that is typically overlooked is that it again invokes the Collapse.[32] Russell observes that the target complex is not only distinct from the postulated second-level complex we seek; is not even a constituent of the latter complex (as it is of ^{m}Russell has memorized the first line of Gray's *Elegy*^{m}, and of ^{m}the content of the first line of Gray's *Elegy*^{m}). Here Russell pursues the obvious question: Given that the indirect quotation '^{m}the first line of Gray's *Elegy*^{m}' must express a second-level complex that determines our target complex, which second-level complex does it express? The best way to identify the sought after second-level complex would be to provide a definite description of the form 'the determining

'believes that') that shift expressions in their scope into *ungerade* mode in favor of fully extensional operators applied to univocal names of senses: Suppose for a *reductio* that the true proposition that Bela believes that Opus 132 is a masterpiece does not contain a second-level complex that determines the proposition that Opus 132 is a masterpiece, and that instead the latter proposition represents itself in the former proposition. In accordance with Church's methodology, we introduce an artificial extensional two-place operator '**Believes**' for the binary relation of belief (between a believer and the object believed), so that 'Bela **Believes** (^{m}Opus 132 is a masterpiece^m)' expresses that Bela believes that Opus 132 is a masterpiece. Then according to Frege's theory, the quasi-artificial expression E, 'Bela **Believes** (Opus 132 is a masterpiece)', expresses the bizarre proposition that Bela believes a particular *truth-value*—to wit, the truth value that is truth if Opus 132 is a masterpiece, and is falsity otherwise. But by our *reductio* hypothesis, E expresses a content consisting of the very components of the proposition that Bela believes that Opus 132 is a masterpiece, composed the very same way. By Compositionality, E therefore expresses our target proposition. (This collapse is obtained, in effect, from the *reductio* hypothesis by Synonymous Interchange.) On Frege's extensional semantics, substitution in E of any sentence materially equivalent with 'Opus 132 is a masterpiece' preserves truth-value. Since E expresses that Bela believes that Opus 132 is a masterpiece, it follows on Frege's theory that if Bela believes that Opus 132 is a masterpiece, he believes every materially equivalent proposition, which is absurd.

Striking evidence that the central thrust of the "Gray's *Elegy*" argument has been lost on Russell's readers is provided by Burge's remark (at p. 280n8) that to his knowledge, the argument presented above was nowhere explicitly stated before. Burge's argument employs a sentence in place of a definite description, but this difference from Russell's examples is completely inessential to the general argument. Burge also frames his argument in terms of a Fregean conception whereby an artificial notation should be used to avoid natural-language ambiguities produced by *ungerade* devices (e.g., '**Believes**' in place of 'believes that'). This introduces additional complexity, also inessential to the general point and leading to an unnecessarily restricted conclusion. Burge's argument may be strengthened as follows: Suppose for a *reductio* that the proposition that ^{m}the center of mass of the Solar System^m is a sense does not contain a second-level complex that determines ^{m}the center of mass of the Solar System^m, and that instead the complex ^{m}the center of mass of the Solar System^m represents itself in the proposition. The English sentence S, 'The center of mass of the Solar System is a sense'—which contains no artificial notation—expresses a proposition consisting of the very components of the proposition that ^{m}the center of mass of the Solar System^m is a sense, and composed the very same way. By Compositionality, S therefore expresses our target proposition. This conflicts with the fact that S is false in English.

[32] A notable exception is Kremer, *ibid.*, at pp. 287–288. Though my analysis of the argument differs from his, I have benefited from his meticulous probing and careful analysis of the passage.

complex that is such-and-such' which is fully understood (independently of indirect-quotation), and which is synonymous with '"the first line of Gray's *Elegy*". Given Compositionality, it might be hoped that the suitable definite description will incorporate something expressing the designated target complex itself. We would thus construct the postulated second-level complex using the target complex. However, the desired description cannot be 'the complex that determines the first line of Gray's *Elegy*', for there are infinitely many and varied complexes each of which determines the words 'The curfew tolls . . .'. Let us try a different tack. Let '*c*' name the target complex, and consider: *the determining complex that is c*. Russell observes that this will not do either. Indeed, no description of the form 'the determining complex that bears relation *R* to *c*' will succeed. Or to put the same point somewhat differently, our postulated second-level complex cannot be ^{M}the determining complex that bears *R* to c^M, for some binary relation *R*. (Note the indirect-quasi-quotation marks.) For the Collapse occurs with determining complexes just as it does with propositions. The content of the description collapses into: '"the determining complex that bears *R* to the first line of Gray's *Elegy*". The problem here is that there is no "backward road" from the words 'The curfew tolls . . .' to their particular representation by '"the first line of Gray's *Elegy*", and likewise no backward road from the Solar System's center of mass to its particular representation as such. That is, there is no relevantly identifiable binary relation *R* whose converse is a "choice" function that selects exactly our target complex, to the exclusion of all others, and assigns it, and only it, to its determinatum. If *R* is taken to be the relation of *determining*, then the collapsed second-level complex fails to determine a unique complex because there are too many complexes (infinitely many, in fact) that bear this relation to the first line of Gray's *Elegy*. And if *R* is taken to be the relation of identity, then the resulting second-level complex fails to determine a unique complex because there are too few complexes that bear this relation to the first line of Gray's *Elegy*. More generally, if *c* is our target complex, the postulated second-level complex cannot be of the form $^Mf(c)^M$, where '*f*' designates a choice function that selects a distinguished or privileged determining complex from the class of all complexes that determine a given object. It is important to notice that the missing choice function *f* goes not at the level from the target complex to the second-level complex, but at the bottom level from the determinatum to the complex itself. A "low" backward road might enable us to construct the postulated second-level complex from the target complex. But high or low, no backward road is forthcoming.

So ends stage (*VI*). Because there is no backward road from 'The curfew tolls . . .' to '"the first line of Gray's *Elegy*", it follows *via* the Collapse that the second-level complex '" '"the first line of Gray's *Elegy*" " is not constructed from the target complex '"the first line of Gray's *Elegy*". Indirect quotations thus constitute a restriction on a principle of *Strong Compositionality* (also endorsed by both Frege and Russell), according to which the content of a compound expression is not only a function of, but is in fact a complex composed of, the contents of the contentful components.

Russell might have taken the argument a step further. Continuing and embellishing the argument on Russell's behalf, although the content quotation ‴the first line of Gray's *Elegy*‴ expresses, and thereby uniquely fixes, the postulated second-level complex, the target complex designated by the indirect quotation does not itself uniquely single out the second-level complex. It is a serious mistake, for example, to suppose that ″ ‴the first line of Gray's *Elegy*‴ ″ can be described as the content of ‴the first line of Gray's *Elegy*‴.(Russell believes he has shown that on *ST*, this description designates the target complex itself, whereas the description actually designates nothing. The alternative phrase, 'the content of 'the first line of Gray's *Elegy*'' *does* designate the target complex itself. Still, we do not get at the postulated second-level complex.) But neither can ″ ‴the first line of Gray's Elegy‴ ″ be described as *the* complex that determines ‴the first line of Gray's *Elegy*‴. For any given object there are infinitely many complexes that determine it. Our target complex is also determined by such second-level complexes as ‴the determining complex occurring in the second of Russell's instances‴ and ‴the determining complex that has given Russell's readers more headaches than any other‴—neither of which is suited to be the content expressed by ‴the first line of Gray's *Elegy*‴. Thus not only is it the case, as Russell explicitly argues, that the target complex is altogether different from the postulated second-level complex. The target complex does not even uniquely fix the second-level complex. Never mind the Collapse. If there is no backward road from determinata to determining complexes, then not only is there no low road from the first line of Gray's *Elegy* to ‴the first line of Gray's *Elegy*‴; there is likewise no high road from ‴the first line of Gray's *Elegy*‴ to ″ ‴the first line of Gray's *Elegy*‴ ″. We have no way to go from the content of a definite description to the content of its indirect quotation. Our indirect quotation marks thus yield a restriction also on the weaker principle of Compositionality: The content of an indirect quotation is not even a computable function of (let alone a complex composed partly of) the content of the expression within the quotes. This result is stronger than the conclusion that Russell explicitly draws. If the target complex were a constituent of the postulated second-level complex, presumably it would single out the latter complex. But the mere fact that the target complex is not a constituent of the second-level complex does not yet rule out the possibility that the target complex uniquely fixes the second-level complex in some other manner. The fact that there is a multiplicity of complexes determining any given object seems to do just that. (By contrast, the indirect quotation ‴the first line of Gray's *Elegy*‴ singles out the second-level complex, as its English content.)[33]

[33] The argument just given on Russell's behalf purports to prove that, in Frege's terminology, the sense of an indirect quotation is not an effectively computable function of the *customary* senses of the expressions within the content quotes. Frege concedes that the sense of a compound expression is not always composed of the customary senses of the component expressions. Frege would insist, however, that indirect quotation marks do not violate Compositionality, or even Strong Compositionality as he intends these principles, since an expression does not have its customary sense when occurring within indirect quotation marks and instead expresses its indirect sense, which *does* uniquely fix the sense of the indirect quotation. He says something analogous in connection with direct quotation. Direct quotations of customary synonyms are not themselves synonyms.

V

Although Russell does not explicitly argue for the stronger conclusion, he seems to have it very much in mind. Stage (*VII*) proceeds as if the stronger conclusion has just been established. Sub-paragraph (G_i) requires little rewriting:

(G'_i) Thus it would seem that $^{m\ m}D^{m\ m}$ and c are [altogether] different entities, such that $^{m\ m}D^{m\ m}$ determines c; but this cannot be an explanation [of $^{m\ m}D^{m\ m}$], because the relation of $^{m\ m}D^{m\ m}$ to c remains wholly mysterious; and where are we to find the determining complex $^{m\ m}D^{m\ m}$ which is to determine c?

Here—at last, and with breathtaking brevity—Russell points to a *defect*, the fatal flaw, in the theory that definite descriptions are singular terms. So brief is the presentation that several distinct interpretations, some largely unrelated to each other, have been offered. Some of Russell's defenders, as well as his critics, reconstruct the argument in (*F*) and (G_i) with the result that it is remarkably weak.[34] This

[34] Blackburn and Code (*ibid.*) interpret the "Gray's *Elegy*" passage as arguing primarily that in order to introduce and justify his notion of sense, Frege must find a way to "specify" the sense of an expression recognizably—e.g., by constructing a definite description for the sense or explicitly defining an indirect quotation—using, but not mentioning, the very expression whose sense is to be specified, while also guaranteeing a logical connection between the expression and the term for its sense; and this he cannot do, because any such term for the sense will have its own sense which must also be designated recognizably while guaranteeing its logical connections, and so on *ad infinitum*, generating an infinite regress. This interpretation bears at most a superficial resemblance to mine. Blackburn and Code interpret Russell's assertion that "the meaning cannot be got at except by means of denoting phrases" as meaning that the theory cannot meet the demand that the required sense specification not mention any expression whose sense is in question (p. 72)—rather than that the sense cannot be designated by a logically proper name. They do not make clear why Russell (or anyone else) should insist that it is illegitimate for Frege to introduce his notion of sense by pointing out that, for example, 'the center of mass of the Solar System' and 'the point of intersection of lines a and b' share a common designatum yet differ in sense. (I believe Blackburn's and Code's interpretation stems from a serious misreading of Russell's assertion that "the relation of meaning and denotation is not merely linguistic through the phrase." See notes 17 and 24 above.) Other commentators (e.g., Pakaluk) have followed Blackburn and Code in interpreting Russell as objecting to the content/designation distinction on the ground of an infinite regress, though there is no clear evidence of such an objection in the passage. Only later, in 'Knowledge by Acquaintance and Knowledge by Description' *Proceedings of the Aristotelian Society*, 11 (1910–1911), pp. 108–128 (reprinted in N. Salmon and S. Soames, eds., *Propositions and Attitudes*, Oxford University Press, 1988, pp. 16–32, at 28–29) does Russell give a similar objection based on an infinite regress. Like Blackburn and Code, Noonan (pp. 92–97) sees Russell as insisting that determining complexes, were there to be any, would have to be specifiable without mentioning expressions that express those complexes. Noonan interprets Russell as arguing that nevertheless, no complex is specifiable except by mentioning an expression whose content it is, since the Collapse precludes naming complexes, and a complex cannot be specified as a function of its determinatum; since there are no other possibilities, it follows that no determining complexes exist. Noonan admits that this argument is strikingly weak. Worse, there is no clear evidence in the passage that Russell believes these are the only possibilities for designating a complex. On the contrary, he evidently believes they are not; witness Russell's example: 'the determining complex occurring in the second of the above instances'. Makin's interpretation (which appeared some years after I wrote the present essay) depicts Russell as objecting to the theory of determining complexes on the grounds that when we wish to form a proposition about a given determining complex, the theory requires us to obtain an appropriate determining second-level complex from the target complex itself, whereas

is none too surprising. The actual wording seems more rhetorical than profound, more of a complaint than an argument. This is unfortunate. I believe Russell may have had in mind a strikingly forceful argument, which builds upon the considerations expressed in the foregoing paragraphs in a way that proves their importance (especially that of the Collapse) to the debate concerning the logico-semantic status of determiner phrases.

We seek an explanation of how to express a proposition about a determining complex c using an indirect quotation or other name for c—an explanation, for example, of the content of a sentence like (4). What we are able to determine from *ST* is that, because of the Collapse, the indirect quotation is not a logically proper name and instead expresses a second-level complex $^{m\ m}$the center of mass of the Solar System$^{m\ m}$ which represents ^{m}the center of mass of the Solar System^{m} in the proposition. But we have as yet no idea which determining complex $^{m\ m}$the center of mass of the Solar System$^{m\ m}$ is of the infinitely many second-level complexes that determine ^{m}the center of mass of the Solar System^{m}. We know what determining complex the indirect quotation '^{m}the center of mass of the Solar System^{m}' designates, but we do not know *how* the indirect quotation designates it. We know the indirect quotation's designatum but not its content. It turns out that we are at a loss even to *understand* (4). At best, we know that the sentence somehow expresses something *about* that complex—some proposition or other to the effect that it is a point—but we know not which of the infinitely many propositions that do this is actually expressed. What is worse, because of the nonexistence of a high backward road, our prior knowledge, arrived at through a commonplace human process of semantic computation, that the definite description 'the center of mass of the Solar System' expresses the particular content ^{m}the center of mass of the Solar System^{m}, together with our knowledge of exactly which determining complex this is—i.e., our "understanding" of the phrase, in this sense—is not sufficient to enable us to compute the content of the sentence. The problem is not so much to *locate* the postulated second-level complex. (Russell: 'Where are we to find the denoting complex "C" which is to denote C?') It resides in the class of second-level complexes that each determine ^{m}the first line of Gray's *Elegy*^{m}, alongside its neighbors

the same theory fails to provide any systematic way of doing this (*op. cit.*, pp. 31–32, and *passim*); hence "by the theory's own strictures," determining complexes cannot be thought or spoken of even in principle, nor can anything be true or false of them (pp. 22–23). Aside from the scant evidence that Russell believes the theory of determining complexes requires us to obtain the needed second-level complex from the target complex, the argument attributed to Russell is clearly invalid. The theory in question in fact provides for a multitude of general propositions about any given determining complex.

Hylton (pp. 250–252) interprets (G_i) as an expression of incredulity regarding the Fregean hierarchy, while echoing Searle's reading (albeit more sympathetically than Searle—see note 27 above) on which Russell insists that if there are determining complexes, then there must also be singular propositions about them. Hylton also says that Russell rejects the Fregean hierarchy as a vicious infinite regress. Kremer (*ibid.*, pp. 284–287) sharply criticizes Hylton's interpretation, showing that on Russell's view at the time, the infinite "regress" (if one is to call it that) is not vicious. Kremer's interpretation of (F_{iii}) and (G_i) (pp. 287–290) is similar in important respects to my own (as is Makin's). It is not exactly the same, though, and I shall endeavor here to strengthen and sharpen Russell's argument significantly.

^{m}the determining complex occurring in the second of Russell's instances^m and ^{m}the determining complex that has given Russell's readers more headaches than any other^m. The problem is one of *identification*: Which of the infinitely many complexes in this equivalence class is it?

This identification problem is no mere pebble in *ST*'s shoe. It is a theoretical crisis. The problem looms larger when examining everyday contexts in which we actually designate contents by means of indirect quotations: contexts attributing modality or propositional attitudes. Ordinary English has the functional equivalent of indirect-quotation marks, at least when they flank an English sentence: the word 'that'.[35] The attribution 'Albert believes ^{m}the center of mass of the Solar Syste^m is a point^m' translates into ordinary English as

(5) Albert believes that the center of mass of the Solar System is a point.

Russell may be interpreted as objecting to Frege's hierarchy of indirect senses on the grounds that the customary sense of an expression does not determine the indirect sense (let alone higher-level indirect senses), so that one's ability to understand a sentence ϕ does not automatically enable one to understand $\ulcorner\alpha$ believes that $\phi\urcorner$, in which ϕ expresses its indirect sense. Suppose we utter (5) in conversation with Smith. When Smith apologizes that he does not understand the phrase 'center of mass', we accommodate him by defining the term. But on the doctrine of indirect senses (and hence on the theory that definite descriptions are singular terms), this is not sufficient for Smith now to understand (5). For though he now knows the customary sense of 'center of mass', he does not know the indirect sense. His knowing the customary sense of (3) without also knowing its indirect sense gives him the information that (5) in some way expresses *about* the proposition ^{m}the center of mass of the Solar System is a point^m that Albert believes it. But for want of a backward road, Smith does not thereby know, and has insufficient information to be able to determine, by what sense the proposition said to be believed by Albert is designated. Consequently, without further, independent information specifying the sense of the 'that'-clause, $\ulcorner$that (3)$\urcorner$, Smith does not, and cannot, actually understand (5) itself. So ends stage (*VII*), and with it the heart of the 'Gray's *Elegy*' argument.

This is a genuine, and difficult, philosophical problem, rediscovered more recently by Donald Davidson.[36] One may be tempted to suppose that the English

---

[35] See my *Frege's Puzzle* (Atascadero, Ca: Ridgeview, 1986, 1991), at pp. 5–6.

[36] Davidson, 'Theories of Meaning and Learnable Languages,' in Y. Bar-Hillel, ed., *Logic, Methodology, and Philosophy of Science: Proceedings* (Amsterdam: North-Holland, 1965), pp. 383–394, at 393–394. Even before Davidson, Carnap had complained, in *Meaning and Necessity* (note 29 above, §30, pp. 129–133), that "Frege nowhere explains in more ordinary terms what this third entity is." Neither Carnap nor Davidson credit Russell.

Dummett dismisses the "Gray's *Elegy*" argument as "extremely confused," in *Frege: Philosophy of Language*, at p. 267. Dummett nevertheless extracts this same extension of the stage (*VII*) objection to indirect senses—or an objection very close to this one—saying that it constitutes a *reductio ad absurdum* of Frege's entire theory. Dummett adds, "There is, however, a simple emendation which can be made to the doctrine [of indirect sense], which, with only a small perturbation in the system, dispels the objection." His proposed emendation consists in two claims: It is not the sense alone, but the sense together with a position within a sentence—what Dummett calls a *context*—that determines designation; and expressions have the same sense (though not the same designatum)

indirect sense of an expression invokes the expression itself, for example that the English indirect sense of 'center of mass' (the English customary sense of the indirect quotation '"center of mass"') is the customary sense of the definite description 'the English customary sense of "center of mass"'. This would yield the result that no two distinct synonyms could be *thoroughly synonymous*, i.e., sharing the same entire hierarchy of indirect senses. Customary synonyms—expressions with the same customary sense—will automatically differ in indirect sense (and therefore also in doubly indirect sense and every higher-level indirect sense). It would also provide a shortcut backward road, not from designatum to sense nor from sense to indirect sense, but directly from expression to indirect sense. Reflection reveals, however, that this cannot be correct. If it were, Smith would understand (5) even *without* being told the English customary sense of 'center of mass'. For he already knows the customary sense of the 'customary English sense of 'center of mass''; it is its designatum he does not know. Moreover, as Church famously argued, if (5) mentioned the particular English phrase 'center of mass' (perhaps by mentioning the entire English sentence (3)), then its translation into another language, say German, would be; not what it is normally taken to be, but instead a German sentence that quotes the English phrase 'center of mass', and that therefore fails to identify in German exactly what Albert is said to believe (specifying it instead perhaps as *whatever proposition is expressed in English by the particular words 'The center of mass of the Solar System is a point'*).[37]

when occurring in an *ungerade* linguistic context as they do when occurring in an ordinary ('transparent') context. See note 29 above. Ironically, the second part of this proposed emendation is precisely what was ruled out at stage (*V*) *via* the Collapse. Dummett does not address this earlier stage of the argument, though (as I interpret Russell) it is the central argument of the passage. In particular, Dummett's emendation seems to have the peculiar consequence that the proposition that '"the center of mass of the Solar System"' is a point = the proposition that the center of mass of the Solar System is a point. (This is the Collapse.) It would also have the consequence that this single proposition has no truth-value apart from an English context for the particular words 'the center of mass of the Solar System' (or a German context for the description's German translation, or etc.).

Dummett's acknowledgment of the problem noted by Russell at stage (*VII*) does not extend to the further problem to be noted two paragraphs below in the text. I criticize Dummett on this issue in 'The Very Possibility of Language: A Sermon on the Consequences of Missing Church,' in C. A. Anderson and M. Zeleny, eds., *Logic, Meaning and Computation: Essays in Memory of Alonzo Church* (Boston: Kluwer, 2001), pp. 573–595.

[37] In this sense it may be said that the relation of sense to indirect sense is not merely 'linguistic through the phrase,' though I believe this departs from Russell's meaning for those words; see note 17 above. That the indirect sense of an expression involves designation of the expression itself is suggested by Church's remarks concerning the paradox of analysis, in his famous review of the Black-White exchange, in *Journal of Symbolic Logic*, 11 (1946), pp. 132–133. Church's remarks there seem inconsistent, however, with his later writings concerning what has come to be called *the Church translation argument*, for example, 'On Carnap's Analysis of Statements of Assertion and Belief,' *Analysis*, 10, 5 (1950), pp. 97–99. This was noted by C. Anthony Anderson in his in-depth critical review of George Bealer's *Quality and Concept*, in *Journal of Philosophical Logic*, 16 (1987), pp. 115–164, at 162n27, and independently in my 'A Problem in the Frege–Church Theory of Sense and Denotation,' *Noûs*, 27, 2 (1993), pp. 158–166. Dummett has defended the exegetical thesis that Frege identified the indirect sense of α with the customary sense of ⌜the customary sense of 'α'⌝, in *The Interpretation of Frege's Philosophy* (Cambridge, Mass.: Harvard University Press, 1981), at pp. 89–100. (This represents a turnabout for Dummett, who had earlier dismissed the

As serious as this difficulty is, the problems with the theory that definite descriptions are singular terms do not end there. Russell argues, in effect, that *ST* is forced to claim, on pain of incoherence, that the contents of definite descriptions are (to use a notion that figures in 'On Denoting' and that Russell will develop in later work) knowable only *by description*, never *by acquaintance*. As noted, this corner is the very place where one prominent sub-group of *ST* theorists—*viz.*, Frege and some of his followers—have willingly chosen to call home. For Frege, *all* knowledge of things is of a sort that Russell will classify as knowledge by description, including our knowledge of senses. By Russell's lights, this renders the very phenomenon of our understanding language altogether impossible. For understanding an expression entails knowing what the content (for Frege, the *Sinn*) of the expression is. Understanding 'the first line of Gray's *Elegy*' evidently requires (indeed consists largely in) knowing of the determining complex ^{m}the first line of Gray's Elegy^m (*de re*) that the phrase expresses it. By virtue of the Collapse (and the stage (V) argument), the linguistic proposition that the phrase expresses ^{m}the first line of Gray's *Elegy*^{m} cannot be a singular proposition about the complex, and instead incorporates the postulated second-level complex ^{m} ^{m}the first line of Gray's *Elegy*^{m} ^{m}. The required *de re* knowledge is of the form: '*The first line of Gray's Elegy' expresses the determining complex that is such-and-such.* (More exactly, it is knowledge of the proposition ^{M}'the first line of Gray's *Elegy*' expresses c_1^{M}, where c_1 is the postulated second-level complex.) But on Russell's epistemology, knowing merely that 'the first line of Gray's *Elegy*' expresses the complex that is such-and-such—even if this knowledge is properly arrived at by an appropriate semantic computation—cannot qualify as genuine *understanding* of the definite description. For it is *de dicto* knowledge and not *de re*; it is only knowledge by description. The fact that 'the first line of Gray's *Elegy*' expresses the determining complex that is such-and-such begs the question: Which complex is *that*? Only by *identifying* the complex in question— i.e., by providing direct acquaintance with it—do we achieve the special sort of *de re* knowledge that constitutes genuine understanding of the description in question. Thus not only are we in no position to gain an understanding of a belief attribution like 'Albert believes that the first line of Gray's *Elegy* is beautiful'; a slight extension of the 'Gray's *Elegy*' argument appears to show that on *ST*, we cannot understand any definite description. And since the Collapse applies to any expression for which there is a content/designation distinction of the sort *ST* ascribes to definite

---

idea as 'rather implausible,' in *Frege: Philosophy of Language*, see the previous note above.) Both the thesis concerning the indirect sense of α and the exegetical thesis that Frege held the former thesis are defended in Gary Kemp, 'Salmon on Fregean Approaches to the Paradox of Analysis,' *Philosophical Studies*, 78, 2 (May 1995), pp. 153–162. I criticize this interpretation in 'The Very Possibility of Language,' note 36 above, §2. (See also §3, note 30.) The general idea that the indirect sense of an expression invokes the expression itself is also found (in various forms) in Herbert Heidelberger's review of Dummett's *Frege: Philosophy of Language*, in *Metaphilosophy*, 6, 1 (January 1975), pp. 35–43, at 37; Joseph Owens, 'Synonymy and the Nonindividualistic Model of the Mental,' *Synthese*, 66, 3 (March 1986), pp. 361–382, at 376–379; and C. Anthony Anderson, *ibid.* at pp. 141–143, and recently in 'Alonzo Church's Contributions to Philosophy and Intensional Logic,' §2.2, in C. A. Anderson and M. Zeleny, eds., *Essays in Memory of Alonzo Church* (Boston: Kluwer, 2001).

descriptions, on Russell's epistemology the theory that there are any expressions with contents that determine their designata—whether they be definite descriptions, sentences, or something else—inadvertently renders these expressions in principle unintelligible. This situation is indeed philosophically intolerable, in many respects, analogous to the derivation of Russell's Paradox about sets.[38]

Curiously, Russell.does not take the argument to this further stage, deriving a truly untenable consequence from *ST*. He seems determined, nevertheless, that the argument shall end with not a whine but a solar flare. Still discussing the connection between the target complex c and the postulated second-level complex $^m{}^mD^m{}^m$, the remainder of (G) reads as if to compensate for the relative weakness of (G_i):

(G_{ii}) Moreover, when C occurs in a proposition, it is not *only* the denotation that occurs (as we shall see in the next paragraph); yet, on the view in question, C is only the denotation, the meaning being wholly relegated to 'C.' This is an inextricable tangle, and seems to prove that the whole distinction of meaning and designation has been wrongly conceived.

Here an additional complication in translation arises. In previous paragraphs, I have everywhere replaced Russell's variable 'C' either with our metalinguistic variable 'α' or with our determining-complex variable 'c.' Where 'C' functions as a schematic letter standing in for a definite description (as suggested, for example, by the particular phraseology 'C is only the denotation'), I have replaced it with our schematic letter 'D'. A new complication concerns Russell's use of the phrase 'occur in a proposition'. Using my notion of *representation* (Section II above), and using specific instances instead of a schema, Russell evidently means to argue as follows, repeating the very circumstances that lead to the Collapse:

When the determining complex ^{m}the center of mass of the Solar System^m occurs in a proposition (as the subject), both the complex itself and its determinatum are involved in the proposition; yet we have seen that on the view in question, whenever ^{m}the center of mass of the

---

[38] Previous interpreters (e.g., Kremer, Noonan) have noted that, if it is assumed that we can designate anything with which we are acquainted by a "genuine name in the strict, logical sense" (and that we apprehend propositions expressed with the help of definite descriptions), then the explicit conclusion of this stage of Russell's argument—that "the meaning cannot be got at except by means of denoting phrases"—flatly contradicts a principle, usually called *the Principle of Acquaintance*, which is fundamental to Russell's epistemology and which is in fact explicitly enunciated in the closing paragraph of 'On Denoting' (and hinted at in the second paragraph): "Thus in every proposition that we can apprehend (i.e. not only in those whose truth or falsehood we can judge of, but in all that we can think about), all the constituents are really entities with which we have immediate acquaintance." The principle is restated more succinctly in Russell's 'Knowledge by Acquaintance and Knowledge by Description' (note 34 above, at p. 23 of Salmon and Soames): "Every proposition which we can understand must be composed wholly of constituents with which we are acquainted."

Though this point is closely related to the argument just given in the text, that argument does not rely on the assumption that any object of our acquaintance can be genuinely named nor on the Principle of Acquaintance. The very existence of the Collapse casts serious doubt on the former assumption. The argument employs instead a premise that is significantly more certain: that understanding a definite description requires *knowing which* complex it expresses. And in lieu of Acquaintance the argument employs a premise that is at least as certain: that in order to know which determining complex is such-and-such (as opposed merely to grasping the complex in question), one must know the singular proposition that it is such-and-such.

Solar System^m occurs in a proposition, it represents only the center of mass of the Solar System, which is its determinatum, the representation of the complex itself being wholly relegated to the occurrence of $^m\,{}^m$the center of mass of the Solar System$^m\,{}^m$ in a proposition. And similarly when the complex ^{m}the first line of Gray's *Elegy*^{m} occurs in a proposition, when ^{m}the author of *Waverley*^{m} occurs, and so on. Therefore, the view in question has been wrongly conceived.

The remainder of the passage, which constitutes a supplementary final stage of the argument, may thus be recast, without undue violence to Russell's apparent intent, as follows:

(G'_{ii}) Moreover, when c occurs in a proposition, it is not *only* the determinatum that occurs (as we shall see in the next paragraph); yet, on the view in question, c [represents] only the determinatum, the content [i.e., the representing of c itself] being wholly relegated to $^m\,{}^mD^m\,{}^m$. This is an inextricable tangle, and seems to prove that the whole distinction of content and designation has been wrongly conceived.

(H') That the content is relevant when a determiner phrase occurs in [a sentence expressing] a proposition is formally proved by the puzzle about the author of *Waverley*. The proposition ^{m}Scott is the author of *Waverley*^{m} has a property not possessed by ^{m}Scott is Scott^m, namely the property that George IV wished to know whether it was true. Thus the two are not identical propositions; hence the content of 'the author of *Waverley*' must be relevant [to the proposition] as well as the designatum, if I we adhere to the point of view to which this distinction belongs. Yet, as we have seen, so long as we adhere to this point of view, we are compelled to hold that only the designatum can be relevant. Thus the point of view in question must be abandoned.

The inextricable tangle does indeed seem to prove that the whole distinction of content and designation has been wrongly conceived . . . by Russell. Assuming stages (*IV*)–(*VI*) have been successful, on the theory that definite descriptions are singular terms, though the proposition is *about* the description's designatum and not about the content, the content itself is still relevant to the proposition's identity, and especially to its distinctness from other propositions involving determining complexes with the same determinata. This is the very point of the theory. To be sure, Russell knows this. He seems to be arguing in stage (*VIII*) more like a debating politician seeking votes, than the great philosopher that he is (and indeed that he proves himself to be in 'On Denoting').

VI

The heart of the "Gray's *Elegy*" argument comprises stages (*IV*)-(*VII*), in paragraph (*F*) and sub-paragraph (*G_i*). This portion is philosophically important. It deserves a thoughtful reply or, if a plausible reply cannot be found, nothing less than our endorsement.

On this reconstruction, the crux of Russell's objection to the theory that definite descriptions are singular terms is the Collapse: The attempt to form a singular proposition about a determining complex results instead in a general proposition about the complex's determinatum. The Collapse precludes "preserving the connection of content and designatum while preventing these from being one and the same, unless the content cannot be got at except by means of determining phrases." And this leads to the unsolvable mystery of second-level determining complexes (and higher-level complexes), Frege's *ungerade Sinne*. The "connection" of content and designatum may be given by the following:

P: The content of a singular term represents the term's designatum in propositions expressed by means of sentences containing the term.

If this principle *P* is respected, then the proposition expressed by '″′The center of mass of the Solar System′″ is a determining complex' will incorporate the content of '″the center of mass of the Solar System″′. If this proposition is a singular proposition about ″the center of mass of the Solar System″ (as was our intent), then the content of '″the center of mass of the Solar System″′ just *is* ″the center of mass of the Solar System″ representing itself. Equivalently, if we disallow the content of '″the center of mass of the Solar System″′ from being simply the designatum, then '″the center of mass of the Solar System″′ will have a separate content, ″ ″the center of mass of the Solar System″ ″. If there are singular propositions about determining complexes, then this separate content is completely idle, with no role to play in the, singular propositions expressed using '″the center of mass of the Solar System″′, in violation of *P*. It would appear, then, that if *P* is preserved *and* the content of an indirect quotation is prevented from being the designatum, then: (*i*) there cannot be singular propositions about determining complexes; (*ii*) '″the center of mass of the Solar System″′ must be a disguised definite description; and (*iii*) determining complexes cannot be named *in the strict, logical sense*. But then there is, according to Russell, a further difficulty that stems from the fact that "content cannot be got at except by means of determiner phrases": We have insufficient information to fix which determining complex ″ ″the center of mass of the Solar System″ ″ is, and hence, we do not even so much as understand the indirect quotation.

There is a viable reply to this argument. Recall our attempt to inform Smith of Albert's view by uttering (5). We noted that on Frege's theory, Smith needs to know the indirect sense of 'center of mass' in order to understand (5). But contrary to the argument that knowledge of the customary sense alone is insufficient, it would appear to be exactly this knowledge—nothing more and nothing less—that Smith needs in order to understand (5).[39] This suggests that there is indeed a backward road, not generally from designatum to sense but from customary sense to indirect sense. A thoroughgoing Fregean does not agree with Russell that we are *directly* acquainted with our concepts. A Fregean might nevertheless hold out the prospect that concepts are epistemologically special in that we grasp or apprehend them. It may be suggested that our very apprehension of a concept provides a distinguished second-level concept that presents the former concept in an epistemologically special, *de re* manner. Consider an analogy: The sentence 'Jane's dress is the same color as my hair' fails to identify the color that is in question. It is perfectly sensible to

---

[39] The best way to see this point is to undergo the process for oneself. I have invented a new word: 'nosdog'. Suppose the following belief attribution is true: 'Vito believes that his nosdog is loyal'. What does Vito believe? Hint: Vito's belief is not about a pet. Still do not know? Very well, let me specify the customary sense of the mystery word: it is ″godson″. Now try again: What does Vito believe?

respond with 'But what color is that?' By contrast, the sentence 'Jane's dress is black' preempts any such further query. The phrase 'the color of my hair' does not specify the color in the same definitive manner as the adjective 'black'. A Fregean should acknowledge that the adjective expresses a concept that determines the designated color in a uniquely identifying way, a special manner of presentation with respect to which the question 'But which one is thus presented?' does not arise. Call this special manner of presentation *Sinnful identification*. The particular second-level concept $^{m\ m}$the first line of Gray's *Elegy*$^{m\ m}$ that is postulated by Frege would have to be similarly privileged among second-level concepts that determine ^{m}the first line of Gray's *Elegy*^{m}, enjoying this more intimate relationship to its determinatum than do its equivalence-classmates ^{m}the determining complex occurring in the second of Russell's instances^m and ^{m}the determining complex that has given Russell's readers more headaches than any other^m. The target complex is uniquely Sinnfully identified by the postulated second-level concept for one who correctly understands 'the first line of Gray's *Elegy*' and thereby apprehends the content expressed. Knowledge by Sinnfully identifying description is acquaintance Frege-style, the next best thing to Russellian direct acquaintance.[40] It generates a special choice function on concepts: for each concept c that we can apprehend, there is a distinguished second-level concept that is the Sinnful identifier of c. The Sinnful identifier function would also provide a solution to the problem of how it is that we understand definite descriptions: Understanding 'the first line of Gray's *Elegy*' would consist in knowing (as the result of an appropriate semantic computation) that the description expresses the determining complex that is *such-and-such*, where this knowledge invokes the postulated second-level complex c_1 which not only represents but Sinnfully identifies the complex in question, i.e., it would consist in knowing: ^{M}'the first line of Gray's *Elegy*' expresses in English c_1^{M}.[41]

This does not defeat Russell's stage (*VI*) argument. Even if a Sinnful identifier choice function were found that selects a distinguished second-level complex from the equivalence class of complexes that determine ^{m}the first line of Gray's *Elegy*^{m}, unless this function also works (or provides another function f that works) at the bottom level, it is of no help in constructing the postulated second-level complex from our target complex, because of the Collapse. The moment we put the target complex into a larger complex, at best the Sinnful identifier function will be applied to the determinatum rather than to the complex itself. If the Sinnful identifier function exists, it yields the high backward road. But to defeat the argument at stage

---

[40] I argue in 'The Very Possibility of Language,' §4, that Church, and probably Frege, are committed to an epistemology of just this sort. Frege appeared to believe that certain indexicals, especially 'I', are typically used with a special identifying sense. The central point of Church's 'On Carnap's Analysis of Statements of Assertion and Belief,' is that an ordinary propositional-attitude or assertion attribution like 'Seneca said that man is a rational animal' differs from such surrogates as 'Seneca asserted the proposition expressed in English by "Man is a rational animal"' precisely in that the former "conveys the content of what Seneca said" (in Linsky, ed., p. 169). The latter, by contrast, merely specifies what Seneca said by describing it as the content of a certain string of words in a certain language. See note 37 above.

[41] The discussion in this paragraph has benefitted from remarks made by Kripke in a seminar, though he may not entirely agree with the reconstruction proposed here.

(*VII*) Frege does not need to *construct* the second-level complex from the target complex; it is enough simply to single out the second-level complex given the target complex, by Sinnfully identifying the latter. The high road leads directly from where we are to where Frege needs to go.

The Fregean hierarchy is generated by the following schema, which we may call *Frege's Rule* (for English), where α may be any meaningful English expression:

The English n-fold indirect sense of $\alpha =$ the English customary sense of $\ulcorner {}^n\alpha^n \urcorner$,

where the superscript 'n' represents a string of n occurrences of the indirect-quotation mark 'm'. Thus, the indirect sense of 'the first line of Gray's *Elegy*' is the customary sense of '^{m}the first line of Gray's *Elegy*^{m}', the doubly indirect sense is the customary sense of '^{m} ^{m}the first line of Gray's *Elegy*^{m} ^{m}', and so on.[42] Below these is the customary sense, which may be identified with the 0-fold indirect sense. If one is given only the designatum of a definite description α, one cannot determine what the customary sense is, but if one is given that customary sense, using Frege's Rule one can discover the n-fold indirect sense for any n—provided that one can derive the customary sense of an arbitrary indirect quotation $\ulcorner {}^m\beta^m \urcorner$ given the customary sense of β, i.e., provided that, contrary to the stage (*VII*) argument, indirect-quotation marks dot not constitute a restriction on the weaker version of Compositionality. The derivation of the sense of $\ulcorner {}^m\beta^m \urcorner$ from that of β will be possible if, but only if, one's apprehension of a sense provides one with a special manner in which that sense is presented, i.e. iff there is a backward road of the sort envisaged. The procedure for working out the n-fold indirect sense of α from its customary sense proceeds as follows: In understanding α, one thereby knows its customary sense c_0. The very knowledge that α expresses c_0 is of the form: α *expresses the determining complex that is such-and-such*, employing the particular second-level concept c_1 that Sinnfully identifies c_0. By cognitively attending to the special manner in which the customary sense c_0 is presented in one's very understanding of α, one *gleans* the Sinnfully identifying complex c_1. This enables one to understand the content quotation $\ulcorner {}^m\alpha^m \urcorner$ as expressing c_1—which, by Frege's Rule is the indirect sense of α. (Gleaning c_1 from one's knowledge that α expresses c_0 is tantamount to computing the *identifier* function for the apprehended complex c_0 as argument.) By attending to the special manner in which c_1 is presented in one's newly acquired understanding of $\ulcorner {}^m\alpha^m \urcorner$, one gleans the third-level complex c_2 that Sinnfully identifies c_1. This now enables one to understand $\ulcorner {}^m \, {}^m\alpha^m \, {}^m \urcorner$ as expressing c_2 (by Frege's Rule, the doubly indirect sense of α), and so on. In this manner, one works out the sense of a nested indirect quotation not in one fell swoop, but from the innermost indirect quotation out, climbing Frege's hierarchy one rung at a time. Frege's Rule utilizes the high backward road, enabling one to generate any level indirect sense from the customary

---

[42] See note 28 above. In 'Reference and Information Content: Names and Descriptions,' in D. M. Gabbay and F. Guenthner, eds., *Handbook of Philosophical Logic IV: Topics in the Philosophy of Language* (Dordrecht: D. Reidel, 1989), pp. 409–461, at 440–441, 455n11, I propose Frege's Rule as a solution to Davidson's challenge to Frege (see note 36 above) to state the rule that gives "the individual expressions that make up a sentence governed by 'believes'... the meanings they have in such a context."

sense as the situation demands ('Smith heard that Jones said that he believes that Salmon said that Russell believed that Frege thought that...'). Notice that on this reconstruction of Frege's theory, any pair of synonyms will be thoroughly synonymous, i.e., they will share the same indirect sense, the same doubly indirect sense, the same triply indirect sense, and so on all the way up.[43]

In short, for largely independent reasons, Frege should have countenanced a high backward road even while denying the existence of a low backward road. If stage (*V*) of the "Gray's *Elegy*" argument is correct that *ST* is committed to disavowing singular propositions about determining complexes, then even if the stage (*VI*) argument is also correct and Strong Compositionality fails for embeddings within *ungerade* contexts, the high backward road provides exactly the escape route that the theory needs to evade stage (*VII*). The "Gray's *Elegy*" argument thus does not succeed in refuting Frege's version of *ST*.

VII

The defense of *ST* invoking acquaintance Frege-style, though it may be the ticket for Fregeans, is not adequate for those, like myself, who wish to allow that definite descriptions are singular terms while retaining singular propositions about their contents. The defense does not contest stage (*V*), allowing the "Gray's *Elegy*" argument to score an early point by showing that the theory is indeed committed to rejecting singular propositions about determining complexes. Non-Fregean versions of *ST* must insert a wedge before stage (*V*). Indeed, our ground must be held at stage (*II*), in which the Collapse first appears. For non-Fregeans, it is the Collapse itself that must be defeated.

One obvious component of any viable non-Fregean defense against the Collapse (other than capitulating to it, as with the Theory of Descriptions) is to distinguish the propositions expressed by (3) and (4) by distinguishing two different ways in which the determining complex ^{m}the center of mass of the Solar System^m occurs therein. In fact, one finds exactly such a distinction of modes of occurrence in posthumously published writings by that most resourceful of all neo-Millians, Russell. Repeatedly in 'On Fundamentals,' written just prior to 'On Denoting' (see note 24 above), no sooner is one conceptual apparatus proposed than it is modified and replaced. In the course of his discursive explorations, Russell eventually discovers, and opts for, a rudimentary version of Theory of Descriptions. But before he does, he distinguishes

[43] As I argued in 'A Problem in the Frege–Church Theory of Sense and Denotation,' note 37 above, Church seems committed to accepting that expressions that are customarily synonymous are thoroughly synonymous, in his 'Intensional Isomorphism and Identity of Belief,' *Philosophical Studies*, 5 (1954), pp. 65–73; reprinted in N. Salmon and S. Soames, *Propositions and Attitudes* (Oxford University Press, 1988), pp. 159–168. I have also speculated, in 'The Very Possibility of Language,' §4 (see especially note 39), that Church may have believed in some such semantic computation of the sort described here. See note 40 above. Indeed, since the procedure amounts to repeated applications of the *identifier* function by attending to the value at one step and gleaning the value at the next, the procedure parallels the sort of effective computation relevant to Church's Thesis.

six modes of occurrences of propositional constituents, the two most significant of which he calls *primary occurrence* and *secondary occurrence*. He writes:

> When a *denoting* complex A occurs in a [propositional] complex B, it may occur in such a way that the truth-value of B is unchanged by the substitution for A of anything having the same denotation. (For the sake of brevity, it is convenient to regard anything which is *not* a denoting complex as denoting itself.) This is the case with 'the author of *Waverley*' in 'Scott was the author of *Waverley*', but not in 'people were surprised that Scott was the author of *Waverley*.'... We will call A a *primary constituent* of B when only the denotation of A is relevant to the truth-value of B, and we will call the occurrence of A a *primary occurrence* in this case; otherwise we will speak of A as a *secondary constituent*, and of its occurrence as a *secondary occurrence*.[44]

Roughly, then, a determining complex is here said by Russell to have *primary occurrence* in a containing complex (e.g., in a proposition) if it represents its determinatum in that occurrence—as ^{m}the center of mass of the Solar System^m occurs in the proposition expressed by (3)—and it is said to have a *secondary occurrence* if it represents itself, as in (4) and (5). The particular terms 'primary occurrence' and 'secondary occurrence' are conscripted in 'On Denoting' for a different distinction altogether: that of scope. I shall continue to speak instead of what is *represented* by an occurrence of the complex in a containing complex. What Russell in 'On Fundamentals' calls a *primary occurrence* in a proposition is a determinatum-representing occurrence, and what he calls a *secondary occurrence* is a self-representing occurrence. (A single complex may be self-representing in one occurrence and determinatum-representing in another in the same proposition, as in '^{mm}The center of mass of the Solar System^m determines the center of mass of the Solar System'.)

The distinction between determinatum-representing and self-representing occurrences, though it is surely part of the solution, does not of itself solve the problem of the Collapse. In fact, it is *after* Russell develops this distinction (and other related distinctions of modes of occurrence) in 'On Fundamentals' that he presents the Collapse as a problem yet to be solved. It is assumed that a proposition is fully determined by its components and their mode of composition. Earlier in the essay, Russell states that when one complex occurs in another, the kind of occurrence is determined by the nature of the containing complex and the position that the contained complex occupies therein (pp. 369–370, and *passim*). The problem is that, as Russell views the situation, ^{m}the center of mass of the Solar System^m occupies the same position in the propositions expressed by (3) and (4), and therefore is determinatum-presenting in both, hence the Collapse (pp. 381–382). To illustrate: it

---

[44] Page 374. In the preceding pages Russell instead calls these *occurrence as entity*, or as *being*, and *occurrence as meaning*. He says, 'When a complex occurs as being, any other complex having the same denotation, or the denotation itself, may be substituted without altering the truth or non-truth of the complex in which the said complex occurs" (p. 369), and goes on to say that ^{m}the author of *Waverley*^{m} occurs "as entity" in ^{m}Scott was the author of *Waverley*^{m}, and occurs "as meaning" in ^{m}people were surprised that Scott was the author of *Waverley*^{m} (p. 370). The connotations of these terms are—frustratingly—exactly the reverse of the concepts they express. The likely reason is that Russell here distinguishes among a complex, the complex's determinatum, and the complex's content, and he thinks of the complex as somehow going proxy for one or the other of these two attributes in the proposition. The terminology is scrapped just a few pages later, when these same terms are used for a different distinction altogether.

is now standard practice to represent propositions as sequences of proposition components. This allows one to distinguish the proposition that the author of *Waverley* is ingenious from the singular proposition about the author that he is ingenious. The latter proposition is identified with the ordered pair <Scott, ingenuity>, whereas the former proposition results by replacing Scott with ^{m}"the author of *Waverley*"^{m}. Now let *c* be ^{m}"the center of mass of the Solar System"^{m} and let *d* be ^{m}"is a point"^{m}. We then represent the proposition formed from these two concepts, appropriately composed, by the ordered pair <*c, d*>. But which proposition is this, a general proposition about a point or a singular proposition about a determining complex? Suppose we stipulate that if *c* occurs as determinatum-representing then this is the true proposition that the center of mass of the Solar System is a point, whereas if *c* occurs instead as self-representing, then this is the false singular proposition about *c* itself that it is a point. This is no solution. In each case, we have the same proposition composed of the same two concepts in the same way. How these concepts occur in the proposition seems a result of pragmatics—of speaker's intentions or the like. It is irrelevant to the identity of the proposition.

One ingenious line of defense against the Collapse has been proposed by another particularly resourceful neo-Millian, Kaplan. He writes:

The solution to the difficulty is simple. Regard the 'object' places of a singular proposition as marked by some operation which cannot mark a complex. (There always will be some such operation.) For example, suppose that no complex is (represented by) a set containing a single member. Then we need only add {...} to mark the places in a singular proposition which correspond to directly referential terms. We no longer need worry about confusing a complex with a propositional constituent corresponding to a directly referring term because no complex will have the form {*x*}. In particular, [^{m}"the center of mass of the Solar System"^{m} $\neq$ {^{m}"the center of mass of the Solar System"^{m}}]. This technique can also be used to resolve another confusion in Russell. He argued that a sentence containing a [nondesignating] directly referential term (he would have called it a nondenoting 'logically proper name') would be meaningless, presumably because the purported singular proposition would be incomplete. But the braces themselves can fill out the singular proposition, and if they contain nothing, no more anomalies need result than what the development of Free Logic has already inured us to. ('Demonstratives,' note 6 above, at 496n23.)

The general idea is to distinguish the two modes of occurrence as constituents of propositions by actually *marking* some constituents so as to indicate that they represent themselves in the proposition. The singular proposition about Scott that he is ingenious is now represented by the ordered pair: <{Scott}, ingenuity>. This evidently requires some modification in Synonymous Interchange. If it is conceded that 'the center of mass of the Solar System' has the same content as its indirect quotation (or any other name for its content), then some synonyms do not designate the same thing, and substitution of one expression by a synonym cannot be allowed when the two do not share the same designatum. Even substitution of co-designative expressions may involve more than mere substitution of one proposition component by another— as when ^{m}"the first line of Gray's *Elegy*"^{m} is substituted for the grammatical subject in 'The determining complex occurring in the second of Russell's instances has given Russell's readers more headaches than any other complex'. For Kaplan, this substitution of a determinatum-representing complex by its determinatum is automatically accompanied by a mark transforming the position occupied into a self-representing position. Here the restriction on Synonymous Interchange comes into play, since we cannot go on to substitute 'the first line of Gray's *Elegy*' without altering the content Kaplan proposes extending his marking procedure to the occurrence of nondesignating names, thereby providing semantic content where Russell finds none.

Russell explicitly considers a similar proposal in 'On Denoting,' where he dismisses any such solution as being essentially Meinongian. Immediately after criticizing Meinong in 'On Denoting,' Russell says:

> Another way of taking the same course (so far as our present alternative is concerned) is adopted by Frege, who provides by definition some purely conventional denotations for the cases in which otherwise there would be none. Thus, 'the king of France' is to denote the null-class . . . But this procedure, though it may not lead to actual logical error, is plainly artificial, and does not give an exact analysis of the matter.

Russell would surely say the same about a more restrictive proposal that confines itself to names instead of descriptions. And he would be correct. There is something artificial about Kaplan's representation of the content of 'Nappy is a despot'[45] as $\langle\{\}$, ^{m}is a despot$^m\rangle$, something that is equally plainly artificial about his representation of singular propositions about Scott as containing {Scott} in subject position instead of Scott.

There is a more liberal interpretation possible for Kaplan's proposal. It might appear as if Kaplan is backpedaling, modifying the offending version of *ST* so that the content of a logically proper name is held to be not simply its designatum but the unit set of its designatum. But this may be to place undue weight on an artifact of the particular marking system he suggests. One might take the basic idea to be, rather, that the content of an indirect quotation is just the complex, which typically represents its determinatum when occurring in a proposition but which is marked instead for self-representation in the false singular proposition expressed by (4), analogously to the way in which the definite description itself is marked by indirect-quotation marks in (4). Even so, whatever the mark of self-representation is, it must be an actual feature of the proposition, else the Collapse. Indeed, the "proposition" that Kaplan provides in the case of a sentence with a nondesignating name as grammatical subject has no actual representing component in subject position, but instead only the mark. One suspects that Russell would resist this proposal on the same grounds that though it may not lead to actual logical error, it is plainly artificial and does not give an exact analysis of the matter. And it is by no means obvious that his complaint would be entirely misplaced. The proposal does seem a bit airy fairy. Are we really to suppose that a singular proposition about Mont Blanc contains not only the mountain with all its snowfields but also the mountain with the hypo-thesized "mark"? What exactly is the mark? What portion or aspect of the sentence (e.g., 'Scott is ingenious') actually contributes the mark?

It remains true that a self-representing occurrence of ^{m}the center of mass of the Solar System^m in a proposition is very different from a determinatum-representing

---

[45] I have invented the name 'Nappy' for the present emperor of France. There is no such person.

occurrence. This much, by itself, is not an *ad hoc* stipulation; it is a factual observation. The problem is to clarify this distinction in such a way as to distinguish (3) and (4) in its terms without making the distinction merely a matter of syntax and pragmatics, and without resorting to artificial and *ad hoc* alteration of the content of a name.

There is a way to do this. Though I came upon the idea independently (and used it extensively in my book, *Frege's Puzzle*[46]), it comes as little surprise to find the same idea in 'On Fundamentals.'

There Russell says that ^{m}the author of *Waverley*^{m} is an *analyzable* constituent of ^{m}Scott was the author of *Waverley*^{m} whereas the latter's occurrence in ^{m}people were surprised that Scott was the author of *Waverley*^{m} is *unanalyzable*, in that the determinatum-representing proper constituents of the former proposition (e.g., ^{m}the author of *Waverley*^{m}) are self-representing rather than determinatum-representing constituents of the latter proposition (pp. 375, 378, 379).[47] Analyzable and unanalyzable occurrences are both contrasted with a third mode of occurrence, *occurrence as meaning*. Something occurs in a proposition in this third way if it "can only be replaced [without loss of significance] by an entity of a certain sort, e.g. a proposition" (pp. 374, 378). Russell has in mind occurrences like a conditional proposition's antecedent, which must be a proposition (and not, e.g., a person) for the conditional to be meaningful. According to Russell, when a determining complex *A* occurs in this way in a complex *B*, *A* is not so much analyzable as it is *analyzed* in *B*, in that it "is not a constituent of the complex *B* in which it is said to occur, but its constituents occur in *B*, and occur in that relation to each other which constitutes the meaning of *A*" (p. 378).

Russell's notion of an *analyzed* (as opposed to an *analyzable*) occurrence provides for a mode of occurrence in a manner other than as a *constituent*. He stipulated that the proposition ^{m}Scott was the author of *Waverley*^{m} occurs in just this manner in ^{m}if Scott was the author of *Waverley*, then he combined the talents of a poet and a novelist^m (p. 375). There is no reason why the determining complex ^{m}the author of *Waverley*^{m} itself should not occur in the proposition ^{m}Scott was the author of *Waverley*^{m} in this very same manner: not as an analyzable constituent, not as a constituent at all, but analyzed (in Russell's senses of these terms). Instead Russell explicitly says that ^{m}the author of *Waverley*^{m} is an analyzable, determinatum-representing ("primary") constituent of ^{m}Scott was the author of *Waverley*^{m} (p. 375).[48]

One should distinguish sharply between a determining complex "occurring in" a proposition as a *concept-component* and its occurring as what I call a *sub-concept*— analogous to the two ways in which one set might occur within another: as an element or as a subset. (At the very least, one should draw an analogous distinction

---

[46] In Appendix *C*, pp. 143–151; see especially pp. 145–147, clauses 16, 23–24, 28–29, 32–36. (See also pp. 20–21.)

[47] Russell appears to believe that the proposition ^{m}Scott was the author of *Waverley*^{m} determines itself (and is therefore determinatum-representing in ^{m}people were surprised that Scott was the author of *Waverley*^{m}). This is highly dubious, however, since substitution of 'Scott' for 'the author of *Waverley*' in 'Scott = the author of *Waverley*', though it does not preserve the proposition expressed, should yield a proposition with the same determinatum. Frege relied on considerations like this to argue that a proposition determines its truth-value.

[48] *Cf. The Principles of Mathematics*, pp. 64, 502.

for the occurrence of a determining complex within a proposition if determining complexes are, as Russell's terminology suggests, *complex*, i.e., non-simple.) This distinction of modes of occurrence corresponds not to Russell's distinction between *analyzable* and *unanalyzable*, but to a Russellian distinction for which he introduces terms but of which he otherwise takes no special notice, that between *constituent* and *analyzed*. The determining complex ^{m}the center of mass of the Solar System^m analyzes into two concept-components: ^{m}the^m and ^{m}center of mass of the Solar System^m. (The latter concept-component is what Russell, in *The Principles of Mathematics*, called a *class-concept*; it is a concept of a unit class of points in real space. In *Frege's Puzzle*, the former concept-component is identified with the *operation* of assigning to any unit class its sole element.) To treat these two as concept-components also of the singular proposition about the complex that it is intriguing, and of the proposition expressed by (4), is to misunderstand the fundamental nature of a singular proposition. Here these concept-components are like the occurrence of arms and hands in the singular proposition about Scott that he is ingenious. The entire complex ^{m}the center of mass of the Solar System^m is a concept-component ("constituent") of the singular proposition about it that it itself is intriguing, and likewise of the singular proposition expressed by (4), whereas the same complex is not a concept-component, in this sense, but a sub-concept of ("occurs analyzed in") the proposition that the center of mass of the Solar System is intriguing and of the general proposition expressed by (3)—just as $<a, b>$ is a sequence-element of $<<a, b>, e>$ and a sub-sequence of $<a, b, e>$.[49] Using the sequence representation for propositions, we may let $a = {}^m$the^m; $b = {}^m$center of mass of the Solar System^m; $e = {}^m$is intriguing^m. Then the complex ^{m}the center of mass of the Solar System^m is represented by $<a, b>$, the proposition that the center of mass of the Solar System is intriguing by $<a, b, e>$, and the singular proposition about ^{m}the center of mass of the Solar System^m by $<<a, b>, e>$. No marks, no pragmatic clutter, and no collapse—and any remaining artificiality (e.g., the representation of complexes by sequences) is reduced to a minimal level that ought to be acceptable, at least for the purpose of rescuing a non-Fregean version of *ST* from the 'Gray's *Elegy*' argument.

The distinction between occurrence as concept-component and occurrence as sub-concept violates the principle *P* mentioned above. It is true that the moment we put a determining complex in a proposition as a sub-concept, the proposition is about the determinatum of the complex; but this is not true when we put the complex in as a concept-component. The distinction also shows that Compositionality does not

---

[49] A sequence s is a *sub-sequence* of a sequence s' if there are positive whole numbers j, m, and n such that s is an m-ary sequence, s' is an n-ary sequence, $m \leq n$, and for each whole number i, $1 \leq i \leq m$, the ith sequence-element of s is the $(j + i)$th sequence-element of s'. In this sense, s "is not a constituent of s' in which it is said to occur, but its constituents occur in s', and occur in that relation to each other which constitutes s." The notion of *sub-concept* should be understood analogously in terms of *concept-component*.

To forestall misinterpretation: I am not suggesting that a proposition is best represented as a sequence of concept-components, let alone that it *is* such a sequence. What I am proposing is that, whatever the real structure of propositions may be (e.g., perhaps a tree structure), one should distinguish these two modes in which entities might be said to "occur in" a proposition—as component, or alternatively as sub-concept—and that this distinction provides a promising solution to the central problem posed in Russell's 'Gray's *Elegy*' argument.

directly yield Synonymous Interchange. Let us assume that sentences like (3) and (4) are mere sequences of words (rather than tree-structures or the like). The proposition represented by $<a, b, e>$ is the value of a computable function applied to the contents of the contentful component words and phrases of (3), just as $<<a, b>, e>$ is the value of a computable function applied to the contents of the contentful component words and phrases of (4). One may suppose that it is the same computable function, defined by cases (e.g., treating indirect quotations differently from definite descriptions). Even a version of Strong Compositionality is upheld, though the content of the description 'the center of mass of the Solar System' occurs as sub-concept rather than concept-component. It is precisely this feature of the definite description that prevents substitution for it by its indirect quotation or by a name of the complex expressed. For though their contents are the same object, that object occurs differently in the content of the sentence, depending on whether its concept-components are contributed *en masse*, by the indirect quotation or name, or individually by the definite description's components.

Though forceful and important, the reasoning of the 'Gray's Elegy' argument is mistaken at each stage. The alleged Collapse of (4) into (3) is a myth; hence *ST* is not committed to the Fregean hierarchy, though Millian versions of *ST* are committed to a restriction on Synonymous Interchange. Those who voluntarily undertake the commitment to Frege's hierarchy may concede that the indirect sense is not constructed from the customary sense, so that indirect-quotation marks and 'that' constitute further restrictions on Strong Compositionality. But they may also follow the high backward road to derive the indirect sense from the customary in compliance with the weaker version of Compositionality.

Ironically, had Russell seen that a determining complex occurs *analyzed* in a proposition rather than as a *constituent*, in his sense, he might not have discovered the Theory of Descriptions—at any rate, not as the stream of consciousness flows in 'On Fundamentals.' It follows from nothing I have said that the Theory of Descriptions is wrong and that English is WRL rather than IRL. On the contrary, it was extremely fortunate for Philosophy that Russell was prompted by the threat of the Collapse to discover that paradigm of philosophy. Without it, the IRL hypothesis might never have been discovered and those of us who ponder content might forever have dreamed that we know which language we speak.

APPENDIX: ANALYTICAL TRANSLATION OF THE OBSCURE PASSAGE

On Russell's terminology, a *denoting phrase* is a singular noun phrase beginning with what linguists call a *determiner*, like 'every', 'some', or 'the'. Both definite and indefinite descriptions are denoting phrases, in Russell's sense. A definite description of a given language is said to *mean*—in a more standard terminology, it *expresses*—a *denoting complex c* as its *meaning*. The denoting complex *c*, in turn, *denotes*—in Church's terminology, it is a concept of—an object as its *denotation*. I here translate Russell's term 'meaning' as 'content'. Russell does not use any special term for the binary relation between a definite description and the object of which the expression's content in the language is a concept. Instead Russell speaks of "the denotation of the meaning," saying that a definite description α "has a meaning which denotes" an object x. Sometimes he says that α itself (as opposed to its content) denotes x. Here I avoid Russell's term 'denote' altogether. Instead I use 'determine' for the relation between a complex c and the object x of which c is a concept, and I call x the 'determinatum' of c. I use 'designate' for the relation between the expression α and x, and I call x the 'designatum' of α.

Russell uses 'C' as a variable ranging over determining complexes, and sometimes instead as a metalinguistic variable ranging over determiner phrases. Frequently he uses 'C' as a schematic letter (a substitutional variable), sometimes standing in for an arbitrary definite description, sometimes for a term designating an arbitrary determining complex. Any sentence in which 'C' occurs as schematic letter is strictly speaking a *schema*, of which Russell means to assert every instance. Fortunately, with a little finesse, Russell's intent can usually be captured by taking 'C' as a variable either ranging over definite descriptions or ranging over determining complexes. I here use 'α' as a metalinguistic variable, and upper case 'D' as a schematic letter standing in for an arbitrary definite description. I use lower-case 'c' as a determining-complex variable. I use Quine's quasi-quotation marks, '$\ulcorner$' and '$\urcorner$' in combination with 'α'. In quasi-quotation, all internal expressions are quoted, i.e., mentioned (designated), except for metalinguistic variables, whose values are mentioned. I use single quotation marks for direct (expression) quotation. Following Kaplan, I use superscripted occurrences of 'm' as indirect-quotation marks, and superscripted occurrences of 'M' as indirect-quasi-quotation marks.[i] In indirect-quasi-quotation, the contents of all internal expressions are mentioned, except for concept variables, whose values are mentioned. Here I avoid double quotation marks, except as scare-quotes when using another's words. Departures from the original appear in **boldface**.

(A') The relation of the **content** to the **designatum** involves certain rather curious difficulties, which seem in themselves sufficient to prove that the theory which leads to such difficulties must be wrong.

(B') (*I*) When we wish to speak about, *i.e.*, **to designate**, the **content** of a **determiner** phrase, *i.e.*, **of a definite description**, as opposed to its **designatum**, the **present** mode of doing so is by **indirect-quotation marks**. Thus we say:

The center of mass of the Solar System is a point, not a **determining** complex;

^{m}The center of mass of the Solar System^m is a **determining** complex, not a point.

Or again,

The first line of Gray's *Elegy* **expresses** a proposition.

^{m}The first line of Gray's *Elegy*^{m} **does not express** a proposition.

Thus taking any **determiner** phrase, **e.g., taking any definite description** . . . , α, we wish to consider the relation between α and $\ulcorner{}^m\alpha{}^m\urcorner$, where the difference of the two is of the kind exemplified in the above two instances.

---

[i] Kaplan, 'Quantifying In,' in L. Linsky, ed., *Reference and Modality* (Oxford University Press, 1971), pp. 112–144, at 120–121. (Kaplan there calls indirect-quotation marks *meaning-quotation marks*.) The reader who is unfamiliar with these devices is advised to look them up.

(*C′*)   We say, to, begin with, that when **α** occurs it is the ***designatum* of α** that we are speaking about; but when ⌜*ᵐ*α*ᵐ*⌝ occurs, it is the **content**. Now the relation of **content to designatum** is not merely linguistic through the phrase, *i.e.*, it is not merely the **indirect relative product of the semantic relations of *being the content of* a phrase and *designating*:** there must be a direct, non-semantic, logico-metaphysical relation involved, which we express by saying that the **content *determines* the designatum**. But the difficulty which confronts us is that we cannot succeed in *both* preserving the connection of **content to designatum** *and* preventing them—**the content and the designatum**—from being one and the same; also that the **content** cannot be got at except by means of **determiner** phrases.[ii] This happens as follows.

(*D′ᵢ*)   The one phrase **α** was to have both **content** and **designation**. But if **in an effort to designate the content**, we speak of ⌜**the content of α**⌝, that gives us the **content** (if any) of the **designatum of α**. 'The **content** of the first line of Gray's *Elegy*' **designates** the same **complex** as 'The **content** of *ᵐ*The curfew tolls the knell of parting day*ᵐ*', and . . . not the same as 'The **content** of *ᵐ*the first line of Gray's *Elegy*ᵐ*'. Thus in order to get the **content** we want, we must speak not of ⌜**the content of α**⌝, but of ⌜**the content of *ᵐ*α*ᵐ*⌝, which **designates** the same as ⌜*ᵐ*α*ᵐ*⌝ by itself.[iii]

(*D′ᵢᵢ*)   Similarly ⌜**the determinatum of α**⌝ does not **designate the determinatum** we want, **the determinatum of α's content**, but means something, *i.e.*, **expresses a determining complex**, which, if it **determines anything** at all, **determines** what is **determined** by the **determinatum** we want. For example, let **α** be 'the **determining** complex occurring in the second of the above instances'. Then ⌜α = *ᵐ*the first line of Gray's *Elegy*ᵐ*⌝ and ⌜**The determinatum of α** = 'The curfew tolls the knell of parting day'⌝ **are both true**.[iv]

[ii] It might have been more perspicuous for Russell to formulate his objection this way: We cannot succeed in both preserving the connection of content to designatum and *allowing* the content and the designatum to be one and the same. Moreover we cannot even succeed in both preserving the connection of content to designatum and *disallowing* the content and the designatum from being one and the same, *unless* the content cannot be got at except by means of determiner phrases. That is, if we preserve the connection whereby the designatum of a definite description is determined by the description's content which is distinct from the designatum itself, then the content cannot be designated by means of a "genuine name in the strict, logical sense."

[iii] This yields the awkward result that ⌜*ᵐ*α*ᵐ* = the content of *ᵐ*α*ᵐ*⌝ is true. I am here attributing to Russell a serious equivocation, resulting from his dual use of inverted commas both as direct quotation marks and as indirect-quotation marks. He appears to believe that he has derived from the theory that definite descriptions have a content/designation distinction the consequence that in order to designate *ᵐ*the center of mass of the Solar System*ᵐ*, rather than using the inappropriate phrase 'the content of the center of mass of the Solar System' we must use 'the content of *ᵐ*the center of mass of the Solar System*ᵐ*' (which Russell fails to distinguish from the perfectly appropriate 'the content of 'the center of mass of the Solar System' '), thus ascribing a content to a determining complex itself. As a criticism of the content/designation theory, or even as a neutral description, this is a red herring. Instead the theory entails that one may designate *ᵐ*the center of mass of the Solar System*ᵐ* using the functor 'the content of' in combination with 'the center of mass of the Solar System' and direct quotation, not indirect quotation. Russell has a stronger criticism to make of the theory, though, his presentation is colored somewhat by this red herring.

[iv] In the original text Russell here uses '*C*' as a schematic letter standing in for a term designating a determining complex. The preceding two sentences should read:

For example, let '*C*' [stand in for] 'the determining complex occurring in the second of the above instances'. Then *C* = *ᵐ*the first line of Gray's *Elegy*ᵐ*, and the determinatum of *C* = 'The curfew tolls the knell of parting day'.

I have reformulated this in the metalinguistic mode using 'α', quasi-quotation, and the predicate 'is true'.

But what we *meant* to have as the **determinatum** was ^{m}the first line of Gray's *Elegy*^{m}. Thus we have failed to get what we wanted **from** ⌜**the determinatum of** α⌝.[v]

(E′ᵢ)   **(II)** The difficulty in speaking of the **content** of a **determining** complex, *i.e.*, in using a phrase of the form ⌜**the content of** $^m\alpha^m$⌝, may be stated thus: The moment we put the complex in a proposition, the proposition is about the **determinatum**;[vi] and hence if we make a proposition in which the subject **component** is ^{M}**the content of** c^M, **for some determining complex** c, then the subject **represents the content** (if any) of the **determinatum of** c, which was not intended.[vii]

(E′ᵢᵢ)   **(III)** This leads us to say that, when we distinguish **content** and **determinatum** of a **determining complex, as we did in the preceding paragraph,** we must be dealing **in both cases** with the **content: the content has a determinatum** and is a **determining** complex, and there is not something other than the **content**, which can be called ⌜**the complex** $^m\alpha^m$⌝, and be said to *have* both **content** and a **determinatum**. The right phrase**ology**, on the view in question, is that some **contents** have **determinata**.

(F′ᵢ)   **(IV)** But this only makes our difficulty in speaking of **contents** more evident. For suppose c is our **target** complex, **and let 'D' represent in what follows a determiner phrase that expresses** c (for example, let c be ^{m}**the center of mass of the Solar System**^{m} **and let 'D' stand in for the phrase 'the centre of mass of the Solar System'**); then we are to say that $^mD^m$, *i.e.*, c *is* the content of the phrase 'D', **instead of saying that** $^mD^m$ itself **has a content**. Nevertheless, whenever 'D' occurs without **indirect-quotation** marks, what is said is not **about** $^mD^m$, the content of 'D', but only **about** D, the designatum of 'D', as when we say:

The center of mass of the Solar System is a point

(F′ᵢᵢ)   **(V)** Thus to speak of $^mD^m$ itself, *i.e.*, to **express** a proposition about the **content of** 'D', our subject **component** must not be $^mD^m$ *itself*, but something **else, a new determining complex, which determines** $^mD^m$.[viii] Thus ^{m} $^mD^m$ ^{m}—which iterated indirect quotation is what we use when we want to speak of the **content of** '$^mD^m$'— must be not the **content of** 'D', *i.e.*, **not** $^mD^m$ itself, but something which **determines** the **content**.

(F′ᵢᵢᵢ)   **(VI)** And $^mD^m$, *i.e.*, c, must not be a constituent of this **higher-level** complex ^{m} $^mD^m$ ^{m} (as it is of ^{M}**the content of** c^M); for if $^mD^m$ occurs in the complex, it will be its **determinatum**, not the content of 'D', *i.e.*, **not** $^mD^m$ itself, that will **be represented**

---

[v] *Pace* Russell, his apparent observation that in order to designate the designatum of α we should use ⌜the determinatum of $^m\alpha^m$⌝ rather than ⌜the determinatum of α⌝, though correct, provides no support whatever to his apparent conclusion that in order to designate the content of α, rather than using ⌜the content of α⌝ we must use ⌜the content of $^m\alpha^m$⌝, which is in fact equally inappropriate. Instead we can designate α's content by using ⌜the content of 'α'⌝ or ⌜$^m\alpha^m$⌝. Analogously, we can designate α's designatum by using ⌜the designatum of 'α'⌝ or α itself.

[vi] That is, as soon as we put a determining complex in a proposition, by using a singular term whose content is the complex, the proposition is about the complex's determinatum. This generates what I call *the Collapse*. As Russell will argue below, this same phenomenon arises even when designating the complex by using the simple indirect quotation ⌜$^m\alpha^m$⌝.

[vii] Roughly, a proposition component *represents* an object x in a proposition p if p is about x in virtue of that component. This marks the first use by Russell of his variable 'C' as ranging over determining complexes rather than definite descriptions. Moreover, the quotation marks here are indirect-quasi-quotation marks. The quotation ^{M}the content of c^M designates the determining complex consisting of the content of the functor 'the content of' joined with the complex c.

[viii] In this sence, the content cannot be got at except by means of determiner phrases; it cannot be genuinely *named*, in the strict, logical sense.

and there is no backward road from **determinata** to **contents**, because every object can be **designated** by an infinite number of different **determiner** phrases.

(G'_i)   (**VII**) Thus it would seem that $^{m}{}^{m}D^{m}{}^{m}$ and $^{m}D^{m}$ are **altogether** different entities, such that $^{m}{}^{m}D^{m}{}^{m}$ **determines** $^{m}D^{m}$; but this cannot be an explanation **of** $^{m}{}^{m}D^{m}{}^{m}$, because the relation of $^{m}{}^{m}D^{m}{}^{m}$ to $^{m}D^{m}$ remains wholly mysterious; and where are we to find the **determining** complex $^{m}{}^{m}D^{m}{}^{m}$ which is to **determine** $^{m}D^{m}$?

(G'_{ii})   (**VIII**) Moreover, when $^{m}D^{m}$ occurs in a proposition, it is not *only* the **determinatum** that occurs (as we shall see in the next paragraph); yet, on the view in question, $^{m}D^{m}$ **represents** only the **determinatum**, the content (*i.e.*, the representing of c itself) being wholly relegated to $^{m}{}^{m}D^{m}{}^{m}$. This is an inextricable tangle, and seems to prove that the whole distinction of **content and designation** has been wrongly conceived.

(H')   That the **content** is relevant when a **determiner** phrase occurs in **a sentence expressing** a proposition is formally proved by the puzzle about the author of *Waverley*. The proposition ^{m}Scott is the author of *Waverley*^{m} has a property not possessed by ^{m}Scott is Scott^{m}, namely the property that George IV wished to know whether it was true. Thus the two are not identical propositions; hence the **content** of 'the author of *Waverley*' must be relevant **to the proposition** as well as the **designatum**, if we adhere to the point of view to which this distinction belongs. Yet, as we have seen, so long as we adhere to this point of view, we are compelled to hold that only the **designatum** can be relevant. Thus the point of view in question must be abandoned.

16

A Problem in the Frege–Church Theory of Sense and Denotation (1993)

There is an inconsistency among claims made (or apparently made) in separate articles by Alonzo Church concerning Frege's distinction between sense and denotation taken together with plausible assertions by Frege concerning his notion of *ungerade Sinn*—i.e., the sense that an expression allegedly takes on in positions in which it has *ungerade Bedeutung*, denoting its own customary sense.[1] As with any inconsistency, the difficulty can be avoided by relinquishing one of the joint assumptions from which contradiction may be derived. Yet what seems the most plausible resolution, in light of Church's own arguments, involves abandoning the theory of sense and denotation, in the form in which it has been staunchly advocated by both Frege and Church. That theory has come under sustained criticism from several quarters.[2] Whereas the present difficulty supplements the case against the theory, it is unlike more familiar criticisms, since it is not framed from the perspective of an alternative theory (or picture) but is based instead on an internal conflict, and therefore has special force.

I

The difficulty can be illustrated by assuming (solely for the sake of the illustration) that the word 'brother' has exactly the same customary sense in English as the phrase 'male sibling', and that, consequently, so do the following two sentences:

(1) Holmes has an older brother
(2) Holmes has an older male sibling.

One version of the so-called Paradox of Analysis can then be set out by noting that the following analysis of the proposition that Holmes has an older brother is

I am grateful to Anthony Brueckner and Matthew Hanser for their helpful comments.

[1] I follow Church in translating Frege's use of '*Bedeutung*' as 'denotation' rather than 'meaning', and Frege's use of '*Gedanke*' as 'proposition' rather than 'thought'. I also use the word 'concept' in Church's sense, which is very different from Frege's use of '*Begriff*'.

[2] I have summarized and integrated the most influential aspects of that criticism in part I of my book, *Reference and Essence* (Princeton University Press, 1981).

informative, or can be, even for someone who correctly understands both of the English sentences (1) and (2):

> (*PA*) The proposition that Holmes has an older brother is the proposition that Holmes has an older male sibling.[3]

Extrapolating from remarks in Church's review of the famous Black/White controversy concerning the Paradox of Analysis, he would evidently claim that the informativeness of (*PA*) is explained, along familiar lines, by the fact that the English phrases 'the proposition that Holmes has an older brother' and 'the proposition that Holmes has an older male sibling', while they have the same (customary) denotation, differ in (customary) sense.[4]

Consider now the following English sentences:

> (3) Watson believes that Holmes has an older brother
> (4) Watson believes that Holmes has an older male sibling.

According to the Frege–Church theory of sense and denotation, relative to their positions in these sentences, respectively, (1) and (2) denote their (shared) customary English sense—the proposition that Holmes has an older brother—rather than their truth-value. Both (3) and (4) thereby attribute to Watson belief of the very same proposition, and therefore cannot differ in their truth-value in English.

Furthermore, according to the theory, sentence (1) denotes its customary sense in the English sentence (3) by there expressing its *indirect sense*, which is a concept of (i.e. which determines) the proposition that Holmes has an older brother. In his seminal '*Über Sinn und Bedeutung*,' Frege says that the indirect sense (in English) of a sentence like (1) is the customary sense (in English) of the phrase 'the proposition that Holmes has an older brother'.[5] Taken together with Church's proposed solution to the Paradox of Analysis, this entails that, whereas they have the same customary English sense, the English sentences (1) and (2) above differ in indirect sense, i.e. they express differing senses in English when positioned within the scope of an '*ungerade*' operator, as in (3) and (4) or in (*PA*).[6]

Some philosophers—notably Tyler Burge—criticize the assertion that (3) and (4) cannot differ in truth-value in English.[7] Imagine that Watson readily accepts the truth of (1), as a sentence of English, yet because of uncertainty as to the exact

---

[3] The alleged informativeness of analyses might be seen more vividly in the case of nontrivial philosophical analyses, such as have been proposed for the concepts of knowledge, perception, nonnatural meaning, and for propositions expressed by means of definite descriptions, etc.

[4] *Journal of Symbolic Logic*, 11 (1946), pp. 132–133. The suggested interpretation is probably standard. It has been questioned by Terence Parsons. See his 'Frege's Hierarchies of Indirect Senses and the Paradox of Analysis,' in P. French, T. Uehling, Jr., and H. Wettstein, eds., *Midwest Studies in Philosophy VI: The Foundations of Analytic Philosophy* (Minneapolis: University of Minnesota Press, 1981), pp. 37–57, at p. 53n7. See note 10 below.

[5] See Frege's *Collected Papers*, B. McGuinness, ed. (Oxford: Blackwell, 1984), at p. 166.

[6] *Cf.* Morton White, 'On the Church–Frege Solution of the Paradox of Analysis,' *Philosophy and Phenomenological Research*, 9, 2 (December 1948), pp. 305–308; and Joseph Owens, 'Synonymy and the Nonindividualistic Model of the Mental,' *Synthese*, 66, 3 (March 1986), pp. 361–382, at pp. 376–379.

[7] Tyler Burge, 'Belief and Synonymy,' *Journal of Philosophy*, 75, 3 (March 1978), pp. 119–138.

meaning in English of 'sibling', hesitates over (2). Whereas the truth in English of (3) is beyond reasonable doubt, the philosophers in question, on careful reflection of the issue, express doubt concerning (4) (under the current supposition), in consideration of Watson's hesitation over (2). Adding an interesting wrinkle to the debate, Benson Mates brought the very existence of this controversy to bear on itself, arguing, in effect, that the mere possibility of the stance taken by philosophers like Burge demonstrates that expressions sharing the same English sense cannot always be inter-substituted in attributing propositional attitude.[8] We consider for this purpose the following complex sentences:

(5) Burge doubts that Watson believes that Holmes has an older brother
(6) Burge doubts that Watson believes that Holmes has an older male sibling.

Many philosophers, in addition to Burge, would follow Mates in his suggestion that even if (1) and (2) in fact share the same English sense, (6) is true in English whereas (5) is false. Indeed, perhaps the most natural way of reporting Burge's position in English is precisely to assert (6) while denying (5).

In criticism of Mates, Church argued (in effect) to the contrary that (5) and (6) can both be correctly translated (preserving sense) from English into a language lacking a single-word translation for 'brother' by means of a single sentence of that language employing translations for the English words 'male' and 'sibling'—thereby establishing that (5) and (6) are alike in (customary) sense, and hence, contrary to Mates and company, alike in truth-value.[9]

Church's criticism of Mates is plausible and seems true to the spirit of Frege's theory. It is impossible, though, to be certain how Frege himself would have responded to the Mates problem. One of Frege's explicit doctrines is directly relevant. Frege held that any expression already having *ungerade Bedeutung* (by occurring within the scope of an operator like 'Watson believes that'), when positioned within

[8] 'Synonymity,' *University of California Publications in Philosophy*, 25 (1950); reprinted in L. Linsky, ed., *Semantics and the Philosophy of Language* (University of Illinois Press, 1952), pp. 11–136, at p. 125. Mates's actual conclusion is that the mere existence of the stance taken by philosophers like Burge "seems to suggest" that any adequate explication of synonymy will be incorrect. An "adequate" explication of synonymy is understood by Mates (p. 119) to be one according to which any pair of expressions are synonymous in a language *L* if and only if they are inter-substitutable without altering truth-value in any sentence of *L*.

[9] 'Intensional Isomorphism and Identity of Belief,' *Philosophical Studies*, 5 (1954), pp. 65–73; reprinted in N. Salmon and S. Soames, eds., *Propositions and Attitudes* (Oxford Readings in Philosophy, 1988), pp. 159–168. Church would add that both (5) and (6) are false in English, and that, "whatever he himself may tell us," Burge does not doubt the proposition expressed in English by (4), but instead something like the meta-theoretic claim that (4) is true in English. (Church attributes instead a doubt that Watson satisfies the English sentential matrix '*x* believes that Holmes has an older male sibling', with free '*x*', or rather the analogue for the example he considers.) It should be noted, however, that these assertions are essentially supplementary and not fundamental to Church's criticism of Mates. One might embrace the core of that criticism while plausibly asserting instead that, whatever Burge himself may tell us, (5) is true in English as well as (6). *Cf.* Saul Kripke, 'A Puzzle about Belief,' in N. Salmon and S. Soames, eds., *Propositions and Attitudes*, Oxford Readings in Philosophy, 1988, pp. 102–148, at pp. 109–110, 140n15, 147–148n46; and my response in 'Illogical Belief,' in J. Tomberlin, ed., *Philosophical Perspectives, 3, Philosophy of Mind and Action Theory, 1989* (Atascadero, Ca.: Ridgeview, 1989), pp. 243–285, especially at pp. 265–266, 279n23.

the scope of a further *ungerade* operator ('Burge doubts that'), will shift still further to denoting its indirect sense instead of its customary sense. Frege would claim that the sentences (1) and (2), as they occur embedded in (5) and (6), thus denote their indirect senses in English, and must therefore express yet other senses, their *doubly indirect* senses, which are concepts of their (singly) indirect senses. Church shares Frege's doctrine that an expression occurring in a doubly *ungerade* context denotes a sense other than its customary sense and expresses yet a third sense. It is precisely this that leads to the infinite hierarchies of senses of the sort Church explored and clarified in his classical papers on the logic of sense and denotation.[10]

[10] 'A Formulation of the Logic of Sense and Denotation,' in Henle, Kallen, and Langer, eds., *Structure, Method, and Meaning: Essays in Honor of Henry M. Sheffer* (New York: Liberal Arts Press, 1951), pp. 3–24; 'Outline of a Revised Formulation of the Logic of Sense and Denotation,' Part I, *Nous*, 7 (March 1973), pp. 24–33; Part II, *Nous*, 8 (May 1974), pp. 135–156; 'A Revised Formulation of the Logic of Sense and Denotation. Alternative (1),' *Nous*, 27, 2 (June 1993).

Terence Parsons recently shared with me a brief note that Church wrote, while the present article was in press, in response to a query by Parsons whether Church had invoked Frege's notion of indirect sense in the 1946 review of the Black/White controversy. (See note 4 above.) Church says that the notion of indirect sense is, at best, a very vague notion which, as far as it makes sense, is concerned with natural language and not with the formalized language of his Logic of Sense and Denotation (LSD). He explicitly recognizes that the sense of a given expression may be denoted by another expression which will have its own sense, and so on *ad infinitum* (as is the case in LSD), but adds that this is not the same as saying that a *single* expression has in addition to its denotation and its sense a *third* semantic value, which one might want to call its 'indirect sense.'

The exact import of Church's highly compressed remarks is somewhat obscure. It is an essential component of Fregean theory that any expression will denote its own sense in a variety of English constructions, such as the phrase 'Holmes's older brother' in each of the following: 'Watson believes that Holmes's older brother lives in London'; 'Watson is seeking Holmes's older brother'; 'The property of being more intelligent than Holmes's older brother has no instances', etc. Even if this much is regarded as settled, there is a question, over which Fregean theorists differ, whether the phrase 'Holmes's older brother' expresses a sense in English other than its customary sense in such constructions. If the answer is that it does (as Frege himself held), there remains a further question whether the phrase expresses in English the very same sense in all of these constructions. And even if it does, it might still be possible to add an artificially stipulated device to the English lexicon, designed to insure the result that a single expression does not always express the same sense in the expanded language in constructions where it is induced to denote its own sense. There is no clear indication in his reply to Parsons that Church no longer holds, with Frege, that an expression occurring in an English *ungerade* context (such as (1) as it occurs in (3)) there expresses as its sense a concept of the expression's customary sense, and that such a concept is denoted by the expression when it occurs in a suitable doubly *ungerade* context ((1) as it occurs in (5)). I believe that what Church is concerned to deny is instead that there is for any (unambiguous) expression of English a *single* concept which determines (i.e. which is a concept of) the expression's sense and which can appropriately serve as the sense expressed when the expression occurs in an *ungerade* context (or as the denotation when the expression occurs in a doubly *ungerade* context). Rather, as I interpret his remarks, Church contends that for any expression there *may* be a plurality of (perhaps even infinitely many) such concepts, no one of which can be correctly singled out as the indirect sense in English of the expression—i.e., as *the only* sense the expression expresses in English when it is induced by the context to denote its own sense. If this is so, it would be better to speak in a relativized manner of the indirect sense in the language of a given expression *with respect to* a particular *ungerade* construction, or with respect to a particular choice from among various paths up a tree of Fregean hierarchies rooted in the expression's customary sense, etc. (Such, for example, might be the sense of the expression's "first ascendant" in LSD.) But on Church's view (as I interpret him), one should not allow such a relativized manner of speaking to promote the confusion that there is for any given expression a level of semantic content beyond sense. (Thanks to C. Anthony Anderson for correspondence concerning this issue.)

The doctrine of infinite hierarchies of sense is not sufficient by itself, however, to yield an answer to the question of whether substitution of customarily synonymous expressions (i.e. those sharing the same customary sense) will fail in English in doubly embedding *ungerade* sentences like (5) and (6). It must first be settled whether customarily synonymous expressions are also *fully synonymous* in the sense that they share the same entire hierarchy of indirect senses (the same indirect sense, the same doubly indirect sense, the same triply indirect sense, and so on). If expressions alike in customary sense differ in the senses they express in *ungerade* contexts, then those same expressions differ in denotation when occurring in a doubly embedded *ungerade* context.[11]

The inconsistency in Church's theory of sense and denotation is now apparent: Given that the sentences (1) and (2) denote their indirect senses in (5) and (6), respectively, the claim that (5) and (6) are customarily synonymous is incompatible with the earlier claim that (1) and (2) do not have the same indirect sense. If (1) and (2) differ in indirect sense, it should be incorrect to translate both (5) and (6) by means of a single sentence of another language. Any sentence of that language that might be put forward as a translation for both (5) and (6) could preserve denotation, within the sentence, of at most only one of the differing indirect senses for (1) and (2).

Doubly embedding *ungerade* sentences like (5) and (6) are not required to generate the contradiction. If Church's apparent solution to the Paradox of Analysis, as set out above, is correct, and Frege's claim about the indirect senses of sentences like (1) and (2) is also correct, then those very sentences, as they occur embedded in the singly embedding *ungerade* English sentences (3) and (4), differ in the senses they express there. Yet, on the assumption that (1) and (2) have the same customary English sense, Church also claims that one may correctly translate not only (4) but also (3), while preserving its English sense, into a language lacking a single-word translation for 'brother' simply by using translations for 'male' and 'sibling'. Since the sentences (3) and (4) would thus both be translated into the very same sentence of the target language, this would establish their customary synonymy in English. But (3) and (4) cannot express the same proposition in English if those sentences contain corresponding components that differ in the senses they express in those sentences. Whereas both (3) and (4) attribute to Watson belief of the same

If my interpretation is at least roughly correct, then Church agrees with Frege that the English sentence (1) occurring in (5) there denotes in English neither its truth-value (customary denotation) nor its sense but a concept of its sense. In any event, it is nearly certain that Church would agree that the English phrase 'that Holmes has an older brother' expresses the same sense in (*PA*) that it expresses in (3), and similarly that the English phrase 'that Holmes has an older male sibling' expresses the same sense in (*PA*) that it expresses in (4). This is sufficient to generate the contradiction to be discussed. Indeed, the same problem can be reinstated by substituting for the phrase 'the indirect sense in English of the sentence "…"' instead a suitably relativized-phrase, or even the phrase 'the sense in English of "that…"' (*mutatis mutandis*).

[11] Parsons supports the view that customarily synonymous expressions are invariably fully synonymous. Owens argues instead that phenomena like the Mates problem may be seen as indicating that expressions sharing the same customary sense will typically differ in indirect sense. C. Anthony Anderson defends the position taken by Owens. See his in-depth critical review of George Bealer's *Quality and Concept, Journal of Philosophical Logic*, 16 (1987), pp. 115–164, at 141–143.

proposition—that Holmes has an older brother—if (1) and (2) differ in the senses they express therein, then (3) and (4) specify the attributed proposition by means of differing senses, and must therefore themselves express differing propositions (one of which may be doubted while the other is not).[12]

Consider also translating the English sentence (*PA*) above, preserving its sense. If one translates in the manner suggested, the translation will have the logical form of a reflexive identity, $\ulcorner \alpha = \alpha \urcorner$, and will therefore lack (*PA*)'s status as a potentially informative analysis.

II

The problem can be posed in the form of an apparently inconsistent triad: (*i*) Frege's assertion that the indirect sense in English of a sentence like (1) is the customary sense of the corresponding phrase 'the proposition that Holmes has an older brother'; (*ii*) a Fregean solution to the Paradox of Analysis, along the lines suggested by Church, according to which the English phrases 'the proposition that Holmes has an older brother' and 'the proposition that Holmes has an older male sibling' differ in customary sense; and (*iii*) Church's claim that the English sentences (1) and (2), even as occurring in positions in which they express their indirect senses, can be correctly translated, preserving sense, by means of a single sentence of another language. (Other assumptions are involved, of course, but they are plausible to the point of being beyond reasonable dispute.) A Fregean resolution of this problem could shed light on a controversial aspect of orthodox Fregean theory that has long seemed obscure.

Resolution requires the rejection of one (or more) of the triad's components. Properly understood, perhaps the first component is the most compelling of the three—or at least, so is the conjunction of the particular instances involved in deriving the present contradiction. It amounts to the claim that the English sentences (1) and (2), as they occur embedded in (3) and (4), respectively, express the same senses there that the English phrases 'the proposition that Holmes has an older brother' and 'the proposition that Holmes has an older male sibling' express, respectively, in (*PA*). This claim involves Frege's well-known relativization of the semantic relation between an expression and the sense it expresses (in a given language) to a position within a sentence. One and the same univocal (unambiguous)

---

[12] Owens at p. 381n26, argues that Church failed to recognize that his proposed solution to the Paradox of Analysis amounts to the claim that (1) and (2) differ in indirect sense, and that this failure is shown by his claim that the doubt that gives rise to the temptation to assert (6) is actually a metalinguistic doubt. (Owens uses another example.) The point I am making is different: Church's apparent solution to the Paradox of Analysis not only makes his rejection of (6) unnecessary. (Indeed, rejection of (6) is unnecessary regardless; see note 9 above.) Given the plausible Fregean doctrine cited, the solution to the Paradox of Analysis actually *contradicts* Church's independent claim that (3) and (4) have the same English sense. That solution does indeed make it unnecessary to treat (5) and (6) as equivalent; it does so precisely by making the assertion of the strict synonymy of (3) and (4) logically impossible. I learned while the present article was already in press that Anderson, at p. 162n27, also recognizes the tension between Church's review of the Black/White exchange and his later critique of Mates's discussion of substitution.

expression, if it recurs in a single sentence, may, according to Frege, express one sense in one of its positions and another sense in another of its positions—as, for example, the two occurrences of (1) in the English sentence 'Holmes has an older brother, although Moriarity does not realize that Holmes has an older brother'.[13] Frege's relativized notion is not employed in contemporary philosophical semantics; instead, one speaks in absolute terms of the sense (or 'content,' 'intension,' etc.) of an expression (in a language *L*). Nevertheless, it seems likely that Frege's more discriminating notion may be explained or understood in terms of concepts familiar in the philosophy of semantics—for example, as the ternary relation that obtains among an expression, a semantic content, and a position of the expression in a particular sentence, when the second of these relata is the component contributed (in language *L*) by the occurrence of the expression in the position in question to the proposition expressed (in *L*) by the sentence in question. In the particular case at hand, the proposition expressed in English by (3) will essentially involve the semantic content (customarily) expressed in English by its complement clause 'that Holmes has an older brother'. The latter must also be essentially involved in the sense (customarily) expressed in English by the phrase 'the proposition that Holmes has an older brother', and hence in the proposition expressed in English by (*PA*).[14] Once Frege's notion of *expressing in such-and-such position* (in language *L*) is properly defined, and once the *ungerade* operator 'that' occurring in both (*PA*) and (3) is properly seen as merely an indirect–quotation device, exactly analogous to a pair of ordinary quotation marks (except grammatically restricted in its application to whole sentences), (*i*) seems to emerge as something that is trivially true.

Church's own defense of (*iii*) is also very persuasive. That defense turns on strong and widely shared intuitions concerning what a particular language, given its resources, is or is not capable of semantically expressing. If the word 'brother' expresses exactly the same sense in English as the phrase 'male sibling', then, as Church points out, it seems that whatever can be expressed in English by means of the former can also be expressed in another language lacking a single-word translation for 'brother' simply by using translations for 'male' and 'sibling'. Assuming the customary synonymy of the English expressions 'brother' and 'male sibling', the

---

[13] Frege's relativization of the relation between an expression and the sense it expresses to positions within a sentence yields perhaps the most straightforward interpretation of his earlier principle that "it is only in the context of a sentence that words have any meaning" (*Grundlagen der Arithmetik*, J. L. Austin, ed., Blackwell, 1950, 1958, at pp. 71, 73).

[14] *Cf.* my 'Reference and Information Content: Names and Descriptions,' in D. Gabbay and F. Guenthner, eds., *Handbook of Philosophical Logic IV: Topics in the Philosophy of Language* (Dordrecht: D. Reidel), pp. 409–461, at pp. 440–441. One may assume that the words 'the proposition' in the phrase 'the proposition that' stand in grammatical apposition to the 'that' clause that follows them. The 'that' operator may be regarded as the paradigm *ungerade* operator. *Cf.* my *Frege's Puzzle* (Atascadero, Ca.: Ridgeview, 1986, 1991), at pp. 5–6. Indeed, (*PA*) could be reformulated more succinctly (albeit somewhat more peculiarly) as 'That Holmes has an older brother = that Holmes has an older male sibling', with no effect on its status as a (potentially) informative analysis of the proposition that Holmes has an older brother. There can be little doubt that if the two expressions flanking ' = ' differ in the senses they express in English, then those same expressions likewise differ in their contributions to the propositions expressed in English by (3) and (4). (*Cf.* note 10 above.)

presence of the former surely does not extend the expressive capabilities of English; anything that can be expressed in English by its means—including the proposition expressed by (5)—can also be expressed using 'male sibling' instead. As far as the expressive resources of English are concerned, the word 'brother' seems to be entirely superfluous, "a dispensable linguistic luxury."[15] Taking multiply embedded *ungerade* contexts into account, this observation seems to have the consequence that the customary sense of an expression determines its n-fold indirect sense, for $n \geq 1$. With indirect senses of any level above customary sense, there is a "backward road" from denotation to sense. This is made all the more plausible by the further observation that knowing the customary sense of an expression is both necessary and sufficient for understanding occurrences of that expression in multiply embedded *ungerade* contexts, assuming one already understands the surrounding context.

My own favored resolution of the inconsistency is to reject (*ii*). Although either of the other components of the inconsistent triad might be rejected instead, such rejection seems significantly less plausible than accepting that if the expressions 'brother' and 'male sibling' share exactly the same semantic content in English, then so likewise do the phrases 'the proposition that Holmes has an older brother' and

---

[15] The present writer regards Church's arguments in this connection as nearly decisive (modulo the qualification described in note 9 above). Those arguments are, however, philosophical in nature, and not everyone is persuaded. (See note 11 above.) Burge argues that Church's reliance on translation is inappropriate, on the following grounds:

Good translation should preserve truth-value. But Church and Mates disagree about the truth-value of [⌜(6) but not (5)⌝]. Church takes it to be a contradiction, whereas Mates regards it as true. Until this difference is resolved, one surely cannot decide whether Church's proposed translation of [⌜(6) but not (5)⌝] (in the relevant context) as an *explicit contradiction* is correct. Obvious truths and falsehoods are normally used in arriving at a translation—not vice versa (p. 122)

Perhaps obvious truths and falsehoods are appropriately relied upon in Quine's special project of so-called radical translation. It is important therefore to note that Church is engaged in an entirely different enterprise, one that explicitly relies on antecedent knowledge of inter-language synonymies among sub-sentential words and phrases. Church's concern *in the present context* is to translate in such a manner as to preserve the proposition semantically expressed—rather than preserving, for example, the point being illustrated (if necessary at the expense of preserving sense). Church calls this 'literal translation'. Not only is it possible to provide such translation without first determining truth-value; given the sole objective of preserving semantic content, it would be highly irregular to proceed as Burge seems to suggest, only by first settling the question of truth-value. When one correctly understands each of two languages, one can normally provide a literal translation for a given sentence, in the sense of one preserving semantic content, even without having any opinion as to its truth-value. Indeed, contra Burge, knowledge of truth-value seems irrelevant to the task. Providing a literal translation for (5) into a language containing literal translations for the English words 'male' and 'sibling' poses no special problems (on the operative assumption that 'brother' has exactly the same English sense as 'male sibling'); a radical departure from normal practice would not be justified.

Burge further dismisses as begging the question Church's argument that if the target language can properly translate the English words 'male' and 'sibling', then the absence of an alternative translation for the English word 'brother' cannot be regarded as a deficiency that makes literal translation of (5) into that language impossible (*ibid.*, p. 122n4). The present writer fails to see that Church's argument genuinely begs the question (Burge does not elaborate beyond the passage quoted above); indeed, it would seem closer to the facts to say instead that the argument genuinely refutes Mates by exposing an implausible consequence of his claims.

'the proposition that Holmes has an older male sibling'. The customary synonymy of the two phrases is supported by the now familiar translation test.[16]

Rejecting (*ii*) does carry a certain price: it requires one to seek an alternative solution to the Paradox of Analysis. I have suggested such a solution elsewhere, while rejecting the Frege–Church theory of sense and denotation.[17]

If Church were also to resolve the inconsistency by rejecting (*ii*) and seeking an alternative solution to the Paradox of Analysis, his doing so would immediately raise the question of why he does not embrace an exactly parallel alternative solution to Frege's original puzzle about the informativeness of 'Hesperus is Phosphorus'—a solution that, by hypothesis, does not involve distinguishing co-denotational proper names as regards semantic content. Adopting such an alternative solution would seriously threaten the Frege–Church theory. For once it is agreed that the apparent informativeness of an identity statement like (*PA*) is to be explained in some way other than by postulating a distinction between the senses of the singular terms involved, Church's and Frege's original argument for the theory of sense and denotation collapses. The apparent inconsistency in the Frege–Church theory thus goes to the heart of that theory.

---

[16] This might be taken to indicate that Church's remarks pertaining to the Paradox of Analysis have been misinterpreted. (See note 4 above.) If they have been, then the difficulties raised in the next two paragraphs are particularly pressing for Church.

[17] *Frege's Puzzle*, especially around pp. 57–60, 78–79. The neo-Russellian theory defended there avoids infinite hierarchies of indirect sense while also affording an alternative explanation for the fact, mentioned above, that knowing the customary semantic content of an expression is both necessary and sufficient for understanding occurrences of that expression in multiply embedded *ungerade* contexts: The semantic content of an expression in any *ungerade* context, no matter how deeply embedded, is identical with the customary content.

17

The Very Possibility of Language (2001)

A Sermon on the Consequences of Missing Church

I

An English speaker in uttering the words, (0) 'The earth is round', says, or asserts, the same thing as a French speaker uttering the words, (0') '*La terre est ronde*'.[1] The thing asserted is a proposition, the proposition that the earth is round. That there are propositions, as distinct from the sentences that express them, is a commitment of psychology and other human sciences, which ascribe beliefs and other propositional attitudes. The existence of propositions is an integral part of our ordinary conceptions of consciousness and cognition, and therewith of our ordinary conception of what it is to be a person.

The evidence for this commitment to propositions, qua extra-linguistic entities expressed by intra-linguistic entities, is compelling. No one has done more to bring that evidence to the attention of philosophers than Alonzo Church, and nowhere does he do so with more force than in his elegant and farsighted paper 'On Carnap's Analysis of Statements of Assertion and Belief.'[2] That deceptively brief note presents a sharp and telling criticism of one possible attempt to do away with propositions (in the sense that Church intends) in favor of the cognitive dispositions of speakers *vis-à-vis* particular sentences of a language ("semantic system"). The argument has a

As a student, I had the privilege and distinct good fortune to take numerous courses from Alonzo Church, one of the truly great analytical thinkers of this century. My own intellectual development has benefitted enormously from the masterful tutelage of this extraordinary logician and philosopher, in whose honor this essay was written, shortly before his death. I am grateful to my audiences at UCLA in 1994 and at UC Berkeley in 1996 for their comments, and to C. Anthony Anderson and Saul Kripke for discussion.

[1] These sentences are to be taken in the usual sense throughout, as expressing that the earth is spherical.

[2] *Analysis*, 10, 5 (1950), pp. 97–99; reprinted in L. Linsky, ed., *Reference and Modality* (Oxford University Press, 1971), pp. 168–170. See also Church's 'A Formulation of the Logic of Sense and Denotation,' in Henle, Kallen, and Langer, eds., *Structure, Method, and Meaning: Essays in Honor of Henry M. Sheffer* (New York: Liberal Arts Press, 1988), pp. 3–24 at 5–6n; 'Intensional Isomorphism and Identity of Belief,' *Philosophical Studies*, 5 (1954), pp. 65–73, reprinted in N. Salmon and S. Soames, eds., *Propositions and Attitudes* (Oxford University Press, 1988), pp. 159–168; and *Introduction to Mathematical Logic I* (Princeton University Press, 1956), p. 62n.

broad, generic sweep; it is equally applicable to any of a wide range of theories that posit a reference to sentences or other intra-linguistic items in the semantic content of a variety of constructions, especially attributions of propositional attitude, even including such theories as may be proposed that do this while simultaneously embracing propositions. (The particular theory Church criticizes, as Carnap intended it, arguably does just this.) The argument, which invokes the translation of various sentences between languages, has come to be called *the Church Translation Argument*.[3]

Some philosophers of language, many of them in pursuit of a propositionless world, have attempted to rebut the Translation Argument.[4] Numerous writers today dismiss the argument as weak, fallacious, or otherwise underwhelming, or they simply ignore it. Where Church wasted few words, some of his critics have minced even fewer. Michael Dummett, who does not himself reject propositions, nevertheless said that "it is difficult to treat this objection very seriously."[5] Peter Geach labeled the argument "frivolously bad."[6] In the judgment of the present author, the current dismissive attitude toward the Church Translation Argument constitutes a quantum leap backward, and is, from the point of view of the formal study of semantics, regrettable in the extreme.[7] The point at issue is by no means narrowly confined to the question of whether attributions of propositional attitude involve a

---

[3] In all of his writings on the subject, Church reminds the reader that the basic insight of employing translation as a test for determining whether an expression is being used or mentioned is due to C. H. Langford. See also footnote 12 below.

[4] The following is a partial list: Tyler Burge, 'Self-Reference and Translation,' in F. Guenthner and M. Guenthner-Reutter, eds., *Translation and Meaning* (London: Duckworth, 1977), pp. 137–153, and 'Belief and Synonymy,' *Journal of Philosophy*, 75, no. 3 (March 1978), pp. 119–138; Rudolf Carnap, 'On Belief-Sentences: Reply to Alonzo Church,' in Carnap's *Meaning and Necessity* (University of Chicago Press, 1947, 1956), pp. 230–232; Donald Davidson, 'The Method of Extension and Intension,' in P. A. Schilpp, ed., *The Philosophy of Rudolf Carnap* (La Salle, Ill., 1963), pp. 331–349, at 344–346; Michael Dummett, *Frege: Philosophy of Language* (Cambridge, Mass.: Harvard University Press, 1973, 1981), at pp. 372–373, and *The Interpretation of Frege's Philosophy* (Cambridge, Mass.: Harvard University Press, 1981), at pp. 90–94; Peter Geach, *Mental Acts* (London: Routledge, 1957), at pp. 89–92, and 'The Identity of Propositions,' in Geach's *Logic Matters* (Oxford: Blackwell, 1972), pp. 166–174; Steven Leeds, 'Church's Translation Argument,' *Canadian Journal of Philosophy*, 9, no. 1 (March 1979), pp. 43–51 (I thank Mark Richard for providing this reference); Brian Loar, *Mind and Meaning* (Cambridge University Press, 1981), pp. 29–30, 152; Hilary Putnam, 'Synonymy, and the Analysis of Belief Sentences,' *Analysis*, 14, no. 5 (April 1954), pp. 114–122, reprinted in N. Salmon and S. Soames, eds., *Propositions and Attitudes* (Oxford University Press, 1988), pp. 149–158; W. V. Quine, 'Quantifiers and Propositional Attitudes,' reprinted in L. Linsky, ed., *Reference and Modality* (Oxford University Press, 1971), pp. 101–111, at 110; Mark Richard, *Propositional Attitudes* (Cambridge University Press, 1990), at p. 156ff; Israel Scheffler, 'An Inscriptional Approach to Indirect Quotation,' *Analysis*, 14, no. 4 (March 1954), pp. 83–90, and 'On Synonymy and Indirect Discourse,' *Philosophy of Science*, 22, no. 1 (January 1955), pp. 39–44, at 43–44n. While no attempt is made here to respond adequately to each of these critiques, much of what will be said here is applicable to a number of them.

[5] Frege, *Philosophy of Language*, p. 372.   [6] 'The Identity of Propositions,' p. 167.

[7] More generally, it is my considered view that the attempt to avoid an ontology of extra-linguistic abstract entities by an appeal to intra-linguistic substitutes is philosophically misguided. The reasons for this judgment are complex. As an excessively brief summary, I mention that the ontology of everyday discourse is replete with abstract entities other than propositions. The philosophical security that is supposed to be afforded by replacing propositions with sentences is largely an illusion, since sentences, no less than propositions, are abstract entities. Many sentences—infinitely many, in fact—are too long to be written or uttered by any conceivable

commitment to propositions. Those who reject the Translation Argument have typically failed to comprehend the more general point on which it is based, and have thereby failed to appreciate one of the most fundamental facts concerning the phenomenon of understanding. This failure is especially dramatic in the case of Dummett. As I shall argue, Dummett's failure to grasp the larger import of Church's argument has led him and his followers to defend a seriously distorted version of Frege's theory, one that has the consequence (clearly unintended) that language, as a mode of communication and a vehicle of cognition, is altogether impossible. I shall endeavor here to explain the main thrust of the Church Translation Argument, especially in regard to those aspects of the argument that are misunderstood by its detractors. I shall do so by reference to a particular lacuna in Frege's philosophy of semantics, showing how Church's valuable insights help to resolve a longstanding controversy concerning Frege's notion of indirect sense.

Generalizing slightly on Church's presentation, consider the theory that the first of the following two English sentences is analyzable (definable with full preservation of meaning) by means of the second:[8]

(1) Chris believes that the earth is round.
(2) Chris accepts 'The earth is round'.

The analysans (2) may be expanded if necessary to focus on a particular meaning for the sentence it mentions, perhaps by adding a phrase like 'as a sentence of English', 'as a sentence of the same language as this very sentence', or 'as I, the present speaker of this very sentence, would mean it'.[9] It should be noted that any possible expansion of (2) that apparently mentions the proposition that the earth is round, or otherwise apparently logically entails the existence of a proposition, would not be suitable as part of an attempt to relieve the author of (1) of his or her apparent commitment to propositions, although it may be appropriate for other purposes.[10] The particular

---

creature. Moreover, principles concerning the identification of sentences are not nearly as "extensional" as is sometimes supposed. This last difficulty often manifests itself in the need to resort not merely to sentences as such, but to *sentences as sentences of a particular language*, or to *sentences as meaning that such-and-such*, etc.

[8] For many applications, the requirement of full preservation of meaning (whereby, as a consequence, one believes what is expressed by the analysandum if and only if one also believes what is expressed by the analysans) may be weakened to mere logical equivalence, and in some applications, to such wider equivalence relations as modal equivalence or *a priori* equivalence, with little effect on the overall force of the argument.

[9] Church's conception of linguistic expressions and their semantics is such as to require that such semantic attributes as sense, denotation, and truth-value always be relativized to a particular language. Others favor a conception according to which relativization to a language is unnecessary or even inappropriate. *Cf.* Peter Geach's protests in *Mental Acts*, pp. 88–89; and David Kaplan, 'Words,' *Proceedings of the Aristotelian Society*, 64 (1990), pp. 93–116. Although Church's presentation of the Translation Argument assumes his view on this issue, the argument can also be presented with the opposite view presupposed, or with neutrality (as it is here).

[10] One addendum that would obviously be inadmissible for the purpose of eliminating commitment to propositions is the phrase 'as expressing the proposition that the earth is round', or more simply 'as meaning that the earth is round'. (*Cf.* footnote 7 above.) Church explicitly considers a possible expansion of (2) that logically entails this inadmissible one, admitting that such an expanded version may yield (1) as a logical consequence. He does not note that the expansion in

word 'accepts' is used schematically; any of a variety of transitive verb phrases may be substituted. As an example, one may replace 'accepts' with a carefully formulated phrase like 'is disposed, on reflection, when sincere and nonreticent, to assent to some sufficiently understood translation or other of'. Alternatively, one may substitute Quine's word 'believes-true'[11] or even the phrase 'believes the proposition expressed by'. The latter cannot be used if one's objective is to avoid commitment to propositions, but might be used, for example, by one (such as Dummett) who supposes that a 'that'-clause is to be understood by reference to its contained sentence. Moreover, the pair of words, 'believes' and 'accepts', may be replaced by other pairs of suitably related terms, e.g., 'asserted'-'uttered', 'disbelieves'-'rejects', etc.

We demonstrate that the proposed analysis fails as follows: Translating both analysandum and analysans into French, we obtain,

(1') *Chris croit que la terre est ronde.*

(2') *Chris accepte* 'The earth is round'.

(The word *'accepte'* is used here schematically for the literal French translation of whatever English phrase replaces 'accepts', subject to the same possible variations mentioned earlier.) We pause to note that the proper translation for (2) is not

(3') *Chris accepte 'La terre est ronde'.*

question would not be suitable for the elimination of propositions. (It may even lead to circularity, if the proposed analysis is extended to such constructions as 'Sentence *S* means in language *L* that the earth is round' in addition to (1).) Instead he notes, correctly, that the particular expansion of (2) he considers does not preserve the meaning of (1). Again he utilizes translation to crystalize the point. In addition, he considers embedded constructions like 'Jones believes that Chris believes that the earth is round', arguing that alleged analyses of this and of its translation may even differ in truth-value in their respective languages. (*Cf.* footnote 8 above.) Carnap says in response (p. 230, in a highly compressed paragraph) that he intended precisely such an expansion of (2), while conceding that Church's objection is correct.

Carnap's overall response to Church is unclear and puzzling. In *Meaning and Necessity*, pp. 63–64, scarcely a page after presenting his analysis of statements of belief, Carnap says of analysis in general that although analysandum and analysans must be logically equivalent, they need not be intensionally isomorphic—or as Carnap also puts it, the analysis must preserve intension but need not preserve intensional structure. Davidson and Putnam argue, in effect, that Carnap's analysis of statements of assertion and belief in particular, therefore, is not intended to capture their meaning but only something logically equivalent—thus making Church's objections inapplicable. In sharp contrast, Carnap concedes not only Church's objection, but furthermore that (1) is strictly not even a logical consequence of the intended version of (2) (pp. 230–231). Curiously, Carnap also endorses Putnam's response (p. 230), while proffering an alternative version of (2) as a scientific replacement (presumably now logically equivalent) for (1) (pp. 231–232). The textual evidence suggests, however, that Carnap confused Putnam's response on this point with Putnam's response to a separate objection by Benson Mates concerning embedded constructions. In 'Intensional Isomorphism and Identity of Belief,' Church extends the Translation Argument against Putnam's response to Mates. See also the introduction to N. Salmon and S. Soames, eds., *Propositions and Attitudes* (Oxford University Press, 1988), pp. 13–14n10.

The issues here are numerous and quite complex. *Cf.* footnote 28 below. Insofar as embedded constructions are involved, the dispute is intimately related to issues concerning Frege's notion of indirect sense. See footnote 25 below.

[11] Quine, at pp. 109–110. The expression 'believes-true' is, however, significantly misleading. For discussion, see my 'Relational Belief,' in P. Leonardi and M. Santambrogio, eds., *On Quine* (Cambridge University Press, 1995).

This sentence mentions a particular French sentence not mentioned in (2), while lacking any mention of the English sentence mentioned in (2). It is thus (2′) rather than (3′) that captures the literal meaning of (2).[12] Likewise, (1) and (1′) are literal translations of one another. But it is evident that the French sentences (1′) and (2′) are not synonymous. For they "would obviously convey different meanings"— indeed, logically independent propositions—to a French speaker having no knowledge of English. Of the two only (1′) conveys the content of what Chris allegedly believes. Sentences (1) and (2) must, therefore differ in meaning in English, contrary to the proposed analysis.

II

As noted above, the scope of the argument is wide. It is equally applicable, for example, against the *redundancy* or *disquotational theory of truth*, according to which the English sentence ' 'The earth is round' is true in English' simply reduces to 'The earth is round'. The argument demonstrates that the two sentences are in fact logically independent. It is also directly applicable to a longstanding controversy in orthodox Fregean theory. Frege held that the English sentence (0) ordinarily denotes its truth-value—in this case, the value truth ("the True")—but that, when occurring in an indirect or oblique (*ungerade*) context in English, as in (1), it instead has its indirect denotation, denoting what is ordinarily its English sense, the proposition that the earth is round.[13] Frege held further that when (0) occurs in any English indirect context, it takes on its indirect sense, which is a concept of its indirect denotation, or ordinary sense. But which of the myriad concepts of the proposition that the earth is round is thereby expressed? Carnap complained that "Frege nowhere explains in more ordinary terms what this third entity is."[14]

The matter remains controversial. Dummett argues that, for Frege, the indirect sense in English of (0) is the ordinary sense in English of the phrase

(4) the ordinary sense in English of 'The earth is round.'[15]

---

[12] *Cf.* G. E. Moore, 'Russell's "Theory of Descriptions",' in his *Philosophical Papers* (New York: Collier Books, 1959), pp. 149–192, at 156–157, where he anticipates Langford's translation test.

[13] 'Über Sinn and Bedeutung,' translated as 'On Sense and Reference,' in R. M. Harnish, ed., *Basic Topics in the Philosophy of Language* (Englewood Cliffs, NJ.: Prentice Hall, 1994), pp. 142–160, at 144. I follow Church in translating Frege's use of '*Bedeutung*' as 'denotation' rather than 'meaning' or 'reference', and Frege's use of '*Gedanke*' as 'proposition' rather than 'thought'. I also use the word 'concept' in Church's sense, which is very different from Frege's use of '*Begriff*'.

[14] *Meaning and Necessity*, §30, pp. 129–133.

[15] *The Interpretation of Frege's Philosophy*, at pp. 89–100. This represents a turnabout for Dummett. In his earlier work, *Frege: Philosophy of Language*, he considered the thesis that the indirect sense of (0) in English is the customary sense of (4), only to dismiss it as "rather implausible" (p. 267). Both this thesis concerning indirect sense, and the exegetical thesis that Frege's theory implies the former thesis, are defended in Gary Kemp, 'Salmon on Fregean Approaches to the Paradox of Analysis,' *Philosophical Studies*, 78, no. 2 (May 1995), pp. 153–162, wherein specific references to Frege's writings are provided (at p. 160) in support of Dummett's interpretation.

Dummett does not support this exegetical thesis by citing any passage from Frege's writings. Instead he provides quite general considerations in favor of the interpretation:

> There is nothing in what Frege says about direct [i.e., ordinary] and indirect sense and reference [denotation] to rule out the possibility that, although distinct expressions, in the same or different languages, may have the same sense, no sense can be given to us save as the sense of some particular expression; such a thesis would fit very well what Frege sometimes says to the effect that *we* can grasp thoughts only via words or other symbols. But, if so, then, if an expression stands for a sense, and does so in virtue of *its* sense, that sense must involve a reference, overt or covert, to some expression—the same or different—whose sense its referent is. (p. 91)

> It is perfectly consistent to combine the thesis that the object of belief is a thought [proposition] with the thesis that we can apprehend a thought only as the sense of a sentence (in a verbal or symbolic language). It is therefore equally consistent to combine the thesis that a clause in *oratio obliqua* [indirect discourse], or an expression within that clause, stands for its ordinary sense with the thesis that, in understanding it as referring to that sense, we apprehend that sense as being the sense of that clause or expression. . . . Frege [adheres] to both these theses. (p. 94)

Dummett adds further on that Frege thought that "we can grasp a thought only as expressed in some way" (p. 98), and that the thesis that the indirect sense in English of (0) is the ordinary sense of (4) "does appear to follow from the two theses, taken together: the thesis that a sense can be given only as the sense of some expression, and the thesis that an expression in *oratio obliqua* stands for its ordinary sense" (p. 95).[16] He continues, saying that "our grasp of the sense of the expression . . . , on Frege's account, . . . leaves us with no access to that sense save as the sense of some expression" (p. 97).[17]

Echoing Carnap, Dummett argues against Frege that it is preferable not to confer on an expression a concept of its ordinary sense to serve as the sense expressed in indirect contexts.[18] Despite his misgivings about the notion of indirect sense, Dummett explicitly endorses the idea that, as he puts it, "a sense can be given to us only as the sense carried by some particular expression." He explains that to say this "implies that the most direct means by which we can refer in English to the sense expressed by, say, "the moon" is by using the phrase "the sense of 'the moon'""

---

[16] Dummett points out that the inference in question is actually invalid, but he allows (pp. 98–99) that it is validated by the addition of a third thesis (which Frege held and which Dummett rejects) as premise, to wit, that "the sense of an expression is the way in which its [denotation] is given to us."

[17] Bishop Berkeley argued, against Locke's doctrine of "abstraction," that one cannot conceive of, for example, a color without also conceiving of some shape or other with that color. According to Dummett, Frege did not hold, in the same spirit as Berkeley, merely that one cannot conceive of a sense in any way without also conceiving of it as the sense of some expression or other. It is not that any conception of a sense we have, must be *accompanied* in cognition by a conception of it as the sense of some expression. The point, rather, is that in conceiving of a sense, we conceive of it only as the sense of *e*, for some expression *e* or other, since we have no conception of the sense other than as the sense of *e*, for some expression *e*, for such a conception to accompany. (This will be made more precise below. I am grateful to Charles Chihara for bringing this distinction to my attention.)

[18] Carnap, at p. 129; Dummett, *Frege: Philosophy and Language*, pp. 266–269.

(p. 95). Dummett says moreover that "we cannot refer to the sense of most expressions save by explicit allusion to the expressions" (p. 90). And he joins with Frege, as Dummett has interpreted him, in holding that

> we apprehend the indirect referent as being the sense of the expression which we perceive as occurring in the *oratio obliqua* clause.... our way of grasping what the sense of an expression is, renders us incapable of detaching the sense from every actual or hypothetical means of expressing it.... when we take the expression in *oratio obliqua* as standing for its own sense, we are conceiving of that sense as the sense of that very expression. (pp. 97–98)

Although Dummett does not share Frege's belief in the need for indirect senses, it is clear from the foregoing passages that Dummett maintains the following thesis (which he cites in support of his interpretation of Frege on indirect sense): In order for us to conceive of any sense at all (in order to form a belief about it, or to speculate about it, or even merely to entertain a thought about it, etc.), there must be some expression *e* (of some language *l*) such that we conceive of the sense in question (or as Dummett also puts it, the sense is "given to us") *as* the ordinary sense of *e* (in *l*); we are unable to conceive of a sense in any way other than as the ordinary sense of *e* (in *l*), for some expression *e* (of some language *l*).[19] Let us call this *Dummett's Thesis*.

The considerations cited by Dummett in favor of his interpretation of Frege are unconvincing, especially in light of Frege's explicit pronouncement (which both Carnap and Dummett may have overlooked) that the indirect sense in English of (0) is rather the ordinary sense in English of the alternative phrase

(5) the proposition that the earth is round.[20]

One may wonder whether the phrases (4) and (5) are not themselves synonymous in English. In fact, Geach explicitly argued that on Fregean theory, such phrases are completely interchangeable (pp. 168–169). And Dummett evidently treats such phrases as synonyms.[21] Furthermore, Dummett's interpretation depicts Frege as having held that the ordinary sense of (5) in English presents the proposition in question as the ordinary sense of some particular linguistic expression. The only plausible candidate for that expression is the English sentence (0).[22] This would make (5) a mere English paraphrase of (4)—even if it is a "less direct means" of denoting the proposition denoted by each. If (4) and (5) are indeed synonymous in English, then Dummett's formulation of Frege's thesis concerning indirect sense is simply another way of saying the same as Frege.

Any suspicion that (4) and (5) are synonymous may be dispelled, however, by the Translation Argument. Of course, (4) and (5) denote the same proposition in

---

[19] Dummett does not explicitly speak in a relativized manner of the sense of an expression *in a language*. The parenthetical references to the language *l* are included here for the benefit of those whose view of linguistic expressions and their semantics requires for propriety the relativization to a language. See footnote 9 above.   [20] '*Uber Sinn und Bedeutung*,' at p. 149 of Harnish.

[21] In *The Interpretation of Frege's Philosophy*, at p. 89, there occurs an otherwise inexplicable switch, wherein the discussion, suddenly and without notice, changes its focus from an identification of the indirect sense of a sentence like (0) with the ordinary sense of the corresponding analogue of (5), to an identification of the indirect sense of 'Aristotle' instead with the customary sense of 'the sense of "Aristotle"'.

[22] *Cf.* the argument given by Dummett, p. 95, top paragraph. See also Kemp.

English, but their literal French translations—'*le sens ordinaire en anglais de* "The earth is round"' and '*la proposition que la terre est ronde*', respectively—clearly carry different meanings for the French speaker who knows no English. Hence, (4) and (5) are not ordinarily synonymous in English, i.e., they differ in ordinary English sense.

Furthermore, the Translation Argument demonstrates that the thesis Dummett erroneously attributes to Frege is in any case incorrect. For just as (0) expresses its English indirect sense in (1), (0') expresses its French indirect sense in (1'). Yet unlike (2'), (1') evidently makes no mention of (0). It is probable, furthermore, that the particular linguistic item creating the indirect context in (1) is not the English word 'believes' but 'that'.[23] For terms denoting the same proposition are typically interchangeable, with no affect on truth-value, following occurrences of 'believes', 'asserted', 'doubts', etc. Consider for example the following inferences:

Carnap believed Frege's central doctrine in the philosophy of mathematics.
Frege's central doctrine in the philosophy of mathematics was logicism.
Therefore, Carnap believed logicism.

Church doubts logicism.
Logicism is the doctrine that mathematics is reducible to logic.
Therefore, Church doubts that mathematics is reducible to logic.

By contrast, the word 'that' is equally involved in substitution failures that do not involve belief ('Bert asserted *that*...') and even in substitution failures that do not concern attitudes of any kind, for example in contexts concerning modality ('It is a necessary truth *that*...'). The word 'that' is plausibly regarded as a device of indirect–quotation, which when attached to an English declarative sentence forms the standard English name for the proposition ordinarily expressed by that sentence (in a manner analogous to that in which direct quotation marks form the standard name of the expression enclosed within). As such, 'that' would be a paradigmatic *ungerade* device ('oblique operator') of English, with the phrase 'the proposition' occurring in (5) functioning as a grammatical appositive to the 'that'-clause.[24] This hypothesis on Dummett's proposal implies that, since (0) is induced by the 'that' prefix to express its English indirect sense in (1), (1) itself may be rewritten without alteration of meaning in a form dispensing with any *ungerade* device (beyond ordinary quotation marks), simply by substituting (4) for the shortened version of its alleged synonym (5) within it:

(6) Chris believes the ordinary sense in English of 'The earth is round'.

---

[23] It must be admitted that the construction 'Chris believes the earth is round', without the word 'that', is perfectly grammatical English, and (0) occurs nonextensionally therein. This phenomenon, however, does not immediately yield the result that 'believes' is a nonextensional *(ungerade)* operator. It is arguable that (0) is induced to shift to the indirect mode here by other (perhaps pragmatic) factors. (Indeed, linguists commonly refer to the phenomenon as '"that" deletion.')

[24] *Cf.* my *Frege's Puzzle* (Atascadero, Ca.: Ridgeview, 1986, 1991), at pp. 5–6; and 'Reference and Information Content: Names and Descriptions,' in D. Gabbay and F. Guenthner, eds., *Handbook of Philosophical Logic IV: Topics in the Philosophy of Language* (Boston: D. Reidel, 1989), pp. 409–462, at 440–441.

Since this is a sentence of precisely the form of (2), the Translation Argument, as originally given, disproves the theory that it is an English paraphrase of (1). Again by contrast, the hypothesis that the English word 'that' is a device for indirect-quotation strongly supports Frege's actual claim concerning the indirect sense of a sentence like (0).[25]

III

A few years after Church's paper appeared, Geach protested,

> Very often, what we count as correct translation will include translation of quoted expressions; a translator of *Quo Vadis* would not feel obliged to leave all the conversations in the original Polish, and we should count it as perversely wrong, not pedantically correct, if he did so.[26]

Others have since echoed Geach's complaint, notably Tyler Burge and Dummett.[27] It must be observed that each of Burge, Dummett, and Geach offers a reply different in various respects from the other two—and it is not obvious that any of the three agrees entirely with any other—but they share an emphasis on divergences between translation in actual practice and the special, sense-preserving translation proposed by Church. Translators would very likely proffer (3′) rather than (2′), they argue, as a correct rendering of the English (2) into French. No one denies that (3′) fails to preserve (2)'s mention of (0); (3′) mentions different words of a different language altogether. Insofar as preservation of meaning, or sense, requires the preservation of denotation, rendering the English (2) into French by means of (3′) does not preserve meaning.[28] But Burge, Dummett, and Geach each deny that correct translation must

---

[25] The Translation Argument is not supportive of all aspects of Fregean theory. As is shown in my article 'A Problem in the Frege–Church Theory of Sense and Denotation,' *Noûs*, 27, no. 2 (1993), pp. 158–166, while the argument supports Frege's thesis concerning indirect sense, it thereby leads to an inconsistency when combined with a Fregean solution to the Paradox of Analysis, of a sort advocated by Church in his review of the Black/White exchange concerning the Paradox of Analysis, *The Journal of Symbolic Logic*, 11 (1946), pp. 132–133. I argue in the article that relinquishing the Fregean solution to the Paradox of Analysis threatens the Frege–Church theory, by collapsing Frege's and Church's original argument for the pivotal distinction between the sense and denotation of an expression. (Whereas this difficulty exposes a potentially serious weakness in the Frege–Church theory of sense and denotation, it does nothing to weaken the force of the Translation Argument.)

[26] *Mental Acts*, pp. 91–92. (I thank Saul Kripke for providing this reference.)

[27] Burge, 'Self-reference and Translation,' especially pp. 141—144; Dummett, *loc. cit.* Burge's response to the Translation Argument is also endorsed by James Higgenbotham, in 'Linguistic Theory and Davidson's Program in Semantics,' in E. Lepore, ed., *Truth and Interpretation: Perspectives on the Philosophy of Donald Davidson* (Oxford: Basil Blackwell, 1986), pp. 29–48, at 39n. (I thank Higginbotham for providing the last reference.)

[28] This point is explicitly acknowledged by Dummett *(Frege: Philosophy of Language*, p. 372; *The Interpretation of Frege's Philosophy*, p. 90). It is more or less acknowledged by Burge (p. 141), although his overall response to the Translation Argument is explicitly part of a program to avoid commitment to propositions (pp. 152–153). Geach espouses an extreme skepticism regarding the notion of synonymy. He argues that (3′) is "of the same force as" (his version of) (2), and that (3′) and (2) are "reasonably equivalent," but specifically stops short of declaring that they are either the same, or different, in meaning. By the same token, Geach does not propose (2) as a

preserve meaning—insofar as the preservation of meaning requires the preservation of denotation. Thus Dummett writes, "There is no ground for the presumption that the practical canons of apt translation always require strict synonymy. On the contrary, translations of fiction and, equally, of historical narrative (including the Gospels) always translate even directly quoted dialogue."[29] Amplifying the argument, Burge says, "translation of foreign quoted material aims at conveying the "point" of the passage that contains it" (p. 145). And according to Burge, what is crucial to the point of sentences like (2)

> is not part of the grammar or semantics of the sentences themselves. It is better seen as involved in a convention presupposed in the use and understanding of such sentences.... What is involved in rightly construing the expressions that are mentioned in problem sentences like [(2)] is...the ability to understand those expressions as they would be intended if they were used by the person who uses the relevant token of the sentence in which they are mentioned. (p. 146)

Burge argues that the operative nonsemantic, pragmatic convention in connection with (his version of) the English (2) directs one to interpret the sentence it mentions in the specified manner, and that this yields the result, contrary to Church, that (3′) is a better translation of (2) into French than is (2′).

This general line of criticism was cogently refuted independently by Herbert Heidelberger, Casimir Lewy, and Leonard Linsky.[30] It is completely inessential to

meaning-preserving analysis of (1). It is unclear therefore why he does not concede that any author of (1) is committed to the existence of the proposition that the earth is round (this being what the Translation Argument is aimed at demonstrating), and let this be his reason for recommending that the author substitute (2), which lacks any such commitment. (*Cf.* Quine, and my 'Relational Belief' for discussion.) In any event, Dummett's reply has the advantage over Geach's (and Quine's) that it does not depend (at least not to the same extent) on any implausible or otherwise controversial skeptical theses concerning synonymy.

Burge claims that the sentence he proposes for (2) involves self-denotation, in such a way that the best translation will preserve this feature at the expense of denotation. The details of Burge's argument will not be pursued here. One minor correction should be noted, however. Contrary to Burge's initial claim (which he credits to W. D. Hart) that translation of a self-denoting sentence either preserves self-denotation or denotation but not both, translations may be given that preserve neither one. (For whatever it is worth, it is even probable that such translations have been given in actual practice.) Burge's argument requires only the weaker claim that no translation of a self-denoting sentence preserves both denotation and self-denotation.

[29] *Frege: Philosophy of Language*, p. 372. But see also *The Interpretation of Frege's Philosophy*, p. 90.

[30] Heidelberger, Review of Dummett's *Frege: Philosophy of Language*, in *Metaphilosophy*, 6, no. 1 (January 1975), pp. 35–43, at 42–43; Lewy, *Meaning and Modality* (Cambridge University Press, 1976), at pp. 64–66; Linsky, *Oblique Contexts* (University of Chicago Press, 1983), at p. 8. (I thank C. Anthony Anderson for providing the last two references.) See also Saul Kripke, 'A Puzzle about Belief,' reprinted in N. Salmon and S. Soames, eds., *Propositions and Attitudes* (Oxford University Press, 1988), pp. 102–148, at 142n25.

In his discussion in *The Interpretation of Frege's Philosophy*, Dummett attributes both the thesis that the indirect sense of (0) in English is the ordinary sense of (4), and the exegetical thesis that Frege held the former thesis, to Heidelberger. Dummett also there accuses Heidelberger of inconsistently conjoining these theses with an endorsement of the Translation Argument (pp. 91, 94). These attributions are dubious. Although Heidelberger defends the Translation Argument against Dummett's criticism, he explicitly declines to endorse the argument and instead expresses sympathy for the alternative criticisms of it by Davidson and Putnam (p. 43n). Moreover, he does

the Translation Argument whether (2') is deemed a correct translation into French of the English (2). The claim that an actual translator or interpreter would offer (3') instead is similarly irrelevant. The Translation Argument is concerned exclusively with the semantics of (1) and (2), and not with any pragmatic "conventions presupposed in their use" or with any resulting "practical canons of apt translation" of texts containing either. As Heidelberger correctly notes, the construction '*S*' is a translation into *L*' of the *L* expression *S*' may even be replaced uniformly throughout the argument by '*S*' has the same meaning in *L*' that *S* has in *L*', thereby eliminating any allusion to translation. Any controversy concerning translation (in particular, whether apt or correct translation must preserve meaning) is thus seen to be entirely irrelevant.

Dummett appears to have conceded the irrelevance of the issue of whether the English (2) would be translated into French in actual practice by (2') rather than (3'). Yet (1') is clearly not synonymous in French with (2'), which explicitly mentions the English sentence (0). Once it is conceded that (2') has the same meaning in French that (2) has in English, the critic of the Translation Argument has no alternative but to challenge the remaining premise, that (1') is a sense-preserving French translation of the English (1). In response to unspecified critics (presumably including at least Heidelberger, Lewy, and/or Linsky), Dummett does just that.[31] And indeed, Dummett's interpretation of Frege implies that Frege should have rejected this premise. For according to that interpretation, Frege is supposed to have held that (1) is synonymous in English with (6), which mentions the very expression (0), whereas the French (1') instead mentions (0'). In the general case, the proponent of (2) as an English analysis of (1) will contend that (1') is synonymous in French with (3'), which explicitly mentions (0'), and therefore does not have the same meaning in French that (1) has in English. Such a proponent might even enlist the support of translation at this point, since the sense-preserving translation of (3') into English bears little resemblance to (1).[32]

Though the argument's appeal to sense-preserving translation may be thus thwarted by controversy, Church's general point might still be made without appealing to any contested translation. Church supports the premise that (1') and

not straightforwardly propose either of the theses in question. Instead he correctly attributes to Frege the thesis that the indirect sense of (0) in English is the ordinary sense of (5), while mis-identifying this thesis with the alternative thesis which Dummett had branded "rather implausible" (p. 37; see footnote 15 above). As noted earlier, Dummett also fails to distinguish between these two theses concerning indirect sense, and therefore fails to distinguish properly between the corresponding exegetical theses concerning Frege on indirect sense. (It should also be noted that whereas Heidelberger explicitly attributes to Frege the thesis that the indirect sense of (0) in English is the ordinary sense of (5), he also attributes to Frege a fallacious argument for that thesis which Frege does not give, and which is in fact inconsistent with his views.)

[31] *The Interpretation of Frege's Philosophy*, pp. 90–91. The premise is explicitly rejected by Kemp and Stephen Leeds Curiously, Dummett ultimately endorses the premise (p. 94), on the ground that (1) has the same "conventional significance" in English that (1) has in French (p. 99). It is unclear why Dummett insists nevertheless that it is illegitimate for Church to assert this premise, on the same or very similar ground, in the course of his argument against the proposed analysis.

[32] For more on this sort of issue, especially as it relates to Burge's response to the Translation Argument, see my 'A Problem in the Frege–Church Theory of Sense and Denotation,' at p. 166 n15.

(2′) are not synonymous in French by observing that they "obviously convey different meanings" to a French speaker who knows no English, with only (1′) conveying the content of what Chris is supposed to believe. In a similar vein, one might object to the proposal that (1) is synonymous in English with (2) on the ground that different information is conveyed to an English speaker by (1) than is conveyed to a French speaker by (2′)—which, it has now been conceded, is a sense-preserving French translation of (2).

In response to this possible objection, Stephen Leeds objects that

> what information a sentence conveys to a hearer depends not only on what the sentence means but on what background information the hearer has. The mere ability to understand a language can constitute such background information; for example, '*Luther sprach: 'Hier steh ich''* will convey more to someone who speaks German than its strict translation into English: 'Luther said: '*Hier steh ich*' ' will to a monolingual speaker of English. (p. 46)

This last point might also be illustrated by (2) and (2′). The two have the same meaning in their respective languages, yet an English speaker obtains more information on the basis of the former than a French speaker obtains on the basis of the latter. Church himself noted, as part of his argument, that the knowledge of what (0) means in English would enable one to infer from (2′) the content of the belief attributed to Chris. Leeds contends that it is arguably this ancillary knowledge, rather than the content semantically expressed by (1), that likewise accounts for the information conveyed to an English speaker by (1) that is not conveyed to a French speaker by (2′). Indeed, as we have seen, Burge argues that the pragmatics involved in the use of (2) (and therefore also in the use of its alleged paraphrase (1)) directs one to interpret the mentioned sentence (0).

It is here that this general response to the Church Translation Argument betrays a failure to grasp the central point of the argument—or perhaps I should say, at least one of the central points of the argument—and in a sense, one of the main points also of Frege's philosophy of language.

IV

Just as the "practical canons of apt translation" are entirely irrelevant to the Church Translation Argument, so also is the information obtained on the basis of an utterance. To use a terminology I introduced in previous work, the information obtained from an utterance can involve not only *semantically encoded information*, but also *pragmatically imparted information*.[33] (What counts as apt translation, for that matter, may also be concerned to some extent with information of both kinds.) The Translation Argument, by contrast, is concerned exclusively with the former. One who knows the English language is able to infer additional information from an utterance of (2) not semantically contained within (2) itself. While this additional information is thereby pragmatically imparted (at least indirectly) to an English

[33] *Frege's Puzzle* (footnote 24 above), pp. 58–60 and elsewhere (especially pp. 78–79, 84–85, 100, 114–115).

speaker by the utterance, it is not directly 'conveyed' by (2) in the sense relevant to the Translation Argument. Rather, it is inferred from the semantically contained information taken together with the ancillary knowledge of what (0) means in English. When Church argues that (1') and (2') convey different information to a French speaker who knows no English, he is speaking of the information semantically encoded in each, the propositions that the French sentences convey to the French speaker solely in virtue of their literal French meanings. He explicitly contrasts this with information that may be inferred from this together with knowledge of English. And indeed, the very conclusion of the argument (the denial of which Leeds seeks to defend) is that (1) and (2) semantically contain different information, despite the fact that the content of (1) is easily inferred from an utterance of (2) given knowledge of the English meaning of (0).

Translation between languages is invoked merely as a device to facilitate our seeing the difference in semantic content that exists between (1) and (2)—or as a special case, between (1) and (6)—despite the ease with which one is inferred from the other, relying on our knowledge of English. The merely auxiliary role of translation in the Translation Argument was first noted explicitly by Church himself:

> The existence of more than one language is not usually to be thought of as a fundamental ground for the conclusions reached by this method. Its role is rather as a useful device to separate those features of a statement which are essential to its meaning from those which are merely accidental to its expression in a particular language, the former but not the latter being invariant under translation. And distinctions (e.g., of use and mention) which are established by this method it should be possible also to see more directly.[34]

In the application of the Translation Argument to the question of indirect sense, the distinction that one should be able to see more directly is a special distinction between the meanings of (4) and (5). This same distinction accounts for the difference in meaning between (1) and (2).

What exactly is this special distinction, and how are we supposed to see it without resorting to translation? The answer to this is what I take to be the crucial point, and the very point that Church's detractors have failed to appreciate. Church puts this point by noting that the proposed analysis of (1)

> must be rejected on the ground that [(2)] does not convey the same information as (1). Thus (1) conveys the content of what [Chris believes] ... it is not even possible to infer (1) as a consequence of [(2)], on logical grounds alone—but only by making use of [an] item of factual information, not contained in [(2), that (0) means in English that the earth is round].
> ('On Carnap's Analysis of Statements of Assertion and Belief,' pp. 168–169 of Linsky)

Consider (6), as a special case of (2), and the purely semantic differences that Church is limning between it and (1). Church's main point is that (1) gives the

---

[34] 'Intensional Isomorphism and Identify of Belief,' in Salmon and Soames, p. 168n22. In a similar vein, Church had written in 'A Formulation of the Logic of Sense and Denotation,' at p. 5n: "This device is not essential to the explanation, but is helpful in order to dispel any remnants of an illusion that there is something in some way necessary or transparent about the connection between a word or a sentence and its meaning, whereas, of course, this connection is entirely artificial and arbitrary."

content of the belief attributed to Chris in a special manner, a manner in which (6) does not. In short, (1) *identifies* that content. To be sure, both (1) and (6) specify the content, but (6) does so only by describing it in the manner of (4), as *whatever sense* (0) *ordinarily expresses in English*. This is indeed a way of conceiving of the English ordinary sense of (0)—it is a concept of the proposition, in Church's terminology— but it is a concept of that sense that even one who has no understanding of (0), as an English expression, may possess with perfect mastery, provided he or she knows only that (0) is a meaningful English expression. For such a person is in a position to infer that (0) ordinarily expresses in English its own English ordinary sense. This inferred knowledge is trivial; it does nothing to further the quest to learn what, by contrast, one who understands (0), as a sentence of English, thereby knows, *viz.* that (0) specifically means *this* proposition in English: that the earth is round.

This is essentially a special case of Russell's more general distinction between *knowledge by acquaintance* and *knowledge by description*.[35] The latter is a distinction between two kinds of knowledge of things, as opposed to knowledge of facts (in French, two kinds of *connaissance* as opposed to *savoir*). Knowledge of a thing by acquaintance might be explained as a conception of the thing *qua* "that *F*," perhaps perceptually ostended or otherwise demonstratively selected, for a particular sortal '*F*' (which might even be the universal sortal, 'thing'). Knowledge of a thing by description, by contrast, is a correct conception of the thing *qua* "whatever uniquely satisfies *C*," invoking some purely descriptive condition *C*. In Church's terminology, knowledge of a thing by description is exactly the conceiving of that thing through the apprehension of a concept of it.[36]

---

[35] Russell, 'Knowledge by Acquaintance and Knowledge by Description,' reprinted in N. Salmon and S. Soames, eds., *Propositions and Attitudes* (Oxford University Press, 1988), pp. 16–32.

[36] In calling a condition 'purely descriptive,' I mean to preclude its being such a condition as might be expressed in the form 'the condition of being [identical with] that very *F*'. It is assumed here that Church's notion of a *concept* likewise excludes such conditions. *Cf.* my *Reference and Essence* (Princeton University Press and Basil Blackwell, 1981), pp. 14–23 (where the term 'descriptional' is employed instead of 'descriptive').

Russell construed acquaintance in a very strict sense which excluded the possiblity of acquaintance with particulars other than oneself or mental items directly contained in one's consciousness. The distinction itself can be drawn independently of this severe restriction, however, and is clearly legitimate with regard to more familiar notions of acquaintance. One such notion is that of having perceptual, or other natural or "real," cognitive contact with a particular person or object— the sort of connection that is sufficient to enable one to form beliefs or other attitudes *about* the object (in an ordinary sense). A somewhat stricter notion imposes the further condition of *knowing who or what* the object is, in an ordinary sense. (Some philosophers, having evidently overlooked the possibility of perceiving an object without knowing who or what the object is, have confused these two broader notions of acquaintance. See my 'How to Measure the Standard Metre,' *Proceedings of the Aristotelian Society*, NS, 38 (1987/88), pp. 193–217, especially at 200–201n, 213ff.)

Throughout I use the term 'identification' for a notion of acquaintance implying knowledge of who or what the object is. Some contemporary neo-Russellian theories of meaning deny that one who knows the content of (1) automatically thereby knows what proposition it is that Chris believes (i.e., automatically thereby knows at least one proposition that Chris believes). Such theories may hold instead that one who knows the content of (1) is thereby acquainted with the believed proposition in some less familiar way, and may not know exactly what proposition is in question. Knowing what *F* so-and-so is (as special cases, knowing what proposition Chris is hereby held to believe, or knowing what person—or who—so-and-so is) may be a matter knowing of so-and-so, *de re*, that so-and-so is it (him/her), believing this fact about so-and-so while conceiving of it in a

Russell thought of the two kinds of knowledge as mutually exclusive. To be sure, the very same thing may be simultaneously known in each of the two ways, but on Russell's conception of the distinction, no knowledge of a thing by description is also acquaintance with that same thing. Other philosophers embrace a strict representational epistemology according to which all knowledge of things is achieved only through the apprehension of concepts (in Church's sense), so that all knowledge of things is ultimately knowledge by description (in Russell's sense). Any knowledge that can be called 'acquaintance', on such a view, is merely a peculiar kind of knowledge by description, one in which the relevant descriptive condition or concept is of a special sort. It is arguable that Frege in particular held a strict representational epistemology. And indeed, this epistemological stance may lie behind the principal divergence between broadly Fregean and Russellian semantic theories.[37]

There is an infinite-regress argument against the tenability of this strict representational sort of epistemology: If conceiving of a thing invariably invokes a concept of that thing, then in order to conceive of any particular thing x, one must, in that very act of conceiving, apprehend some antecedently understood concept c_1 which is a concept of x. But by the same token, in order to know c_1, one would have to apprehend some further antecedently understood concept c_2 which is a concept of c_1, and so on. It seems to follow that in order to conceive of anything at all, one would have to apprehend each of an infinite sequence of antecedently understood concepts. One is invited to conclude from the threat of this infinite regress that all knowledge of things ultimately rests on 'direct' knowledge of things, knowledge that is not mediated through concepts of those things.[38]

Textual evidence suggests that, in a sense, Frege instead embraced the infinite regress, via his infinite hierarchies of indirect senses (ordinary sense, indirect sense, doubly indirect sense, and so on).[39] It is a possibility also that Church holds a similar

special, identifying way. (See my *Frege's Puzzle*, pp. 103–118, on the notion of believing a proposition while taking it a particular way; see also footnote 43 below.) Even such theories, however, will generally recognize an important epistemological difference between the contents of (1) and (6), such that knowing the fact described by (6) falls well short of knowing that fact described by (1). It may be acknowledged, for example, that one who knows the content of (1)—by contrast with one who merely knows the content of (6)—*ipso facto* knows something *de re* about the proposition that the earth is round, namely, that it is something Chris believes (even, perhaps, without knowing exactly what proposition is in question). This is sufficient for my primary purpose in the discussion to follow. For related discussion, see Mark Richard, 'Articulated Terms,' in J. Tomberlin, ed., *Philosophical Perspectives*, 7: *Language and Logic* (Atascadero, Ca.: Ridgeview, 1993), pp. 207–230.

It is possible that there is a gradation of notions of acquaintance. This would not make Russell's distinction between knowledge by acquaintance and knowledge by description untenable; on the contrary, it would make for a multiplicity of legitimate Russellian distinctions. The distinction on which I rely in the discussion to follow need not be made completely precise, and will be sufficiently obvious to support the conclusions reached by its means.

[37] As explained in the previous note, Russell himself held a respresentational epistemology with regard to all particulars other than oneself and the mental contents of one's consciousness. Contemporary Russellians have typically favored a less restrictive epistemology on which one knows various concrete particulars "directly," i.e., without appealing to individuating qualitative concepts of those particulars.

[38] *Cf.* the infinite-regress argument in Russell, at pp. 28–29 of Salmon and Soames.

[39] One may not straightforwardly conclude from the infinite-regress argument that according to the strict representational sort of epistemology in question, in order to conceive of a thing x, one

epistemological view.[40] Even so, both Frege and Church doubtlessly recognized that knowledge of a thing by acquaintance has a very different cognitive flavor from mere knowledge by description (i.e., from knowledge of the thing not by acquaintance).

The distinction is made evident in the familiar contrast found in pairs of color terms like 'white' and 'the color of snow'.[41] The former identifies the color in question in a way that the latter does not. One who, because of limited experience, is ignorant of both the color of snow and the color of Church's hair, may still know that Church's hair is the color of snow, i.e., that Church's hair has the same color that snow has, whatever color that may be. If such a person may be said to know what color Church's hair is, then he or she knows it merely by description. Just as he or she knows that Church's hair is the color of snow, he or she also knows that snow is the color of snow. What such a person lacks is the knowledge of *which color* that is, the identifying information normally taken to be contained in the words: 'Snow is *white*'. A person who has been deprived of sight since birth may be incapable of knowing any color except merely by description (e.g., as the property, visually manifested in some manner or other, of reflecting light of such-and-such wavelengths.) The legitimacy of this

must *in that very act of conceiving* apprehend each of infinitely many concepts. For although the epistemology requires that the act of conceiving of x necessarily involves an act of apprehending a concept c_1 of x, it does not require that the act of apprehending c_1 necessarily involves conceiving of c_1. One might even label the act of apprehending a concept without conceiving of it a kind of "direct acquaintance" with the concept.

One may not even conclude from the infinite-regress argument that according to strict representational epistemology, in order to conceive of anything one must already apprehend each of infinitely many concepts. What is required on Frege's doctrine of the hierarchy is that one be able to acquire an apprehension of any one of the infinitely many concepts on demand, so to speak, in order to comprehend a sentence that embeds an expression within a sufficiently large number of *ungerade* operators. Strict representational epistemology nevertheless yields a possible answer to Russell's famous "no backward road" observation and the difficulty it is supposed to raise for Frege's doctrine. It is true that on Frege's theory, for anything x there are countless concepts of x, no one of which can be singled out as privileged or as the "designated" or "standard" concept of x. But according to strict representational epistemology, in conceiving of a concept c_1 through one's acquaintance with it, one is thereby apprehending a special identifying concept c_2 of c_1. By attending to what one is apprehending, one can conceive of c_2 through one's acquaintance with it, and hence through one's apprehension of a special identifying concept c_3 of c_2, and so on. Thus it seems that one need only attend to what one is apprehending to generate a proper Fregean hierarchy starting from a single concept. Even if there is no "backward road" (privileged branch) from a thing that is not a concept to a concept of the thing, it seems there may be a backward road from a concept to a concept of the concept. (I am indebted here to remarks made in a seminar by Saul Kripke and to later discussion with C. Anthony Anderson.) *Cf.* my 'Reference and Information Content: Names and Descriptions,' and 'A Problem in the Frege–Church Theory of Sense and Denotation,' at p. 163.

[40] It must be noted, however, that Church rejects Frege's notion of indirect sense. See 'A Problem in the Frege–Church Theory of Sense and Denotation,' pp. 164–165n10.

[41] A number of philosophers have noted differences of meaning beween such terms. For a sample of the relevant literature, see D. M. Armstrong, 'Materialism, Properties and Predicates,' *Monist*, 56, no. 2 (April 1972), pp. 163–176, at 174; Jaegwon Kim, 'On the Psycho-Physical Identity Theory,' *American Philosophical Quarterly*, 3, no. 3 (July 1966), pp. 227–235, and 'Events and Their Descriptions,' in N. Rescher, ed., *Essays in Honor of Carl G. Hempel* (Dordrecht: D. Reidel, 1969), pp. 198–215, at 205–206; Bernard Linsky, 'General Terms as Designators,' *Pacific Philosophical Quarterly*, 65 (1984), pp. 259–276; N. L. Wilson, 'The Trouble with Meanings,' *Dialogue*, 3, no. 1 (June 1964), pp. 52–64. (The last is evidently the ancestor of the other discussions.)

distinction between two different ways of knowing the color white (or of knowing the color of Church's hair, etc.) seems sufficiently obvious that it will be readily recognized even by those who hold that the knowledge that snow is white is ultimately knowledge to the effect that snow has whatever color it is that uniquely satisfies a certain, special visual condition (perhaps a phenomenological condition).

The analogy between the pair of contrasting color terms and (4)–(5) is striking. In particular, knowing the English meaning of (0) by the description (4) is not a way of *understanding* (0), in any ordinary sense. As noted above, someone who speaks no English, upon learning only that (0) is a meaningful expression of English, is thereby given its meaning by this description. The person still lacks information specifying what that meaning is—to wit, the identifying information that (0) expresses in English the proposition that the earth is round. (Compare again knowing what color snow is only by the description 'the color of snow' vs. knowing that snow is this color: white.)

Earlier we applied the Translation Argument against Dummett's apparent hypothesis that (4) and (5) are ordinarily synonymous in English. A more direct application of the argument is possible. The translations of the following meta-linguistic sentences reveal a fundamental difference in meaning:

(7) 'The earth is round' ordinarily expresses in English the proposition that the earth is round.

(8) 'The earth is round' ordinarily expresses in English the ordinary sense in English of 'The earth is round'.

The meta-English sentence (8) is tautologous, or virtually so. By contrast, (7)—or more simply '(0) means in English that the earth is round'—"conveys the content," in Church's terminology, of (0) in English; it identifies the English meaning of (0), semantically specifying it in a way that (8) does not even come close to doing.

Translation into another language of both (7) and (8), and likewise the translation of both (1) and (2), is merely a pedagogical aid which more clearly reveals their divergent semantic properties. We have already seen that the question of whether the strict sort of translation that is invoked in The Translation Argument conforms with the practice of actual translators and interpreters is quite irrelevant to the purpose for which translation is pressed into service. What is essential for that purpose is that the translation be what Church calls 'literal', i.e., sense-preserving.[42] The relevant differences in meaning between the English (4) and (5)—which is the principal point of the argument—can be seen independently of translation, for example by appealing to the striking analogy with 'white' and 'the color of snow'. And as Church says, it should be possible also to see the point directly.

V

Recall Leed's contention that it is arguably not the semantic content of (1) in English but the understanding of what (0) means (which, according to Burge, is pragmatically

---

[42] 'Intensional Isomorphism and Identity of Belief,' footnote 25 (p. 168 of Salmon and Soames).

required by (1)), that accounts for the additional information that an English speaker obtains from (1) but a French speaker does not obtain from the sense-preserving translation of (6). This observation is meant to isolate the claim that, semantically, (1) specifies the content of the belief attributed to Chris (as does (6)) in precisely the manner of (4). But this claim flies in the face of Church's main point, that (1) semantically "conveys the content" of Chris's alleged belief, identifying that content in a special manner exhibited by neither (6) nor its French translation. The content of Chris's belief is not merely pragmatically imparted to an English speaker by an utterance of (1) *via* an inference. Contrary to Leeds, the content of Chris's belief is semantically encoded by (1). Indeed, Leed's rejoinder is nearly enough self-defeating. For it implicitly recognizes that there is a special way of thinking of the proposition that the earth is round—a way of being acquainted with it—such that one who knows that (0) in English expresses that proposition conceived in that way, knows what (0) means in English, whereas one who knows only that (0) in English expresses the English ordinary sense of (0) (conceived in that way, by that description) does not know what (0) means. This special identifying "way of thinking" of the proposition seems to be carried in English by (5), and it would seem to be precisely this that so markedly distinguishes (5) from (4). It is natural to assume, in fact, that the special way of thinking of the proposition is nothing less than the concept semantically expressed in English by (5). It is difficult to imagine how else one might express it.[43]

The foregoing considerations reveal the reasons for the failure of the theory that Dummett mistakenly imputes to Frege. For the hypothesis that the indirect sense of (0) in English is the ordinary sense of (4) yields the erroneous conclusion that one who understands no English beyond the words 'Chris believes that', and who is informed that (0) is a meaningful English sentence without being given its actual meaning, may thereby know what (1) means in English. In fact, it would seem that what he or she still needs in order to know the meaning of (1) is to be given the meaning in English of (0) *qua* the proposition that the earth is round, i.e., via the concept that is ordinarily expressed in English by (5) rather than that ordinarily expressed by (4). It is thus possible to see directly, without resorting to translation, the superiority of Frege's thesis concerning indirect sense over the thesis Dummett erroneously attributes to him.

The foregoing also dramatically exposes a fatal error in Dummett's Thesis that the only way in which we can conceive of any sense is as the sense of some particular linguistic expression. Using Church's terminology (in combination with some of Dummett's), the thesis may be stated more precisely thus:

For every concept c_1, if someone conceives of c_1, then there is some concept c_2 of c_1 such that that very act of conceiving of c_1 consists in apprehending c_2; and furthermore, for every concept c_2 of c_1 that we can apprehend, there is some expression e (of some possible language l)

---

[43] Presumably understanding (0), as a sentence of English, entails knowing what (0) means in English, but it is arguable that understanding, in a strict sense, requires more than this (perhaps acquiring the knowledge of the meaning of (0) in a special computational manner). There are delicate issues, on which the present discussion is neutral, concerning the extent to which the English meaning of (5) captures the way of conceiving the proposition in question that is possessed by one who correctly understands (0) as a sentence of English. See footnote 36 above.

such that: (*i*) c_1 is the ordinary sense of *e* (in *l*); and (*ii*) c_2 presents c_1 as the ordinary sense of *e* (in *l*), i.e., to apprehend c_2 is exactly to conceive of c_1 as the ordinary sense of *e* (in *l*).[44]

Although Dummett attributes this thesis to Frege, it is in fact deeply out of sync with the fundamental character and structure of Frege's philosophy of language. Frege does say that we apprehend propositions through words.[45] And it seems clearly true that we do this with at least a great many propositions. It by no means follows, however, that we are unable to conceive of the proposition except as whatever sense it may be that those words ordinarily express. Frege would certainly have insisted, against Dummett, that there are infinitely many ways to denote the proposition that the earth is round without mentioning particular linguistic expressions, either explicitly or implicitly: 'the proposition that Columbus set out to prove by sailing westward to India', 'the proposition that Aristotle proved on the basis of the shape of the earth's shadow on the moon', 'Chris's favorite proposition', 'the first thing Columbus asserted upon sighting the mainland of America', etc. These unremarkable phrases, and many others, express graspable concepts that "give us" the proposition in ways other than as the sense of an expression.[46] More important, the very apprehension of a proposition, even by means of the words through which we apprehend it, crucially involves an identifying conception of the proposition, a knowledge of it by acquaintance and not merely as whatever it is that these words ordinarily express. This is true in fact of understanding in general; there is no comprehension without identification.

Dummett's Thesis precludes the possibility of a language that works the way Frege thought all language worked, and even the very possibility of language itself. On Dummett's view, in taking (0) to express such-and-such, one must, in that very act of cognition, conceive of the concept in question as *whatever sense is ordinarily expressed by e*, for some particular linguistic expression *e*—there being no other way for us to conceive of any concept. This theory makes all of language unintelligible for us in principle. Dummett's Thesis leaves our grasp of language in a state of ignorance exactly analogous to someone who, from birth, sees the world only in black and white and shades of grey. A person who has always been completely color-blind may know that physical objects are colored, and that certain of them have the same color as certain others (snow and Church's hair, grass and emeralds, etc.), but in some sense has no way of learning what color anything is. Dummett's Thesis reduces us all

---

[44] See footnotes 19 and 36 above. The first conjunct expresses strict representationalism with regard to concepts. On a Fregean theory the word 'as' occurring in Dummett's constructions '... is given to us as —' and 'conceives of ... as —' must be itself regarded as an *ungerade* operator. Dummett's Thesis, as formulated here and as given by Dummett himself, thus involves quantification into a nonextensional context. (I am not claiming that Dummett would accept my specific formulation of his thesis, only that he explicitly endorses the thesis itself, which I formulate thus, and attributes the same thesis to Frege. The textual evidence for these claims is clear.)

[45] For example, in 'On the Scientific Justification of a Conceptual Notation' (reproduced in his *Conceptual Notation and Related Articles*, T. W. Bynum, ed. (Oxford University Press, 1972), pp. 83–89), Frege says that "we think in words ..., and if not in words, then in mathematical or other symbols" (p. 84). See footnote 15 above.

[46] In light of this, Frege undoubtedly rejected even the weaker, Berkeleyan thesis mentioned in note 17 above.

to the state of the international traveler who knows that the words he or she sees and hears have meaning, but is completely ignorant of what those meanings are. Indeed, the theory renders us considerably worse off than the traveler. A tourist can identify the foreign meanings by consulting a phrase book. Dummett's theory has the consequence that we are unable even to understand expressions by translating them into our native language. For the only knowledge we have of the meanings of *our own* words is by the description: whatever it is that those words mean. On Dummett's theory, there is no identification of meanings, no knowledge of meaning by acquaintance, only knowledge by description. This makes the veil of syntax utterly opaque, and the wall of unintelligibility impenetrable even in principle. Since there can be no comprehension without identification, Dummett's theory has the unintended consequence that we comprehend nothing.[47]

The fundamental flaw in Dummett's theory can also be seen through the theory of definition, by means of a variation of the infinite-regress argument considered above. According to Dummett's Thesis, in knowing that the ordinary sense of an expression e_1 (in a language l_1) is such-and-such, one must conceive of that sense as the ordinary sense of some expression e_2 (of a language l_2). This is tantamount to the claim that every meaningful linguistic expression that the speaker understands is understood by means of a kind of verbal definition: The ordinary sense of e_1 is the same as the ordinary sense of e_2, or as it is sometimes written, $e_1 =_{def} e_2$.[48] The definiens e_2 would likewise be understood by means of an analogous definition, $e_2 =_{def} e_3$, and so on. It is well known, however, that not all expressions of a language may be understood by means of verbal definition. There has to be a stock of primitives, whose sense is learned in some way other than by verbal definition (by ostensive definition, for example). Dummett's Thesis leads ultimately to a vicious circularity among the definitions. And this makes all understanding impossible even in principle.

The root problem with Dummett's Thesis is that it restricts all knowledge of meaning to knowledge by description, precluding even the possibility of our identifying the ordinary sense of any expression. Since there is no comprehension without identification, Dummett's Thesis makes comprehension utterly unattainable. And this, I submit, excludes the very possibility of the phenomenon we call *language*.

If I am correct, the main point of the Church Translation Argument is exactly the antithesis of Dummett's Thesis. The 'that'-clause in English expressions like (1) and

---

[47] It is arguable that a person completely color-blind from birth may nevertheless learn of the color green (*de re*) that grass and emeralds are *that color*, by learning that they reflect light of such-and-such wavelengths under visually normal conditions. Even so, there still seems to be some knowledge that those of us who see green (as green) have, and that the completely color-blind person lacks, concerning the color of grass. In some sense, the completely color-blind person still does not know how grass looks, phenomenologically, with regard to color. By contrast, if Dummett's theory were correct, none of us could know *of* the proposition that the earth is round (*de re*), that (0) expresses it in English (let alone could we understand what (0) means in English— see footnotes 36 and 43 above).

[48] This notation is normally used for definitions within a single language. For present purposes we may think of the union of all of the separate languages spoken by a particular speaker as constituting a single comprehensive language. (Any resulting lexical ambiguities may be resolved by means of disambiguating subscripts.) Alternatively, the notation is easily extendible to accommodate inter-language definitions, for example by writing: $[e_1, l_1] =_{def} [e_2, l_2]$.

(7) carries with it a special way of conceptualizing the content of the sentence following 'that', an identifying way of thinking of the proposition which constitutes acquaintance rather than mere knowledge by description. Church's appeal to translation serves to illuminate this fundamental point. Frege's explanation of the indirect sense of (0) in English as the ordinary sense of (5) rather than that of (4) almost certainly reflects his own grasp of this same fundamental point, and with it a repudiation of Dummett's Thesis.

Insofar as understanding requires acquaintance, what is it that we are required to be acquainted with? If there is no comprehension without identification, what is it that we are identifying? Not just sentences in a language, as we have seen. But if not just sentences in a language, then what else?

The Translation Argument has been with us a long time—longer even than I have. Yet many language theorists today have missed its principal point. If nothing else, there is an important lesson to be learned from the failure of the argument's critics to appreciate that point, and from the decisive collapse of at least one theory that has been proffered in defiance of the argument.

18

Tense and Intension (2003)

The radical philosopher of flux, Cratylus of Athens, is said to have spurned the use of language altogether in part because, like everything else, our words' meanings are continually changing, making it impossible to convey what we intend. Scholars in the age of 'publish or perish' know that language has uses that do not require successful communication, but this seems a weak answer to Cratylus. Whereas diachronic change is inevitable, change in lexical meaning usually takes place over a long enough period that we manage during the interim, now and then, to get our thoughts across. I have come to believe, however, that any viable theory of the semantic content of language—whether Fregean, Russellian, or neither, or both—must accommodate the fact that, in a significant sense, the content or sense of most terms ('red', 'table', 'tree', 'walk') is indeed different at different times. I present here an account of semantic content that is philosophically neutral with respect to the sorts of issues that dominated twentieth-century philosophy of semantics, but that entails this kind of content shiftiness and other interesting consequences concerning the relationship between content and the empire of Time.

SEMANTIC CONTENT

The primary presupposition of any philosophical theory of semantic content is that the (or at least one) semantic function of declarative sentences is to express a proposition.[1] A declarative sentence may be said to *contain* the proposition it

Portions of my book *Frege's Puzzle* (Atascadero, Calif.: Ridgeview, 1986, 1991) and of my chapter 'Tense and Singular Propositions,' in J. Almog, J. Perry, and H. Wettstein, eds., *Themes from Kaplan* (Oxford: Oxford University Press, 1989), pp. 331–392, have been incorporated into the present chapter. Where those presentations presuppose a Millian (or neo-Russellian) semantic theory, this presentation, by contrast, is deliberately neutral regarding all such issues. I am grateful to Steven Humphrey, Aleksandar Jokic, Takashi Yagisawa, and my audience at the Santa Barbara City College conference "Time, Tense, and Reference" for their comments.

[1] Throughout this chapter, I am concerned with discrete units of information that are specifiable by means of a 'that'-clause—for example, that Socrates is wise. These discrete units are *propositions*. Following the usual practice, I use the verb 'express' in such a way that an unambiguous declarative sentence expresses (with respect to a given possible context *c*) a single proposition, which is referred to (with respect to *c*) by the result of prefixing 'the proposition that' to the sentence. A declarative sentence may express two or more propositions, but if it does so, it is ambiguous. Propositions expressed by the proper logical consequences of an unambiguous sentence are not themselves expressed, in this sense, by the sentence. The proposition that snow is white and grass is green is

semantically expresses, and that proposition may be described as the *semantic content*, or more simply as the *content*, of the sentence. Propositions are, like the sentences that express them, abstract entities. Many of their properties can be "read off" from the containing sentences. Thus, for instance, it is evident that propositions are not ontologically simple but complex. The proposition that Frege is ingenious and the proposition that Frege is ingenuous are both, in the same way, propositions directly about Frege; hence, they must have some component in common. Likewise, the proposition that Frege is ingenious has some component in common with the proposition that Russell is ingenious, and that component is different from what it has in common with the proposition that Frege is ingenuous. Correspondingly, the declarative sentence 'Frege is ingenious' shares certain syntactic components with the sentences 'Frege is ingenuous' and 'Russell is ingenious'. These syntactic components— the name 'Frege' and the predicate 'is ingenious'—are separately semantically correlated with the corresponding component of the proposition contained by the sentence. Let us call the proposition-component semantically correlated with an expression the *semantic content* of the expression. The semantic content of the name 'Frege' is that which the name contributes to the proposition contained by such sentences as 'Frege is ingenious' and 'Frege is ingenuous'; similarly, the semantic content of the predicate 'is ingenious' is that entity which the predicate contributes to the proposition contained in such sentences as 'Frege is ingenious' and 'Russell is ingenious'. As a limiting case, the semantic content of a declarative sentence is the proposition it contains, its proposition content.

Within the framework of so-called possible-worlds semantics, the *extension* of a singular term with respect to a possible world w is simply its *referent* with respect to w, that is, the object or individual to which the term refers with respect to w. The extension of a sentence with respect to w is its truth-value with respect to w—either truth or falsehood. The extension of an n-place predicate with respect to w is the class of n-tuples to which the predicate applies with respect to w, or rather the characteristic function of the class, that is, the function that assigns either truth or falsehood to an n-tuple of individuals, according as the predicate or its negation applies with respect to w to the n-tuple. (Assuming bivalence, the extension of an n-place predicate may simply be identified instead with the class of n-tuples to which the predicate applies.) The content of an expression determines the *intension* of the expression. The intension of a singular term, sentence, or predicate is a function that assigns to any possible world w the extension that the expression takes on with respect to w.

Since ordinary language includes so-called indexical expressions (such context-sensitive expression as 'I', 'here', 'now', 'this', 'she'), the semantic content of an expression, and hence also the semantic intension, may vary with the context in which the expression is uttered. This means that content must in general be "indexed" (i.e., relativized) to context. That is, strictly one should speak of the semantic content of an expression *with respect to* this or that context of utterance, and similarly for the

---

different from the proposition that snow is white, though intuitively the latter is included as part of the former. The sentence 'Snow is white and grass is green' expresses only the former, not the latter.

corresponding semantic intension of an expression. This generates a higher-level, nonrelativized semantic value for expressions, which Kaplan calls the *character* of an expression. The character of an expression is a function or rule that determines for any possible context of utterance *c*, the semantic content that the expression takes on with respect to *c*. An indexical expression is then definable as one whose character is not a constant function.[2]

The systematic method by which it is secured which proposition is semantically expressed by which sentence (with respect to a context) is, roughly, that a sentence semantically contains that proposition whose components are the semantic contents of the sentence-parts, with these semantic contents combined as the sentence-parts are themselves combined to form the sentence.[3] In order to analyze

[2] Whereas Kaplan introduces his notion of character in connection with his version of a direct reference theory, the general idea of relativizing content to context, and the resulting notion of the character of an expression, can easily fit within a Fregean (or "anti-direct reference") conception of content.

Throughout this chapter, I use a quasi-technical notion of the *context* of an utterance which is such that for any particular actual utterance of an expression, if any facts had been different, even if only facts entirely independent of and isolated from the utterance itself, then the context of the utterance would, *ipso facto*, be a different context—even if the utterance is made by the very same speaker in the very same way to the very same audience at the very same time in the very same place. To put it another way, although a single utterance occurs in indefinitely many different possible worlds, in every possible world in which the same utterance occurs it occurs in a new and different context—even if the speakers, his or her manner of uttering, the time of the utterance, the location of the speaker, the audience being addressed, and all other such features and aspects of the utterance reamin exactly the same. Suppose, for example, that it will come to pass that a Democrat is elected to the US presidency in the year 2000, and consider a possible world *w* that is exactly like the actual world in every detail up to January 1, 1999, but in which a Republican is elected to the US presidency in 2000. Suppose I here and now utter the sentence

(i) Actually, a Republican will be elected to the US presidency in 2000 AD.

In the actual world, I thereby assert a proposition that is necessarily false. In *w*, on the other hand, I thereby assert a necessary truth. In uttering the very same sequence of words of English with the very same English meanings in both possible worlds, I assert different things. If we were to use the term 'context' in such a way that the context of my utterance remains the same in both worlds, we would be forced to say, quite mysteriously, that the sentence I uttered is such that it would have expressed a different proposition with respect to the context in which I uttered it if *w* had obtained, even though both its meaning and its context of utterance would remain exactly the same. The content of the sentence would emerge as a function not only of the meaning of the sentence and the context of utterance but also of the apparently irrelevant question of which political party wins the US presidency in the year 2000. Using the term 'context' as I do, we may say instead that although I make the very same utterance both in *w* and in the actual world, the context of the utterance is different in the two worlds. This allows us to say that the sentence I utter takes on different information contents with respect to *different* contexts of utterance, thereby assimilating this phenomenon to the sort of context sensitivity that is familiar in cases of such sentences as 'A Republican is presently US president'.

[3] The latter clause is needed in order to distinguish 'Bill loves Mary' from 'Mary loves Bill', where the sequential order of composition is crucial. This succinct statement of the rule connecting sentences and their contents is only an approximation to the truth. A complicated difficulty arises in connection with the latter clause of the rule and with quantificational locutions. Grammatically the sentence 'Someone is wise' is analogous to 'Socrates is wise', though logically and semantically they are disanalogous. In 'Socrates is wise', the predicate 'is wise' attaches to the singular term 'Socrates'. As Russell showed, this situation is reversed in 'Someone is wise', wherein the restricted quantifier 'someone' attaches to the predicate 'is wise'. Thus, whereas grammatically 'someone' is combined with 'is wise' to form the first sentence in just the same way that 'Socrates' is combined

the proposition contained by a sentence into its components, one simply decomposes the sentence into its contentful parts, and the semantic contents thereof are the components of the contained proposition. In this way, declarative sentences not only contain but also codify propositions. One may take it as a sort of general rule or principle that the semantic content of any compound expression, with respect to a given context of utterance, is made up of the semantic contents, with respect to the given context, of the contentful components of the compound. This general rule is subject to certain important qualifications, however, and must be construed more as a general guide or rule of thumb. Exceptions arise in connection with quotation marks and similar devices. The numeral '9' is, in an ordinary sense, a component part of the sentence 'The numeral "9" is a singular term', though the semantic content of the former is no part of the proposition content of the latter. I shall argue below that, in addition to quotation marks, there is another important though often neglected class of operators that yield exceptions to the general rule in something like the way quotation marks do. Still, it may be correctly said of any English sentence free of any operators other than truth-functional connectives (e.g., 'If Frege is ingenious, then so is Russell') that its proposition content is a complex made up of the semantic contents of its contentful components.

THE SIMPLE THEORY

The *simple theory* is a theory of the semantic contents of some, but not all, sorts of expressions. Specifically, the simple theory is tacit on the controversial question of the semantic contents of proper names and similar sorts of singular terms. According to the simple theory, the semantic content of a predicate (or common noun or verb), as used in a particular context, is something like the attribute or concept semantically associated with the predicate with respect to that context. For example, the content of a monadic predicate may be identified with the corresponding property, while the content of an *n*-adic predicate, $n > 1$, may be identified with the corresponding *n*-ary relation. On the simple theory, the content of the sentence 'Frege is ingenious' is to be the proposition consisting of the semantic content of 'Frege'—whatever that may be (man, representational concept, or whatever)—and ingenuity (the property of being ingenious). More generally, an atomic sentence consisting of an *n*-place predicate Π attached to an *n*-ary sequence of singular terms, $\alpha_1, \alpha_2, \ldots, \alpha_n$, when evaluated with respect to a particular possible context, is held to express the proposition consisting of the attribute or concept referred to by Π and the sequence of semantic contents of the attached singular terms. A sentential connective may be construed on the model of a predicate. The semantic content of a sentential connective would thus be an attribute—not an attribute of individuals like Frege,

with 'is wise' to form the second sentence, the semantic contents of 'someone' and 'is wise' are combined very differently from the way the contents of 'Socrates' and 'is wise' are combined. A perhaps more important qualification to the general rule is noted in the next paragraph of the text. Yet another important qualification concerns overlaid quantifiers. For details, see *Frege's Puzzle*, pp. 155–157.

Top level: *character*
                + context *c*
                ↓

Middle level: *content* with respect to *c* → *intension* with respect to *c*
                                           + possible world *w* and time *t*
                                             ↓

Bottom level: *extension* with respect to *c*, *w*, and *t*

Figure 18.1 Semantic values on the simple theory

but an attribute of propositions. Similarly, the semantic content of a quantifier might be identified with a property of properties of individuals, and so on.

One may be tempted to hold that a sentence is a means for referring to its proposition content by specifying the components that make it up. However, a familiar argument due primarily to Alonzo Church and independently to Kurt Gödel establishes that the closest theoretical analogue of singular-term reference for any expression is its extension.[4] Accordingly, the simple theory will be understood to make room for the thesis that any expression refers to its extension, and for a resulting distinction between reference and semantic content.

The simple theory thus recognizes three distinct levels of semantic value. The three primary semantic values are *extension, content,* and *character.* On the same level as, and fully determined by, content is *intension.* Semantic values on the simple theory, and their levels and interrelations, are diagrammed in Figure 18.1. (Of course, these are not the only semantic values available on the simple theory, but they are the significant ones.) Within the framework of the simple theory, the *meaning* of an expression might be identified with the expression's character, that is, the semantically correlated function from possible contexts of utterance to semantic contents. For example, the meaning of the sentence

(1) I am writing

may be thought of as a function that assigns to any context of utterance *c* the proposition composed of the semantic content of 'I' with respect to *c* (whether that content may be the agent of *c*, a Fregean sense, or something else) and the property of writing.

PROPOSITIONS AND PROPOSITION MATRICES

Compelling though it is, the simple theory is fundamentally defective and must be modified if it is to yield a viable theory of semantic content. The flaw is illustrated by the following example: Suppose that at some time in 1890 Frege utters sentence

---

[4] See A. Church, 'Review of Carnap's *Introduction to Semantics,' The Philosophical Review,* 52 (1943), pp. 298–304, at pp. 299–301; K. Gödel, 'Russell's Mathematical Logic,' in P. A. Schilpp, ed., *The Philosophy of Bertrand Russell* (New York: Tudor, 1944), pp. 125–153, at pp. 128–129. The general argument is applied to the special case of monadic predicates in my *Frege's Puzzle,* pp. 22–23, and in greater detail to the special case of common nouns in my *Reference and Essence* (Princeton, N.J.: Princeton University Press, 1981 and Amherst, N.Y.: Prometheus Books, 2005), pp. 48–52.

(1) (or its German equivalent). Consider the proposition that Frege asserts in uttering this sentence. This is the proposition content of the sentence with respect to the context of Frege's uttering it. Let us call this proposition '$p*$' and the context in which Frege asserts it 'c^*'. The proposition p^* is made up of the semantic content of the indexical term 'I' with respect to c^* and the semantic content of the predicate 'writing' with respect to c^*. According to the simple theory, the latter semantic content is the property of writing. Thus, p^* (the semantic content of the whole sentence with respect to c^*) is a complex abstract entity made up of the semantic content of 'Frege' and the property of writing. Let us call this complex 'Frege writing', or 'fw' for short. Thus, according to the simple theory, $p^* = fw$. But this cannot be correct. If fw is thought of as having a truth-value, then it is true if *and when* Frege is writing and false if and when he is not writing. Thus, fw vacillated in truth-value over time, becoming true whenever Frege began writing and false whenever he ceased writing.[5] But p^*, being a proposition, has in any possible world (or at least in any possible world in which something is determined by the semantic content of 'Frege') a fixed and unchanging truth-value throughout its existence, and never takes on the opposite truth-value. In effect, a present-tensed sentence like (1) expresses the same eternal proposition on any occasion of utterance as does its temporally modified cousin

(2) I am writing now.

In this sense, propositions are *eternal*.

Not just some; all propositions are eternal. The eternalness of a proposition is central and fundamental to the very idea of a proposition, and is part and parcel of a philosophically entrenched conception of proposition content. For example, Frege, identifying the cognitive proposition content (*Erkenntniswerte*) of a sentence with what he called the 'thought' (*Gedanke*) expressed by the sentence, wrote:

> Now is a thought changeable or is it timeless? The thought we express by the Pythagorean Theorem is surely timeless, eternal, unvarying. "But are there not thoughts which are true today but false in six months' time? The thought, for example, that the tree there is covered with green leaves, will surely be false in six months' time." No, for it is not the same thought at all. The words 'This tree is covered with green leaves' are not sufficient by themselves to constitute the expression of thought, for the time of utterance is involved as well. Without the time-specification thus given we have not a complete thought, i.e., we have no thought at all. Only a sentence with the time-specification filled out, a sentence complete in every respect, expresses a thought. But this thought, if it is true, is true not only today or tomorrow but timelessly. ('Thoughts,' in Frege's *Logical Investigations*, P. T. Geach, ed., New Haven, Conn.: Yale University Press, 1977, pp. 1–30, at pp. 27–28)

The same sort of consideration is used by Richard Cartwright to show that the meaning of a present-tensed sentence is not its proposition content when uttered with assertive intent, or what is asserted by someone who utters the sentence.

---

[5] This forces a misconstrual of the intension of sentence (1) with respect to Frege's context $c*$ as a two-place function that assigns to the ordered pair of both a possible world w and a time t a truth-value, either truth or falsehood, according as the individual determined by the semantic content of 'Frege' is writing in w at t or not.

Cartwright's argument exploits the further fact that the truth-value of a proposition is constant over space as well as time:

> Consider, for this purpose, the words 'It's raining'. These are words, in the uttering of which, people often (though not always) assert something. But of course *what* is asserted varies from one occasion of their utterance to another. A person who utters them one day does not (normally) make the same statement as one who utters them the next; and one who utters them in Oberlin does not usually assert what is asserted by one who utters them in Detroit. But these variations in what is asserted are *not* accompanied by corresponding changes in meaning. The words 'It's raining' retain the same meaning throughout . . . [One] who utters [these words] speaks correctly only if he [talks about] the weather at the time of his utterance and in his (more or less) immediate vicinity. It is this general fact about what the words mean which makes it possible for distinct utterances of them to vary as to statement made . . . They are used, without any alteration in meaning, to assert now one thing, now another. ('Propositions,' in R. Butler, ed., *Analytical Philosophy*, Oxford: Basil Blackwell, 1968, pp. 81–103, at pp. 92–94)

Similar remarks by G. E. Moore make essentially the same point about propositions expressed using the past tense:

> As a general rule, whenever we use a past tense to express a proposition, the fact that we use it is a sign that the proposition expressed is *about* the time at which we use it; so that if I say twice over 'Caesar was murdered,' the proposition which I express on each occasion is a different one—the first being a proposition with regard to the earlier of the two times at which I use the words, to the effect that Caesar was murdered before *that* time, and the second a proposition with regard to the latter of the two, to the effect that he was murdered before *that* time. So much seems to me hardly open to question. ('Facts and Propositions,' in *Philosophical Papers*, New York: Collier, 1966, pp. 60–88, at p. 71)

Consider again Frege's "thought" that a particular tree is covered with green leaves. Six months from now, when the tree in question is no longer covered with green leaves, the sentence

(3) This tree is covered with green leaves,

uttered with reference to the tree in question, will express the proposition that the tree is *then* covered with green leaves. This will be false. But that proposition is false even now. What is true now is the proposition that the tree *is* covered with green leaves, in other words, the proposition that the tree is *now* covered with green leaves. This is the proposition that one would currently express by uttering sentence (3). It is eternally true—or at least true throughout the entire lifetime of the tree and never false. There is no proposition concerning the tree's foliage that is true now but will be false in six months. Similarly, if the proposition p^* that Frege asserts in c^* is true, it is eternally true. There is no noneternal proposition concerning Frege that vacillates in truth-value as he shifts from writing to not writing. The complex fw is noneternal, neutral with respect to time. Hence, it is not a complete proposition; that is, it is no proposition at all, properly so-called.

The truths truthsayers say and the sooths soothsayers soothsay—these all are propositions fixed, eternal, and unvarying. Eternal are the things asserters assert, the things believers believe, the things dreamers dream. Eternal also are the principles we defend, the doctrines we abhor, the things we doubt, the things we cannot doubt. The truths that are necessarily true and those that are not, the falsehoods that are necessarily false and those that are not—these are one and all eternal propositions. None of this is to say that the noneternal complex *fw* is not a semantic value of the sentence Frege utters, or that *fw* has nothing to do with proposition content. Indeed, *fw* is directly obtained from the sentence Frege utters in the context *c** by taking the semantic content of 'I' with respect to *c** and the property associated with 'writing' with respect to *c**. Moreover, *fw* can be converted into a proposition simply by *eternalizing* it, that is, by infusing a particular time (moment or interval) *t* into the complex to get a new abstract entity consisting of the semantic content of 'Frege', the property of writing, and the particular time *t*. One may think of the noneternal complex *fw* as the matrix of the proposition *p** that Frege asserts in *c**. Each time he utters sentence (1), Frege asserts a different proposition, expresses a different "thought," but always one having the same matrix *fw*. Similarly, in some cases it may be necessary to incorporate a location as well as a time in order to obtain a genuine proposition, for example, 'It is raining' or 'It is noon'. A proposition does not have different truth-values at different locations in the universe, any more than it has different truth-values at different times. A proposition is fixed, eternal, and unvarying in truth-value over both time and space.

To each proposition matrix there corresponds a particular property of times (or, where necessary, a binary relation between times and places). For example, the time property corresponding to the proposition matrix *fw* is the property of being a time at which Frege is writing. It is often helpful in considering the role of proposition matrices in the semantics of sentences to think of a proposition matrix as if it were its corresponding property of times.

It has been noted by William and Martha Kneale, and more recently and in more detail by Mark Richard, that this traditional conception of semantic content is reflected in our ordinary ascriptions of belief and other propositional attitudes.[6] As Richard points out, if what is asserted or believed were something temporally neutral or noneternal, then from the conjunction

(4) In 1990, Mary believed that Bush was president, and she has not changed her mind about that,

it would be legitimate to infer

(5) Mary still believes that Bush is president.

Such an inference is an insult not only to Mary but also to the logic of English, as it is ordinarily spoken. Rather, what we might infer is

(6) There is some time *t* in 1990 such that Mary still believes that Bush was president at *t*.

[6] See W. Kneale and M. Kneale, 'Propositions and Time,' in A. Ambrose and M. Lazerowitz, eds., *G. E. Moore: Essays in Retrospect* (New York: Humanities Press, 1970), pp. 228–241, at p. 235; Mark Richard, 'Temporalism and Eternalism,' *Philosophical Studies*, 39 (1981), pp. 1–13.

The reason for this is that what Mary is said by sentence (4) to have believed in 1990 is not the noneternal proposition matrix, Bush being president, but the eternal proposition that Bush is president throughout a particular time period. The point is bolstered if 'know' is substituted for 'believe'.

The length of the time period is a vague matter. For many purposes, it may be taken to be the entire year of 1990. When the time interval involved in a proposition is significantly long, the proposition may mimic its noneternal matrix—for example, in contexts like 'Mary once believed that Bush was a Republican, and she still believes that'—as long as one stays within the boundaries of the time interval in question. Relatively stable properties (like being a Republican, as opposed to being US president) tend to lengthen the time interval in question.[7] (They need not invariably do so.) This point is crucial to the proper analysis of inferences that seem to tell against the argument just considered. Mark Aronszajn, for example, objects to the argument by citing formally similar but evidently valid inferences like the following:

(7) In 1976, experts doubted that AIDS was transmitted through unprotected heterosexual intercourse, but no experts doubt that today.
Therefore, today no experts doubt that AIDS is transmitted through unprotected heterosexual intercourse.

(8) In 1990, Mary believed that Bush was president, and in 1992, she still believed that.
Therefore, in 1992, Mary still believed that Bush was president.[8]

The modes by which AIDS is transmitted among humans are presumed to be invariant over a very long period of time (perhaps for eternity). Likewise, a natural interpretation of the second inference has its author ascribing to Mary the belief that

---

[7] This is similar to a point made by Kneale and Kneale, 'Propositions and Time,' pp. 232–233. Compare my *Frege's Puzzle*, p. 157n3. On the most natural interpretation of past-tensed belief attribution sentences ⌜α believed that φ⌝, such a sentence is true with respect to a particular time t if and only if there is a salient time t' earlier than t and a salient interval t'' including t' such that the referent of α with respect to t' believed at t' the proposition expressed by φ with respect to t''. (This semantics involves a slight departure from that proposed by Richard.)

[8] See M. Aronszajn, 'A Defense of Temporalism,' *Philosophical Studies*, 81 (1996), pp. 71–95. Aronszajn's actual examples invoke the past progressive in place of the simple past tense (specifically, 'AIDS was spreading among heterosexuals' in place of 'AIDS was transmitted through unprotected heterosexual intercourse', and the attribute of being up to no good as president in place of merely being president. Aronszajn's examples strike me as significantly less plausible than the ones provided here. If experts in 1976 believed that AIDS was not spreading among heterosexuals, but they have since changed their minds about that, then what they no longer believe is that AIDS was not spreading in 1976 among heterosexuals. It is logically possible, and even consistent (albeit irrational), for such experts to believe that AIDS was spreading among heterosexuals in 1976 (having changed their minds in exactly the manner described) and at the same time to believe that as a result of recent educational efforts AIDS is no longer spreading among heterosexuals. Likewise, though Mary in 1990 believed Bush to be up to no good, and though she held fast about that two years later, she may well have believed by then that Bush was no longer up to no good. Imagine, for example, Mary saying the following: 'In 1990, I believed on the basis of reliable sources that Bush was abusing the power of his office through illegal wiretaps, directing the IRS to persecute his enemies, and more. Two years later, I received confirmation of that very same abuse in the 1990 White House and so continued to believe that, though I also believed that Bush had cleaned up his act by then and was finally behaving properly. I have just received evidence that such abuse in fact continued through 1992.'

Bush was president during the presidential term encompassing the years 1990–1992 (as he in fact was). Indeed, if the attributed belief is presumed instead to be merely that Bush was president throughout some shorter period of time (e.g., the year 1990), the inference becomes obviously invalid. In each case, insofar as the inference receives an interpretation on which it is clearly valid, the proposition attributed incorporates a time interval encompassing the indicated passage of time.

CONTENT AND CONTENT BASE

Let us call the proposition matrix that a sentence like (1) takes on with respect to a particular context *c* the *content base* of the sentence with respect to *c*. More generally, we may speak of the *content base* with respect to a context of any meaningful expression (a singular term, a predicate, a connective, a quantifier, etc.). The content base of an expression is the entity that the expression contributes to the proposition matrix taken on by (i.e., the content base of) typical sentences containing the expression (where a 'typical' sentence containing an expression does not include additional occurrences of such devices as quotation marks or the 'that'-operator).

The content base of a simple predicate, such as 'writes', with respect to a context *c*, is the attribute semantically associated with the predicate with respect to *c* (the property of writing). The content base of a compound expression, like a sentence, is (typically) a complex made up of the content bases of the simple parts of the compound expression. In particular, the content base of a definite description is a complex made up partly of the property associated with the description's constitutive predicate. Since ordinary language includes indexical expressions such as 'this tree', not only the semantic content but also the content base of an expression is to be relativized to the context of utterance. An expression may take on one content base with respect to one context, and another content base with respect to a different context. An indexical expression is properly defined as one that takes on different content bases with respect to different possible contexts.

The simple theory is at odds with the eternalness of propositions. There remains a question of how best to accommodate this feature of propositions within a framework like that of the simple theory. While alternative accounts are available, what is perhaps the path of minimal mutilation from the simple theory centers on its notion of *character*.[9] As defined by Kaplan, the character of an expression is the function or

---

It should be noted that the anaphoric pronoun 'that' in examples like those under consideration here need not always refer to the proposition referred to by its antecedent. In some uses, it may refer instead to another proposition related to the antecedently referred to proposition by having the same matrix. Analogously, the conjunction 'Johnny believes that he is the strongest boy in the class and so does Billy' may be used to report agreement between Johnny and Billy concerning who is strongest, or alternatively to report a disagreement between them. On the latter reading, the anaphoric pronoun 'so' does not refer to the act of believing the particular proposition referred to in the first disjunct, but to the act of believing the proposition expressed by 'I am strongest'. (Compare 'Naturally, Johnny believes that he is the strongest boy in the class. At that age, nearly every boy believes that'.)

[9] A somewhat different approach is adopted in my *Frege's Puzzle*, pp. 24–43, and in 'Tense and Singular Propositions.' Compare M. Richard, 'Tense, Propositions, and Meanings,' *Philosophical*

rule that takes one from an arbitrary context of utterance to the expression's semantic content with respect to that context. This may be identified with the expression's *meaning* only insofar as the content is misidentified with its noneternal matrix. Let us now reconstrue character as the function or rule that determines for any possible context c the content base (rather than the content) that the expression takes on with respect to c. This transmutation of the old notion of character forms the heart of a corrected version of the simple theory. An indexical expression is now redefined as one whose character, as here reconstrued, is not a constant function; it is one whose content base varies with context.

The content base of an expression with respect to a context c determines a corresponding function that assigns to any time t (and location l, if necessary) an appropriate content for the expression. (In fact, the function also determines the corresponding content base.) For example, the proposition matrix *fw* (the content base of 'Frege is writing') determines a function that assigns to any time t the proposition that Frege is writing at t. (This is the propositional function corresponding to the property of being a time at which Frege is writing.) Let us call the function from times (and locations) to contents thus determined by the content base of an expression with respect to a given context c the *schedule* of the expression with respect to c. Since the semantic content of an expression determines its intension, the content base of an expression with respect to a context c also determines a corresponding function that assigns to any time t (and location l, if necessary) the resulting intension for the expression. Let us call this function from times (and locations) to intensions the *superintension* of the expression with respect to c. Accordingly, we should speak of the semantic content, and the corresponding intension, of an expression *with respect to a context c and a time t (and a location l,* if necessary). The simple theory must be modified accordingly. Specifically, the notion of semantic content, by contrast with that of content base, is doubly relativized (in some cases, triply relativized). Significantly, the time to which the content of an expression is relativized need not be the time of the context, although of course it can be. Thus, for example, the expression 'my car' refers with respect to my present context and the year 1989 to the Honda that is formerly mine. The same expression refers with respect to my present context and the year 1996 to the Toyota that is presently mine.

We should also like to speak (as we already have) of the content of an expression (e.g., of the proposition expressed by a sentence) with respect to a context *simpliciter,* without having to speak of the content with respect to *both* a context and a time.

Studies, 41 (1982), pp. 337–351. The burden of this chapter is to show that one can consistently hold that propositions are eternal while temporal sentential operators operate on noneternal semantic values of sentences, by holding that temporal sentential operators operate on two-place functions from contexts and times to eternal propositions. These two-place functions are similar to (and determined by) sentence characters. Indeed, Richard calls his two-place functions the 'meanings' of sentences. The claim that temporal operators operate on the 'meanings' of expressions, however, is at best misleading. When each of Richard's two-place functions is replaced by its corresponding one-place function from contexts to one-place functions from times to eternal propositions, it emerges that temporal operators operate on something at a level other than that of character.

This is implicit in the notion of the character of an expression, as defined earlier. How do we get from the content base of an expression with respect to a given context to the content with respect to the same context *simpliciter* without further indexing, or relativization, to a time (and location)?

In the passage quoted above, Frege seems to suggest that the words making up a tensed but otherwise temporally unmodified sentence, taken together with contextual factors that secure contents for indexical expressions such as 'this tree', at most yield only something like what we are calling a 'proposition matrix', that is, the content base of the sentence with respect to the context of utterance, which is 'not a complete thought, i.e., . . . no thought at all.' He suggests further that we must rely on the very time of the context of utterance to provide a 'time-specification' or 'time-indication'—presumably a specification or indication of the very time itself—which supplements the words to eternalize their content base, thereby yielding a genuine proposition or 'thought.' Earlier in the same article, Frege writes:

> [It often happens that] the mere wording, which can be made permanent by writing or the gramophone, does not suffice for the expression of the thought. The present tense is [typically] used . . . in order to indicate a time. . . . If a time-indication is conveyed by the present tense one must know when the sentence was uttered in order to grasp the thought correctly. Therefore the time of utterance is part of the expression of the thought. ('Thoughts,' in *Logical Investigations*, p. 10)

On Frege's view, strictly speaking, the sequence of words making up a tensed but otherwise temporally unmodified sentence like (3), even when taken together with a contextual indication of which tree is intended, does not yet bear genuine cognitive content. Its content is incomplete. Presumably, on Frege's view, the sequence of words together with a contextual indication of which tree is intended has the logico–semantic status of a predicate true of certain times—something like the predicate 'is a time at which this tree is covered with green leaves' accompanied by a pointing to the tree in question—except that (3) thus accompanied may be completed by a time, serving as a specification or indication of itself, rather than by something syntactic, like the term 'now'. Accordingly, on Frege's theory, the content, or "sense" (*Sinn*), of (3) together with an indication of the intended tree but in abstraction from any time would be a function whose values are propositions, or "thoughts" (*Gedanken*).[10] Only the sequence of words making up the sentence together with an

Richard also apparently misconstrues to some extent what Kaplan (and others) mean in saying that an operator 'operates on' such-and-such's. In general, to say that a given operator operates on the such-and-such of its operand is to say that an appropriate extension for the operator would be a function from such-and-such's appropriate to expressions that may serve as its operand to extensions appropriate to the compounds formed from the operator together with the operand. For example, to say that a modal sentential operator operates on the content or on the intension of its operand sentence is to say that an appropriate extension for a modal operator would be a function from propositions or from sentence intensions (functions from possible worlds to truth-values) to truth-values.

[10] On Frege's theory, the domain of this function would consist of senses that determine times, rather than the times themselves.

There is no reason on Frege's theory why the time-indication or time-specification that supplements the incomplete present-tensed sentence could not be verbal, as in 'At 12:00 noon on

indication of which tree is intended and *together with* a time-indication or time-specification, as may be provided by the time of utterance itself, is "a sentence complete in every respect" and has cognitive content.

It is not necessary to view the situation by Frege's lights. Whereas Frege speaks of the cognitive thought content (or *Erkenntniswerte*) of the words *supplemented by* both a contextual indication of which tree is intended and a "time-indication," one may speak instead (as I already have) of the content of the sequence of words themselves *with respect to* a context of utterance and a time. The content of sentence (3) with respect to a context c and a time t is simply the result of applying the schedule, with respect to c, of the sequence of words to t. This is a proposition about the tree contextually indicated in c, to the effect that it is covered with green leaves at t. In the general case, instead of speaking of the content of an expression supplemented by both a contextual indication of the referents of the demonstratives or other indexicals contained therein and a "time-indication," as may be provided by the time of utterance, one may speak of the content of the expression *with respect to* a context and a time (and a location, if necessary). Still, Frege's conception strongly suggests a way of constructing a singly indexed notion of the content of an expression with respect to (or supplemented by) a context of utterance c *simpliciter*, without further relativization to (or supplementation by) a time, in terms of the doubly indexed locution: we may define the singly relativized notion of the content of an expression with respect to a context c as the content with respect both to c and the very time of c (and with respect to the very location of c, if necessary).

In particular, then, the semantic content of a sentence with respect to a given context c is its content with respect to c and the time of c (and the location of c, if necessary). Consequently, any temporally unmodified sentence or clause expresses different propositions with respect to different contexts of utterance (*simpliciter*). For example, sentence (3) (more accurately, the untensed clause 'this tree be covered

July 4, 1983, this tree is covered with green leaves'. This aspect of Frege's theory allows for a solution to the problem of failure of substitutivity of coreferential singular terms in temporal contexts—a solution very different from Frege's solution to the parallel problem of failure of substitutivity in propositional attitude contexts. Consider the following example. The expressions 'the US president' and 'Bill Clinton' refer to the same individual with respect to the time of my writing these words, but the former cannot be substituted *salva veritate* for the latter in the true sentence 'In 1991, Bill Clinton was a Democrat'. The result of such substitution is 'In 1991, the US president was a Democrat', which is false on the relevant reading (the Russellian secondary occurrence or narrow scope reading). Frege may solve this problem, not implausibly, by noting that the expression 'the US president' is incomplete and requires supplementation by a time-specification, such as may be provided by the time of utterance, before it can refer to an individual. The description 'the US president', supplemented by the time of my writing these words, refers to the same individual as the name 'Bill Clinton'. Supplemented by the year 1991, or by a verbal specification thereof, it refers to George Bush. The result of the substitution includes a verbal time-specification, 'in 1991', which, we may assume, supersedes the time of utterance in completing any expression occurring within its scope in need of completion by a time-specification. Compare Frege's treatment of substitutivity failure in propositional attitude contexts. On Frege's theory, a propositional attitude operator such as 'Jones believes that' creates an oblique context in which expressions refer to their customary contents ("senses") instead of their customary referents. On the Fregean solution to substitutivity failure in temporal contexts presented here, by contrast, the referent of 'the US president', as occurring within the context 'in 1991, __', is just its customary referent.

with green leaves') contains different propositions with respect to different times of utterance even though the speaker is pointing to the same tree. Uttered six months from now, it expresses the proposition about the tree in question that it is then covered with green leaves. Uttered today, it contains the proposition that the tree is covered with green leaves, that is, that it is now covered with green leaves. The existence of this linguistic phenomenon is precisely the point made by Frege and echoed by Moore and Cartwright in the passages quoted in the section on Propositions and Proposition Matrices.

Let us call this adjusted version of the simple theory the *corrected theory*. The corrected theory is the simple theory adjusted to accommodate the eternalness of semantic content. The adjustment involves only the temporal nature of content. The corrected theory remains neutral with respect to the dispute among Fregeans, Millians, and others concerning the question of what constitutes the semantic content of indexicals and similar expressions.

Within the framework of the corrected theory, the meaning of an expression is identified with its character, now construed as a function from contexts to content bases. This allows one to distinguish pairs of expressions like 'the US president' and 'the present US president' as having different meanings, even though they take on the same contents (or at least trivially equivalent contents) with respect to the same contexts. Their difference in meaning is highlighted by the fact that the latter is indexical while the former is not. More accurately, the character of an expression is the primary component of what is ordinarily called the 'meaning' of the expression, though an expression's meaning may have additional components that supplement the character.[11]

The corrected theory's notion of the content base of an expression with respect to a given context, and the resulting reconstrual of the character of an expression, impose a fourth level of semantic value, intermediate between the level of character and the level of content. The four primary semantic values, from the bottom up, are *extension*, *content* (construed now as necessarily eternal), *content base*, and *character*. There are also two additional subordinate semantic values. Besides intension (construed now as a one-place function from possible worlds) there are *schedule* and *superintension*, both of which are on the same level as, and fully determined by, the content base. Semantic values on the corrected theory, and their levels and interrelations, are diagrammed in Figure 18.2. (Notice that character now takes one from a context c to a content base, which still needs a time t in order to generate a content.)

The referent of a complex definite description like 'the wife of the present US president' with respect to a context of utterance c, a time t, and a possible world w is semantically determined in a sequence of steps. First, the character of the expression is applied to the context c to yield the content base of the expression with respect to c.

---

[11] For example, the meaning of the term 'table' might include, in addition to its character, some sort of conceptual content, such as a specification of the function of a table. If so, it does not follow that this sort of conceptual entity is any part of the semantic content of the term. Nor does it follow that it is *analytic*, in the classical sense, that tables have such and such a function. What does follow is that in order to know fully the meaning of 'table', one would have to know that the things called 'tables' are conventionally believed to have such and such a function.

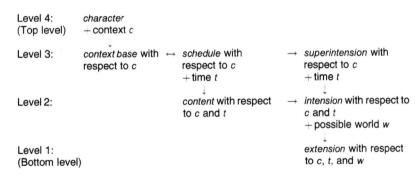

Figure 18.2 Semantic values on the corrected theory

The latter is something like the time-neutral concept of uniquely being a wife of whoever is uniquely US president at c_T, where c_T is the particular time of the context c. (The temporal indexing to c_T is provided for by the term 'present', which is interpreted here in its indexical sense.) This yields the schedule of the expression with respect to c, which assigns to any time t' the concept of uniquely being at t' a wife of whoever is uniquely US president at c_T. This schedule is applied to the particular time t to give the eternal semantic content of the expression with respect to both c and t. This semantic content, in turn, yields the expression's intension with respect to c and t, which assigns to any possible world w' the individual who is uniquely a wife at t in w' of whoever is uniquely US president at c_T in w'. (Since this is not a constant function, the description is not a rigid designator.) Finally, this intension is applied to the particular world w to yield the wife at t in w of the US president at c_T in w. On the corrected theory, the extension of an expression with respect simply to a given context of utterance, without further relativization to a time or a possible world, is the result of applying the intension of the expression with respect to that context (which in turn is the result of applying the super-intension of the expression with respect to that context to the very time of the context) to the very possible world of the context. Thus, where c_W is the possible world of c, the referent of 'the wife of the present US president' with respect to c itself is none other than the wife at c_T in c_W of the US president at c_T in c_W.

TENSE VERSUS INDEXICALITY

It may appear that I have been spinning out semantic values in excess of what is needed. We need a singly indexed notion of the semantic content of an expression with respect to a context and, as a special case, a notion of the content of a sentence with respect to a context. This led to the simple theory's identification of meaning with a function from contexts to contents. But we have just seen that this function has no special role to play in determining the semantics for an expression like 'the wife of the actual US president'. In getting to the content, and ultimately to the extension, we are now going by way of the content base instead of the content.

With regard to 'the wife of the actual US president', and similarly with regard to an entire sentence like (1) or (3), the content base with respect to a context is neutral with respect to time whereas the content with respect to the same context is eternal, somehow incorporating the time (and location, if necessary) of the context. If the rule of content composition is that the content of a complex expression, like a sentence, is constructed from the contents of the simple contentful components *together with* the time (and location, if necessary) of utterance, then why bother mentioning those partially constructed propositions I am calling 'proposition matrices'? Singling out content bases as separate semantic values generates the doubly indexed notion of the content of a sentence with respect to both a context c and a time t, and thereby the new construal of character. What is the point of this doubly indexed notion, and of the resulting reconstrual of character? Are we not interested only in the case where the time t is the time of the context of utterance c? Why separate out the time as an independent semantic parameter that may differ from the time of utterance?

Semantic theorists heretofore have gotten along fine by indexing the notion of content once, and only once, to the context of utterance, without relativizing further and independently to times. For example, in discussing the phenomenon of tense, Frege also considers various indexicals—'today', 'yesterday', 'here', 'there', and 'I'—and suggests a uniform treatment for sentences involving either tense or indexicals:

> In all such cases the mere wording, as it can be preserved in writing, is not the complete expression of the thought; the knowledge of certain conditions accompanying the utterance, which are used as a means of expressing the thought, is needed for us to grasp the thought correctly. Pointing the finger, hand gestures, glances may belong here too. ('Thoughts,' in *Logical Investigations*, pp. 10–11)

Following Frege, it would seem that we can handle the phenomena of tense and indexicality together in one fell swoop, with tense as a special case of indexicality, by simply relativizing the notion of semantic content once and for all to the complete context of utterance—including the time and location of the utterance as well as the speaker and his or her accompanying pointings, hand gestures, and glances. Any aspect of the complete context of utterance may conceivably form "part of the expression of the thought" or contribute to the content. Once content is relativized to the complete context, including the time of utterance, gestures, and so on, there seems to be no need to relativize further and independently to times.

It has been known since the mid-1970s that the phenomenon of tense cannot be fully assimilated to temporal indexicality and that the presence of indexical temporal operators necessitates "double indexing," that is, relativization of the extensions of expressions—the reference of a singular term, the truth-value of a sentence, the class of application of a predicate—to utterance times independently of the relativization to times already required by the presence of tense or other temporal operators.[12] (Something similar is true in the presence of an indexical modal operator such as 'actually' and in the presence of indexical locational operators such as 'it is the case

---

[12] The need for double indexing was apparently first noted in 1967 by Hans Kamp in unpublished material distributed to a graduate seminar while Kamp was a graduate student at UCLA. See his 'Formal Properties of "Now",' *Theoria* 37 (1972), pp. 227–273. Kamp's results were reported in A. N. Prior, ' "Now",' *Noûs* 2 (1968), pp. 101–119.

here that'.) Here is an illustration: The present perfect tense operator functions in such a way that for any untensed clause S (e.g., 'Frege be writing'), the result of applying the present perfect tense operator to S ('Frege has been writing') is true with respect to a time t (roughly) if and only if S is true with respect to some time t' earlier than t. Similarly, the nonindexical operator 'on the next day' + future tense functions in such a way that the result of applying this operator to any untensed clause S is true with respect to a time t if and only if S is true with respect to the day next after the day of t. For example, suppose that instead of uttering sentence (1), Frege speaks the following words (perhaps as part of a larger utterance) in his context c^*:

(9) I will be writing on the next day.

This sentence, in Frege's mouth, is true with respect to a time t if and only if Frege writes on the day after the day of t—whether or not t is the time of c^*. Indeed, our primary interest may be in some time t other than that of c^*—for example, if Frege's complete utterance in c^* is of the sentence

(10) Regarding December 24, 1891, I will be writing on the next day.

On the other hand, the indexical operator 'tomorrow' + future tense functions in such a way that the result of applying it to any untensed clause S is true with respect to a context c and a time t if and only if S is true with respect to c and the day after c, forgetting about the time t altogether. If in c^* Frege had uttered the sentence

(11) I will be writing tomorrow,

the sentence, in Frege's mouth, would be true with respect to any time if and only if Frege writes on the day after c^*.

To illustrate the need for double indexing, consider how one might attempt to accommodate 'on the next day' + future tense using relativization only to possible contexts of utterance, without independent relativization to times. Let us try this: Say that the result of applying this operator to S is true with respect to a context c if and only if S is true with respect to some possible context c' just like c in every respect (agent, location, etc.) except that the time of c' is one day later than that of c. For example, 'I will be writing on the next day' will be regarded as being true with respect to a context c if and only if its untensed operand

(1′) I be writing

is true with respect to a possible context c' whose day is the day after c, but which involves the same agent as c to preserve the referent of 'I'. (We assume for the time being that an untensed clause such as (1′) is a mere surface grammar variation of its present-tensed counterpart, so that (1) and (1′) share the same semantics.) This singly indexed account seems to yield the correct results until we consider sentences that embed one temporal operator within the scope of another. Consider the following sentences:

(12) The US president is a Republican,
(13) The present US president is a Republican,
(14) Sometimes, the US president is a Republican,
(15) Sometimes, the present US president is a Republican.

Sentences (14) and (15) result from applying the temporal operator 'sometimes' to sentences (12) and (13), respectively. According to the singly relativized account, (15) is true with respect to a context of utterance c (roughly) if and only if there is some time t', which need not be c_T (the time of c), such that the US president at t' is a Republican at t' (in the possible world of c). But this is the wrong truth-condition for the sentence. In fact, it is the correct truth-condition for the wrong sentence, to wit, the *nonindexical* sentence (14).

Sentences (14) and (15) differ in their truth-conditions. Suppose both sentences are uttered in 1996, when the US president is a lifelong Democrat though previously the presidency had been held by the Republicans. Sentence (14) is then true whereas sentence (15) is false. Sentence (15) is true with respect to a context of utterance c (roughly) if and only if there is some time t' such that the US president at c_T (the time of the context c) is a Republican at t' (in the possible world of c). The temporal operator 'sometimes' directs us to evaluate its operand clause with respect to all times t'. The operand clause (13) is true with respect to the same context c and a time t' if and only if the description 'the present US president' refers to something with respect to c and t' to which the predicate 'is a Republican' applies with respect to c and t'. In computing the referent of the description with respect to c and t', the indexical operator 'present' directs us to seek an object to which its operand phrase 'US president' applies with respect to c_T, the very time of the context of utterance itself, forgetting about the time t'. Thus, in evaluating sentence (15) with respect to a time of utterance c_T, we are concerned simultaneously with the extension of 'US president' with respect to c_T and the extension of 'is a Republican' with respect to a second time t'. The truth-value of the whole depends entirely and solely on whether the unique object to which the phrase 'US president' applies with respect to c_T is something to which the predicate 'is a Republican' applies with respect to t'. It is for this reason that a systematic theory of the extensions of the expressions of a language containing indexical temporal operators requires double indexing; that is, in general the notion of the extension of an expression (e.g., the truth-value of a sentence) is relativized to both a context and a time, treated as independent semantic parameters.

A systematic singly indexed theory gives the wrong results. Frege's theory, for example, must regard the indexical description 'the present US president' as extensionally semantically equivalent to the nonindexical 'the US president'. Both would be regarded as expressions that are incomplete by themselves (hence, refer by themselves, in abstraction from any context, to functions), but that when completed by a "time-specification" or "time-indication" (as may be provided by the time of utterance) refer to the individual who is US president at the specified or indicated time. Using extensional semantic considerations alone, Frege's theory is unable to find any difference with respect to truth or even with respect to truth-conditions between the indexical sentence (15), taken as uttered at a certain time, and the nonindexical (14), taken as uttered at the very same time.[13]

---

[13] This is partly a result of Frege's principle of compositionality (or interchange) for reference. (See note 1.) On Frege's theory of tense and indexicality, both 'the US president' and 'the present US president' refer, in abstraction from context, to the function that assigns to any time t the individual who is US president at t—like the functor 'the US president at time___'—except that the

This example illustrates that where an indexical temporal operator occurs within the scope of another temporal operator within a single sentence, the extensions of expressions are to be indexed both to the time of utterance and to a second time parameter, which may be other than the time of utterance and not even significantly related to the time of utterance. Temporal operators determine which time or times the extension of their operands are determined with respect to. In the special case of indexical temporal operators, the time so determined is a function of the time of the context of utterance. What is distinctive about indexical expressions ('I', 'this tree', or 'the present US president') is not merely that the extension with respect to a context c varies with the context c, or even that the intension or semantic content with respect to a context c varies with c. That much may be true of even a non-indexical expression, such as 'the US president' or 'Frege is writing'. What makes an expression indexical is that its extension with respect to a context c and a time t and a possible world w varies with the context c even when the other parameters are held fixed. This is to say that its superintension, and hence its content base, with respect to a context c varies with c. It is precisely this that separates 'the present US president' from its nonindexical cousin 'the US president'.

Though it is less often noted,[14] it is equally important that double indexing to contexts and times (or triple indexing to contexts, times, and locations, if necessary) is required at the level of semantic content as well as at the level of extension. For illustration, consider first the sentence

(16) At t^*, I believed that Frege was writing.

By the ordinary laws of temporal semantics, this sentence is true with respect to a context of utterance c if and only if the sentence

(17) I believe that Frege is writing

is true with respect to both c and the time t^*. This, in turn, is so if and only if the binary predicate 'believe' applies with respect to c and t^* to the ordered pair of the referent of 'I' with respect to c and t^* and the referent of the 'that'-clause 'that Frege is writing' with respect to c and t^*. Hence, sentence (16) is true with respect to c if and only if the agent of c believes at t^* the proposition referred to by the 'that'-clause with respect to c and t^*. The 'that'-clause in (16) refers with respect to c and t^* to the proposition that is the content of the operand sentence 'Frege is writing'. But which proposition is that?

If content is to be singly indexed to context alone, it would seem that the 'that'-clause 'that Frege is writing' refers with respect to c and t^* to the content of 'Frege is writing' *with respect to c*, forgetting about t^* altogether. This is the proposition that

expression may be completed by a time rather than by a verbal time-specification (the time of utterance acting as a self-referential singular term). By Frege's compositionality principle for reference, it follows that any complete sentence built from 'the US president', without using oblique devices (e.g., 'In 1996, the US president was a Republican'), has the same truth-conditions, and therefore the same truth-value, as the corresponding sentence built from 'the present US president'.

[14] But see Richard, 'Tense, Propositions, and Meanings,' pp. 346–349. The idea of double indexing content to both contexts and times is Richard's.

Frege is writing at c_T, where c_T is the time of c. However, this yields the wrong truth-condition for (16). This would be the correct truth-condition for the sentence

(18) At t^*, I believed that Frege would be writing now.

Sentence (16) ascribes a belief at t^* that Frege is writing *at t^**. Assuming that content is singly indexed to context alone, we are apparently forced to construe the 'that'-operator in such a way that a 'that'-clause ⌐that S⌐ refers with respect to a context c and a time t' not to the content of S with respect to c but to the content of S with respect to a (typically different) context c' exactly like c in every respect (agent, location, etc.) except that its time is t'. (The contexts c and c' would be the same if and only if t' were the time of c.)

This account appears to yield exactly the right results until we consider a sentence that embeds an indexical temporal operator within the 'that'-operator and embeds the result within another temporal operator. Consider the following:

(19) In 2001, Jones will believe that the present US president is the best of all the former US presidents.

This sentence is true with respect to a context c if and only if Jones believes in 2001 the proposition referred to by the words 'that the present US president is the best of all the former US presidents' with respect to c and the year 2001. On the singly indexed account of content, sentence (19) comes out true if and only if Jones believes in 2001 that the US president in 2001 is the best of all the US presidents before 2001. But this is the truth-condition for the wrong sentence, namely,

(20) In 2001, Jones will believe that the then US president is the best of all the former US presidents.

Sentence (19) ascribes, with respect to c, a belief that the US president at c_T is the best of all the US presidents before 2001. In order to obtain this result, the 'that'-clause in (19) must be taken as referring with respect to c and the year 2001 to the proposition that the US president at c_T is the best of all the US presidents prior to 2001 (or to some proposition trivially equivalent to this). This cannot be accommodated by a singly indexed account. It requires seeing content as doubly indexed: to the original context c and to the year 2001.

TEMPORAL OPERATORS

Two sorts of operators are familiar to philosophers of language. An *extensional* operator is one that operates on the extensions of its operands, in the sense that an appropriate extension for the operator itself would be a function from *extensions* appropriate to the operands (as opposed to some other aspect of the operands) to extensions appropriate to the compounds formed by attaching the operator to an appropriate operand. An extensional sentential connective (such as 'not' or 'if...', then...') is truth functional; an appropriate extension would be a function from (*n*-tuples of) truth-values to truth-values, and hence an appropriate semantic content would be an attribute of truth-values. An *intensional* or *modal* operator is one that operates on the intensions of its operands. An appropriate extension for a modal connective like 'it is necessarily the case that' would be a function from (*n*-tuples of) sentence intensions (functions from possible worlds to truth-values) or propositions to truth-values, and an appropriate semantic content would be an attribute of intensions or propositions—for example, the property of being a necessary truth.

David Kaplan forcefully raises an objection to the conventional conception of propositions as eternal in connection with the applicability of intensional operators. He writes:

> Operators of the familiar kind treated in intensional logic (modal, temporal, etc.) operate on contents. . . . A modal operator when applied to an intension will look at the behavior of the intension with respect to [possible worlds]. A temporal operator will, similarly, be concerned with the time. . . . If we build the time of evaluation into the contents (thus . . . making contents *specific* as to time), it would make no sense to have temporal operators. To put the point another way, if *what is said* [i.e., if the proposition asserted by a speaker] is thought of as incorporating reference to a specific time, . . . it is otiose to ask whether what is said [the proposition] would have been true at another time . . . ('Demonstratives,' pp. 502–503)

He elaborates in a footnote:

> Technically, we must note that [temporal] operators must, if they are not to be vacuous, operate on contents which are neutral with respect to [time]. Thus, for example, if we take the content of [(1)] to be [an eternal, time-specific proposition rather than its noneternal, temporally neutral matrix], the application of a temporal operator to such a content would have no effect; the operator would be vacuous. ('Demonstratives,' pp. 503–504 n.)

Continuing this line of thought in the text, he writes:

> This functional notion of the content of a sentence in a context may not, because of the neutrality of content with respect to time and place, say, exactly correspond to the classical conception of a proposition. But the classical conception can be introduced by adding the demonstratives 'now' and 'here' to the sentence and taking the content of the result. ('Demonstratives,' p. 504)

It is not otiose in the least to modify a sentence like (1) by applying a temporal operator, like 'yesterday' + past tense. The attached operator is anything but vacuous. It does not follow, however, that the content of (1), with respect to a given context, is something temporally neutral. Claiming that temporal operators operate on contents, and having defined the content of a sentence as the proposition asserted by someone in uttering the sentence, or *what is said*, Kaplan is forced to construe the proposition expressed by a sentence like (1) as something that may change in truth-value at different times and in some cases even at different places. But this yields an incorrect account of propositions. Propositions, qua objects of assertion and belief, are eternal. As Frege, Moore, and Cartwright pointed out—and as Kaplan seems to acknowledge—propositions do not vacillate in truth-value over time or space.

Consider the temporal operator 'sometimes'—or more accurately, 'sometimes' + present tense, which applies to an untensed clause S to form a new sentence. Is this an extensional operator? Certainly not. With respect to my actual present context, the sentences 'It is cloudy' and '2 + 2 = 5' are equally false, though 'Sometimes, it is cloudy' is true whereas 'Sometimes, 2 + 2 = 5' is false. Nor is the 'sometimes' operator intensional, in the above sense. As with (1) and (2), sentences (12) and (13), uttered simultaneously, have precisely the same intension—indeed, they share the same proposition content (or at least trivially equivalent contents that are very nearly the same). But their temporal existential generalizations, (14) and (15), uttered simultaneously, have different contents, even different truth-values. On the relevant reading (the Russellian secondary occurrence or narrow scope reading), (14) is true whereas (15) is false. (In fact, (15) is false on both the narrow scope and wide scope readings.) Thus, 'sometimes' is not a content operator either. As Kaplan points out, a temporal operator, if it is not to be vacuous, must operate on something that is temporally neutral. Contrary to Kaplan, what follows from this is that temporal operators do not operate on propositions. When a temporal operator is applied to (12), it is the matrix of the proposition expressed by (12), not the proposition itself, that is the proper object upon which the operator operates. In short, temporal operators like 'sometimes' are superintensional operators.[15] An appropriate extension for 'sometimes' with respect to a context c, a time t, and a possible world w would be the function that assigns truth to a proposition matrix (or to its corresponding schedule or superintension) if its value for at least one time (the resulting proposition or sentence intension) itself yields truth for the world w, and that otherwise assigns falsehood to the proposition matrix.

Kaplan comes close to recognizing that the objects of assertion and propositional attitude are eternal propositions when he shows ('Demonstratives,' p. 500) that *what is said* in uttering a temporally indexical sentence like (2) at different times is different. His argument for this is that if such a sentence is uttered by me today and by you tomorrow, then

> [if] what we say differs in truth-value, that is enough to show that we say different things. But even if the truth-values were the same, it is clear that there are possible circumstances in which what I said would be true but what you said would be false. Thus we say different things.

This is indeed correct. But the same argument can be made with equal force for a nonindexical tensed sentence. Thus, it is not surprising to find the following analogous argument given earlier by G. E. Moore:

> It seems at first sight obvious that, if you have a number of judgements [i.e., utterances] with the same content, if one is true the rest must be.
>
> But if you take a set of judgements [i.e., utterances] with regard to a given event A, [using words to the effect] either that it is happening, or that it is past, or that it is future, some of each set will be true and some false, which are true and which false depending on the time when the judgement [i.e., utterance] is made.
>
> It seems a sufficient answer to say that a judgement [i.e., an utterance of a sentence of the form] 'A is happening' made at one time never has the same content as the judgement [i.e., an utterance of the sentence] 'A is happening' made at another. ('The Present,' Notebook II.

---

[15] Modal operators on the so-called branching worlds (or 'unpreventability') interpretation emerge as superintensional operators.

[*c.* 1926], in *The Commonplace Book 1919–1953*, Casimir Lewy, ed., New York: Macmillan, 1962, p. 89)

Consider again sentence (1). Mimicking Kaplan, and following Moore, one may argue that if Frege utters it at t^* and again on the next day, and if what he asserted on the two occasions of utterance differ in truth-value (across time), as indeed they may, that is enough to show that he asserted different things. This is precisely because it is known that what is asserted is not the sort of thing that can switch back and forth in truth-value from one moment to the next. Since what is asserted on the one occasion is different from what is asserted on the other, it is not this content but its matrix, *fw*, upon which temporal operators operate.

In order to obtain the correct results, one must regard a sentential temporal operator such as 'sometimes' as operating on some aspect of its operand clause that is fixed relative to a context of utterance (in order to give a correct treatment of temporally modified indexical sentences like (15)) but whose truth-value typically varies with respect to time (so that it makes sense to say that it is *sometimes* true, or true at such and such time). Once it is acknowledged that content is eternal, there simply is no such semantic value of a sentence on the simple theory's three-tiered array of semantic values. Nothing that is fixed relative to a context is also time sensitive in the required way. In order to find an appropriate semantic value for temporal operators such as 'sometimes' + present tense to operate on, one must posit a fourth level of semantic value.

The result of applying 'sometimes' to a sentence S may be regarded as expressing, with respect to a given context c, a proposition concerning the content base of the operand sentence S with respect to c. For example, the sentence

(21) Sometimes, I am writing

contains, with respect to Frege's context c^* (or any other context in which Frege is the agent), the proposition about the proposition matrix *fw* that it is sometimes true. Accordingly, an appropriate semantic content for a temporal operator such as 'sometimes' would be a property of proposition matrices—in this case, the property of being true at some time(s).

PREDICATES AND QUANTIFIERS

An important point about predicates, quantifiers, and certain other operators emerges from the four-tiered corrected theory, and from the distinction between semantic content and content base in particular. The content base of a predicate with respect to a given context of utterance c is a concept or attribute (property or relation). This, together with a time t, determines the semantic content of the predicate with respect to c and t. In turn, the semantic content of a predicate with respect to c and t, together with a possible world w, determines the extension of the predicate with respect to c, t, and w. It follows that the semantic content of a predicate such as 'writes' (or 'be writing') with respect to a context c and a time t is not just the concept or property of writing (or anything similar, such as the function that assigns to any individual x the proposition matrix x *writing*). The concept or property of writing, together with a possible world w, cannot determine the extension of 'writes' with respect to both the world w and the time t, that is, the class of possible individuals who are writing at t in w. The property of writing, together with a possible world w, determines only the class of possible individuals who are writing *at some time or other* in w (or at most, the function that assigns to any time t the class of possible individuals who are writing at t in w). The semantic content of 'writes' with respect to a time t must be such as to determine for any possible world w the class of (possible) individuals who are writing *at the given time t* in w. Only some sort of complex consisting of the concept or property of writing *together with the given time t* will suffice to determine for any possible world w the extension of 'writes' with respect to both w and t. The semantic content of 'writes' with respect to a given time t is not merely the concept or property of writing but a *temporally indexed* concept or property: the concept or property of *writing at t.*

In general, the semantic content of a predicate with respect to a time t (and a location l, if necessary) is not the same attribute as the content base of the predicate but is the temporally indexed attribute that results from taking the content base of the predicate together with the time t (and location l, if necessary). Semantic content for predicates like 'writes' thus varies with time. Exactly analogous remarks apply to quantifiers, other second-order predicates, the definite-description operator 'the', and a variety of other operators.

This usually unrecognized fact about predicates allows us to retain, at least as a sort of general guide or rule of thumb, the principle that the semantic content of a compound expression, such as a sentence or phrase, is a complex made up solely and entirely of the semantic contents of the contentful components that make up the compound. In particular, the content of sentence (1) with respect to a context of utterance c may be thought of as made up of the semantic contents of 'I' and 'am writing' with respect to c. There is no need to introduce the time of the context as a third and separate component, for it is already built into the semantic content of the predicate (the property or concept of writing-at-c_T, where c_T is the time of c).

Since the semantic content of an expression with respect to a context c *simpliciter* is the semantic content with respect to both c and the time of c (and the location of c, if necessary), it follows that the semantic content of a typical predicate varies with context—even the content of nonindexicals like 'writes', 'red', 'table', 'tree'. To this extent, Cratylus was right on the money. It is this usually unnoticed feature of predicates that accounts for the fact that the sentence 'Frege is writing' takes on not only different truth-values but also different contents when uttered at different times, even though the sentence contains no indexicals and is not itself indexical. It is also this feature of predicates that accounts for the fact that certain noneternal (i.e., temporally nonrigid) definite descriptions, such as 'the US president', take on not only different referents but also different semantic contents when uttered at different times even though the description is not indexical. Recall that the distinctive feature of an indexical like 'I' or 'the present US president' is that it takes on different content bases in different contexts. The semantic contents of the definite description 'the US president', of the word 'writes', and of the sentence 'The US president is writing' each varies with context. Yet none of these expressions is indexical; each retains the same content base in all contexts.[16]

The account of the semantic contents of temporal operators as properties of proposition matrices (or other content bases) makes for an important but usually unrecognized class of exceptions to the general principle that the semantic content of a compound expression is made up of the contents of its contentful components. Where T is a monadic temporal sentential operator (e.g., 'sometimes' + present tense or 'on July 4, 1968' + past tense), the content of the result of applying T to a clause S is made up of the content of T together with the content base rather than the content of S. In general, if T is a temporal operator, the content of the result of applying T to an expression is a complex made up of the semantic content of T and the content base rather than the content of the operand expression. Ordinarily, the content of an expression containing as a part the result of applying a temporal operator T to an operand expression is made up, in part, of the content base of the operand expression rather than its semantic content. (For complete accuracy, the notion of semantic content with respect to a context, a time, and a location, for a language L should be defined recursively over the complexity of expressions of L.)[17]

It is instructive to look at how the four-tiered corrected theory treats a simple, untensed clause, such as (1′) and various complex sentences built from it. The character of (1′) is given by the following rule:

(22) For any context c, the content base of (1′) with respect to c is the proposition matrix c_A *writing*, where c_A is the agent of c. This proposition matrix is made up of the content bases of 'I' and of 'be writing' with respect to c. The latter may be taken to be the property or concept of writing.

---

[16] On this account, the sentence 'Rain is falling' typically expresses, with respect to a context of utterance c, the proposition that rain is falling at c_L at c_T, where c_L is the location of c and c_T is the time of c. (An exception arises if, for example, the sentence is used as a shorthand for 'Rain is falling there', with implicit reference to some location other than that of the context.) No actual reference is made, however, either explicitly or implicitly, to either c_L or c_T. Instead, assuming that the sentence is subject-predicate, the predicate 'is falling' expresses as its semantic content the spatially and temporally indexed concept or property of falling at c_L at c_T, and the extension determined is the class of things that are falling at c_L at c_T in the world of the context. This contrasts with the account proposed by Mark Crimmins and John Perry. See their 'The Prince and the Phone Booth: Reporting Puzzling Beliefs,' *Journal of Philosophy* 86 (December 1989), pp. 685–711, at pp. 699–700; and Crimmins's *Talk about Beliefs* (Cambridge, Mass.: MIT Press, 1992), pp. 16–18.

[17] The content base of the result of attaching a content operator (such as 'necessarily' or the 'that'-operator) to a sentence is a complex made up of the content base of the operator and the content base of the sentence, rather than its content. Thus, for example, the content base of the 'that'-clause 'that Frege is writing' with respect to any context c does not involve the content of 'Frege is writing' with respect to c (which is the proposition that Frege is writing at c_T). Instead, it is something like the ordered pair of two elements: (a) a certain abstract entity, analogous to a property, which is the operation of assigning any proposition to itself (this operation—call it 'O_p'— is the content base of the 'that'-operator); and (b) the proposition matrix fw. Thus, the content base of 'that Frege is writing' has the structure $\langle O_p, \langle \text{Frege, writing} \rangle \rangle$. The content of 'Sometimes, Frege believes that he is writing' has the following structure, where 'Σtimes' designates the property of proposition matrices of being true at some time(s):

(i) $\langle \langle \text{Frege}, O_p, \langle \text{Frege, writing} \rangle, \text{believing} \rangle, \Sigma \text{times} \rangle$.

(For further details, see appendix C of *Frege's Puzzle*.)

The schedule of $(1')$ with respect to a given context c is thus given by the following rule:

> (23) For any time t, the semantic content of $(1')$ with respect to c and t is the proposition made up of the content of 'I' with respect to c and t (i.e., the result of applying the schedule of 'I' with respect to c to the particular time t) and the property of writing-at-t (the result of applying the schedule of 'be writing' to t). This may be taken to be the proposition that c_A is writing at t, where c_A is the agent of c.

The semantic content of $(1')$ with respect to a context c *simpliciter* is therefore the proposition that c_A is writing at c_T, where c_T is the time of c.

We may contrast this with the indexical sentence (2). Its character is given by something like the following rule:

> (24) For any context c, the content base of (2) with respect to c is the higher-order proposition made up of the content bases of $(1')$ and of 'now' + present tense with respect to c. The former may be taken to be the proposition matrix c_A *writing*, and the latter the property of proposition matrices of obtaining (or being true) at c_T, where c_A is the agent of c and c_T is the time of c.

This rule reveals the fact that the content base, of the eternal sentence (2) is in fact already a full-fledged, eternal proposition, rather than a noneternal proposition matrix. The schedule of (2) with respect to a context c is thus a constant function from times to the higher-order proposition about the proposition matrix c_A writing that it obtains at c_T. The content of (2) with respect to a context c *simpliciter* is this same higher-order singular proposition, whereas the semantic content of the simpler $(1')$ with respect to c is the proposition that c_A is writing at c_T. Since c_A is writing at c_T if and only if the proposition matrix c_A *writing* obtains at c_T, the semantic contents of $(1')$ and (2) with respect to any context of utterance are trivially equivalent. If we assume that sentence (1) is merely a surface transformation of $(1')$, then *what is said* by a speaker uttering either (1) or (2) at the same time is very nearly the same, as long as the speaker is the same. Still, the content bases are very different. With respect to any context c, the content base of (1) is noneternal, neutral with respect to time, whereas the content base of (2) is eternal. As Kaplan notes, only the former can be felicitously operated upon by temporal operators.

Contrary to Kaplan, since the contents, *what is said*, are trivially equivalent, the function of 'now' cannot be primarily to affect what is said in context. Its effect on content is in fact nil (or virtually so). Rather, the function of 'now' is primarily to affect the content base of its operand, eternalizing it and thereby sealing it off from the influence of external occurrences of temporal operators. For example, attaching 'sometimes' to sentence (1), whose content base with respect to any context is noneternal, aptly yields sentence (21), whose content base is eternal. By contrast, 'sometimes' is at best superfluous in

> (25) Sometimes, I am writing now.

Compare also the role of 'present' in (15).

Analogously, the schedule of a sentence like 'I will be writing tomorrow', as uttered by a speaker c_A at time c_T, is the constant function that assigns to any time t the eternal proposition that c_A *writing* obtains on d^+, where d^+ is the day after the day of c_T. The schedule of the sentence 'I will be writing on the next day', with respect to the same context, is a nonconstant function that assigns to any time t the proposition that c_A *writing* obtains on the day next after t_D, where t_D is the day of t. Despite the close similarity between the contents of the two sentences with respect to any context (*what are said*), the schedules are very different, and only the latter sentence may be felicitously operated upon by temporal operators. Compare 'On December 24, 2001, I will be writing on the next day' with 'On December 24, 2001, 1 will be writing tomorrow'.

PURE TENSES

A considerably richer semantic theory of temporal operators may be obtained by drawing a three-way distinction among *quantificational* or *general* temporal operators, *specific* or *singular* temporal operators, and *pure tense* operators such as simple past or future tense. Quantificational or general temporal operators include such operators as 'sometimes', 'always', present perfect tense (as in 'I have been writing' in the sense of 'I have sometimes been writing'), 'it will always be that' + present tense, 'twice before' + past tense, and so on. Specific or singular temporal operators include 'it is now the case that', 'on December 24, 2001' + future tense, 'when Frege wrote "Thoughts" ' + past tense, and so on. (Compare 'possibly' with 'actually'.) The difference between these two sorts of temporal operators lies in their accompanying semantics. Roughly, a specific sentential temporal operator T is one such that there is some specific time t semantically associated with T, with respect to a context (and a time and a possible world), in such way that the result of applying T to a sentence S is true with respect to a time t' if and only if S is true with respect to t, and t stands in some appropriate temporal-order relation to t'. For example, 'On December 24, 2001, I will be writing' is true with respect to a context c and the year 1996 if and only if both of the following conditions obtain: (a) clause (1') (or sentence (1)) is true with respect to c and December 24, 2001; and (b) 2001 is later than 1996. A general sentential temporal operator T is a nonspecific temporal operator such that there is some specific property P of classes of times semantically associated with T (with respect to semantic parameters) in such a way that the result of applying T to a sentence S is true with respect to a time t' if and only if the class of times with respect to which S is true and that stand in some appropriate temporal-order relation to t' has P. For example, in the case of the present perfect tense, the property P is that of being nonempty, and the appropriate temporal-order relation is the earlier-than relation.[18]

---

[18] These explications of the notions of specific and general temporal operators cannot be regarded as strict definitions and are intended only to convey a general idea. The operator 'when Frege wrote "Thoughts" ' + past tense is to count as a specific temporal operator even if it should turn out that Frege did not write 'Thoughts.' Also, given a sufficiently liberal notion of a property

Now consider ordinary past or future tense, as in 'Frege was writing' or 'Frege will be writing'. Past tense is often treated as though it were a quantificational temporal operator, so that the displayed sentence is regarded as being true with respect to a time t if and only if 'Frege is writing' is true with respect to some time or other earlier than t. (See, for example, the quotation from G. E. Moore two sections back.) While a simple past-tensed sentence is sometimes used in this way (roughly, as equivalent to the corresponding present-perfect-tensed sentence), it generally is not. Ordinarily, a simple past-tensed sentence like 'Frege was writing' is used with implicit reference to a specific (though perhaps vaguely delineated) time, so that if Frege was not writing at the relevant time, then what is said is false even if Frege was writing at some time or other prior to the utterance. Compare 'I asked Frege to come along, but he was writing' with 'I have sometimes asked Frege to come along, but he has sometimes been writing'. Analogous remarks apply to future tense.

Most simple sentential temporal operators require, in idiomatic English, an appropriate adjustment in the tense of the operand. For example, if I wished to apply the temporal operator 'at 3:00 p.m. on August 24, 1996' to sentence (1), at the time of my writing these words—which happens to be 2:55 p.m. on August 24, 1996—I must accompany it with a shift from present to future tense. If I wait six minutes and forever thereafter, I must instead use past tense. It is not sufficient to say when my writing occurs; I must also specify whether the time of my writing is now, or previously, or still to come. The content base of each sentence is eternal, and the same proposition (or at least very nearly the same propositions) would be asserted at each time, and yet grammar compels me to indicate besides the indicated time, the temporal direction of that time—either earlier or later—from the time of utterance. What I say is that (a) my writing occurs at 3:00 p.m. on August 24, 1996; and (b) 3:00 p.m. on August 24, 1996, is future (or present or past, depending on the tense used). It is not enough simply to date the described state of affairs. One is linguistically required also to place the state of affairs described within what J. M. E. McTaggart called the *A-series*—the everchanging manifold divided into past, present, and future, in which each element in the third of these three categories eventually finds itself temporarily in the second before coming to rest in the first. In this sense, the specific temporal operator 'at 3:00 p.m. on August 24, 1996' is *incomplete*. Simple past tense and simple future tense are complementary incomplete temporal operators, which modify an untensed, temporally unmodified clause like (1′) to form a sentence that may now be modified by an incomplete specific or incomplete general temporal operator. The tense operator primes the atomic clause for the application of a specific or general (incomplete) temporal operator. An

of a class, some precaution must be taken if a specific temporal operator is to be precluded from being a general temporal operator. It may be appropriate to define a general temporal operator as a *nonspecific* temporal operator of a certain sort. (A similar difficulty is encountered in defining ordinary quantifiers in such a way as to preclude ordinary singular terms.) More importantly, the explications provided here are appropriate for what I shall call *complete* temporal operators below, although the terminology of 'specific' or 'singular' and 'quantificational' or 'general' temporal operators will be used also for the components of these, which I shall call 'incomplete' temporal operators below (e.g., 'when Frege wrote "Thoughts"' without an accompanying tense operator). These various notions can be made precise, though it is preferable to leave them at an intuitive, informal level in motivating the account under consideration here.

incomplete specific or general temporal operator combines with a pure tense operator to form a complete temporal operator. The complete temporal operator applied to (1′) is 'at 3:00 p.m. on August 24, 1996' + future tense. The extension of a complete temporal operator is a function from proposition matrices (or minimally, from sentence superintensions) to truth-values, and the content of a complete temporal operator is accordingly a concept or property of proposition matrices.

It is instructive to regard ordinary past tense as a superintensional operator with the following distinguishing property: its extension with respect to a time t and a possible world w is the function that assigns to any proposition matrix m (alternatively, to any sentence schedule or superintension—i.e., any function from times to sentence intensions) not a truth-value, but the class of times $t′$ earlier than t at which m obtains in w (or equivalently, the characteristic function of this class of times). An analogous construal is possible for the future tense operator, replacing 'earlier' by 'later'. A past-tensed or future-tensed but otherwise temporally unmodified sentence would thus have as its extension not a truth-value, but a class of times. For example, the extension of the simple past-tensed sentence

(26) I was writing,

with respect to a context c, a time t, and a possible world w, would be the class of times $t′$ earlier than t such that the component untensed clause (1′) is true with respect to c, $t′$, and w. An unmodified past-tensed sentence like (26) may be represented formally as

(27) *Past Tense*[*Be Writing*(*I*)].[19]

Such a sentence essentially stands in need of completion by an incomplete temporal operator, either specific or general, in order to achieve truth-value. The extension (with respect to a context, a time, and a possible world) of an incomplete specific temporal operator, like 'at 3:00 p.m. on August 24, 1996', may be taken to be simply the indicated time, rather than the corresponding function from proposition matrices (or sentence schedules or superintensions) to truth-values. Where T is any incomplete specific temporal operator without an accompanying tense operator, the result of applying T to a past-tensed sentence such as (26) is representable as

(28) *T*(*Past Tense*[*Be Writing*(*I*)]).

This is a complete sentence, whose extension is a truth-value. The sentence is true (with respect to semantic parameters) if and only if the extension of T is an element of the extension of the operand past-tensed clause *Past Tense*[*Be Writing*(*I*)]. It is thus as if the past tense operator in (26) transformed its operand clause (1′) into the corresponding predicate

(29) is a past time at which I be writing.

[19] The naked infinitive phrase 'be writing' might be represented further as

(i) *Progressive Tense* (*Write*).

The word 'writing' itself is functioning here adjectivally.

An incomplete specific temporal operator such as 'at 3:00 p.m. on August 24, 1996' attaches to the tensed sentence as if the operator were a singular term to which a monadic predicate attaches. The complete temporal operator 'at 3:00 p.m. on August 24, 1996' + past tense is a one-place connective. Its extension may be regarded as a function from proposition matrices to truth-values.

In ordinary use, a past-tensed but otherwise temporally unmodified sentence like (26), standing alone as a declarative sentence in a piece of discourse, may be regarded as involving an implicit, specific, demonstrative temporal operator 'then', or 'at that time', in order to obtain a complete sentence, 'I was writing then'. This ordinary sort of use of (26) would thus be represented formally as

(30) *Then(Past Tense[Be Writing(I)])*

and would be taken to mean something like *That time is a past time at which I be writing*. If the time implicitly designated in an utterance of (26) (standing alone as a declarative sentence in a piece of discourse) is not one at which the speaker writes, what is said is false even if the speaker has written at other times prior to the utterance. Analogous remarks apply to 'I will be writing'.[20]

Taking the extension of an incomplete specific temporal operator like 'at 3:00 p.m. on August 24, 1996' without an accompanying tense operator to be simply the indicated time, in order to obtain a complete sentence whose extension is a truth-value from an incomplete specific temporal operator and an untensed clause like (1') as operand, a tense operator must be supplied as a bridge connecting the content base of the operand clause with respect to a context c to the extension with respect to c of the temporal operator, thereby achieving truth-value. Which tense operator is appropriate will depend on the direction of the indicated time, earlier or later, relative to the time of c. This account thus accommodates the fact that the appropriate complete temporal operator typically shifts its constitutive tense from future to past with the passage of time.

On a Fregean approach, incomplete specific temporal operators like 'now' and 'at 3:00 p.m. on August 24, 1996' would be taken as expressing as the operator's semantic content (*Sinn*), a certain concept or property of the time so designated. On a Millian approach, by contrast, the semantic contents of these operators may again be regarded as simply the indicated time. On either approach, the content of a specific temporal operator like 'when Frege wrote "Thoughts" ' may plausibly be regarded as analogous to that of the corresponding definite description 'the past time at which Frege writes "Thoughts" '. (The word 'when' in such constructions is the temporal analogue of the definite-description operator 'the'.) To repeat, the corrected theory is completely neutral regarding such issues and is consistent with either approach.

In earlier work, I have advocated a Millian version of the corrected theory, on which the semantic content of 'now' with respect to a context is taken to be the time of the context itself rather than a concept or property (*presentness*) of that time (see *Frege's Puzzle* and 'Tense and Singular Propositions'). It does not follow, contrary to

---

[20] See W. V. O. Quine, *Word and Object* (Cambridge, Mass.: MIT Press, 1960), pp. 170–171.

an argument of Quentin Smith,[21] that my nonneutral approach is committed to a rejection of McTaggart's A-series of time in favor of the B-series—in which any element is past, present, or future not *per se* but only relative to some (another or the same) element of the series—and hence to a 'tenseless' theory of time, according to which the distinction among past, present, and future is unreal, illusory, relational (to a particular speech act or thought act), merely subjective, or carries no special metaphysical or cosmological significance.[22] Nor does it follow that tensed sentences like (1), (2), and (26), on my approach, locate particular states of affairs within the B-series but not within the A-series. On the contrary, even the corrected theory, which is itself neutral with regard to the contents of specific temporal operators— and of which my Millian account is a special version—explicitly recognizes, for example, that (26) places the speaker's writing in the past. On a Millian version of the corrected theory, this is not accomplished by the implicit 'then' in (26). On any version of the corrected theory, it is accomplished by the explicit 'was'. The A-property of pastness is overtly expressed in (26), by the very presence of past tense. Similarly, futurity is expressed by future tense.[23]

Just as an incomplete specific temporal operator may be plausibly treated as a singular term, so an incomplete quantificational temporal operator may be plausibly

---

[21] See Q. Smith, *Language and Time* (Oxford: Oxford University Press, 1993), especially pp. 44–48; L. N. Oaklander and Q. Smith, eds., *The New Theory of Time* (New Haven, Conn.: Yale University Press, 1994), especially pp. 12–19, 51–54, 136–153.

[22] Those (such as myself) who accept the A-series as veridical need not deny that the dating of an event or state of affairs within the series, or indeed that the whole series itself, is relativized to a 'frame of reference.' They may hold that, relative to one's frame of reference, the division among past, present, and future is real, with the present enjoying a special metaphysical status and each time eventually having its turn at it.

[23] Furthermore, even if the particular word 'now' does not express any concept as its semantic content, a relevant concept of presentness may be semantically contained elsewhere in other expressions. In my 'Existence,' in J. Tomberlin, ed., *Philosophical Perspectives*. Vol. 1, *Metaphysics* (Atascadero, Calif.: Ridgeview, 1987), pp. 49–108, I suggest that the English word 'current', as in 'the current US president', exemplifies an ambiguity analogous to David Lewis's distinction between the primary (indexical) and secondary (nonindexical) English senses of 'actual'. (Consider 'In 1989, current interest rates were higher than present rates'.) The secondary sense of 'current' is a concept of precisely the sort that Smith misinterprets me as rejecting (note 21 above).
On the other hand, on the corrected theory a tensed sentence is translatable, in some relevant sense, into an untensed sentence that places the described state of affairs in the B-series. According to the corrected theory, in uttering the sentence 'At t^*, Frege was writing', one asserts that (a) fw obtains at t^*, and (b) t^* is past. This is an A-determination, rather than a B-determination, in virtue of the second conjunct. But since propositions are eternal, the second conjunct is not the proposition matrix t^* *being past* (which obtains only after t^*, not at t^* itself or at any earlier time), but the eternal proposition that t^* is past *at* c_T, where c_T is the time of utterance. And this proposition is tantamount to the B-determination that t^* is earlier than c_T. For this reason, it is a conceptual mistake to pose the question of whether "time is tensed" (i.e., whether the A-series is cosmologically veridical or objective, etc.) in terms of the untranslatability of tensed A-statements into tenseless B-statements. And indeed, it is a philosophical mistake to infer from the translatability (in this sense) of A-statements into B-statements that the A-properties of pastness, presentness, and futurity are somehow unreal or illusory, and so on. Doing so is analogous to claiming to have discovered a cure for baldness, which consists in paraphrasing any statement ascribing baldness to Jones into a statement asserting the binary relation of *being bald at*—not a property—to hold between Jones and the time of utterance. Though Jones may rejoice in his loss of the property of baldness, he still has no need of shampoo. (Hegelians, who love a synthesis, will probably conclude that he wears a wig.)

treated as a corresponding quantifier. The extension of 'sometimes', for example, may be taken to be the class of all nonempty classes of times (or equivalently, the characteristic function of this class), and its semantic content may likewise be taken to be the corresponding higher-order property of being a nonempty class of times. A quantificational temporal operator thus also requires an accompanying tense as a bridge connecting the superintension of its operand clause to its own extension. The result of applying a quantificational temporal operator to a tensed sentence is true if and only if the extension of the tensed sentence (which is not a truth-value but a class of times) is an element of the extension of the quantificational temporal operator. Thus, for example, the sentence 'Sometimes, Frege was writing' is true with respect to a time t if and only if the class of times earlier than t at which Frege is writing (the extension of 'Frege was writing' with respect to t) is nonempty—that is, if and only if some time t' is a time earlier than t at which Frege is writing. (The complete quantificational temporal operator 'sometimes' + past tense provides a roughly correct, albeit somewhat strained, definition of one use of the present perfect tense, as in 'Frege has been writing', as well as of language theorists' alternative use of simple past tense.) Incomplete quantificational temporal sentential operators such as 'sometimes', 'always', and 'twice before' are thus regarded as attaching to tensed sentences in the way that quantifiers such as 'something', 'everything', and 'exactly two smaller things' attach to monadic predicates, whereas incomplete specific temporal operators such as 'on August 24, 1996' and 'when Frege wrote "Thoughts"' are regarded as attaching to tensed sentences in the way that singular terms are attached to by monadic predicates.[24]

There are complications involved in extending this account of temporal operators to cases in which temporal operators such as 'sometimes', 'always', 'now', and 'today' are applied directly to present-tensed sentences, as in any of the examples (2), (14), (15), and (21). The account would suggest that such instances of present tense be regarded as instances of a pure tense operator, analogous to past or future tense except that its extension with respect to a time t and a possible world w is the function that assigns to any proposition matrix m the class of times t'—whether earlier than, later than, or overlapping with t—at which m obtains in w. Such an operator is required, on the account being considered here, in order to prime a temporally unmodified clause such as (1′) for an operator such as 'sometimes' or 'today', to bridge the super-intension of the unmodified clause with the extension of the incomplete specific or general temporal operator.

Strictly speaking, (1) probably should not be regarded as the atomic sentence formed by attaching the temporally unmodified predicate corresponding to the naked infinitive phrase 'be writing' to the term 'I', as represented formally by

(31) *Be Writing* (I).

---

[24] A problem for this account arises in connection with such constructions as 'Frege always was busy', which does not mean that every time is a past time at which Frege is busy. The sentence seems to mean instead that every past time is a time at which Frege is busy. But on the account proposed here, the past tense operator operates on the value base of the untensed clause 'Frege be busy' and the incomplete operator 'always' attaches to the result (i.e., to the past-tensed 'Frege was busy'), apparently resulting in the incorrect former reading for the sentence. The alternative reading would seem to require seeing the past tense operator as somehow modifying the 'always' rather than the untensed clause.

What this represents is not (1) but (1′). Although (1′) is not a grammatical sentence of English, it is complete in itself. Its extension (with respect to appropriate semantic parameters) is a truth-value; it is true with respect to a context *c*, a world *w*, and a time *t* if and only if the agent of *c* is writing at *t* in *w*. What, then, becomes of (1)?

On the account of temporal operators under consideration, the result of applying present tense to (1′), represented formally as

(32) *Present Tense*[*Be Writing*(*I*)],

is not a complete sentence of English, capable of truth-value standing alone. Its extension is a class of times rather than a truth-value. Yet surely one who wishes to assert what is encoded by a simple, atomic clause like (1′) uses a tensed sentence, namely, (1). How are we to accommodate the fact that (1) is capable of achieving truth-value when standing alone as a declarative sentence without an additional temporal operator?

On this theory, such uses are regarded as involving an implicit specific, indexical temporal operator such as 'now'. For example, sentence (1) standing alone would be seen as elliptical for (2), represented formally as

(33) *Now*(*Present Tense*[*Be Writing*(*I*)]).

This account of simple present tense is exactly analogous to the treatment suggested above of simple past tense according to which a simple past-tensed sentence such as (26) or 'Frege was writing', standing alone as a declarative sentence in a piece of discourse, is elliptical for a temporally indexical completion, for example, 'Frege was writing then'. We may call this the *ellipsis theory of present tense*.[25] It is not my

---

Whereas the latter reading of the sentence is closer to the actual meaning than the former (clearly a misreading), it also does not seem exactly correct. The sentence in question generally is not used with this meaning (although, of course, it *can be* so used). As with a simple past-tensed sentence, a sentence such as 'Frege always was busy' is ordinarily used with implicit reference to a particular (perhaps vaguely delineated) period or interval of time in mind, so that what is said is true as long as Frege is busy throughout that period even if at some other times he is not busy. This feature of such constructions can be accommodated on the present account by taking incomplete quantificational temporal operators, such as 'always', to involve implicit reference to a particular period or interval—very much in the manner of implicitly relativized uses of quantificational constructions in English (such as the 'everything' in 'Everything is in order' or the 'everyone' in 'Is everyone here?'). A sentence such as 'Frege always was busy', standing alone as a declarative sentence in a piece of discourse, may thus be taken to mean something like the following: Every time during *that period* is an earlier time at which Frege is busy (with reference to a contextually indicated period of time).

[25] One alternative to the ellipsis theory is the theory that the English construction represented by '*Writing*(*I*)' is simply sentence (1). Indeed, it is commonplace in most discussions concerning logical form to assume that (1) is, at least as typically intended, an atomic sentence constructed from the singular term 'I' and the simple predicate 'am writing', while regarding the present tense of the latter not as a separate component of the sentence but as somehow built into the predicate. In an effort to facilitate understanding of the general theory of temporal operators presented here, much of the preceding discussion was based on the presumption of some such theory. However, if verb tenses are to be taken seriously in accordance with the general theory of temporal operators presented here—as semantically significant contributions to sentences in themselves—this alternative theory ultimately requires the postulation of a systematic semantic ambiguity in the present tense, so that a simple, present-tensed sentence like (1) is ambiguous between the complete

(i) *Writing*(*I*)

purpose here to fill out the details of the ellipsis theory or to cite linguistic evidence either in favor of or against this general account of the simple tenses. It is adequate to my purpose merely to indicate the richness of the apparatus of the corrected theory for dealing with complete and incomplete temporal operators.[26]

It is interesting to note that on the ellipsis theory, a present-tensed sentence such as (3) is taken to be an incomplete sentence standing in need of completion, much as if it were the corresponding predicate 'is a time at which this tree be covered with green leaves'. At the level of semantic content, the present tense operator thus converts the content base of its untensed operand clause into something like its corresponding property of being a time at which the tree in question is covered with green leaves. This theory of the pure tenses thus mimics Frege's construal of a present-tensed sentence as standing in need of completion or supplementation, typically provided by the time of utterance. Frege's theory works remarkably well as a theory of tense. Unfortunately, as we saw above, it fails as an account of temporal indexicality.

---

and the incomplete (in need of supplementation by an incomplete specific or general temporal operator)

(ii) *Present Tense*[*Writing*(I)].

The first would be an instance of the *tenseless* use of present tense, the second of the *tensed* use. The tenseless (1) has a truth-value for its extension and would be an appropriate operand for any complete temporal operator, whereas the tensed (1) would be the result of applying a certain tense operator (*viz.*, present tense qua tense operator) to the tenseless (1). The more complex logical form of the latter would have to be regarded on this theory as going entirely unrepresented in the surface grammar. We may call this the *ambiguity theory of present tense*.

Certain general considerations tend to favor the ellipsis theory over the ambiguity theory of present tense. In general, when attempting to explain apparently divergent uses of a single expression or locution, if an ellipsis account is available, it is to be preferred over the postulation of a systematic semantic ambiguity—although, of course, some third alternative may be preferable to it. See S. Kripke, 'Speaker's Reference and Semantic Reference,' in P. French, T. Uehling, and H. Wettstein, eds., *Contemporary Perspectives in the Philosophy of Language* (Minneapolis: University of Minnesota Press, 1979), pp. 6–27, especially p. 19.

[26] It is important for a full theory of the simple tenses to take account of the fact that the proper operands of tenses in English seem to be not whole clauses but simple predicates (or, more accurately, verbs). It is largely a simple problem of formal engineering to transform the theory of pure tenses presented here into a theory of tenses as operators on the content bases of simple predicates rather than on the value bases of whole clauses. For example, in accordance with the spirit of the general theory of tenses presented here, a past-tensed predicate such as 'was writing'— which results from applying the past tense operation to the simple predicate (naked infinitive) 'be writing'—may be regarded as having for its extension, with respect to a possible world w and a time t, not a class of individuals (or its corresponding characteristic function from individuals to truth-values), but the function that assigns to each (possible, past, present, or future) individual i the class of times before t at which i is writing in w.

It may also be important to recognize that the 'that'-operator, which transforms a sentence into a singular term (typically) referring to the sentence's semantic content, may be attached in English to a tensed but apparently otherwise temporally unmodified sentence, for example, 'When Frege wrote "Thoughts," he knew that he was writing'. It may be necessary to regard such 'that'-clauses as involving an implicit 'then' or 'now' operator. See note 17.

19

Pronouns as Variables (2005)

I

The English sentence,

(1) Every male soldier overseas misses the only woman waiting for him back home

may be seen as having an underlying logical form given by the following—where items in boldface correspond to explicit elements in the surface form:

(1′) [**every** x: **male soldier**(x); **overseas**(x)] (x **misses** [**the only** y: **woman**(y)](y **is waiting for** x **back home**)).

The expression '[every x: male soldier(x); overseas(x)]' is a *restricted universal quantifier phrase*; '[the only y: woman(y)](y is waiting for x back home)' is an open definite description.[1] The variable 'x' is bound in (1′) by the restricted universal quantifier; so the 'him' in (1) may be said to be bound by 'every male soldier overseas'.

Peter Geach holds that, with one kind of exception, anaphoric pronouns in general are bound variables.[2] The exceptions are the *pronouns of laziness*, which go proxy for another expression that the speaker wishes not to repeat. Indeed, aside from pronouns of laziness, and aside also from deictic (non-anaphoric) uses of pronouns—which correspond in some respects to free variables under an assigned value—typical pronoun-occurrences in English appear to function as bound variables. As Geach puts it, "It is very important to notice that the relation of bound variables to the binding operator in symbolism *strictly* corresponds to the relation of pronoun to antecedent in the vernacular."[3] One of the most valuable insights in Alan Berger's study, *Terms and Truth*, is his critique of the

I thank Alan Berger for comments and discussion. I am also grateful to the UCLA Workshop in Philosophy of Language during Spring 2004 for their initial reactions to some of the material presented here.

[1] I remain neutral concerning whether a definite description is a singular term or a uniqueness-restricted quantifier.

[2] Geach, *Reference and Generality* (Ithaca, NY: Cornell University Press, 1962), at pp. 125–126, and *passim*.

[3] Geach, 'History of a Fallacy,' *Journal of the Philosophical Association* (Bombay), 5, 19–20 (1958); reprinted in Geach's *Logic Matters* (Oxford: Basil Blackwell, 1972), pp. 1–13, at 12–13. See also Geach's 'Quine's Syntactical Insights,' *Synthese*, 19, 1/2 (1968–1969); reprinted in *Logic*

increasingly popular view that certain anaphoric pronouns are, contrary to Geach, unbound.

A standard view is that free variables (and occurrences of compound designators containing free variables) designate, whereas bound variables range over a universe of values and do not also designate. An analogous view is generally assumed with regard to natural-language pronouns: deictic occurrences and some laziness occurrences designate; bound-variable anaphoric occurrences do not. Geach criticizes "the lazy assumption that pronouns, or phrases containing them, can be disposed of by calling them 'referring expressions' and asking what they refer to."[4] He says of anaphoric pronoun-occurrences, "It is simply a prejudice or a blunder to regard such pronouns as needing a reference at all" (*Reference and Generality*, p. 126). This attitude betrays a lack of analytical vision. The prejudice or blunder, I contend, is on Geach's side. He is not alone.

It is essential in what follows that the reader be ever vigilant, paying extremely close attention to the distinction between expressions themselves and their occurrences.[5]

II

Geach's contention that anaphoric pronoun-occurrences (other than pronouns of laziness) are bound variables, and his insistence that bound variables do not designate, are independent. In fact, perhaps most theoretical linguists and philosophers of language maintain with Geach that bound variables do not designate, while also maintaining with Gareth Evans that some pronoun-occurrences anaphoric upon a quantifier (besides laziness occurrences) designate, or at least have semantic extension.[6] Following Evans, an anaphoric pronoun-occurrence whose grammatical antecedent is a quantifier-occurrence within whose scope that pronoun-occurrence does not stand is often called an *E-type pronoun*.[7] It is generally held that an *E*-type pronoun-occurrence is an occurrence of a definite description recoverable from the antecedent quantifier—or alternatively, an occurrence of a rigid singular term whose reference is fixed by the recoverable definite description. (See note 1.) *E*-type

---

Matters, pp. 115–127, at 118. For present purposes I am ignoring reflexive pronouns like 'himself', although Geach's thesis extends to these. *Cf.* my 'Reflexivity,' *Notre Dame Journal of Formal Logic*, 27, 3 (July 1986), pp. 401–429, reprinted in N. Salmon and S. Soames, eds., *Propositions and Attitudes* (Oxford Readings in Philosophy, 1988), pp. 240–274; and 'Reflections on Reflexivity,' *Linguistics and Philosophy*, 15, 1 (February 1992), pp. 53–63.

[4] Geach, 'Ryle on Namely-Riders,' *Analysis*, 21, 3 (1960–1961); reprinted in *Logic Matters* (Oxford: Basil Blackwell, 1972), pp. 88–92, at 92.

[5] For most purposes, an expression-occurrence may be regarded as the expression *together with* a position that the expression occupies within a larger expression. With some trepidation, I follow the common vernacular in speaking of "bound variables" where what are mentioned are actually bound *occurrences*.

[6] *Cf.* Evans, 'Pronouns, Quantifiers, and Relative Clauses (1),' *Canadian Journal of Philosophy*, 7 (1977), pp. 777–797; 'Pronouns,' *Linguistic Inquiry*, 11 (1980), pp. 337–362.

[7] In the vernacular of theoretical linguistics, the term '*E*-type pronoun' is used for an anaphoric pronoun-occurrence whose grammatical antecedent is a quantifier-occurrence that does not *c-command* that pronoun-occurrence. (See note 5 above.)

pronoun-occurrences, according to Evans, are "assigned a reference and their immediate sentential contexts can be evaluated independently for truth and falsehood."

Those familiar with classical first-order logic typically treat the 'it' in

(2) If any man has a home, it is his castle.

as a variable bound by the phrase 'a home' functioning as a prenex restricted universal quantifier:

(2G) [any x: man(x)] [any y: home(y)] (if x has y, then y is x's castle).

Evans argued in opposition to Geach that the phrase 'a home' is an existential quantifier. Furthermore, according to Evans, its scope does not extend beyond (2)'s antecedent, and so does not bind the E-type pronoun 'it'. Evans hinted at one sort of consideration that counts against a treatment of the 'it' as a bound variable.[8] The analogous sentence,

(3) If any man has several homes, they are his castles

is clearly not equivalent to (2G). Neither is it equivalent to

[any x: man(x)] [several y: home(y)] (if x has y, then y is x's castle).

The latter is true even if (3) is false, merely because for any man there are several homes he does not have. The anaphoric occurrence of 'they' in (3) is therefore not a variable-occurrence bound by its antecedent. By analogy, neither is the 'it' in (2) a variable bound by its antecedent.

Evans takes the 'it' in (2) to be a rigid singular term whose reference is fixed by the description 'the home that he has', bound only by the initial restricted universal quantifier 'any man'. He might have represented (2) as having the following logical form:

(2E) [any x: man(x)] (if [a y: home(y)](x has y), then *dthat*[[the z: home(z)](x has z)] is x's castle).[9]

An E-type pronoun can also occur in a separate sentence from its antecedent. Consider the following discourse fragment:

(4) (*i*) A comedian composed the musical score for *City Lights*. (*ii*) He was multi-talented.

---

[8] 'Pronouns, Quantifiers and Relative Clauses (I),' at §IV*B*(*a*).

[9] Kaplan, 'Dthat,' in P. Cole, ed., *Syntax and Semantics 9: Pragmatics* (New York: Academic Press, 1978), pp. 221–243. Here I treat *dthat* as a rigidifying operator complete in itself, and into whose scope it is possible to quantify (contrary to Kaplan's intentions). Presumably Evans would offer a similar analysis for (3), perhaps

(3E) [any x: man(x)] (if [several y: home(y)] (x has y), then *dthose*[[the z's: home(z)](x has z)] are x's castles).

where '[the z's: home(z)](x has z)' is a *plural definite description* (representing 'the homes that he has') and '*dthose*' is a plural rigidifier.

Evans's theory encounters a serious difficulty (indeed, a counterexample) with the more natural variant of (2) obtained by replacing 'any man' with 'a man'.

The particular sentence (4*ii*) is ordinarily regarded as an open formula, with 'he' a free variable. As Geach has noted, the pronoun evidently functions differently *as it occurs in (4)*. Geach takes the 'he' to be a variable-occurrence bound by a prenex occurrence of the restricted existential quantifier 'a comedian', as in the following:

(4*G*) [a *x*: comedian(*x*)] (*x* composed the musical score for *City Lights* & *x* was multi-talented).[10]

Evans's evidence that 'a comedian' in (4*i*) does not bind the 'he' in (4*ii*) comes by considering an analogous discourse fragment like

(5) Just two actors starred in *City Lights*. They were both multi-talented,

which is not equivalent to the quantified generalization,

Just two actors both: starred in *City Lights* and were multi-talented.

Many writers, including several critics, have followed Evans in concluding that the pronoun 'they' in (5) is an occurrence of a closed expression. By analogy, the 'he' in (4) appears to be a free occurrence of a closed definite description or, as Evans maintained, a rigidified variant. Evans thus represents (4) as having the following logical form:

(4*E*) (*i*) [a *x*: comedian(*x*)] (*x* composed the musical score for *City Lights*).
         (*ii*) *dthat*[[the *y*: comedian(*y*)](*y* composed the musical score for *City Lights*)] was multi-talented.

The full '*dthat*'-term (a closed expression) is alleged to be the formal counterpart of the 'he' in (4*ii*).

III

Persuaded that *E*-type pronouns are not bound variables, some writers have mis-cataloged certain directly referential singular terms as non-rigid definite descriptions, partly as a result of a failure to distinguish sharply between the term and its occurrence. Michael McKinsey, Scott Soames, Stephen Neale, and others argue that the 'he', as it occurs in (4), is synonymous with 'the only comedian who composed the musical score for *City Lights*'.[11] Consider a possible world *W* in which Buster Keaton composed the musical score for Chaplin's classic silent film. The discourse fragment (4) is true with respect to *W* iff Keaton is a multi-talented comedian in *W*, never mind Chaplin.[12] With respect to *W*, it is argued, the 'he' in (4) designates

[10] *Reference and Generality*, at pp. 129*ff*, and 'Quine's Syntactical Insights,' at pp. 118–119 of *Logic Matters*.
[11] McKinsey, 'Mental Anaphora,' *Synthese*, 66 (1986), pp. 159–175, at 161; Soames, review of Gareth Evans's *Collected Papers*, in *The Journal of Philosophy*, 86 (1989), pp. 141–156, at 145; Neale, 'Descriptive Pronouns and Donkey Anaphora,' *The Journal of Philosophy*, 87 (1990), pp. 113–150, at 130, and *Descriptions* (Cambridge, Mass.: MIT Press, 1990), p. 186.
[12] Insofar as the modal truth-conditions for (4) yield this result, the 'he' does not function in (4) as a demonstrative. The sentence '*Dthat*[the comedian who composed the musical score for *City*

Keaton. The entire discourse fragment is thus depicted as having the following logical form, in contrast to (4E):

(4M) (i) [a x: comedian(x)] (x composed the musical score for *City Lights*).

(ii) [the y: comedian(y)](y composed the musical score for *City Lights*) was multi-talented.

The full definite description in (4Mii) is alleged to be the formal counterpart of the 'he' in (4).

That the pronoun 'he' (the expression) is in fact rigid is confirmed in the present instance by positioning it in the scope of a modal operator-occurrence:[13]

A comedian composed the musical score for *City Lights*. That he was multi-talented is a contingent truth.

The second sentence here does not impute contingency to the fact that whichever comedian composed the music for *City Lights* was multi-talented. (If it did, it would presumably be false.) Instead it expresses something about Chaplin himself: that although in fact multi-talented, he might not have been.

This does not mean, however, that Evans was right and Geach wrong concerning *E*-type pronouns.

IV

Classical semantics does not abide by Frege's admonition that *one should never ask for the designation or content of an expression in isolation, but only in the context of a sentence*. Classical semantics imputes semantic designation to expressions (under assignments of values to variables), not to their occurrences in formulae. Yet Frege's Context Principle has a point. One reason for departing from classical semantics—and one possible motivation for the Context Principle—is the desire for universal principles of extensionality for designation and of compositionality for semantic content. Even more important is our intuition concerning what is actually being mentioned in a particular context. Consider, for example, the following fallacious inference:

In 1999, the President of the United States was a Democrat.
The President of the United States = George W. Bush.
Therefore, in 1999, George W. Bush was a Democrat.

The invalidity is partially explained by noting that whereas the definite description in the second premise designates Bush, there is no mention of Bush in the first premise. Though perhaps incomplete, the explanation is intuitive, even satisfying.

Lights] was multi-talented' is true with respect to a context c and a possible world w iff the comedian who *in the possible world of c* (rather than w) composed the musical score for *City Lights*, was multi-talented in w.

[13] This is also pointed out by Alan Berger in his book, *Terms and Truth* (Cambridge, Mass.: MIT Press, 2002), pp. 171–178. *Cf.*, my 'Demonstrating and Necessity,' *The Philosophical Review*, 111, 4 (October 2002), pp. 497–537, at pp. 536–537n52.

Frege regarded the attributing of semantic values to expressions *simpliciter* as legitimate only to the extent that such attribution is derivative from semantic attribution to those expression's occurrences in sentences. One need not adopt Frege's attitude in order to make sense of attributing semantic values to an expression-occurrence. Semantic attribution to occurrences may be regarded as derivative from the metalinguistic *T*-sentences (and similar meta-theorems) derived from basic semantic principles. Thus, we may choose to say that whereas 'the President of the United States' *customarily* designates Bush, the *occurrence* of 'the President of the United States' in the major premise above designates the function that assigns to any time *t*, the person who is President of the United States at *t*. The semantic value of the description that bears on the truth-value of the sentence is not Bush, but this function.

It is indeed a mistake to treat a bound variable (or other bound expression-occurrence) as having its customary, or default, designatum.[14] The value of a variable, under an assignment of values to variables, is what free occurrences of the variable designate. Does a bound variable have a non-standard designatum? It does; it has what I call the variable's *bondage designatum*. In a properly developed semantic theory applicable to expression-occurrences, the occurrences of '*x*' in (1′), and the 'him' in (1), each designate the identity function on the universe of individuals over which those variables range.[15]

A similar situation obtains with regard to *E*-type pronouns. As Berger remarks,

Usually in linguistic literature when it is argued that an anaphoric pronoun should not be analyzed as a bound variable, what is argued [i.e., what is actually shown] is simply that the immediate anaphoric antecedent does not bind the variable occurrence representing the pronoun... But it does not follow that the pronoun is not to be analyzed as a bound variable. For it is possible to analyze the pronoun as a bound variable without regarding it as bound by the immediate anaphoric antecedent. (p. 166)

The pronoun-occurrence in (4) is plausibly regarded as a variable-occurrence bound by a restricted quantifier implicit in (4*ii*). The entire discourse fragment is plausibly regarded as having a logical form more like the following:

(4′)　(*i*)　[a *x*: comedian(*x*)] (*x* **composed the musical score for** *City Lights*).
　　　(*ii*)　[a *y*: comedian(*y*); *y* composed the musical score for *City Lights*] (*y* **was multi-talented**).

The open formula '*y* was multi-talented' occurring in (4′*ii*) makes an explicit appearance in the surface form, as (4*ii*). The rest of (4′*ii*) does not. On this analysis, an *E*-type pronoun-occurrence is a species of bound-variable occurrence, as Geach has long maintained. In fact, (4′) is equivalent to (4*G*). Contrary to Geach, however, the anaphora between an *E*-type pronoun and its antecedent is not the same relation as that between a bound variable and its binding operator. Instead the *E*-type pronoun is bound by an absent operator recoverable from the antecedent.

---

[14] When a quantifier (or other variable-binding operator) "quantifies into" an open expression, I say that the external quantifier-occurrence, in addition to binding the variable occurrence, also binds the containing open-expression occurrence itself.

[15] A justification for this claim is offered in my 'A Theory of Bondage' (forthcoming).

One important advantage of this analysis over both (4*E*) and (4*M*) is that the mere grammar of (4) does not support an inference to a uniqueness claim of the sort presupposed or otherwise entailed by the use of '*the only* comedian that scored the music for *City Lights*'. This is obvious with the following discourse:

A comedian panned the musical score for *City Lights*. He was jealous. Another comedian also panned the musical score for *City Lights*. He wasn't jealous; he was tone-deaf.

Another important difference is that there is no definite description in (4′) to be regarded as a formal counterpart of the 'he' in (4). There is no designation at all of Chaplin in (4′), except by the variables 'x' and 'y' under appropriate value-assignments. The rigidity of 'he' suggests that its formal counterpart in (4′) is simply the last occurrence of 'y'.[16]

It is extremely important here to distinguish sharply between the English *sentence* (4*ii*) and its *occurrence* in the discourse-fragment (4). The former is the natural-language analog of an open formula. That is the sentence itself, whose logical form is given, nearly enough, by 'y was multi-talented'. The occurrence of (4*ii*) in (4) is a horse of a different color. Here the surface form of an occurrence is not a reliable guide to the logical form. The occurrence of (4*ii*) in (4) corresponds not merely to 'y was multi-talented' but to the whole of (4′*ii*), in which a quantifier binds the open formula. Though superficially an occurrence of an open formula, the underlying logical form is that of a closed sentence, one that "can be evaluated independently for truth and falsehood." In effect, the second sentence-occurrence in (4), though syntactically an occurrence of (4*ii*), is semantically an occurrence of (4′*ii*). One could say that the *sentence* (4*ii*) itself is bound in (4), though not by any element of (4*i*)— indeed, not by any element of the surface form of (4). One might say that the occurrence of (4*ii*) in (4) is a *pro-clause of laziness*; it has the logical form of the whole consisting of (4*ii*) *together with a binding quantifier phrase*. The quantifier phrase itself, though invisible, is present behind the scenes.[17]

---

[16] Likewise, (2) is plausibly seen as having the following logical form:

(2′) [any x: man(x)] (if [a y: home(y)] (x has y), then [any z: home(z); x has z] (z is x's castle)).

The boldface occurrence of 'z' corresponds to the *E*-type pronoun 'it' in (2). This more long-winded alternative to (2*G*) is equivalent to it. A similar analysis may be given for (3).

The analysis Berger provides for discourse-fragments like (4), *ibid.*, at pp. 159–189, 203–227, looks to be similar to (4′) but for a difference in presupposition.

Both anaphoric pronoun-occurrences in 'If a man has a home, it is his castle' are naturally taken as variable-occurrences bound by restricted-universal-quantifier occurrences. The sentence is plausibly regarded as having the following logical form:

If [a x: man(x)] [a y: home(y)] (x has y), then [any x': man(x')] [any y': home(y'); x' has y'] (y' is x''s castle).

[17] The discourse fragment (5) is plausibly regarded as having the following logical form:

(5′) (*i*) [just two x: actor(x)](x starred in *City Lights*).
(*ii*) [every y: actor(y); y starred in *City Lights*] (y was multi-talented).

See the previous note. Consider, in contrast, the discourse fragment:

(*i*) A man and a woman starred in *City Lights*. (*ii*) The man was multi-talented.

If the occurrence of '*y* was multi-talented' in (4'*ii*) is to be regarded as having an extension, its extension is not a truth-value, but rather the function that maps individuals in the range of '*y*' who were multi-talented to truth, and maps those who were not to falsehood. The whole of (4'*ii*)—and hence the occurrence of (4*ii*) in (4)—is true iff the class characterized by this function includes a comedian who composed the musical score for *City Lights*. The occurrence of (4*ii*) in (4) is thus true with respect to the possible world *W* iff Keaton was multi-talented in *W*.

The very fact that the occurrence of (4*ii*) in (4) has these modal truth-conditions despite the rigidity of 'he' indicates that, contrary to Evans and several of his critics, the 'he' in (4) is a bound variable. One can say with some justification that the 'he' in (4)—the occurrence—is a non-rigid designator. This is not because the occurrence designates Chaplin with respect to one world and Keaton another. It does neither. Where it occurs free (e.g., a deictic use), 'he' is a rigid designator of its customary extension under a designatum-assignment. If the pronoun-occurrence in (4) is to be regarded as designating at all, it has its bondage designatum. Insofar as the occurrence is non-rigid, it is so because it ranges over different universes with respect to different worlds.

If this does not entail that only one man starred in *City Lights*, its logical form is arguably given by,

(*i*) [a *x*: man(*x*)] (*x* starred in *City Lights*) and [a *x*: woman(*x*)] (*x* starred in *City Lights*).
(*ii*) [a *y*: man(*y*)]; *y* starred in *City Lights*] ([the *z*: man(*z*)](*z* = *y*) was multi-talented).

Bibliography of Nathan Salmon, 1979–2005

BOOKS

Essentialism in Current Theories of Reference (1979 UCLA doctoral dissertation, University Microfilms International, 1980).

Reference and Essence (Princeton University Press, 1981; and Basil Blackwell, 1982).

Frege's Puzzle (Cambridge, Mass.: Bradford Books, MIT Press, 1986).

Propositions and Attitudes (co-edited with Scott Soames) (Oxford: Oxford University Press, Oxford Readings in Philosophy, 1988).

Frege's Puzzle (Second Edition) (Atascadero, Ca.: Ridgeview, 1991).

Reference and Essence, Korean translation by Joonho Park, Chonbuk National University, Korea (Korea: Hankook, 2000).

Reference and Essence (Second Edition) (Amherst, NY: Prometheus Books, 2005).

ARTICLES

Critical Review of Leonard Linsky, *Names and Descriptions, The Journal of Philosophy*, 76, 8 (August 1979), pp. 436–452.

'How *Not* to Derive Essentialism from the Theory of Reference,' *The Journal of Philosophy*, 76, 12 (December 1979), pp. 703–725.

†† 'Assertion and Incomplete Definite Descriptions,' *Philosophical Studies*, 42, 1 (July 1982), pp. 37–45.

'Fregean Theory and the Four Worlds Paradox: A Reply to David Over,' *Philosophical Books*, 25, 1 (January 1984), pp. 7–11; reprinted in *Reference and Essence (Second Edition)* (Prometheus Books, 2005), pp. 265–271.

† 'Impossible Worlds,' *Analysis*, 44, 3 (June 1984), pp. 114–117.

†† 'Reflexivity,' *Notre Dame Journal of Formal Logic*, 27, 3 (July 1986), pp. 401–429; reprinted in *Propositions and Attitudes* (Oxford Readings in Philosophy, 1988), pp. 240–274.

'Modal Paradox: Parts and Counterparts, Points and Counterpoints,' in Peter French, Theodore Uehling, Jr., and Howard Wettstein, eds., *Midwest Studies in Philosophy XI: Studies in Essentialism* (Minneapolis: University of Minnesota Press, 1986), pp. 75–120; reprinted in *Reference and Essence (Second Edition)* (Prometheus Books, 2005), pp. 273–344.

† 'Existence,' in James Tomberlin, ed., *Philosophical Perspectives, 1: Metaphysics* (Atascadero, Calif.: Ridgeview, 1987), pp. 49–108.

† 'The Fact that $x = y$,' *Philosophia* (Israel), 17, 4 (December 1987), pp. 517–518.

† Critical Review of David Lewis, *On the Plurality of Worlds, The Philosophical Review*, 97, 2 (April 1988), pp. 237–244.

†† 'How to Measure the Standard Metre,' *Proceedings of the Aristotelian Society* NS, 88 (1987/1988), pp. 193–217.

'Introduction' to *Propositions and Attitudes* (co-authored with Scott Soames, Oxford Readings in Philosophy, 1988), pp. 1–15.

† 'The Logic of What Might Have Been,' *The Philosophical Review*, 98, 1 (January 1989), pp. 3–34.

'Reference and Information Content: Names and Descriptions,' in Dov Gabbay and Franz Guenthner, eds., *Handbook of Philosophical Logic IV: Topics in the Philosophy of Language* (Dordrecht: Springer, 1989), Chapter IV.5, pp. 409–461.

'How to Become a Millian Heir,' *Noûs*, 23, 2 (April 1989), pp. 211–220.

'Tense and Singular Propositions,' in Joseph Almog, John Perry, and Howard Wettstein, eds., *Themes from Kaplan* (Oxford University Press, 1989), pp. 331–392.

†† 'Illogical Belief,' in James Tomberlin, ed., *Philosophical Perspectives, 3: Philosophy of Mind and Action Theory* (Atascadero, Calif.: Ridgeview, 1989), pp. 243–285.

†† 'A Millian Heir Rejects the Wages of *Sinn*,' in C. Anthony Anderson and Joseph Owens, eds., *Propositional Attitudes: the Role of Content in Logic, Language, and Mind* (Stanford, Calif.: Center for the Study of Language and Information, Stanford University, 1990), pp. 215–247.

'Temporality,' in William Bright, ed., *Oxford International Encyclopedia of Linguistics* (Oxford University Press, 1990).

'Singular Terms,' in Hans Burkhardt and Barry Smith, eds., *Handbook of Metaphysics and Ontology* (Munich: Philosophia Verlag, 1990).

†† 'How *Not* to Become a Millian Heir,' *Philosophical Studies*, 62, 2 (May 1991), pp. 165–177.

†† 'The Pragmatic Fallacy,' *Philosophical Studies*, 63, 1 (July 1991), pp. 83–97.

†† 'Reflections on Reflexivity,' *Linguistics and Philosophy*, 15, 1 (February 1992), pp. 53–63.

† 'On Content,' *Mind*, 101, 404 (October 1992; special issue commemorating the centennial of Gottlob Frege's '*Über Sinn und Bedeutung*'), pp. 733–751.

†† 'Relative and Absolute Apriority,' *Philosophical Studies*, 69 (1993), pp. 83–100.

† 'This Side of Paradox,' *Philosophical Topics*, 21, 2 (Spring 1993), pp. 187–197.

† 'A Problem in the Frege–Church Theory of Sense and Denotation,' *Noûs*, 27, 2 (June 1993), pp. 158–166.

†† 'Analyticity and Apriority,' in J. E. Tomberlin, ed., *Philosophical Perspectives, 7: Language and Logic* (Atascadero, Ca.: Ridgeview, 1993), pp. 125–133.

'Sense and Reference,' in Robert M. Harnish, ed., *Basic Topics in the Philosophy of Language* (Prentice-Hall and Harvester Wheatsheaf, 1994), pp. 99–129.

'*Frege's Puzzle* (excerpts),' in Robert M. Harnish, ed., *Basic Topics in the Philosophy of Language* (Prentice-Hall and Harvester Wheatsheaf, 1994), pp. 447–489.

†† 'Being of Two Minds: Belief with Doubt,' *Noûs*, 29, 1 (January 1995), pp. 1–20.

†† 'Relational Belief,' in Paolo Leonardi and Marco Santambrogio, eds., *On Quine: New Essays* (Cambridge University Press, 1995), pp. 206–228.

'Reference: Names, Descriptions, and Variables,' in Marcelo Dascal, Dietfried Gerhardus, Kuno Lorenz, and Georg Meggle, eds., *Handbuch Sprachphilosophie: Volume 2* (Berlin: Walter De Gruyter & Co, 1996), pp. 1123–1152.

'Trans-World Identification and Stipulation,' *Philosophical Studies*, 84, 2–3 (December 1996), pp. 203–223; reprinted in *Reference and Essence (Second Edition)* (Prometheus Books, 2005), pp. 345–36.

† 'Wholes, Parts, and Numbers,' in J. E. Tomberlin, ed., *Philosophical Perspectives, 11: Mind, Causation, and World* (Atascadero, Ca.: Ridgeview, 1997), pp. 1–15.

† 'Nonexistence,' *Noûs*, 32, 3 (September 1998), pp. 277–319.

†† 'Is *De Re* Belief Reducible to *De Dicto*?' in A. A. Kazmi, ed., *Meaning and Reference (Canadian Journal of Philosophy*, Supplementary Volume 23, 1997, (University of Calgay Press, 1998), pp. 85–110.

'Kripke,' entry in the *Cambridge Dictionary of Philosophy, Second Edition* (Cambridge University Press, 1995, 1999), p. 476.

'Preface' to the Korean Translation of *Reference and Essence*, Korean translation by Joonho Park (Korea: Hankook, 2000).

† 'The Limits of Human Mathematics,' in J. E. Tomberlin, ed., *Philosophical Perspectives, 15: Metaphysics, 2001* (Oxford: Blackwell, 2001), pp. 93–117.

† 'Mythical Objects,' in J. Campbell, M. O'Rourke, and D. Shier, eds., *Meaning and Truth*, Proceedings of the Eastern Washington University and the University of Idaho Inland Northwest Philosophy Conference on Meaning (Seven Bridges Press, 2002), pp. 105–123.

'Puzzles about Intensionality,' in Dale Jacquette, ed., *Blackwell Companion to Philosophical Logic* (Oxford: Blackwell, 2002), pp. 73–85.

† 'The Very Possibility of Language: A Sermon on the Consequences of Missing Church,' C. A. Anderson and M. Zeleny, eds., *Logic, Meaning and Computation: Essays in Memory of Alonzo Church* (Boston: Kluwer, 2001), pp. 573–595.

† 'Identity Facts,' in C. Hill, ed., *Philosophical Topics*, 30, 1 (Spring 2002), pp. 237–267.

†† 'Demonstrating and Necessity,' *The Philosophical Review*, 111, 4 (October 2002), pp. 497–537.

'Naming, Necessity, and Beyond,' *Mind*, 112, 447 (July 2003), pp. 475–492; reprinted in *Reference and Essence (Second Edition)* (Prometheus Books, 2005), pp. 377–397.

† 'Tense and Intension,' in A. Jokic, ed., *Time, Tense, and Reference* (Cambridge University Press, 2003), pp. 107–154.

'Reference and Information Content: Names and Descriptions' (revised), in Dov Gabbay and Franz Guenthner, eds., *Handbook of Philosophical Logic, Second Edition, 10* (Boston: Kluwer, 1989, 2003), pp. 39–85.

†† 'The Good, the Bad, and the Ugly,' in A. Bezuidenhout and M. Reimer, eds., *Descriptions* (Oxford University Press, 2004), pp. 230–260.

†† 'Two Conceptions of Semantics,' in Zoltan Szabo, ed., *Semantics and Pragmatics* (Ithaca, NY: Cornell University Press, 2004).

'Semantics *vs.* Pragmatics,' in Richard Schantz, ed., *What is Meaning?* (New York: de Gruyter, forthcoming, 2004).

†† 'Are General Terms Rigid?' *Linguistics and Philosophy*, 2004 .

'Proper Names and Descriptions,' in Donald M. Borchert, ed., *Encyclopedia of Philosophy* (Second Edition) (New York: Macmillan, forthcoming 2005).

† 'On Designating,' in S. Neale, ed., *Mind*, special issue celebrating the centennial of 'On Denoting' (forthcoming 2005).

† 'Personal Identity: What's the Problem?' in J. Berg, ed., Proceedings of the University of Haifa International Conference on the Work of Saul Kripke: *Naming, Necessity, and More* (forthcoming).

' "Must" and "Might",' for a chapter on modal logic to appear in D. Kalish, R. Montague, G. Mar, and N. Salmon, *Logic: Techniques of Formal Reasoning (Third Edition)*, Oxford University Press.

'Quantifying Into the Unquantifiable: The Life and Work of David Kaplan,' to appear in a Festschrift for David Kaplan edited by J. Almog and P. Leonardi, eds., available online at http://www.humnet.ucla.edu/humnet/phil/Lectures/DavidFest/DavidFest.htm.

†† 'The Resilience of Illogical Belief,' *Noûs* (forthcoming 2005).

† 'Pronouns as Variables,' forthcoming in a 2005 symposium in *Philosophy and Phenomenological Research* on Alan Berger's *Terms and Truth* (Cambridge, Mass.: MIT Press, 2002).

'Three Perspectives on Quantifying In,' forthcoming in *Pacific Philosophical Quarterly*.

Index